D1399824

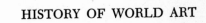

HISTORY OF WORLD ART

History of World Art

EVERARD M. UPJOHN
Associate Professor of Fine Arts
Columbia University

PAUL S. WINGERT
Assistant Professor of Fine Arts
Columbia University

JANE GASTON MAHLER
Associate in Fine Arts
Columbia University

NEW YORK

Oxford University Press

1949

Preface

THE purpose of this work is to interpret the arts in terms of their historic backgrounds. We are not presenting an integrated and comprehensive philosophy of art. We have, however, given as many concrete examples as possible of the accepted concepts of criticism in our interpretation of the works discussed.

The enormous mass of material collected by scholars of the history of art cannot be compressed into one volume, nor can it be absorbed by even the most brilliant student in the space of a single introductory course in art. For the beginner we believe it is wiser and more rewarding to concentrate on a relatively small number of objects, and the facts and ideas pertinent to them, than to lose himself in a maze of names and dates.

With this in mind we have concentrated on the painting, sculpture, and architecture of civilized peoples in Europe, North America, and Asia from the birth of history in Egypt and Mesopotamia to the present time; the many branches of the minor arts have been treated more briefly. The examples chosen for discussion have stood the test of time and criticism. Almost all of them are illustrated, many with full-page photographs. A short discussion of the major historical facts serves to introduce each of the principal art periods to help set the stage on which the artists played their parts. Not all centuries are examined with equal thoroughness; on the contrary, emphasis is laid on the art of those generations or centuries that appear to fulfil most completely the ideals of the longer cultural periods, in so far as the variety of the latter can be said to have single ideals or philosophies. Thus, we have preferred in the chapters on antiquity to devote more space to the sculpture and architecture of Periclean Athens than to preceding or succeeding generations because the later Greeks and Romans themselves felt that that age had best expressed the classic spirit and because that age has been of exceptional significance for much of later art. Likewise the Romanesque, the Gothic of the thirteenth century, the Italian Renaissance, and the Baroque deserve relatively intensive treatment.

At the same time, we who live in twentieth-century America are naturally concerned with our own art and its more immediate background. Therefore the successive changes in the arts during the nineteenth century, when our present industrial and urban culture was growing apace, call for a more comprehensive treatment than is usually accorded them. Consequently we have devoted three chapters to the arts in nineteenth-century Europe and one long chapter to the nineteenth and twentieth centuries in America.

The vast field of oriental art calls for a slightly different approach since its historical, religious, and philosophical background is unknown to most of us. We believe it necessary, for example, to present more of the unfamiliar life of Buddha than of the familiar one of Christ. Still, even in Mrs. Mahler's chapters on the four great cultures of Asia more space has been accorded to Achaemenid sculpture and architecture, Persian miniatures, the paintings at Ajantā, T'ang sculpture, Sung painting, and Japanese prints than to some of the many other fascinating eras and topics within these cultures.

Contrary to the custom of most histories of art, we have grouped the illustrations together, rather than spread them throughout the text, because we feel that for many people the pictures in themselves will offer a graphic record of the arts. This separation of text and illustrations has made possible the use of a special manufacturing technique that offers improved quality in the illustration of books of this kind. Larger and clearer pictures, too, have been the result, every attempt having been made to avoid the 'postage-stamp' size plate so often required if a picture is to be placed on or near the page where it is discussed in the text. The text, similarly, has been printed in a manner and on paper that insure maximum readability, unencumbered by breaks and 'runarounds.'

Finally, a word to those who, like us, are teaching introductory courses in art. No doubt you have felt, as we have, the inexorable pressure of time in such courses, and the need of a single reliable volume to cover those periods that should be known to your students but that you would willingly omit from the class to devote more time to men and matters particularly congenial to you. One purpose of this book is to provide the basic facts and interpretations for the major periods and artists so that in class the teacher can expand where he likes, relying on the text to fill in the gaps. A glossary of technical terms, a selected list of supplementary reading (in English since very few college students in America can command any other language), art maps of Europe and the Orient, chronological charts of art periods, artists, and monuments, and a thorough index are included. The chronological charts are designed not so much to list the artists and their dates, as to present visually the relation in time of the arts in the several centuries and countries.

Although we as authors must take full responsibility for this volume, our thanks are due to our distinguished colleagues Professor William B. Dinsmoor and Professor Emerson H. Swift for their many helpful comments on the classical and medieval portions of the text, to Professor Ralph Fanning of Ohio State University and Mr. Peyton Boswell of the *Art Digest* for their constructive criticisms of the chapters on western art, to Mr. John Pope and Dr. Richard Ettinghausen of the Freer Gallery in Washington, D. C., and Miss Pauline Simmons of the Metropolitan Museum in New York for their careful reading of and suggestions for the chapters on oriental art. We want further to express our appreciation of the care and imagination taken in the design of this volume by Mr. John Begg, of the Oxford University Press, and of the exceptionally careful editorial guidance given us by the staff of the Publishing Department of that organization. Acknowledgment of the courtesy of the many museums and private individuals from whom photographs have been obtained will be found in the list of illustrations, and in this regard special mention must be made of the kindness of Mr. Joseph Powers.

Columbia University   E.M.U.
New York, N. Y   P.S.W.
1 October 1948   J.G.M.

Table of Contents

List of Illustrations

ILLUSTRATIONS

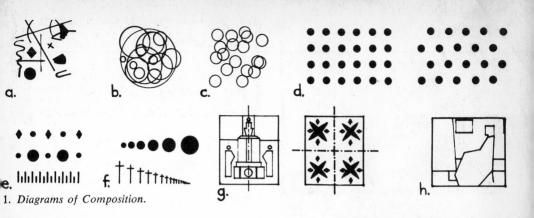

1. *Diagrams of Composition.*

2. *Stonehenge,* near Salisbury, England (*c.* 1500 B.C.).

3. *Typical Mastaba.*

4. *Pyramids and Sphinx,* Gizeh (*c.* 2700-2600 B.C.) Limestone; heights 218′, 471′

5. *Temple of the Sphinx*, Gizeh (*c.* 2700-
2600 B.C.) Limestone and granite; *c.* 260'
long x 40' high.

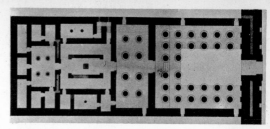

6. *Temple of Khonsû*, Karnak (*c.* 1200 B.C.)
Plan, section.

7. *Temple of Horus*, Edfû (237-57 B.C.) Pylon *c.* 250' wide x 145' high.

8. *Hypostyle Hall*, Temple of Amon Ra, Karnak. Model, Central columns *c.* 70' high, 12' diameter.

9. *Mortuary Temple of Queen Hatshepsût*, Deir-el-Baharî (*c.* 1480 B.C.) *c.* 275' wide x 625', total length.

10. *Temple of Rameses II*, Abû Simbel (1257 B.C.) Façade 119' wide x 100' high; cut back into rock 148'.

12. *Khafra*, from the Temple of the Sphinx (*c.* 2700-2600 B.C.) National Museum, Cairo. Diorite; 5′6″ high.

13. *Ranefer* (*c.* 2500 B.C.) Cairo Museum. Limestone, painted yellowish red; 6′1″, total height.

11. *Seated Scribe* (*c.* 2500 B.C.) Louvre, Paris. Limestone, painted red; 21″ high.

14. *Seti I Offering to Osiris*, Abydos (*c.* 1300 B.C.). Limestone.

15. *Tomb of Nakht*, Thebes (*c.* 1410 B.C.). Width of rear wall 4′11″.

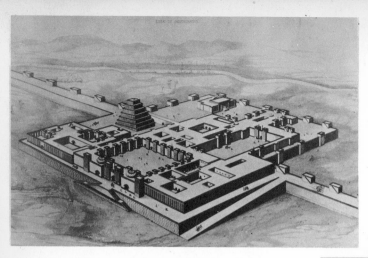

16. *Palace of Sargon*, Khorsabad (722-705 B.C.) Perspective.

17. *Palace of Sargon*, Khorsabad (722-705 B.C.) Plan. 1050' wide x 1140' deep.

18. *Gudea, Patesi of Lagash* (*c.* 2400 B.C.) Louvre, Paris. Diorite.

19. *Ashur-nasir-pal Storming a City,* from Palace at Nimrud (884-859 B.C.) British Museum, London. 3' x 5'7".

20. *Wounded Lioness,* from Palace of Ashur-bani-pal, Ninevah. (668-626 B.C.) British Museum, London. Alabaster; 2'1" x 3'4".

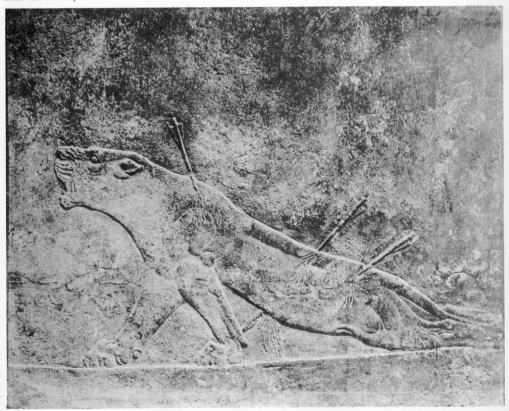

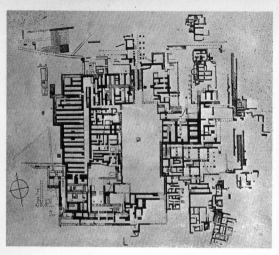

21. *Palace at Cnossus* (*c.* 1800-1600 B.C.) Plan. *c.* 375' wide x 465' deep.

22. *Palace at Cnossus* (*c.* 1800-1600 B.C.) Stair-hall, Restored.

23. *Bull Leapers,* from Palace at Cnossus. Candia Museum. Fresco; *c.* 5'4" x 2'.

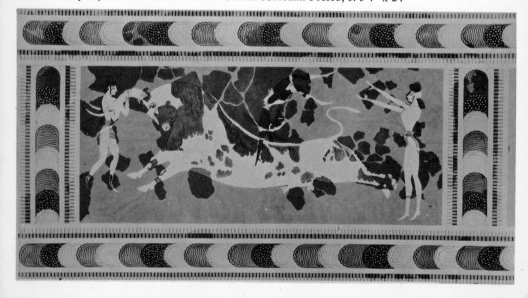

24. *Cretan Snake Goddess* (16th cent. B.C.) Museum of Fine Arts, Boston. Gold and ivory; 7″ high.

25. *Gold Cups from Vaphio* (*c.* 16th-12th cent. B.C.) National Museum, Athens. *c.* 3¼″ high.

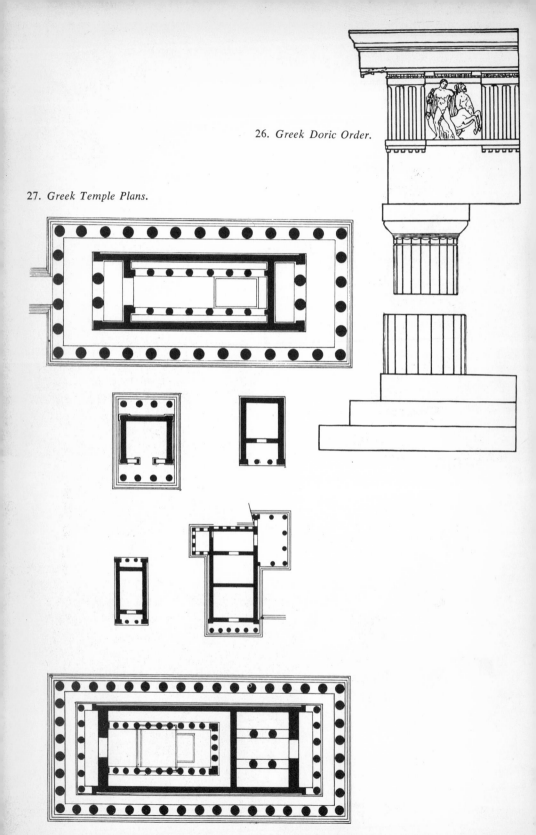

26. *Greek Doric Order.*

27. *Greek Temple Plans.*

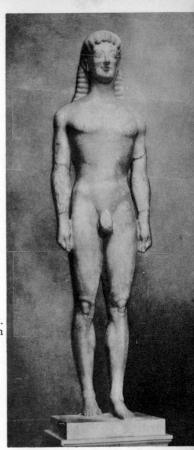

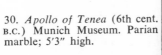

29. *Greek Ionic Order.*

30. *Apollo of Tenea* (6th cent. B.C.) Munich Museum. Parian marble; 5'3" high.

28. *Temple of Poseidon*, Paestum (*c.* 460 B.C.) Limestone; 79'7½" wide x 196'9" long.

31. *Hera of Samos* (*c.* 550 B.C.) Louvre, Paris. Marble; *c.* 5′3″.

32. *Chares of Branchidae* (late 6th cent. B.C.) British Museum, London. Marble; 5'9".

34. *Seated Gods*, Frieze, Treasury of Siphnians, Delphi (550-520 B.C.) Museum, Delphi. Marble; 9'5" long x 2'1½" high.

33. Micciades and Archermus, *Nike of Delos* (550-520 B.C.) National Museum, Athens. Marble; 3' high.

35. Execias (active 6th cent. B.C.)
Dionysus (*c.* 530 B.C.) Black-figured vase, Museum, Munich.

36. Euphronius (active 6th cent. B.C.) *Heracles and Antaeus* (*c.* 510 B.C.) Red-figured vase.

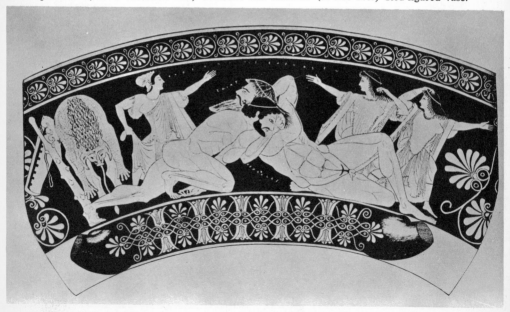

37. *Maiden from the Acropolis* (*c.* 530 B.C.) Acropolis Museum, Athens. Marble; 4′ high.

38. *Statuette from Ligourio* (*c.* 460 B.C.) Bronze; 5″ high.

39. *Athena and Warriors*, West Pediment, Temple of Aphaia, Aegina (*c.* 480 B.C.) Marble; figure of Athena 5' high.

40. *Wounded Warrior*, West Pediment, Temple of Aphaia, Aegina (*c.* 480 B.C.) Marble; 4'5½".

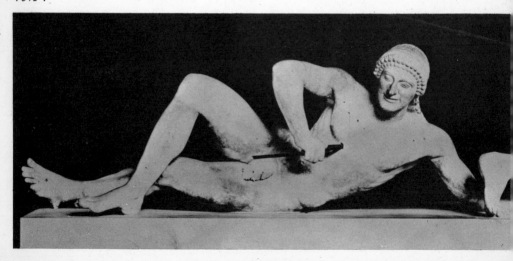

41. *Pediments Restored*, Temple of Aphaia, Aegina (*c.* 480 B.C.).

42. *Pediments Restored*, Temple of Zeus, Olympia (*c.* 460 B.C.).

43. *Centaur and Lapith*, West Pediment, Temple of Zeus, Olympia (*c.* 460 B.C.) Marble; 6'9" high.

44. *Apollo*, West Pediment, Temple of Zeus, Olympia (*c*. 460 B.C.) Marble; *c*. 10′ high.

45. *Head of Apollo*, West Pediment, Temple of Zeus, Olympia (*c*. 460 B.C.) Marble; 17″ high.

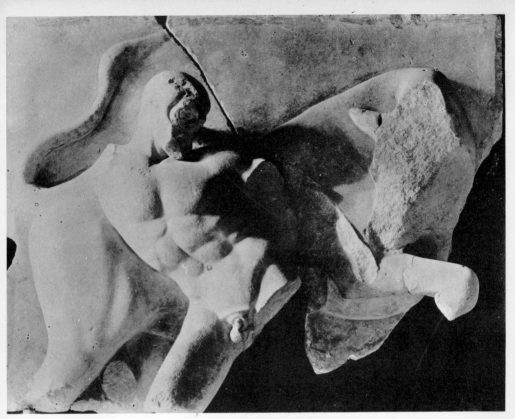

46. *Heracles and the Cretan Bull*, Metope, Temple of Zeus, Olympia (*c.* 460 B.C.) Marble; 5'3" high x 5' wide.

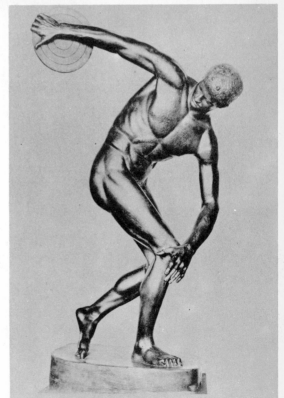

47. Myron (*c.* 490-430 B.C.) *Discobolus* (*c.* 460 B.C.).

48. *Charioteer of Delphi* (*c.* 470 B.C.) Museum, Delphi. Bronze; 5′11″ high.

49. Ictinus and Callicrates, *Parthenon, Athens* (447-432 B.C.).

50. *Athena Lemnia* (*c.* 450 B.C.) Over 6' high.

51. *Centaur and Lapith,* Metope, Parthenon, Athens. Marble;
3'11" x 4'2".

52. *Horsemen*, West Frieze, Parthenon, Athens, British Museum, London. Marble; 4'4" high.

53. *Seated Gods*, East Frieze, Parthenon, Athens. British Museum, London. Marble; 4'4" high.

54. *Demeter, Persephone, and Iris,* East Pediment, Parthenon, Athens. Marble; Demeter and Persephone: 4'10½" high; Iris: 5'8" high.

55. *Theseus,* East Pediment, Parthenon, Athens. British Museum, London. Marble; 5'8" long.

56. *Erechtheum, Athens* (c. 421-406 B.C.) North Porch.

57. Mnesicles, *Propylaea, Athens* (437-432 B.C.).

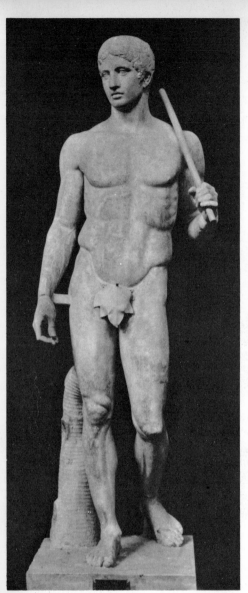

58. Polyclitus (active 450-420 B.C.) *The Dory-phorus.* 7' high.

60. *Corinthian Capital*, Tholos, Epidaurus (*c.* 350 B.C.) Museum, Epidaurus.

59. *Slaughter of the Niobids* (5th cent. B.C.) vase. Museum, Orvieto.

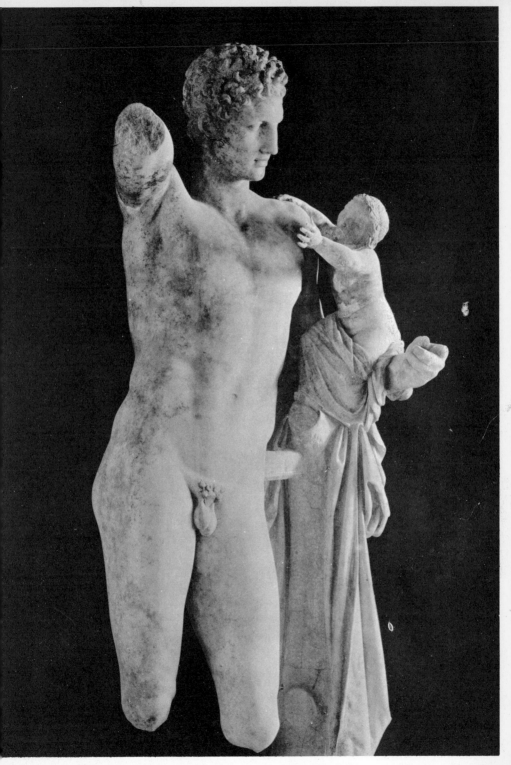

61. Praxiteles (active *c.* 390-330 B.C.) *Hermes Carrying the Infant Dionysus.* Museum, Olympia.
Parian Marble; 7'8" high.

62. Praxiteles (active *c.* 390-330 B.C.) *Aphrodite of Cnidus*. Over life size.

64. Lysippus (active *c.* 370-325 B.C.) *Agias*.

63. *Greeks and Amazons*, Frieze, Mausoleum, Halicarnassus (*c.* 350 B.C.) British Museum, London. Marble; 2'9" high.

65. *Aphrodite of Melos* (3rd-2nd cent. B.C.)
Louvre, Paris. Marble; *c.* life size.

66. *Nike of Samothrace* (*c.* 306 B.C.) Louvre,
Paris. Marble; 9′3″ high.

67. *Dying Gaul,* Pergamum (*c.* 225 B.C.) Capitoline Museum, Rome. Marble; 6'3" long.

68. *Gods and Giants,* Frieze, Altar of Zeus, Pergamum (197-159 B.C.) Berlin, Museum. Marble; 7'10" high.

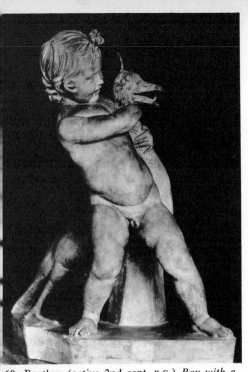

71. *Portrait of Unknown Roman* (1st cent. B.C.) Museum of Fine Arts, Boston. Terra cotta; life size.

69. Boethus (active 2nd cent. B.C.) *Boy with a Goose* (*c*. 200 B.C.) Munich Museum. *c.* 3′ high.

70. *Farmer Driving His Bull to Market*. Munich Museum. Marble relief; 11″ x 12″.

72. *Augustus, Prima Porta* (c. 156 B.C.) Vatican Museum, Rome. 7'3" high.

73. *Frieze*, Ara Pacis Augustae, Rome (13-9 B.C.) Uffizi, Florence.

4. *Spoils of Jerusalem*, Arch of Titus, Rome (A.D. 81). Relief.

75. *Trajan's Campaign Against the Dacians*, Column of Trajan, Rome (A.D. 117) Bronze; height of column: 97'; length of frieze: 656'.

6. *Cupids as Wine Dealers*, House of the Vettii, Pompeii (*c.* A.D. 50-79).

DORIC IONIC CORINTHIAN COMPOSITE

77. *Roman Orders.*

78. *Maison Carrée,* Nîmes (16 B.C.) 59′ x 117′ total dimensions; podium 11′ high; columns 30½′ high, 2′9″ diameter.

79. *Pont du Gard*, Nîmes (*c.* A.D. 50) *c.* 880′ long x 155′ high.

80. *Structure of an Arch*. Diagram.

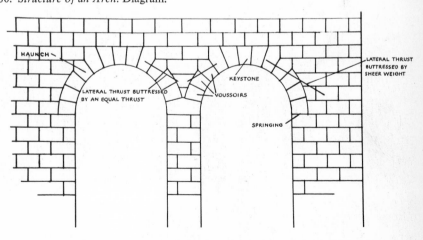

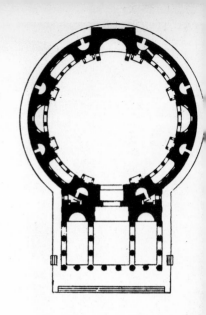

81. *Pantheon*, Rome (*c*. A.D. 120-124) Plan and section.

82. *Pantheon*, Rome (*c*. A.D. 120-124) 142′ interior diameter; 140′ interior height; walls 20′ thick; portico 101′ x 59′.

3. *Colosseum,* Rome (A.D. 75-82) 620′ on long axis; 513 on short axis; 160′ high.

84. *Arch of Constantine,* Rome (A.D. 312) dimensions of central arch: 37′3″ high; 21′6″ wide.

85. *Basilica of Constantine*, Rome (A.D. *c.* 310-*c.* 320) 266′ long; 195′ wide; 120′ high.

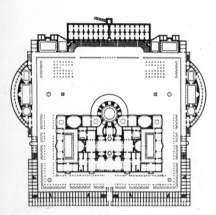

86. *Baths of Caracalla*, Rome (A.D. 211-17) Plan. Central hall 184′ long x 72′ wide x 108′ high.

87. *Baths of Caracalla*, Rome (A.D. 211-17) Hall Restored. 184′ long x 72′ wide x 108′ high.

89. *San Clemente*, Rome (6th cent., rebuilt 12th cent.)
Nave. 115′ long x 71′ wide.

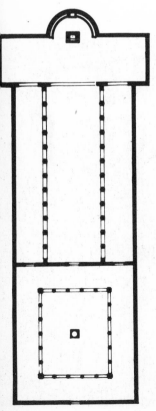

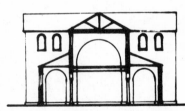

88. *Early Christain Roman Basilica.* Typical
Plan and Section.

90. *Jonah and the Whale*, sarcophagus (3rd cent.) Lateran Museum, Rome. 7′2″ x 2′3″ x 2′2″.

91. *Mosaic, Santa Costanza*, Rome (4th cent.).

92. *Apse Mosaic,* Santa Pudenziana, Rome (4th cent.).

93. *The Vatican Virgil* (4th cent.)
Vatican, Rome.

94. Anthemius of Tralles and Isidorus of Miletus, *Hagia Sophia*, Constantinople (532-37) Isometric.

96. Anthemius of Tralles and Isidorus of Miletus, *Hagia Sophia*, Constantinople (532-37).

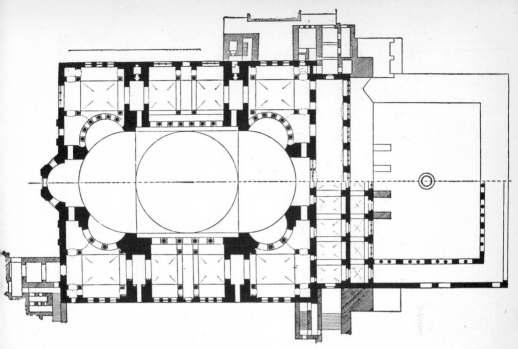

95. Anthemius of Tralles and Isidorus of Miletus, *Hagia Sophia*, Constantinople (532-37) Plan. 256'4" x 235'6".

97. Anthemius of Tralles and Isidorus of Miletus, *Hagia Sophia*, Constantinople (532-37) Interior. Dome 183'8".

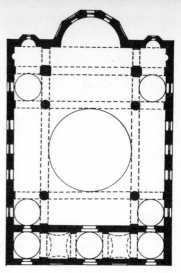

98. *Capital and Impost Block*, Hagia Sophia, Constantinople (532-37).

99. *Typical Byzantine Plan*. Second Golden Age.

100. *Little Metropolitan Church*, Athens (12th cent.).

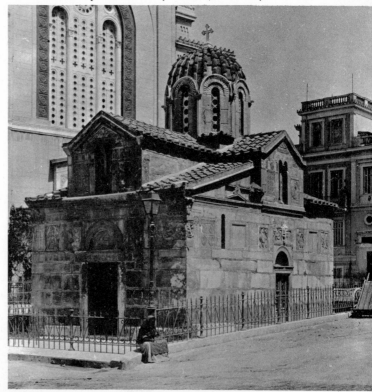

101. *Throne of Maximianus,* Cathedral, Ravenna (546-56) Wood and ivory.

102. *Christ Crowning the Emperor Roman IV and Eudoxia* (11th cent.?) Ivory.

103. *Apse Mosaic,* San Vitale, Ravenna (*c.* 530).

104. *Chastity*, Mosaic, St. Mark's, Venice (11th cent.).

105. *Initial Page of the Gospel of St.
Matthew, Book of Kells* (8th cent.).

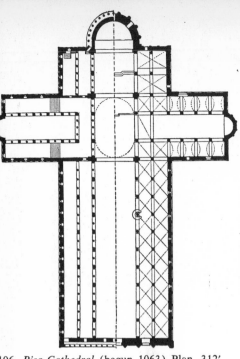

106. *Pisa Cathedral* (begun 1063) Plan. 312′ x 106′.

107. *Pisa Cathedral* (begun 1063) Nave.

108. *Pisa Cathedral* (begun 1063).

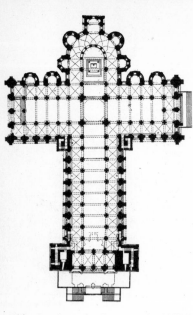

109. *Santiago de Compostela* (1075-1128) Plan.

110. *Santiago de Compostela* (1075-1128) Nave. *c.* 164′ long x 65′ wide x 79′ high.

111. *St. Sernin*, Toulouse (begun 1080) Exterior of Apse.

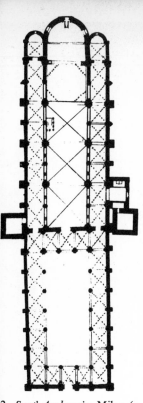

113. *Sant' Ambrogio*, Milan (*c.* 1077-12th cent.) Transverse Section.

12. *Sant' Ambrogio*, Milan (*c.* 077-12th cent.) Plan.

114. *Sant' Ambrogio*, Milan (*c.* 1077-12th cent.) Nave. *c.* 128' long x 44' wide x 62' high.

115. *Sant' Ambrogio*, Milan (*c.* 1077-12th cent.) Exterior.

117. *St. Étienne*, Caen (1064-*c.*1135) Nave 157½' x 32'10".

116. *St. Étienne*, Caen (1064-*c.*1135) Plan. *c.* 360' x 73'.

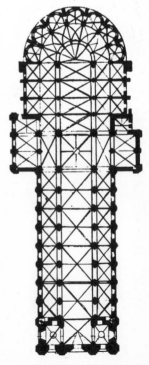

118. St. *Étienne*, Caen (1064-*c.* 1135) Façade. Towers 295′ high.

119. *Durham Cathedral* (*c.* 1096-1133) Nave. 201′ long x 60′ wide x 72′ high.

120. *Portal*, St. Trophîme, Arles (*c.* 1150) *c.* 40′ wide x 46′ high.

121. *Apostles,* portal, St. Trophîme, Arles, (*c.* 1150).

22. *St. Peter*, St. Pierre, Moissac (early 12th
nt.) 5′ high.

3. *Tympanum*, St. Pierre, Moissac (12th cent.)
8″ wide.

124. *Tympanum,* La Madeleine, Vézelay (*c.* 1130) 31′4″ wide x 35′6″ high.

26. *Cain and Abel*, Capital, Moutier St. Jean (12 cent.) Fogg Museum, Cambridge, Mass. 26″ high x 25″ wide at top x 16″ wide at bottom.

125, *Temptation of Christ*, Capital, Autun (12th cent.).

127. *Liber Vitae*, Newminster (11th cent.).

128. *Apsidal Vault*, Morienval (*c.* 1120).

129. *Romanesque and Gothic Vaults.* Diagram.

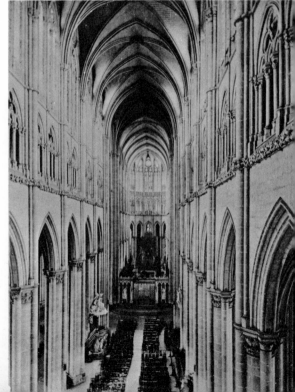

130. *Amiens Cathedral* (1220-88) Nave. 150'10" long x 46'1" wide x 138' high.

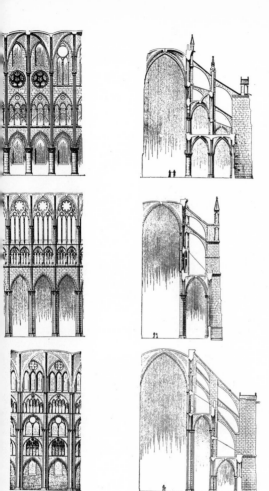

131. *Notre Dame,* Paris (1163-1235) Nave.
c. 147′ long x 48′ wide x 112′ high.

133. *Ste. Chapelle,* Paris (1242-47) 99′6″
long x 32′ wide.

132. *Gothic Buttresses.* Diagram.

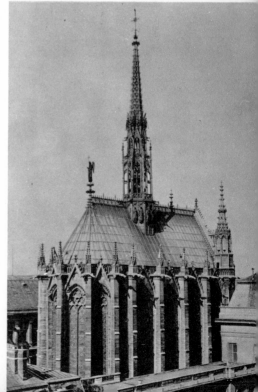

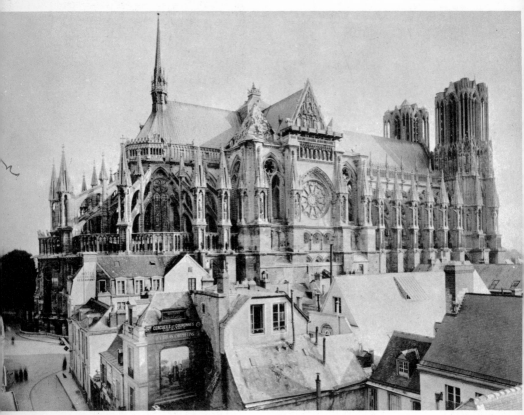

134. *Rheims Cathedral* (1211-90) Side View. *c.* 455′ long x 125′ high.

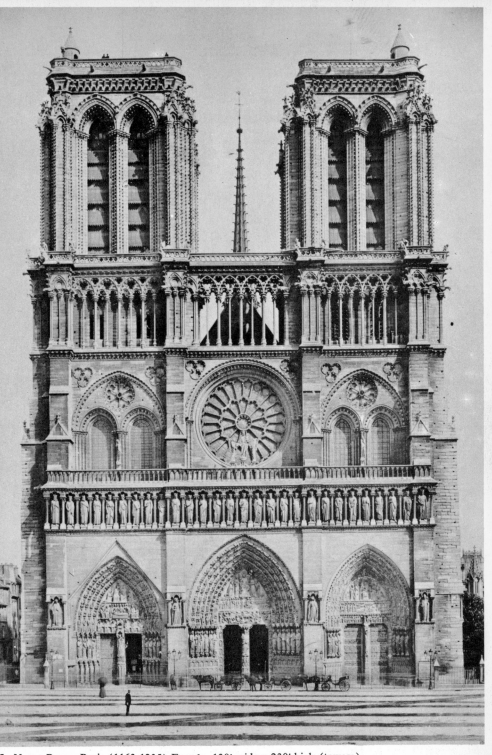

35. *Notre Dame*, Paris (1163-1235) Façade. 130′ wide x 230′ high (towers).

137. *Chartres Cathedral* (*c.* 1194-1260) Nave. *c.* 130′ long x 55′ wide x 120′ high.

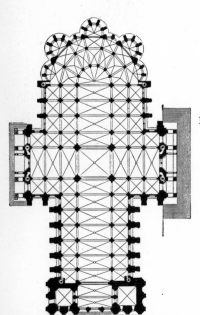

136. *Chartres Cathedral* (*c.* 1194-1260) Plan.

138. *Chartres Cathedral* (*c.* 1194-1260) Façade. 157′ wide x 377′ high (north tower); 157′ wide x 344′ high (south tower).

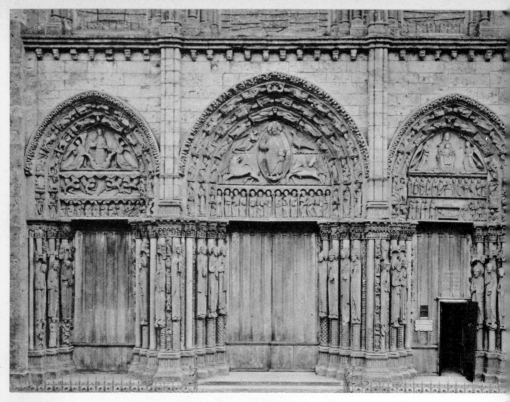

139. *West Portals*, Chartres Cathedral (1145-70).

140. *Kings and Queens*, West Portal, Chartres Cathedral (1145-70) 20′6″ high.

141. *Coronation of the Virgin*, North Tympanum, Notre Dame, Paris (1163-1235) 23'3" high.

142. *Beau Dieu*, Amiens Cathedral (*c.* 1225). 24'6"
height of trumeau.

143. *Annunciation and Visitation*, Rheims Cathedral (*c.* 1280) 10′2″ height of Visitation.

144. *Signs of the Zodiac*, West Façade, Amiens Cathedral (*c.* 1225) 2′6″ size of single relief.

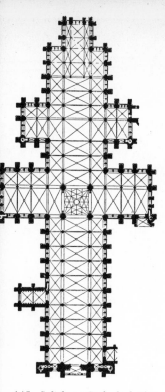

145. *Salisbury Cathedral*. Plan.

146. *Salisbury Cathedral* (1220-58; 1290-1375) Nave. 229′6″ x 51′9″ wide x 81′ high.

47. *Salisbury Cathedral* (1220-58; 1290-1375) Side View. 473′ total length.

148. *Gloucester Cathedral* (1351-1412) Cloisters. *c.* 147′ long x 12′ wide x 18′ high.

149. *St. Maclou*, Rouen (1437-1521) Façade.

150. *Cloth Hall,* Ypres (1200-1304) 440′ long x 230′ high.

151. *Bodiam Castle,* Sussex, (1386).

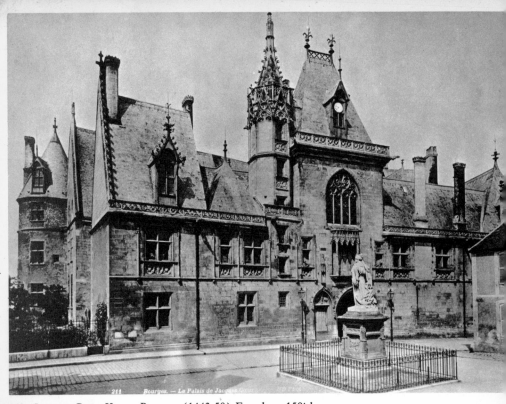

152. *Jacques Cœur House*, Bourges (1443-50) Façade *c.* 150′ long.

153. *Compton Wynyates*, Warwickshire (begun *c.* 1505) Façade *c.* 135′ long.

154. *Vierge Dorée,* South Transept Portal, Amiens Cathedral (*c.* 1280) 19'9" total height of trumeau.

156. *Female Saint* (15th-16th cent.) Museum of Historic Art, Princeton University. Limestone; 3'10" high.

155. Claus Sluter (active 1375-1405) *Moses,* Well of Moses, Champmol (1395-1403) Stone; 5'8" high.

157. Nicola Pisano (*c.* 1206-80) *Nativity*, Detail, Pulpit, Pisa Baptistry (1260).

158. Giovanni Pisano (*c.* 1250-1320) *Nativity*, Detail, Pulpit, Siena Cathedral.

159. Andrea Pisano (*c.* 1270-1349)
South Doors, Florence Baptistry
(1330-39) Bronze; 18'6" high.

0. Andrea Pisano (*c.* 1270-1349)
ast of Herod, Detail, South Doors,
orence Baptistry (1330-39) Bronze;
½" x 20".

161. *Metz Pontifical* (14th cent.).

quam metuendus est locus iste

Vere non est hic aliud nisi domus

dei et porta celi. Benedictus dominus

sum patris et cum Gloria patri. Reptendo. a'.

164. Duccio di Buoninsegna (c. 1255-1319) *Corruption of Judas*, Detail, Majestas, Cathedral of Siena (1308-11).

165. Duccio di Buoninsegna (c. 1255-1319) *Three Maries at the Sepulchre*, Detail, Majestas, Cathedral of Siena (1308-11).

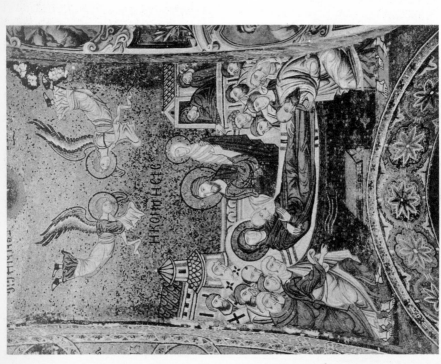

162. *Death of the Virgin*, La Martorana, Palermo. Mosaic.

163. Duccio di Buoninsegna (c. 1255-1319) *Majestas*, Cathedral of Siena (1308-11) Tempera on wood; 6'11" x 13'10".

166. Simone Martini (*c.* 1283-1344) *Sant' Ansano Annunciation*, Uffizi, Florence (1333).
Total dimensions 9'10" x 8'7"; dimensions of central panel 5'4" x 4'.

167. Simone Martini (*c.* 1283-1344) *Guidoriccio da Fogliano* (1328) Palazzo Pubblico, Siena.
Fresco; figure life size.

168. Giovanni Cimabue (*c.* 1240-1301) *Madonna Enthroned* (1270-85) Uffizi, Florence.
7′4″ x 12′6″.

169. Giotto di Bondone (*c.* 1266-1336) *Return of Joachim to the Shepherds,* Detail, Arena Chapel, Paduá (1303-6). Fresco.

170. Giotto di Bondone (*c.* 1266-1336) *The Bewailing of Christ,* Detail Arena Chapel, Padua (1303-6). Fresco.

171. Giotto di Bondone (*c.* 1266-1336) *Death of St. Francis,* Detail, Bardi Chapel, Santa Croce, Florence (after 1317). Fresco.

172. Bernat Martorel, *St. George Killing the Dragon* (*c.* 1430) Art Institute, Chicago. 4'8" x 2".

173. Pol de Limbourg (active *c.* 1400-1455) *February, Chantilly Hours* (early 15th cent.) Musée Condé, Chantilly. 11½" x 8".

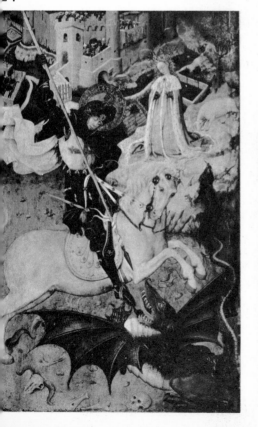

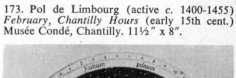

174. Hubert van Eyck (*c*. 1366-1426) and Jan van Eyck (*c*. 1385-
1440) *Singing Angels*, Ghent Altarpiece (1432) St. Bavon, Ghent.
5'4" x 2'3½".

175. Jan van Eyck (*c.* 1385-1440) *Madonna of the Canon van der Paele* (1434) Town Gallery, Bruges. 4′ x 5′2″.

176. Roger van der Weyden (*c.* 1399-1464) *Deposition* (1440) Escurial, Madrid. 7′ x 8′5″.

178. Hans Memling (c. 1430-94) *Martin van Nieuven-hoven* (1487) Johanneshospital, Bruges. 17″ x 13″.

177. Hugo van der Goes (c. 1435-82) *Portinari Altarpiece* (c. 1475) Uffizi, Florence. 8′ x 9′7½″.

179. *Florence Cathedral* (1296–1462). Total length 508'; height of dome 367'.

180. Filippo Brunelleschi (1377-1446) *Pazzi Chapel*, Florence (*c.* 1429) 59′9″ x 35′8″.

181. Filippo Brunelleschi (1377-1446) *San Lorenzo*, Florence (*c.* 1420) Nave. 200′ long x 75′ wide, including aisles.

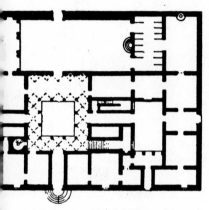

182. Michelozzo (1396-1472) *Riccardi Palace*, Florence (1444-59). Plan.

183. Michelozzo (1396-1472) *Riccardi Palace*, Florence (1444-59) Façade. *c.* 225′ long x 80′ high.

184. Leon Battista Alberti (1404-72) *Rucellai Palace*, Florence (1451-5) 69′ high.

185. Leon Battista Alberti (1404-72) *San Francesco*, Rimini (1447-55). Façade 97′ wide.

186. *Certosa*, Pavia (late 14th-late 15th cent.) Façade. Marble; *c*. 125′ long x 100′ high in center.

187. Jacopo della Quercia (*c.* 1374-1438) *Temptation*, Detail, Portal, San Petronio, Bologna (1425-38).

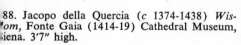

88. Jacopo della Quercia (*c* 1374-1438) *Wisdom*, Fonte Gaia (1414-19) Cathedral Museum, Siena. 3'7" high.

190. Lorenzo Ghiberti (1378-1455
Story of Abraham, Detail, Eas
Doors, Florence Baptistry. Bronze

189. Lorenzo Ghiberti (1378-
1455) *East Doors*, Florence
Baptistry (1425-52). Bronze;
18'6" high.

191. Donatello (1386-1466) *David* (1411) Bargello, Florence. Bronze; 5′½″ high.

192. Donatello (1386-1466) *Lo Zuccone* (1423-
) Campanile, Florence Cathedral. Marble; *c.*
′8″ high.

193. Donatello (1386-1466) *Gattamelata* (1443-6) Padua. Bronze; total height 10′6″.

194. Andrea della Robbia (1435-1525) *Annunciation* (1490-1500) Ospedale degli Innocenti, Florrence. Glazed terra cotta; 5′½″ x 9′4″.

195. Desiderio da Settignano (1428-64) *Madonna and Child*. Turin Museum.

196. Bernardo Rossellino (1409-64) *Tomb of Leonardo Bruni* (1444) Santa Croce, Florence.

197. Antonio Pollaiuolo (1432-98) *Hercules and Antaeus* (c. 1460) Bargello, Florence. Bronze; 17¾″ high.

198. Andrea del Verrocchio (1435-88) *Colleoni*. Venice. Bronze.

199. Domenico Ghirlandaio (1449-94) *Giovanna degli Albizzi*. J. Pierpont Morgan Collection, London. Tempera on panel.

200. Antonello da Messina (*c.* 1422-79) *Il Condottiere* (1475) Louvre, Paris. Oil on panel; 1'1" x 11".

201. Masaccio (*c.* 1401-28) *Expulsion from the Garden* (*c.* 1426) Brancacci Chapel, Sta. Maria del Carmine, Florence. Fresco; 6'6" × 2'9".

202. Masaccio (c. 1401-28) *Tribute Money.* Brancacci Chapel, Sta. Maria del Carmine, Florence. Fresco; 19'8" x 8'4".

203. Paolo Uccello (*c.* 1397-1475) *Battle of Sant' Egidio* (1432) National Gallery, London. Tempera on wood; 10'5" x 6'.

205. Luca Signorelli (1441-1523) *The Damned*. San Brixio Chapel, Orvieto Cathedral. Fresco.

104. Piero della Francesca (*c.* 1420-92) *Resurrection*. Palazzo Communale, Sansepulcro. Fresco.

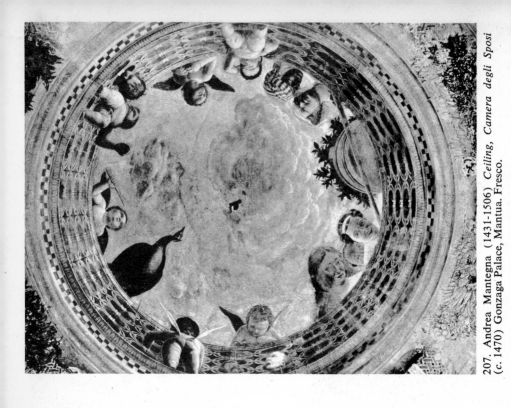

207. Andrea Mantegna (1431-1506) *Ceiling, Camera degli Sposi* (c. 1470) Gonzaga Palace, Mantua. Fresco.

206. Andrea Mantegna (1431-1506) *St. James Led to Execution* (1448-52) Eremitani, Padua. Fresco.

208. Fra Angelico (1387-1455) *Annunciation* (c. 1438-45) Chapter House, San Marco, Florence. Fresco; 7'6" x 10'5".

209. Fra Filippo Lippi (1406-69) *Madonna and Child* (1452) Pitti Palace, Florence. 4'3" diameter

10. Sandro Botticelli (1444-1510) *Birth of Venus* (1486-7) Uffizi, Florence. Tempera on canvas; '1″ x 5′8″.

1. Sandro Botticelli (1444-1510) *Primavera* (c. 1478) Uffizi, Florence. Tempera on wood panel; 10″ x 5′8″.

212. Perugino (1446-1523) *Crucifixion* (c. 1495) Sta. Maria Maddalena dei Pazzi, Florence. Fresco.

214. Bramante (1444-1514) *Tempietto* (1501) San Pietro in Montorio, Rome. *c.* 15′ in diameter.

213. Giovanni Bellini (c. 1430-1516) *Madonna* (1488) Sta. Maria Gloriosa dei Frari, Venice. 2′7″ x 6′.

215. Antonio da San Gallo, the Elder (1455-1534) *San Biagio, Montepulciano* (*c.* 1518-37) Interio c. 120' x 120' x 160' to top of dome.

216. Bramante (1444-1514) *Cancelleria Palace*, Rome (1495-1505) Façade; *c.* 298' x 80'.

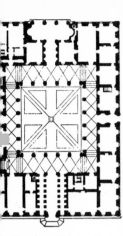

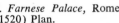

. *Farnese Palace*, Rome 218. *Farnese Palace*, Rome (*c.* 1520) Façade. *c.* 185′ x 95′.
1520) Plan.

. *Farnese Palace*, Rome (*c.* 1520) Court. *c.* 78′

220. Leonardo da Vinci (1452-15
Madonna of the Rocks (14:
Louvre, Paris. Canvas, transfer
from wood; 6'6" x 4'.

221. Leonardo da Vinci (1452-15
Last Supper (1495-98) Sta. M
delle Grazie, Milan. 28¼' x 14'5".

22. Leonardo da Vinci (1452-1519) *Madonna and St. Anne* (1506-10) Louvre, Paris. 4′7″ x 4′2″.

223. Michelangelo (1475-1564) *Pietà* (1498-1500) St. Peter's, Rome. Marble; 5'9" high.

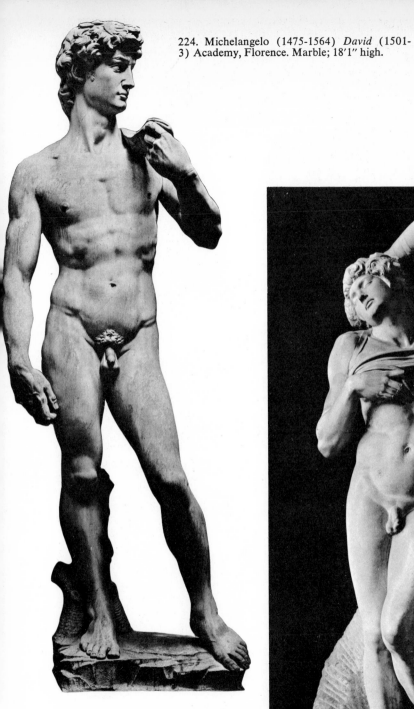

224. Michelangelo (1475-1564) *David* (1501-3) Academy, Florence. Marble; 18′1″ high.

225. Michelangelo (1475-1564) *Bound Slave* (1513-16) Louvre, Paris. Marble; 7′2½″ high.

228. Michelangelo (1475-1564) *Creation of Man,* Detail, Sistine Chapel, Rome (1508-12) Fresco, over life size.

230. Michelangelo (1475-1564) *Decorative Figure*, Detail, Sistine Chapel, Rome (1508-12) Fresco, over life size.

229. Michelangelo (1475-1564) *Jeremiah*, Detail, Sistine Chapel, Rome (1508-12) Fresco, over life size.

231. Raphael (1483-1520) *Madonna del Cardellino* (1505-6) Uffizi, Florence. 3'1" x 2'5".

232. Raphaël (1483-1520) *Baldassar Castiglione* (1516) Louvre, Paris. 1'8" 2'1".

233. Raphael (1483-1520) *School of Athens* (1508-13) Camera della Segnatura, Vatican, Rome. Fresco; *c.* 26' x 18

34. Giorgione (*c.* 1478-1510) *The Tempest*. Palazzo Giovanelli, Venice. 2′6″ x 2′4″.

235. Giorgione (*c.* 1478-1510) *Sleeping Venus* (*c.* 1508-10) Museum, Dresden. Oil on canvas; 3'6" x 5'8".

237. Titian (1477-1576) *Bacchus and Ariadne* (1523) National Gallery, London. 5'9" x 6'2".

236. Titian (1477-1576) *Assumption of the Virgin* (1516-18) Academy, Venice. 11′8″ x 22′6″.

240. Correggio (1494-1534) *Madonna of St. Jerome* (c. 1523) Gallery, Parma. 6'9" x 4'7".

238. Titian (1477-1576) *Young Englishman* (1540-45) Pitti, Florence. 3'7" x 3'.

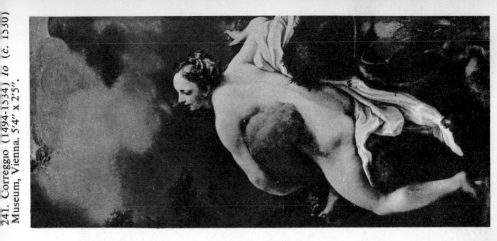

242. Tintoretto (1518-94) *Presentation of the Virgin* (1551-6) Sta. Maria dell' Orto, Venice. 14'1" x 15'9".

243. Tintoretto (1518-94) *Marriage of Bacchus and Ariadne* (1577-8) Sala del Anticollegio, Ducal Palace, Venice. 4'9" x 5'5".

4. Veronese (1528-88) *Marriage at Cana* (*c.* 1560) Museum, Dresden. 15′ x 6′9″.

5. Jacopo Sansovino (1477-1570) *Library*, Venice (1536) *c.* 290′ long x 60′ high.

48. Caravaggio (1573-1610) *Death of the Virgin* (1607) Louvre, Paris. 12'11" x 8'.

251. Giovanni da Bologna (c. 1524-1608)
Rape of the Sabines, Loggia dei Lanzi,

250. Giovanni da Bologna (c. 1524-1608)
Flying Mercury (After 1574) Bronze,

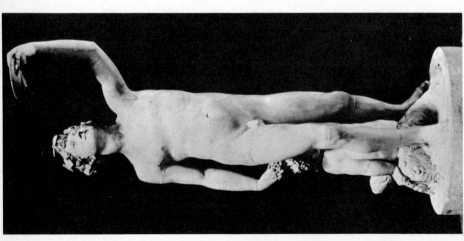

249. Jacopo Sansovino (1477-1570) *Bacchus* Bargello, Florence

254. Michelangelo (1475-1564) *St. Peter's*, Rome. West End (begun 1546).

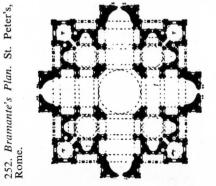

252. *Bramante's Plan.* St. Peter's, Rome.

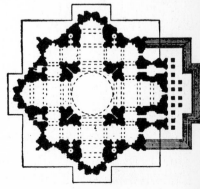

253. *Michelangelo's Plan.* St. Peter's, Rome.

255. Carlo Maderna (1556-1639) *St. Peter's*, Rome (1606-26) Façade. 374′ wide x 147′ high.

256. Carlo Maderna (1556-1639) *St. Peter's*, Rome (1606-26) Nave.

57. Andrea Palladio
(1518-80) *Villa Rotonda,*
Vicenza (1552-3) 80'
width on each side; 32'6"
height of porticoes; 70'
height of dome.

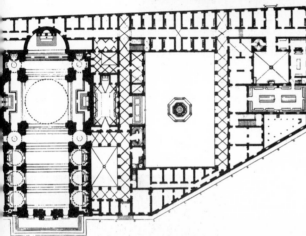

258. Giacomo Barozzi da Vignola
(1507-73) *Il Gesù,* Rome (1568-84)
Plan.

259. Giacomo Barozzi da
Vignola (1507-73) *Il
Gesù,* Rome (1568-84)
Nave. 225' long x 115'
greatest width.

260. Giacomo della Porta (1537-1604) *Il Gesù*, Rome (1568-84) Façade. *c.* 115′ wide x 105′ high.

261. *Fountain of the Organ* (begun 1550) Villa d'Este, Tivoli.

62. *Francis 1 Wing*, Château, Blois. (1515-19) *c.* 150′ long.

63. *Château*, Chambord (1523-6) *c.* 425′ long.

264. Pierre Lescot (c. 1510-78) *Lescot Wing,* Louvre Paris (1541-48) c. 175' long x 95' high.

265. Pierre Bontemps (c. 1510-71) *Urn for the Heart of Francis I* (1550-55) St. Denis, Paris. c. 4' high.

66. Jean Goujon (*c.* 1510-68) *Nymphs* (1547-9) Fountain of the Innocents, Paris. 2′4″ x 6′4″.

67. Germain Pilon (1535-90) *Christ of the Resurrection* (*c.* 1583) Church of St. Paul-St. Louis, Paris. 5′7″ high.

268. Albrecht Dürer (1471-1528) *Adoration of the Magi* (1504) Uffizi, Florence. 3'2" x 3'8".

269. Albrecht Dürer (1471-1528) *Four Saints* (1526) Museum, Munich. 2'5" x 6'8".

70. Hans Holbein the Younger (1497-1543) *Georg Gisze* (1532) Museum, Berlin. 3'2" x 2'9".

272. François Clouet (c. 1505-72) *Elizabeth of Austria.* Louvre, Paris. c. 14" x 11".

271. Hans Holbein the Younger (1497-1543) *Jane Seymour* (1536) Museum, Vienna. 22" x 17".

274. Francesco Borromini (1599-1667) *San Carlo alle Quattro Fontane*, Rome (1638-67) Façade.

275. Gian Lorenzo Bernini (1598-1680) *Apollo and Daphne* (1622-5) Villa Borghese, Rome. Marble; life size.

276. Gian Lorenzo Bernini (159?–1680) *Francesco d'Este*.

278. Gian Lorenzo Bernini (1598-1680) *Tomb of Alexander VII* (1672-8) St. Peter's, Rome. 19'4" wide x 24'2" high.

77. Gian Lorenzo Bernini (1598-1680) *Vision of St. Theresa of Avila* (1644-7) Sta. Maria della ittoria, Cornaro Chapel, Rome. Marble.

281. Giovanni Battista Tiepolo (1696-1770) *Institution of the Rosary,*
Gesuati, Venice.

279. Guercino (1591-1666) *Burial of St. Petronilla*
(1621) Capitoline Museum, Rome. 237″ x 13′10″.

280. Fra Andrea
Pozzo (1642-1709)
Ceiling, Sant' Igna-
zio, Rome (c 1702).

282. El Greco (Domeni-
kos Theotokopoulos) (c.
1545-1614) *Purification of
the Temple* (after 1577)
Minneapolis Institute of
Arts. Oil; 56" x 59".

284. El Greco (c. 1545-1614) *Resurrection* (c. 1597-1604) Prado, Madrid. 9¼" x 42".

1545-1614) *Burial of the Count of Orgaz* (1586) S. Tomé, Toledo. 15'9" x 11'9".

285. El Greco (*c.* 1545-1614) *Niño de Guevara* (*c.* 1596-1601) Metropolitan Museum, New York. 5'7½" x 3'6½".

286. Velásquez (1599-1660) *Innocent X* (1650) Palazzo Doria, Rome 4'7" x 3'11".

. Velásquez (1599-1660) *Las Meninas* (1656) Prado, Madrid. 10′4″ x 9′.

288. Bartolomé Esteban Murillo (1617-8
Immaculate Conception (1678) Louvre, Par
9'11" x 6'3".

289. Peter Paul Rubens (1577-1640)
Descent from the Cross (1611-14) Cathedral, Antwerp. 13'10" x 10'1".

90. Peter Paul Rubens (1577-1640) *Rape of the Daughters of Leucippus* (c. 1618) Museum, Munich. 3″ x 6′10″.

291. Peter Paul Rubens (1577-1640) *Helena Fourment* (c. 1631) Hermitage, Leningrad. 6'1" x 2'.

292. Anthony van Dyck (1599-1641) *Maria Louisa van Tassis* (c. 1629) Liechtenstein Gallery

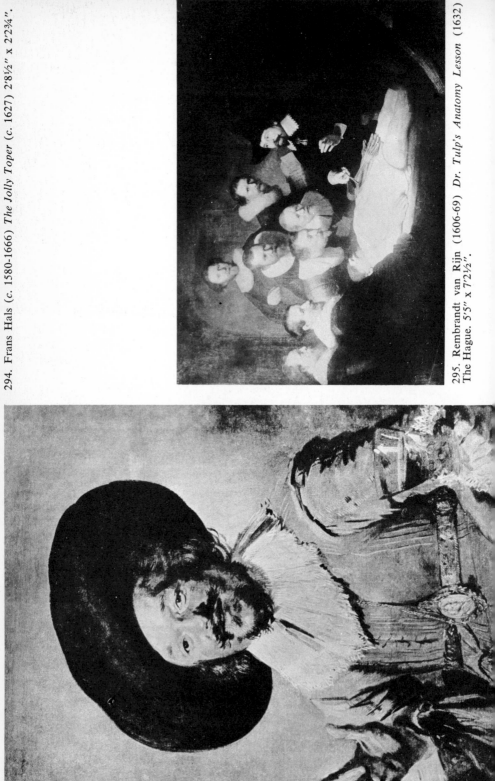

294. Frans Hals (c. 1580-1666) *The Jolly Toper* (c. 1627) 2'8½" x 2'2¾".

295. Rembrandt van Rijn (1606-69) *Dr. Tulp's Anatomy Lesson* (1632) The Hague. 5'5" x 7'2½".

296. Rembrandt (1606-69)
The Night Watch (1642)
Rijks Museum, Amsterdam.
11'9" x 14'3¼".

297. Rembrandt (1606-69) *The Rabbi* (1657) National Gallery, London. 2'5½" x 2'1¾".

298. Rembrandt (1606-69) *Rembrandt Laughing Before the Bust of a Roman Emperor* (*c.* 1668) Museum, Cologne. 2'8½" x 2'1".

9. Jan Vermeer (1632-75) *Girl with a Water Jug*, Metropolitan Museum, New York. 1'6" x 1'4".

300. Jakob van Ruysdael (1628-82) *The Mill*. Rijks Museum, Amsterdam. 2'9" x 3'4".

301. Nicolas Poussin (1594-1665) *Kingdom of Flora* (*c.* 1635) Museum, Dresden. 4'3" x 5'10½"

2. Nicolas Poussin (1594-1665) *Et in Arcadia Ego* (1638-9) Louvre, Paris. 2′9″ x 3′11″.

3. Claude Lorrain (1600-1682) *Marriage of Isaac and Rebecca* (1647) National Gallery, London. 1″ x 6′7″.

304. Claude Perrault (1613-88) *Louvre*, Paris (1667-74) East Façade. *c.* 600′ long.

305. *Palace of Versailles*. Plan.

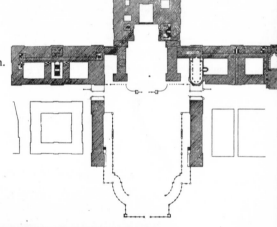

306. Charles le Brun (1619-90), decorator, and Jules Hardouin Mansart (1645-1708), designer. *Hall of Mirrors*, Palace of Versailles (1678-84) 240′ long x 34′ wide x 43′ high.

307. Jules Hardouin Mansart (1645-1708) *Garden Front*, Palace of Versailles. Total length 935'.

308. Pierre Puget (1620-94) *Milo of Croton* (1672-82) Louvre, Paris. 8'10" high x 4'7" wide.

309. Antoine Coysevox (1640-1720) *Le Brun* (1679) Louvre, Paris. 2'2" high.

310. Inigo Jones (1573-1652) *Banque*
ing House, Whitehall, London (1619
1622) 110′ long.

311. Christopher Wren (1632-1723
Steeple of St. Mary-le-Bow, Londo
(1671-80). Total height 216′1″; steepl
104′6″.

12. Christopher Wren (1632-1723) *St. Paul's Cathedral*, London (1675-1710).

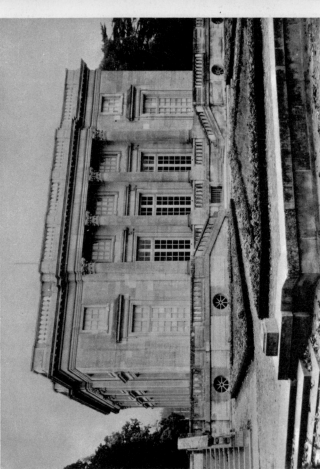

313. Germain Boffrand (1667-1754) *Salon de la Princesse*, Hôtel de Soubise, Paris (c. 1740) *c.* 33' x 26'.

314. Jacques Ange Gabriel (1698-1782) *Petit Trianon*, Versailles (1762-8).

315. Jacques Germain Soufflot (1709-80) *The Panthéon (Ste. Geneviève)* (1764-90) Total

318. François Boucher (1703-70) *Vulcan Presenting to Venus the Arms of Aeneas* (1757) Louvre, Paris. 10'6" x 10'6".

320. Jean Honoré Fragonard (1732-1806) *The Swing* (c. 1766-9) Wallace Collection, London. 2'8" x 2'1½".

321. Jean Baptiste Greuze (1725-1805
The Return of the Prodigal Son. Louvr
Paris. 4'3" x 5'3".

324. Jean Baptiste Pigalle (1714-8
Tomb of Marshal Saxe (1756-70
Church of St. Thomas, Strasbourg.
15'11" high.

2. Étienne Maurice Fal-
net (1716-91) *The Bather*
1757) Louvre, Paris.
arble; 2'8" high.

323. Clodion (1738-1814) *Nymph and Satyr*. Metropolitan Museum, New York. 1'11" high.

?5. Jean Antoine Houdon (1741-1828)
oltaire (1781) Théâtre-Français, Paris.
fe size.

326. John Wood (*c.* 1704-54) *Prior Park* (1735-43) Near Bath. 147′ long; columns 32′ high.

327. Robert Adam (1728-92), James Adam (1730-94) *Lord Derby's House,* London (1773).

8. William Hogarth (1697-1764) *Marriage à la Mode I* (finished 1744) Tate Gallery, London.
3″ x 2′11″.

329. Joshua Reynolds (1723-92) *Dr. Johnson* (1772) National Gallery, London. 3'5½" x 2'1".

331. *Parson Capen House*, Topsfield, Mass. (1683) *c*. 43' long x 20' wide.

333. John Copley (1737-1815) *Mr. Jeremiah Lee* (1769) Collection of Thomas Amory Lee Topeka, Kansas. 7'11" x 4'11".

335. Thomas Jefferson (1743-1826) *State Capitol*, Richmond Va. (1785-98) 146' long x 84'6" wide x 53' high.

34. Gilbert Stuart (1755-1828) *Thomas Jefferson* (1799) Bowdoin College, Brunswick, Maine. 3′10½″ x 3′2¾″.

36. Barthélemy Vignon (1762-1829) *La Madeleine*, Paris (1804-42) 350′ long x 147′ wide.

337. Antonio Canova (1757-1822) *Perseus*.
Vatican Museum, Rome.

339. Jacques Louis David (1748-1825) *Charlott
de Val d'Ognes* (*c.* 1795) Metropolitan Museum
New York. 5'3½" x 4'2½".

338. Jacques Louis David (1748-1825) *Death of Socrates* (1787) Metropolitan Museum, New York
4'11" x 6'6".

40. James Wyatt
(1748-1813) *Fonthill
Abbey* (1796-1814) In-
terior. *c.* 245′ long x
5′ wide.

41. Sir Charles Barry
(1795-1860) *Houses
of Parliament*, London
(1840-60) 940′ long.

342. François Rude (1784-1855) *Departure of the Volunteers*, Arc de Triomphe, Paris (1836) 41'8" x 26' wide.

343. François Rude (1784-1855) *Marshal Ney* Luxembourg Gardens, Paris. Bronze.

344. Antoine Louis Barye (1796-1875) *Jaguar Devouring a Hare* (1851) Louvre, Paris. Bronze; 3'5" long x 17" high.

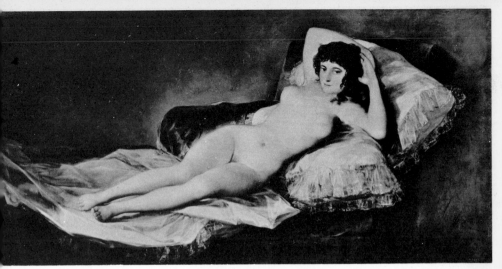

45. Goya (1746-1828) *Maja Desnuda* (before 1802) Prado, Madrid. 3'1" x 6'2".

46. Goya (1746-1828) *Execution of Madrileños* (1808) Prado, Madrid. 8'8" x 11'4".

347. Goya (1746-1828) *Hasta la M*‹
erte (Los Caprichos) Etching; 7½"
5¼".

348. Baron Gros (1771-1835) *Nap*‹
leon in the Pest House at Jaffa (1804
Louvre, Paris. 17'6" x 23'7".

49. Théodore Géricault
(1791-1824) *Raft of the
Medusa* (1818-19)
Louvre, Paris. 16'2" x
23'3".

50. Eugène Delacroix
(1798-1863) *Massacre of
cio* (1824) Louvre,
Paris. 13'11" x 11'8".

351. Eugène Delacroix (1798-1863) *Liberty Leading the People* (1831) Louvre, Paris. 8′6″ x 10′10″.

52. Eugène Delacroix (1798-1863) *Algerian Women* (1834) Louvre, Paris. 5′9″ x 7′5″.

53. Jean Auguste Dominique Ingres (1780-1867) *Odalisque* (1814) Louvre, Paris. 3′ x 5′4″.

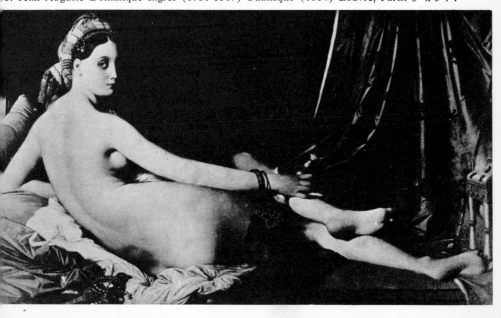

354. John Constable (1776-1837) *Hay Wain* (1821) National Gallery, London. 4'2¾" x 6'1".

355. J. M. W. Turner (1775-1851) *The Fighting Téméraire* (1838-9) National Gallery, London.
2'11½" x 3'11½".

56. Théodore Rousseau (1812-67) *The Oaks*. Louvre, Paris. 2'1" x 3'3".

357. Jean Baptiste Camille Corot (1796-1875) *La Matinée* (1850) Luxembourg Museum, Paris. 3'2" x 4'3".

358. Corot (1796-1875) *Honfleur Houses on the Quay* (c. 1830) Mme. E. Staub-Terlinden, Männedorf. 1'3" x 1'11".

359. Jean François Millet (1814-75) *The Sower* (1850) Museum of Fine Arts, Boston. 3'4" x 2'8½".

60. Henri Labrouste (1801-75) *Bibliothèque Ste. Geneviève,* Paris (1843-50) Reading Room.

61. Charles Garnier (1825-98) *Opera House,* Paris (1861-74) Façade *c.* 200′ wide x 95′ high.

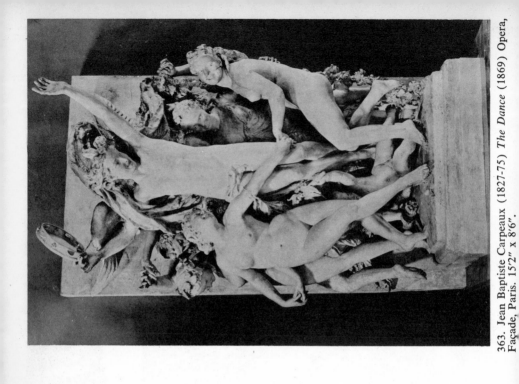

363. Jean Baptiste Carpeaux (1827-75) *The Dance* (1869) Opera, Façade, Paris. 15′2″ x 8′6″.

362. Charles Garnier (1825-98) *Opera House,* Paris (1861-74) Interior stairway.

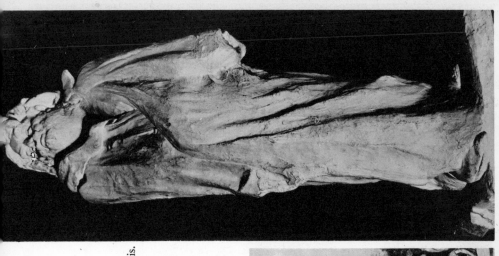

364. Auguste Rodin (1840-1917) The Kiss (1898) marble; 61 ins. high.

365. Auguste Rodin (1840-1917) *Balzac* (1892-7) Rodin Museum, Paris. 9′10″ high.

366. Honoré Daumier (1808-79) *Gargantua* (1831) Lithograph; 12″ x 8½″.

367. Honoré Daumier (1808-79) *Washwoman* (*c.* 1863) Louvre, Paris. 1'7" x 1'1".

68. Gustave Courbet (1819-77) *Burial at Ornans* (1849) Louvre, Paris. 10'3" x 20'10".

69. Gustave Courbet (1819-77) *The Wave* (1865-9) 2'1¾" x 2'10¾".

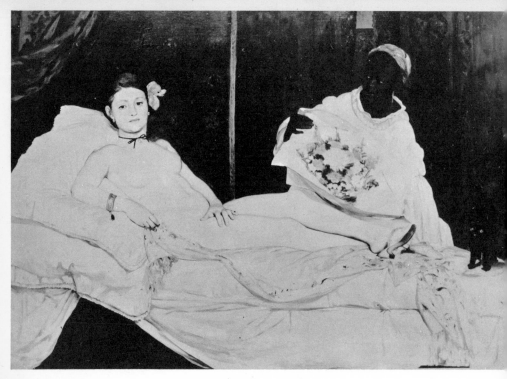

370. Edouard Manet (1832-83) *Olympia* (1863) Louvre, Paris. 4'3¼" x 6'3".

371. Edouard Manet (1832-83) *Bar of the Folies Bergères* (1882) Courtauld Collection, London. 3'1¾" x 4'2".

372. Claude Monet (1840-1926) *Haystacks* (1891) Museum of Fine Arts, Boston.
2′1¾″ x 4′2″.

373. Auguste Renoir (1841-1919) *Moulin de la Galette* (1876) Louvre, Paris. 2′7″ x 3′8″.

576. Georges Seurat (1859-91) *Sunday on the Grande Jatte* (1884-6) Chicago Art Institute. 83 × 1072 .

377. Paul Gauguin (1848-1903) *Manao Tu Papua* (1892) A. Conger Goodyear Collection, New York.

378. Paul Gauguin (1848-1903) *Mahana No Atua* (The Day of the God) (1894) Chicago Art Institute. Oil on canvas; 26½" x 35½".

379. Vincent van Gogh (1853-90) *La Berceuse* (1889) Chicago Art Institute. 3′ x 2′4″.

0. Vincent van Gogh (1853-90) *Landscape at Auvers* (1890) Museum, Munich. 2′5″ x 3′¼″.

381. Paul Cézanne (1839-
1906) *Still Life* (c. 1887)
Louvre, Paris. 2'1½" x 2'7½".

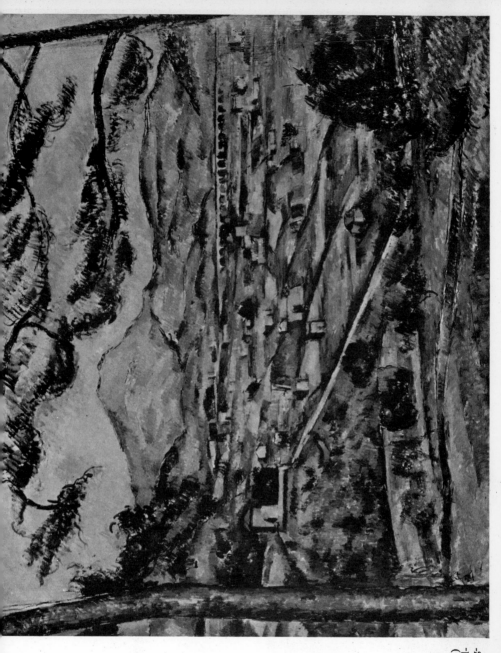

382. Paul Cézanne (1839-1906)
Mt. Ste. Victoire (1885-7) Phillips Memorial Gallery, Washington. 1'11½" x 24½".

383. Paul Cézanne (1839-1906) *Bathers* (189?-1906) J. V. Pellerin, Paris. 6'10" x 8'2½".

384. Bouguereau (1825-1905) *Birth of Venu?* (1879) Luxembourg Museum, Paris. 9'10" ?7'1½".

5. Thomas U. Walter (1804-88) *Andalusia, Pa.* (1836).

6. Horatio Greenough (1805-52) *Wash-ington* (1832-42) Smithsonian Institution, ashington. 11'4" high.

387. Richard Upjohn (1802-78) *Trinity Church,* New York (1839-46) 200' x 75'.

389. John Rogers (1829-1904) *Coming to the Parson* (1870). 17" long x 22" high.

388. Henry Kirke Brown (1814-86) *Washington*, Union Square, New York. (1856) Over life size.

390. Asher Brown Durand (1796-1886) *In the Woods*, 1855 Metropolitan Museum, New York. 5'¾" x 4'½".

91. George Inness (1825-94) *Autumn Oaks*. Metroplitan Museum, New York. 1'8" x 2'5½".

92. Winslow Homer (1836-1910) *Northeaster* (1895) Metropolitan Museum, New York. 2'10½" 4'2¼".

393. Henry H. Richardson (1838-86) *Trinity Church*, Boston (1872-7) Façade *c.* 96′ wide.

394. Henry H. Richardson (1838-86) *Marshall Field Warehouse*, Chicago (1885-7) Façade 325′ long x 120′ high.

5. McKim, Mead, and White *Agricultural Building,* World's Columbian Exposition, Chicago 1893). 800′ long x 500′ wide.

6. Louis Sullivan (1856-1924) *Transportation Building,* World's Columbian Exposition, Chicago 1893). 960′ long x 256′ wide.

397. Henry Bacon (1866-1924
Lincoln Memorial, Washingto
(1923). *c.* 188′ x 118′ x 80′.

399. James McNeill Whistle
(1834-1903) *Old Battersea Bridg*
(*c.* 1872) Tate Gallery, Londor
2′2″ x 1′7¾″.

98. Augustus St. Gaudens (1848-
907) *Admiral Farragut Monument,*
Madison Square, N. Y. (1880) Bronze.

100. John Singer Sargent (1856-1925)
Daughters of Asher Wertheimer (1901)
Tate Gallery, London. 6'1" x 4'3½".

402. Louis Sullivan (1856-1924) *Wainwright Building*, St. Louis (1890-91). 127′

401. Leroy S. Buffington (1847-1931) *Skyscraper Design* (1887-8).

405. Eliel Saarinen (1873-) *Chicago Tribune Tower.* Competition (1922) Second Prize.

404. Hugh Ferriss (1889-) *Zoning Law Diagram* New York (1916).

403. Cass Gilbert (1859-1934) *Woolworth Building,* New York (1913). 60 stories; 800' high.

406. Holabird and Root, *Chicago Daily News Building* (1928).

407. McKenzie, Voorhees Gmelin, *Barclay-Vesey Telephone Building,* New York (1924-6). 29 stories high.

408. Howe and Lescaze, *Philadelphia Savings Fund Society Building,* Philadelphia (1931-2). 3. stories high.

409. Frank Lloyd Wright (1869-   ) *Unity Church*, Oak Park, Ill. (1903).

410. Frank Lloyd Wright (1869-   ) *Coonley House*, Riverside, Ill. (1908).

1. Frank Lloyd Wright (1869-   ) *Kaufmann House,* Bear Run, Pa. (1937-9). *c.* 64′ deep x
′ wide.

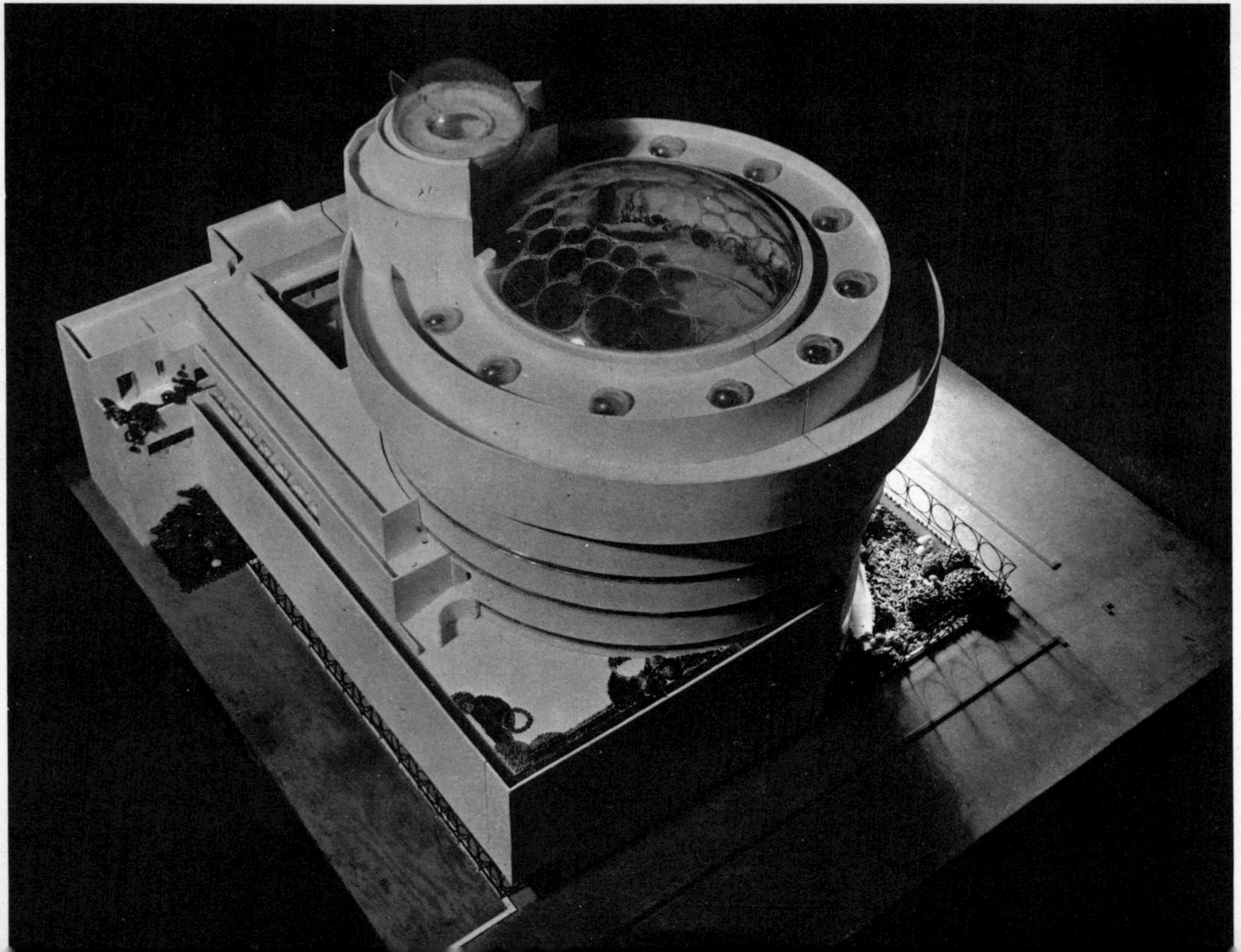

412. Frank Lloyd Wright (1869-) *Modern Gallery* (1945) Project.

Statue of a Woman (1912-27) J. A.
Dunbad Collection, N. Y. Bronze;
5'8" high.

414. William Zorach (1887-)
Mother and Child (1927-30) Marble; 5'6" high.

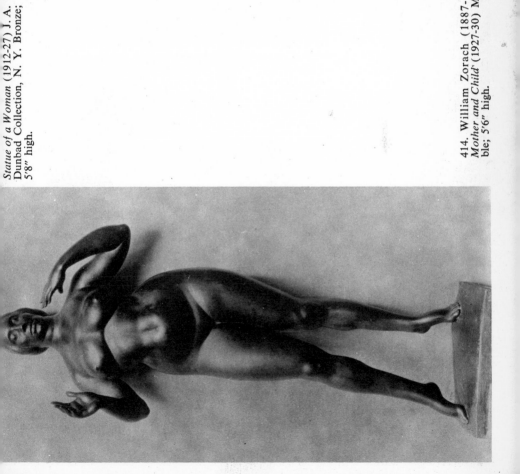

415. George Bellows (1882-1925) *Dempsey and Firp* (1924) Whitney Museum N. Y. 4'3" x 5'3".

416. Edward Hopper (1882-) *Lighthouse* (1929). 2'5" x 3'7".

417. Thomas Benton (1889-) *Arts of the West*, Whitney Museum, New York. 7'5" x 13'3".

18. Henri Matisse (1869-   ) *The Dance*, Museum of Modern Western Art, Moscow. 8'5½" x 2'9½".

19. Pablo Picasso (1881-   ) *The Spring* (1921-2) Private Collection.

420. Pablo Picasso (1881-)
Fernande (1908) Museum of
Modern Art, New York, on loan
from Henry Church. 2'½" x
1'4¾".

422. Piet Mondrian (1872-1944
*Composition in White, Black, an
Red* (1936) Museum of Moder
Art, New York. 3'4¼" x 3'5

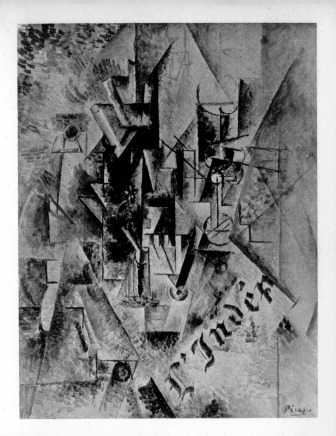

22. Pablo Picasso (1881-) *Still Life.*

23. Salvador Dali (1904-) *Persistence of Memory.* Museum of Modern Art, New York. 10″ x 14″.

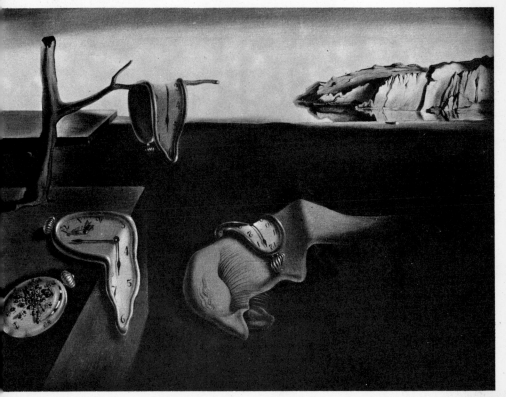

424. Aristide Maillol (1861-1944) *Seated Woman* (c. 1901) Tuileries, Paris. Marble; over life size.

425. Émile Antoine Bourdelle (1861-1929) *The Dance* (1912) Théâtre des Champs-Elysées, Paris. Stone; figure life size.

26. Ivan Meštrović (1883-   ) *The Maiden of Kossovo* (1908).

27. Alexander Archipenko (1887-   ) *Medrano*.

430. Alvar Aalto (1898-) *Plywood Chairs.*

431. Walter Gropius (1883-) *Bauhaus Dessau (1925-6).*

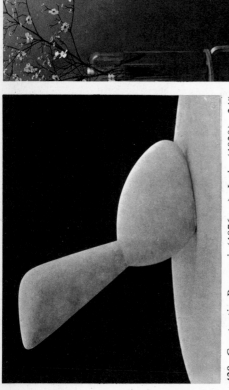

428. Constantin Brancusi (1876-) *Leda* (1920). 24"
high.

429. Hans Arp (1888-) *Human Concretion* (1935).
19½" high.

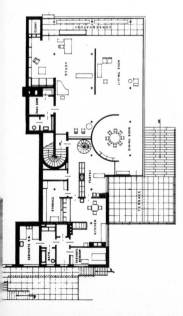

432. Miës van der Rohe (1886-) *Tugendhat House*, Brno, Czechoslovakia (1930-31) Plan.

434. Miës van der Rohe (1886-) *Tugendhat House*, Brno (1930-31) Interior.

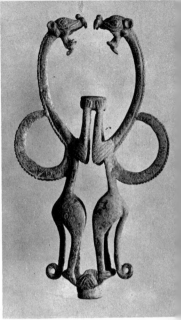

435. *Painted Jar with Conventionalized Ibex* (*c.* 3500 B.C.) Oriental Institute, Chicago. Pottery.

436. *Finial* (*c.* 2700 B.C.) Museu[m] of Fine Arts, Boston. Bronze; 6¼ high.

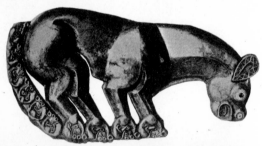

437. *Pectoral of Lioness from Ke[l]ermes* (*c.* 500 B.C.) Hermitag[e] Moscow. Gold, inlaid with amber.

438. *Tomb of Xerxes*, Naqsh-i-Ru[s]tam, near Persepolis (*c.* 465 B.C[.]) Stone.

439. *Tomb of Cyrus,* Pasargadae (*c.* 530
.C.) Stone; interior 10' long x 7' wide.

440. *Apadana of Xerxes with Palace of
?arius in the Distance,* Persepolis (*c.
?65* B.C.) Stone.

441. *Gate of Xerxes,* Persepolis (486-465 B.C.) Stone.

?42. *Bactrian Leading
?amel,* Stairway, Palace
f Xerxes, Persepolis
?485-465 B.C) Stone; 3'
?igh.

443. *Lion Attacking Bull*, Stairway, Palace of Xerxes, Persepolis (485-465 B.C.) Stone.

444. *Double Bull Capital*, Palace of Artaxerxes II, Susa (404-358 B.C.) Louvre, Paris. Stone; 10′ high

445. *Column Base*, Palace of Artaxerxes II, Susa (404-358 B.C.) Louvre, Paris. Stone; base, 2′ high.

446. *Tachara of Darius*, Persepolis (521-485 B.C.) Stone.

447. *Winged Ibex Handle* (4th cent. B.C.) Louvre, Paris. Gilded bronze; 11″ high.

. *Tāq-i-Kisrā*, Ctesi-
n (A.D. 242-72) Brick;
' wide x 112' high.

. *Investiture of Ar-
ḥīr I*, Naqsh-i-Rustam,
r Persepolis (A.D. 224-
Stone.

450. *Peroz I Hunting* (457-63). Metropolitan Museum, New York. Gilded Silver; 8½" high.

451. *Shroud of St. Colombe*, Cathedral, Sens (6th-7th cent.) Silk.

452. *Detail of Frieze*, Mschatta (743-4 Staatliche Museum, Berlin. Stone.

454. *Interior of North Dome*, Congreg tional Mosque, Isfahan (1088). Brick.

453. *Carved Wood Panels*, Al-Aqsa Mosque, Jerusalem (8th cent.) Wood; *c.* 3′ high.

5. *Northwest Īwān,* Congregational Mosque, ahan (12th cent.). Brick.

457. *Bowl with Polychrome Painting* (1242) Victoria and Albert Museum, London. Pottery; 7¾″ high.

458. *Physicians Cutting Plant,* from *Materia Medica of Dioscorides* (1224) Freer Gallery, Washington. Opaque color and gold on paper; 5″ high x 7″ wide.

6. *King Hunting and Holding Audience,* etails of Silver Ewer (1232). British Museum, London. Inlaid; medallions 1½″ high.

459. *Stag and Doe* from *Manāfi' al-Hayawān* (1297) Morgan Library, New York. Painting on paper.

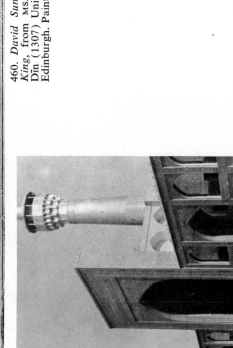

461. Bihzād, *Sultān Husayn Mīrzā Revelling*, from a Būstān MS.
(1488). Royal Egyptian Library, Cairo. Painting on paper, 12″

460. *David Summoned to Be King*, from ms. of Rashīd-al-Dīn (1307) University Library, Edinburgh. Painting on paper.

462. *The Old Court* (15th cent.) and Minaret (*c.* 1730) Shrine

Rustam, from a Shāh-nāmah MS. (15th cent.) Fogg Museum, Cam-bridge, Mass. Painting on paper; 8¼″ high x 4½″ wide.

464. Bihzād, *King Da-rius and Herdsman*, from a Būstān MS. (1488) Royal Egyptian Library, Cairo. Painting on paper; 12″ high x 8½″ wide.

466. *Queen of Sheba*, School of Bokhara (16th cent.) Anet Collection, Paris. Ink on paper.

465. *Bookbinding* (14th cent.) A. Chester Beatty Collection, London. Leather.

467. *Layla and Majnūn* (c. 1600) Museum of Fine Arts, Boston. Silk; repeat; 9½" high.

468. *Painted Jar from Chandu-Daro* (c. 3000 B.C.) Museum of Fine Arts, Boston. Pottery.

470. *Torso from Harappa* (*c.* 3000 B.C.) Archaeological Museum, Mohenjo-Daro. Sandstone.

471. *Dancing Girl from Mohenjo-Daro* (*c.* 3000 B.C.) Archaeological Museum, Mohenjo-Daro. Bronze.

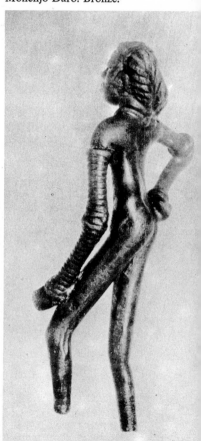

472. *Aśokan Capital* (322-185 B.C.)
Archaeological Museum, Sārnāth. Sandstone; 7' high x 2'10" wide.

473. *Stūpa No. 1*, Sānchī (70-25 B.C.)
Stone; 54' high, 120' diam.

474. *Yakshī, East Gate, Stūpa No. 1,* Sānchī (70-25 B.C.) Stone.

475. *Yakshī,* Buddhist Railing Bhārhut (185-80 B.C.) Stone.

476. *Conception of the Buddha,* Buddhist Railing, Bhārhut (185-80 B.C.) Stone; medallion 20″ high.

477. *Sūrya*, Buddhist Railing, Bodhgayā (185-80 B.C.)
Stone.

478. *Chaitya Hall,
Kārlī* (185-80 B.C.)
Stone.

479. *Chaitya Hall*, Kārlī (185-8
B.C.) Interior. Stone; 124' long x 45
high.

480. *Casket of Kanishka* (A.D. 2nd cent.) Provincial Museum, Peshāwar. Gilded metal; 8" high.

481. *Buddha* (1st-5th cent.) Guides'
Mess, Hotī-Mardan. Stone.

82. *Bodhisattva from Sahri Bahlol.* Stone.

483. *Māra from Hadda* (5th cent.) Musée Guimet, Paris. Stucco; 11½" high.

84. *Colossal Buddha*, Bāmiyān, Afghanistan (5th cent.) tone; 175′ high.

488. *Buddha and the Elephant, Nalagiri*
Stūpa No. 1, Amarāvatī (A.D. 150-300) Government Museum, Madras. Stone; 31½" high.

485. *Bodhisattva, Dedicated by Friar Bala* (A.D. 131-2) Archaelogical Museum, Sārnāth. Sandstone, 8'1½" high.

486. *Heracles and the Nemean Lion* (A.D. 50-320) Indian Museum, Calcutta. Stone; 29½" high.

487. *Representation of a Stūpa,* from Amarāvatī (A.D. 150-300) Government Museum, Madras. Marble; 6'3" high.

489. *Buddha Preaching in the Deer Park* (320-600) Archaeological Museum, Sārnāth. Sandstone; 5'3" high.

490. *Cave* XIX, Ajantā (320-600) Façade. Stone; 38' high x 32' wide.

492. *Details of Ceiling*, Cave I, Ajantā (320-600) Fresco.

491. *The Beautiful Bodhisattva*, Cave I, Ajantā (320-600) Fresco; 5' 9½" high.

493. *Dancing Śiva* (13th cent.) Government Museum, Madras. Bronze; 47″ high.

494. *Pārvatī* (11th-12th cent.) Freer Gallery, Washington. Bronze; 3′4″ high.

495. *Kālī*, Nelson Gallery, Kansas City. Bronze.

496. *Descent of the Ganges*, Māmallapuram (600-850) Stone; 28′ high.

7. *Kailāsa Temple*, Elūrā (600-850) Stone; 200′ deep x 100′ wide x 100′ high.

8. *Rāvana under Mt. Kailāsa*, ilāsa Temple, Elūrā (600-850) Stone.

499. *Śaiva Trinity*, Hindu Temple, Elephantā (8th cent.) Stone; 12′ high.

500. *Mahābodhi Temple* (restored
Bodhgayā (4th cent.) Brick; 180' hig

501. *Temple No.* 17, Sānchī (32
600) Stone.

2. *Durgā Temple,* Aihole (320-600) Stone; 84′ long x 36′ wide x 30′ high.

3. *Paraśurāmeśvara Temple,* Bhuvaneśvara (8th cent.) Stone; 48′ long x 44′ high.

504. *Lingarāja Temple*, Bhuvaneśvara (10th cent.) Stone; *c.* 150′ high.

505. *Black Pagoda*, Sūrya Temple, Konārak (13th cen
Stone; 100′ long x 100′ wide x 100′ high.

506. *Wheel*, Black Pagoda, Sūrya Temple, Konārak (13th cent.) Stone; 10′ high.

7. *Gopuram, Great Temple,* Madura (17th cent.) Brick, stucco; *c.* 200′ high.

8. *Jain Temple,* Mt. Ābu (11th-
2th cent.) Marble.

509. *Tāj Mahall*, Agra (17th cent.
Marble; 186′ long x 186′ wide 18
high.

510. *Pearl Mosque*, Agra (1646-53)
Marble; court 150′ sq.

511. *Rājput-Rājasthānī*, Todī Rāginī (17th cent.)
Museum of Fine Arts, Boston. Painting on paper;
8″ high x 6″ wide.

513. *Jahāngīr* (*c.* 1615) Museum of Fine Arts, Boston. Painting on paper; 1½″ high x 1½″ wide.

12. *Illumination,* from Hamza-āmah (17th cent.) Metropolitan useum, New York. Painting on otton.

515. *The Hour of Cow Dust* (18th cent.) Museum of Fine Arts, Boston. Painting on paper; 10½″ high x 8½″ wide.

14. *Ināyat Khān* (17th cent.) Museum of Fine rts, Boston. Ink on paper; 3¾″ high x 5¼″ wide.

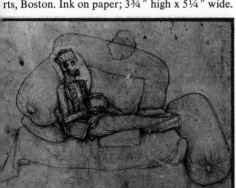

516. *Buddha Nirvāna*, Gal Vihār
Polonnāruva (13th cent.) Stone, 4
long.

517. *Buddha Nirvāna with Ānand*
Gal Vihāra, Polonnāruva (13th cent.
Granite; 23' high.

518. *Dancing Śiva from Polonnāruva* (13th cent.) Museum, Colombo. Copper.

519. *Great Stūpa*, Bara-dur (8th cent.) Stone; 00′ high.

520. *Dhyāni Buddha*, Barabudur (8th cent.
Stone.

521. *Bath of the Bodhisattva; Hīru Land
in Hīruka.* Reliefs, First Gallery, Barabudu
(8th cent.) Stone.

522. *Hari-Hara* (5th-7th cent.) Musée Albert Sarraut, Phnom-Penh. Stone; 6'3" high.

523. *Head of Divinity* (11th cent.) Sandstone; 11" high.

524. *The Bayon*, Angkor Thom (1112-52) Stone; face 9′ high.

526. *Dancing Girls*, Angkor Vat (12th cent.) Stone.

528. *Palace Courtyard*, Bangkok (19th cent.).

525. *Angkor Vat,* (12th cent.) General View. Stone; central tower 200′ high.

527. *Buddha* (15th-16th cent.) Museum of Fine Arts, Boston. Bronze.

529. *Jeweled Buddha* (10th-11th cent.) Museum of Fine Arts, Boston. Stone.

530. *Nepalese Vajra Tārā* (15th cent.) Museum of Fine Arts, Boston. Gilt copper, 5″ high.

531. *Painted Pot from Kansu.* Museum of Far Eastern Antiquities, Stockholm. Pottery; 17″ high.

532. *Carved Bone from Anyang* (1400-1100 B.C.) Art Institute, Chicago. Bone; 6½" high.

533. *Owl from Anyang* (1400-1100 B.C.) Academia Sinica, Nanking. Stone.

534. *Beaker, Type Ku* (12th cent. B.C.) Nelson Gallery, Kansas City. Bronze; 11" high x 6¼" wide.

536. *Ceremonial Tripod Vessel, Type Ting* (1400-1100 B.C.) Art Institute, Chicago. Bronze.

35. *Ceremonial Wine Vessel, Type Chüeh* (1400-900 c.) Freer Gallery, Washington. Bronze; 10″ high x ′ wide.

37. *Tuan Fang Altar with Vessels* (1100-900 B.C.) Metropolitan Museum, New York. Bronze; altar 7″ gh x 35″ wide.

538. *Bell, Type Chung* (600-25 B.C.) A. Stoclet Collection, Brussels. Bronze.

539. *Mirror* (600-250 B.C.) Art Institute, Chicago. Bronze.

540. *Disk, Type Pi* (600-250 B.C.) Nelson Gallery, Kansas City. Jade; 8½″ high.

541. *Horse Trampling Barbarian Warrior*, Tomb of Ho Ch'ü-ping, Shensi (117 B.C.) Stone.

542. *Funerary Pillar of Shên*, Ch'ü-hsien, Szechwan (2nd cent.) Stone.

543. *Red Bird, Funerary Pillar of Shên*, Ch'ü-hsien, Szechwan (2nd cent.) Stone.

544. *Visit of Mu Wang to Hsi Wang Mu*, Tomb of Wu Liang Tzū, Shantung (2nd cent.) Stone.

545. *House Model* (2nd cent.) Nelson Gallery, Kansas City. Unbaked clay; 52″ high.

546. *Mirror, TLV type* (206 B.C.-A.D. 221) Metropolitan Museum, New York. Bronze.

547. *Bears* (206 B.C.-A.D. 221) Gardner Museum, Boston. Bronze, with traces of gold.

549. *Colossal Buddha,* Yün-kang, Shansi (A.D. 5th cent.) Sandstone; 32′ high.

550. *Bodhisattva,* from Lung-mên (6th cent.) Metropolitan Museum, New York. Black marble.

51. *Empress as Donor*, Pin Yang Cave, Lung-mên (6th cent.) Stone.

552. *Tuan Fang Shrine of Amitābha Buddha and Attendants*
(593) Museum of Fine Arts, Boston. Bronze.

553. *Kuan Yin* (6th-7th cent.) Museum of Fine Arts, Boston. Stone.

554. *Demons and Apsarases,* Cave 120 N, Tun-huang (6th cent.) Painting.

555. *Camel and Driver.* Palmer Collection, Chicago. Glazed pottery.

56. *Amitābha Paradise,* Cave 139 A, Tun-huang (9th cent.) Painting.

557. *Adoring Bodhisattva,* from Tun-huang (8th cent.) Fogg Museum, Cambridge. Clay.

558. *Avalokiteśvara as the Guide of Souls* (10th cent.) British Museum. Painting on silk.

559. *Colossal Vairocana Buddha,* Lung-mên, Honan (672-6) Stone; 85′ high.

560. *Guardians*, Lung-mên, Honan (672-6) Stone; 50′ high.

561. *Buddha* (7th cent.) Metropolitan Museum, New York. Gilt bronze.

562. *Painted Case,* from Lo-lang, Korea (Han Dynasty) Lacquer; 8″ high.

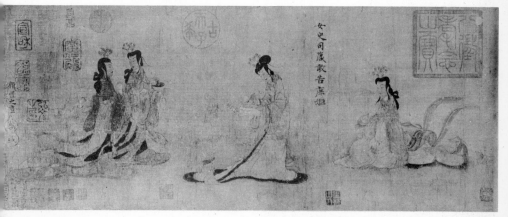

563. Ku K'ai-chih (*c.* 350-400) *Admonitions of the Imperial Preceptress*. British Museum, London. Painting on silk; 10″ high.

564. Hui-tsung (1082-1135) *Ladies Preparing Newly Woven Silk*. Museum of Fine Arts, Boston. Painting on silk; scroll 14½″ high x 4 9″ long.

565. Hui-tsung (1082-1135) *The Five-Colored Parakeet*. Museum of Fine Arts, Boston. Painting on silk.

66. Fan K'uan (act. 990-1030) *A Temple Among the Snowy Hills*. Museum of Fine Arts, Boston.
ainting on silk; 10″ high x 10″ wide.

67. Tung Yüan (10th cent.) *Detail of Clear Weather in the Valley*. Museum of Fine Arts, Boston.
nk on paper; scroll, 1′3″ high x 5′11″ wide.

568. Liang K'ai (act. 12th cent.) *The Poet Li T'ai-po*. Count Matsudaira Collection, Tōkyō. Ink on paper.

569. Liang K'ai (act. 12th cent.) *The Priest Hui-nêng*. Count Matsudaira Collection, Tōkyō. Ink on paper; 30″ high.

570. Mu Ch'i (13th cent.) *Persimmons*, Ryūkōin Temple, Kyōto. Ink on paper.

571. Ma Yüan (act. 1190-1225) *Bare Willows and Distant Mountains*. Museum of Fine Arts, Boston. Painting on paper; 9½" high x 9½" wide.

572. Hsia Kuei (act. 1195-1224) *Rain Storm*. Baron Kawasaki Collection, Kobe. Painting on paper.

573. Mi Fei (1051-1107) *Misty Landscape*. Freer Gallery, Washington. Painting on silk; 4'11" high x 2'7" wide.

574. Li T'ang (act. 1100-30) *Man on a Water Buffalo*. Museum of Fine Arts, Boston. Painting on silk; 10" high x 11" wide.

575. Ma Lin (act. 1215-25) *Ling Chao-nü Standing in the Snow*. Museum of Fine Arts, Boston. Painting on silk; 9½" high x 10" wide.

576. *Return of Lady Wen-chi to Ying Ch'uan* (12th cent.) Museum of Fine Arts, Boston. Painting on silk; 10″ high x 22″ wide.

577. Ch'ên Jung (act. 1235-55) *Detail of Nine Dragon Scroll.* Museum of Fine Arts, Boston. Ink on paper; scroll 36′ long x 1′5½″ high.

579. Hsi-chin Chü-shih (13t
cent.) *One of the Ten King
of Hell.* Metropolitan Museun
New York. Painting on silk
3'8" high x 1'7" wide.

30. Lin T'ing-kuei
(act. 1160-80) *Arhats
Giving Alms to Beg-
gars*. Museum of Fine
Arts, Boston. Painting
on silk; 3'8" high x
1'9" wide.

581. Lu Hsin-chung (13th cent.) *Vanavāsi Gazing at a Lotus Pond*. Museum of Fine Arts, Boston. Painting on silk; 31½″ high x 16″ wide.

82. Li Kung-lin ? (11th-12th cent.) *Realms of the Immortals*. Freer Gallery, Washington. Ink on paper; scroll 31′ long x 16½″ high.

83. *Ting Ware Bowl* (10th-13th cent.) Museum of Fine Arts, Boston. Pottery.

584. Kuan Tao-shêng (14th cent.) *Bamboo* (1309) Museum of Fine Arts, Boston. Ink on silk; 11″ high x 53½″ wide.

585. Ni Tsan (1301-74) *Landscape* (1362) Freer Gallery, Washington. Ink on paper; 12″ high × 20″ wide.

587. *Altar of Heaven*, Peking.

586. Yen Hui, *An Immortal*, Chion-ji, Kyōto. Painting on silk.

588. Tai Chin (act. 1430-50) *Detail of Breaking Waves and Autumn Winds*. Freer Gallery, Washington. Ink on paper; scroll 36'6" long x 12" high.

589. Chu Tuan
Man and Boy in
Boat under Tree
(1518) Museum o
Fine Arts, Bostor
Ink on paper; 48
high x 24½″ wide

591. Chu Ta (act. 1630-50) *Kingfisher on a Lotus Stalk*. Kuwara Collection, Kyōto. Ink on paper.

592. *The Great Shrine,* Izumo, Shimané Prefecture (bef. A.D. 552) Wood.

593. *Hōryū-ji Temple,* Nara Prefecture (7th cent.) Wood, plaster, tile.

594. *Kōdō*, Tōshōdai-ji (8th cent.) Wood, plaster, tile.

595. *Kwannon*, Yumedono Hall,
Hōryū-ji Temple (6th-7th cent.)
Wood; 6' high.

596. Tori Busshi, *Shaka and Two Bosatsu*, Golden Hall, Hōryū-ji
Temple (623) Bronze; central figure, 34" high; attendants, 36" high.

597. *Kudara Kwannon*, Hōryū-ji Temple (7th cent.) Wood; 6′8″ high.

598. *Guardian Figure Bishamonten*, Golden Hall, Hōryū-ji Temple (7th cent.) Wood; 4′4″ high.

*isattva in Medita-
...ūgū-ji Nunnery,
...emple (7th cent.)
...* high.

600. *Base of Tamamushi Shrine,* Golden
Hall, Hōryū-ji Temple (7th cent.) Painting on wood; 25" high.

...e of Lady Tachibana, Golden Hall, Hōryū-ji Temple (7th cent.) Bronze.

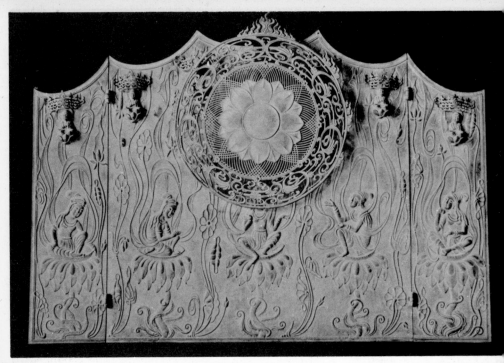

602. *Screen and Halo of Lad[y]
Tachibana's Shrine*, Golden Hal[l]
Hōryū-ji Temple (7th cent.[)]
Bronze; screen, 21"; halo, 11½[".]

603. *Amida Enthroned*, Golde[n]
Hall, Hōryū-ji Temple (7th cent.[)]
Fresco; 10' high.

504. *Yakushi*, Kondō, Yakushi-ji Temple, Nara Prefecture (7th-8th cent.) Bronze; 7′4″ high.

606 *Pagoda*, section. Yakushi-ji Temple, Nara Prefecture
(8th cent.)

605. *Pagoda*, Yakushi-ji Temple, Nara Prefecture (8th cent.)
Wood plaster, tile.

608. *Bodhisattva*, Shōsōin, Nara (8th cent.) Painting on hemp; 5' high x 5' wide.

32" high.

609. *Deer*, Shōsōin, Nar (8th cent.) Ink on pape.

610. *Bonten*, Hokkedō, Tōdai-ji Temple, Nara (8th cent.) Clay; 6'7" high.

611. *Shikkongōjin*, Hokkedō, Tōdai-ji Temple, Nara (8th cent.) Clay; 5'6" high.

12. *Thousand-Armed Kwannon*, Tōshōdai-ji Temple, Nara (8th cent.) Dry lacquer; 17′6″ high.

613. *Aśura*, Kōfuku-ji Temple, Nara (8th cent.) Dry lacquer; 5′ high.

614. *Red Fudō*, Myōōin Temple, Mt. Kōya (9 cent.) Painting on silk; 5′1″ high x 3′2″ wide.

6. *Phoenix Hall, Hōōdō,* Byōdōin Temple, Uji, Kyōto Prefecture (1053) Wood, plaster, tile.

617. Jōchō (d. 1057)
Amida of Hōōdō, Byōdōin
Temple, Uji, Kyōto Pre-
fecture. Gilded wood; 9′
8″ high.

618. Takayoshi? (12th
cent.) *Illustration of Genji
Monogatari*. Tokugawa
Collection, Tōkyō. Paint-
ing on paper; 8½″ high.

19. Toba Sōjō (12th cent.) *Hare Chasing a Monkey*, Kōzan-ji Temple, Kyōto. Ink on paper; 12" high.

20. *Kichijōten*, Jōruri-ji Temple, Kyōto Prefecture (12th cent.) Wood; 35" high.

621. *Detail of the Burning of the Sanjō Palace* (13th cent.) Museum of Fine Arts, Boston. Painting on paper; scroll 16" high x 22'11" wide.

623. Nobuzané (1177-1265) *Detail of Scroll of the Thirty-six Poets.* Formerly Marquis Sataké Collection. Painting on paper; scroll 14″ high.

622. *Imperial Mounted Guard* (1247) Ōkura Collection, Tōkyō. Painting on paper; 11½″ high.

625. *Jizō* (12th-14th cent.) Metropolitan Museum, New York. Painting on silk.

624. En-i, *Detail of Scroll of the Life of Ippen Shōnin*, Kankikō-ji Temple, Kyōto (1299). Painting on silk; scroll 15″ high.

626. Kōshun, *Hachiman as a Priest* (1328) Museum of Fine Arts, Boston. Wood.

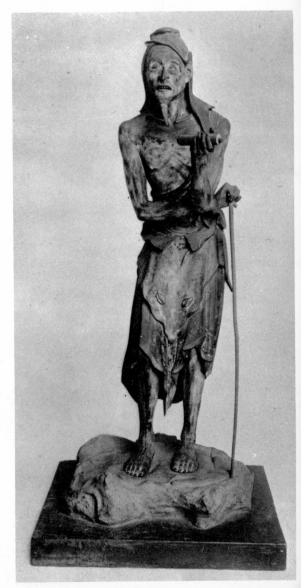

627. Unkei, *Hossō Patriarch Muchaku*, Hokuendō, Kōfuku-ji Temple, Nara (1208). Wood; 6′2″ high.

628. School of Unkei (13th cent.) *Basu-sennin*, Sanjūsangendō Temple, Kyōto. Wood; 5′3″ high.

629. Jōkei (13th cent.) *Kongō-rikishi*, Kōfuku-ji Temple, Nara. Wood.

630. *Red Fudō*, Hokkēdō (13th cent.) Wood.

631. *Benzaiten*, Tsurugaoka Hachi-mangū Shrine, Kamakura (1266). Wood; 38″ high.

632. *Uesugi Shigefusa*, Meigetsuin Temple, Kamakura (13th cent.) Wood 27″ high.

633. *The Great Buddha*, Kamakura (1252) Bronze; 33′ high.

634. *The Golden Pavilion*, Rokuon-ji Temple, Kyōto (1397) Wood.

635. Sō-ami, *Chinese Landscape Screen* (late 15th cent.) Rockefeller Collection, New York. Ink on paper.

636. Jōsetsu (act. 1394-1408) *Catfish and Gourd*, Taizōin Temple, Kyōto. Painting on paper; 30″ high x 47″ wide.

637. Shūbun (15th cent.) *Landscape*. Museum of Fine Arts, Boston. Ink on paper.

638. Sesshū (1420-1506) *Winter Landscape*, Manjuin Temple, Kyōto. Ink on paper; 18″ high x 11½″ wide.

39. Sesson (16th cent.) *Boat Returning in a Storm*. Nomura Tokushichi Collection, Ōsaka. Ink on paper; 12" high x 9" wide.

40. Tosa School (15th cent.) *Detail of Screen of Tethered Horses and Figures*. Museum of Art, Cleveland. Painting on paper; 5'4½" high x 12'1" wide.

641. Kanō Sanraku (1559-1635) *Peonies, on Sliding Screen Panels*, Daikaku-ji Temple, Kyōto. Painting on paper; 3'3" high x 6'1" wide.

642. *Castle*, Nagoya (1611).

43. Sanraku (1559-1635) *Uji Bridge*. Mizoguchi Munehiko Collection, Tōkyō. Painting on paper; 6" high x 11'2" wide.

44. Hasegawa Tōhaku (1539-1610) *Screen with Gibbons*. Museum of Fine Arts, Boston. Ink on paper; 1'11" high x 5' wide.

645. Kōrin Ogata (1658-1716), designer, and Kenzan Ogata (1663-1743) *Plate*. Museum of Fine Arts, Boston.

646. Kenzan Ogata (1663-1743) *Flower Baskets*. Han Tomitarō Collection, Yoko hama. Painting on paper; 44 high x 19½″ wide.

647. *Yōmeimon Gate,* Tōshōgu Shrine, Nikkō, Tochigi Prefecture (17th cent.) Wood.

648. Torii Kiyomasu (1679-1763) *Actor Matsumoto Shigemaki as a Woman*. Museum of Fine Arts, Boston. Wood-block Print.

649. Suzuki Harunobu (1725-70) *The Crow and the Heron.* Louis V. Ledoux Collection, New York. Woodblock print; 11″ high x 8″ wide.

650. Torii Kiyonaga (1742-1815) *The Debarkation.* Art Institute, Chicago. Wood-block print.

551. Kitagawa Utamaro (1754-1806) *Three Geisha*. Art Institute, Chicago. Wood-block print.

652. Tōshūsai Sharaku (18th cent.) *Ichikawa Ebizō IV as Washizuka Kwandayū* (1794) Metropolitan Museum, New York. Wood-block print.

553. Katsushika Hokusai (1760-1849) *Thirty-six Views of Fuji: The Wave*. Museum of Fine Arts, Boston. Wood-block print; 10″ high x 15″ wide.

654. Andō Hiroshigé (1797-1858) *Fifty-three stages of the Tōkaidō: Shōno*. Museum of Fine Arts, Boston. Wood-block print.

HISTORY OF WORLD ART

In General

ART is the response to a fundamental human demand. Its primary purpose is to add to the interpretation and completeness of life. It may be, and at times has been, made to serve other ends, the glorification of religion, propaganda, symbolism, and so on, but in the last analysis these aims, whether laudable or not, are foreign to its main goal. They may even hinder its achievement of artistic results. These results do not contribute in themselves to the necessities of being. Mankind cannot live without food, shelter, and clothing; it can exist without art. Under frontier conditions, since art has no immediate and practical value, it must be subordinated to more pressing needs, if not indeed eliminated. Nevertheless, man's craving for art is very deep rooted; it has appeared continuously since prehistoric days. All that we know of early man, except what may be gleaned from his bones, is learned from his handicrafts. These reveal his desire to add something to his tools beyond pure utility. To adorn them cost him time and effort, but only under the lash of necessity has humanity been willing to forego the pleasure it gains by seeing and handling well-made objects that not merely satisfy their primary practical purpose but in addition delight the hand and eye.

Few activities of man offer such a variety of legitimate interpretations as his artistic expression. From the most limited acquaintance with the literature of the field, or even in conversation, one cannot but perceive that art has a different meaning to everyone. To an Aristotle, it suggests the formulation of an aesthetic theory; to a Spengler, the reflection of a civilization. A scientist or an engineer may be concerned with its technical processes; a poet with its personal expression or interpretation. Perhaps it is an opportunity for intellectual organization in painting, sculpture, or architecture. Its decorative beauty may enhance man's pleasure in the objects with which he surrounds himself. With equal legitimacy, the sensitive creator or observer may find here room for emotional expression.

The existence of these, and many other, paths to the enjoyment of art, or any conceivable combination of them, implies the necessity of tolerance. This matter of aesthetic creeds is like customs; each has validity in its time and place. So long as mankind is composed of individuals, each will take the way he finds most congenial. Some avenues are open to everyone, regardless of training; others require experience or information or both. But that person will receive the richest satisfaction to whom the greatest number of approaches is available.

A work of art is like a triangle whose sides are content, expression, and decoration. These three factors are interdependent, but not necessarily equal. In any given example the artist may choose, or circumstances may compel him, to develop one phase beyond another. Since none of these elements is inherently more important or fruitful than its companions, to emphasize decoration rather than content and expression is neither better nor worse than to stress expression more than the others. Nor does concentration on one side of the triangle always result from conscious choice by the artist. It is quite possible that although in some cases the creator deliberates about his purpose, his arrangement, or a dozen different matters, in other instances his instinct may direct his selection.

The sides of our triangle are distinct from the artistic vehicles, such as line, mass, volume, space, color, and texture, which may serve the purpose of the designer in developing content, expression, and decoration. Let us examine each side in turn, beginning with content. Almost all examples of painting and sculpture have definite subject matter; they represent something, although in recent times some artists have minimized if not eliminated this factor. In Las Meninas (fig. 287), Velásquez records an incident of the Spanish court. He draws the figures as volumes existing in the space his brush creates; the color of the costumes is that of the cloth itself; the light is made to appear in the painting as it is in the artist's studio wherein the scene is laid. The means available to the painter are here utilized in large part to convey to the spectator the content or representational aspects of the design. To recognize the dominance of the representational side in this instance is not to deny other values in the work. Because the color, for example, of the Infanta's dress records that fact, it is not necessary to conclude that it has no decorative or expressive value; on the contrary, these factors amplify and reinforce the content. The Apollo and Daphne (fig. 275), by Bernini, avails itself of the means of sculpture to describe that incident of classic mythology. Each contrast of texture in flesh, hair, textile, or foliage is rendered by the artist; the movement dramatizes the chase, however much it contributes to the decorative or expressive possibilities.

By its very nature, representation cannot exist in architecture and in many of the so-called minor arts; the corresponding element in these categories is function, the utilitarian need the building or object is designed to meet. One point at which architecture diverges from the representational arts is the importance of this factor. In painting and sculpture, content, as we have used the term to refer to illustrative possibilities, may be primary or it may be negligible. With very few exceptions, function is vital in architecture. Adequate provision for the use of a building is a prerequisite; if the edifice is not necessarily successful because it fulfils its function, it is unsuccessful if it fails to do so.

By expression, we mean the artist's comment on, or interpretation of his theme. Theoretically an artist may attempt a dispassionate statement in paint or stone of what he sees; a colored photograph, so to speak, of an object or event. Practically, such impersonality does not exist. The portrait of Georg Gisze (fig. 270) by Holbein is objective, but its very strength of characterization is in effect the artist's analysis of his sitter's personality. Even the selection of subject involves some comment by the artist, since it indicates what seems to him important or of aesthetic interest. Usually much more than this is involved. Two artists rarely react to the same event in the same way. An incident of daily life may be humorous to one artist, a human tragedy to another, or an opportunity for biting appraisal of society to a third. These varied interpretations may reflect individual reactions; they may also reveal the artist's personality. At times this is highly individual, and therefore susceptible of complete understanding only by others of similar temperament. Since personality is unique, its extreme expression may be comprehensible only to the artist, but such a possibility is of only theoretical interest.

The Sienese painter, Simone Martini, takes advantage of the expressive potentialities of pure line. The painters of China and Japan use pure line as a means of expression to a greater extent than any European artist. In Simone's portrait of Guidoriccio da Fogliano (fig. 167), the fortified towns, the spears and pennons, and the palisade not only represent the military activity of the little man but intensify it by their spiky angularity of silhouette. To Simone, the mobility of a horse is one of its outstanding qualities. Repeated curves in both horse and rider create a suggestion of motion as vivid in its conventionality as it could be in the most scientific record of a horse in movement, though the latter might reveal a more equine, less undulating action. In the Seated Woman (fig. 424) by Maillol, the mass and weight of the figure have the greatest significance and are so emphasized. In this instance, the expressive aspect of the insistence on mass is foremost, but the mass contributes to the stony feeling appropriate to the material. Color also can be made interpretive. The color of the gaunt ascetic figures of Picasso's 'blue period' enhances this poignancy. At the time, 1901–3, this Spaniard's life darkened his feeling for the tragedies of existence. He experimented with painting in a single color, blue, which to him best conveyed a somber view. Evidently the prevailing tone was not chosen for representation, since the subjects would be clearer if painted with a wider palette, nor does the unity of color add to the decorative aspect. We must consider it, then, as an emotional reflection of Picasso's ideas of life.

Allied to expression, and at times identical with it as we have used the term, is artistic character, applicable especially in connection with architecture. The phrase refers to the revelation of the purpose of an edifice in its design. We expect a church to look like a church, a bank like a bank, and so on. Function should mold the plan, which involves the size, shape, and disposition of the several apartments in a building. In so far as the plan adheres to these requirements, it must reflect them, and since it in turn governs the exterior of the building, it reveals its character. Thus, in theory at least, the proper character of any structure results from adequate planning. In practice, character tends to become recognizability, which is conditioned by what we happen to know. We expect a school to look not merely like a school, but like schools familiar to us. Such a situation may be unfortunate if the buildings we identify as schools do not happen to function well as such. Moreover, we may expect the design to admit spirituality in a church, entertainment in a theater, or in a bank the stability and security we hope it has. Of course, we may, by extension, consider character as applying to painting and sculpture. A carved or painted altarpiece is presumed to be devotional in intent, and different in expression from a picture intended for a boudoir, or a statue designed for a hall of state.

Decoration in a work of art is the third side of our triangle. The term refers to a formal organization of the parts of any design, over and above that which may be demanded by content or the exigencies of expression. It is not essential to narrative or illustrative clarity; indeed, it may act in opposition to representational clearness. Nor does it, of itself, extend the expressive possibilities. It may include such matters as composition, proportion, scale (at times), and other qualities which are in themselves pleasing to the eye. If it is sometimes difficult to separate content from expression, it is impossible wholly to distinguish decoration from the other two. Nevertheless, in Gauguin's painting, Mahana No Atua (fig. 378), the lines limiting shapes in the water are essentially decorative. These watery lines have some illustrative value in conveying the liquid nature of this placid sea, but their decorative rhythms predominate. It would be easy to conceive a method, even through line alone, that would more clearly depict that particular subject matter, and perhaps one that would better express its limpid surface; to find a more telling decorative passage might be hard. The rich color of medieval stained glass is highly decorative. A window in Chartres makes no pretense to accurate representation of objects. In the Parable of the Sower from Canterbury, the trees and plants are golden yellow, blue, or purple, not because green was not available — it exists in the same window — nor because the designer saw purple bushes, but because those tones in their particular combination afford a rich decorative ensemble. Many Japanese prints appeal to us because of their decorative beauty.

These three possibilities then, content, expression, and decoration, always exist. The artist may select one of them, or any combination that suits his needs of the moment; or, in many ages, historical formulation of the problem may determine the combination. In any case he must try to achieve such unity that his primary purpose will be impressed on the observer without boring him. Though several aims may be included, like plot and sub-plots in a novel, one must dominate. Introduction of foreign subject matter, by contradiction or confusion, no matter how expressive or decorative such extraneous material may be, is apt to weaken the concentration on the main theme. To take an extreme case, imagine a still life depicting a bowl of fruit on a table. A knife and fork lying beside the bowl may seem appropriate, but if the artist were to substitute a sword or an ax, one's mind would rebel. The sword might provide just the right shape, size, and color the work demanded, but one would still feel it to be a disintegrating element. Conversely, pertinent material can enrich a theme. By painting Georg Gisze (fig. 270) in his office surrounded by his business equipment, Holbein helps to characterize the man for us. The artist may also deliberately introduce contrasting objects to heighten the effect, but in that case the material is not extraneous.

Aesthetic unity in a work of art is achieved through composition or design; that is, a visual co-ordination of the parts whereof it is made. Composition has three factors, though not all need be exploited in a single example. The first, *harmony,* refers to the creation of a sense of order by repetition of aesthetic motives. Figure 1,*a,* illustrates lack of harmony in size, shape, value, and arrangement of the lines or areas. With *b,* a simple motive, the circle, is adopted and a vague pattern appears. The sense of order, though minor, is due to the repetition of a series of circles. In size and arrangement, however, there is still no harmony. Make all the circles of the same size, as in *c,* and a contributory factor enhances the harmony; place them in some specific relation to one another, for example, at the corners of squares, triangles, hexagons, or any other fundamental system, and a recognizable pattern results, *d.* Not only is the familiar polka dot design so created, but most all-over patterns of textiles and wallpapers adopt this foundation.

Sequence, or rhythm, the second element of composition, may be defined as regularity of change. While not always distinguishable from harmony, which also involves regularity, sequence is nevertheless distinct. It has two forms. In *e,* the regularity of change is that of alternation of long and short, large and small; it may be of different tones and colors, contrasting motives, and so on. Such schemes can be considered as two patterns illustrating harmony superposed on one another. Or a motive may show a sequence of progression, *f.* Applied to size, it results from repeated forms seen in perspective, as when one looks along a line of telegraph poles, or down a railway track. We know the distant ties are as large as those in the foreground, but they appear to diminish in length. A spiral, like a mathematical progression, shows regularity of change in direction, as in an Ionic capital (fig. 29). Or again, a sequence of direction exists in a group of curves becoming successively flatter, or a series of angles more and more acute. The anthemion motive forming a band below the capitals of the north porch on the Erechtheum in Athens (fig. 56) is an application of this device.

The third of our factors, *balance,* again has two types. Axial balance, or symmetry, refers to the duplication of motives on either side of an imaginary central line or point, *g.* One of our diagrams might apply to many late fifteenth-century or early sixteenth-century Italian paintings, such as the Castelfranco Madonna by Giorgione. What we define as asymmetrical or occult balance is the arrangement of motives unlike in shape, size, color, and so on, but whose visual sum creates a sense of equilibrium around a point. For example, *h* is based on Whistler's painting of his Mother. Furthermore, diagonal lines might be made equal and regular, but a series of diagonals moving in one direction can be balanced by another series, not identical, moving in the opposite direction. Or again, in Titian's painting, called the Duke of Norfolk (fig. 238), the central line of the canvas passes through the left eye of the subject, so that the head is slightly to the left, as is the right hand. But, though small, the cuff of the left hand is placed so far to the right that a sense of equilibrium is established between the three light areas in the design. Perhaps the majority of Far Eastern paintings are based on occult balance.

These elements of composition are so broad as to admit of no exceptions, even though it would be absurd to think that in most periods the artist gave conscious thought to them. Order can be analyzed in these terms, not only in the visual arts, but in other forms of artistic expression as well, and even in nature herself. The organization of nature in general is so complex as to defy ready analysis, but in her component parts, she affords countless illustrations of harmony, sequence, and balance. The symmetry of a pine and the balanced distribution of leaves on either side of a stem in certain plants are homely illustrations. The color sequence of a rainbow, the radial arrangement of the petals in a daisy, the progressive length of feathers in a bird's wing come to mind at once. Harmony is so universal that one needs cite only the billowing masses of cumulus clouds or the broken wisps of cirrus to prove the point. Occasionally through some cataclysm, nature destroys her own organization; more commonly the activities of man accomplish the same result, but everyone recognizes such matters as deplorable. The disorder resulting from a forest fire, a timber cutting, or a hurricane destroys the beauty of a landscape.

In the sister arts, too, these elements, though perhaps called by other names, are present. Rhythm and meter in poetry are harmony; rhyme often shows sequence of alternation. The repetition of phrases or variations on a theme in music accomplish the same end. For the dance, as also in music, the time factor leads to an emphasis on sequence, rhythm, which may be greater than that in painting or sculpture. Such parallels afford a realm for speculation.

Although the application of these elements will recur in the following chapters, three examples may be analyzed here as demonstrations. Owing in part to its purpose, and in part to its materials and methods of construction, the Chicago Daily News Building (fig. 406), by Holabird and Root, consists of a harmony of cubical masses. Like most public buildings, it is symmetrical, the masses, voids, and solids balanced on either side of an axis. Most of the windows are identical separated units, but at both ends of the main front two vertical rows are united in a projecting mass as continuous strips. That projection and those strips convey to the eye a termination of the design from side to side, but the same projecting feature also includes a row of normal windows like those in the large area of the front, not tied together in bands and so repeating the motive of the central treatment. Moreover, beyond these terminal sections, the plane of the wall is recalled in a single windowed bay. A *bay* is a unit of architectural design extending from the axis of one column or section of wall to the center of the next support. See, too, how those terminals are repeated with variations on the end of the building, so that from most points of vision the front and sides of the structure act together as parts of a single design. In themselves, the vertical strips of windows might form an element of contrast, but they are not so left. Over the main area, the windows of the second, third, and fourth floors from the top of the principal mass are again tied together in short vertical bands, serving not only to recall the vertical accents of the end pavilions, but also providing a warning of vertical termination. Once more the plain window form recurs in a single row above that. Then the first setback takes up the theme again. At or near the bottom of the building, the voids and solids are larger; at the top also that scheme is reintroduced as a crowning member. Such an analysis, however incomplete, takes many words; but the unity of effect is perceived instantaneously, even when the observer does not take the pains to examine the way in which that unity is achieved.

Equally open to analysis is Bourdelle's relief, The Dance (fig. 425), on the Théâtre des Champs Elysées in Paris. A double harmony of curves in the fragments of drapery and of angularity in the figures is superposed. In the male figure, a sequence of alternation is apparent in the similar angles in which the various parts of the body are conceived with respect to one another. The shapes flow readily so that the movement of the lower left leg of the man passes on through the right thigh of the woman and *vice versa*. The two figures balance without repeating the shapes. In each part of the drapery, the folds create a pattern-like repetition of lines, varied just enough to prevent monotony.

Lastly, consider the Purification of the Temple (fig. 282), by El Greco. First of all, the artist depicts Christ in the center of a compact knot of figures. That group forms a rectangle the proportions of which are similar to the shape of the whole canvas. Another area of like proportions is found in the portraits of four artists in the lower right corner, a clear example of harmony of shape. In the mother and child to the right of the main characters, and in the men of the extreme background, the general movement tilts to the right. The vertical standing figures limit the principal theme on its right edge, followed by Christ, whose action causes the upper part of His figure to shift to the left. As the traders try to escape His lash, their bodies lean more and more to the left, until they reach the diagonal motive of the woman dealing in doves. El Greco recalls that diagonal in the seated man at the right corner of the group, and again in the infant lying on the steps. Such a sequence toward the diagonal needs something to terminate it; hence the strong vertical of the woman's arm, and of the man behind her.

El Greco accents Christ as the principal figure. His head centers on the opening to the piazza against the front of one of the distant palaces. For dramatic interest, Jesus, though in the center, is distinct from the group. Compact elsewhere, it opens up in V-shaped voids to His right and left, more apparent in the original than in any reproduction because of the color. The latter, too, contributes its share to the compositional unity. Each major tone of red, blue, yellow, or green is echoed again and again through this design.

If one is to speak or think precisely about color, one must realize that the word covers three considerations that together are better called *tone*. The three elements of tone have many names. The first is *color* properly speaking, the redness, blueness, or yellowness of any passage. That tone may vary when modified by other colors; for instance, addition of yellow changes blue to green. One may produce two tones, both pure blue unaffected by any other color, but one a bright blue and one a gray blue. This vividness or dullness of tone is known as *intensity*. Finally, tone may change in lightness or darkness, that is in *value*.

This triple division offers certain opportunities to the artist. The complete range of tone is infinite, but an artist in any particular work can select his palette, limiting himself but achieving thereby possibilities of harmony. Van Gogh may prefer tones of maximum or nearly maximum intensity, and reach harmony by that means. In many of his landscapes, Corot does just the opposite, choosing to employ only low intensities, and further avoiding very high and very low values. The richness of Venetian painting is due in part to its *tonality*; that is, the sense of a general tone dominating the several colors. In this school, a transparent yellowish glaze, spread over the strong local colors, leaves them in the same relation to one another, but pulls them all toward the tone of the glaze. Thus a white dress may seem to be white in relation to a red passage next to it, whereas in actuality if we isolate the 'white' area, we shall find it to be yellow in color. A similar consequence stems from nature in Monet's painting of the mists at Giverny, where all tones are drawn toward the tone of the fog.

In such matters as composition and tone, a contemporary artist finds himself remarkably free. In the past, the creator has by no means controlled what he should do. His client decided on the subject; the Church dictated its arrangement; and often the very pigments were specified in advance. Today, the artist limits himself when he selects the problem, and further through the demands of composition. The medium or material chosen restricts him in two further directions. Every substance at his disposal offers only a certain range of possibilities because of its physical properties — the strength and weight of stone, the lightness and workability of wood, the toughness of metal. Some designs, feasible in bronze, would be impossible in stone. Giovanni da Bologna's Flying Mercury (fig. 250) illustrates this. The small cross section through the wind from the mouth of Aeolus would hardly support the weight of a stone figure. Neither could marble be carved into the flowing wings or attenuated shapes of the caduceus. This is obvious, but critics agree that indefinite limits, narrower than those imposed by the physical properties, exist in any material, and these the sensitive designer will respect.

For example, the range of color, value, and intensity available for fresco painting is more restricted than that at the disposal of a painter in oils. The possibilities of brush work in oils are not identical with those in water color. In sculpture, the choice of stone compels some compactness of conception. The actual limits are however very wide. In his Apollo and Daphne (fig. 275), Bernini shows what technical dexterity can do in manipulation of this substance. But it may also be true here that the sculptor forces stone to produce effects which are not appropriate to it; that by thinking in pictorial terms, he exceeds the proper limits of his medium. The sculpturesque diorite portrait of Khafra (fig. 12) has far more respect for stone. Its design conveys a sense of the weight of material; its compactness confines our attention within the mass of the block, instead of leading our eye out of it, as do the extended arms of the Apollo or the Daphne. A clever imitation of textures by Bernini tries to convince the observer that marble has ceased to be stone; their absence in the Khafra allows full expression to the texture of the stone itself.

Though the effect on design in architecture is no greater than in sculpture or painting, the results are easier to isolate. Wood, a fibrous material strong in proportion to its weight, can be cut into long members for beams or columns. A slender wood post supporting long beams results in a rectangle longer than it is high. Most oriental architecture, like the

Kōdō (fig. 594) at Tōshōdaiji, is founded on wood construction, and therefore is composed of such horizontal rectangles, not only in its proportions, but even in the smaller units of decorative detail. The weight of stone produces a different form. A stone beam as long and thin as the wood members of the Kōdō would break of its own weight and certainly could not support the additional load of a roof or floor upon it. These considerations enforce a short length for stone beams, and frequent supports. Similar factors suggest heavier proportions for stone columns. Therefore, if stone supports must be themselves heavier and more closely spaced, the result must be a vertical rectangle, much taller than it is wide.

The earliest examples of architecture, such as prehistoric Stonehenge (fig. 2), illustrate this stone aesthetic. The design of this ring of monoliths, with short beams of stone spanning the openings, is built on repeated vertical rectangles. Broadly speaking, Western architecture, based in essence on stone construction until recent times, displays this fundamental result. Such styles as the eighteenth-century colonial in America may often be built in wood, but both proportion and architectural vocabulary derive from styles worked out in masonry. In cases like this, details may be adapted to the new material by sympathetic craftsmanship; columns, whose elements correspond to those developed for stone, may be attenuated to a point where they could not be executed in marble.

The bearing of material on design is not only apparent in the broad distinction of wood and stone, but may be narrowed to the different treatments appropriate to oak or mahogany, to granite or marble. The hardness of granite suggests that design in this material should rely on simple proportions with little surface interruption. The Temple of the Sphinx at Gizeh (fig. 5) speaks with solemn grandeur through its prismatic blocks supporting plain beams, devoid of moldings. In a marble building such as the Parthenon in Athens (fig. 49), greater detail is possible because of the comparative ease of cutting marble. The same is true in sculpture. The diorite portrait of Khafra (fig. 12) is highly simplified as compared with the marble figure of Michelangelo's Night (fig. 227) on the Medici Tomb.

The matters discussed so far are inherent in the artistic problem. If the artist lived in a void, only such considerations would be pertinent. Since that cannot be the case, other forces bear on any specific creation. These stem from the time and place in which the work is born. They shape the problem confronting the artist; they also mold his mentality.

Geography, though its effect is often overrated, does have some bearing especially on architecture, in both specific and more general ways. First, the site chosen for a building should help to determine its direction and character. Except for taking advantage of sunlight, a structure on a plain might face in any direction. On the other hand, a sloping plot restricts such freedom. Moreover, a design that suits an open treeless country may be inappropriate for wooded, mountainous terrain.

Second, assuming an architecture to be indigenous, we might expect to find a low pitched roof in southern countries, a high pitched roof in northern. The gentle slope of the roof of the Parthenon (fig. 49) suffices to void any rainfall, but would be less suitable if snow were a serious consideration in Athens. The steep roof of the Parson Capen House in Topsfield, Massachusetts (fig. 331), implies the rigorous New England climate. Architecture in a desert exhibits a flat roof, as in the Indian pueblos of the Southwest or in Egyptian temples (fig. 8). However, so many other considerations exist, such as the type and materials of construction, or the transfer through tradition of an architecture from one region to another, that climate is not a paramount factor.

A third and more important effect of geography, especially in the past with its primitive methods of transportation, is the supply of local materials. Where wood is plentiful, it will be used and so will shape the design. Greece, because of its abundant marble quarries, developed a stone architecture. Mesopotamia, lacking both stone and wood, had perforce to resort to clay, and a style in brick with all its implications came into being. Finally, geography often accounts for the spread of artistic styles from one land to another. Trade routes as well as propinquity bear on the history of art more than is often realized.

Economic conditions are even more influential. A continued period of economic chaos can eliminate the arts. The Hundred Years War in France, which brought to an end the epoch of cathedral building, was, by comparison, artistically barren. The Thirty Years War blighted those parts of Germany touched by it. The centuries of poverty and confusion in Western Europe following the collapse of the Roman Empire nearly extinguished the creative flame. A few insignificant buildings, some manuscripts and ivory carvings, enamels and other small objects are all that remain in the West from this time.

It does not follow that a period of economic prosperity will be great in the arts; merely that some surplus beyond the minimum needs of man is essential for aesthetic activity. Moreover, it is so common as to be almost a rule that cultural expression lags a generation or more behind an economic or political rise — quite naturally, since it may take years to train men to the appropriate expression.

In another sense, economics impinges on art. Methods of production of the requisite materials affect the problem of making some products plentiful and others to be had only with some difficulty. The change from a handicraft to a machine technique in the production of building materials is one of the causes for the course taken by nineteenth- and twentieth-century architecture. Similarly, labor bears on the question; the higher the cost of skilled labor, the less can one afford its products.

Although the form of government in itself may not be important, nevertheless by preserving order a strong state can foster the conditions suited to artistic growth. In minor instances, it may directly affect the arts. For example, taxation based on the number or size of windows may tempt builders to limit themselves in these respects; or, if levied on the number of stories in the wall of a house, may have prompted the development of the Mansard roof, a device to add a story, almost of full height throughout, but within the roof. More important are the possibilities of patronage. The great wealth of the Church in the Middle Ages accounts for the primarily ecclesiastical art expression of that time. Official support and encouragement of the Academy in France since the seventeenth century is responsible for the leadership she has held in the world of art from that time almost to the present. This does not mean that the results achieved by the Academy have been admirable; on the contrary, the progressive work of the nineteenth century was done in protest against the official stand. Still, though its aims were sometimes misdirected, its efforts have been beneficial in contributing a stimulus to the general field.

Even more vital is the broad social structure of an age, since that in the last analysis establishes its problems. The power of imperial Rome created a civilization, and therefore an art, to reflect itself, immense in scale, sumptuous in colored marbles, crass in effect. The aristocratic democracies of Greece nourished refined consideration of philosophical and aesthetic matters, and were bound to develop an expression in art of balance, delicacy, and refinement. The importance of the salon in eighteenth-century France produced a boudoir art, small in scale, playful, lawless, but never crude.

Finally, religion has, in most centuries, taken the lead in artistic development, in part because of the identification of religion and government in many civilizations. Egyptian architecture, as we know it, exists chiefly in the temple and the tomb, and the bulk of sculpture and paintings was produced to adorn these structures or to be contained in them. Most Greek sculpture is also religious in purpose, either votive or associated with temples. The nature of the belief calls for a specific expression toward which the artist must strive. The roots of the contrast between Greek temples and Gothic cathedrals lie in the different conceptions of God held by these two cultures; they required a different character. Most directly of all, the usages of any liturgy write the programs for the artist to follow.

In so far as any period is itself a historical unit, the government, religion, and form of society act to produce a unity of expression. Hence we may speak of a Gothic age, or the epoch of the Renaissance or the Baroque, to indicate thereby the existence of some similarities in contemporary production. But though several of these factors may hold good at any moment in history over large geographical areas, others may not, or may be of differing degrees of significance within smaller regions. Consequently, we have to take into account not only the Gothic or Renaissance styles, but also the dissimilarities of English as contrasted with French Gothic, of Flemish with Italian Baroque. Finally, any individual artist may respond differently to the same conditions of time and place. A Michelangelo and a Raphael do not react to their times in the same way. Both are characteristic of the High Renaissance in Italy, but as personalities their work is distinct. It is because of the interaction of these three components of individual, time, and place upon the artistic problem that the history of art through the centuries is so infinite in variety.

II

The Pre-Classical Arts

OUR Western tradition and its subsequent growth in the history of art begins in Egypt. From the limitless stretches of prehistoric time, a pitifully meager handful of works remain. Some of them, like the cave paintings of Altamira and Font de Gaume, rank high as direct expression through pure line and color, perhaps more accomplished than many products of later cultures. Stonehenge (fig. 2), whose massive blocks were brought from a considerable distance, offers problems for speculation. To effect such an undertaking, to raise these weighty stones into position, postulates more extensive group action than one ordinarily associates with so remote a past. But however remarkable be these remains in themselves, their bearing on the growth of European traditions is negligible. The very existence of the Cro-Magnon paintings was unguessed by later inhabitants of those regions until recent times; nor had Stonehenge and the dolmens of northern France any connection with the birth of architectural traditions in Europe.

HISTORY, as we know it, starts in the eastern Mediterranean area along the valley of the Nile, or possibly that of the Tigris-Euphrates. The balance of evidence gleaned from recent archaeology indi-
EGYPT
cates that Mesopotamian civilization may have begun at least as early as, and perhaps before, the Egyptian. There is not much to choose between these two regions in date, however, and since through large parts of its history Egypt was self-contained, one may consider its development first. To be sure, Egyptian isolation is a comparative term; Egyptian pottery has been found in Crete, and, through trade and war, the Nile valley had some contact with neighboring countries. Still, whereas these relations have an influence on other regions, such as the effect of Egyptian sculpture on early Greek art, little influence from other cultures upon the Egyptian is perceptible.

That civilization should flower early in the Nile valley was inevitable. Herodotus described Egypt as the gift of the river; by simplifying existence in many ways and by complicating it in a few, the Nile stimulated culture as does a hothouse. Primitive methods of agriculture sufficed in a soil whose fertility the river renewed by layers of silt deposited from annual inundations. Irrigation by water wheels or by a device like a well-sweep was essential after the floods had subsided, since rain was unknown and one hot cloudless day followed another. Not only did the Nile irrigate the land and through its floods fertilize it, but the river also provided an avenue for communication and transportation, binding the country together. The cliffs that flank the valley provided stone; if need arose this could be ferried up or down the Nile. Clay, too, was available for less permanent buildings, such as houses, and for unimportant tomb figures. Satisfactory timber was scarce; the palm was not a desirable building material. Although at the outset the Egyptians relied on reeds of the lotus or the papyrus bundled together and matted with clay, when the buildings became monumental the earlier system of construction came to be adapted to stone.

These geographical advantages were balanced by a few difficulties. The floods of the Nile obliterated landmarks and so compelled an early development of surveying to re-establish boundaries. Disputes were bound to arise, however, and a legal system must have been devised to care for them. During Egypt's long history of over three thousand years, four periods of strong government rose and fell, to be separated by centuries of weakness. These periods coincide with the times of artistic activity, presumably because they imposed settled conditions in which the arts could flourish. During the third century before Christ, an Egyptian priest named Manetho listed the rulers of Egypt according to dynasties, thereby providing a convenient chronological system.

The earliest epoch of strong government is often called the Old Kingdom, comprising Dynasties III–VI, which flourished about 3000–2500 B.C. The power of the rulers, whose capital was at Memphis, declined during the VI Dynasty, and Egypt subsided into chaos and artistic inactivity after the brilliant achievements of early sculpture and the building of the pyramids, a condition from which the strong rulers of the Middle Kingdom (2160–1785 B.C.) of the XI and XII Dynasties rescued her. Then the feudal system set up by these kings at Thebes in turn decayed into weakness. The warlike Pharaohs of the XVIII Dynasty established the Empire or New Kingdom, as it is sometimes called (1580–1100 B.C.). It grew in power through the XIX Dynasty, pushing its conquests into

Nubia in the south and into Mesopotamia or the Fertile Crescent to the northeast; these were the Pharaohs who accomplished the bondage of Israel. Though still fairly strong, the XX Dynasty lacked the energy of its predecessors; its wars were defensive, and it was followed by another time of weakness and foreign domination when the Assyrian warrior kings captured the land. Finally, the XXVI Dynasty formed the Saite period (663–525 B.C.), named from its capital at Sais in the Nile delta, whose rulers drove out the Semitic invaders and returned to purely Egyptian forms of expression. Still later, Egypt was ruled in turn by the Greek Ptolemies and by Rome, but in these later centuries, the fact that Egyptian art clings to its native character as that of no other country has ever done to the same extent, demonstrates the force of tradition in the Nile valley.

On close inspection Egyptian art shows slight differences in each of these eras of history; the sculpture of the Old Kingdom, for example, is realistic by comparison with the conventionality of the Middle Kingdom, or with the elegant or colossal works of the Empire, but such sweeping generalizations, however sound, admit of many exceptions. A broader view shows not divergence but uniformity. The art of no other country, even over shorter stretches of time, displays such adherence to established forms.

This continuity was a consequence of Egyptian social and religious customs. The Pharaoh was the head of the state both in religion and politics. As priest and prince, from being the representative of the god on earth, he was soon to be himself deified, at first after death, and later even while alive. The very name Pharaoh, meaning 'great house,' indicated his sanctity by so oblique a reference to his sacred person. It did not follow that the Pharaoh was free; the priesthood, of which he was the figurehead, controlled him. They and the nobility were unwilling to jeopardize their position by allowing change of any kind. Early in their civilization, the Egyptians developed an expression in art so satisfactory to them that, from their point of view, any change could not but be for the worse. It is significant that the one period in Egyptian art of experimentation and comparative freedom occurred during the reign of Ikhnaton in the XVIII Dynasty, when the ruler turned from polytheism to monotheism — a departure from tradition that was defeated by the priesthood.

The most important aspect of Egyptian religion in its bearing on art was the nature of the belief in the after life. Four components were present in every human being: the *ka* or double, a dematerialized replica of the body, analogous to our conception of a ghost; the *ba*, which approximates the soul in Christianity; the *khû*, or spark of divine fire; and the body. All four of these had to be preserved for the individual to attain immortality. The *ba* and *khû*, as spiritual elements, could be sustained by prayers and did not profoundly affect art. Preservation of the body, however, involved mummification and, what is still more important, protection of the mummy from damage. Hence, the Egyptians defended their tombs from desecration. This was even more essential, since the *ka* lived in the tomb. As the *ka* was identical with the deceased, save in its lack of substance, the tomb was conceived as a house for the dead, equipped to support life after death and to make it enjoyable. Foreseeing the possibility of damage to or disintegration of the mummy, the Egyptians placed one or more effigies of its owner within the tomb. As substitutes that the *ka* might inhabit in case the body were destroyed, these portrait statues were likely to be made in hard materials. Granite might be expected to outlast wood or limestone, and was preferable in that respect, though the difficulty of working granite restricted its use, and its hardness militated against realism in portraiture.

If the *ka* could exist in the mummy, or in the portrait statues, and live in the tomb, it must be fed. The offerings of pious descendants supplied this want, but within a few generations this duty might be neglected. Since the *ka* was itself immaterial, its food and drink could be carved or painted on the walls. From this, it was but a step to represent food in preparation, its production, and eventually all the activities of life. Thus the tomb came to be a picture book of Egyptian life in all its variety.

The characteristic tomb of the nobility in the Old Kingdom is the mastaba (fig. 3), to be found in numbers clustered around the pyramids at Gizeh, the necropolis of ancient Memphis. This simple rectangular mass is *oriented*; that is, laid out according to compass directions. Its sides face north, south, east, and west. The outer walls are not vertical, but slope inward in the form called a *batter*. Such a battered wall is more stable than a vertical one, and was adopted no doubt because of the greater permanence ensured thereby. From the top of the mastaba, a shaft descends through its mass into the rock below, leading to the burial chamber where the sarcophagus is placed. This shaft, which at times is more than a hundred feet deep, is filled with rubble after the coffin receives its mummy and the opening is sealed to disguise it as part of the roof. Little of value is interred with the body, but a second chamber, called the *serdab*, also is embedded in the mass without communication from the outside. Though often undecorated, this room contains the portrait of the owner, as well as the treasure and utensils to sustain the *ka* in his ethereal existence.

The only opening in the outer walls of the mastaba leads to the chapel in which the living could place offerings for the dead. On one wall of the chapel is cut a false door, often carved with a relief of the owner coming through it to welcome his descendants. Perhaps above or to one side of this door, the owner may be seen again, this time at table, partaking of the offering made to him. Scenes in paint or low relief cover the other walls of the chapel, and show the activities of the owner, and his wife, his children, his servants, his ox, and his ass, and everything that is his. Through these decorations, the *ka* could enjoy in death what he had possessed in life.

The far more imposing pyramids are royal tombs. Whatever their origin, whether in a mound of stones or in a superposition of mastabas, they are the outstanding monuments of the Old Kingdom. The largest, those at Gizeh (fig. 4), are the sepulchers of the IV Dynasty Pharaohs. The pyramids are more precisely oriented than the mastabas. Since the structure is intended to be closed, the funerary chapel has to be separate and thus develops an independent existence; it contains the serdab. One of several openings in the center of the mass is the burial chamber. A series of passages too complex to be described in detail leads to these rooms. After the burial, blocks of stone are slid into the passages leading to the burial chamber from the outside world, and the only opening concealed with the utmost care. In spite of these precautions, entrance to the pyramids had been forced even in antiquity.

The bulk of these great piles is composed of colossal blocks of stone, cut with metal tools, and heaped step upon step to the apex. In proportion of width at the base to height, they are almost precisely 11 to 7, which suggests that these numbers had special significance even at that time. To accomplish so huge an undertaking — the base of the Great Pyramid of Khûfû is about 750 feet square — presupposes an army of slaves acting under the king's foreman. It has been calculated that ten thousand men must have worked for twenty years to achieve this result. To support, administer, and direct such an army of laborers argues organizing ability of a high order.

These pyramids have always captured the imagination. Although today we see them composed of flights of colossal steps, those were not visible in antiquity. A smooth coating of limestone sheathed the whole mass, each face of which presented one unbroken plane to the observer.

This strict adherence to geometric form appeals to man's sense of organization, just as does a crystal ball; nothing interrupts or detracts from
the unity. But equal completeness may be observed in a small model,
capable of resting on the hand, without stimulating the observer to awe.
Surely it is the size of this simple form that makes it imposing. We
measure ourselves against it and feel overwhelmed by our insignificance. To a lesser degree the Perisphere at the New York World's Fair
of 1939 gained distinction from the same source — reliance on geometric
form, infinitely enlarged.

The shape of the pyramid is also appropriate to its purpose. Except
perhaps for the cone, a pyramid is the most stable of geometric forms,
more so than a rectangular prism of similar height and width. Its immobility of mass is the essence of permanence; it comes as near to eternity
as any man-made object can. Not without reason have the pyramids
come to be associated in the popular mind with changelessness.

The cost of the pyramids in labor forbade their being undertaken by
any but powerful monarchs, at least on so imposing a scale. The Middle
Kingdom abandoned the form, in favor of tombs cut into the rock of
the cliffs along the Nile valley. The best preserved are at Beni Hasan.
Here the chapel is preceded by a small colonnaded portico as an entrance.
These columns, like those within, are not constructed, but allowed to remain when the surrounding rock is cut away. The functions of the serdab
seem to have been combined with those of the chapel, forming a niche
or sanctuary in it. A shaft to the burial chamber might be cut through
the chapel floor, or into the cliff from in front of the portico.

By the Empire period, it had become obvious that no strength of
blocked passages within a tomb would avail to exclude thieves. The
visibility of the tomb itself, by its admission of treasure concealed
within, was a challenge not overlooked by robbers of Egyptian days
despite severe laws against desecration. Yielding to necessity, the Pharaohs of the Empire period, who dug their tombs in the Valley of the
Kings near Thebes, sacrificed the advertisement of a visible tomb to
security. They chose to drive a shaft into the foot of the cliffs. The
existence of the tomb itself, when occupied, they concealed by broken
stone, such as might have fallen from the cliffs. The effectiveness of
this step is testified by the fact that the last of these tombs, that of
Tutankhamen, remained intact until the twentieth century of our era,
defying searchers for more than three thousand years. The corridor-
like shaft, sometimes more than four hundred feet long, led to one or
more decorated chambers, furnished with models of all that the soul

could desire. Although these deep rock-cut tombs add another step in the development of sepulchral design, and although the treasures of Egyptian art preserved in them are invaluable, as architecture they are negligible. To elaborate an architectural setting not to be seen by a living eye would be absurd, at least to the modern mind. By this time, the chapel, placed near the river, was removed from the tomb, with no connection to it.

However much they tell of Egyptian life through their decoration, the tombs as architecture do not compare with the Egyptian temples. One of the earliest preserved is the IV Dynasty Temple of the Sphinx at Gizeh (fig. 5), connected with the pyramid of Khafra by a covered causeway. Exceptional in plan and in severity of design, its granite monoliths support unadorned granite beams, impressive through the austerity of their geometric form and their reliance on beauty of material. Moreover, in order to light the interior, the roof section is raised above the side aisles, to give space for small windows, which send shafts of light within to play around the square piers. In this design, we may recognize the first known example of the clearstory, an architectural device that reaches its apogee thousands of years later in the Christian church.

The Temple of Khonsû at Karnak (fig. 6), from the Empire period, on the other hand, illustrates the normal features of the Egyptian temple. An avenue lined with sphinxes announces the axis along which the principal elements follow in sequence. The first part of the temple proper is the *pylon*, a monumental gateway composed of two tall masses of masonry flanking the door. The Pharaoh who finished the building placed his obelisks and statues to either side in front of the pylon, which was further enlivened by flagpoles set in narrow grooves. Behind the pylon is the *peristyle*, an open court bounded by colonnades on three sides. This leads to the *hypostyle hall*, where files of columns support a roof. The last principal component of the plan, the *sanctuary*, lies behind the hall.

Sequence of composition is illustrated in these four elements, pylon, peristyle, hypostyle, and sanctuary. As we see in the cross section, the top or roof of each part becomes lower from the entrance to the sanctuary. In answering movement, the hypostyle floor is a few steps above that of the peristyle, the sanctuary a step above the hypostyle. The height of each unit, therefore, lessens as one proceeds. Moreover, though the open peristyle is brilliantly lighted, the hypostyle hall gets its light only through the doors leading from the peristyle, and is dark in consequence, while the sanctuary, lighted only from the hypostyle, is still darker. This progressive darkening must have enhanced the mystery associated with the abode of the god. The mystery was further increased by the fact that the laity had access only to the peristyle and hypostyle, whereas the sanctuary was reserved for the consecrated attendants of the god, the priestly class, and of course the Pharaoh as head of the state religion; thus the ceremonial was but dimly perceived by the people.

The Egyptian temple was always adorned with sculpture and painting, perhaps too richly, since every surface was so covered as to lose the value of contrast. For example, the Temple of Horus at Edfû (fig. 7) of Ptolemaic times shows the battered walls of the pylon covered with low relief sculpture. This depicts the prowess of the king capturing and slaying his enemies. The royal person is drawn at larger scale than the others to emphasize his superiority. Similar scenes may line the walls of the peristyle in Egyptian temples, but in the hypostyle hall the action is less violent. This chamber is conceived as a microcosm of the world; around the lower walls and at the bottom of the columns luxuriant plants flourish in low relief, birds flutter above them, and gold stars sparkle on a blue ceiling. Prayers in hieroglyphics and representations of ceremonial enrich the sanctuary and the rooms around it, whose precise purpose is unknown, but which Egyptologists believe were designed to house the equipment and treasure of the temple.

The desire for permanence revealed in the pyramids is once more illustrated in the temple by the battered walls of the pylon, as though to emphasize stability, as does the same device in the mastaba. Pier and lintel construction is almost universal, because of its stability and simplicity, though the arch is known and occasionally employed in utilitarian structures. In this rainless climate, the simplest of all coverings, the flat roof, is inevitable. Where the hypostyle is too large to be even dimly lighted from the peristyle, the central part of the roof is elevated, as in the great Temple of Amon Ra at Karnak (fig. 8) in the XIX Dynasty, an enlargement of the clearstory first adopted during the Old Kingdom in the Temple of the Sphinx. Interruption of the wall surface by moldings is rare, but a plain *cornice*, curving outward at the top, terminates the wall and is indeed standard in Egyptian architecture.

Most column forms derive from plants. The top of the column, called the *capital*, in the type used for the larger columns at Karnak, flares outward like an inverted bell decorated with petals and sepals resembling the open flower of the lotus, which grows in profusion along the banks of the Nile. On the smaller lateral columns of the hypostyle, the bud capital appears, so named from its correspondence to the closed bud of the lotus or papyrus. More rarely, and in much later times under Greek influence, the Egyptians adopted a capital with carved leaves complicating the surface of the bell-shaped form. Close inspection of the shafts of the columns at Karnak shows them to be constricted at the base, like the stems of certain flowers just above the root. That source is betrayed by painted leaves growing up around the base. In many instances elsewhere, including some of the earliest, the shaft is not a plain cylinder, but a bundle of reed-like shapes bound together just below the capital by horizontal withes. Such forms reflect primitive construction in which papyrus or lotus reeds were tied together, possibly around a clay core, or perhaps strong enough in themselves to support light loads. These materials are not durable, but when stone came to be employed, architects retained the familiar shapes. Through simplification, those forms were adapted to the new material, but with only partial success, and these columns never attained the directness or expressiveness of columns thought out in terms of stone.

Moreover, the several types of Egyptian capitals are never wholly satisfactory in either structure or design. The aesthetic purpose of a capital is to afford a transition for the eye from the vertical shaft to the horizontal beam above. The bell-shaped capital itself does this well, but here the presence of a tall square block above it interrupts and destroys this transition. On the other hand, in the bud capital, no attempt at all is made to perform this function; on the contrary, by its constricting lines, it accentuates the change from vertical to horizontal, so that the beam appears to be impaled on the shaft. Structurally, the purpose of the capital is to provide a larger surface to support the ends of beams than that afforded by the top of the shaft. Here again the bud capital, whose bearing surface may be smaller in diameter than the shaft, fails, and although the bell capital and the similar palm-leaf type may seem to be satisfactory, their thin rims are too fragile to give even the appearance of adequate support. Thus neither the bell nor the bud types, the commonest forms of Egyptian capital, can be judged successful, though the bell shape is the better of the two.

Temples composed of such walls, roofs, and columns as these constitute the bulk of Egyptian architecture. In the hemi-speos temple, illustrated by the Mortuary Temple of Queen Hatshepsût of the XVIII Dynasty at Deir-el-Baharî (fig. 9), the sanctuary and hypostyle are entombed in the rock, but the open courts, corresponding to the peristyles in constructed temples, rise one above another as terraces. Here we may see employed the sixteen-sided shaft. This form is a more direct solution of the problem of support than the common types of Egyptian column. It was developed by cutting off the corners of square piers, such as those in the Temple of the Sphinx, and then again cutting the corners. The repeated vertical lines so produced dramatize the idea of support, of upward or downward movement in the column; and the simplicity of the courts surrounded by such shafts commands a respect that is hardly attained in the sumptuous architecture of the usual temple.

In the speos temples, such as that of Rameses II of the XIX Dynasty at Abû Simbel (fig. 10), not only the sanctuary and hypostyle but also the peristyle are cut out of the living rock. The arrangement and the architectural vocabulary are not substantially different from those already discussed. In this instance, carved figures of Osiris, god of the underworld, stand before and in part supplant the columns, but this somewhat exceptional motive is known in normal temples. Externally, the only visible unit is the pylon, with its gigantic guardian statues, cut from the face of the cliff.

The human craving for permanence, more pronounced in Egypt than elsewhere, is confined to her religious architecture. The immortality of the gods dictated this need in their homes, while a belief in the after life, immeasurably longer than man's sojourn on earth, called for a similar timelessness in the tomb. Houses for the living, even the royal palace, need be no more than temporary. Mud brick, not stone, sufficed for them, and as a consequence they have vanished, though the type and method of construction have affected Egyptian building.

At its best, the scale of Egyptian architecture and its instinct for geometric mass endow it with an imposing but austere character, as in the pyramids, even if it lacks the clarity, delicacy, and sophistication of the Greek, or the complex organization of the Roman. Though some of its forms, like the clustered column and the bud capital, derive from plants, the forms themselves are with some success adapted to the stone medium, while other units, such as the pylons, are conceived in stone, with a monumentality rarely equaled and never surpassed by later civilizations. In the smaller temples, organization dominates the ordered sequence of one element after another. However, in some of Egypt's greatest buildings, the Pharaohs sacrificed unity to their desire to outstrip their predecessors in size, by adding to a plan already complete in itself, other hypostyle halls, other peristyles, and especially other pylons, thereby destroying its unity. The largest temples, those of Karnak and

Luxor, are the worst offenders; in consequence, they seem to sprawl. Finally, the inordinate love of decoration defeats one of its important functions: if decoration be for accent, too much of it results in equal emphasis everywhere, leaving an accent nowhere.

Naturally the same religious factors mold Egyptian sculpture that play so large a part in shaping the architecture. It is customary to speak of Egyptian sculpture of the Old Kingdom as realistic, or of the Middle Kingdom as conventional, but one must realize at the outset that these are relative terms. If by realism we understand an attempt to reproduce nature, and by conventionalism a willingness to accept certain shapes as symbolical or typical of natural forms, then we must admit that the most realistic Egyptian statue is conventional when compared with a Roman portrait (fig. 71). Moreover, statues of Pharaohs are usually idealized; that is, their individuality is minimized and their features carved in general terms to suggest their power and immortality.

Certain traits persist from dynasty to dynasty. The desire for permanence dictates the choice of materials and the dimensions of the sculpture. The love of size, apparent in the pyramids, is obvious in the Sphinx (fig. 4). This monster's head, with an ear larger than a man, is an idealized portrait of the Pharaoh Khafra of the IV Dynasty, with whose pyramid the Sphinx is connected. Or again, in the colossi of Rameses II at Abû Simbel (fig. 10) from the Empire period, about 65 feet high, the effectiveness results from their enormous scale. Size in itself may not ensure permanence but at least it suggests it. The selection of obdurate materials, however, is a more effective way of assuring durability. Though such soft media as limestone and sandstone, and even wood, are employed, the harder stones like granite, basalt, and diorite are common in Egyptian sculpture, in spite of the difficulties involved in working them.

The use of an effigy as a substitute for the body, in case it should be destroyed, created a demand for portraits. This required a moderate realism, most pronounced in the Old Kingdom, where it appears especially in the heads. However, such realism is apt to be present in inverse ratio to the social position of the subject. The Seated Scribe (fig. 11) from the Old Kingdom, now in the Louvre, betrays his sedentary occupation by the rolls of flesh on his torso. In naive fashion, his toes appear to have sunk into the limestone block so that only three are visible. But in the head, the artist displays his power of observation. He well renders the bony structure of the skull; the eyes and mouth reveal the scribe's close attention to the dictation of his master. As on most Egyptian statues, the male flesh is painted red, but the inlaid eyes are colored white with a black pupil and iris, to enhance the effect of life.

The Seated Scribe belongs to the servant class. On the other hand, Ranefer (fig. 13) in the V Dynasty represents the dominant priesthood. His pose, the commonest in Egyptian sculpture, shows him walking, the right foot forward, the weight evenly distributed between the feet, the axis of the body erect. While some concern for the details of nature is manifest in the articulated toes and knees, and in a few indications of the torso, nevertheless, the treatment of the sharp shin, narrow hips, broad shoulders, and the absence of much anatomical detail prove that for such a person a generalized representation was preferred. By this stately pose, and above all by the head, the artist has portrayed a person independent and accustomed to command. Ranefer at once depicts an individual and the class to which he belongs. We must regard some of the conventions as expressions of the material. For instance, the original size of the block of stone from which the figure was hewn is preserved in the base and in the slab at his back, which adds strength to the statue. The body follows the original limits of this block; the shoulders extend as far as they may, the arms hang vertical, and therefore the hips are small to permit room for the arms within the prism of stone.

If the statues of the lower classes are carved with moderate realism, those of the Pharaohs, because of their semi-divine character, are idealized, with a regularity of feature and absence of individuality as though to create an ideal and perhaps imaginary personage. Such a result is reached even at colossal size in the Sphinx at Gizeh; it is more striking in the diorite Khafra (fig. 12). This masterpiece of the Old Kingdom is outstanding for its related masses, for its sculpturesque repose, its feeling for the material, and its detail selected with an eye to expressive and decorative value, rather than to its representative function, though that also is served to some extent. The simplified forms may be due in part to the obdurate material, but it seems probable that the idealization is an attribute of the royal sitter, and therefore deliberate.

In spite of occasional masterpieces, such as the seated Khafra or the Ranefer, and in spite of the simplification and feeling for the material, any considerable number of Egyptian figures in the round, when seen together, appear monotonous. This uniformity is the more obvious because of the limited number of types the sculptor was allowed to develop. The most common is the standing or walking type with one foot forward. The figure may also sit on a block, or cross-legged on the floor, or more rarely kneel on both knees. Beyond these possibilities the sculptor seldom experimented. This repetition of pose is the more pronounced since all these attitudes respect the law of frontality: that is, a rigid verticality of the body which allows no deviation of its axis from side to side, no bending of the body, and but little animation. These types, established early in Egyptian history, are retained to the end through the force of convention. But tradition enforced a uniformity in Egypt even beyond the poses. A comparison of the Ranefer (fig. 13) and the colossi of Rameses II (fig. 10) is illuminating here. There is, to be sure, convention in both, but in the former the narrow hips, sharp shins, and simplified forms may be deliberate, so largely do they enhance the design. In the latter, the legs and arms, the puffy cheeks, the pharaonic headdress seem perfunctory. Absorbed by the scale at which he is working, the sculptor is content with these conventions because by the XIX Dynasty they have become molded by a weight of tradition that was seldom raised.

Although tradition plays a large role in sculpture in the round, it is even more obvious in sculpture in relief or in painting, two modes of expression that in Egypt are basically one, since the relief is almost flat and was regularly painted. Indeed, painting was a handmaid to relief sculpture, or a cheap substitute for it. Three methods were in common use. The first, low or bas-relief proper, consists of figures carved with a slight projection from the background. In sunk relief also, the figures are modeled but the surrounding background is not cut away to allow them to project; consequently, each object is embedded behind the surfaces around it. The third and cheapest method, scratch relief, engraves the outline of its figures but makes no attempt to model them within the limits of that outline.

The exquisite bas-relief of Seti I Offering to Osiris (fig. 14), from the XIX Dynasty, in his mortuary temple at Abydos, shows the same subtlety of detail as does the figure of Khafra. No amount of convention can destroy the delicacy of the planes that indicate the light garment worn by the Pharaoh, the bodily forms seen through it, or the elegance resulting from these refinements. Such a relief bespeaks a sculptor of real sophistication, sensitive to the decorative possibilities of line and of subtle changes of surface.

It is with such reliefs as this that the temple walls were adorned, not to mention the walls of the chapels in tombs. As we have seen, these reliefs were practical in purpose, to record and glorify the exploits of the kings, to depict religious practices, or to perpetuate by representa-

tion human activities necessary to the life hereafter. As such, they become pictographs whose legibility is of cardinal importance. Their over-
abundance as decoration is due to this purpose: the more recorded, the
better. The apparent Egyptian fear of blank walls is to be explained by
a desire to tell as much as possible; they may add hieroglyphics to
whatever spaces are not filled by figures or other represented objects.
To this need for exposition, aesthetic considerations must of necessity
be subordinated.

Many of the conventions of Egyptian reliefs are also traceable to this
cause. The peculiar angularity of the figures results from each part being drawn in its most easily recognizable shape, its most characteristic
attitude. So, in the painting of the XVIII Dynasty Tomb of Nakht at
Thebes (fig. 15), the feet are drawn in profile, regardless of the pose
of the figure. To draw a shape that will be immediately recognized as a
foot is easier in profile than when seen from in front, a point of view
from which the foot would have to be foreshortened or rendered in perspective. The profile view is maintained from the feet through the hips,
but at the waist the body half turns so that the shoulders are represented
facing front, again because they are readily identified in that position.
For the same reason, the head is in profile, but the eye in full front.
Thus, the figure consists of an alternation of the facing and profile positions, each designed to be legible, even if the result seems incongruous
to eyes conditioned by realistic painting.

Such figures, and indeed all objects in the scene, are painted in a few
standard tones, laid on in flat washes; that is, within an outline, no
change of color or value occurs. We must not expect shadows in Egyptian painting, except in so far as they are created by the slight changes
of surface in the sculpture to which the paint is applied, a very minor
exception in view of the flatness of the relief. The available palette was
simple, too. A brick-red tone distinguishes the flesh of men; ochre-yellow
of women. Hair and the pupil and iris of the eye are black, though the
ball of the eye is white. These tones, with green, blue, and a few others,
may depict details of necklaces or the varied tones of such natural phenomena as birds, animals, trees, and water. It is a primitive method,
naive, but clear through its conventions.

Certain other arbitrary devices must also be described. An obvious
way of emphasizing one figure in a group is to enlarge that figure. Here
Nakht and his wife are several times as large as their servants. Often,
indeed, the husband is drawn at a bigger scale than his wife; for example, the queen of Rameses II at Abû Simbel (fig. 10) stands between his

legs. Of course, the smaller size of subordinates permits a greater number of them within any area. Rather than break up the wall into separate scenes, the Egyptian artist treats his minor figures in bands, allowing one incident to carry over into the next with nothing like a frame to separate them. A further result of the small size of minor characters is that several bands of them are possible, one above another. A modern painter, by applying perspective, may arrange one action behind another with the plane of the ground receding into the distance. The Egyptian painter, without perspective, draws a single line to represent the ground, scatters his figures along it, and then repeats another ground line above their heads.

The absence of perspective has several other consequences. If a number of persons are engaged in the same action, or if more than one identical object is to be recorded, instead of representing each one behind another, the artist draws one of them in the required action, and then repeats the front half of his outline as often as may be necessary. This serves well for things that stand on the ground, but what of things that parallel the plane of the ground? Two solutions are possible. A lake or a river may be painted in cross section with fish swimming in the blue water. Or it may be represented as though seen from above — fundamentally the same profile full-front device used in figures. Thus, we see a lake as though from the air, but the trees on its banks and even the figures within the pond are drawn from the side. Finally, in the details of nature, the artist reduces many things to patterns: the lotus or papyrus stems in a marsh, the zigzag lines on a blue background to indicate water, and so on.

The bulk of Egyptian decoration consists of these formulae, established early and followed by generation after generation of artists. Rigid though they are, a wide variety of action can be indicated within them. Indeed they form a script less limited in its possibilities of expression than many languages. Moreover, this conventionality was imposed on the artist by his patrons; it is unreasonable to suppose that he adhered to it through inability to observe nature. Convention is more pronounced in the human figure than in other objects, where we may suppose conservatism was less necessary to preserve the *status quo*. Even in the figure, there are some departures from the norm. Semitic captives are distinguished from Egyptians not only by their costumes, but by their bearded faces and prominent noses; Nubians, by their color and their negroid features. Rarely the profile full-front tradition is abandoned; for example, a painting of dancing girls and the musicians who play for them is a clear attempt at naturalism, created during the reign of Ikhnaton, when the power of priestly conservatism was momentarily broken.

A genuine love of nature impels the painter to observe and record some of her minutiae. If papyrus in a swamp tends to become a pattern, its details are precise. The famous Geese from Medum, a masterpiece dating from the Old Kingdom, repeats the colors and outlines of those fowls with great fidelity; the shrike and other birds on the walls of the tomb of Khnumhotep at Beni Hasan, from the Middle Kingdom, are no mere symbols; they are readily identifiable. In part, this naturalism may be attributed to the artist's desire to make them recognizable for what they are, but in any case he has not reduced them to a formula.

Egyptian reliefs and paintings as a whole, despite their conventions, are more interesting than the sculpture in the round, for the same reason that the figurines once buried in the tombs but now displayed in museums arouse the curiosity of visitors. They provide a panorama of a rich and varied culture, and bring us close to the very existence of the past. Such an interest may not be aesthetic, but it is none the less legitimate. Like the more imposing sculpture in the round, an occasional relief, such as the Seti I (fig. 14), is beautiful in its mastery of technique, its subtle drawing and design, quite aside from its legibility and its subject interest. But the bulk of this work is of primary value in the history of culture, and only secondarily as art.

LIKE the Egyptian civilization, that of Mesopotamia began in the fourth millennium before Christ. Born in the .Tigris-Euphrates valley, it spread through the whole of the Fertile Crescent, which bounds the deserts of Arabia on the north and west. By 3000 B.C., the non-Semitic Sumerian tribes were already settled in city kingdoms, and had begun to make the contributions of this region to civilization. These kingdoms struggled with each other for survival, and also with the Semitic Akkadians, who conquered them about 2750 B.C., but through the rest of the millennium the balance of power in Babylonia shifted back and forth between Semitic and non-Semitic tribes. During the second millennium, the Semitic Assyrians were slowly rising to power and laying the foundations for their empire, which flourished under strong rulers from the ninth to the seventh centuries. Finally, at the end of the seventh century, the Assyrian capital at Nineveh was utterly destroyed by the Chaldeans from Babylonia, who were themselves in the next century to fall before the might of Persia.

MESOPOTAMIA

Whereas Egyptian architecture at its outset was hampered by a lack of timber suitable for building, the lower part of the Tigris-Euphrates valley provided neither wood nor stone. These materials had to be brought from a distance; on the other hand, clay pits abounded. Consequently an architecture in brick developed, with a different character from the stone architecture of Egypt. The relative absence of stone hampered sculpture even more, since although clay is easily modeled, its products are neither monumental nor durable. Thus, the corpus of Mesopotamian art is limited compared to that of Egypt.

Like the Egyptians, the Sumerians believed in a life after death, but in their religion the after life was not dependent on the preservation of the body, or on the sustenance of the spirit by physical objects or representations of them. Since the religious motive, which in Egypt had demanded an illustration of existence, was absent, we find no such total record of life here as we did in the Nile valley. In its place, the artists celebrate the king and his exploits in hunting and warfare; the more so since most of the sculpture preserved to us appears to have been executed at the royal command. Divinities are represented either as protectors of the king or worshiped by him. However, it may be fair to say that the contributions Mesopotamia has made to world civilization are less important in the arts than in other fields. In the history of religion, the Near East gave birth to three of the great faiths of the world— Christianity, Judaism, and Mohammedanism. Our system of chronology and the source of astronomy are traceable to Mesopotamia; its cuneiform writing, by means of wedge-shaped marks, evolved into an alphabet that served as the origin of all Western written languages.

One result of the difference of religion from that of Egypt is that the tomb ceases to be an architectural problem. In its place is the palace; and, of course, the temple, or at least the temple tower, is prominent. The latter, present as one element of the Palace of Sargon at Khorsabad (fig. 16), built during the eighth century B.C., in mass is like the Egyptian pyramid. Here it was only part of the palace chapel, but in large independent examples, the temple consisted of six or seven huge stages, whose vertical faces were laced by ramps that gave access to the shrine of the god on the top. This tower, called a *ziggurat*, was exactly oriented with its angles facing the cardinal points of the compass. Built of a mass of unbaked brick, perhaps faced with glazed brick, each section was colored, the tones increasing in brilliance as they approached the summit. Herodotus describes the city walls at Agbatana, which was inspired by the Mesopotamian culture, as having the battlements colored white, black, scarlet, blue, orange, silver, and gold in that order, a sequence of tones arising to a climax of brilliance.

Because of their material, these ziggurats have disintegrated into mounds of clay, but they must have had a garish audacity in antiquity. However, it seems doubtful that they could ever have rivaled the pyramids in grandeur. For one thing, the material lacks the implication of permanence that stone gives us; for another, the stepped form has not the austerity of the Egyptian geometric monuments.

The palaces of the Assyrian kings were semi-military rather than purely domestic in purpose. The huge platform, which at Khorsabad served as a bastion in the city fortifications, raised the palace 60 feet above the level of the city (fig. 16). The immense task involved in building this mass of brick, 1140 by 1050 feet in dimensions, staggers the imagination, and could only have been accomplished by slave labor, the unwilling service of war captives. To void any moisture that might find its way into this pile, it was honeycombed with drains. These were arched to carry the weight above them. In the absence of other materials, brick was also employed for the single-story palace. Probably the roof was used as a terrace in the cool of the evening, as it certainly was in Palestine at the other end of the Fertile Crescent. Several Biblical incidents refer to this use of the roof, such as the story of David and Bathsheba.

The plan of the Palace of Sargon at Khorsabad (fig. 17) consists of several courts surrounded by long and narrow rooms. One large court formed the nucleus of the service quarters; another, the men's portion, accommodated the king and his retainers; and a third corresponded to the harem. The presence of a ziggurat indicates that a temple was incorporated in the palace complex, like the chapels of medieval fortresses. The multiplicity of chambers and courts offered opportunities in design, which were only partly seized. In so far as the courts expressed the purposes of the palace, we may characterize the design as functional. It is less successful in the lack of relation between the parts, and the seemingly indiscriminate location of the rooms around the courts. The units of the Egyptian temple were related to one another; the rooms here are not. However, before we condemn these builders, let us remember two things. With their knowledge of the purposes of these parts, they may have had more reason for this apparent disorder than we can guess. Secondly, the problem they were facing was more complex than that offered in the Egyptian, or for that matter the Greek, temple.

The awkward shape of the rooms results from the material and the system of construction it imposed. Sunbaked brick is not strong; it does not lend itself to a columnar system, like that of the Egyptians, although remains show that columns were employed in rare cases. Instead, it suggests thick walls with as few openings as possible: precisely what we see in this plan. Still more important, since a brick is too small to serve as a beam, and since the region provided no adequate timber nearer than the cedars of Lebanon, the Mesopotamian builders were compelled to develop the arch and vault as a means of covering space. The drains in the platform show that several forms of vault were known. It seems certain that the long rooms were so planned partly to facilitate covering them with semicylindrical, or barrel, vaults. No doubt some, if not all, of the square chambers were domed. These vaults might have been visible externally, but the evidence indicates that the roof above them was generally level, with a solid filling of brick or clay between the vaults. The weight of this form of roofing provided a further reason for the solid walls.

The description of such a palace sounds forbidding, but textile hangings and carpets, sumptuous in color, mitigated its severity on the interior. That part of the world has always been famous for its rugs. Indeed, the slab that paved the entrance to the Palace of Sennacherib at Kouyunjik was carved with a pattern derived from rugs, but transmuted into stone because of the wear to be expected in this location. Also brick, glazed and painted with patterns or figure or animal designs, gave accent to doorways and other important features. But the most interesting decoration was by sculpture. Monsters carved in stone guarded the portals, while friezes or bands of sculpture in low relief adorned the interiors and recounted the prowess of the monarch in arms or in the hunt.

As in Egypt, though to a different extent, the early sculpture in Mesopotamia assumed a degree of realism absent in later work. The fragmentary figures from Tellô, carved in the twenty-fourth century B.C., especially that of Gudea, Patesi of Lagash (fig. 18), are the best known. Whether standing or seated with the hands folded in deference, these statues adhere to the law of frontality as do the Egyptian. One consideration, not present in Egypt, hampered any tendency the sculptor may have had toward anatomical realism: Egyptian men were clad only in a loin cloth; both sexes in Babylonia and Assyria encased their bodies in robes of heavy stuffs. The cylindrical mass produced by these garments adds to the sense of weight and of simplified form to produce a sculpturesque result. Nevertheless, the garment blocks the sculptor's opportunity to study the human form. That these artists were capable of observation and considered some accuracy of anatomy worthy of attainment appears in those parts of the body that escape from the clothing. The feet, for instance, emphasize the joints of the toes, the toenails, and the sinews of the foot. The fleshy arms are by no means conventional, and the bony structure of the head is clearly perceived. The tendency to indicate detail in terms of pattern, common to the early stages of art in so many countries, accounts for several of the conventions. The heavy eyebrows, a racial trait, form a herringbone pattern of lines engraved in the stone; the hair is reduced to a formula; and fringes of drapery open the door to like abstractions. None the less, the squat proportions, large heads, and simplification endow the best of these statues with a sculptural feeling that almost rivals the best of Egyptian work.

In later Assyrian times, examples of sculpture in the round are even less common. The ninth-century Ashur-nasir-pal in the British Museum demonstrates that the incipient realism of the Gudea had not borne fruit. Cut from a thin slab of stone, the linear conventions are more pronounced than heretofore. A formal beard is arranged in rows of artificial curls alternating with zigzag bands. Robes cover the body more than before, and their pattern-like details absorb the sculptor's attention. The bulging eyes of the figure have been accentuated by ringed ridges. In general, the artistic impetus of the early phases of Mesopotamian art has faded into formalism.

One peculiar conception is illustrated by the creatures who guard the entrances to the Assyrian palaces. These are not cut in the round, since they do not stand free of the wall, nor are they in relief in the ordinary sense of that term, since the slab is carved at one end as well as on the side. Because of their architectural position, they are carved in the three-quarter round. These curiosities have the body and feet of a lion, or sometimes of a bull, the wings of a bird, and a human head crowned with the horned headdress peculiar to deities in Mesopotamia. The primitive love of pattern comes out here, not only in the hair and eyes, but in the pattern-like treatment of the feathers that form the wings, and in a diagrammatic indication of the muscles. One naive detail results from their being viewed from the front as well as from the side. As one approaches the entrance, the monster appears to be standing still, its weight carried on the two forelegs, while from within the portal, it seems to be walking, with all four legs visible; consequently, it has five legs in all, one of the front legs being represented twice. Such details though amusing, are not important. In general, these monsters form monumental accents in the architectural ensemble, and their sculpturesque masses, recalling the original planes of the block of stone, give them an artistic integrity worthy of their prominent position in the palace.

But the largest body of Assyrian sculpture consists of friezes in low relief, which lined the lower part of the walls in the important rooms of Mesopotamian palaces. The sculptor faces the same problem here as the Egyptian sculptor had in his reliefs, and some at least of the conventions are the same, though modified by the traditions of the region. The slab of Ashur-nasir-pal Storming a City (fig. 19), of the ninth century, treats the hair and drapery in the usual Assyrian manner, but tends, as in Egypt, to alternate full-front and profile aspects for the several parts of the body. The eye, for example, is rendered full front in a profile head; the legs are in profile, but the shoulders are not always twisted around so fully as they had been along the banks of the Nile, and therefore the result is less angular. Where not hidden by drapery, the anatomy, as in the calf, is symbolic, each muscle defined as an area with rounded edges, and ridges between indicative of tendons. Thus the leg becomes the basis of a pattern as formal as the reduction of a flower to a rosette. For emphasis, the royal figure and his attendant deities are exaggerated in scale, and, similarly, landscape features are introduced to explain the setting without regard for their comparative size. The defenders of the fortress can hardly be contained within it; they are too large to pass through the gates of their own city or to enter its buildings. If this discrepancy in size occurred only in the king or in the Assyrian soldiers, one might conclude that the artist imagined them to be nearer to the observer, and therefore that their size was an indication of distance, but the soldiers within the walls prove that this is not the case. It must rather be a means of emphasis, to call attention to what the sculptor or his audience considered important. As in Egypt, water is represented by a series of wavy lines.

Though human beings in Assyrian art are conventionalized, animals are drawn with greater freedom. The Wounded Lioness (fig. 20) from the Palace of Ashur-bani-pal in the seventh century is brilliantly conceived. Here the sculptor grapples with a problem involving representation and expression. In the solution of the former, he only half succeeds. The head and forequarters convey its appearance, but because the dragging hindquarters, paralyzed by the arrows that transfix her, are too difficult for him to represent, he resorts to the Assyrian conventions for muscles. On the other hand, the artist is more successful from the point of view of expression. To him, the strength and courage of the lioness are outstanding. Though wounded to the death, she still drags herself forward snarling to the attack. A more realistic version might interpret her spirit less vividly than this simplified design. The forward movement is not achieved by the posture alone, but more by the flowing curves, which really create it. To find a clearer example of the expressive possibilities of line in sculpture would be difficult.

Though less completely than in Egypt, these reliefs shed light on the civilization that produced them. Because the subjects are restricted to royal activity, they yield little information about the general conduct of life. Instead, they depict the military caste, headed by the ruler and his court, whose occupation was warfare and whose diversion the hunt. They confirm the reputation for ferocity that caste has won in literature. The heads of the king's enemies are impaled on spikes, their headless bodies strewn over the ground. When Ashur-bani-pal dines with his favorite queen — almost the only instance in which a woman is represented in Assyrian sculpture — the food is served in the palace garden. His majesty, dressed in embroidered robes, half reclines on a couch and drinks from a bowl brought to him by his attendants. Perhaps his wine was the sweeter for the heads of foes impaled in a tree in his line of vision.

The civilization of this region, through conquest and trade, spread in all directions. Persia, for instance, which ultimately conquered Mesopotamia, was an artistic province, except in architecture, where the use of stone enabled a columnar style to develop. The same three-quarter-round monsters we have already seen in Assyria, but without the fifth leg, have been discovered at Persepolis (fig. 441); the Frieze of Archers from the Palace of Darius at Susa in glazed brick adopts a technique and a style developed in Mesopotamia. Here, and in the Frieze of Lions, also in glazed brick, the repetition of stylized forms in rich color results in a decorative magnificence derived from the art of the Fertile Crescent.

THE Aegean culture, third and last of the great cultures of the Mediterranean area previous to the classical, was unknown and its existence
THE AEGEAN   unsuspected until about a century ago. Even now, everything we know of this civilization is deduced
from its art. In Egypt, the hieroglyphics, deciphered a century ago by Champollion, provide us with a mass of recorded history; the clay tab-

lets of Babylonia and Assyria, first read by Layard, document its past; but in the Aegean, few inscriptions have come to light, and these have not yet yielded their secrets. The enthusiasm of the one-time indigo merchant, Heinrich Schliemann, by his excavations at Troy, Tiryns, and Mycenae, first brought proof of a pre-Greek civilization. However, when early in the present century Sir Arthur Evans discovered the Cretan remains at Cnossus, it became clear that the Aegean civilization had developed and reached its apogee in Crete, and that the Mycenaean age on the mainland was merely the afterglow, a barbaric imitation of a higher culture.

Thus the island Palace of Cnossus, its present remains dated in the middle of the second millennium, outshines the mainland fort at Tiryns. Its plan (fig. 21) has as many rooms as a Mesopotamian palace, but in several ways is more advanced. The elements are grouped around one principal court, and although their purpose is not certain, at least some of the rooms form a suite, one chamber leading to another with a definite order in their disposition. Also, the Cretan palace had at least two stories and perhaps three or four. Therefore, stairs were essential, and because a staircase is an element of two or more stories, the relation of the stairs to the second and third floors had to be visualized before the ground story was built. In itself, this requirement postulates a more than rudimentary architectural training. Furthermore, the upper stories compelled the inclusion of courts or light wells to illumine the ground floor. The stair wells were built with columns, tapered toward the bottom as seen in paintings, and of the type adopted in tombs on the mainland of Greece. Made of wood, the columns have vanished, but the stone sockets in which they rested are preserved and make it possible to restore the hall (fig. 22). The peculiar bulging capital of these columns has some resemblance to the later Greek Doric form, though any historic connection between them is conjectural. In other ways besides its advanced plan, the palace of Cnossus bespeaks a high state of civilization. Extensive piping and a flush toilet provided sanitation. The latter invention, so essential in modern life, was not destined to reappear in European civilization until the seventeenth century after Christ, a lapse of over three thousand years. Cnossus in its heyday was unfortified; evidently the sea kings of Crete relied on their navy for protection. In fact, one suspects that the late fortifications indicate that, toward the end of her long history, Crete lost control of the sea and had to provide land defenses, which during her prime had been superfluous.

The Palace at Tiryns on the mainland of Greece, built somewhat later

than that at Cnossus, in contrast is fortified, like a medieval castle, with
thick walls of huge stones laid together without mortar, and with its
gates defended by additional walls. The sequence of gates, courts, and
rooms probably comes from Crete, as does the type of column used in
the entrances to the palace proper. The principal chamber, entered
from the portico, is doubtless to be identified as the 'megaron,' familiar
to us from the Homeric poems; it has an open hearth in the center. A
second suite of rooms, presumably the 'thalamus' or women's quarters,
connects with the megaron by a circuitous route easy to control. The
various rooms of this, as of the Cretan palace, were roofed with timber,
but such contemporary tombs as the Treasury of Atreus at Mycenae
adopt the so-called corbel vault. Built underground, its single chamber
is shaped like a beehive, which looks like a true vault; but whereas in
a true vault the stones are wedge shaped and the joints between each
course or layer of stone radiate from a point within the void covered
by the vault, in the corbel system the stones are laid with the joints
horizontal, so that each block lies flat on the one below it, its interior
surface projecting further into the void.

The discovery of Egyptian pottery in Crete proves that there had
been some trade with Egypt, a conclusion corroborated by the abundant
paintings of the region. The design, called the Bull Leapers, from the
Palace of Cnossus (fig. 23), like Egyptian painting, is executed in line
and flat tone, the several parts of the composition outlined, and each
area then filled with a single tone. In Crete, however, a slight modification of the major tone may appear along the edges of each area, which
mitigates the stiffness characteristic of Egyptian work. The red-brown
men and the pale yellow women recall a similar color scheme in the
Nile valley. Even the conventions of the body have some parallels; the
eye is full front in a profile head, the hips even narrower than in Egyptian painting, and the shoulders broader, but the profile full-front alternation is not quite so regular.

In spite of these points of correspondence, Cretan painting is different
in appearance from Egyptian and more pleasing to many people today.
The less precise blocking out is partly responsible, but more important
is the remarkable sense of selection; instead of crowding the composition with a host of details, the Cretan artist realizes the value of open
space; he stresses the fundamentals and ignores the rest. The movement of the bull and the figures in linear rhythms is cardinal; all that
is needed to dramatize that action is included, and, of equal significance,
nothing else is permitted. Extraneous material, however delightful, is

eschewed, its elimination so pronounced that it gives the painting an oriental effect. The bull strikes an attitude that is, to say the least, improbable from a naturalistic point of view, but one which lends itself to design and to the suggestion of movement. Its curves are simplified to make them expressive. Moreover, such drawing is not the work of an amateur, or of a primitive artist, if by primitive we understand a craftsman who is feeling his way toward a goal that he does not know quite how to reach. These curves are swept in with consummate assurance. With such artistic success, the fact that we cannot surely interpret the scene is of small significance; whether these figures vaulting over the back of the bull are to be interpreted as acrobats, as performers of a dance, or as engaged in some religious rite, one does not know. The frequency with which the bull recurs in Aegean art colors the supposition that the animal was connected with religion, but just how is still a matter for archaeology to determine.

Painting in Crete takes the place occupied by sculpture in Egypt and Mesopotamia. Except for the Lion Gate at Mycenae, which comes from the bitter end of this civilization, no monumental carving has been discovered. In the minor arts, sculpture on a small scale does exist, such as the exquisite Snake Goddess in the Boston Museum (fig. 24), with her body and dress of ivory, but the nipples of her breasts, the flounces of her skirt, and the writhing snakes held in her hands of gold. Though only about seven inches high, she conveys the impression of a larger figure, freely modeled and highly idealized in her aristocratic features. The narrow waist and the elaborate costume, both of which occur in paintings, follow the fashion of their day.

In the famous Gold Cups from Vaphio (fig. 25), the Cretan demonstrates his skill in metalwork. Bulls again form the subject; on one cup they are grazing, while on the other they are captured in nets. Though some realistic shortcomings are evident, the result shows remarkable observation of nature, but the artistic quality comes from the creative selection, the rhythm, and the technique with which the material is handled.

Though much remains unknown about this civilization, its general course is clear. It rose slowly through the third millennium before Christ, until the sea kings of Crete brought their culture to its apex during the second millennium, when the Palace at Cnossus with its masterpieces of painting was created. At this time, Crete controlled some of the islands in the Aegean Sea, and spread her style to them. Then during the second millennium, barbarian Greeks from the north began to arrive in the

Peloponnesus, to touch the outskirts of this culture and to learn its elements. These people, who form the Mycenaean civilization, catch a
provincial reflection of the sophisticated island development; for example, a version of the Bull Leapers in Tiryns is the same in subject
as the masterpiece from Cnossus, but its technique is amateurish. Presumably, these people undermined the power of the sea kings until
they forced the addition to Cnossus of the late fortifications.

That these Mycenaeans were the Greeks who fought the Trojan War,
and of whom Homer wrote, seems undeniable. The sites of the Homeric
poems, Troy, Tiryns, Mycenae 'rich in gold,' as the poet says, which
yielded over a ton of gold objects to the excavations of Heinrich Schliemann, are the sites modern archaeology has found most fruitful of
Mycenaean remains. Homer speaks with wonder of the walls of Tiryns,
of Crete and its ninety cities. The poems mention only one statue, but
describe in detail several objects of the minor arts, such as the cup of
Nestor and the shield of Achilles. If one allows for poetic exaggeration,
these descriptions offer a similarity to the metalwork of Mycenaean days.
But pale reflection of Crete though this be, it was yet superior in culture to anything known to the new waves of barbarian Greeks who
began to arrive in the Peloponnesus toward the end of the second millennium. The Homeric Greeks had learned something from Crete, but
had not had time themselves to become fully civilized; for the newcomers, Dorian, Ionian, and Aeolian tribes, overthrew the long-haired,
mail-clad Achaeans of whom Homer wrote. Centuries were to elapse
before these new tribes, the Greeks as we know them, were to find
their own manner of artistic expression, one that was to be distinct
from the Mycenaean or any other civilization that had preceded them.

III

The Beginnings of Greek Art

ACCORDING to tradition, the historic Greeks arrived in the Peloponnesus in 1100 B.C. To accept this literally is absurd; the Greeks did not arrive on schedule like a conducted tour. The process was slower and less simple, one of infiltration by successive waves of migration by these peoples from the north, like the barbarian invasions that centuries later upset the Roman Empire. Like that later and better-known movement, the Greek migration was followed by several centuries of the 'Dark Ages,' so-called partly because we know little about them, and partly because they cover the time when these primitive peoples were taking the first toddling steps toward what would one day emerge as a glorious culture.

The land in which the newcomers found themselves was very different from either Egypt or Mesopotamia. Odysseus said of his native Ithaca that it was 'a rugged land but a good nurse of men,' and the phrase might apply to all Greece. Life was not so easy here as in the Nile valley, but the Greeks' very struggles for existence may have stimulated their innate energy, their resourcefulness, their willingness to experiment and to adventure on untried lines of endeavor. The mountains that break up the country and the arms of the sea that penetrate the land fostered small city states, often at war with their neighbors, but intensely proud of themselves. Although the Homeric poems were read throughout the Greek world and helped to give the Greeks a feeling of brotherhood distinct from the barbarian or non-Greek world of the older civilizations, still it required the danger of a Persian invasion to compel one city even partly to co-operate with another. However, the smallness of the city state, which enabled every citizen to play an active part in civic life, promoted public spirit and an atmosphere of free discussion stimulating to the individual. The artists of older civilizations knew when they were doing good work and, human nature being what it is, must have been proud of it. We may assume that this was true in Mesopotamia and Egypt; in Greece, the individual, even the humblest potter, parades his pride of creation in dozens of inscriptions, while the prominent sculptors win reputations that have lasted to this day.

Moreover, this land supplied all the materials necessary for sculpture and architecture. Good timber could be had and was used for domestic building as well as for the roofs of temples, and at the beginning probably for the whole temple. But above all, the quarries yielded the fine-grained marbles of Paros and Pentelicus, stones hard enough to wear well, yet workable under the sculptor's chisel. Given an intellectual people stimulated by their surroundings, with the raw materials of architecture and sculpture at hand, a brilliant artistic development was bound to occur.

The first of the visual arts to emerge was architecture. Sometime during the Dark Ages, the Greek temple and the two principal *orders* or systems of Greek architecture developed. The more important of the orders is the Doric (fig. 26), which, when matured in the fifth century, was to exhibit a rare balance of delicacy and strength, a perfect relation of the parts to the whole and of the parts to their purposes, which has never been surpassed. Any structural member in architecture may be classified according to function in one of three types: a base or foundation member, a supporting member, or a crowning or terminating member. In the Doric order, these functions are expressed in the three principal divisions, the same triple memberships carrying through even the minor units. A base or *stereobate* serves as and expresses the foundation of the temple; the *columns* rest on it; and they in turn support an *entablature* that reflects the roof and crowns the edifice. Several steps, generally three, compose the stereobate. Since the Doric column has no individual base, the *stylobate* or top step serves a double function: it terminates the stereobate and it serves as a foundation to the colonnade. This combination of purposes in the stylobate links the stereobate and the colonnade. The *shaft* of the column, which gives the height necessary for the temple, has its essential movement emphasized by narrow vertical grooves or *flutes* (collectively *fluting*). In the Doric order, these are shaped as elliptical curves and meet one another in an edge. The shaft is not quite cylindrical; it tapers toward the top, a logical device in that the bottom of the shaft must support all the weight carried by the top and, in addition, the mass of the column itself. This tapering is not uniform but is cut in a flat curve, called *entasis*, which gives the shaft a vigorous beauty.

The column terminates with a *capital*, which likewise consists of three parts: the fluted *necking*, separated from the shaft by a narrow groove; the bulging cushion-like molding, the *echinus;* and, at the top, a square block, the *abacus.* Through its similarity to the shaft, the necking merges that part with the capital. The strong freehand curve of the echinus is admirable in that it offers an enlarged area to help in supporting the beams, and both in appearance and actuality is strong enough to hold considerable weight. The abacus completes the transition from the circular plan of the shaft and echinus to the rec-tangular shapes of the entablature above, and yet is not too high to break the transition from the vertical to the horizontal line afforded by the echinus.

The abacus not only terminates the capital; it also serves as a base for the lowest of the three members of the entablature, the *architrave*, a plain beam that spans the void from column to column. This, in turn, is topped by a narrow molding, that links it to the *frieze*, the middle member of the entablature. The Doric order is peculiar in that the frieze, a continuous band in the other orders, alternates vertical triple bars called *triglyphs,* and almost square slabs, either plain or sculp-tured, the *metopes.* The alternation of verticals and plain areas in the frieze recalls the alternation of vertical columns and open spaces in the colonnade, though there are almost twice as many triglyphs as columns. Above the frieze, horizontal moldings compose the *cornice,* the third member of the entablature, analogous to the eaves of a wooden house; it reflects the roof and causes rainfall to drip away from the stonework below, rather than to trickle down the face of the lower members and so, in time, damage them. The lower or bed moldings of the cornice serve to support the upper projecting members, on whose sides above each triglyph and each metope appear flat blocks, called *mutules.* These recall the divisions below, and so establish the harmony between the frieze and the cornice. Peg-like ornaments, *guttae,* decorate the under surface of the mutules. Finally, since the climate of Greece is not rainless, a low gable roof is necessary to shed moisture. That roof produces a triangular space at either end of the temple, the *pedi-ment.* The entablature, except the top molding of the cornice, contin-ues as a horizontal band across the front and back of the temple, but most of the cornice must be duplicated to follow the slope of the roof, where it is called the *raking cornice.* Most of these terms apply to other orders besides the Doric and recur through later architectural history.

Two questions arise in connection with the Doric order. Did this system, which in developed instances seems so perfectly adapted to stone, originate in that medium? To what extent, if at all, was this architecture influenced by previous civilizations? The vaulted architecture of Mesopotamia was foreign to the Greeks; for although they knew the principle of the arch and used it for unimportant structures and in inconspicuous positions, its dynamic implications contradicted the serenity and quietness they considered essential in monumental buildings. However, the colonnaded architecture of Egypt might have suggested a colonnaded style to the Greeks, but this assumption involves several difficulties. For one thing, while Egypt during the Saite period welcomed the Greeks, that period postdates the earliest steps in the formation of the temple and the Doric order. Secondly, the Egyptian temple is an internal form; its colonnades line the walls of the peristyle, and support the roof of the hypostyle hall; only the pylon is enriched externally, but that member has no parallel in Greek architecture. With the Greek temple, however, the converse is true. Essentially a shrine and a monument to the god, it is designed to be seen from without more than from within. Finally, the only type of Egyptian column at all resembling the Doric is the sixteen-sided column (fig. 9). Although at first glance the similarity is striking, closer examination suggests that these parallels are fortuitous. Nothing in Egypt corresponds to the entablature of the order and, although the shafts look alike, many details do not correspond. The Egyptian column has an abacus but no true capital. Most significant, the Egyptian shaft is light in proportion, like that of the developed Greek Doric of later days, but different from the heavy proportions of the early Doric. If Egypt suggested the pier and lintel system to the Greeks, that was all it did. Even that seems doubtful, since that method is so elementary as probably to be indigenous in any region, like Greece, in which appropriate materials are available.

Geography implies, however, that the Aegean area might well have influenced the early Greeks. The portico, restored as an entrance to the Palace at Tiryns, resembles the colonnaded porches of smaller Greek temples. Moreover, the cushion-like Doric echinus vaguely suggests the capital of Aegean columns, and there are some details in Aegean architecture that may have prompted the triglyph and metope system of the Doric. On the other hand, the Minoan column tapers toward the bottom, exactly opposite to the Greek solution. It is conceivable that some memories may have persisted of the earlier architecture of the Aegean area into the later Doric forms, but if so, they were so slight that we may speak of the Doric order as a purely Greek development.

Less difficult is the question whether the Doric order originated in wood or stone. Advocates of the latter theory maintain, among other things, that its details and proportions are so expressive of stone that they could hardly have been developed in wood, which implies different relationships. Especially the column itself and its spacing support this argument. As we have seen in the first chapter, timber construction tends to produce a horizontal rectangle with slender, widely spaced supports. The Doric column, notably in the early examples, is heavy and squat. It could be true that the early Greeks took the trunks of trees for their first columns, but nevertheless it seems absurd to suppose that they would have chosen such large trees and spaced them so closely.

In reply to this, the proponents of a wooden origin assume that, when the order was translated from wood to stone, a complete change of proportions in the column was effected. They rest their case on the evidence of the order itself and on certain historical indications. First, it is not wise to expose the cross section of a wood beam to the weather. Moisture and consequent decay penetrate deeper into the ends of such timbers than through the sides. The triglyphs look like cleats placed for protection over the ends of beams which might have supported the ceiling of the temple. Second, the guttae attached to blocks below the triglyphs resemble wooden pegs intended to hold the triglyphs in place. It is hard to imagine what else can have suggested them. Finally in a wooden roof, the rafters must be covered with planks on which tiles, shingles, slate, or some other form of protection is fixed. Are not the mutules reminders of the projecting ends of these planks, again pegged into position with guttae?

One of the earliest large temples is the Heraeum (Temple of Hera) at Olympia. In its present form it is not earlier than about 600 B.C. In this temple, there is no doubt that the columns were built originally of wood and that, as they rotted, they were replaced from time to time in the current style of stone columns. As one might expect under these circumstances, they differ from one another in their details. Pausanias, who wrote a guide book of Greece during the second century after Christ, tells us that one column in the back porch was still of wood in his day. If the columns were originally of wood, then the entablature must also have been of wood. This building, therefore, would seem to settle the argument; and so it would, if we could prove that the existing stone members were like the wooden shafts they replaced, and if we could demonstrate that the vanished wood entablature was Doric.

The presumption is strong that it was, but final proof is impossible. Still, the Heraeum, coupled with the evidence of the order itself, makes so clear a case for a wooden origin of the Doric that one can only assume that when the more permanent material was chosen, the column proportions were adapted to it.

The Greeks crystallized the arrangement of the temple early in their history. In plan (fig. 27), the temple consists of a rectangular chamber, the *cella* or sanctuary, ringed by a free-standing colonnade. This scheme, sometimes elaborated by the addition of one or two chambers behind the cella as storage rooms, was followed in all the larger Greek temples from the seventh or eighth century before Christ to the end of Greek history. Smaller examples include only the cella with a columned portico at one or both ends. To refine and perfect this simple plan, the Greeks devoted their architectural energies for the next few centuries. So long a period of experimentation and adjustment, in matters that must seem to the layman mere details, alone made possible the exquisite balance of the Parthenon. In general, this development followed certain clear lines. The Heraeum is, in plan, about three times as long as it is wide. Mature examples such as the Parthenon are more compact with a length just over twice the width. Developed temples usually have on the side one column more than twice the number that they have across the front. Thus the Parthenon has eight columns in front and seventeen on the side; the contemporary Theseum in Athens has six and thirteen columns. On the other hand, the Heraeum shows six and sixteen columns.

Moreover, with the passing centuries, the entablature lightened as compared with the total height of the temple or that of the columns. In early examples, it was a crushing mass almost half as high as the column and therefore a third of the height of the building above the stylobate; but by the fifth century, the entablature became about a third as high as the column, and so a quarter of the total building height. Meanwhile, the shaft grew taller in proportion to its width at the base, often referred to as its lower diameter. The early examples might be only four lower diameters in height; when the Parthenon was designed, they were almost five and a half lower diameters. These figures, of course, tell us nothing of the actual height of the column, which must depend on the size of the temple, but simply the proportions of the column. The last development to be mentioned is found in the echinus. In the early capitals of the Heraeum, this member flared out from the shaft, with a bulging curve, which, as time went on, became less marked and rose at an angle of approximately 45 degrees. This flatter curve and sharper rise is both more powerful in support and more subtle in appearance than the crude early type.

The fifth-century Temple of Poseidon at Paestum (fig. 28) in southern Italy, while not perfected in detail, forms a fitting illustration of the type, though the emphasis still is more on robustness than on refinement. The sense of compact form, held in such high esteem by the Greeks and illustrated in Greek tragedy, here has its exact architectural expression. To this form nothing is lacking, and from it nothing can be subtracted; its unity is outstanding. Furthermore, the decoration is restrained. Though not in this instance, in some examples sculpture in the round filled the triangular pediments, the metopes were carved in high relief, and groups placed above the angles of the pediment served to accent those parts. All this decoration was restricted to the top of the temple, leaving simpler forms below. Color added a final grace; tones of bright red and blue gave contrast to the smaller moldings of the entablature, which otherwise could hardly be seen from the ground. Any patterns applied to these moldings, either in color or by carving, repeat on their surfaces the shape of the moldings in cross section. For example, a molding that is rectangular in section may be adorned with a device composed of straight lines and right angles, such as a fret; one whose profile forms a quarter circle, in curved shapes. Thus the pattern repeats in design the shape of the surface on which it is placed.

To the Greeks, the Doric order was masculine because of its strength; the grace of the Ionic was feminine. Developed at the same time as the Doric, the less simple and less bold Ionic order was popular in the islands of the Aegean and on the mainland of Asia Minor, but less so in the Peloponnesus and in southern Italy. Its first point of difference (fig. 29) is the individual *base* under each column. A square *plinth* or block of stone may serve as a foundation (though not in the Athenian buildings), above which convex and concave moldings are combined in several ways. The shaft, more slender than even the developed Doric shaft, tapers less than the Doric. The semicircular flutes are deeper, and are separated from one another by a narrow band. The dominant feature of the capital is the pair of flanking *volutes* or scrolls connected by curving lines. It is as though paper had been rolled up from either end, the edges of these rolls visible on the front and back of the capital. Charming as the result is, it contains several problems. Since the front and side of the capital contrast, it must be adjusted at the corner of the building, lest either the front or side colonnade exhibit one capital different in appearance from the others in the same range. The Greek solution before Hellenistic times was to twist the volute on the corner capital outward to a 45° angle, and so to force an approximate similarity of appearance on the neighboring faces of the capital. Though this device has been praised as showing the ingenuity of the Greeks, it is in fact awkward. This lopsided capital does not look well from any point of view; its resemblance to its neighbors is superficial, while its irregularity betrays it as a makeshift. The Hellenistic Greeks were to solve the problem of the corner capital of the Ionic order by changing its shape. The canted volute was repeated at all four corners of the capital; this made it symmetrical and so adapted for use both on the corner and in the center of a colonnade. The truth is that the earlier Greek Ionic, though graceful in itself, can be effective only where the colonnade does not turn a corner.

The Ionic entablature, like the Doric, has three principal divisions, but the architrave is broken into three bands by small moldings. The continuous frieze is sometimes adorned with sculpture. A distinguishing element in the Ionic cornice is the *dentil range*, broken into square blocks like a row of teeth, which supports the overhanging parts of the cornice.

That the Ionic order developed from wood is universally admitted. The dentil range, for instance, derived from the ends of rafters, and the earliest examples show proportions in the column hardly possible except in wood. When the order was converted to stone, these proportions became more robust, but never rivaled the massiveness of the Doric. The early capital allowed its scrolls to grow out of the shaft; only later were they connected with one another. Like the Doric, the most splendid examples of the order occur in the fifth century.

Whereas architecture begins to exhibit its characteristic, if still archaic, forms at least as early as the seventh century, sculpture becomes important only toward the end of that century. That this art reached a high level in Hellenic times is the universal testimony of ancient authors. Their comments are valuable in two ways: first, their descriptions identify some of the famous statues and connect them with sculptors whom antiquity regarded as masters; and second, their criticisms and comparisons allow us to imagine what the original beauty of the statues may have been. In this connection, much depends on how we value the judgment of ancient critics; some, like Pliny, confused fame with artistic merit and admired some statues for reasons modern critics do not consider of aesthetic importance. Others, such as Lucian, appear to have been more sensitive to qualities beyond mere verisimilitude. From the period that antiquity, including so discerning a critic as Lucian, regarded as the culmination of Greek sculpture, few, if any, of the famous originals are preserved. We know approximately what many of these statues looked like, because they were copied for the Roman market, just as photographs or casts of 'old masters' are available today.

These late Greek or Roman copies hardly warrant the praise bestowed on them by the nineteenth century. Their quality varies but often is dull and uninspired. One would not dream of trying to evaluate the painting of Titian, for example, on the basis of copies, even if they were made by men of recognized talent, since the hand of the copyist must alter the subtle relations established by the original master; and yet this is what one must do with the famous masters of Greek sculpture. Two courses, therefore, remain open today. The first is to deflate the prestige of Greek sculpture, at least during its period of maturity, on the ground that the copies do not justify a high opinion. To accept this position is to reject the testimony of classic critics (who saw the originals) as based on the outmoded idea that art must hold the mirror up to nature. The other and fairer approach is to withhold judgment, to admit the shortcomings in extant copies, and, in the absence of other evidence, to accept the dicta of the more discerning critics of antiquity. We should prove these dicta so far as possible by comparisons, but must make charitable allowance for qualities that may have been present in the original, but which the copyist might have lost, partly through inability and partly through copying in marble a statue designed by the master in bronze — a profound modification to be remembered in most of the famous copies.

However, there is extant some original Greek work of two sorts. First, archaic sculpture was not sufficiently esteemed by the Romans to be carted away by them; much of it, too, had been buried by accident, or, after the Persian wars, deliberately, among the debris of that struggle during which it had been damaged. Second, architectural sculpture, the metopes and friezes and the figures in the pediments of Greek temples, remains to us. The marbles of the Parthenon, for example, are undoubted Greek originals of the fifth century and, in the absence of more famous statues, must establish for us the character of the period. The slightest comparison of these originals with Roman copies from other contemporary work demonstrates the vitality of the former and the dullness of the latter. But in antiquity, architectural decorations like

these were secondary or tertiary in importance, worth only a passing
mention by critics, and often the product of less celebrated artists working under the direction of a master — what, in other epochs, are called
'school' works. If these originals are so superior to the copied masterpieces, how much more allowance we should make for the discrepancy between those copies and the lost masterpieces on which they
were based.

Though unproductive of sculpture, the Dark Ages laid the foundations of civilization in Greece. During this time, Greece came into contact with the older cultures of the Mediterranean region. Then, too, the
Homeric poems received their definite form. The poet looks back
longingly from his own day to the heroic past — that is, to the Mycenaean
civilization. In *The Iliad*, Homer says Ajax picked up a large stone to
cast at his adversary; no one in the poet's time could lift such a stone.

This pessimism may be an instinctive tendency to admire 'the good
old times,' but comparison of the Vaphio Cups with geometric vases
of the eighth century goes far to explain Homer's attitude. The Aegean
proficiency of technique has vanished. Most of the surface of these large
funerary vases is banded with patterns, but in a few of the wider bands
the craftsman drew 'memory pictures.' The figures these contain are
diagrammatic, their legs shaped like those of wasps, their torsos inverted triangles, and their heads circles. No less primitive is the drawing of horses. In many vases of this period, and even more so in the
seventh-century vases from Rhodes, oriental animal motives testify to
the contact with Egypt and particularly with Mesopotamia. Wherever
space permits among the figures, horses, and chariots, the craftsman
inserts decorative motives. Nothing remains of the beauty of technique
or of the sophistication of the Vaphio Cups, and yet the geometric vases
have a primitive vigor. Their patterns are well adapted to the surfaces
they decorate. The fact is that these vases are not crude attempts to
preserve Mycenaean tradition; on the contrary, they illustrate the birth
of a promising Hellenic culture.

Perhaps the most important result of the Homeric poems was to
clarify and vivify the gods of the Olympic pantheon. No one after
reading *The Iliad* can think of Zeus and Hera, Ares and Aphrodite as
abstract conceptions; they are too individual and human. Unlike the
deities of Egypt and Mesopotamia, these gods are envisioned in human
form, though more perfect physically and more powerful than ordinary
mankind. To overemphasize the importance of this anthropomorphism
in religion is impossible. When the Greeks began to carve statues of

their gods, they found the whole force of religion behind them, impelling them to seek a result that would incorporate this human conception. No conventionalized version could long prove satisfactory. Since gods were like men, their statues must be reasonably realistic. But once the sculptor acquired the ability to carve a realistic figure, he was under pressure to conceive and render forms more perfect than any to be found on earth, shapes that might be at once human and superhuman. Hence on a basis of realistic knowledge, the Greek sculptor molds his idealized conceptions of the Olympic pantheon until, a century later, he eliminates the individual, the incidental, and the accidental.

Naturally, this idealism could not be reached over night. The first century and a half of Greek sculpture, called the archaic period, extends from the late seventh century to the end of the Persian wars in 480 B.C.; it is an epoch of experimentation, of observation of the body and its possibilities, of struggle for mastery over stone — all calculated to reach this realistic first goal. Especially at the beginning, the sculptors were hampered by ignorance of how to render the body accurately, and how far it was safe to cut into the block of stone. In lieu of these skills, at least in part, the instinct for pattern common among primitive peoples provided an outlet for the creative energies of the craftsmen. This concern with design produced some masterpieces of high quality, possibly a purer expression than might have been reached had the sculptor been more sophisticated. That the trend of Greek sculpture is away from convention and toward realism is historical fact. For better or worse, the Greeks regarded these limitations, which may result in a sculptural mass and a design based upon the sense of pattern, as restrictions to be escaped as soon as possible. Consequently the Greek sculptor experimented constantly. Recognizing the realistic defects of his own or his master's works, he sought to rectify them. Many failures resulted, of course, from the point of view both of design and of realism, but static this art could never be.

The sculpture of the first seventy-five years (625–550 B.C.) exhibits a limited number of types or poses, the most important of which is the standing nude male figure. Though called the 'Apollo' type, such as the Apollo of Tenea (fig. 30), these figures are not all identified. Some may be statues of that god, but some are statues of athletes, victors in the Olympic games or one of the other festivals. The similarity to the Egyptian priest, Ranefer (fig. 13), is striking. Like him, the Apollo walks forward, the weight carried on both feet; the erect body respects the law of frontality; the shoulders are broad and, since the arms are locked to the sides, the hips are narrow. Clearly the material dominates the conception. Perhaps the sculptor started with a prismatic block of stone, drew the silhouette of his figure first on the front of the block and then chiseled away the parts that were not within that outline. The procedure was repeated on the sides of the block. When the edges of this rough mass were rounded off, an approximation of the human form resulted, but the planes of such a figure tended to mirror the original planes of the block and so expressed the material. Moreover, details show that the craftsman was afraid to cut deeply into the stone. The hands are not free from the body, and indeed in the earliest examples almost the whole length of the arm is attached to the torso. The long hair, which falls over the shoulders, strengthens the neck at its weakest point by adding to the cross section of stone. Instead of cutting into the stone to force the eyes to recede beneath the brows, the eyes bulge out to preserve the ovoid mass of the head. The compact sculpturesque result of the early archaic figures comes in part from these considerations.

But if the 'Apollos' parallel Egyptian standing or walking figures, the differences are even more prophetic. The slab of stone that served as a background for Ranefer is gone. The Greek figure is nude, innocent even of the loin cloth, which almost universally appears in Egypt and points to the Greek concern with the body as the primary vehicle of sculpture. Significant is the willingness to experiment with anatomy. The sculptor of the Apollo of Tenea indicates the muscular divisions of the torso, articulates the kneecap, and represents the bony structure of the body, as in the shoulder blades. Some errors in realism, such as the proportions of the lower legs, make this man look as though he were standing on tiptoe. The characteristic archaic smile creates a stilted, even irritating, impression of complacency; the hair is reduced to patterns, with snail-shell curls over the forehead and repeated wavy lines for the mass of the hair. As a work of art, the Apollo of Tenea is not equal to the Ranefer; it lacks the assurance, the competence, and the strength of the Egyptian. The Greek sculptor does not yet equal his predecessors in technique. But if the statue itself is less successful, it contains the germ of progress.

The standing female type of the Hera of Samos (fig. 31), dated about 550 B.C., is almost as common as the 'Apollo' type. Its cylindrical mass presupposes earlier statues in wood, images carved from trunks of trees; and although the sculptor is here working in stone, he preserves the familiar shape. No parts separate themselves from the mass; the arms join the body through their entire length. Until much later, the female figure in Greek art is always clothed; therefore, the sculptor seizes the opportunity offered by the drapery for design in pure pattern. Small parallel folds compose the skirt as though it were accordion pleated, and contrast with another system of lines in the upper garment that sweep down from the left shoulder and spread outward over the breast. The sequence in direction of these wider folds serves as a foil to the vertical harmony below, at once enhancing and being enriched by it. Unrealistic though she is, the compactness and the pattern make the Hera of Samos a masterpiece comparable with any.

Other early figure types are less common. If the 'Apollo' type recalls ⤿ the contact Greece had with Egypt during the seventh century, the seated Chares of Branchidae (fig. 32) has Mesopotamian qualities. Like the Gudea (fig. 18), it is draped so heavily that little of the underlying body can be perceived. The folds of the garment, indicated by lines, are flattened on the surface rather than modeled with any considerable projection and recession. So block-like is this figure and so intimately connected with its chair, that it could not rise without taking the throne with it. Although compact, the result seems heavy.

The archaic Greek artist rarely essayed bolder problems. The winged Nike or Victory of Delos (fig. 33) is the oldest Greek statue ascribed, however doubtfully, to known sculptors, Micciades and Archermus of Delos. The literary evidence indicates that the Nike was carved early in the sixth century. This kneeling figure parallels Egyptian methods of representation, as though an Egyptian relief were converted into sculpture in the round. The head and shoulders are viewed from in front, but at the waist the figure half turns so that the legs are seen in profile. In short, Micciades and Archermus transferred to sculpture in the round, where it appears unnecessary, a convention understandable in relief. They conceived of their statue not as something the spectator may walk around and inspect from all sides, but as something to be seen from a single point of view, like relief sculpture. If the result is not quite successful, to attempt the Nike of Delos at all took courage. These sculptors were eager to conceive a pose, untried before, that was still beyond their technical ability.

These early sculptors laid the foundations and established the traditions to be developed in the next seventy years, from 550 to 480 B.C. The frieze of the Treasury of the Siphnians at Delphi (fig. 34) represents a struggle of gods and giants; it complicates the decorative possibilities inherent in earlier work. These artists seem not to have concerned themselves with the possibilities of the body. Most of the figures are draped, and the body serves more as a frame to hold the patterns of clothing than as something interesting in itself, although the drapery is often pulled forward so that it outlines the back of the figure. The bodies are heavy in proportion, puffy rather than muscular, with the archaic smile, patterned hair, and bulging eyes still prominent. On the other hand, a field for rich design opened in the draperies themselves. If the folds are not cut too deep to disguise the mass of the stone, they are arranged with a superb feeling for rhythm and variety. These changes by the sculptor may indicate differences in the costumes, but also display a love of design and fertility of imagination.

The archaic decorative sense predominates in the vases of the mid-sixth century, such as that by Execias (fig. 35). Within the bowl, Dionysus sails through a school of porpoises. The setting is symbolic, with no indication of the sea save for the presence of the fish. These and the grapevine that Dionysus brings to man approximate a scalloped pattern around the rim of the vase to echo and harmonize with its shape. Up to this time, Greek vases retained the black-figured style, wherein the motives are glazed in black, sometimes with other colors added, on the red ground of the baked clay.

However, the late sixth century reversed this technique to the red-figured style, which allowed greater freedom to the artist. This is illustrated in the vase by Euphronius, whose theme is the struggle of Heracles and Antaeus (fig. 36). Once more the elimination of landscape details enables the painter to concentrate his whole attention on the human figures. This preoccupation with man could be explained in sculpture by the nature of the medium, which does not lend itself to the indication of landscape, except in low relief. When one observes the same omission in painting, one can only interpret it as a testimony of the Greek belief in the preponderant importance of humanity as an artistic motive. The figures, drawn in line alone, show many of the same conventions in drapery and the same eagerness to experiment with pose that characterize archaic sculpture.

The type illustrated by the Hera of Samos became more elaborate in the *Kore* or Maiden from the Acropolis (fig. 37), one of many similar figures dedicated in Athens in late archaic times, damaged during the Persian wars, and buried on the Acropolis when the Athenians returned to their city after its sack by the Persians. Posed as quietly as the Hera, the right arm extends forward from the elbow, bearing an offering in its hand. This part of the figure is carved from a separate stone fitted into a socket on the main block; on most figures of this type, these arms have disappeared but the sockets are still visible. The draped folds end with a zigzag line, which reduces to pattern the edge of cloth. Details of this late sixth-century dress show an advance in realism over the Hera of Samos, as the extended arm bespeaks an increased mastery of the material.

The most remarkable point about these figures is the color. We have become accustomed to think of sculpture as monochromatic and executed chiefly in white marble. Such a view results from the fact that most of us have our first impressions of sculpture formed by colorless Roman copies of Greek statues, by carvings of modern sculptors who choose uncolored marble or limestone, and by white plaster casts. In actuality, most great ages of sculpture have known the value of color judiciously employed. Many of the earliest Greek works were painted in strong tones of red and blue, or less frequently with other hues. Probably their effect was garish, but in these Maidens only details of the figure are picked out in color, black for the hair, red lips, black eyes, and above all patterns as of embroidery on the hem of the garments. Far from being crude, these well-selected touches of color enhance the loveliness of the work, and in no way conceal the texture of the stone and its own inherent beauty as had the more completely painted earlier examples.

The bronze Statuette from Ligourio (fig. 38) reflects the athletic style of Ageladas of Argos; derived from the 'Apollo' type, it progresses beyond that type, if by progress we understand historical development. Though few examples in bronze are extant, it is important to remember that most famous later artists preferred to work in bronze rather than in marble. The freer handling of this figure is partly attributable to the material. In the first place, the law of frontality is broken. The weight is not evenly distributed between the feet; therefore the axis of the torso is no longer vertical, and a transverse line through the hips ceases to be horizontal but slopes downward to the left, while a line through the shoulders tips down to the right. Unlike the earlier figures, this statue stands at ease, not at attention. Moreover, the sculptor's observation of the human form has begun to bear fruit. The arms are no longer fixed to the side but fall naturally, or move forward or backward. The salient points of anatomy are perceived; the divisions of the torso are not scratched in line on its surface but are presented as plastic masses, modeled to approximate the body.

Since the Ligourio statuette suggests the figure of an athlete, sculpture of this type is sometimes called the school of athletic art. The athletic festivals in Greece, such as the Olympic games and the preparation for them must account for these athletes. In the palaestra, the youth of Greece trained in the nude for the contests; constant observation of young men running, jumping, wrestling, and throwing the discus or the javelin gave the Greek artist an opportunity enjoyed by sculptors of no other country. He had continually before him the spectacle of the body in action. Through long familiarity, a knowledge of the figure must have become second nature to him and to his critical audience. Unlike the artists of our own day, who must base their work on a few models in the privacy of the studio, these artists had as their models the flower of Greek youth. That the Greeks should have developed their study of the male figure beyond that of the female is illuminating. Woman in sculpture remains archaic long after man has become natural. Indeed, the Greeks themselves realized the disadvantage under which the sculptor labored in representing the female figure. When, in the fourth century, the people of Croton ordered a painting of Helen by Zeuxis, they tried to compensate for this deficiency by affording him as nearly parallel an opportunity as possible to observe the figures of the fairest maidens of the city.

The sculpture of the pediments from the Temple of Aphaia at Aegina (fig. 39), at the beginning of the fifth century, restored a century ago by Thorvaldsen, points this contrast. The goddess Athena in the center of the group is more conservative in style than the warriors on either side. Like the 'Kore' figures from the Acropolis, she is clothed in a patterned garment, but the male figures take advantage of the new freedom. The sculptor, possibly Onatas, who was then the leader of the school of Aegina, has posed them with extraordinary freedom: they lie wounded on their elbows, crouch in defense behind shields, stoop forward to assist a fallen comrade, or spear in hand await the attack of an enemy. The action of these figures is far removed from the conventional pose of the 'Apollos.' These are athletic types too, hard muscular figures that betray hours of exercise. The planes of the figures are blocked out, sharp and crisp, and do not flow into one another as in later and more facile productions. The sculptor has mastered his medium, but that control has been so recently acquired that he has not forgotten the demands of stone; he is aware that it is hard to carve, his new technical skill is not taken for granted, and consequently a certain stony quality creeps into his design. Only in the heads are the conventions of archaism still obtrusive. The hair on the scalp is engraved in wavy lines, with a row of curls over the forehead; the eyes, not yet sunk under the brows, do not rival the realism of the bodies; and the archaic smile still predominates. The latter contrasts with the freedom of the figures, as it did not in the 'Apollos,' where it had shared in the general formalization. To see a warrior (fig. 40), wounded no doubt to the death, smile while he pulls a javelin from his breast is incongruous.

The problem of design within the low triangle of the pediment offered a difficult challenge to the artist. In the early pediments, such as that of the Treasury of the Siphnians at Delphi, the sculptor had allowed the action to progress from left to right. But since the pediment established an axis, it demanded in sculpture a balanced, not a continuous, design. Moreover, grouped figures must all approximate the same scale; therefore, if figures stand erect to fill the center of the pediment, it follows that those designed for the outer angles cannot also be posed standing. This axiom was not grasped by the earlier designers, and the lateral figures of the Siphnian pediments are midgets alongside of the principal characters.

In these and other respects, the Aegina pediments (fig. 41) are superior. The subject, the Trojan Wars, appears to have been arranged as two lines of battle, opened out like the leaves of a book. Athena, who directs the fortunes of war, stands in the center; warrior balances warrior; each pose duplicates the figure opposite. And yet, much remains to be solved. Though the balance is complete, it is achieved by means too obvious to sustain the interest of an observer. The axis, too, is emphasized more than necessary. Though some rhythmic relation of the figures exists, their connection is not strong enough to unite the design. The carving of each individual figure has so absorbed the artist that little creative energy remains to solve the larger problem of the whole pediment.

The century and a half that separates the earliest 'Apollos' and the Aegina pediments witnesses the sculptor's acquisition of the technical knowledge to enable him to carve stone with freedom though he retains great respect for his medium. Progressing from crude attempts at representation in the beginning, the latest works show remarkable skill. If the hinges of creation creak a little, the fundamental problems have been solved, and the doors opened to facility of rendition. One problem remains — that of the head. Even at Aegina, the conventions of the head obtrude themselves as archaisms in those otherwise advanced works.

To previous generations, this century and a half, if known at all, had a merely archaeological interest; the absence of anatomical realism betrayed inability. Many of these statues do solve only in part the twin problems of design and representation, but the best welcome comparison with the greatest productions of more sophisticated ages. Though the goal of Greek sculpture had not been reached, the sense of pattern and design, the feeling for the material and for sculpturesque mass, provide these immature works with an artistic quality that needs no apology.

IV

Greek Art during the Fifth and Fourth Centuries B.C.

THE end of the Persian Wars in 480 B.C. loosed a surge of creative energy in Greece to flow in all directions. To have repulsed the unmeasured forces of the Achaemenid empire with their own small numbers and resources must have confirmed the Greeks' confidence in themselves and their pride in being Greeks. Surely the gods approved their civilization and had protected it. In literature, this date introduces the flowering of Greek drama at the hands of Aeschylus, Sophocles, and Euripides, while in the visual arts it marks the inception of that era the later Greeks at least were to deem the climax of their sculptural and architectural history. The Persians had destroyed much, especially in Athens, and so had cleared the ground for new undertakings. Also the spoils of war helped provide the wealth for new creations: the colossal bronze Athena Promachos by Phidias was made from the spoils of the battle on the plains of Marathon. Athens in particular enjoyed a generation or more of great prosperity, partly due to the Delian League; the smaller cities of this league, which had banded together during the Persian Wars under Athenian leadership, contributed money to construct and man a navy for mutual defense. When peace returned, the Athenians assumed that, so long as protection was provided, they might use the funds of the League for their own ends. The civic works program undertaken by Pericles in Athens, an extraordinary effort considering the size of the city, could hardly have been completed without this source on which to draw. However, the full effects of the new wealth and the new self-confidence did not at once reveal themselves. About a generation had to elapse before these conditions bore fruit.

The largest corpus of sculpture from this generation is that from the Temple of Zeus at Olympia, dated about 460 B.C. It includes two pedimental groups and twelve metopes. The former (fig. 42) at once demand comparison with the earlier pediments at Aegina. In the east pediment, which deals with the chariot race of Pelops and Oenomaus, the traditional origin of the Olympic games, chariots separated the principal characters from the subordinate. Consequently, some concentration on the major characters replaces the distributed interest at Aegina. In the Battle of Centaurs and Lapiths in the west pediment, the figures are grouped in twos and threes. Here, group balances group but only approximately, not with the duplication of figure and even of action that marked the late archaic example. However, a few matters in design remain to receive their final polish. The central group in the east pediment is monotonous, because of the repeated verticals of five standing figures; in both pediments a single erect form too openly strikes the axis; and, finally, the transitions from group to group leave something to be desired.

As regards the separate figures, a corresponding change appears. The sculptor of the Centaur and Lapith (fig. 43) is no longer so conscious of his hard material. The two or three extra decades of experience enable him to take it more for granted that he can execute in stone whatever conceptions his mind evolves. While it is not yet true that he has lost respect for his medium, he leaves his marble with less of the stony feeling than did his Aegina predecessors. Perhaps this is to say that he has become more realistic. Few statues have ever reached a finer balance between conception and execution than the Apollo (fig. 44) of the west pediment. This godlike figure guides the fortune of battle by his presence alone, calm and majestic, with outstretched hand and quiet glance. Muscular masses are still in evidence, but a little rounder and less defined than hitherto; as if to emphasize their flowing contours, a wisp of drapery falls over his shoulder and wrist; its plain lines and surfaces enrich and are enriched by contrast with the body.

The obvious archaisms present at Aegina vanish here (fig. 45); the hair is less patterned, the eyes lose their protrusion and the mouth its archaic smile. In many figures details are slurred over. The hair, for example, is suggested by a raised surface like a skull cap, a summary treatment possible because of the height above the ground at which these figures must be seen, and because of the use of paint to distinguish such parts as needed to be visible. A uniformity of expression in the faces tempts one to conclude that the artist had not yet realized the possibility of conveying emotions through the human face, but a further glance at the Centaur and Lapith (fig. 43) proves that such a conclusion is unwarranted. The Centaur's distorted features convey his anger and excitement, his bestiality in the heat of battle as he bites the Lapith's arm, but the latter can hardly have been so stoical as this. The statue demonstrates the Greek feeling that such higher beings as Lapiths, the gods, and the Greeks themselves must not yield to even a normal emotional display, though that may be permitted to inferior beings like Centaurs.

The metopes, placed not on the outside of the temple but over the porches front and back, within the colonnade, recount the twelve labors of Heracles. The finest in design, that of Heracles and the Cretan Bull (fig. 46), through the opposed action, produces a dynamic tension adjusted to a sense of balance. In this location, diagonals are the more desirable since they contrast with the vertical lines of the triglyphs to either side and with the horizontal direction of the other parts of the entablature. These metopes are better preserved than the pediments, because of their protected situation in the temple; but after all allowances have been made for weathering of the pedimental figures, it is apparent that the metopes are more carefully finished. In so large a body of sculpture, it seems probable that even if the work were designed and controlled by a single artist, more than one man must have shared in the execution. Such an assumption may account for the variation in style between the pediments and metopes at Olympia.

At about this time, Myron reached the full power of his creative life. He was famed in antiquity for the realism of his bronzes; his Heifer, set up on the Acropolis in Athens, so closely imitated nature that cows used to low at it as they passed — or so it was said. His most famous statue today, the Discobolus or Discus Thrower (fig. 47), must have been popular in antiquity to warrant the number of copies still preserved. Since the original bronze has vanished, it is hard to judge the quality of Myron's work in most respects; but from the pose and proportions of the copies, we can recognize his preference for athletic figures in violent movement, or, more precisely, in a moment of rest between two periods of action. This youth is modeled at just the moment when the backward swing of the discus has been completed and the forward revolutions of the exercise have not yet commenced. In consequence, a certain poise is preserved, and the muscles are still not strained to the utmost. The free pose, with the head looking backward toward the hand that holds the discus, as Lucian describes it, consists of a series of curves that turn the spectator's attention back into the figure. Conceived in bronze, it need not be block-like, as in the archaic figures, but one can still refer to the contained or enclosed quality of the composition.

The inadequacy of Roman copies to convey the beauty of the original may be measured by turning from the Discus Thrower to the Charioteer from Delphi (fig. 48), dated about 470 B.C., whose sculptor is unknown, though on tenuous evidence the name of Calamis of Athens has been associated with it. That an increased realism need not hinder design is evident here; the deep folds of the garment below the waist, different one from another in depth and spacing, develop into smaller rhythmic folds over the shoulders. A compactness and sculpturesque simplification form the basis of this masterpiece. At the same time, a love of realism is evident in the modeled toes, the fluffy curls escaping from the fillet that binds the hair over the temples, the soft half-grown sideburns of youth untouched as yet by a razor, and in the eyes, which are inserted in white paste with a black disk to imitate pupil and iris. Such matters are easy to observe, but we must also recognize that the proportions, the crisp articulation of the features, and the broad modeling of the surfaces are elements of continuity from earlier times. These works illustrate the final steps toward freedom taken by the Greek artist. By this time, near the middle of the fifth century, he controls his resources; his medium, whether bronze or stone, continues to influence his designs, but it no longer dominates and restricts them; his ability to conceive is not hampered by an inability to execute; and, if he chooses to avail himself of it, an accurate knowledge of the human figure is at his disposal.

When Pericles rose to power in Athens during the sixties, a time of great prosperity, he was able to adopt a program designed to make Athens the cultural and artistic center of Greece. The group of buildings on the Acropolis, of which the Parthenon is the largest, combined with others constructed elsewhere in the city and in Athenian territory at this time, constitute a civic effort unparalleled elsewhere in history and the more remarkable in view of the size of this city state of 300,000 inhabitants, including slaves. Pericles entrusted the supervision of these undertakings to Phidias, then the leading sculptor in Athens; but for the architecture of the various buildings other men were responsible.

In the Parthenon, begun in 447 and completed by 432 B.C., Ictinus and Callicrates undertook to create the most splendid temple in Greece, one that should be worthy of Athena and a fit shrine for her image. Though not the largest Greek temple, its size is exceptional, approximately 228 by 101 feet, measured along the stylobate. Consequently, the usual six-column front is here expanded to eight columns, with seventeen along each side. Built of Pentelic marble throughout, the Parthenon marks the culmination of the Greek Doric temple. The adjustment of all its parts is the fruit of centuries of experiment by Greek architects. Where the earlier temples had emphasized weight and power in proportions, the Parthenon (fig. 49) balances strength and grace. The columns, about five and a half lower diameters in height, look sturdy but not ponderous, and require a lighter entablature, approximately one fourth the height of the building.

If the Parthenon has a completeness and perfection of form rarely found elsewhere, we must remember that it is a simple problem, by comparison with the complex requirements of a Roman forum on the one hand, or a medieval cathedral on the other. The form seems expressive of Greece. The deities of the Olympic pantheon, though more powerful than men, and though immortal, were subject to human passions — to anger, jealousy, and love. Greek religion was not of the spirit, as is Christianity. It might be crudely described as a system of barter; if an individual respected certain customs and performed sacrifices, he might expect protection or favor from the god. Emotion, love, adoration had little place here. A rational attitude dictated this architecture, which seems to cling to the earth. Moreover, unlike a church, worship took place outside a Greek temple, at an altar in front of it. The temple was a shrine in which the statue of the god might be housed, and although people could enter it to see the statue, it was not intended to accommodate crowds. Consequently, its effectiveness was greater on the exterior than the interior.

Furthermore, the care lavished on the structure shows itself not only in the larger aspects of design, but also in the processes of construction. While the columns seem to be vertical and evenly spaced, careful measurements show that the central openings are wider than those at the corners, both on the front and the sides of the temple. Moreover, the columns tilt inwards. The variations in spacing and the departure from verticality are so minute as to be almost invisible, but they contribute to the impression of stability. The eye seems to demand in stone buildings some hint of greater strength at the corners — a desire that in the last analysis is rooted in sound construction. But the most curious feature of the Parthenon lies in the curvature of its main horizontal lines; the stylobate is not a dead level but curves upward slightly, 2½ inches in a length of 101 feet on the front, and on the side 4¼ inches in 228 feet. This refinement is visible when one sights along the line of the top step. That the regular curves are due neither to accident nor to time is certain; the Greeks felt it worth while to incur the trouble and expense of such careful construction to counteract an illusion of sagging, said to be produced when a series of vertical lines rested on a long horizontal line, or, in other words, columns based on a stylobate. Whether such an illusion might exist or not, the refinements prevented a mechanical or machine-made appearance in the building.

To the Greeks, man was incomparably the subject most worthy of their study. The purpose of the Greek sculptor, in the century and a half after the Persian Wars, was to achieve a version of the figure that should be not necessarily like the individuals of his experience, but rather an embodiment of their possibilities, an ideal concept worthy to represent the gods of Olympus. This goal is manifest both in what he chose to do, with the consent of his patrons, and in how he did it. With all of the new knowledge at his disposal, the sculptor still limited himself to a few types. His males may be adolescents, boyish forms of fifteen or sixteen, slight and graceful, but without the malproportions that so often mark that stage in a man's development. A few years older is the type of the young man (fig. 58) in his early twenties, now physically developed; and beyond that in turn, the type adopted for the older gods, Zeus and Poseidon, still in the prime of life and physical vigor, full bearded, the muscles hardened by years of exercise. The young woman, such as the Athena Lemnia (fig. 50), in age and growth is a fit sister to the young man, adult and sturdy; her type also matures, as in the Demeter of the Parthenon east pediment (fig. 54), heavier but with no signs of age yet apparent. To the Greeks of this period, since infancy is immature, it was unworthy the sculptor's study, whereas age, with its attendant physical decline, was also avoided. Only ideal types were suitable.

Furthermore, the artist presented not what the body is, but what it ought to be. His treatment was generalized, selective in the extreme; he eliminated all minor and accidental details that might detract attention from his broad purpose. He thus created an intellectual and objective analysis of the human figure. Through this approach, the figures and their parts involve a clarity of definition, a unity of structure, a formal description that transcends reality and endows them with an Olympian detachment.

The sculpture of the Parthenon is more basic today for an understanding of the art of Periclean Athens than it would have been for one of Phidias' contemporaries, who could examine his huge gold and ivory Athena Parthenos and the still larger Zeus at Olympia, statues on which rested Phidias' reputation in antiquity. But the intrinsic worth of the materials of these statues invited their destruction, and the copies of them have only an archaeological interest, whereas the Parthenon sculpture is original. Although Phidias had charge of that sculpture, its quantity is too large to have been the product of a single chisel. Its harmony of design and its adaptation to the architecture exhibit a unity postulating some guiding spirit, but to carve 92 metopes, some 520 feet of frieze, and the monumental figures of the pediments called for the work of many hands. One may imagine, though one cannot prove, that the opportunities drew to

Athens in these years many artists — some of them of an older generation, whose artistic style crystallized about the time of the Aegina pediments, others who grew up with the sculptors of Olympia, while there were doubtless many men, still in the formative stage of their careers, whose methods of expression might have been shaped by Phidias himself.

The metopes, completed before the frieze and pediments, confirm this supposition. Their position on the building proves that they were in place by 438 B.C., by which time the building was roofed. The best-preserved examples deal with the struggles of Centaurs and Lapiths. They exhibit striking differences of hand; some are mediocre, reminiscent of the angularity but devoid of the quality of the Aegina marbles; others look Myronic. A few are wholly Phidian in style (fig. 51). Opposing diagonals, provided by Centaur and Lapith as they pass each other in the fight, give the design best suited to its location between the verticals and horizontals of the architecture. The Lapith's robe slips from his shoulders and contrasts its pattern to the broad expression of the body. To believe that this metope was carved by the master is quite legitimate, since he probably executed one or two himself as models for his assistants.

The frieze illustrates the Panathenaic procession, the culmination of the quadrennial celebration in honor of Athena, which carried to her in the Parthenon the robe embroidered during the preceding four years by maidens of Athens. In this ceremony, all the citizenry of Athens are represented: maidens, magistrates, and young men come to pay honor and make sacrifice to the patron of their city. In the west frieze, youths form the procession, stand beside their horses or mount them (fig. 52). The parade moves along each side toward the east, so that it accompanied, so to speak, the visitor to the Parthenon; as he proceeded, he glimpsed it at the top of the cella wall inside the colonnade. At the east end, a group of seated gods (fig. 53), guests at Athena's celebration as it were, form a divine reviewing stand, and look backward toward the procession as it approaches.

To treat without monotony a band of sculpture so long and narrow — it measures over 520 feet in length but only 3 feet 4 inches in height — called for fertility of imagination. The figures vary in pose, in their draped or undraped condition, in their relation to the horses, mounted or on foot, in front or behind, active or quiet. Chariots, sheep and cows for the sacrifices, youths on foot bearing water jugs, magistrates, maidens, and gods add to the wealth of material filling the frieze without crowding it. Its location on the building under the ceiling of the porch, where light could not reach it directly but had to be reflected from the floor of the porch or the ground outside, demanded an exceptional technical scheme. Ordinarily in low-relief sculpture, the parts of the figure project from the background in proportion to their roundness or mass in the human figure; thus, the calf would have more projection than the ankle, the head more than the neck. However, with the light coming from below, a normal projection of feet and legs would allow them to cast heavy shadows, and so draw overmuch attention to themselves at the expense of the head and torso. Therefore, Phidias invented a system of sloping outward the planes of relief. The boldest projection of the upper parts of the relief may reach 2¼ inches, while those in the lower part are restricted to a maximum of 1¼ inches. Also, to indicate several planes, as when a man stands behind a horse, or in a four-horse team, he lets the planes overlap like shingles, to create more apparent depth than would ordinarily be possible with this amount of relief.

The pediments form the climax of this sculptural scheme. In the east pediment, Phidias depicts the Birth of Athena; in the west, the Contest of Athena and Poseidon for the patronage of the land of Attica. Though the central groups of both pediments have now vanished, it is possible, through sketches made centuries ago and from descriptions, to reach some idea of their arrangement. Their composition is the culmination of the line of development in pedimental sculpture that began back in archaic times. First, the single figure, which overstressed the axis of the pediment, is replaced here by a group of two figures to create a dynamic contrast of action. In the west pediment, for example, Poseidon's movement to the right answers that of Athena, who draws away to the left. Second, on either side group echoes group but without duplication; in any pair, Phidias varies the pose, sex, or costume without losing the larger balance. Third, a sequence of action leads the eye from the angles up to the climax in the center, and fourth, individual figures and groups alike exhibit a series of beautiful transitions from one to another. For example, in the three figures identified as Demeter, Persephone, and Iris (fig. 54), the first leans against the second, whereas Iris is more independent. However, the extended arm of Persephone overlaps that of Iris to carry the eye from one to the other. Moreover, the deep fold of drapery that sweeps back from Iris' shin leads over in one direction to the lap of Persephone, and in the other develops into reversed curves to complete the action of Iris.

In the drapery of these figures, Phidias selects his detail to emphasize those folds and movements that help explain the meaning of each character; for instance, the flowing curves of Iris' costume express her haste to spread the news of Athena's birth. Minor folds, which might be accurate in a realistic sense, would have no artistic validity here, and are sup-pressed by the sculptor, lest they destroy the effect of ideal intellectual-ized conceptions in godlike form. The so-called Theseus (fig. 55) illus-trates the same method applied to the figure. The principal masses are firmly defined; veins, wrinkles, minor changes of surface are ignored, not because Phidias and his associated artists were unaware of them, but be-cause, in their intellectual analysis of the figure, such minutiae seemed incidental. Such elimination of detail, if carried to an extreme, may result in lifeless generalization, as it does at the hands of Roman copyists, but judiciously employed it produces epic conceptions. As a nineteenth-century sculptor remarked on first seeing these marbles, 'They look like human beings, but where is one to find such models?' Such models do not, and never did, exist; given a thorough knowledge of the body, one must then analyze it, distinguish the important from the incidental, and give form to the significant parts. The Theseus is particularly interesting, since it alone of all the figures of the pediments has the head preserved. The broad skull and rounded cheeks appear to indicate the type of head pre-ferred by Phidias, since these characteristics also exist in the copies of the Athena Parthenos.

Great as is the artistic effort represented by the Parthenon and its sculpture, it was only one of the Periclean undertakings for the beautifi-cation of Athens. If, in the Parthenon, the apogee of the Greek Doric order is reached, the Ionic order comes to its summit in the Erechtheum. The asymmetrical, not to say amorphous, plan of this edifice as built is unique in Greek architecture, which makes it more than probable that the conception of the architect was not completed. The north porch (fig. 56), exquisite in its proportions, is graceful but has only as much strength as this lighter order permits. The Ionic never lends itself to an expression of austere power, as does the Doric. The door of the north porch is sump-tuous, the size of the jambs and of the cornice at the top proportioned to the scale of the opening. On the south front of the Erechtheum, in the small Porch of the Maidens, the architect substituted six female figures for columns to support the superstructure. In theory, it is dubious whether such a motive is desirable, but one must admit that the device handled with tact on a small scale adds a charming variant to the customary portico. The sturdy figures look capable of carrying the weight above, which is lightened by the omission of the frieze from the entablature.

The Acropolis, as the ceremonial center of Athens, needed a suitable gateway. Mnesicles designed the Propylaea (fig. 57) for this purpose, and although circumstances prevented his ambitious plan from being carried out in its entirety, even the part that was built exhibits a monumentality of scale fit for an entrance to this great center. The principal colonnades are Doric, but to line the central passage Mnesicles selected the slender Ionic, which left a more open interior. This passage is accented by the large portico, flanked by smaller colonnades on either side, one of which gives access to the little Ionic Temple of Wingless Victory on a bastion in front of the Acropolis. A sculptured frieze or parapet surrounded this eminence, adorned with low reliefs of Victories driving cows to sacrifice. The style is similar to but more developed than that of the Parthenon, the clinging drapery thinner and with less elimination of detail.

A second sculptor of this generation, almost as famous in antiquity as Phidias, was Polyclitus. The uninspired copies from late Greek and Roman days of his best-known statue, the Doryphorus or Spearbearer (fig. 58), give little idea of his ability. Pliny implies that much of the beauty in the bronzes of Polyclitus lay in the surface treatment, always the first quality lost in a copy. However, we see here the so-called walking motive of Polyclitus. Like the Statuette from Ligourio (fig. 38), the Spearbearer rests his weight on one foot, hardly touching the ground with the other. Therefore, the axis of the body assumes a slight reversed curve, with one hip higher than the other, but the torso bent enough to balance the figure. The ease of posture realized in this way was carried further by the succeeding century. Polyclitus modeled the Doryphorus to illustrate his theory of the ideal proportions of the human body. He himself said, 'Successful attainment in art is the result of minute accuracy in a multitude of arithmetic proportions.' With parts of the body as units of measurement, Polyclitus worked out his arithmetic of the figure. The head, for example, was one seventh the height of the figure; the foot, three times the length of the palm of the hand; the lower leg to the kneecap, six palms; from the kneecap to the middle of the abdomen, six palms; and so on.

Polyclitus defines each part of the figure with a clarity of shape that leaves it an integral and yet independent unit of the larger whole. Indeed this tendency is characteristic of Greek thought at this time on all matters. The Doric column is a defined entity in itself, and yet, for all its own unity, it subordinates itself to the larger unity of the temple. The singleness of purpose and expression of the temple is composed of the sum of its parts. Similarly, the choruses in Aeschylus and Euripides are poems, independent entities, and yet essential to the larger expression of the whole drama. This craving for clarity of form was deep-rooted in the Greek mind. It is suggestive that Greek mathematics, far as it was developed, found no place for the concept of infinity; that, by definition, is unformed, amorphous, intangible, and thus incomprehensible to the Greek mind. This clarity of form applied to sculpture derives from the linear structure of archaic figures, whose forms attain greater breadth and more idealism in the fifth century. Polyclitus gave perfect form to the ideal toward which the Greek sculptors had been moving for centuries.

By this time, vase painting also had freed itself of the last traces of archaism. Although the figures are still indicated in line, the Slaughter of the Niobids (fig. 59) on the Orvieto vase shows how free the painter is to represent his characters in any posture he may wish. Some of the types are idealized and reminiscent of statues by Phidias; the drawing and composition, on the other hand, reflect the manner of Polygnotus, the foremost painter of the time of Pericles. At least as significant as the new-won freedom is the irregular ground line on which Apollo and Artemis and the children of Niobe stand or lie. Whereas in archaic vases, such as the Heracles and Antaeus (fig. 36), the lower border of the scene sufficed for both support and setting, the later painter feels it necessary to indicate uneven ground and to suggest by repetition of the ground line the existence of two or more planes in depth. That such an innovation is a step in the direction of realism of setting is undeniable; but this needless complication destroys the clarity of design and the adaptation of the figures to the surface. The gain in reality hardly compensates for the decline in decorative value and the indifference to the medium. The great period of vase painting had passed; and as realism advanced, the art declined to a craft, its place being taken by the celebrated painters whose works have vanished.

Toward the end of the fifth century, the Peloponnesian War developed from the struggle for supremacy between Athens and Sparta and, before it ended, involved and weakened most of the Greek city states. It foretells the uninspiring history of the fourth century, a dismal series of petty wars, when one city after another, singly or in coalition, rose to pre-eminence for a few years, only to fall before the jealousy of its neighbors. The spectacle was hardly edifying; it tended to lower the prestige of the state. In Pericles' time, the state had been the great patron of the arts. The Parthenon and the Temple of Zeus, with their sculpture, were civic undertakings, grand in scale, and public in purpose; so, too, were the gold and ivory Athena and the Olympian Zeus of Phidias, as well as Polyclitus' Hera at Argos of the same materials. In the fourth century, the cities, impoverished by war, could not afford such enterprises, and the citizens, partly inspired by the philosophers, developed their own individualism, and no longer submerged their personalities as before in the collective expression of the city.

Inevitably, the artists, who worked more than hitherto for private individuals, tended to smaller concepts. At least by comparison, they began to turn from idealism to reality, although they did not yet carry that quality to an extreme. They concerned themselves with the minor gods, or with intimate aspects of the greater deities. The Olympian divinities lose their abstract grandeur, their serene dignity; within limits, they display more human emotions. The artist and his patrons began to approach the work subjectively, and substituted sentiment and prettiness for grandeur. Portraits become commoner and more literal than the generalized fifth-century examples. None of these changes are carried to excess, but they point the new direction for art, and introduce some of the tendencies that, after the death of Alexander, became more pronounced.

In architecture, a feature of the late fifth century and early fourth century is the invention or development of the Corinthian order, in detail the richest of the three Greek orders. Somewhat similar to the Ionic, the column has a more elaborate base. Its capital, the easiest identification card of the order, is illustrated in the Tholos at Epidaurus (fig. 60); its inverted bell-shaped mass is encircled with two rows of acanthus leaves, whose tips curl away from the bell; above them paired tendrils coil like watch springs under the corners of an abacus, concave on all four sides. Such a capital, less austere and less functional than the Doric, seems analogous to the subjectivity of its contemporary sculpture. An entablature, richer than the Ionic, is characterized by a cornice, supported on *modillions,* brackets of stone whose under surface is formed by a curling acanthus leaf. However, the Greeks seem to have used this order sparingly, and mainly in small buildings, such as the Choragic Monument of Lysicrates in Athens; whereas its richness was to bring it popularity in Roman times.

Three sculptors rose to fame at this time, namely, Praxiteles, Scopas, and Lysippus. The two first were active early in the fourth century, but of Scopas little is known. Classic authors mention twenty-five works by him. Of these, only the very fragmentary sculpture from the pediments of the Temple of Athena Alea at Tegea reflects his style, and even this bears the same relation to Scopas that the Parthenon marbles do to Phidias. His most famous statue, the Meleager, was often copied. One of the best versions is that in the Fogg Museum in Cambridge, Massachusetts, but the discrepancies among existing replicas are so pronounced that few trustworthy conclusions about Scopas can be deduced from them. This wandering artist seems to have concerned himself with the stormier, more emotional aspects of life, an interest suggested by the wide-open eyes, the lips parted as though the figure were breathing heavily, and the tragic implications of much of his subject matter.

Praxiteles, on the other hand, preferred the cheerful and pleasant side of existence. The list of his works cited in ancient literature exceeds that of Scopas', and testifies to his popularity. He was exceptional among the great sculptors of Greece in that he preferred marble to bronze. Consequently the designs of his statues, such as the Hermes Carrying the Infant Dionysus (fig. 61), an original Greek work, take into account, within limits, the material. Extant marble copies of the Discus Thrower and the Doryphorus (fig. 58) derived from originals in bronze; since the cross section of stone at the ankles seemed weak, the copyist introduced the ungainly tree stump to support and scratch the legs of these unfortunate athletes. But Praxiteles used the support as part of the motive, so that, no longer extraneous, it became an integral unit of the design. In this instance, Hermes, at rest for a moment on his journey, lounges against the tree stump over which his drapery falls.

The pose of the figure involves a reversed curve in its axis, what is often called the S-curve of Praxiteles. This device developed from Polyclitus' walking motive, but is softer and more relaxed. The head with its dreamy eyes suggests the introspective, as though Hermes' thoughts were far away. This effect comes from lids drawn half over the eyeball, the lower lid barely indicated. The beauty of finish, for which ancient writers extol the work of Praxiteles, is illustrated in the textures of the drapery, which simulates cloth with remarkable success; of the hair, which looks far more like hair than the formal versions of earlier designs; and of the flesh, which has a subtle sensuousness. The modeling rebels against the fifth-century sculptors' technique. Definition has yielded to a softer, filmier approximation of reality. No longer do we see each muscular mass separated, and the whole figure composed of the sum of its parts; instead, the parts fuse, one plane melts into another; for Praxiteles was more concerned than Polyclitus, for example, with the visual effect of the figure, and consequently less interested in an intellectualized statement of its structural parts.

These changes entail a decline in sculpturesque quality and open the path to the softness and sentiment of later times. The Hermes itself, however, retains, because of its strength and idealism, much nobility of conception. The effeminacy, often observed in copies of Praxiteles' work and in statues influenced by him, must have resulted from an overemphasis by the later craftsmen of qualities that he himself kept under control. The wide difference in quality between the Hermes and the Aphrodite of

Cnidus (fig. 62) testifies to the inadequacy of Roman copies. The former is unique as the only extant example carved by the chisel of an artist whom antiquity ranked among the great. The latter, far more famous than the Hermes in classic times, seems to have been the first rendering of the female nude in Greek sculpture in the round. The motive, Aphrodite preparing for the bath, permits the goddess to drop her clothing on a vase beside her, which gives the same kind of support within the composition as that provided by the stump on which Hermes leans. This theme, though subjective and sensuous, avoids sensuality; the goddess is unaware of or indifferent to the presence of spectators, and is in fact as dreamy as the Hermes. By analogy with the latter, it seems only fair to conclude that the extraordinary fame in the past of this Aphrodite was partly owing to a beauty of finish in the original, and possibly in part to the sensational nature of the motive.

The death of Mausolus, Satrap of Caria, in the middle of the fourth century, gave his widow Artemisia the opportunity to build the Mausoleum at Halicarnassus as his tomb and memorial. Its scale and the quantity of its sculpture made it renowned as one of the seven wonders of the ancient world. Three friezes in high relief, a chariot group, and many individual statues enriched it. One frieze showed a chariot race, with figures influenced by Scopas; another the Battle of Centaurs and Lapiths; while the third dealt with the struggle of the Greeks and Amazons (fig. 63), and at once invites comparison with the Parthenon frieze. In the Mausoleum, the characters, rendered in bolder relief, are widely spaced, thus creating an emphasis on each individual figure. The violence of action demanded by the subject permits repeated insistence on the diagonal line, as the fighters attack or withdraw from their adversaries. The drapery of many of the Amazons is so disposed that the figures are seen virtually in the nude, another case of the fourth-century interest in the female figure already displayed by Praxiteles.

The story of fourth-century sculpture closes with the career of Lysippus, a younger man than Praxiteles or Scopas, and one of the court portraitists of Alexander the Great. Tradition says that Lysippus worked in a bronze foundry, and, though he did not restrict himself to that medium, he seems to have preferred it to marble. The lighter proportions of the figure favored in his generation are emphasized by his new canon of proportions, in which the head is one eighth the height of the figure rather than the one seventh that Polyclitus deemed ideal. The statue called the Apoxyomenos, of an athlete, who after exercise scrapes from his skin the dust and the oil with which young men anointed themselves, is extant only in later copies; it seems to illustrate these taller proportions. The Agias, on the other hand, is a Greek statue (fig. 64), probably produced by the workshop of Lysippus himself and, if so, under his personal supervision. The academic quality of the Apoxyomenos is less obvious here, as though Lysippus' new formula had not yet been developed, but the approach to a more visual rendering is evident. Pliny tells us that 'while others had made men as they were, he had made them as they were seen to be [*quales viderentur esse*].' The statement characterized the direction taken by fourth-century sculpture culminating in Lysippus, namely a decline in the intellectual analysis of the figure, replaced by a softer articulation of the body, less definition of its separate parts, and hence a greater naturalism. The old clarity of structure is no longer sought; in its place, there is a looser organization, paralleling the change in Greek drama between the tragedies of Euripides and the comedies of Aristophanes.

During these two centuries, the Greeks first acquired such knowledge and skill as enabled them to be fairly accurate in their version of the figure. That information was no sooner available than they turned to superhuman figures, conceived as intellectual ideals worthy to express the Greek conception of the dignity of Olympian gods. Then, the austerity and nobility of those concepts yielded, under the baleful influence of fratricidal wars, to more intimate and human conceptions, which inevitably led to a realism that was to grow and flower only after the death of Alexander.

The Character of Later Classic Sculpture

SHORT-LIVED though it was, the empire of Alexander the Great created a profound change in Greek life and ideals. For the two previous centuries, Greek culture had exhibited a completeness within itself. HELLENISTIC The archaic influences from Egypt and Mesopotamia had dissolved or had been absorbed, to permit the Greek or Hellenic civilization its purest expression. With the armies of Macedonia, Hellenic culture overflowed the geographic limits of Greece, affecting the art of other countries as remote as India; but as it spread, Hellenic culture itself was modified by the ideals of the conquered lands, thus producing a Hellenistic, or Greek-like world. Some of its characteristics grow from seed planted in the fourth century. The old confidence in the Olympic pantheon was already waning, partly under the influence of the philosophers and partly in the normal course of history, when Greece was brought into closer contact with the religions of Egypt and the Near East. Oriental cults, some of them mystic, rose to momentary or permanent consequence: for example, the Oriental conception of Artemis as the earth mother. As in modern times, many shades and varieties of belief existed simultaneously.

Moreover, the Hellenistic age gave birth to criticism and erudition, one cannot quite say at the expense of creative and imaginative energy, but supplementary to it and modifying it. Libraries were founded, such as that at Pergamum, and especially the one at Alexandria which contained half a million scrolls. Scholarly editions of the writings of 'old masters' were compiled, just as today we study annotated versions of Shakespeare and Chaucer. After all, Homer was as remote from the Greeks of the third century as Chaucer is from us in the twentieth century. With scholarship came a development of science. Aristotle, after the middle of the fourth century, tended to base his philosophy more on the world as he found it than did Plato, who early in the same century dealt with the world as he would have liked it to be. Plato's *Republic* describes an ideal state; in *The Poetics*, Aristotle examines tragedy, for instance, by an analysis of the elements that appear in successful tragedies. During the third century, Archimedes had diverse interests in many branches of science; he experimented with the lever, discovered the principle of specific gravity, and contributed also to astronomy. Euclid developed his theorems of geometry, for centuries the basis of that division of mathematics. Eratosthenes measured the earth, computed its diameter and circumference, and came remarkably close to the truth.

Such a complex background is apt to produce an art period without the consistency characteristic of earlier Greek epochs. Strains and counterstrains weave a diverse texture, difficult of compact treatment. An art of the connoisseur appears, with the variety of delicate figurines from Tanagra and elsewhere — statuettes in terra cotta made from molds in which the head, the body, and perhaps other elements might be united in different combinations. A wider range is now permitted the sculptor; no longer is he restricted to a limited series of types, but rather he may turn at his discretion to figures of old age or infancy, to genre scenes based on incidents of daily life, and even to narrative or descriptive topics handled as pictures in relief sculpture.

These tendencies gain momentum during the third century, but reach their climax only after the conquest of Greece by Rome, that is, about 146 B.C., the date of the fall of Corinth. Then the Greek cities were pillaged of their art treasures. Some generations earlier the Roman conquest of the Greek cities in southern Italy and Sicily had stimulated Roman admiration for Greek art. But with the growth of Rome, there were not enough originals to satisfy the demand and a thriving trade in copies of famous originals sprang up, analogous to our production of casts and copies of paintings or even photographs of masterpieces. These copies, often made by Greek craftsmen of Hellenistic or Roman date, provide much of our information about noted Greek statues. However, through most of its history, the Roman taste was realistic and measured the success of a work of art by its fidelity to nature; this taste helps to explain not only the naturalism of their own sculpture, but also the avidity with which the Romans sought copies of Greek originals from the time of the Parthenon and later, but paid slight attention to the archaic period. Occasionally, but only occasionally, do we find artists who recognized the beauty of pattern in archaic art enough to use it for inspiration. From the more sophisticated generations the later designers borrowed freely, sometimes from one man, sometimes from another, or stole ideas from Lysippus to combine with others more likely to be found in the fifth century. This free borrowing from the past, called eclecticism, like so many other characteristics of late classic sculpture, is echoed in recent times.

One of the finest examples of Hellenistic sculpture is the Aphrodite of Melos (fig. 65), to which archaeologists have assigned many dates from the fifth century on. But so far as is known, the fifth century avoided the nude female figure in art, and while the fourth century accepted it, such statues as the Aphrodite of Cnidus (fig. 62) are completely nude. It remained for later times to try the effect of a partly draped figure. The small head exaggerates the lighter proportions instituted by Lysippus, again an indication of late work, and the cryptic motive also seems unlikely in earlier times. But although in all probability a late work, the Aphrodite of Melos has a beauty about which no doubt can exist; its idealization and its sense of form rank it with the masterpieces of any epoch.

The one thread that leads through the maze of these later centuries is the emphasis on realism, the precise record of the visible, the individual, and even the accidental, in contrast to a concern with the imaginary or the ideal in form. Such a purpose demands a technical dexterity that at times approaches virtuosity. At the close of the fourth century, the Victory of Samothrace (fig. 66), reconstructed from many fragments, is conceived sensationally as she lands on the prow of a ship to sound the trumpet of victory. The whole figure is made to convey movement. A thin flowing costume, reminiscent of late fifth-century statues, gathers here and there in heavy masses, as it might have toward the middle of the fourth century. However, these eclectic features merge with the Hellenistic desire for intricacy when this drapery sweeps around from the front to the side, drawing with it the attention of the spectator. The front seems incomplete in itself; so too does the side; and only when the work is seen from several points of view can the artist's conception be fully grasped. In short, he insists that his admirer walk around the work. This attitude, at the opposite extreme from the method of archaic sculpture, had been growing steadily since then, until here it reached its full possibilities.

The purest realism of the time characterizes the first school of Pergamum, represented by the dedications of Attalus I, late in the third century. This ruler commemorated his defeat of the Gauls by sculptured groups, some of which dealt with the subject itself, while others, like the struggles of the Gods and Giants, of the Greeks and Amazons, or of the Greeks and Persians, implied comparison of his success with the epic and historic contests of civilization and barbarism. The Dying Gaul (fig. 67) enhances the impression of physical prowess, with his superb body, whose anatomy is thoroughly observed and recorded, no part overemphasized and none neglected. The hair, matted with grease, follows the customs of the Gauls. His calloused feet are cut and scratched on the soles, as though by sharp stones. Gore drips from the wound in his side, while on the ground litter of the battlefield creates a similar reality of setting. However, it is his courage, his reluctance to accept defeat while he yet breathes, that gives vitality to the figure, qualities vividly in contrast to the Dead Persian of the same series of statues, who seems soft even in death. This latter, dressed in trousers that the Greeks considered effeminate, has crooked his arm under his head as though to welcome death as an escape from the lash of his masters. The contrast of these figures implied that to defeat the vigorous Gauls was even more difficult than it had been two and a half centuries before to repulse the Persians.

If these dedications of Attalus I form the first school of Pergamum, the chief monument of the second school of Pergamum under Eumenes II, early in the second century before Christ, is the Altar of Zeus at Pergamum. The altar itself, surrounded on three sides with Ionic colonnades and on the fourth approached by a flight of steps, was placed on a high platform, on whose walls a frieze of figures in high relief sculpture (fig. 68) depicted the time-honored, if not hackneyed, theme of the struggle of gods and giants. The designer's concept of his subject typifies the scholarship of his own day. To represent only the well-known gods of the Olympic pantheon would not provide enough figures to fill this length of over 400 feet. It seems as though the sculptor had read all the available sources in literature to compile as complete a catalogue of gods as possible, together with all attributes, whether objects or attendants, that could be associated with them. Many of these characters did not enter into the common knowledge of the people of his day; therefore, the sculptor had to label each figure. In the Parthenon, such an expedient was unnecessary, since the principal figures would be recognized instantly by any Greek, whereas it made little difference whether the minor individuals were identified or not; their decorative and expressive bearing on the major theme was too clear to need comment. That this later sculptor felt it necessary so to label his characters indicates an atmosphere of research rather than of imaginative creation, as though a Shakespearean actor paused in the midst of his lines to deliver a footnote to his audience on the interpretation of 'miching mallecho.'

The many figures in the Pergamene relief are well united, partly because the legs of the giants change into serpents whose coils wind in and out among the characters to bind them together. Like the Parthenon frieze, but unlike that from the Mausoleum, figures fill the space, but in other respects the contrast is marked. These figures exaggerate reality, if such be possible, and so insist on the muscular structure that each independent mass in the torso clamors for attention. Heavy though the muscles are, one feels less real strength in these gods or giants than in the Dying Gaul; in fact they look like professional strong men, muscle-bound in every part. Thus as representation, they leave something to be desired; in other respects, they are even less satisfactory. Emphasis on everything results in emphasis on nothing; the protrusion of each small mass in the figures creates a monotony of small lights broken by deep shadows. A sense of strain and of striving for effect results from the exaggerated muscular structure, the agitation, and the sensational treatment. The sculptor is a remarkable technician, not to say a virtuoso, but he lacks that supreme gift of the artist, a knowledge of when to stop. In literature, the concept of Zeus, king of gods and men, enthroned on Mt. Olympus, and able to enforce his will by the thunderbolt only he can wield, is grand and vivid. But a thunderbolt hardly lends itself to definition in stone; to render it as a torch, spiked at one end, which could be twirled in the hand like a tomahawk, or could project, splinter-like, from a leg, destroys that concept. Admirable in some respects, and typical of its generation, the Pergamene frieze, nevertheless, grows tiresome, whereas the beauties of the Parthenon frieze increase with familiarity.

This Hellenistic advance in realism involves a decline or disappearance of idealism. If that is true of style in the Dying Gaul and the Pergamene altar, the abandonment of idealized subjects further exemplified it. While not unknown before, genre figures — that is, characters taken from daily life whose interest lies more in their action than in their abstract implications — now acquired wide popularity. The tendency of the fourth-century sculptors toward humanization and the growth of emotion and sentiment prepared the way. In subject, these genre figures are diverse, but a passion for realism binds them together in treatment. For example, we find a Drunken Old Woman singing in her cups, her knees clasping the wine jar, her scrawny neck like that of a plucked chicken, her features haggard, her skin loose, and the physical decline of old age apparent in every detail. Such a work reaches its realistic goal but, though clever, is ugly. Equally literal is the Old Market Woman in the Metropolitan Museum, even to the indication of feathers on the fowl she carries to market in her basket; if she is less disgusting than the previous example, one should observe that in each case it is the subject and its associations, not sculptural considerations, that dictate one's reaction. Aside from the virtuosity of technique, the artist was content to rest his case on his subject, presented as vividly as possible. Some of these genre figures, such as the second-century Boy with a Goose (fig. 69) by Boethus, are humorous and mock heroic. To be convincing in its comedy, the figure must have the proportions of infancy, the large head and the plump arms and legs. Even when a child was a part of the subject, as in Praxiteles' Hermes Carrying the Infant Dionysus (fig. 61), the earlier artists had avoided the character of infancy. That character, inherently human, is here essential to the effect.

Reality again predominates in the pictorial reliefs, also called pastoral, Hellenistic, and Alexandrian reliefs. They correspond in spirit as well as in date with the Idylls of Theocritus and his associates. Some of them may have come from the workshops in Alexandria in Egypt; they first appear in Hellenistic times, though they continue to be produced much later; frequently their subjects are pastoral, reflecting an urban dweller's attraction to the simplicity and peace of country life and nature; and there is a strong tendency to design the relief as though it were a painting. Typical is the Farmer Driving his Bull to Market (fig. 70). The same technical skill is in evidence here as in the genre figures. The sculptor presents a picture in stone, remarkable as representation or narrative, even to the inclusion of landscape elements, such as buildings and trees in the background. Such details of setting may descend from the litter of the battlefield on the bases of the dedications of Attalus I (fig. 67), or from the pictorial features that helped to fill the great frieze from Pergamum. The artist keeps some of these features in very low relief, and allows others to project boldly; thus, he implies depths that do not exist and prepares the way for the illusionism sometimes present in Roman sculpture. But he attains his success in these matters at the cost of sculptural design and disregard for his medium. However dexterous, it remains a *tour de force* to push stone beyond its appropriate limits.

WITH the growth of realism and individualism, an objective attitude in portraiture is inevitable. Such portraits as exist from the fifth century in Greece and many even from the fourth century are idealized ROMAN and generalized. The Hellenistic sculptors, however, turned eagerly to portraiture and have left us many individualized statues of such men as Demosthenes. By Roman times, the patron demanded of his artist a description of his features as precise as an official report. The matter of fact, practical spirit of the Romans dwelt in reality, not in an imaginative sphere. Consequently, their architecture deals with specific problems; their sculpture records the men who for centuries ruled the Western world. The Unknown Roman (fig. 71) of the first century before Christ is a speaking likeness. One can imagine this stern individual debating in the senate, or leading the legions to fresh conquests; one cannot picture him enraptured by art or literature. For his portrait, he would expect that the individual bony structure of his skull, the worried furrows of his brow, all his facial peculiarities would be present in true proportion. He would expect to compare his bust to himself. And yet this portrait reveals his character through his features.

Realism as an artistic goal is no less evident in the series of painted portraits from Fayum in Egypt, mostly from the first and second centuries of the Christian era. These paintings were made during the lifetime of their subjects. After death, these life-size portraits were held in place over the head of the mummy by wrappings so arranged that the painting would be visible. The medium selected was encaustic, in which a considerable range of pigment suspended in melted wax could be applied to a surface of wood. The artist devoted his greatest attention to the head, delineated in light and shade, with unusually large eyes, and with much success in characterization. The costumes, on the other hand, are indicated in a broad or impressionist manner.

The purpose of a state portrait is different, but only slightly. The Augustus from Prima Porta (fig. 72) not only resembles Augustus as a man, but also indicates his position as emperor. Again the head is realistic; it tells us exactly how this ruler looked. His oratorical pose, as though he were addressing his troops, bespeaks his position. Virgil traces the ancestry of the Julian line of emperors back through Aeneas to Venus, and the cupid and dolphin beside Augustus allude to this compliment. The statue represents a great man, accustomed to command, and idealizes his position.

The procession on the frieze of the Ara Pacis Augustae (fig. 73) contains a double file of portraits, including those of Augustus and Livia, and between them her son. The same individuality reigns here, though Augustus appears rather as a citizen than as a ruler. The foreground figures are in high relief, those of the background in low relief. This method, like that in the pictorial reliefs, indicates distance and reminds one of the spatial effects in Roman architecture. In this case, the sculptor restricts himself to long quiet rows of figures, with no landscape in the background to distract attention from the procession or to contradict the material, but nevertheless the Ara Pacis Augustae looks forward to illusionism.

The panels from the Arch of Titus (fig. 74) in the Roman Forum illustrate that quality. The Roman legionaries in A.D. 71 carry the spoils of

Jerusalem in triumph, and are about to pass through an arch. Ignorance of perspective makes the illusion less convincing than it might be otherwise, but the planes of high relief for the foreground figures, contrasted with low relief for those in the background, and coupled with the landscape elements beyond them, betray a love of fact. The Romans did not trust the imagination; all circumstances must be specific and as descriptive as possible.

The motive in the Arch of Titus was a single isolated event, but at times the Romans wanted to tell a continuous story in sculpture. A spiral band in relief winds around the shaft of the Column of Trajan. In what is called the method of continuous narration, the sculptor recounts Trajan's campaigns against the Dacians (fig. 75) early in the second century. The incidents arrange themselves in sequence, but are not separated by means of a frame or any other device, though the action of the figures, like those in Egyptian reliefs or wall paintings, serves to describe each scene adequately. This band records the campaign; the soldiers build a bridge or a camp, attack the enemy or are attacked, the emperor addresses his troops or offers sacrifices. A clearer picture of Roman military life and methods would be hard to imagine; indeed, its fascination lies in what it depicts of the past rather than in the sculpture itself.

Aside from the encaustic portraits, the largest single group of Roman paintings are from Pompeii though parallel work exists elsewhere. Archaeologists establish the chronology of these murals in four groups. The incrustation or architectonic plastic style extends down to 80 B.C. Panels of unbroken color or diaper patterns divide the wall into horizontal zones, as though in imitation of marble slabs or other features of architectural decoration. The architectural style occupies the next seventy years. Perhaps under the influence of stage design, painted columns, arches, entablatures, and pediments appear to recede to enframe landscape and figure compositions, and to obliterate the surface of the wall. Nevertheless, the scenes around which this architectural setting is disposed convey some idea of the achievements in painting during the reign of Augustus. The Odyssey Landscapes once illustrated eight incidents, of which six are preserved, of the wandering of Ulysses as told in the tenth and eleventh books of *The Odyssey*. These panels, linked by painted red pilasters or flattened columns, contain small figures set within imaginary landscapes. The purpose of the artist seems not to attempt to render specific scenes, but to create a decorative setting. The indication of atmosphere and of perspective, and the sense of depth given by contrasting color, duplicate the tendency in sculpture toward illusionism in its depth and spatial sense.

The architectural style yielded about 10 B.C. to the ornate style. The semblance of architectural construction hitherto preserved tended to become subordinate to decoration and of minor importance. The paintings within its borders gain in prominence as though imitating easel pictures. Decorative devices, Egyptian in origin, recall the Roman conquest of that country not long before the ornate style began. Finally, most Pompeian paintings date from the intricate style, which began about A.D. 50 and came to an end with the burial of the city in A.D. 79 by the eruption of Mt. Vesuvius. The painted architectural settings become fantastic, with reed-like colonnettes and arabesques in abundance. Extensive panels of flat color, perhaps a vivid red or black, enclose diminutive scenes. Those from the House of the Vettii, such as the Cupids as Wine Dealers (fig. 76), are playful in character, but not inappropriate as wall decorations. Many murals from Pompeii have been preserved, but it is well to remember that that city was not a fashionable center and therefore its paintings are at best pallid reflections of the quality of Roman painting.

The estimation of late Greek and Roman art has changed radically through the centuries. During the Renaissance, when Greek art of the earlier periods was as yet unknown, the kind of sculpture reviewed in this chapter was considered supreme, the acme of skill, and the ultimate to which a sculptor might hope to approach. Even Michelangelo felt it to be the great source of inspiration, however much he might differ from it when he conceived his own sculpture. But with the discovery of the earlier phases of Greek art in the late eighteenth and early nineteenth centuries, this judgment was reversed. The new wave of enthusiasm rated the Hellenic as supreme, almost beyond criticism, and came to regard Roman art as degenerate Greek, to castigate its lack of taste, its want of ideals, its arrogant and vulgar realism. More recently, we have modified that estimate in turn with a saner realization that although Roman art owes much to Greek, it is the expression of a different civilization, one that is by no means inferior to the Greek in all matters. Generally, this later sculpture is weakest where most it follows or tries to follow Hellenic precedent. Less imaginative — one might almost say less creative — certainly less intellectual and abstract in thought than Greek art of the time of Pericles, Roman sculpture has a straightforward matter-of-fact character, developed from later Greek work but in its essence peculiarly Roman. Its realism, its interest in illusionism, and its desire to tell a story in the method of continuous narration are all fruits of the practical Roman genius, the same mentality that made their architecture the most grandly organized in space up to their time, if not indeed of all time.

VI

Roman Architecture

THE character of the Romans inevitably led them to greater success in architecture than in sculpture or painting. The direct applicability of architecture to human needs brought it into accord with their factual spirit, which had called forth those realistic portraits. One thinks of the Romans as soldiers, not as imaginative poets; as ambitious and efficient administrators and statesmen, rather than as artists. Theirs was a world of affairs, not the abstract realm of the mind and spirit. Virgil himself recognized and admitted this characterization.

Others shall beat out the breathing bronze to softer lines . . . shall draw living lineaments from the marble . . . be thy charge, O Roman, to rule the nations in thine empire; this shall be thine art, to ordain the law of peace, to be merciful to the conquered and beat the haughty down. [Aeneid, Book vi, J. W. Mackail translation, p. 126, Modern Library.]

Roman architecture grew from Roman needs. Its engineering accomplishments are stupendous; its sense of planning hitherto not even approached. Its weakness, as might be expected, lies on the decorative side; minor elements, such as moldings, are carved as applied decoration rather than developed as aesthetic growths; never do the Romans approximate that sensitiveness and restraint, that perfect sympathy of design and form in these details, which typifies the Parthenon and Erechtheum. They confuse the ornate with the rich. Their aim is an imperial magnificence, capable at its best of grandeur, but, when less inspired, of grandiosity or vulgarity.

To imagine that Roman architecture, any more than Roman sculpture, is degenerate Greek is to mistake its significance. Nevertheless, the admiration of the Romans for things Greek made inevitable a strong influence from Greek forms, if not from the Hellenic spirit; for example, the orders of Roman architecture derive from those of the earlier civilization, although even here changes are evident. In the first place, the three Greek orders increase to five in number; secondly, the Romans modify even those most traceable to the Greek (fig. 77). Though Vitruvius, a Roman architect of the first century before Christ, codified rules of design for the several orders, existing remains show that no rigid system of proportions prevailed. He prescribed seven lower diameters for the column height of the simplest Roman order, called the Tuscan, a plainer version of the Doric. The Doric itself rises to eight lower diameters, a result of the tendency to reduce its bulk, evident in Greek times and continued by the Romans; in addition to other changes of detail, the Roman Doric has individual bases for each column. Nine diameters are normal for the Roman Ionic, and straight lines unite the volutes of the capital, instead of the graceful curves exemplified in the Erechtheum. The Corinthian, the most popular of the orders in Rome thanks to its richness, and the Composite orders are ten diameters in height. The latter, of still more elaborate design than the Corinthian, derives its name from its capital, in which the scrolls of the Ionic are superposed on the acanthus leafage of the Corinthian order. While the Romans effect dozens of modifications in smaller matters in each of these systems, in general they prefer opulence and discard the restraint of Hellenic detail.

The Romans borrowed the form of their buildings sometimes from the Greeks and sometimes from the Etruscans. The latter had already developed a civilization of their own, strongly influenced by Greece, while Rome was still a small city state. Their use of the arch and vault as forms of primary architectural value may well have affected Roman architecture, while Etruscan temples, many of them constructed of wood and terra cotta on a raised platform allowed the cella to expand to the entire width of the temple, and the porch, restricted to the front, to deepen to the extent of two or three intercolumniations. The Roman rectangular temple, for example the Maison Carrée at Nîmes (fig. 78) in the south of France, dating from the age of Augustus, is an amalgam of Greek and Etruscan influences. This small building is beautifully proportioned and, though sumptuous in detail, especially in the entablature with its carved modillions and scroll design in the frieze, free from ostentation. The plan of the Maison Carrée is more Etruscan than Greek in derivation. The cella increases in width; therefore, although the colonnade remains, much of its length consists of *engaged columns*: that is, of columns attached to the wall rather than standing free in front of it. It is often said that the Romans used the column less as a structural member than for decoration, and it may be true that if these columns were removed, the walls and roof of the Maison

Carrée would still stand, whereas no column of the typical Greek temple could be taken away without causing that part of the building to collapse. To that extent, the engaged column is not a vital structural element. Nevertheless, it stiffens and thereby strengthens any wall to which it is applied, and thus makes it possible to build a wall thinner than would be safe without it. This additional strength cannot be expressed quantitatively in simple figures, but the critic should recognize its presence, rather than indulge in a sweeping condemnation of the engaged column.

Whereas the Greek temple with its free-standing colonnade and continuous porch may be approached on all sides, the cella of the Roman temple extends the full width of the building and rests on a pedestal or *podium,* another indication of Etruscan influence. This arrangement lacks that close connection with the ground that the Greek temple maintains through its unbroken lines of steps; instead, the Maison Carrée seems set up for display, as though to link it to the Roman love for show. The use of the podium and of the engaged order permits a flight of steps as wide as the front of the building, which leads to a deep porch. Since access is possible at one end only, the Maison Carrée has a more explicit direction than the Greek temple, whose two ends are almost identical.

The greatness of Roman architecture, however, is not due to its debt to the Greeks or to the Etruscans; it comes in spite of it. Roman engineering testifies to the practical character of this people. The permanence of their roads is proverbial; built for the ages, the foundations are in some instances still in use today. Roman bridges and especially Roman aqueducts, such as the Pont du Gard at Nîmes (fig. 79), have a stark grandeur; when solving problems like these, the Romans concentrated on their purpose, not on architectural effect, and indeed the beauty of the Pont du Gard lies in its directness. The sturdy masonry of its plain arches, their austerity not mitigated by even a molding, and the sense of scale derived from the contrast of the large arcades with the smaller arches at the top, which carried the water channel to feed ancient Nîmes, dignify this monument.

The cardinal achievement of the Romans in architecture, however, is their planning of vast and complex edifices. To say that the Parthenon is not well planned would be absurd, but the Greek temple with its single chamber is a simple problem. The Greeks might have developed planning, but their life did not call for complicated buildings, since they lived largely out of doors. In the Roman buildings, the architects had to provide enormous spaces to shelter the crowds of such vast cities as Rome, and so relate these interior volumes to one another that the building would seem open and coherent.

These interiors need uninterrupted spaces. To carry the roof of a large hall by the pier and lintel system of the Greeks would mean that the supports would interrupt that space; columns could not be placed far apart, and the sense of interior volume would be lost in the forest of columns, as it is in the hypostyle hall of the Egyptian temples (fig. 8). Before the days of steel construction, such spaces could be obtained only through vaulting. The Romans early became proficient in building arches, perhaps — but by no means certainly — under Etruscan inspiration. In some instances, including most of the aqueducts, the arches are of stone, but the concrete arch and vault are commoner in the best-known Roman buildings. Vaulted architecture involves problems unknown in the pier and lintel system. An arch (fig. 80) is composed of wedge-shaped blocks, called *voussoirs.* The blocks near the center, though pulled downward by gravity, cannot fall unless they can push their neighbors so far apart that the wider dimension of the block at the top can squeeze through the narrower space at the bottom. Therefore, the lateral pressure of the contiguous blocks holds each voussoir in position. This outward pressure of the central stones, called *thrust* or more precisely lateral thrust, must be counteracted, for clearly if it is not resisted or *buttressed,* the central blocks will push aside their neighbors and fall. Buttressing may be effected in two basic ways. Another arch of the same size may be erected beside the first, as in an arcade; then, the thrust of one arch will meet and balance the thrust of the next. Secondly, a mass of material can be provided by a thick wall or otherwise, so heavy that the thrust of the arch or vault cannot push it over or move it. Moreover, the weight of a masonry vault, far greater than that of a wooden roof, necessitates heavier supports, larger walls, or bigger piers.

Finally, we must consider how an arch can be built. Once the blocks are in position and given sufficient buttressing, they will hold themselves there, but as the stones are placed upon one another, although those at the sides might be held in place by friction on the blocks below them, those nearer the center must have some temporary support, or centering. This is usually of timber, and calls for more or less elaborate carpentry. If a series of like arches are to be erected, a single form of centering may be constructed and moved from one arch to another as each is completed. Similarly, since a vault is composed of arched surfaces, a repetition of similar shapes in vaulting will perhaps effect great economy in centering. Because the shape of the centering determines the under surface of the vault, a series of sunken panels or coffers could all be formed from a single piece of centering, and thus through using repetitive shapes in their buildings the Romans economized on skilled labor.

The geometry of the Pantheon, dated A.D. 120–24, one of the most famous of Roman vaulted structures, is a sphere. A vast dome (fig. 81) rests on, and its lower part is contained within, a cylindrical wall of masonry thick enough to support and buttress its weight and thrust. Above the wall, concrete steps in rings surround the lower visible parts of the dome in order to tie in and counteract the thrust. At present, thrust in the Pantheon is probably small, since the concrete of the dome appears to be monolithic; if so, as in an inverted tea cup, no thrust exists. However, until the concrete had hardened, thrust would have been present. The placement of the dome partly within the walls allows the cylindrical outer mass the utmost visibility, since it is crowned only by a low saucer-like form (fig. 82). The Romans felt that concrete should be covered by some more finished surface and therefore, originally, they sheathed the exterior of the Pantheon with marble, which has now vanished; but the austere cylinder of brick-faced concrete may even have gained in impressiveness thereby. Such a mass is imposing through its size and through the simplicity of its shape. The colonnaded portico, splendid though it be in itself, seems out of place by contrast, like an excrescence on so colossal a mass.

The unity and spaciousness of the Pantheon derive from the dome, which dramatizes the geometry and enforces comprehension of the enclosed volume. Extensions of the interior space into the thickness of the walls produce seven niches or chapel-like areas at intervals, but always as arms of the main spatial area rather than as separate volumes. The under surface of the dome is marked off in squares, or more exactly in trapezoids, by horizontal rings crossed at regular intervals by bands radiated from a single opening in the center of the dome, which lights the whole building. The coffers or sunk panels within these trapezoids are repeated around the dome in every horizontal row. More than a single form was certainly constructed, but such a system might be built with a small group of centers, moved around the dome as one part after another was completed. The floor and walls of the Pantheon were originally sheathed in thin slabs of marble; that surfacing did not pretend to be structural, like the solid marble blocks of Greek temples; rather it was treated frankly as a veneer, almost like wallpaper, to add the beauty of color of the veined marble to the wall surfaces. To use marble thus seems legitimate, so long as it does not suggest that the surface is doing structural work. So splendid a wall covering reflects imperial Roman power, able to draw its materials from the length and breadth of the empire, and to concentrate limitless wealth and resources of labor.

The remarkable preservation of the Pantheon, in contrast to the ruins of most Roman buildings, is the result of its having been converted into a Christian church. The interior finish and a section of the exterior of the Colosseum (fig. 83) have disappeared. This huge bowl, designed in the first century of the Christian era to accommodate some 50,000 people, served the same purpose as our football stadia today: a setting for public entertainments, gladiatorial combats, and the like, to be attended by throngs of people. The three stories of arcades, to which a fourth story was added later, by their horizontal continuity echo the elliptical plan and support tiers of seats rising above the arena. To permit so large a crowd readily to find their places and as easily to leave them, multiple stairways and exits are needed. The complex arrangement of those stairs leads through the arcades on each level to the seats, and of course on the ground floor possible ingress and egress through all the arches simplified the handling of such throngs.

The Roman combination of arch and column, known as the Roman arch order, is nowhere better illustrated than in the Colosseum. The structure rests on the arches, but those are enframed by an engaged column on each pier, which supports an entablature; thus the columns and entablature create a rectangle around the arch. This use of the orders, like the engaged columns of the Maison Carrée, if not wholly decorative, is less structural than the Greek. It does, however, hold in check the visual movement created by the arches, and balances their dynamic appearance with the repose of the pier and lintel system. In the three lower stories, these orders are superposed. In such a design, the sturdiest order is placed at the bottom, the lightest at the top; thus the Tuscan serves on the ground floor, the Ionic on the second, and finally, the Corinthian terminates the series. Each order supports above its entablature a parapet, which also acts as a pedestal or base for the order above, and thus serves as a link between the stories.

Many Roman buildings exemplify this combination of arch and column, such as the triumphal arches intended to commemorate the victories of Roman emperors. Some earlier examples, like the first-century Arch of Titus in the Roman Forum, have but a single opening;

but the more elaborate Arch of Constantine, rebuilt in the fourth century (fig. 84), near the Colosseum, is triple, a large passage in the center flanked by smaller ones. Though the columns in this case are free standing, they perform the same purpose in design as if they were engaged. Here at last, one really finds the decorative use of the column; they support nothing but the statues, which in turn look as though they were added to give some excuse for the columns. Since they do not touch the mass, the columns can add nothing to its stability, which, in any case, is patently sufficient. But to consider this and similar designs as demonstrations of construction is preposterous. As monuments, they must look imposing; in that, the Arch of Constantine succeeds, thanks to its size and scale, its bold proportions, and its decorative richness both of architectural features and of sculpture. He is dull indeed who does not perceive in such a monument the pomp and circumstance of imperial Rome.

The Roman feeling for space is nowhere more evident than in the Basilica of Constantine (fig. 85), more accurately known as the Basilica of Maxentius, since that Emperor began the project between A.D. 306 and 312. What is preserved, colossal though it be, represents less than a third of the original building. For more complex problems like this, the simpler vault forms no longer suffice. A hemispherical dome suggests a circular building like the Pantheon. A semi-cylindrical barrel vault covers a rectangular area like the passages through a triumphal arch, but since it requires continuous support on each long side, as well as continuous buttressing, it tends to be heavy and difficult to light, best adapted to tunnels and hence often called a tunnel vault. The *groined* or cross vault obviates these difficulties; if two equal barrel vaults intersect at right angles, their groins or lines of intersection will form a diagonal cross in the square covered by their intersection. If that square, then, be taken as a unit, it need be supported and buttressed only at the corners, and therefore may be lighted from all four sides or any combination of them, and for the same reason it can be combined with other groined vaults or barrel vaults. The three groined vaults of the central aisle in the Basilica of Maxentius covered an enormous volume, which was extended on each side by three barrel vaults. Since each of these barrel-vaulted compartments corresponded to one of the major bays or sections of groined vaulting, the connection between the two was unmistakable, and the impression of organized space was inescapable. Though the Basilica of Maxentius, like most Roman ruins, has long since lost its surface treatment, the pattern of octagonal coffers still enlivens the under surface of the vault; but most impressive is the scale of this fragment, which commemorates the Roman engineering genius and the wealth and administrative power necessary to carry to completion such a project.

The Roman genius for planning might be expected to display itself in such civic centers as the forums. However, the most celebrated of them all, the Forum Romanum, grew slowly through the centuries, one building after another added to it, rather than the whole planned as a unit. Magnificent though it was, restorations of it leave an impression of confusion, owing no doubt to its slow and accidental growth. As a meeting place, the Roman Forum satisfied the needs of the city while it was still small, but with its growth under the Empire to a population estimated at well over a million, the Forum Romanum exhausted its available space and still remained inadequate. Therefore, emperor after emperor built his forum adjoining the old center to accommodate the overflow, and since these imperial forums were designed as units, one can look to them for examples of the Roman ability in planning. In the Forum of Trajan, dedicated in A.D. 113, a single principal axis gave unity and clarity to the whole. First, a large court, flanked by colonnades and with curved shapes, called *exedrae,* to conclude the transverse axis, provided meeting places in which the businessmen of Rome might conduct their activities. Doubtless small shops found room within the colonnade. The further side of the court was blocked by the Basilica Ulpia, again a common meeting place, whose axis once more crossed the major axis at right angles, and again was terminated by exedrae. Beyond that in turn was the column of Trajan, still on axis, and finally, in the center of yet another axial court, the Temple of the Divine Trajan completed the whole coherent scheme.

Certainly the most remarkable instances of Roman planning are found in the great imperial bathing or thermal establishments. Bathing became a ritual under the Roman Empire, and the building provided not only for hot, medium, and cold baths, dressing rooms, and halls, but also for all sorts of conveniences that might be associated with them: small shops around the perimeter, libraries where the more studious patrons could relax before or after bathing, palaestra in which exercise might prepare the visitor for his ablutions, gardens where he might stroll after they had been completed, and so on. With the bath as a primary excuse, all and more than all the functions of a modern country club were combined in one vast composition.

The plan of the Baths of Caracalla (fig. 86), built early in the third

century, shows a characteristic organization, developed on the basis of
a complex pattern of crossed axes. The principal structure is placed
within a rectangle of subsidiary buildings, on axis with an entrance and
again with the stadium at the rear. Each major axis is adequately
terminated. Consider the long axis of the central hall; not only are the
three bays of the hall based upon it, but it is prolonged at either end
by a vestibule-like chamber, only partly separated from the hall by
colonnades, but enough so to prepare the visitor for something different
beyond. Each of these vestibules leads to colonnaded courts, still on
the same axis. On the further side of these courts within the colonnades,
niches, intended to enframe statues, give termination to this axis, which
is finally recalled in the outer structure beyond the lawns by another
pair of niches. Moreover, it is apparent that most of the units placed
upon this axis have secondary axes, less developed but sufficient to
bring coherence and clarity to the complex of rooms and services demanded by the bath.

The importance of this type of axial planning does not lie in the
pattern of crossed axes; one cannot see the plan of a building except
on paper, and in fact most visitors are unaware of its existence. Nevertheless, such a plan, which is fundamentally the organization of a succession of volumes, leaves its mark, almost subconsciously, on the mind
of a visitor in the impression of order and of openings where openness
is required. A sequence of vistas results from the forethought and
imagination of the architect who envisages these multiple requirements
in relation to one another. The layman is soon aware of inconvenience
in a building not adequately planned, even though he fails to recognize
the reason; but the design of the Baths of Caracalla suggests where to
find the services needed.

The main hall of these baths (fig. 87) was roofed by three groined
vaults like those which once covered the central aisle of the Basilica
of Maxentius. From the lunettes, or semicircular windows, at the sides
as well as from either end, light streamed in to flood the space. The
vaults appeared to rest on Corinthian columns supporting blocks of
entablature, but these really served less to hold the weight of the vault,
which was carried by the solid mass of masonry behind them, than to
give visual intimation of that support, a declaration, so to speak, of the
structural forces. Since these columns could have been removed without causing the concrete vaults to collapse, they were decorative, but
their expressive value more than compensated for their lack of structural consequence; it made them a vital feature in the design. The scale

and impressiveness of this hall, its adequacy of space and light, made it a source of inspiration to architects of much later periods. The concourse of the Pennsylvania Station in New York is inspired by it, and gains much of its impressiveness from the Roman system of design.

Roman architecture has exerted a greater direct influence than the Greek on later European and American developments. For one building that traces its ancestry to Greece today, there must be a hundred that descend from Rome. To some extent, this must be attributed to geography; aside from the vast extent of the Roman Empire, Italy lies nearer the center of the European circle than Greece, and was consequently more familiar through subsequent history. Moreover, the differences of religion between Western or Roman Catholicism and the Eastern or Orthodox Church, coupled with the centuries of domination of the Greeks by the non-European Turks, removed Greece from the main stream of Western culture to whose origin she had given so much. Such classic elements as may be discovered in Western medieval art were Roman. When, in the fifteenth century, the new energy called the Renaissance welled up in Italy, the Italians naturally sought guidance from the Roman style, and as that movement spread north of the Alps, it carried with it the enthusiasm for Roman classic forms, which, though modified, remained the only sources of inspiration until the end of the eighteenth century. At that time, Greek art was rediscovered by western Europe and, from then on, occasional examples of direct Greek influence occur, but even then the restricted scope of Greek architecture could not replace the flexibility of the Roman principles of planning and their applicability to later problems.

The extent of this influence of Rome on later times is a matter of historic fact, fortunate in its results. Though no single Roman building is so exquisite as the Parthenon, the Greek delicacy of proportions and moldings is less significant to the space art of architecture than principles of organization. The Parthenon is perfectly organized as far as it goes; it could not be the success it is were this not so; but its problem is too simple to need a complex plan. When varied problems of design arose in the nineteenth century, the academies of the European countries turned to Rome, the one previous civilization that had had to face comparable problems of interior space design.

VII

The Arts of the Early Church

THE year 476, when the last of the Roman emperors in the west was displaced by his German soldiers, is merely a central point in a long economic and political decline. It used to be believed that the barbarian Goths, Franks, Vandals, and other peoples, who had poured across the frontiers of the empire during the fifth century in waves, were responsible for its collapse. Further study has shown that the picture is less simple, that the barbarians did no more than give the final push to an empire already riddled by the economic troubles of the third and fourth centuries. It is highly doubtful, indeed, whether the disappearance of the last Roman emperor from Rome would have seemed a violent change to the people of the time. They had been accustomed for a century or more to the elevation and deposition of ruler after ruler, the steady decline in power of the central government and its subservience to an unruly army. The latter was recruited from among the barbarians who exerted pressure in the West at this time, because of the unsettled conditions in Asia, where the Han Empire in China was breaking up and northwest India was being sacked by Nomadic invaders.

EARLY CHRISTIAN ART

Toward the end of the third century, Diocletian had divided the empire for administrative convenience into two halves, east and west. Though not intended to have such an effect, the step resulted in almost independent histories for the two. While the empire in the west disappeared, later to be revived, at least in theory, as the Holy Roman Empire, the eastern branch persisted for centuries as the Byzantine Empire, and was not finally destroyed until the Turkish conquest in 1453. With the removal of the last figurehead from the imperial throne in Rome, the Christian Church was left to assume the dominance earlier exercised by the state. During its early years, Christianity had grown very slowly. At the beginning, it was merely one of many Oriental cults that led a wavering existence in Rome. Probably most scholars of the third century, if told that one of these cults would become the dominant religion of Europe, would have guessed it to be the cult of Mithras. However, Christianity prevailed, its triumph signalized by the conversion of the Emperor Constantine and official toleration of Christianity by the state early in the fourth century. The earlier rivalry with Mithraism is reflected and symbolized beneath the church of San Clemente in Rome, where the house of that Christian saint still exists facing a Mithraic temple across the narrow Roman pavement.

To assume that the Christians of the fourth and fifth centuries in Rome were hostile to Roman civilization is absurd. They were none the less Romans because they were Christians, and their modes of thought and expression remained Roman. Their art differs from that of imperial Rome, but the changes may be traced to changed economic circumstances and new problems. The imperial magnificence of Roman baths, the Colosseum, triumphal arches, and forums presupposes a wealthy central government, able to command vast resources of labor and materials, which Rome could no longer supply during the fourth and fifth centuries. If the Christian buildings were, in some respects, plainer in design and simpler in construction than the earlier Roman monuments, so too were contemporary pagan structures.

The breakdown of the classic canons of design, so evident in the early Christian buildings, is equally clear in late Roman monuments. The systems of proportion followed by the designers of the first and second centuries, and their conception of the purpose and relationship of architectural elements gave way during the fourth century to greater liberty, especially in the combination of arch and column. In the Colosseum, the standard arch order is one device; another appears in the Baths of Caracalla, where the columns seemed to support the vaults above. But the classic columns are designed to carry an entablature, whose architrave rests its ends upon the column. Therefore, if the architects of the earlier Empire need to support an arch on a column, they insert an entablature between them. On the other hand, in the Palace of Diocletian at Spalato, late in the third century, the architects play all sorts of tricks; in one part, the whole entablature is bent into an arch; elsewhere, arches rest directly on the capitals, which are ill adapted to support them. In other cases, the column itself is treated as a decorative device; it stands free of the wall and, since it is supported on a bracket, obviously can carry no important weight. Aside from its value as a demonstration of the freedom in handling classic elements in late pagan buildings, which also typifies early Christian churches, the Palace of Diocletian at Spalato symbolizes the growing danger to the Empire. Planned on the lines of a Roman camp, the palace is a fortress and suggests a possible need for defense.

With the toleration of the Church, first granted by Galerius in 311, and its subsequent recognition by Constantine in 313, the Christians could venture to build themselves churches of some size. In Rome the type, already well established in the fourth century, is known as the Early Christian basilica. A new problem, none of the many types of Roman building would serve its needs. Its origin is one of the most debated matters in all the history of art. Possibly some ideas were borrowed from the Roman private house, in which the Christians had often gathered for worship; others may have come from the pagan civil basilica; but in any case the solution called forth by the Christian liturgy is simple. The plan (fig. 88) includes first an *atrium* or forecourt, open to the sky but surrounded by covered walks. The walk next to the church may be developed more than the others, to serve as a vestibule or *narthex*. Beyond the atrium on the same axis is the basilica proper, divided into *aisles,* the wider central one known as the *nave.* The nave and aisles, designed to house the congregation, lead to a cross member, at right angles to the main axis, which may project beyond the aisles to each side as *transepts.* Finally, beyond the transepts, and usually as wide as the nave, is a semicircular exedra known as the *apse.* In the apse and to a lesser extent in the transepts, the clergy performed the services of the ritual. Some larger churches have five aisles rather than the customary three; in some, the transepts terminate with the walls of the aisles, but in general these features are standardized and provide the fundamental elements in plan of almost all later church architecture.

The cross section is equally standard. A wooden roof supported by thin walls covers the nave, which rises above the roof of the aisles to become a *clearstory*. These walls may then be pierced with windows to give abundant light to the nave. Below the clearstory, an area of plain wall corresponds to the height of the lean-to roof over the aisles; this zone is in later architecture to be developed into the *triforium*. A colonnade permits free access from nave to aisles, and supports beams in some of the earlier churches, or arches in the later examples. Finally, a half dome over the apse is the one exception to the generality that these churches are unvaulted.

At the beginning of Christian church architecture, orientation had not become fixed; some churches placed the altar near the west end of the building, so that the priest stood behind the altar and faced east, and therefore the congregation faced west. During the fifth century, this custom changed, so that the congregation and the priest both faced toward the east, and the priest at the altar now had to turn his back on the people at significant points in the service. Thus the altar was so regularly located at the east end and the entrance at the west that these points of the compass can be used to indicate the corresponding parts of churches throughout the later course of the Middle Ages.

The church of San Clemente (fig. 89), though not built in its present form until the twelfth century, and though without transepts, illustrates the type. Externally, the walls are as drab and unadorned as any shed. It has even been suggested that this unpretentious exterior recalls the days of persecution, when to advertise themselves was to court suppression. More probably, the need for economy dictated this plainness. At San Clemente, the atrium is the only one preserved in Early Christian basilicas. Within the church, the drabness of the exterior disappears. Floors patterned in marble, mosaic of colored stone or glass in the apse vault and sometimes on the walls, and marble columns produce a magnificent polychromy. Files of columns, rows of clearstory windows, and the beams of the ceiling (here replaced) all serve to lead the attention to the altar as the focal point of the edifice. Above it, the half dome of the apse forces the eye downward to that point again. Thus the architecture enhances the concentration on the ritual center of the building.

As a corollary to the poor economic conditions of the times, craftsmanship declined, and the temptation arose to use materials already at hand whenever possible. The changed religion and the falling population left many Roman buildings deserted, and to them the Christians, like the Romans before them, turned for materials. Fragments of entirely different design are often combined in a haphazard manner; in the church of San Clemente some columns are fluted, others plain; in the fifth-century church of San Lorenzo, the beams over the columns near the east end are carved, but the designs on neighboring stones vary from one another, which makes it evident that blocks were borrowed from wherever they could be found. The patterns in the floor and the furniture are arranged around disks of red, green, yellow, or black marble, which probably were sliced from Roman columns, as ready sources of such costly substances. Light though its construction is, the Early Christian basilica was admirably adapted to its purpose. If its roof should be burned in the frequent fires of medieval towns, it could be replaced at slight cost. Simple and naive though the basilica is, its effectiveness is testified by the persistence of that form in the city of Rome from the time of Constantine in the fourth century almost to the Renaissance, a thousand years later. The changes on medieval architecture were to be rung elsewhere.

Much of the largest corpus of Early Christian sculpture is the sarcophagi, whose fronts and more rarely whose lids are carved with small figures in high relief. In a sense, these are examples of late Roman sculpture, but a decay in technical ability as compared to earlier Roman standards is evident throughout these works. The clumsy heads retain little of the topical realism of older Roman times. For example, the Jonah Sarcophagus (fig. 90) of the third century deals in episodic fashion with a number of incidents: with Jonah thrown overboard by the sailors into the gaping mouth of a sea monster, spewed up by his host on the shore, at rest under the vine; Moses striking water from the rock; the raising of Lazarus; and so on. As in the Column of Trajan, several incidents find room in a single frame. These subjects are for the most part scriptural and symbolic in interpretation, but, except for their lack of realism, they also have some of the pictorial interest of such reliefs as that of the Farmer Driving his Bull to Market (fig. 70). The presence of such landscape features as the vine or the water, or ships and architecture, can be traced to this source.

Pagan motives are retained but given different and specifically Christian interpretation. After all, these themes were part of the artistic vocabulary of the late Roman world, of which the Early Christians formed a part. Moreover, during the hard times before the recognition of Christianity, to select motives that only the initiated would identify as Christian was safer, and protected the mysteries of the church. The meaning and derivation of some of these symbols are obvious, but others are more involved. The Good Shepherd in the Lateran, from the middle of the third century, one of the few large works of Early Christian sculpture, comes from the type of a man carrying a calf, sheep, or ram on his shoulders, a motive that goes back to the beginning of Greek sculpture, but here is probably derived from the bucolic genre figures similar to those in the pictorial reliefs. That the Christians should identify such a figure as Christ, the Shepherd of His flock, is easy to understand. So, too, the fisherman suggests Christ, the Fisher of Men. On the other hand, the fish itself is often used as a cryptogram of Christ, because the initial letters of the Greek words for Jesus Christ Son of God Saviour spell the Greek word for fish.

Of course, these motives are also present in mosaics. The fourth-century vault of Santa Costanza in Rome shows the vine pattern, amplified along the sides by small scenes; laborers gather the harvest in carts and bring it to the press, where the feet of men tread juice from the grapes (fig. 91).

This vine theme had been common for tavern floors and for other Roman buildings, but since wine plays a part in the Eucharist, the Christians did not hesitate to identify the vine with the sacrament. The art of mosaic was common enough in Roman times. At the outset, small cubes or tesserae of colored marbles were set in patterns, or figures and other pictorial subjects were depicted. Though mosaic is a highly architectural method of decoration, to create a realistic representation in this medium is impossible; subtleties of linear expression cannot be achieved with tesserae. The color may be rich, though its scope is limited by the tones of available marbles. However, the 'palette' of the mosaic worker expanded in the fourth century with the substitution of tesserae of colored glass for marble. The possibilities inherent in this substitution were not immediately exploited. Here in Santa Costanza, even though the mosaic is made of glass, the white background, gray-green vine pattern, and dull yellow or ochre in the figures and other parts, all repeat tones available in stone. Obviously the designer, accustomed to white marble backgrounds, continued to use them in spite of the new material, and failed to avail himself of the wider color range.

The climax of the mosaic scheme in the basilica is the half dome of the apse. At Santa Pudenziana (fig. 92) in the late fourth century, Christ is enthroned in the center, flanked by seated apostles. The cross above Christ marks the axis of a semicircle composed of the four beasts emblematic of the evangelists, which parallel the semicircle below. This repetition of shapes serves to adapt the composition to the shape of the half dome, and to achieve its own harmony; the motive was to become a source of inspiration to Raphael centuries later. The treatment of figures is still classic. In spite of the limitations of the medium, the figures are not conventional; on the contrary, modeling by gradations of tone adds a classic sense of form and mass to the apostles; a pronounced individuality distinguishes the heads, though these were restored in the nineteenth century; and even the buildings, which doubtless symbolize the heavenly Jerusalem in terms of the earthly city, display the Roman bent toward realism.

The more hieratic and stylized Byzantine style modified this classic spirit soon after the disappearance of the Roman Empire in the west. Even in Rome itself, the sixth-century apse mosaic of SS. Cosmo and Damiano adopted linear patterns and forsook the indication of weight and dignity in the figures obtainable through modeling. The color is equally formal: a path of reddish clouds, against which Christ stands, splits the gorgeous dark-blue background of heaven. A new vigor animates faces of a type unknown to classic art, as though the barbarians had infused their vitality into the weary individuals of late Roman days. This mosaic does not attempt the realism of the fourth- and fifth-century designs, but in such artistic matters as decoration by simplified and powerful color, the apse of SS. Cosmo and Damiano grasps the real possibilities of the medium.

Roman tradition persists also in manuscript illumination. The Vatican Virgil of the fourth century (fig. 93), to be sure, is classic; it contains illustrations of the *Georgics* and of the *Aeneid*, enframed in bands of solid color, and extending the full width of the page. The best of these bucolic scenes retain something of Roman illusionism in their depth and naturalistic setting, the classic style and pose of the figures, and in their rich but heavy color. By the sixth century, the classic traditions had faded both in Rome and elsewhere. The purple pages and silver lettering of the Vienna *Genesis* bespeak its East-Mediterranean origin, as do details of costume, though traces of classic tradition remain in the personification of natural phenomena. In most of the miniatures, the setting is eliminated to compel the crude but vivacious figures to tell their story without any assistance from landscape.

WHILE the new social, economic, and religious conditions in Rome were destroying or transforming the imperial Roman style, Constantinople or Byzantium presented an entirely different story. If Rome

BYZANTINE ART itself dwindled from a city of millions to one with a mere fraction of its former population, Byzantium retained and even increased its power. Far from being overthrown, the East Roman Empire survived varying fortunes for a thousand years, until its conquest by the Ottoman Turks in 1453. The civilization it produced had its religion in common with the Christians of the West, though interpreted somewhat differently in the Greek Church than in the Roman. On the other hand, the presence of the emperor with a concentration of wealth and power in the court resulted in an imperial architecture, vaster in scale and more sumptuous than the Early Christian Roman productions. This empire, because of its geographical location, tended to become a semi-oriental despotism, Eastern in its hieratic approach to life and art, colorful to a degree seldom approximated by the West, with a passion in art for surface patterns illustrated alike in the use of marble, in crisp undercut carving, and in the mosaics. The Byzantine style first flowered during the reign of Justinian in the sixth century, and was spread far by his conquests, and farther by his prestige as successor to Rome. His general,

Belisarius, conquered Sicily, to impose over the classical cultures of that island a layer of Byzantine culture that made itself felt for centuries. At Ravenna in the north of Italy, another center of the Byzantine style appeared, illustrated by the churches of Sant' Apollinare in Classe, and Sant' Apollinare Nuovo, both Byzantine versions of the basilica, and above all by San Vitale, with its celebrated and influential architecture and mosaics.

Although the Byzantines retain, in Ravenna and elsewhere, the unvaulted design of the Early Christian basilica, their more typical monuments are vaulted. The increased sense of space, the added monumentality, and the fireproof nature of vaulted buildings as compared to the wooden-roofed basilicas dictated the adoption of that system of construction. The greater difficulty of vaulting and its higher cost could be overcome by the imperial power of Byzantium. The chief type of vault with which the Byzantines experimented was the dome, though other shapes were occasionally employed by them; it was part of their Near Eastern heritage, used with great magnificence by the Sassanian Persians at this time and earlier. As a hemispherical shape, the dome appears to require a circular wall, or supports arranged in a circle; such a plan, as represented by the Pantheon (fig. 81), is satisfactory when the dome covers almost the whole interior space. If, however, as usually happens, the dome is to cover only part of the interior and is to be combined with other domes or with some different type of roof, the circular support may be inconvenient. The circle does not combine readily with other shapes. It was necessary to contrive some method by which the dome could be carried on four piers placed at the corners of a square, and thus permit combination with other shapes.

The principal means developed to solve this problem was the *pendentive*. In shape pendentives are spherical triangles, four of which unite to support a dome. These four pendentives, one of which is visible in the drawing of Hagia Sophia (fig. 94), rest their lower points on the main piers; their other angles touch the neighboring pendentives, and so produce along their upper edges a circular form upon which the dome can be built. The pendentive, like other Byzantine motives, existed in Roman buildings, but a good deal of experimentation during the fourth and fifth centuries led to the full development of the dome on pendentives in the sixth century. So adequate was this solution of the problem that the Byzantines retained it through their long subsequent history, and even after the end of medieval architecture the builders of Western Europe found it useful.

The Byzantine architects of the sixth century tried in many ways to adapt the dome to the problems of church architecture. The Church of the Holy Apostles in Constantinople, now destroyed, was laid out as a Greek cross with four arms of equal length, and five domes, one in the center and the other four over the arms of the cross. In SS. Sergius and Bacchus in Constantinople, and in San Vitale in Ravenna, a single dome covers most of the area, but is surrounded by an aisle, so that in the one case the building is approximately square, in the other case octagonal. Such buildings are often described as the central type: that is, the composition develops around a central vertical axis rising through the dome, rather than to either side of a horizontal axis dividing the church lengthwise into two equal parts. Architecturally, this type lends itself to concentration, since it forces the whole building to focus on the dome, to which all else is subordinated. It permits the building to be symmetrical on all four sides, which cannot be true of the Early Christian basilica. However, a small apse often projects from the eastern side of the structure without any attempt to duplicate it on the other three sides.

One serious flaw is inherent in the form: the dominance of the dome and the subordination of the aisle to it create an architectural focus under the center of the dome. To place the altar at that point is bad, for the Christian liturgy demands that the congregation shall be in front of the altar; it is most undesirable to force any considerable part of the congregation during a service to occupy space at the sides of the altar, or still worse behind it. Therefore, the altar should not be placed beneath the center of the dome; instead, a small apse with a chancel or sanctuary is needed to the east. But to place the altar in such a location involves a separation of the architectural and liturgical climaxes of the building. In the Early Christian basilica, on the other hand, the long horizontal lines of the building lead to the east end, where the altar is logically placed, the architecture quite properly stressing the primary purpose of the building.

Perhaps this prompted the experimentation that produced what is called the domed basilica, whose greatest expression is found in Hagia Sophia. The earlier church of Hagia Sophia was destroyed during the Nika sedition of 532. Justinian immediately directed his architects to rebuild along more magnificent lines. Except for the atrium, this great church was built with extraordinary rapidity, and dedicated in 537; and although part of the structure collapsed in 558 as the result of an earthquake, it was rebuilt on stronger buttressed supports by 563. Such an accomplishment postulates the backing of the emperor; indeed all the evidence points to the interest Justinian took in his new edifice. The plan (fig. 95), developed by Anthemius of Tralles and his assistant Isidorus of Miletus, is almost square.

A single dome ensures unity, but the necessary length is gained to the east and west by half domes, lower than the main dome, but of the same diameter. Although a dome may have less outward thrust than other types of vault, because of the way in which the units are laid, still that thrust may be presumed to push out in all directions. On the east and west, the half domes of Hagia Sophia begin to transfer the thrusts from the main dome outward and downward toward the outer walls of the building. These half domes are in turn buttressed by domical niches and other vaulted forms. To the north and south, sections of barrel vault, or thick arches, bound the main dome. Much later, in 1317, four huge blocks of masonry were added, for further security, behind the piers that uphold the pendentives of the main dome.

The result of this complex system is that the exterior builds up to the central dome, as waves of masonry lap the rim of the culminating feature (fig. 96). One mass after another prepares the way for the climax in the great dome. Only a part of the curve of the dome is visible externally, since the lower part is concealed behind smaller buttresses between each pair of the multiple windows that pierce its base. While the dome of Hagia Sophia is not embedded in the mass of the building, like that of the Pantheon, its effect is achieved more by the complex mass design than by a full revelation externally of the domical form. In this respect it is unlike the later domes of the Italian Renaissance, the Cathedral of Florence or St. Peter's in Rome, for example. However effective Hagia Sophia may be in its mass, little or no decoration appears on the drab masses of the exterior.

The full splendor of Hagia Sophia is evident only in the interior (fig. 97). Immediately on entrance, the affirmation of spatial unity is apparent. The combination of domes and half domes, illuminated by the ring of windows at the base of the dome, at once catches the eye and creates an impression of monumentality and, at the same time, of lightness. It has been well said that the dome looks as though it were suspended from heaven, not supported from earth. The sense of scale, the result of permitting the smaller volumes to lead insensibly to the larger, is further emphasized by the columns, which separate nave from aisles, and by the smaller columns and arcades in the gallery. Red and green porphyry shafts contribute to a rich polychromy, amplified by polished marble slabs on the lower walls and a complete incrustation of mosaic on the higher surfaces. The veined marble slabs themselves create rich patterns. A block of stone is cut in half and opened out like the leaves of a book, so that the pattern of the veins is repeated in reversed form; these two in turn may be divided in half and similarly treated to create the same pattern of veins in four neighboring slabs.

The carved architectural members contribute to the richness of this design. Extensive use of the drill, sharp undercutting, and a reliance on patterns on the surface relieved against deep shadows create a lacelike effect (fig. 98), contrary to the plastic type of moldings developed by the Greeks and Romans. Such patterns are less modeled surfaces than flat designs emphasized by the shadowed incisions, sometimes picked out by gold leaf on a ground of deep blue to ensure a contrast — another indication of the kinship between Byzantine art and Near Eastern. The same technique transforms the capitals of antiquity. The modeled form of the Corinthian capital with its projecting leafage gives way to designs sometimes of foliate origin, sometimes of pure pattern, which adhere to the cushion-like mass. The decorative possibilities of such capitals are limitless, and if traces of the older types of capital sometimes remain, the Byzantine fertility in design opened the way to variety. Moreover, the capitals of the older orders were designed to support beams; now they must often carry an arch. This new purpose requires a larger bearing surface, and so compels the inclusion above the capital of an *impost block*, whose function it is to gather the uneasy load of the arches and bring it to rest in more concentrated form on the capital.

The spaciousness of Hagia Sophia and its sumptuousness make it a masterpiece of world architecture. Justinian had cause to be proud, and to feel that his church outshone the temple in Jerusalem. He is said to have exclaimed on entering to dedicate the new church, 'Oh, Solomon, I have surpassed thee.' Indeed the reign of Justinian marks the first climax of the Byzantine style in all the arts. This period, called the First Golden Age, ends with the Iconoclastic controversy of the eighth century. With the rise of the Macedonian dynasty under Basil I in 867, a new epoch of Byzantine art emerges. From this date, the Second Golden Age [1] lasts down to the capture of Constantinople by the fourth crusade in 1204. During these centuries, most churches follow a single type of plan, derived from the lost church, the Nea, built by Basil I before 886. This standard plan (fig. 99) consists of a Greek cross inscribed within a square. A central dome is buttressed by four other domes set in the angles of the square between the arms of the cross, which themselves are roofed with barrel vaults. This scheme offers the advantages of compactness and of logic in

1. While the term First Golden Age to describe Byzantine art before the Iconoclastic controversy is generally accepted, no such agreement exists for the terminology of later periods.

abutment. The barrel-vaulted arms of the cross push out sidewise against the four angle domes; to some extent their thrusts balance. The central dome is secured by the barrel-vaulted arms and the four subsidiary domes, which abut it on all sides. The smaller size of the churches at this period and especially the small size of the central dome minimize the liturgical loss of concentration on the altar inherent in this arrangement.

The exterior of the twelfth-century Little Metropolitan Church in Athens (fig. 100) shows greater richness through moldings and flat decorative sculpture than do churches of the First Golden Age. The angle domes are often invisible from the exterior, but the central dome, raised on a drum or cylinder of masonry, looks like a turret crowned by the fully visible curve of the dome. The small size makes this revelation of the curve possible without serious danger from thrust, such as would exist in a larger building designed in the same way. Though not in this case, arches often echo the barrel-vaulted arms of the cross on the exterior, and further enliven the whole. While good examples of the architecture of this time are found in Constantinople, much building occurred in other parts of the Byzantine Empire, and even in regions influenced by but not under Byzantine control. The most famous Byzantine church of the period, at least to western Europeans, is St. Mark's, Venice, built in c. 1063. This design accords with its period in the polychromatic and dynamic exterior, but in plan represents a throwback to the Church of the Holy Apostles in Constantinople.

The Fourth Crusade overthrew the Byzantine Empire in 1204, and set up a short-lived Latin kingdom in its place. After that in turn had fallen in 1261, a last epoch of the style arose, which we may call the Byzantine Renaissance or the late Byzantine. The metropolis itself never fully recovered from the shock, so that many churches of the last period were built in the provinces, in Greece or in the northern Balkans, for example. Mostly small in size, they follow no one type of plan. Sometimes they retain the five-domed arrangement of the Second Golden Age, sometimes return to the domed basilica, or even to the still simpler form of the unvaulted basilica. A tendency to emphasize height in these buildings is evident in the small domes raised on tower-like drums. These centuries, after all, correspond to the Gothic period in western Europe, though it might be difficult to trace any direct connection in style between them. Their interest lies in the evidence they offer of the longevity of the Byzantine style, which is still later maintained in the architecture of Russia. Even before this, Russian architecture had been an offshoot of Byzantine, modified by local conditions and impulses. This influence from Constantinople remained dominant for centuries in all Russian art, just as the Orthodox Church became the standard religion.

The Byzantine concern with the decorative, though less developed than it was subsequently, is already prominent in the ivory-covered throne of Archbishop Maximianus in Ravenna dating from the sixth century (fig. 101). Apparent in the vine pattern, which contains peacocks and even animals within its scrolls, it also modifies the conception of the figures. If the latter are not yet fully Byzantine, they have ceased to be Roman. Though not purely linear, the drapery verges on convention, and the poses of the figures display a vague angularity and stylization more pronounced in later times. On the other hand, the beauty of execution and the command of his material indicate that the sculptor of these panels had not suffered the technical decline that deadens most Early Christian sarcophagi.

The developed Byzantine style substitutes almost abstract design and symbolism for the realistic classic point of view. The composition of Christ Crowning the Emperor Roman IV and Eudoxia (fig. 102) of the eleventh century is formal and rigidly axial. The drapery of Christ has become linear, while in the human figures the sumptuous costumes have consumed so much attention than any distinction between the sexes has vanished. Reliance is placed on the decorative value of the contrasted patterns, the sensitive placement of the figures within the space, and the fine adaptation of the design to the material.

The Byzantines ordinarily seem to have regarded sculpture as a minor decorative art, though only in the iconoclastic controversy did they reach the point of entire suppression of the graven image, forbidden by the Mosaic code, and then only in religious art. Even then, the monasteries took that prohibition somewhat lightly, and though such hostility was bound to react more or less on all the arts, painting and mosaic were not strictly graven images. The Byzantine apsidal mosaic of San Vitale (fig. 103) of the sixth century contrasts with the fourth-century Early Christian one at Santa Pudenziana (fig. 92). At Ravenna, Christ is seated on a globe flanked by angels and by figures of San Vitale and Archbishop Ecclesius, who carries in his hands a model of the church. Though some indication of ground still remains, the background has now become pure gold with no suggestion at all of depth or setting. If in the faces some trace of individualism still exists, the figures, on the other hand, are elements in a pattern. Both here and in the famous choir mosaics of Justinian and Theodora with their attendants, the old Roman factual sense has disappeared. While some of the heads look like portraits, the artist is much more concerned to develop decoration by a formal linear arrangement of drapery, one fold repeated after another with only a trace of interest in the body beneath them and the merest touch of roundness in them. But what the artist sacrifices in realism, he more than replaces by his distinguished color. Against the glow of a gold background, passages of pure deep color leave an impression of semi-oriental splendor, different from the factual approach of the Santa Pudenziana mosaic and more effective than it as decoration.

The mosaics of San Vitale turn from illustration to decoration, but that ideal becomes more deliberate in later Byzantine mosaics, such as those in St. Mark's, Venice. Here the figure of Chastity (fig. 104) has become a unit of design. The drapery symbolizes rather than represents the body beneath it; concentric dark lines surround oval or tear-drop light areas to create patterns focused over certain parts of the body. In many cases, the proportions of the figures are strikingly elongated, the attitudes sharp and angular. To suppose that the artist saw the figure this way is absurd; he knew that his symbol did not look like a human being, but he was not trying to present man in a realistic image; instead, his purpose was to avoid realism the more clearly to express the superhuman nature of his subject and adapt it to its purpose as architectural decoration. Consequently, if any setting occurs, it too is symbolic, and often the pictographic figure is simply relieved against a pure gold field. Identification of the idea in St. Mark's is aided by lettering, by scrolls held in the hands of the characters, and by well-known emblems, such as the lion for fortitude. Obviously the more these figures are reduced to formulae, the less open they are to charges of transgressing the Mosaic code. Though foreign to the concept of art as representation, held through most Western history, one must admit the legitimacy of such a purpose and its success as decoration.

Manuscript illuminations demonstrate that formalism inherent in the Byzantine conception of art. The opulent color of mosaics mingles with a strong influence from classic tradition, to combine in turn with the conservative and symbolic bent of the Eastern Church, with sometimes one and then another of these factors uppermost. The classical strain predominates in the Joshua Roll of the Vatican in the breadth and free movement of its figures. This manuscript has been variously dated from the seventh to the tenth centuries and may possibly have been copied from a still earlier production. However, the classic influence weakens after the tenth century, to give way, in the late-tenth-century Menology of Basil II in the Vatican, to rigid poses. A monotonous series of figures with upraised hands stand within arcades or between hills silhouetted against gold backgrounds. Still later, in the twelfth century, the Melissenda Psalter of the

British Museum exaggerates the conventions of Byzantine art. The emaciated figures are clad in draperies, the folds reduced to linear patterns analogous to the mosaic figure of Chastity from St. Mark's, Venice.

The significance for Western art of the Byzantine style is immeasurable. Constantinople kept alive a civilization inherited from Rome, but changed the classic modes of expression. The years from about 500 to 1000, commonly called the Dark Ages, may have been less dark than is commonly supposed; the name may perhaps reflect our ignorance rather than the reality. Nevertheless, these five centuries in the West produced little of importance in the major arts, whereas in Asia they were a time of unusual artistic brilliance in India, in the T'ang period in China, and in Japan, where Buddhism had just been accepted and brought with it the cultural impact of the older civilizations.

In the West, more has been preserved in some minor arts. Celtic manuscript illumination discarded representation as an artistic aim, but in its place substituted as rich a vocabulary of decorative ornament as has ever been seen. Such figures as are introduced carry the two-dimensional representation even farther away from nature than does Byzantine art. The initial page of the Gospel of St. Matthew from the *Book of Kells* (fig. 105) of the eighth century runs riot with spirals, rows of red dots, patterns, interlaced ribbons, and lacertines. The last named are bird or animal forms so elongated and intertwined that in this illustration they are hardly distinguishable from ribbons. No other artistic tradition has ever produced such exquisite richness of linear patterns, which are closely related to the Scandinavian arts and to the animal style in Asia.

When a new wave of creative energy swept over western Europe, the emerging peoples turned to the one Christian center that maintained a high level of artistic creation. Therefore, when Charlemagne in the eighth century determined to build a palace chapel at Aachen, his builders journeyed to Ravenna to study the Byzantine design of San Vitale; they did not fully understand the design, but did their best to reproduce it; and even later in the eleventh century, the Western churches satisfied their need for decoration by symbolic figures, partly inspired from Byzantine manuscripts and ivories. So, too, does the Byzantine style play an important role in Carolingian manuscripts, though the latter are also influenced in decoration by Celtic patterns in line. The classic Roman sources likewise played a part in this later revival of art, but the influence of Rome, at least at the outset, is less than the influence of the more conventional and symbolic style of the Eastern Empire. Not only, however, is Byzantium important as a link between the classic civilization and the later culture of western Europe. It is a great independent style, in which the engineering achievements of Rome and its spatial sense are crossed with a semi-oriental love of color, a sense of decoration, and a perfect willingness, nay eagerness, to replace realism by symbolism, and thus to achieve designs obtainable in no other way. No other style has ever reached such splendor without loss of the architectonic flavor.

VIII

Romanesque Art

ALL cultures discussed up to this point have been homogeneous. Though the styles they produced may have been influenced by outside civilizations, as in the case of the Egyptian and Mesopotamian influences on Greek art, and though each style developed within itself, still the expression of the Greek, the Roman, and the Byzantine cultures had in each instance been unified. With the Romanesque period, that ceases to be true. In art, the term Romanesque refers to a group of eleventh- and twelfth-century styles in western Europe, which have some characteristics in common but which also exhibit wide variations. Such divergences reflect the breakdown of such unity as existed in Europe during the Roman Empire. In the second century, one might have journeyed from Italy through Spain, France, and England and found in each town bathing establishments, aqueducts, and temples of much the same form; though a house in Britain might not have been identical with one in Italy, it would have been like enough to cause no great sense of change in passing from one to another. One might have spoken one language in these areas and still have been understood; one would have expected to encounter the same customs, the same ideals, and the same manner of living.

Roman unity broke down after the settlement of the barbarians in western Europe. These peoples, during the so-called Dark Ages from about 500 to 1000, slowly developed differences, reflected in the gradual emergence of Italian, French, Spanish, or Provençal tongues as distinct from Latin, their common source. In art, one can distinguish between the German Romanesque styles and the French or Italian, and one can also differentiate several styles within a country. The art of the Lombard plain contrasts with that of Tuscany to its south, while another type characterizes southern Italy and Sicily. In Germany, the Rhenish buildings are not like those found elsewhere. In France, many

categories suggest themselves; some scholars have distinguished sixteen or seventeen styles of French Romanesque; others limit themselves to seven. Certainly St. Trophîme at Arles in Provence is so different from the domed churches, such as St. Front at Périgueux in
Aquitaine, that to group them together would result in confusion;
Cluny in Burgundy and St. Étienne at Caen in Normandy have some
elements in common, but more divergent features. These local variations within the Romanesque family of styles are partly the architectural consequence of feudalism. Although the great nobility in theory might hold their lands from the king and owe to him the same
feudal duties that their vassals in turn owed to them, still the power
wielded by the Dukes of Normandy even before the conquest of England, by the Dukes of Burgundy, or by the Counts of Toulouse, enabled them to defy the royal power at will. Under these circumstances,
the provinces were virtually independent. Moreover, although pilgrimage and travel were more extensive during the Romanesque period than
one is often led to believe, poor roads tended to throw each region on
its own resources.

Even more than the Gothic, the Romanesque is the great age of the
Church. The papacy through the Dark Ages to some extent took the
place in the West occupied earlier by the Roman Empire. Although
under Charlemagne the imperial idea was partly revived as the Holy
Roman Empire, during the Middle Ages the emperors concerned themselves in fact almost entirely with Germany and Italy, and it was the
power of the Church more than that of the Empire that was felt throughout western Christendom. Perhaps the summit of ecclesiastical power
was reached at Canossa in 1077, when the Emperor Henry IV was
forced to do penance before Pope Gregory VII. That submission, to
be sure, though superficially an abasement of the secular power to
the ecclesiastical, in less obvious ways strengthened the lay power; but
the Church seemed to have brought to its knees her only secular rival.

The religious energy of the age found a dramatic outlet in the Crusades. While the enthusiasm to free the Holy Land from the Sara-
cens may not have been untinctured by a spirit of adventure, a lust
for travel to break the monotony of life at home, one cannot doubt the
primary importance of the religious fervor behind the Crusades. The
first three, in which that spirit is most prominent, all occurred before
the end of the twelfth century. But, if the energy and devotion of the
people vented itself in the Crusades, the Church served the ends of
civilization with greater effect through the monasteries. As centers of

learning at a time when few others were to be found, the monasteries stand out like bright beacons in the intellectual night. Their role might later on be played by others, but during the Romanesque period they reached their greatest height. Though the monks themselves did not, as is commonly supposed, build and decorate all their churches, nevertheless artistic energies centered in and on the artistic problems of the Church to an extent not duplicated in the Gothic.

Succinct definition of the eleventh- and twelfth-century styles is nearly impossible. De Lasteyrie, following Quicherat, defines the Romanesque as 'that architecture which, retaining many elements of the classic, has ceased to be classic, and which, anticipating many elements of the Gothic, has not yet become Gothic.' This statement tends to relegate Romanesque architecture to a mere link between two other styles. Moreover, those styles that have any substantial heritage from antiquity do not foretell the Gothic, and *vice versa*. Nevertheless, this definition calls attention to the genealogy of some branches of the style. To these relationships, one should also add an occasional connection with the Byzantine, as in Aquitaine, with the Saracenic wherever the Romanesque impinged on Mohammedan culture, and of course, at the beginning, with northern elements. Some of these styles are vaulted in a wide variety of forms; others cling to the simpler wooden roof.

One helpful distinction is that between the organic and the inorganic styles. We may define organic architecture as one in which ribbed vaults concentrate their weight and thrust at isolated points, and are logically and visibly supported and abutted. In so far as a style fails to meet these requirements, it can be described as inorganic. Since these specifications are most completely fulfilled in French Gothic, it follows that the organic Romanesque styles are those which De Lasteyrie describes as anticipating the Gothic. These more progressive styles experiment with structure, but, perhaps because the solution of such complex problems in building absorbed much of their creative energies, the organic buildings tend to be more rugged but less finished and less monumental than their simpler inorganic contemporaries. While these terms lead to an understanding of Romanesque architecture, they are only descriptive, not critical; no stigma adheres to inorganic styles as such; on the contrary, they include the finest architectural triumphs of the period.

To discuss all the divisions of the Romanesque in a few pages is neither possible nor necessary. A few examples illustrate the character of the movement, and some of its variety. The Tuscan Romanesque is one instance of an inorganic style. The cathedral group at Pisa, begun in 1063, displays the reliance of that region upon tradition. Of the four structures within this group — the cathedral, the leaning tower or campanile, the baptistry, and the Campo Santo — the first two and part of the third were completed during the eleventh and twelfth centuries. The plan of the cathedral (fig. 106) looks like a development from the Early Christian Roman basilica (fig. 88). Divided into nave and side aisles by colonnades, and lighted by a clearstory, it expands the rudimentary transepts of its ancestor into great salient arms, and prolongs the nave of the church beyond the transepts; it thus becomes a Latin cross in plan. The thin walls and slender supports indicate that, although small vaults exist over the aisles, the nave is still covered by a plain timber roof, less heavy than a stone vault and without its lateral thrust.

Though by no means imperial Roman, the Early Christian basilica represents the tag end of classic architecture, and, in so far as Pisa follows that lead, it retains a classic flavor. The interior (fig. 107), especially in the Corinthian colonnade, follows Roman precedent to an exceptional extent. It is doubtful whether the Middle Ages ever produced elsewhere so classic a feature as this. On the other hand, the arcaded triforium gallery with its paired arches is probably inspired by contemporary work in Lombardy. The Tuscan love of color in architecture shows itself both in the use of marble patterns in the spandrels or triangles between the arches of the nave arcade, and in the alternate bands of light and dark marble in the triforium, and to a lesser extent in other parts of the building. The violent alternation of its strident pattern may not commend itself to all modern eyes, but it suggests the vigor of the eleventh century.

The basilican mass of the church is visible on the exterior (fig. 108), although the transepts and the dome above the *crossing*, as the intersection of transepts and nave is called, complicate the mass. On the other hand, the drabness of the basilica yields to lavish decorative arcading, some of it in the form of shallow galleries behind small columns and arches, but with a blind arcade for the lowest tier, its columns and arches engaged to the wall. Five stories of arcading reflect the divisions of the interior: the blind arcade corresponds in height to the nave arcade within, the lowest open arcade to the triforium, the next to the roof of the triforium gallery, the third to the clearstory, and the last to the pitched roof over the nave. The proportions of the several stories are almost mathematical: the blind arcade occupies a third of the height, while one sixth is devoted to each upper gallery. The love of color, so prominent on the interior, reappears on the façade in restrained banding, and in lozenge-shaped panels enlivened with marble patterns within the arches. The rich shadows, caught by the open arcades, contribute to this sense of color, and, indeed, the marble itself has a strange luminous beauty.

The Middle Ages did not attempt to construct their buildings with the accuracy of the Parthenon. Hardly an arch in the arcade along the sides of the church rises to the same level; some of them almost touch the horizontal molding above, while others are noticeably lower. Builders capable of so large an undertaking as the Cathedral of Pisa were also capable of making arches within the same series rise to a uniform height. Therefore, they must have considered such regularity either undesirable, or, more probably, a matter of indifference. Discrepancies like these in a formal Greek temple would destroy the effect, but in the free and easy medieval design they seem refreshing.

The passion for arcades carries over from the Cathedral to the Campanile at Pisa, constructed a century later, where eight tedious stories of them are superposed. The varied length of the arcades on the Cathedral façade overcomes monotony, but that difference cannot occur in the cylindrical mass of the tower. The latter owes its fame, of course, to its deviation from the perpendicular, a discrepancy present in most Italian towers of the Middle Ages but rarely to the same degree. Details of construction indicate that the tower settled into the ground unequally even while it was being built. The angle of inclination is slightly greater near the bottom than further up, as though the builders tried to overcome the settlement, or at least to mitigate it, as the tower rose. That angle is startling, to be sure, but its implication of insecurity can be very disturbing when one visits Pisa. Though said to be structurally safe at present, the Leaning Tower must be called an architectural aberration.

Quite different from this Tuscan Romanesque, but also inorganic, is the style of Sicily. Few regions so well demonstrate the influence on architecture of layer after layer of civilization. After the classic era, Sicily fell in turn under Byzantine, Saracenic, and, during the Romanesque period, Norman domination, and each of these cultures left its mark. The twelfth-century Cathedral of Monreale, in the hills above Palermo, retains the light construction and wooden roof of the basilica for both nave and aisles, but Byzantium contributed the capitals with their impost blocks, and the mosaics. An oriental luxuriance of polychromy also appears on the exterior; for instance, the golden stonework of the blind arcades in the apse contrasts with the plaster surface of the wall within them. Those arcades interlace as though one series of arches had been placed on another, the supports of the second arcade intermediate between those of the first. This interlacing arcade characterizes Norman architecture, both in northern France and, after the Norman conquest, in England. On the other hand, in Sicily the arches are pointed, after the Saracenic fashion rather than the round arches of the usual Romanesque styles. This use of the pointed arch, inspired by the East, has no connection with its structural use during the Gothic centuries. Indeed, the Romanesque styles exhibit this motive wherever they come into contact with Moslem or Saracenic peoples, as, for example, in Spain. From Normandy, however, come the twin towers that flank the façade of Monreale. For all their simplicity of structure, few Romanesque buildings contain the exotic charm of the Sicilian.

These wooden-roofed styles are completely inorganic, but many vaulted styles of the period fall within this category. A notable group of churches sprang up along the routes to the shrine of St. James, Santiago de Compostela in northwestern Spain. The stream of pilgrims along these roads stimulated intellectual development and the exchange of ideas, and created a demand for monumental churches at intervals along the way. One great function of the monasteries was to afford hospitality to all; but while pilgrims might accept food and lodging at no charge, it was customary to contribute something as a free-will offering, and the gifts of pilgrim hordes helped in the creation of such vast churches as Santiago itself, or St. Sernin at Toulouse in southern France. The standard plan of these churches, which we see at Santiago (fig. 109), begun during the eleventh century, is repeated at least five times in large churches along the roads to Spain. A nave of great length leads to the bold transepts and to the choir to create a cruciform plan. The rich ceremonial of medieval worship, its processions, and its ritual demand this large space. The choir ends in an apse, around which the aisle is bent in a semicircle, with a series of chapels radiating from it. This aisle, called an *ambulatory*, made it possible not only for processions but, even more important, for visiting pilgrims to pass each of the chapels and pay their devotions. Each chapel had its own altar with some relic of the saint to whom the chapel was dedicated, the popularity of these relics dependent at least in part on their supposedly miraculous power. Consequently, a church with a number of such objects of devotion was fortunate indeed, not merely in that they attracted crowds of the devout, but also in the gifts and endowments they might bring to the church. It is suggestive in this connection that the Cathedral of Canterbury was rebuilt and enlarged immediately after the burial there of St. Thomas à Becket. To recognize the financial value of relics is in no way to underestimate their religious significance; that they were venerated with an unquestioning faith is undeniable. It was, in fact, this faith that produced the demand for structures on so magnificent a scale.

The interior of Santiago (fig. 110) shows a nave roofed with a barrel vault partly carried on transverse ribs or arches below the surface of the vault. These ribs, which divide the vault into bays, were probably devised in part to reduce the amount of centering needed while the vault was being built. They dramatize the support for the vault offered by the piers, and visibly connect the pier and vault. On every pier, a colonnette or shaft rises from the floor, apparently to carry to the ground the weight borne by the rib. The arches of the nave arcade also rest on shafts in the main pier, which becomes in consequence a complex of several parts, each designed to serve some specific function. The combination of those parts produces a series of lines on the pier to emphasize its vertical movement and to state visibly its function as a support. A barrel vault, by definition a half cylinder, creates thrust along its full length. In so far as the ribs carry some of the weight of that vault, more lateral thrust collects on them than along the intermediate length; even so, such a vault requires continuous abutment. Therefore, it became necessary to cover the triforium galleries with continuous half-barrel vaults, which partly counteract the thrust and partly carry it over the aisles to the outer wall of the building, where sheer weight of masonry might resist it. Though logical, the failure of this system to concentrate the thrust at isolated points necessitates a suppression of the clearstory. Windows may be present at the end of the nave, or in the aisle walls, but the amount of light that passes across the width of the aisles and through the arches of the nave arcade is inadequate by modern standards. This thick gloom, through which the sonority of the Gregorian chant reverberates, hangs like a pall overhead and half conceals the vaults, but also creates a sense of religious mystery.

The heavy walls, large piers, and plain vault define the major volumes of the church. If smaller volumes exist in the aisles to the right and left, they are perceived rather as parallel voids than as parts of the space contained within the nave. That clear definition of space characterizes the Romanesque style, both inside and out. In St. Sernin at Toulouse (fig. 111), built chiefly in the twelfth century, each unit of the complex mass is separately conceived. Its own roof distinguishes the nave from the aisles with their lower roofs; the apse protrudes above the ambulatory, about which each chapel is a separate bulge. The church is designed as a collection of its parts, each related to the whole but not completely fused with it; every part, though playing its due role, retains its own individuality. This combination of apse, ambulatory, chapels, and transepts builds up to the tower over the crossing, to make the east end of St. Sernin one of the most monumental of all Romanesque buildings. In its expression of unadulterated power, it surpasses the Italian buildings already discussed.

Little importance attaches to the question of priority among the inorganic styles of the Romanesque. Many of them appeared in various parts of Europe simultaneously, and it is unnecessary to assume any direct influence of one upon another. Of the organic styles, on the other hand, the Lombard claims precedence. Though this is disputed, historical evidence points to an influence of Lombardy on the Rhenish and Norman Romanesque churches. Four primary structural features contribute to the organic character of Lombard work. The first is the ribbed quadripartite groined vault, which we may examine in Sant' Ambrogio in Milan (fig. 112), begun in the eleventh century. The area of the nave is divided into a series of square bays, the sides of the square and its diagonals marked by ribs or arches. Three pairs of ribs appear in each bay: two cross the nave and are called transverse ribs, two wall ribs run along the sides of the nave, and two diagonal ribs divide each bay into four triangular compartments. Whether the ribs in fact support these triangles of masonry or simply effect economies in centering, at least they articulate the vault, dramatize the structural forces, and appear to concentrate them at isolated points of support. Since the Lombard ribs are semicircular, it follows that the diagonal ribs, longer than the wall and transverse ribs, must rise to a higher point. Consequently, as one sees in the section (fig. 113), each vaulting bay is domical.

But if the ribs carry any considerable portion of the weight of the vault, as they appear to, it is logical to expect individual support for each rib. To effect this, the membered pier had to be developed. In its complete form, this must include a unit, such as a narrow pilaster or colonnette, to correspond to each rib of the vault; and since each pier supports five ribs of the nave vaults, one transverse, two wall, and two diagonal ribs, therefore five members must appear on the nave side of each pier. Moreover, it would be rational in the design of each colonnette or shaft to indicate the direction taken by the rib it serves. The section of Sant' Ambrogio shows that the shafts carrying the diagonal ribs face diagonally across the nave of the church.

As we look at the interior of Sant' Ambrogio (fig. 114), we see that not all of the piers are of the same size; on the contrary, large piers alternate with smaller ones. To see the reason for this, turn again to the plan (fig. 112). The nave is flanked by side aisles, which are just half its width. If the aisles are also to be vaulted in square compartments (and to vault an oblong rectangle in the Lombard system would be much more difficult), two compartments or bays in each aisle must correspond to one in the nave. These aisle compartments need support at their corners. Therefore, a smaller or intermediate pier is introduced, smaller because it carries a portion of only the aisle vaults, whereas the main piers carry an equal share of the aisle vaults as well as the larger nave vaults. If this intermediate pier were destroyed, theoretically, at least, nothing would happen to the nave vaults; therefore, we do not find on the nave side of the intermediate piers the same complex membering that characterizes the principal piers.

The ribs of these organic vaults bring a considerable thrust to bear against the walls of the church, but only against those points of the wall opposite the pier. To resist that thrust, a solid masonry buttress could have been placed behind the main piers of the nave, but that would have blocked the aisles. Practically, the buttress must be located against the outer wall of the aisle, where it appears as a mass thickening the wall opposite each main pier of the interior (fig. 114). The aisle vaults also thrust outward, but just as the alternate pier is enough to support them, so a smaller buttress is sufficient to care for this thrust. The same alternation we have seen on the interior is also visible on the exterior, which thus reveals the structural system. These pier buttresses, to be effective, must be connected with the nave vaults. The Lombards placed a gallery over the aisles; as we see in the section (fig. 113), arches in these galleries support a wall, which transfers the thrusts from the nave vaults over the aisles to the outside of the church. These four structural features of the Lombard style, the ribbed vault, membered pier, alternate system, and pier buttress, taken together satisfy the definition of an organic style as one in which ribbed vaults concentrate their weight and thrust at isolated points and are logically and visibly supported and abutted.

Such a system is more complex than the scheme of the Cathedral at Pisa, and must have been more costly to construct in proportion to the area enclosed. On the other hand, the heavy masonry of the interior has an appearance of permanence and of monumentality that the Cathedral of Pisa lacks. Though heavy, the structure of Sant' Ambrogio prepares the way for Gothic architecture. Most important among its advantages is that of fire protection. The wooden roof of many inorganic structures was liable to destruction by fire; while it might be replaced without much trouble after such a calamity, the destruction to the interior and its contents caused by the burning timbers could not be so easily repaired. Important as such protection is, it does not follow that the presence of a vault dispenses with the necessity for a roof. The upper surface of a vault cannot be exposed to the weather; rainfall, penetrating the joints between the stones, would soon disintegrate any vault. Consequently, all vaults are covered by some form of wooden roof. The most serious defect of the Lombard system is its lack of light. The galleries and the buttress system limit windows to the outer walls of the aisles and to the end of the nave, and as a result most of the Lombard churches are very dark.

The Lombard style has a robust vigor, but not the finish and sophistication of many inorganic styles. The carving of the capitals is rugged, but on the whole little decoration enlivens the church. Its effectiveness lies in the structural logic and the crude rhythm inherent in the alternate system, though some unity of the interior is lost because of the domical form of the vaults, which suggest separate units rather than continuity. Externally (fig. 115), Sant' Ambrogio is monochromatic, in contrast to the Tuscan and Sicilian styles. Built in brick, with stone reserved for the important architectural members, it makes free use of the arched corbel table, a series of small arches supported on projecting blocks, as decorative bands to accent the principal divisions. Corbel tables in Sant' Ambrogio run along just under the eaves of the church, below the gallery level, and at each story of the tower beside the building. Slight as it is, this feature identifies the spread of the Lombard influence to other countries; it turns up in German Romanesque architecture, in southern Italy, in Normandy, and elsewhere. No single church of the Lombard Romanesque is as distinguished in design as any of the examples of inorganic Romanesque already considered. The Lombard buildings are, indeed, hardly comparable to the inorganic structures in scale, in complexity of mass, or in delicacy of detail. On the other hand, such distinction must not be expected. The solution of the structural problems absorbed so much creative energy that the significance of Lombard buildings is concentrated there.

The connection between Germany and Lombardy, two of the most important regions within the Holy Roman Empire, in part accounts for the spread of the Lombard style northward. During the Dark Ages, to judge from the slight remains, a preference for multiple towers, double apses (one to the west as well as one to the east), and double transepts characterized the buildings. The resulting silhouette was bound to be complex, and the mass composition elaborate to the point of confusion. Something of this spirit, though better controlled, remains in such cathedrals of the twelfth century as Mainz and Worms. At Worms, for instance, apses occur to the east and to the west, each flanked by paired towers, and a lantern rises near each end of the edifice. On the other hand, the quadripartite ribbed vault, the membered pier, the alternate system, and the rudimentary buttresses derive from Lombardy. The German churches are less organic than the Lombard, because they do not always adopt the complete system but are willing to omit one or more of the members of the vault or of the pier. A further indication of Lombard influence, the arched corbel table, recurs even in the inorganic buildings of the Rhineland and in other parts of Germany. But if the German style yields to the Italian in structural logic, it is far ahead in monumentality. The organization of this complexity in design, the combination of vertical and horizontal masses, and the feeling for scale make this Romanesque style the finest architectural achievement of Germany, an indigenous style that commands respect through its power and dignity.

Normandy, on the English channel, also fell under Lombard influence. The energetic Normans were eager to learn from Lombardy, which enjoyed great intellectual prestige throughout western Europe during the eleventh century. Instance after instance occurs of prelates, trained in Lombardy, who brought with them to Normandy a knowledge of Italian architecture. Thus, Lanfranc was born in Pavia early in the eleventh century, entered the monastery of Bec in Normandy in 1042, and became prior of that establishment a few years later. Subsequently, he took charge as abbot of the new Abbaye aux Hommes at Caen, and, as archbishop of Canterbury after the conquest of England, he began the building of a magnificent cathedral. St. Anselm, from Aosta in north Italy, followed Lanfranc in each of his positions and doubtless also drew southern influence in his train.

So energetic a people as the Normans would hardly accept these suggestions in architecture, however good they might be, without trying to improve them. A glance at the plan of St. Étienne at Caen (fig. 116), often called the Abbaye aux Hommes, begun in 1064 though the vaults were added half a century later, reveals the ribbed vault, the membered pier, and the alternate system, but with some differences from the Lombard. Most important, the vault has ceased to be four part or quadripartite; instead, one addition, the intermediate transverse rib, now transversely bisects the square compartment, to halve the lateral triangles and so produces the six part, or sexpartite, vault. Since this intermediate transverse rib in St. Étienne supports part of the nave vault, and since it rests on the intermediate pier, that pier now becomes vital for the support of the nave vault, as well as necessary to hold up the aisle vault. However, it carries less of the nave vault than the main piers, as indicated by the single rib resting upon it, and therefore it follows that the intermediate pier may remain smaller than the main piers and thus preserve the alternate system. The main pier has members to support the main transverse rib and the two diagonal ribs, but the intermediate pier needs only one member for the intermediate transverse rib. The walls in the Norman Romanesque are so massive that they absorb, as it were, the wall rib, which consequently is not visible in the vault or reflected in the pier. These walls are thick enough to be pierced with passages at several levels, for a ready inspection of the building, and to facilitate repairs if necessary.

The Norman church includes a clearstory. As we have seen, this feature, so fundamental to adequate lighting, had been sacrificed to the buttress problem by the Lombards. But in Normandy, the thick walls probably suffice for abutment, though buttresses are often placed against the clearstory wall behind each pier. In the contemporary church of Ste. Trinité, the Abbaye aux Dames, a half arch under the roof of the aisle back of each support is designed to transfer thrust from the nave over the aisles to the outer wall, where the pier buttresses resist it. This expedient, though still rudimentary, affords the germ of the Gothic flying buttress. Moreover, Norman vaults are not domical as are Lombard and occasionally German vaults. Although the transverse ribs remain semicircular, the diagonal ribs are either semi-elliptical or segmental, and thus lower than a full half circle; in this way they reduce the height to which the diagonal arches must rise to the same level as that attained by the transverse ribs. Therefore, the nave of the Norman church (fig. 117) does not show the same interruptions that meet the eye in Sant' Ambrogio. However, this unity is bought at a price. Over any given span, the lower and flatter the arch, the greater is its thrust; and consequently the Norman scheme of flattened diagonal ribs results in a greater thrust than the semicircular Lombard members of the same size.

Austerity pervades the best of these Norman buildings. The sturdy masonry of local stone may be enriched around the arches, and in horizontal bands between the stories, by carved moldings. These do not usually attempt floral, figure, or animal designs; instead, we find the zigzag, the chevron, the billet mold like rows on a checkerboard, and many other geometric patterns. In Normandy itself even these are seldom employed, but they abound in the churches put up by the Normans in England after the Conquest.

That continental severity is pronounced in the façade of St. Étienne (fig. 118), not only in its dearth of detail but in its gaunt proportions. Its design repeats the divisions of the interior, and so becomes a prototype of the Gothic façade. Shallow buttresses divide the façade and correspond to the interior division into nave and side aisles, while three tiers of openings express the vertical sections of nave arcade, triforium, and clearstory. The western towers, whose spires were added later, emphasize the part of the building where the principal entrances are located. Also, they give dramatic interest to the façade, as they rise above the roof level in stages — the lower ones plain in design with few openings or none, and the number of windows and the richness of their treatment increased as the upper stories are reached. Otherwise, however, the Norman façade is bare, its portals and windows small, mere holes pierced through the walls, its buttresses narrow strips, and the dynamic and plastic character of the Gothic nowhere visible.

When the Normans invaded England in 1066, they felt that their architecture surpassed that of the conquered people. During the next century, they built cathedral after cathedral, monastery after monastery, in their own style. However, in England their desire for scale, for ponderous rhythms, and for an overwhelming result to impress their new subjects reduces the amount of structural experimentation that distinguishes their continental buildings. The Anglo-Norman style wins its greatest architectural triumph at the end of the eleventh century in Durham Cathedral (fig. 119). A clear Romanesque definition of volumes in nave and aisles results from the vast size of round columns and alternate membered piers enriched with moldings. Though its vaulted nave is exceptional among English Romanesque buildings, even here the organic Norman scheme is not complete; its diagonal arches above the intermediate piers do not continue to the ground on any colonnette or pilaster. However, Durham does not lack structural interest to the historian; on the contrary, certain features of its vaulting and its buttress system are amazingly advanced when one considers that the nave

vaults were completed by 1133; but its sonorous architecture does not
rely for effect on dramatized structure. Few styles are more imposing
than the Anglo-Norman in the expression of sheer power, and among
the monuments of that style none can equal Durham Cathedral, 'half
house of God, half castle 'gainst the Scot.'

The same variations in style we have reviewed in architecture occur
also in sculpture, and for the same reasons, but it does not follow that
the regions most significant in architecture will be of equal prominence
in the sister art. In general, these styles form a plaid woven of classic,
northern, and Byzantine influences. The last named was the one living
source of inspiration, and even of information in the visual arts to
which Western artists after the Dark Ages could turn. Though Byzantium produced but little monumental sculpture, her minor arts were
brilliant, and her manuscripts and ivories were readily portable. By
their very nature, these arts tend to indicate representational or symbolic
features primarily by outline. That linearism affects much Romanesque
sculpture, even when it is executed on a monumental scale. Few arts
have ever attained so architectonic a flavor. To some extent, this results
from carving stones already set in place in the building, and of the
same material as the architecture. Even further do the angularity of
the forms and the distortion of the figure for the sake of design tend
to bring the sculpture into dependence on the architecture.

In many regions, the sculpture is apt to concentrate around the doorway. In St. Trophîme at Arles (fig. 120), the rich portal contrasts with
the rugged façade. Provence, the once-flourishing Roman province, contained a litter of classic monuments bound to affect subsequent styles.
In this twelfth-century portal, many details, such as the fluted pilasters
for door jambs and the fret molding above, testify to this influence, as
do also the senatorial figures of apostles who flank the door. These
squat figures (fig. 121), heavily robed and full bearded, are not far
removed from the later Roman tradition. The heads are large in proportion to the bodies. Perhaps this massiveness is appropriate to the
location. The multiple folds of drapery are not so deeply cut into the
mass, in spite of the classic influence, as to create a plastic treatment.

A tendency to pattern, vague in the large figures, is more in evidence
in the frieze, which contains seated Apostles in the center, with the
separation of the souls at the sides, the Blessed on the left, and the
Damned to the right. The architecture needs a band in that position;

to provide this, the individual figures are reduced to elements of a pattern; each figure, simple in itself, duplicates its neighbors in pose. The victims chained together on the right, each with his hand on the shoulder of the man in front, march off in lock step with the patterned flames of hell licking around their legs. The subject is clear, and thus the artist is free to turn to the artistic needs of the design.

A different style centers around the pilgrimage routes to the shrine of Santiago de Compostela, though whether the Spanish or French workshops along those roads take precedence remains a point for archaeological debate. If St. Trophîme is related to the classic Roman, the affinities in St. Pierre at Moissac of the twelfth century lie instead with a school of manuscript illumination, ivory carving, and metal work that flourished in western Europe in the ninth and tenth centuries and which was remotely influenced by Byzantium. The figure of St. Peter (fig. 122) on the door jamb has as little correspondence to a human being as it well can. The proportions are attenuated, the head thrown forward at an angle with the body realistically impossible, the neck long; but above all the figure has now become a frame for an arrangement of drapery. The pipe-like legs, especially prominent in the angels of the tympanum above (fig. 123), afford an excuse to change the pattern, not to attempt to represent the leg. The garments fall in flat pleats. Similar patterned drapery and, at least in some examples, a similar indifference to the body, characterized the archaic period of Greek art. This parallel is a coincidence, but the relation to the art of the Dark Ages and to Constantinople is not. Not only the Byzantine ivories, but even the mosaic Chastity in St. Mark's (fig. 104) show the same angularity, attenuation, and kind of design in drapery. However, the sophisticated type and motives from the East receive more emotion from the dynamic spirit and nervous energy of northern and western Europe, manifest in the cross-legged figures and the swirls of drapery.

The composition culminates in the *tympanum,* that is, in the lunette within the arch of the doorway above the openings into the church. There is carved the Christ of the Apocalypse, surrounded by the symbols of the evangelists, angels, and elders (fig. 123). The twenty-four elders, ranged in tiers, gain animation from their crossed legs and varied postures as they look upward to the Saviour. Small in scale, they contrast with the larger central group. Christ dominates by His size, by the larger treatment of His robe, by His crossed halo, and, of course, by His central position. Still, though His figure has some mass, the sculptor refuses to cut into it. Instead, he presses the garment in folds against the figure, and lets the edges end in a zigzag, so that the surfaces rather than the mass create the effect.

Burgundy achieves still more of stylization. The tympanum of the Church of the Madeleine at Vézelay (fig. 124), also from the twelfth century, presents the Pentecost, the descent of the Holy Ghost upon the Apostles. This mystical occurrence is given curiously literal form; Christ in the pointed oval or mandorla shape in the center stretches out His hands to either side; from His finger tips, symbolic rays descend on the head of each of the Apostles. Naive as this may seem, it would be hard to find a more effective method of presenting this mystery, which does not lend itself to treatment in stone. The body has now become, even more than at Moissac, a frame of bent pipe to hold the drapery. In fact, because of the influence from illuminated manuscripts, the whole figure is flattened out; that Christ may have had a body does not concern these sculptors. If their design be effective, and their meaning clear, what need of anything further? For a Romanesque sculptor to be told that his statue did not look like a figure would have meant nothing to him. Aside from the exigencies of design, he might have replied that his figures were not intended to be human; they portrayed spiritual characters and incidents whose actuality had no bearing on their emotional religious significance. To consider them from our realistic point of view is to miss what is more important: namely, their supreme effectiveness as symbolic and didactic illustrations of church dogma and as abstract design.

A second, and yet more extreme, tympanum from Burgundy is that of St. Lazare at Autun, designed by master Gislebertus, whoever he may have been. The characters of the Last Judgment are more elongated, the figure of Christ flatter, and the whole design more diagrammatic and two dimensional than the sculpture at Moissac. The beguiling devils who figure in this subject provide an outlet for the exuberance of the time, but the composition is more confused and less effective than that at Moissac or St. Trophîme.

The character of Italian sculpture, itself varied, presents a solution distinct from these French styles. For one thing, the sculpture is scattered around the church, not concentrated at the doors and in the cloisters. For another, the Italians do not hesitate to carve in marble, regardless of the material of the building. Therefore, the sculpture is less well integrated with the architecture than in the best northern work. Lombardy in the twelfth century borrowed from Provence, as, for example, in the treatment of drapery in the Deposition, a twelfth-century relief from the Cathedral of Modena, possibly by Benedetto of Parma. This formal design fits its rectangle, but without such distortions of the figure as those in Burgundy or Languedoc. Southern Italy, as one might expect, turned to the Byzantine or even to the Roman classic. The former, modified by the Italian love of vivacious narrative, bears fruit in a series of bronze doors, well illustrated at the Cathedral of Benevento. On the other hand, the sculptors of the court of Frederick II at Capua in the early thirteenth century evolved a plastic style so classic in appearance that some of its products, such as the bust of Pier della Vigna or the head of the personified Capua, might easily be confused with Roman art. This school has exceptional importance as the source for the style of Nicola d'Apulia, the outstanding Tuscan sculptor of the mid-thirteenth century.

Outside of Italy, the monumental sculpture of the period is often restricted to the doorways and perhaps to the cloisters. However, the sculptured capitals, though minor, illustrate the character of Romanesque sculpture and are themselves entertaining. The vast majority of these capitals, of course, are plain, molded, or adorned with foliate patterns, sometimes based on Roman precedents, sometimes on Byzantine, but in the aggregate showing a remarkable fertility of invention. Even when the motive is foliate, the Romanesque carver pays little heed to any specific flower or leaf form; instead, he prefers to reduce the suggestions from nature into elements of design, as he does in the figure sculpture elsewhere on the building. A smaller number of capitals deal with figure subjects, but those deserve study. One from Autun (fig. 125) depicts the Temptation of Christ; a fascinating devil, winged and with clawed feet, stands before Christ on top of the temple. The barbaric vigor of the northern imagination is allowed free rein in the demon, who, however, seems unlikely to tempt anyone with success, least of all Christ. Frankly handled as a grotesque, his wrinkled face is deliberately distorted. Christ, on the other hand, His head encircled by a halo inscribed with a cross, exhibits the same angularity and linearism that mark the tympanum figures. From Moutier St. Jean in the twelfth century comes a naive version of the story of Cain and Abel (fig. 126). The older brother can be recognized by his full beard as well as by the sheaf of grain in his hand, while Abel carries a lamb from his flock. The hand of God indicates His preference for the live offering by pointing to it through the cloud presented by repeated wavy lines. Simple as is this arrangement, the story is readable, a primary aim of

the sculptor in days when the lessons of the Church might be incul-
cated through representation on the churches, since books were rare,
and few but the churchmen could read. These narratives filled the place
taken by printing in modern life. For the twentieth-century observer,
in addition to a knowledge of the Bible narrative some imagination is
often necessary to recognize these scenes, but possibly they may have
been more easily identified by those for whom they were made. The
same tendency to distortion is evident here that characterizes the monumental sculpture. Consider the emphasis on the enlarged heads; on the
eyes, by a hole drilled to catch a black shadow, or, in the example from
Autun, by expanding their normal size. One frequently finds this tendency in primitive art, to stress what seemed to the sculptor the significant or identifying features of his subject. Essentially it duplicates the
exaggerated scale in the Christ of the Moissac tympanum. One must
further observe in these capitals the tendency in design, in spite of considerable modeling, to follow the surfaces of the capital rather than to
cut into it. In this way, the design is brought into accord with the
structure of the capital.

As in architecture, so also in manuscript illumination the Germans
retained some of the complexity of Carolingian traditions. The Gospels of Emperor Otto, at the end of the tenth century, display some
Byzantine influence in the figures, with a copious use of gold. On the
other hand, Byzantine influence on the eleventh-century Grimbald Gospels is slight. Distorted, symbolic, and linear though the figures are,
they have a vivacity unknown to their forerunners, but common to the
Winchester school. That sprightliness is apparent in the Newminster
Liber Vitae (fig. 127) early in the eleventh century. The figures, here
sketched in brown ink, depict St. Peter welcoming the elect to heaven
and rescuing a soul by force from the devil, and an angel closing the
gates on the damned in hell. Some distortion remains, but this is insignificant in comparison with the freedom of pose and expression. Much
the same feeling for the grotesque vitalizes the devils here that we
have seen in Romanesque capitals.

The Romanesque style used to be regarded as a crude preparation
for the Gothic; its sculpture was uncouth, because of the ignorance of
the epoch that produced it. Even from this brief review, it should be
obvious that such an attitude is unjustified. While some of its styles are
less refined than the Gothic, in the expression of sheer strength it is

greater. If some of its branches provide the structural experimentation preparatory to the Gothic, many Romanesque styles have no connection with the later French style. In reality, the Romanesque stands triumphant on its own feet, an inevitable expression of the new vigor of western Europe, of its faith, and of its feudal system.

IX

The Early Development of French Gothic Art

In the popular mind, today and for centuries past, medieval art is Gothic art. Though this idea is prejudiced, since it ignores Byzantine and Romanesque art, it has some justification: Gothic art is the most striking manifestation of the whole age; its style or group of styles has the most vivid character, at least in architecture; and in so far as any one style can represent so long and varied a period, the Gothic best does so. The judgment of its success has altered through the years, as its very name, the Gothic, indicates. During the centuries when it was 'modern' and universal, this style, as far as it was called anything, was known as *opus francigenum*, French work, which suggested where its principal motive force lay. Subsequently, in the fifteenth and sixteenth centuries, with the revival of interest in and enthusiasm for antiquity, the Italians maintained that the Middle Ages had been a barbaric period; its most striking product was the style usually characterized by the pointed arch; the Goths were the best known of the barbarians; therefore, the style was Gothic, that is, barbaric. Although for more than a century now the term has ceased to have any stigma attached to it, nevertheless it was coined in the sixteenth century as a term of contempt.

In general, Gothic art is more homogeneous than is Romanesque art. If the style differs in France, England, Spain, and Italy, and if a thorough study of the field uncovers local variations within each country, still those differences are minor when compared with the abrupt contrasts in the architecture and sculpture of neighboring regions during the Romanesque period. To some extent, the greater uniformity of the Gothic may be attributed to the wandering bands of lay workmen who seem to have journeyed from town to town as opportunities for employment arose. More important, however, were the new circumstances of the late twelfth and thirteenth centuries. At this time, the royal government, especially in France, was slowly gaining power. Though the feudal system had by no means disappeared, the royal vassals were not so independent as they had been in the eleventh and early twelfth centuries. The rise of the towns, fostered by the kingship, helped to alter the structure of society. During the thirteenth century under Philip Augustus, France attained a degree of unity unknown before, and even though, subsequently, the English conquered large provinces of France, and in spite of the rival power of the Dukes of Burgundy, the trend was toward increased unity. Moreover, means of communication, though still poor, slowly improved and brought a fuller knowledge to any one region of the activities in other areas. All these changes tended to foster a general French Gothic style rather than individual Norman, Provençal, and Auvergnat styles, with but slight connection between them.

The growth of towns in particular distinguished the Gothic era from the Romanesque, which had been so largely the product of the monasteries. The cathedral was the center of the life of the town, many of whose communal activities took place in it or in front of it; it therefore partook of the character of a civic monument. Each group in the town played a part in building and adorning its great church. The several guilds might donate stained-glass windows, or undertake the responsibility for a chapel, dedicated as a rule to the patron saint of that guild. At Chartres, the townsmen harnessed themselves to carts to draw stone to the cathedral, a contribution of personal service prompted first by religious enthusiasm, but not unmixed with civic pride. The rivalry between towns was intense. Paris built its Notre Dame first, rearing its vaults 115 feet in the clear; Amiens, a little later, as though to outdo Paris, raised its vault 147 feet above the pavement; Beauvais, shortly after Amiens, outdid them both with its cathedral 157 feet high internally. In Beauvais, the zeal to outstrip its rivals in height was carried to such excessive lengths that parts of the building collapsed and had to be replaced. Again, Siena, always jealous of Florence, built its sumptuous cathedral first. When Florence accepted the challenge, her cathedral was made much larger than the Sienese. Not to be outdone, the Sienese determined to convert their new church into merely the transepts of a tremendous structure; to be sure, they never completed more than the foundations, but the intention remains obvious.

This pride of the towns in the cathedrals and the active role taken by the townspeople in their construction has led to a widespread supposition that there were no architects. It is true that the title of architect rarely appeared in the medieval records; the man who performed that function was variously described as master builder, master mason, or clerk of the works. Very surely, too, these craftsmen differed from modern architects in their relation to the process of building, since the master builders combined the functions of architect, contractor, and foreman. But the idea that such complicated designs could be the product of the community is absurd. There must have been some individual whose vision, whose sense of proportion, and whose knowledge of structure made him essentially the architect, the man in whose mind the conception of the cathedral crystallized. That such a person might allow his subordinates greater latitude than is possible today, or that the subordinates developed their own ideas in carving the capitals or other more or less decorative parts of the building, does not mean that no architect took charge. Indeed, the names of many of these master builders have been preserved. What we do not have from the Middle Ages, in contrast to subsequent periods, is any information about the personality of these men. They remain merely names to us. While we may doubt whether they themselves would have welcomed this anonymity, the conception of fame had not yet grown to the point where an architect or artist might take steps to ensure the preservation and dissemination of his reputation.

Even if we recognize the importance of the secular and civic backing of the cathedrals, we must still admit that the prime force behind them was spiritual. That the town should choose to make the cathedral its biggest monument is in itself significant. The soaring lines of the church, its buttresses and pinnacles, its spires reaching heavenward, express a religious enthusiasm and aspiration never reached before or since. No other style has touched that summit of mystical exaltation the Gothic has so perfectly expressed.

Architecturally speaking, the Gothic style is characterized by the pointed arch. It spreads from France over western Europe, beginning late in the twelfth century and lasting until the Renaissance — that is, through the fourteenth century in Italy and into the sixteenth century north of the Alps. C. H. Moore defines Gothic architecture as 'a system of vaults, supports, and buttresses, the supports strong enough to bear the crushing weight only, and the stability maintained by a perfect equilibrium of thrusts.' This definition is as valuable in what it omits as in what it contains. Most surprising to the popular mind is its lack of any reference to the pointed arch. Yet while that feature is prominent in the Gothic style, it is found in other styles, and round arches occur in Gothic buildings. Throughout the Romanesque period, wherever Saracenic influence exists, one may encounter the pointed arch; Monreale Cathedral, for instance, uses it consistently, though the building is Romanesque, not

Gothic. The Spanish Romanesque, also, and even that of Provence not infrequently use pointed arches. On the other hand, in so completely Gothic a building as Chartres Cathedral, the nave clearstory windows, though not their smaller divisions, are round arched, and so too are the diagonal ribs of Notre Dame in Paris. Evidently, this shape is a less certain touchstone of the Gothic than is popularly supposed.

Then, again, Moore's definition rightly mentions no wall, but merely the three great structural elements. In fact, in the developed French Gothic, the wall ceases to exist as a structural member. The building becomes a cage of glass and stone, with windows the full width from pier to pier. If some wall remains, for example below the aisle windows, it plays no role other than to exclude the weather. It is as though the Romanesque wall had been cut into sections, and each section turned outward at right angles to the mass of the building to become a buttress. In essence, the early French Gothic is a structural system composed of the elements mentioned by Moore, and inevitably developed from the organic styles of the Romanesque. Adequate as is this definition in many respects, it has one serious defect. It applies only to early French Gothic; not to Gothic architecture in other countries, or even to later phases of the style in France.

The emphasis on structure implies the desirability of examining the several parts of the Gothic cathedral individually before we attempt to discuss any one monument in its entirety. First in importance is the vault. While logical and organic, the vaulting system of Sant' Ambrogio in Milan (fig. 113) has several shortcomings. The vaults tend to be heavy; the crown or apex of the vault, because of the use of the semicircle for all the ribs, remains domical. This produces a certain amount of outward pressure along the length of the wall rib, and in addition tends to break up the interior into separate units; but above all in Sant' Ambrogio, the elimination of the clearstory results in a very dark church. As we have seen, the Normans in St. Étienne at Caen (fig. 117) and elsewhere reverted to the clearstory, and to a vault with level crowns, but at the expense of heavy walls and of less than semicircular ribs. To meet these objections, the Gothic builders made two fundamental modifications in vaulting. First, to raise the crown of the transverse and wall ribs to the same level as the crown of the diagonal ribs, they adopted the expedient of pointed arches. This step was made only in slow and tentative fashion. At Morienval, in the ambulatory of a very small church, perhaps rebuilt about 1120, the arches were pointed (fig. 128), though in the earlier parts of the same building, they remained the simpler round arches. The pointed arches brought the apex of the ribs around the edges of each area to be covered by the vault approximately to the level reached by the diagonal ribs. Elsewhere, the builders pointed the arches, to be sure, but not enough to give the desired result; consequently, they had to insert above the arch a small section of wall in order to gain the necessary height, as, for example, at Bury. Of course, in the fully developed Gothic, such make-shifts were unnecessary because of the fuller appreciation and bolder use of this device.

The pointed arch could by itself produce a vault with level crowns, that is, one in which all of the ribs rise to the same level. On the other hand, especially in a vault over a rectangular area, if the height is to be achieved simply by pointing wall arches, they must be very sharply pointed indeed. Moreover, the Gothic builders tried to concentrate the thrusts of their vaults as fully as possible along a single line opposite each pier on the outside of the building. The diagram of Romanesque and Gothic vaults (fig. 129) shows that the Romanesque wall arches begin to curve at the same point as do the transverse and diagonal ribs, and therefore cover a triangular area of the outer wall surface. Logically the buttress should cover that triangle, and thus become broader than the Gothic builders desired. In addition to needing a wider buttress, the Romanesque scheme reduces the wall area in the clearstory, which the more open Gothic arrangement converts to window. The Gothic designers *stilt* their wall ribs; that is, instead of allowing the wall ribs to begin to curve at the same point as the diagonal ribs, they insert a colonnette to raise the springing of the wall arches well above that of the others. Therefore, the under surface of the vault assumes a warped form, called the plowshare twist. A second result is the greater window area in the clearstory level; a third, that the wall rib does not need to be so sharply pointed to produce a vault with level crowns; and fourth, the area covered by the vault on the outer wall of the church is restricted to a line instead of a triangle. This type of vault is illustrated in the nave of Amiens Cathedral (fig. 130).

In the matured Gothic of the thirteenth century — for example, at Amiens and Chartres — the designers reverted to the quadripartite system of Lombard origin and abandoned the sexpartite arrangement. This was not true while the style was developing; on the contrary, many twelfth-century Gothic buildings converted the sexpartite system to Gothic structure, as one may see in the nave of Notre Dame at Paris, of the Cathedrals of Laon and Mantes, and many others. But one great advantage of the Gothic vault is its adaptability to any area. Realizing this after the style had been perfected, the builders returned to the uniform quadripartite system and abandoned the alternate arrangement of sexpartite vaults. The domical character of Lombard vaults, prominent in a square plan, would become absurdly emphasized if the plan of the vault were oblong. Clearly the longer the rectangle, the greater the discrepancy between the crowns of round diagonal and wall ribs, if they spring from the same level. With the more flexible Gothic, by pointing and stilting, any height may be reached even over a limited span.

Next to the vault, the second element in the definition of Gothic is the support, which includes not merely the piers of the nave arcade but also the shafts above them in the triforium and clearstory levels designed to carry the vault. Since Gothic structure grows out of the organic Romanesque, one would expect to find a colonnette corresponding to each rib, and so in fact one does, above the level of the capitals in the nave arcade. As the proportions of the building turn toward lightness, these shafts become more attenuated than in the Romanesque, and therefore emphasize verticality. In the piers, however, the story is different. The membered Romanesque pier, however logical, tends to large bulk; it defines and separates the space in the nave from the volumes in the aisles. Though one may pass readily from one to the other, the several parts are conceived as visual units. The first step taken by the Gothic seems retrogressive. The membered pier is replaced by the round column, whose somewhat smaller mass frees the floor area and allows the space to flow from nave to aisles, as though the two were parts of the same volume. However, to use plain columns here means that the apparent support for the vault ribs must stop at the level of the capitals, which, though not structurally objectionable, is weak in appearance. The strong verticality of the colonnettes seems contradicted or at least interrupted by the absence of a similar vertical emphasis in the piers. Therefore, the architects placed a single colonnette in front of the sixth nave pier of Notre Dame in Paris (fig. 131), west of the crossing. Although this one member seems to support three colonnettes, it serves to continue the sense of movement from the vaults to the pavement, or *vice versa*. This pier is lopsided; consequently, in the seventh pier at Paris, similar shafts were applied to the column to support the aisle vaults and under the arches of the nave arcade, as well as on the face of the pier. This symmetrical result proves effective both structurally and visually. The still sturdy piers of Chartres (fig. 137) grow into the elegant shafts of Amiens (fig. 130), as though to suggest the engineering knowledge accumulated through trial and error, and the zeal for height which reaches its culmination in the Cathedral of Beauvais. The increased technical skill of the later builders in the fourteenth and fifteenth centuries permitted a partial return to the elaborately membered pier, but with its component parts so small and delicate that, as a whole, it still remained light.

The buttress is the third and last of the principal structural elements. A Romanesque pier buttress has a massiveness characteristic of the style as a whole. The chief problem lies in connecting the thrusts of the nave vaults with the buttress; if placed against the clearstory, its lower portion will block the aisle. Consequently, the Lombards sacrificed the clearstory to galleries; the latter contain arches, which transfer the thrust of the nave vaults over the aisles to the pier buttresses on the outer wall of the church. The thick walls in Norman churches appear to be heavy enough in themselves largely to care for the problem, but the Gothic walls are thin or nonexistent. The matured Gothic buttress (fig. 132) really has two parts, of which the first, the pier buttress, derived from the Romanesque, is built as a solid mass at right angles to the axis of the church, against the wall of the aisle, and in perfected examples rising high above it. This part through its sheer weight counteracts the outward pressure of the vaults. In such a single-aisled church as the Ste. Chapelle in Paris (fig. 133), this buttress is set, of course, against the body of the building. A series of offsets on its outer edge makes the buttress heavier at the bottom than at the top. This device is effective both as structure and in appearance, since it slopes the buttress inward against the outward pressure of the vault.

The second part, the flying buttress, is peculiar to Gothic, though its germ exists in the church of Ste. Trinité at Caen, where the Normans experimented with a half arch under the aisle roof, as they did also in Durham Cathedral. Although too low at Caen to meet the thrusts of the nave effectively, this engineering expedient was pushed into the open above the aisle roof as the Gothic style grew, and so was brought up to the point where it touched the lower parts of the nave vault. This exposed half arch, which carries a diagonal course of stone, rests its lower end on the pier buttress and its upper against the clearstory of the nave. The flying buttress functions as a prop to transfer the thrusts outward over the aisle roof. Contrary to a common belief, this half arch has very little inward thrust; alone it would be almost valueless to resist the presumably powerful outward pressure of the nave vaults, but as a connective its value is enormous. It is not too much to say that without it French Gothic could never have attained its height and openness. Flying buttresses appear on the flank of Rheims Cathedral (fig. 134), where their soaring lines express both the vertical mass and the skeletal character of the Gothic structure. At first in the evolution of the flying buttress, a single half arch sufficed, but in time the Gothic builders realized that there were two points to be resisted, the vault proper and the pressure upon the walls just above the vault produced by wind on the huge roof that covers the church. Consequently, the flying buttress was doubled, one half arch above another.

In addition to these essential structural components, the Gothic has many elements less fundamental, but very prominent in appearance. To a greater extent than any other style, however, the Gothic avoids applied decoration; its richer details tend to be interwoven with the structure, which itself is made decorative. The large windows, for example, are patterned with *tracery*, bars of stone interlocked like arches. The wind pressure sustained by these vast windows is more than could be borne by stained glass, which is composed of small pieces held in place by pliable lead bars. Although iron rods divide these windows at intervals, some additional support is necessary lest the rods become inordinately heavy. Therefore, vertical stone members, called *mullions*, break the whole window area into smaller units, and support openwork or traceried arches.

As these changes in structure arise, a similar metamorphosis alters the façade. The west front of the Gothic cathedral, derived from such Norman façades as St. Étienne at Caen (fig. 118), reflects the interior. The buttresses of its flanking towers mark the separation of nave and side aisles, and the successive stories echo the interior levels of nave arcade, triforium, and clearstory. It remained to give this division more vivid expression. The façade of Notre Dame in Paris (fig. 135), though still not mature in style, retains these divisions, with the middle section reduced to a row of sculptured figures. The doors are now much larger, and the opening itself expanded by a splayed surface, that is, by a diagonal plane to either side of the doors, which increases the emphasis on them and affords a field for sculpture. The windows, too, are splayed and much larger than in the Romanesque. In later examples, such as the façades of Amiens and Rheims Cathedrals, the corner buttresses of the towers project boldly from the plane of the façades. Therewith, the doors become porches as deep as the projection of the buttresses. In these great salient welcoming portals, the sculpture of the cathedral reaches its culmination.

The Gothic builders preferred to terminate the towers with spires, though in most instances local history prevented their completion. The familiar towers of Notre Dame in Paris were intended to support spires.

The powerful verticals of the buttresses below demand some continuation. At Chartres Cathedral (fig. 138), the magnificent south spire to the right is approximately contemporary with the twelfth-century façade, but the north spire was not constructed until early in the sixteenth century and is consequently different in style. The French felt, at least during the early Gothic, that a spire should grow imperceptibly from the tower. Therefore, in the south spire at Chartres, two transitions were effected: that from the vertical plane of the tower walls to the sloping surfaces of the spire, and that from the square plan of the tower to the octagonal plan of the spire. The soaring dormer windows compose at once the top story of the tower and the lowest stage of the spire, to make so subtle a transition from one to the other that one hardly realizes it has been made. Moldings rise above the center of each dormer and on the angles of the spire to prolong the vertical movement. Most Americans prefer the south spire and are inclined to neglect the north. Only in so far as the south is more in keeping with the façade as a whole is this preference justified.

Many have observed the asymmetry of the Gothic buildings, and undoubtedly that is important. However, in most cathedrals the more obvious asymmetrical features were constructed at different dates. Neither the Gothic nor the Romanesque builders were hostile to symmetry; they simply did not make a fetish of it, and were quite willing to depart from it whenever circumstances afforded some reason to do so. The Gothic castle is usually unsymmetrical and picturesque, but this is because the builders took full advantage of the possibilities of the site. If the ground is level and the fortress built at one time, as at Aigues Mortes, erected by St. Louis in the thirteenth century, tower will balance tower, gate will be echoed by gate, and only the keep will remain as an asymmetrical element. The readiness with which the Gothic builders gave up symmetry, however, allows few Gothic buildings to be absolutely uniform around an axis. Although the façade of the Cathedral of Paris is symmetrical in its larger elements, more than twenty small points of discrepancy can be found between the right and left halves of the design.

Important as are the elements that compose the Gothic cathedral, the whole is still more significant. Each cathedral has its own personality, none more than Chartres (figs. 136–8), dating chiefly from 1194 to 1260. The plan is different from that of all other styles. Because of the elimination of the wall, the plan comprises only a series of points, connected by lines that reflect the presence of ribs in the vault. This lace-like pattern discloses the openness of design, as it points to the vast window area. To credit this openness wholly to a desire for light, however, is not justifiable.

The stained-glass windows of Chartres form a decorative and symbolic expression of the religious exaltation of the Gothic age; but stained glass by its very nature excludes a large proportion of the available light, bathing the church in color whose beautiful tones are too dark to be adequate by modern standards of lighting. For the thirteenth century, the beauty of color more than compensated for the decreased quantity of illumination.

As one enters Chartres Cathedral on a sunny day, shafts of kaleidoscopic color reveal the structural system. The general form of the piers, now fully developed with four colonnettes attached to the central core, is made more subtle by a slight alternation in design. Careful observation shows that where one pier is composed of an octagonal core with four round shafts engaged upon it, its neighbors reverse the scheme, having a circular core with four octagonal shafts. Though most visitors to Chartres are never aware of this alternation, it yet impresses itself imperceptibly by the slight rhythm in design. Moreover, these angular and curved forms add visual interest, since each catches contrasted patterns of shade, the change from a smooth transition of light to shade in the rounded surfaces to the sharper breaks afforded by the octagonal form.

Each pier supports a group of five shafts, to reflect the five ribs of the quadripartite vaults. In those shafts too, a gradual change in size is made from the smallest ones, which respond to the wall ribs, to the largest, which support the transverse ribs. Since the triforium occupies the vertical space marked off by the sloping roof over the aisles, no windows pierce that level; instead, in each bay a group of four arches opens on a narrow passage. On the other hand, the clearstory windows spread from pier to pier, and thus utilize to the full the advantages for stained glass offered by the Gothic system.

Through the piers and their shafts, the builders create a dramatic expression of height, great in itself but even more accented in design. It might be hard to show a necessity for this vast interior space, but from a spiritual point of view its worth is incalculable. As a result, the complex polyphony of the medieval chant reverberates from the vaults above, to fill the church with music and produce an atmosphere that can be gained in no other way. In the last analysis, though, one must regard this height as an expression of civic prestige and of the devotion of the Middle Ages. As one advances through the church, a varying succession of vistas meets the eye. One sees through the nave arcades to the aisles, through them in turn to the transepts; but the culmination of the whole cathedral is the radiant east end, where the aisle winds around the curved apse and gives access to a series of chapels. The curved plan here results in great richness of effect, so that new beauties meet the eye at every step, perspectives change, and the complex patterns of light and shadow flow from one part of the church to another.

The same dramatic verticality governs the exterior. Soaring buttresses march along the flank of the church; each draws the attention upward until, through the crowning pinnacles, the glance merges with the sky. At the west end, towers crowned with spires accent the principal entrance and provide a brilliant climax for the building. Not only through its verticality does the Gothic cathedral differ from the Romanesque; its whole relation to space has altered. These buttresses and spires, unlike the wall in a Romanesque church, do not seem to enclose a given volume; instead they link the building to the surrounding atmosphere. Space flows readily on the interior from nave to aisles, transepts, and ambulatory, with none of the divisions conceived in themselves as definite volumes, but as extensions or ramifications of the same volume. In the same way, the large window area invites that inner space to join with the outer air. The thin sheet of glass hardly interrupts this union. As the buttresses project from the wall plane, they break up any sense of enclosure that plane might otherwise establish, and seem to soften the union with the out-of-doors. Their pinnacles and pointed spires melt into the sky.

This relation of the building to space both inside and out contradicts the method adopted in the Greek temple, as the mystical Christianity of the Gothic age reverses the rational religion of the Greeks. Where the Greek temple clings to earth, the Gothic church springs heavenward. The Parthenon defines its mass; Chartres is less clear and self-contained. It is the difference between the static and dynamic, the intellectual and the emotional. As a whole and in its parts, the Parthenon seems governed by the mind of man, and as complete and reasonable as a proposition in Euclid; whereas the Gothic, like medieval speculation, expresses the intangible, and therefore transcends the human in its hopeful quest for something above and beyond.

The same devotional spirit molds the sculpture, without which the French cathedral is more incomplete than the Greek temple. Like the Romanesque, Gothic sculpture is predominantly ecclesiastical, and, to be understood, it must be approached with some knowledge of medieval interpretation. It is didactic in purpose, calculated to illustrate and emphasize the teachings of the Church. Christ is glorified in all the world, and, therefore, all is worthy of representation in His temple. In his encyclopedia, Vincent of Beauvais groups the knowledge and belief of his day under four divisions, the mirrors of nature, instruction, morals, and history. Thus the sculptor may include plants or animals; he may present symbolic figures of music, astronomy, geometry, and philosophy; or the seven virtues and seven vices; or he may deal with that part of history worthy of remembrance, namely, sacred history.

To understand Gothic sculpture, one must realize that any figure or object may be open to a threefold interpretation. Art is at once a script, a calculus, and a symbolic code. A definite iconography dictates the way in which an artist shall present any given figure. Thus God, the angels, and the apostles are carved with bare feet; other characters will be shod. To represent them otherwise is not merely incorrect; it may almost be heretical. A stalk with a few leaves signifies a tree and therefore indicates that the scene takes place on earth. A tower with a door implies a town; if, however, an angel stands on the tower, it establishes the location as a particular city, the heavenly Jerusalem. The nimbus, or halo, indicates sanctity; when a cross is inscribed within it, the figure is divine. Through such a pictographic script, amounting to a visual language, the identification of the figures and the scene is made clear.

But the subject itself is only a small part of its significance. The place occupied by any figure, with relation to the center of the design where Christ usually appears, has its meaning. In general, the higher the position in the design, the greater is the honor; also, the place on Christ's right hand is more distinguished than that on His left. It must always be borne in mind that, since Christ faces the observer, His right hand is on the left as one looks at the composition. Consequently, the Elect are always placed on the right hand of Christ in representations of the Last Judgment, with the Damned to the left. Some of the clearstory windows in Chartres depict prophets who carry on their shoulders the evangelists. Medieval dogma teaches that although the evangelists rest on the prophets, yet, because they come later in sacred history and have a direct knowledge of the Saviour, they possess a higher spiritual vantage ground and a wider outlook than their forebears. Moreover, certain numbers have precise symbolism. Obviously because of its association with the Trinity, three connotes things spiritual. Four, the number of the elements that compose the world according to the Middle Ages (which in this theory follow antiquity), pertains to the earth. The sum of these two numbers produces seven, the number of humanity and an indication of the dual nature of man, partly spiritual, partly of the earth. Twelve, the product of three and four, explained to the medieval mind the selection of twelve apostles, the twelve lesser prophets, and so on.

Finally, the Middle Ages believed that profound and abstruse meanings are hidden in the Scriptures, allusions and parallels yielding their significance only through analogies. Thus, types or forerunners of Christ stud the Old Testament: the brazen serpent, lifted up by Moses in the wilderness to free the Israelites from a plague of serpents, suggests Christ raised on the cross to expiate the sins of the world. Or again, Melchizedek, as priest and king, prefigures Christ, and his bread and wine given to Abraham foretells the Holy Eucharist. The parable of the Wise and Foolish Virgins not only recalls the account in the Gospels, but also typifies the Elect and the Lost. The lion serves as the emblem of the Resurrection; in medieval belief the lion's cubs were supposed to be as though dead for three days after birth, at the expiration of which period the lion returns and breathes on them and brings them back to life. These three days of apparent death parallel Christ's descent into hell between Good Friday and Easter Sunday.

Because these interpretations are possible, it does not follow that all of them are applicable in every instance. Nor is it certain that these meanings were evident to the uneducated laymen, even in the thirteenth century; doubtless the clergy understood these matters, and on occasion explained them to their flocks, perhaps to illustrate some point in a sermon, but such esoteric meanings were probably hidden from the throng.

The sculpture of the Gothic period differs from that of the Romanesque, even though it grows from it. To be sure, like its predecessor, Gothic sculpture is polychromatic. The colors, at least until the later Gothic, are conventional; they do not imitate tones observed in nature, but instead are conceived as decoration. On the other hand, where Romanesque sculpture seems to have been carved *in situ,* after the stones were placed in the building, the Gothic statues were in most instances carved on the ground, and set in place only when they were finished. Moreover, the sculptor's technique advanced. He no longer turns to ivories and manuscripts for his inspiration; rather he thinks more in terms of stone, and consequently develops a greater roundness in his figures. The folds of drapery are not indicated by line with little change of surface, but become more deeply modeled. The features approximate their normal human proportions and projections, and thus catch a richer pattern of light and shade. The older rigidity of pose relaxes to allow the statues to stand easily. With the full development of Gothic sculpture, idealism dominates. The features and figures, like human beings but without individual traits, are generalized and perfected; conceived as types, they have a certain universality of expression. As a result, the Gothic figures acquire a monumentality well adapted to the new style.

These new qualities, of course, did not appear suddenly. The west portals of Chartres Cathedral (fig. 139), completed in the middle of the twelfth century, are transitional between the two styles, but by common agreement they are classed as Gothic. Frequently the west front contains a series of royal figures; although these are often identified as the kings and queens of France, the Middle Ages would hardly have considered such secular characters worthy of representation in so important a place; thus they must be interpreted as the royal ancestors of Christ, the kings and queens of Judah listed in the first chapter of the Gospel according to St. Matthew.

The most conservative part of the scheme is the tympanum over the central door, where the symbols of the Evangelists surround Christ in hieratic order. His head is backed by a halo inscribed with a cross, though such a symbol here is unnecessary for identification. His drapery is folded in small linear patterns, which hardly indent the mass. Indeed in some parts, such as the raised right arm, the folds swirl so as to bear only a remote resemblance to the body beneath, but a close one to the pattern-like character of Romanesque art. On the other hand, the Christ has a greater roundness of form, more feeling for the mass of the figure than have the earlier conceptions. The head is more natural than the diagrammatic heads in the Romanesque, with more highly modeled features, and perhaps less use of the drill.

However, the kings and queens who line the portal (fig. 140) are remarkably elongated. They seem to grow from the columns on which they rest, and emphasize in design their subordination to the verticality of the architecture; not only are the proportions tall and slender, but the patterns of the clothing reinforce the direction. The long flowing sleeves of the queen, her braided hair, and the folds of her dress create an almost abstract insistence on Gothic movement. Such willingness to subordinate sculpture to architecture and to distort the normal dimensions of the figure continues Romanesque principles. However, where Romanesque sculpture might be applied to door jambs to enrich the architectural design, but with little reference to architectural construction, the new Gothic interest in structure compels a corresponding emphasis on it in sculpture. Also, the heads reveal a pronounced change in the degree of realism. At Chartres, these have considerable individuality, a flash of naturalism, contradicted to be sure by the bodies, but otherwise analogous to the realism of the transitional period in Greek sculpture about the time of Myron. These heads represent an attitude opposed to the stylized, expressive heads of the Romanesque.

The west portals of Chartres Cathedral, dating from the middle of the twelfth century, are at most transitional to the Gothic. Representative of that style in the early thirteenth century in sculpture is the north tympanum on the west front of Notre Dame in Paris (fig. 141). The architectural change between the west fronts of Chartres and Paris produces here a more pointed arch, with a consequent enlargement of the tympanum area. Therefore, instead of treating the tympanum as a single composition, the sculptor breaks it up into three independent bands, and relies on the related subjects to tie the design together. The lowest zone contains six figures, three prophets on our left, three kings on our right. These we may interpret as the spiritual and physical ancestors of Christ, with the spiritual side given the place of honor on the right hand of Christ, whose figure appears above. The middle range depicts the Resurrection of the Virgin. When the last earthly hours of the Madonna arrived, the apostles gathered in her presence from the four corners of the world. Christ reappeared to receive the soul of His Mother and translate it to heaven. He bears in His arms the symbol of the soul, a doll-like creature wrapped in swaddling clothes. The apostles sit or stand around the bier, in meditation on the miracle before them, with St. Peter, the chief apostle in the Western church, significantly at the extreme left, and thus to the right of Christ. Finally, in the top range appears the Coronation of the Virgin. Christ has placed the Virgin on His right, and offers her the scepter in token of His intention to share His power in heaven with her.

These figures project boldly from the background, and if the proportion of the heads is still a little large for the bodies, the discrepancy is by no means so great as previously. The drapery too has changed, even as compared with the carving at Chartres. Large, simple, majestic folds replace the smaller rippling pattern, and lend to the whole concept a monumentality and breadth with more than a touch of idealism about it. A certain ease in pose and restrained freedom of movement animate these figures. The artist conveys his message less through symbolism and more than before through human characters.

The full development of Gothic sculpture, however, is accomplished in Amiens and Rheims Cathedrals. The Beau Dieu at Amiens (fig. 142), from the first half of the thirteenth century, central in the whole scheme of the west front, adorns the post, or *trumeau*, which divides the two halves of the middle door. He is, therefore, isolated from the saints who line the portal where stood the kings and queens at Chartres. While symbolism is still important, it is now subordinate. This is Christ triumphant; He stands on two grotesque animals, and just below two more appear in relief on the pedestal. These four animals are the adder and the basilisk, the lion and the dragon. Since the lion is one of the symbols of antichrist, the dragon of the devil, the basilisk of death, and the adder of sin, this figure commemorates Christ risen from the tomb and triumphant over the powers of darkness. But these symbols are no more needed to convey the message than one needs the crossed halo to identify the figure as Christ. This serene statue is now highly idealized, its features rendered in broad planes, and all marks of individuality and all physical defects eliminated. In fact, we encounter much the same careful selection of details to create a feeling of idealism and impersonality that we have observed in fifth-century Greek sculpture. Indeed, the courses pursued by Greek and by medieval sculpture are curiously parallel; each started with a substitution of convention and symbolism for objective treatment, partly because of an inadequate technique; but later when the material was mastered, each turned to an ideal superhuman conception, only to abandon that in the end in favor of a literal realism.

The Beau Dieu invites comparison with the sculpture of the Parthenon. Each represents the most complete incarnation of the artistic ideals of its epoch. In quality, there is not much to choose between them. Different as they are, each fulfils its purpose on the building. Characteristically, the Gothic figure is clothed, whereas many of the Greek statues are nude. The body had come to be identified with evil during the earlier Middle Ages; at the very least, it was insignificant compared with the soul; the less seen and said about it the better. Any humiliation of the flesh might be counted a gain to the spirit. The fasting, flagellation, use of the hair shirt, and so on, common during these centuries, were directed to that end. Therefore, inevitably the artists avoid the nude whenever possible. When it does appear in medieval art, in scenes of the creation of the world, of Adam and Eve, or of the Resurrection and Last Judgment, the figures were rendered at a small scale, hardly bigger than puppets. Hence, in absolute contrast with antiquity, all of the larger figures of medieval art are fully clothed.

The amount of sculpture on a medieval cathedral is too great to have been executed by a single man. Differences of hand, therefore, are inevitable, but the similarity of expression, not the difference, is remarkable. However, the Annunciation and Visitation groups at Rheims Cathedral (fig. 143), in the second half of the thirteenth century, do vary widely in treatment. The Annunciation figures to the left are youthful, both in face and figure. Their costumes fall in broad expressive folds, analogous to the treatment of the Beau Dieu. Mary and Elizabeth in the Visitation, on the other hand, are more mature; their figures are bulkier, their features more particularized, though still not beyond the limits of idealization. In the head of Elizabeth, a few well-chosen lines in the face and even more the general treatment of the head sympathetically suggest old age. A maze of small folds complicates the drapery. However, instead of reverting to the drapery type of Chartres, these small folds point the way to later developments; they do not create a pattern, but suggest softer stuff with a representational purpose in view. Also, by comparison with the Beau Dieu, these characters in the Visitation are more animated. Their gestures are not so restrained, nor do they stand so quietly as do the slightly earlier figures from Amiens Cathedral. Though it is not yet pronounced, these figures foretell the later trend toward realism, with a consequent partial loss of the union with architecture so clear in earlier medieval sculpture.

The larger statues by no means exhaust the sculptural wealth of the cathedral. Indeed its encyclopedic character is even more evident in the reliefs and in the stained glass. A single example, chosen from the reliefs below the principal figures on the west front of Amiens Cathedral (fig. 144), a series of quatrefoils in two rows, shows in the upper tier the signs of the zodiac and in the lower the activities of the related months. In this particular group the Ram, corresponding roughly to the month of March, is paired with a farmer spading the soil; the Bull, for April, matches a hunter with a falcon on his wrist; and the Twins, for May, parallel a man seated out of doors, basking in the spring sun. These reliefs exhibit the same careful selection of detail as the larger figures; settings are reduced to a minimum; a stalk with a few leaves on it, or the tendrils of a vine suffice to identify the scene. And yet even in these tiny figures, the feeling for roundness is evident. If not masterpieces, such small compositions admirably fulfil their decorative function, and widen our knowledge of the Middle Ages.

Finally, the exuberant spirits of Gothic times find an outlet in the grotesques. Some of them serve as gargoyles, or water spouts, with the figures, especially the legs, contorted to adapt them to this purpose. But most of them balance on the buttresses, peer over the parapet, or crouch on the cornices; an exception to the rule in Gothic, they serve no obvious structural or liturgical purpose. If a few of them are human, or have parts of a human figure, the majority are pure figments of the mind, amusing hybrids of real and imaginary animals. Doubtless God could have made such creatures, but certainly God thought better of it. Carved in the same broad planes as the more serious sculpture, these monsters animate the cathedral to its very top. Such carvings, and in fact all Gothic sculpture, bereft of their settings, are almost meaningless. They are too closely related in interpretation and also in design to the other parts of the sculptural ensemble, as well as to the architectural design, to bear such a separation. When studied in their setting and combined with the cathedral, they contribute to the most complete expression of spiritual exaltation yet produced by Christianity.

X

The Diffusion and Later History of Gothic Art

LITTLE doubt can exist that the focus of Gothic art lies in France. The very name, *opus francigenum*, by which it was known at the time, proves that. But the influence of the French style spread rapidly in all directions, and as each country accepted the new fashion, it modified French Gothic art to meet its own local needs or tastes. Buildings with indigenous variations, moreover, are almost if not quite as early as those that adhere to the French manner. León Cathedral in Spain follows quite closely the style of the thirteenth-century cathedrals of northern France, in plan, structure, and elevation. The vast Cathedral of Seville, on the other hand, has a great many points of contrast with French work, some of them traceable to climatic differences. The flat roof, or at least a roof of but gentle slope, produces a fundamentally different external appearance. Moreover, since a triforium is caused by the sloping roof over the aisle, a flat roof there results in a contraction or even a complete suppression of that internal division. The brilliant southern sun makes it possible and desirable to curtail the window area of French Gothic buildings. Thus in Spanish Gothic architecture, broad wall surfaces, pierced only here and there by windows, supplant the huge glazed areas of French Gothic. Such small openings protect the building from excessive heat in summer, but, in spite of the sun, leave a dark, even gloomy interior. A Spanish interior is apt to be interrupted by a high *coro*, or choir screen, which separates that part of the church from the rest. With these and many other differences in detail, clearly Spanish Gothic architecture is no mere copy of French.

In Italy, a series of monasteries, including San Galgano near Siena, imported a French style. It, however, was the Gothic of Burgundy, more austere and powerful than the better-known architecture of northern France. Nevertheless, climate and the traditional Italian love for the horizontal soon exerted their influence so effectively that the cathedrals of Siena and Orvieto, for example, in spite of a decorative scheme of pointed arches, tracery, pinnacles, and so on, reject the northern version of the Gothic style. The nearly flat roofs, the polychromy inherited from Tuscan Romanesque architecture, the complete indifference to Gothic structure, the small windows and broad wall surfaces, all betray an Italian feeling for the horizontal in contrast to the verticality of the northern style.

Cologne Cathedral in Germany, begun in 1248, though different in many details, is modeled on Amiens. More original are the *Hallenkirchen* or hall churches. Though a similar type may be found in southwestern France, the Germans developed their own form and showed a decided partiality for it and great distinction in handling it. Such churches as St. Elizabeth at Marburg exemplify the system. The aisles are built as high, or almost as high, as the nave itself, and are covered by the same roof. Therefore, the whole interior system of nave arcade, triforium, and clearstory is eliminated. Instead, the piers soar upward to support the vaults directly; this arrangement permits the windows in the aisles sufficient height to light the nave.

The main steps in the history of the Gothic style in France are, of course, duplicated in other countries. Thus, in the late twelfth and early thirteenth centuries, much of the Romanesque spirit was retained; then the local style, under French influence or otherwise, formed itself, and as proficiency in building increased, the expression was further modified during later years. Manifestly, these divergent styles are too numerous to be discussed in detail here; we must be content with one or two examples chosen arbitrarily to demonstrate national contrasts in architecture and the general course taken by Gothic architecture in its later years.

The cathedrals of Amiens and Salisbury were both begun in 1220, but the latter shows the English solution of the problem. In the first place, the plan (fig. 145), in the shape of an archiepiscopal cross, has two pairs of transepts, a large one approximately in the center of the building from end to end, and a smaller one somewhat further to the east. Instead of the complex polygonal apse and ambulatory of Amiens, the English substitute a square east end. The nave is long in proportion, with ten bays instead of the seven customary in France. The façade projects beyond the sides of the church and is treated as a screen, without emphasis on the portals; indeed an English cathedral is normally entered through a porch on the side of the nave, or sometimes through a transept portal. A cloister fits into the corner between nave and transepts.

The interior (fig. 146) is comparatively inorganic, and therefore retains somewhat more of a Romanesque flavor than does the French cathedral. To be sure, the quadripartite vaults recall those across the Channel, but the organic support is not continued to the ground and does not correspond to each of the ribs; instead, at Salisbury a cluster of shafts rests on a bracket in the triforium level. Inevitably, the unbroken horizontal lines of the lower edge of the triforium retain something of the Romanesque spirit. The vaults, too, are relatively low. Where the French vaults rise to well over a hundred feet, the English are rarely more than eighty feet high. One reason is that the ribs of the French vault do not begin to curve until well up in the clearstory; at Salisbury, on the other hand, the ribs spring from the upper level of the triforium, and in many English cathedrals from an even lower point. Moreover, a thick wall, though pierced with more and larger windows than those of the Romanesque period, still helps to support and buttress the vaults. Therefore, the buttress system, as we see on the exterior (fig. 147), does not need to be so fully developed as in France. Some English cathedrals have flying buttresses, but they are meager and less prominent than they are in France. Usually the English cathedral is beautifully set in lawns and foliage, with sufficient open space around it to make it possible to see the building as a whole. Since the structure can frequently be perceived in its entirety from many points of view, the principal tower, with or without a spire, rises from the crossing of the main transept and the nave. If western towers appear, as they generally do — Salisbury is exceptional in this — they are apt to be dominated by the central accent, which pulls the whole design together and culminates it.

The English cathedral is of a type quite distinct from the French. Many of its points of divergence can be credited to its monastic origin. More than half of the English cathedrals, in fact, were built by Benedictines, and even those governed at first by a college of secular canons followed many of the practices typical of monastic buildings. It is significant that English cathedrals are often referred to as minsters (monasteries). Patently the cloister comes from this source. So too does the open setting, a reminder of the monastery grounds. Then the English orders accepted literally the need of orientation. In the French system of radiating chapels, if the altar be placed in its proper architectural position on the axis of the chapel, it cannot face east unless the chapel also faces east. But only one of the chapels around the chevet can be so directed. This consideration apparently prompted the English to abandon the apse in favor of the square east end, so that all the altars might be oriented. Moreover, elaborate processions played a large part in monastic ritual. The route taken by the procession differed in each instance, but it regularly started in the choir, passed around the east end to visit the altars located there, through the transepts where still more altars were found in each bay, out through the cloister, and sometimes even through the churchyard. The need for such ceremonial goes far to explain the particular forms of the English church.

Many have attempted to compare the French and English cathedrals, and have concluded that one is a greater and better architecture than the other. Such a judgment is neither necessary nor desirable. The two styles express different qualities, which must be considered separately; to measure the English by a French yardstick is absurd. In general, the French has a superb energy and an inspiring result, like some triumphant anthem. The English, on the other hand, is reticent, almost private by comparison, calm and restrained. Each, in its own way, is supreme.

The character of Gothic architecture through the early thirteenth century, especially in France but to some extent in the rest of Europe as well, was simple and direct. Absorbed in structural problems, little creative energy remained to devote to an elaboration of design. Even the decoration became a revelation of and an emphasis on structure. But after the structural difficulties were solved, the designers could and did refine the forms and imagine richer variations of solutions already discovered. Piers and tracery were made thinner as experimentation showed it possible to contract their mass. Decorative carving spread over more of the moldings than before. Additional ribs were added to the vaults. In England, the way to this elaboration was easier because of certain peculiarities in laying the stones of the vault. The English method of construction suggested a multiplication of ribs, especially the addition of a ridge rib running down the length of the church at the apex of the vault. Then, as for example in the nave of Exeter Cathedral, intermediate ribs subdivided the four triangles of quadripartite vaults. The reversed curves in the tracery here explain the name Curvilinear Decorated for English architecture of the early fourteenth century.

The English vaulting technique led ultimately to what amounted to new system of construction, which produced the fan vault. The cloister at Gloucester (fig. 148), begun in 1351, where the fan vault is first demonstrated on any considerable scale, shows the ribs radiating from the pier like the ribs of a fan. The ribs look like tracery applied to the under surface of the vault, though in reality cut in the thickness of the vaulting stones; they serve to strengthen the vault much as an engaged column stiffens a wall. An insistent emphasis on the vertical line at this time and for the following century and a half in England, particularly in the tracery, prompts the term Perpendicular style for this phase of Gothic architecture, in which, also, various kinds of pointed arches gain some popularity.

Though by no means identical, the late Gothic style in France, called the Flamboyant, probably borrowed a good deal from England, especially from the Curvilinear Decorated style. It is suggestive that the region in which the Flamboyant most flourished is also the region in closest contact with England. The general course of development in France had been interrupted by the Hundred Years War, fought on French soil. This calamity impoverished the country, and helped to end the earlier Gothic era. It thus opened the way for the Flamboyant style, whose name is derived from the flame-like curves characteristic of its tracery. In St. Maclou at Rouen (fig. 149), begun in 1437, the façade is no longer planned in simple parallel planes. Instead, it bows outward, the central bay normal to the axis of the church, those to the right and left bent back at a slight angle, and finally the two side bays at a greater angle. An openwork gable, whose curved lines of tracery sweep across one another in interlacing patterns, crowns each of its five bays. The old structural emphasis has vanished in favor of a dexterous openness of design, which betrays an exuberant energy without the seriousness and spiritual exaltation of the thirteenth century.

To most people, Gothic architecture is identified with the church, and undoubtedly the major expression of the period does lie in the cathedral. However, to imagine that the church alone represents the age is a mistake. In reality, the style is a vernacular equally applicable to all sorts of problems. Where cities rise to virtual independence, as in Flanders, the town and guild halls are almost as great civic monuments as the cathedrals themselves. The power of the Flemish guilds is evidenced by the size of the Cloth Hall at Ypres (fig. 150), its character established by a great central tower wherein hung the bells to summon the citizens. Naturally, the architectural vocabulary is that of the thirteenth century, when the structure was largely completed. Its distinction depends on the simple majesty of its proportions. Similar in purpose, the municipal buildings of Italy, such as the Palazzo Pubblico in Siena, the Palazzo Vecchio in Florence, and the Ducal Palace in Venice, follow the styles of their respective localities. So, too, does the Knochenhauerampthaus, the butcher's guild hall, at Hildesheim.

In the earlier Middle Ages, domestic architecture reflected the unsettled conditions of the times, which compelled as much fortification as the owner could afford. While the peasantry lived in cottages of wattle and daub, clay matted with green twigs, or more rarely of permanent materials, the characteristic home of the nobility was the castle, one more or less like another all over Europe, picturesque but forbidding, cold and uncomfortable by modern standards, though as time went on it developed a few conveniences. Bodiam Castle (fig. 151) in Sussex, built late in the fourteenth century, is typical and exceptionally complete, at least externally. A moat surrounds the castle to provide the first line of defense. The solid stone walls, punctuated by towers at the corners and around the entrance, and crowned with battlements to protect archers defending the castle against attack, have as few openings as possible, and those only of small size.

Since the castle is built around an open court, the living quarters are more ample and better lighted than might be supposed from the exterior. The principal chamber is the hall, flanked by the kitchen on one side, with its pantries and services, and on the other by the solar and bower, the private chambers of the master and mistress of Bodiam. In a very real sense, the hall is the center of life, where, under the paternalistic system of feudalism, the owner meets and mingles with his retainers. Here are served the meals to the entire household, and here most of the communal activities of life are carried on. In earlier times, the hall had been used as sleeping quarters for the retainers, though that custom had generally disappeared by the fourteenth century. Bodiam reveals a remarkable progress in convenience over earlier medieval castles. Much more living space is enclosed; larger windows on the court are adequate for the rooms they serve; sanitation improves; and a more extensive series of hearths or fireplaces helps to take away the chill. None the less, however picturesque Bodiam may be, and however much one may admire the intimacy between owner and dependents, few of us today would care to live there. Glass, though not unknown, was still a very valuable commodity; probably few, if any, of the windows were glazed. Therefore, one had a difficult option; sufficient light at the expense of free access to wintry winds, or, by closed shutters, few drafts and little or no natural light. Since the sanitary facilities drained into the moat, that charming feature can hardly have been as attractive when the castle was in use as it is today. Moreover, while an open fire is cheerful, it does not provide either the amount or the diffusion of heat to which we are accustomed.

Of course, public safety and peaceful living conditions improved with time. This may be observed in the late fifteenth-century town house of Jacques Cœur at Bourges (fig. 152) in France. Though built around a court, it is entirely without provision for defense, since cities were walled and therefore fortifications of separate buildings within them were unnecessary. Consequently, windows of considerable size appear in the outer wall. This house, in fact, is a splendid example of the Flamboyant style in domestic architecture. A Gothic directness of solution is evident throughout. For one thing, the house is faithful to principles of symmetry only where no reason can be found to abandon them. The central tower has its single large window on axis, filled with Flamboyant tracery, the reversed curves of which form a *fleur de lis* at the top. On the other hand, a stairway in the single turret on one side of the tower gives access to the upper stories of the tower. The entrance to the court provides for both equestrian and pedestrian traffic; it may be desirable at times to admit one kind but not the other. Therefore, two doors of different sizes pierce the wall unsymmetrically below the tower. A traceried parapet emphasizes the junction of the steep roof and the walls. The windows vary in size in proportion to the room they are intended to light. They are composed of multiples of simple units: the openings in a single window are separated from one another by stone mullions and transoms, which form a very plain kind of tracery. In short, all of the architectural elements are characteristic of the time, and all may be found at similar dates in church architecture.

The medieval spirit persisted in the north long after it had disappeared in Italy. As late as the early sixteenth century in England, such a house as Compton Wynyates (fig. 153) is still Gothic, with nothing borrowed from the Italian Renaissance. Though Compton Wynyates is a country residence unlike the Jacques Cœur House, the settled conditions of Tudor England made it possible to dispense with fortifications even in the country. To be sure, a moat used to surround the building, but that was a heritage from earlier and less peaceful days, and was intended less for defense against military operations than to hinder night marauders. Picturesque in its irregularity, the house seems to throw out gables and bay windows wherever the interior demands them. The warm color of brick walls, with a little stone around the doors and windows, contrasts with the blue slate roof and with the brown half-timbered gables. The court is still retained, as is the traditional arrangement of the suite of rooms around the hall. However, the latter has shrunk in size and importance; by this time, the family's comradeship with their retainers at meals and on other occasions was fast disappearing; a new recognition of the conveniences of privacy was growing. Comfort of the occupants increased tenfold. More ample sleeping accommodations have been provided for the dependents as well as for the family. At least every important chamber is now warmed by a fireplace, as the grouped chimney pots attest. Glass for the windows has become general, so that light and warmth are possible at the same time. The result of these advances is a sense of domesticity, informality, and charm, which has attracted the admiration of much later days. While the house lacks 'modern improvements,' it is not wholly foreign to current conceptions of a home. Though we can hardly imagine ourselves living in comfort at Bodiam, and still less so in the earlier castles, Compton Wynyates meets quite closely our ideas of domestic architecture.

By modern standards at least, houses during the Middle Ages were underfurnished, though the quantity and variety of the furniture had increased by the time of Compton Wynyates. Tables, in our sense of the term, were rare. The old phrase, 'to set the board,' meant precisely that: the table top of planks was set on trestles when a meal was in prospect, and removed after the meal was completed. With very few exceptions, family and guests alike sat on stools or benches, though throne-like chairs might be available for the master and mistress. Paintings of the time testify to the existence of massive beds, but the principal object of furniture was the chest, which no doubt served as a bench and at times even as a bed, as well as for storage purposes, and from it in the late Middle Ages developed the cupboard. The few preserved examples of Gothic furniture show the same frank solution of its structural problems, the same respect for its materials, and the same decorative motives, such as tracery and grotesques, that are to be found in late Gothic architecture and sculpture. These examples, built of oak, look and are sturdy.

While architecture and furniture underwent these changes, geographically and chronologically, sculpture did not stand still. On the contrary, just as the house developed its plan and its equipment to meet human needs, so that same concern with a more human quality modified the abstract spiritualization and idealization of mature Gothic statues. Even in the late thirteenth century, the new spirit began to be apparent; the Vierge Dorée at Amiens (fig. 154) betrays a maternal interest tinged with sentiment. Her hip, thrown out to help support the child's weight, gives to the figure more movement than had the Beau Dieu (fig. 142). The drapery, too, becomes complicated and perhaps more realistic, though the latter development is only suggested.

The bare suggestion of realism in the Vierge Dorée leads at the outset of the fifteenth century to such statues as the Moses adorning the well head at Champmol near Dijon, by Claus Sluter (fig. 155). This figure of the patriarch in its voluminous folds of drapery, its flowing beard, and the noble realism of its face conveys the clearest statement of the dignity of man. Thoroughly sculpturesque in mass, the plastic art here dominates the architecture, which serves merely as a setting for the figure; whereas in Chartres, the figures served to enrich a larger architectural composition. This Burgundian work, however, is restrained in its realism when compared with much German sculpture of the fifteenth century. Such artists as Veit Stoss, Adam Krafft, and at times Tilman Riemenschneider display the fullest possibilities of realism in stone, bronze, or wood. Consummate in technique, much of their work turns to pictorial effects that undermine the sculptural massiveness of Claus Sluter.

Such realism provoked a revolt in the movement known as the *détente*, which centered in the Loire valley in the late fifteenth century, and was characterized by a relaxation of extreme realism. Especially the head of the Female Saint (fig. 156) from this epoch is idealized, less spiritual than the distant creations of thirteenth-century art, and not devoid of sentiment, but far from the complete realism of late German Gothic sculpture. The poses at this time are quieter and more restrained, the draperies broad and simple, and the heads ennobled from middle or lower class French types, without individual peculiarities. Nevertheless, the sculptors of the *détente* cannot forget their background. Many details of costume reflect the elaborate fashions of the day, and the accessories show that these artists could have transferred this interest in minutiae to the head had they so desired.

This later development of medieval sculpture curiously parallels the story of classic art after the generation of Phidias. An increased sentiment, coupled with an interest in more human form, characterizes alike the fourth century before Christ and the late thirteenth and fourteenth centuries. Then, in each case, the artists turn toward realism, which after becoming extreme gives way at times to a partial return to idealism. Although one should not attempt to force cyclical patterns upon history, such general similarities do appear to mark certain stages in the history of human culture.

Italy presents a very different story. Even in architecture, the Italians resist the Gothic fashion as something extraneous and foreign to their culture. They divorce the French marriage of sculpture and architecture, and continue to regard sculpture as an independent art. Hence, the Italian preference for marble as a medium for sculpture, regardless of the stone used for the architecture, immediately changes the character from the freestone cathedral statues of the north. Also, in Italy the individual sculptors build reputations and develop personalities, which are remembered through the centuries more than any of the northern sculptors.

Nicola d'Apulia, usually called Nicola Pisano, came to Pisa from the south of Italy, where, it will be remembered, a singularly classic school of sculpture flourished under the Emperor Frederick II and at his court in Capua in the early thirteenth century. If, as seems probable, Nicola was trained in this milieu, it explains the Roman quality in the reliefs of the Nativity (fig. 157) from the pulpit in the Baptistry at Pisa, where his known career centered in the late thirteenth century. Although classed as Gothic, in reality little trace of the Gothic style is discernible in his work, except in some architectural details of the pulpit. The Madonna, half reclining on a couch, Roman fashion, is envisaged as a Roman matron, swathed in large folds of drapery and wearing a tiara. Her features, moreover, are demonstrably classic. The heavy proportions, especially of the heads, of the other figures in this relief, the undercut curly beards of the men, and a plastic approach further betray a similarity to certain phases of Roman sculpture, as does also the plain background. Far from having a Gothic spirituality about them, Nicola d'Apulia's figures are stolid, massive, and mundane. While they have a degree of stark monumentality, they do not equal in technique the best contemporary French sculpture.

In much of his later work, Nicola collaborated with his son, Giovanni Pisano. The younger man, who lacked the south Italian background of his father, had absorbed more of the Gothic feeling, which flooded down from the north like a wave, and, for the moment, extinguished the classic character of Nicola's sculpture. The Nativity (fig. 158) on the pulpit at Siena exhibits a remarkable increase of later Gothic qualities. The composition of this panel is more pictorial than in the Pisan pulpit. Lighter unclassic proportions, a smaller scale, greater movement, and an increased naturalism characterize all these figures, perhaps most obviously the Madonna herself, who has now become a winsome young woman, with none of the massive dignity of Nicola's independent conception. These differences imply the influence of the younger man. In the Visitation group, just to the left of the Madonna, the face of St. Elizabeth is old and haggard, and indeed the whole composition has become looser and more pictorial, like the later stages of Gothic development in the north. These Gothic qualities were yet more pronounced when Giovanni Pisano worked independently of his father, as in the pulpit of Sant' Andrea at Pistoia.

Early in the fourteenth century, Andrea Pisano, who, in spite of his name, was unrelated to the two previous sculptors, modeled the first set of bronze doors for the Baptistry of Florence (fig. 159), the south doors. Twenty-eight square panels enclose quatrefoils to decorate the doors, the small size of the panels according with the architectural scale of the building. It need hardly be said that the shape of these quatrefoils is Gothic, like the similar motives on the Cathedral of Amiens (fig. 144). The upper twenty panels deal with incidents from the life of St. John the Baptist, to whom the building is dedicated. The Feast of Herod (fig. 160) shows that Andrea Pisano was influenced by the paintings of Giotto, in whose circle he belongs. The story is told with directness and simplicity. A Giottesque economy of figures and of setting helps to achieve the architectural quality of these doors. Just enough indication of background, either through landscape elements or by very plain architecture, is included to explain the story, but is not developed in depth to an extent destructive of sculptural values.

Just as she did in architecture, France early in the thirteenth century had assumed the lead in manuscript illumination. At the same time, important changes modify the output of the illuminators, who begin to become professional and known at least by name. The books are written in finer script and in a smaller format than before, perhaps for the benefit of itinerant friars. Architectural enframements of the miniatures, and architectural settings when they appear at all, follow such current details of Gothic buildings as pointed arches, tracery, and pinnacles. A much closer approximation to normal human proportions replaces the Byzantine and Romanesque conventions. As the century progresses, and still more in the early fourteenth century, repetitive or diapered patterns in gold, bright reds, and blues serve as a background for the figures. A page from the *Metz Pontifical* (fig. 161) illustrates this and other characteristics of later Gothic illumination. The figures tend to

sway in pose as did the Vierge Dorée. Moreover, initial letters begin
to sprout pendants, which border and enframe the script. Conventional
or naturalistic foliage grows from these borders at irregular intervals,
while the exuberant fancy of the artists finds an outlet in imaginative
figures and animals, in this case a mermaid and a rabbit playing a harp.
These borders become more elaborate still in the fifteenth century, and
combine with greater naturalism of the miniatures, as painting in northern Europe becomes more independent of books, whereas in Persia, at
this time and for the next few centuries, the miniature continues to be a
major art.

During the early fourteenth century, painting in Italy, as distinct from
manuscript illumination and from mosaics, began to gain importance.
While some painting was produced throughout the earlier Middle Ages
in Italy, the stream trickled very thin, and the artists almost without exception remained anonymous. When the new expansion in painting began,
the artists turned for guidance to the Byzantine mosaics of Sicily. The
Death of the Virgin (fig. 162), in the church of La Martorana in Palermo,
is as Byzantine in style as the mosaics of St. Mark's in Venice. The formal design has an architectural balance. The horizontal movement created by the Madonna on her bier is stopped at either end by groups of
apostles. Christ stands in the center behind the couch with the doll-like
soul of the Madonna in His arms, while from the sky symmetrical figures
of angels sweep down to receive it. The artist substitutes a gold background for any indication of space; he has no interest in, and no knowledge of, perspective; and, since his figures are religious characters, not
ordinary human beings, he is content to indicate them in a conventionally
unreal manner. Figures and drapery alike are defined by flowing lines,
the hands reduced to the simplest of linear patterns, the Madonna's head
to a circle, while the narrow eyes and long aristocratic noses, presented
schematically, have an other-worldly tinge about them. With their sumptuous color and hieratic point of view, these mosaics complete their purpose: they indicate the story with perfect clarity through the diagrammatic rendering, and as decoration they are unsurpassed.

The mosaics of La Martorana are Byzantine, even to the inscriptions
in Greek letters. Soon the Italians begin to adopt this style, and to apply
its lessons to painting. Generally these native works are inferior to the
Byzantine productions in technique and in conception. Moreover, the
dignity of Byzantine art, with its unreality, is undermined by the influence of St. Francis of Assisi. His emphasis on the humanity of Christ,

and his love of nature, call forth a premature attempt to picture this new emotionalism; premature in that the painters' means are not as yet adequate to such an expression, and the results lose the noble Byzantine formality without compensating success in the new venture.

From these mosaics and the styles they inspire spring the two principal schools of Italian fourteenth-century painting. The more conservative is the school of Siena. While it retains much of the Byzantine, it modifies the eastern austerity by a less hieratic attitude, more human figures, and a taste for sprightly narrative. Duccio di Buoninsegna, the real founder of the school, seems to have worked largely, if not entirely, in tempera, one of the two common processes of Italian painting for the next two centuries, and the one preferred by the Sienese, although of course they adopt fresco for mural decorations.

The usual Italian altarpiece is painted on a poplar panel, covered with plaster worked to a smooth hard surface. On this, after making his design, the artist lays sheets of gold leaf wherever that material must appear in the finished picture. Then he sketches the figures with terra verde, a greenish pigment that adds body to the final colors. An apprentice prepared the necessary pigments in a series of small pots or jars, three for each color, and mixed them with egg to bind them to the panel. Since the strongest color in each group is lightened by admixture with white, it follows that any change of tone intended to suggest roundness in the figure or in the folds of drapery will change from red, for instance, in the shadow to white in the lights. To the eye, the most intense red appears in the lights, though not in the high lights, and from there the color becomes less intense as well as lower in value as shadow increases. Thus, the early Italian method reverses this optical effect, but, so long as it is followed consistently, the results in painting are satisfactory. The lower value limits in this medium are restricted, so that tempera tends to produce panels of bright clear color, light in value, and pleasantly decorative, but usually on a small scale.

However, the Rucellai Madonna, in Santa Maria Novella in Florence, proves that tempera can convey considerable scale. This seven-foot panel was ascribed by Vasari to Cimabue, the supposed founder of Florentine painting, but today all critics agree the painting is Sienese, while many believe it a work of Duccio, dated about 1285. This more than life-size Madonna sits on an elaborate paneled throne, her feet on a footstool. The mass of her dark-blue robe strikes the main accent, visible from a distance against the gold background, while to each side in adoration kneel three angels, whose forms extend the central mass laterally. This clear design tells as a two dimensional pattern; in spite of folds of drapery, neither the Madonna nor her throne has great depth; and the flanking angels in the same vertical plane kneel above one another's heads with no visible support needed or indicated.

The one surely dated painting by Duccio is the Majestas, or Madonna in Majesty, made between 1308 and 1311 for the high altar of the Cathedral of Siena. The principal panel depicts the Madonna as the Queen of Heaven surrounded by her court of saints and angels (fig. 163). Mary is a regal figure, but, compared with the Byzantine concepts, less cold and distant, more human, more appealing, a person to whom with due reverence mankind may come to lay its troubles at her feet and receive an understanding human sympathy. The design is clear, as it has to be in order to carry from a distance in the confusing cross lights of the building. The Madonna forms a large vertical mass of strong blue; she is bigger in scale than the figures beside her, partly for emphasis, and partly for design. To the right and left range the saints, each head ringed by its halo, to create several horizontal bands supporting the central vertical. One can perceive the order of the painting from a distance, long before one can distinguish the individual details.

Closer inspection shows much of the Byzantine tradition to be still preserved. Little attempt is made to render natural figures; on the contrary, they are predominantly linear, silhouette playing a major role both in the whole and in the parts. Some shading does occur, to be sure, but it is minor in effect. Traditional conventions define the figure: a circle outlines the head, a linear pattern indicates the hands with their long slender figures, and a beautiful undulating line the hem of the drapery. Aristocratic features marked by a slender nose, narrow slanting eyes, and a small mouth, coupled with the delicate hands give to these sacred characters the distinction the Sienese felt they must have had. The rich quality is further enhanced by the color, sumptuous blues of pounded lapis lazuli, reds, and bronze greens, not to mention the solid gold background and the profusion of gold details.

The back of the Majestas is lined with small panels, which depict incidents from the life of Christ. The Italian instinct for telling a story comes out here. In the Corruption of Judas (fig. 164), Duccio masses his crowd of characters, whose rolling eyes betray their consciousness of wrongdoing as they whisper to one another. But the group also forms a rectangle similar in proportions to the panel and to the rectilinear shape of the simple architectural setting. The loggia set against a gold sky describes the general location of the incident rather than attempting to create much feeling of depth in the design. In reality, these figures, painted more as silhouettes than as solid human beings, need no great depth. Their meaning is clear without it, and a realistic illusion would neither improve the composition nor enhance the narrative force of the painting.

One of Duccio's outstanding merits is his ability in composition. In the panel of the Three Maries at the Sepulchre (fig. 165), a single figure, the angel, balances a group, the three women. This is emphasized in color by the brilliant cinnabar-red mantle of Mary Magdalen, which stands out opposite the white-robed angel. The latter appears to have a red underpainting, not the usual green, which shines through the white to give it a supernatural luminosity, suggesting the Biblical description, 'His appearance was as lightning, and his raiment white as snow.' Again both setting and figures are stylized, the rocks reduced to a pattern on a gold ground, the figures linear with an evident joy in the calligraphic patterns of drapery. That the angel could not for a moment maintain his seat on the tomb is obvious and unimportant. If such an idea had been suggested to Duccio, he would have been astonished that such a need should occur to anyone. He is not dealing with ordinary human beings but with religious types; therefore, to represent them as men and women, even had he been able to do so, would have seemed sacrilegious. If we are to appreciate these panels at their full worth, we must expunge from our minds any notion that an artist must serve the demands of optical realism.

Duccio established the traditions and general manner of early Sienese painting. Though often grouped with the Italian primitives, his paintings belong there only in their historical position in Italian painting. True, the Majestas is not realistic; it is not hampered by scientific perspective, nor does it suggest space; but those are neither the aims of the artist, nor implied in the true meaning of primitive. In actuality, his art stems from the age-long traditions of Byzantine painting. Duccio marks not the beginning of a new line of development but the culmination of an old. His is a highly sophisticated art, produced by a consummate craftsman, who knows what effect he wants to achieve and how to achieve it.

The scanty records give no indication of travel by Duccio. On the other hand, his pupil Simone Martini (c.1283–1344) was anything but a stay at home. His journeys from Siena to Naples in southern Italy and to Avignon in the south of France gave him an opportunity to scatter the ideas and methods of Sienese painting far and wide. Especially important was his sojourn, late in his life, at the papal court in Avignon, since he must have come into contact there with artists from all over western Europe. In most respects, Simone seems not quite the artistic equal of Duccio; for example, his much damaged Majestas, a fresco in the Palazzo Pubblico in Siena, complicates the arrangement of Duccio's Majestas, and thus loses its clarity; but as a draftsman he is supreme. The Sant' Ansano Annunciation (fig. 166), named for that patron saint of Siena, in the left panel carries mastery of line to the point of virtuosity. In his use of line Simone suggests the suavity of the angel whose suspended motion is conveyed by the flowing cape, while the angular lines of the Madonna bespeak her agitation. Nowhere is there a better example of line serving all three sides of the artistic triangle, decoration, representation, and expression. Moreover, the splendid color accentuates the decorative side through the solid-gold background, the customary blues and reds of the Madonna's robes, and the parti-colored wings of the angel. The same decorative quality was no doubt paramount in the original frame (now replaced), which was so integral a part of the picture that it was as much a responsibility of the artist as the painting itself. The same linear expressiveness dominates his portrait in fresco of Guidoriccio da Fogliano (fig. 167).

Through the rest of the fourteenth century and well on into the fifteenth century, this charming style lingered on in conservative Siena, where the new spirit of the Renaissance was accepted reluctantly. Meanwhile, the second important school of Italian fourteenth-century painting arose in Florence. Here were laid the foundations on which European painting of the next five centuries was to build. Especially in Florence, the new energy, the desire for progress, the love of reality rather than of the dreamy mysticism of Siena, fertilized a soil in which new developments flourished. In Giovanni Cimabue of the late thirteenth century, however, the old forms persist at least in externals. His Madonna Enthroned (fig. 168) displays the Byzantinesque types and conventions, the long slender fingers, circular heads, and pointed eyes, but with an undercurrent of fresh vitality. This new energy ill accords with the old forms, and can be felt as a contrast to them, which makes inevitable the development of a concept of painting more adequate to convey this zest for reality.

This original and basically realistic goal is outstanding in the painting of Giotto di Bondone (1266–1336), much of whose work is in the medium of fresco. The small windows of Italian Gothic architecture left large wall areas, which invited the color-loving Italians to mural painting. This could hardly have developed in the north, where, indeed, stained glass provides both color and pictorial expression. Fresco, the second of the media of Italian painting, is in essence the application of pigment to wet plaster. After the design is made, it must be transferred to the dry plaster of the wall. Over that, the artist spreads enough fresh plaster to constitute a single day's work. This obliterates part of the drawing, which must then be reproduced. The pigments, mixed with water, when applied to the wall, sink into the fresh plaster to become an integral part of it. Therefore, no changes or corrections are possible without the arduous process of scraping off the plaster and starting afresh. Although the artist may paint on the wall after it is dry, such additions often flake away. Certain limitations are inherent in this medium. The chemical reactions of the lime in the drying plaster limit the artist to earth pigments, which have not the same brilliance of color possible in the medium of tempera, and are more restricted in both color and value than are oils. Furthermore, the difficulty of change demands a rapid direct procedure. From its very limitations, however, stems much of the mural character of fresco. Its directness forces broad monumental conceptions, an emphasis on the larger elements, and at least a partial suppression of detail. Also, the restrained palette accords with the function of such painting as architectural decoration.

Giotto probably painted three great cycles of frescoes, the first in the church of San Francesco at Assisi, the second in the Arena Chapel at Padua, and the last in several small chapels in Santa Croce in Florence. His mature style is best studied at Padua. This building, lighted from the end wall and from small windows along one side, is lined with Giotto's designs. Three tiers of paintings, separated by decorative patterns, and with a monochromatic design at the bottom in imitation of marble, punctuated by figures of the Virtues and Vices, divide the height. The subjects of the pictures are the lives of Christ and of the Virgin. Incomparably the most important innovation of Giotto is his expression of mass. In the Return of Joachim to the Shepherds (fig. 169), the figures have ceased to be the two dimensional characters of Sienese and Byzantine art. Instead, they appear to have weight, volume, and consequently depth. Through shading, slight though it is, Giotto portrays the roundness of a shoulder, or the mass of a head, and insists on this expression of weight as the most important single factor in his painting. It is an enhanced emphasis on mass as a fundamental reality, which appeals through our eyes to our sense of touch. This step taken by Giotto is the first in Western painting toward an accurate rendering of the phenomena of vision, and yet he is not a complete realist, still less a naturalist. He simplifies his figures to eliminate whatever might hinder his emphasis on weight, and to reduce figure and design alike to fundamentals. As a great innovator, Giotto could hardly develop all the implications of his great discovery. He had to feel his way slowly toward the ideal he had in mind, and in this respect, he is properly called a primitive.

In so far as the expression of mass is concerned, Giotto reaches his goal, but such three-dimensional figures call for a convincing indication of space. While the flat figures of Duccio and Simone rest comfortably on flat thrones, the solid Giottesque characters must exist in front of or behind others. Consequently, Giotto creates a limited space, a shallow box or stage on which his characters can act. Their movement from side to side, rather than from front to back, parallels the plane of the wall and expresses its surface. However, Giotto never invites the spectator to enter his designs. His setting, whether architectural or landscape, is of the simplest, a statement of the locale, not an attempt at a realistic background. The sky, a uniform plane of strong blue, which accords with the simple colors of figures and architecture, serves as a foil for the other parts. A few leaves, twigs, and a stem, or some highly formalized rocks, are enough to show that the scene takes place out of doors. The spectator must supply the rest. Such economy of setting recalls the extremely limited properties and scenery in the original productions of Elizabethan drama. That is all that Giotto feels is needed — and he is right. His primary concern is with the figures and their reactions; to this, everything else is secondary.

Giotto's warm human sympathy enables him to grasp the essentials of character. The Synagogue had rejected Joachim's offering on the ground that, since he and his wife Anna had no children, he was not favored by the Lord and his offering would be unwelcome. Joachim must have been depressed, and, to recover from the shock, he wandered off to his shepherds in the fields. Giotto imagines him strolling along, lost in contemplation, perhaps in self-examination. Joachim's sorrow is revealed not only in himself but in the conduct of his shepherds and his dog. The shepherds know that something is amiss, yet hesitate to break his revery, and merely look at one another in doubt. The dog, with that strange sympathy of animals, pushes up its muzzle toward its master's hand, and yet its tail has not the cheery welcome that might be expected.

The Bewailing of Christ (fig. 170) is often cited to illustrate Giotto's ability to render emotion. But the violence of that painting is not characteristic of Giotto. He feels emotion intensely, but expresses it, as in the Joachim, with restraint. The specific subject in the Bewailing, a lamentation over the body of Christ, permits a display of more extreme emotion than is customary with Giotto, but even here his painting is restrained in comparison with the face-clawing women of his successors.

Giotto's late work in Santa Croce in Florence has been restored, but nevertheless the cycle of six frescoes of the life of St. Francis in the Bardi Chapel shows how far ahead of his contemporaries and immediate followers Giotto is. Although the sense of form is less effective in the Death of St. Francis (fig. 171) than at Padua, doubtless that is due to restoration. The possibilities of line are not abandoned but, even in the silhouette, line is simplified and subordinated to other things. Giotto forces his design to focus on the head of the dying saint. Each of his kneeling figures begins a spiral movement, which coils around the halo of St. Francis and so leads our eye to that point. As at Padua, the action takes place within a shallow box, with any indication of distance limited by the wall in the background.

After Giotto's death even the Florentine school could not maintain his innovations. Its later members in the fourteenth century reverted toward the traditional Sienese style, as the influence of Giotto waned and his feeling for mass faded. Some of his successors realized their inability. Taddeo Gaddi, in the next generation, said that Florentine painting had been declining steadily since the death of Giotto and was still doing so in his day. Though a few artists, like Orcagna, partly stemmed the tide, none were found to wear Giotto's mantle until the appearance of Masaccio, early in the fifteenth century.

Toward the end of the fourteenth, and lasting on into the following century, the Florentine and in general all other schools of painting in Europe had so many qualities in common that the result has been called the International style. This linear style, formulated partly by Siena because of Simone's trip to Avignon, and partly by the calligraphic line of Gothic manuscripts, is enriched with charming if sometimes unreal color. The exuberance of the late Middle Ages and its extravagant chivalry reflected in the romances call forth a fanciful, fastidious, and fairy-like painting, without a trace of seriousness in it. St. George Killing the Dragon (fig. 172), by Bernat Martorel, is Spanish, but its style could be matched in Italian, French, Flemish, or German art. There is an episodic naturalism of details, but no sober concern with reality. The dragon's ferocity we perceive less in the monster himself, in spite of his rows of horrid glistening teeth, than in the spare ribs, skulls, and tibiae of his previous victims strewn around so liberally. These recognizable objects merely provide circumstantial corroborative detail for an otherwise bald and unconvincing narrative. Really the painting tells a fairy story. The kneeling princess wears an ornate crown, St. George's white charger is precisely the steed for a hero of romance, and his armor reflects the light from each polished surface. A Gothic city in the background is equally rich and incredible. In such circumstances, the story can have but one end — St. George must kill the dragon. Indeed, one suspects that if, by accident, St. George should miss his stroke, so polite a dragon would give him a second chance. Such paintings as this cannot be taken seriously, but who can resist their ingenuous charm?

The International style obtains in some of the illuminated manuscripts that provided employment for painters of the time in northern Europe. For example, a Book of the Hours, known as the Chantilly Hours, a pictorial religious calendar painted by Pol de Limbourg and his brothers for the Duc de Berry, depicts the Temptation and Expulsion of Adam and Eve from the Garden of Eden with fairy-tale unreality. However, of the illustrations for each month, that for February (fig. 173), more serious than some others, displays a genuine interest in nature and a desire to copy her, though even here the artist thinks more of the details of nature than of her larger aspects. Therefore, he removes the side of the house in this snowy landscape to let us peep at a woman warming her toes before an open fire. He records with pleasure how a flock of birds in the foreground feeds on grain dropped while foddering the animals. Snow clings to the twigs of a thicket hard by, where a man gathers faggots.

It is from such manuscripts that northern, and especially Flemish, painting grows. Whereas in Italy, mosaics provide a principal origin, and hence a tendency to paint on a monumental scale, the source of Flemish painting in manuscript illumination bequeaths to the artists a small detailed manner. Probably these accurate details also reflect an extensive merchant patronage in the Flemish cities. The good burghers asked for paintings they could examine closely, as they might inspect a piece of cloth to detect flaws in the weave. Their panels must coincide with a Flemish environment, and thus record light and shade cast from definite light sources, often within the picture itself. The types must prove their reality by the presence of wrinkles and other physical defects, or by a selection of ill-favored individuals. Ordinary bric-a-brac furnishes the rooms, or, if the scene is out of doors, towns, rivers, trees, and flowers in microscopic detail lend interest to the landscape. The breadth of fresco could have no charm for Flemish artists or their patrons, nor did the medium of tempera offer the right mode of expression. Therefore, the Flemish evolved an oil technique, which makes it possible to produce panels of enamel-like smoothness. These panels are usually of oak; the pigment, mixed with oil, is applied in layers, with something of the same technique that one finds in Italy of building up the design through under-painting. However, a wider range of color and value is available in the oil medium. Though brilliant in color, a painting in tempera is opaque and does not glisten, since the light and color are reflected to one's eye as from the surface. In the Flemish method, the light seems to penetrate into the paint before it is reflected, which gives great luminosity and polish to panels in this technique.

Though not its inventors, the Van Eyck brothers in the early fifteenth century did much to popularize and spread the oil medium. As the founders of the Flemish school, their work on the Ghent altarpiece is basic. This polyptych, or painting of many panels, was begun by Hubert, the older brother, and completed after his death by Jan. The problem of what parts were done by one brother and what by the other remains unsettled. The principal subject, the apocalyptic Adoration of the Lamb, fills the central panel in the lower half and also the four lower panels on the wings, hinged so as to close over the center. Christ, wearing the triple crown of heaven, is enthroned in the middle of the upper tier. His heavy black beard violates our usual conception of the Saviour, based on Italian paintings. But reflection shows this version to be just as legitimate as the Italian and equally expressive of the power, justice, and mercy of the Son of God. The red-haired Flemish Virgin, in the panel next on the left, is also difficult to accept and for the same reason. She is balanced by the panel of St. John the Baptist, while beyond them are groups of musical angels and finally panels with coarsely realistic representations of Adam and Eve. Portraits of the donors and other sub-jects in monochrome adorn the outside of the wings. To select a single example, the group of the Singing Angels (fig. 174) shows the Flemish realism. These figures are modeled in light and shade, their gowns deeply folded. Light plays over the music stand also to bring prominence to every Gothic detail of its carving. Even in the individuals, the Van Eycks exploit their observations of nature: those angels who sing notes high in the register of their voices contract their brows, a reflex everybody has experienced.

But this realism becomes even more apparent in the Madonna of the Canon van der Paele (fig. 175) by Jan van Eyck (c.1385–1440). The donor kneels to the left, a great hulking man, whose face is scored with wrinkles. Nothing like the Italian sense of physical beauty idealizes this figure, whose strength depends on veracity. The patterned carpet, the brocades of the bishop on the left, the armor of St. George on the right are all presented by the artist to the observer at close range. One needs a magnifying glass to discover all of the detail painted with meticulous care. Moreover, though scientific perspective is not yet known, the artist approximates its effects with sufficient closeness not to contradict the realism of detail. Finally, many tones adopted by the artist fall into the lower value range; as a whole, the painting appears darker than Italian work in tempera.

As court painters, the Van Eycks had few direct pupils, and therefore less personal influence on the Flemish school than had Rogier van der Weyden. Himself at times inspired by the Van Eycks, Van der Weyden does much to spread the Flemish style. In his Deposition (fig. 176), he selects an emotional theme, and handles it with a poignancy that the Van Eycks rarely, if ever, attempt. The weeping and swooning women convey the tragedy and its bitterness. These figures are placed within a box-like setting, reminiscent of the remarkably elaborate Flemish and German late-Gothic wood carvings, which are also suggested by the solidity of the figures.

The scale of most of these Flemish paintings is small. To this generality, the Portinari Altarpiece (fig. 177) by Hugo van der Goes (c.1435–82) forms a notable exception. The central panel, the Adoration of the Shepherds, ranges the figures in a circle around the kneeling Madonna and Child with a consequent indication of depth in the design. The usual Flemish realism is everywhere in evidence; the shepherds crowding in to the right come straight from the fields; their long jaws, unshaven chins, and tousled hair testify to the artist's objectivity by an exaggerated emphasis on homeliness. Or again, in the sheaf of wheat and the jar of flowers we see closely observed passages of still life. This painting has an exceptional position in history. Tommaso Portinari, an Italian businessman who commissioned it, sent his painting back to his native Florence, where it was displayed to an admiring public. The scale of the work forced it on everyone's attention; the realism coincided with Italian taste in the late fifteenth century and surpassed anything the Italians had yet been able to accomplish. Soon after, several Italian paintings plagiarized the unshaven shepherds and the jar of flowers. Not every painting from Flanders would have aroused such enthusiasm; the exceptional scale and monumentality of the Portinari altarpiece proved that these qualities could coexist with minuteness of detail.

The Flemish school was bound to turn to portraiture, not only as parts of religious compositions, such as the Madonna of the Canon van der Paele, but as wholly or semi-independent paintings. A favorite commission was a diptych, one leaf of which represented the Madonna and Child, or possibly a patron saint, and the other a portrait of the donor in an attitude of adoration. So in Hans Memling's (c.1430–94) portrait of Martin van Nieuwenhoven (fig. 178), the subject on the right, his hands clasped in prayer, looks across at the Madonna. Some realism is necessary in portraiture to facilitate recognition, and there is every reason to believe that Memling has rendered accurately this none-too-clever young man. Still that realism affects only detail, not the whole scene. The man looks stiff and hard. We see every knot on his costume and each detail of the room, like the stained-glass window where the young man's patron, St. Martin, divides his cloak with a beggar, with a clarity impossible even if this scene were reconstructed before us. Paradoxically, the Flemish seem to record everything, but fail to reach the effect of reality. This contradiction results from their reluctance to understate some facts in order to emphasize others; therefore, in the absence of any visual focus, the eye roams over the panel from one detail to another. Also, though the distant landscape is often bluish in color, its minutiae stand out with preternatural sharpness, unscreened and unenveloped in atmosphere.

This school of the Van Eyck's and their followers is contemporary not with the medieval Italian painting of Duccio and Giotto, but with the early Renaissance painting of the fifteenth century. It has many of the characteristics of the Renaissance: for example, the love of nature and the desire to represent it in more scientific detail than the early Middle Ages. Indeed, the turn to nature is more obvious in the fifteenth century in the north than in Italy itself, not only in painting but in late Gothic sculpture and in manuscript illumination. Moreover, the Flemish artists and their patrons admit a decline in religious enthusiasm from the earlier Gothic centuries and a corresponding growth in secular interests. The new concern with portraiture implies a growth of individualism entirely absent from the thirteenth century. Nevertheless, this school remains more Gothic than Renaissance. Not only does it issue from Gothic manuscript tradition, but it is innocent of the enthusiastic classicism that heralds the arrival of the new spirit in Italy, an innovation not to affect the north until the sixteenth century, and then only as a fashionable importation from the south. Though the matter is merely one of classification, one should realize that Flemish painting of the fifteenth century has not the same character as contemporary Italian painting, and that its similarity proves only that some elements are common to the century but not basic in the new spirit known as the Renaissance.

XI

The Early Renaissance in Italy

THE Renaissance, or rebirth, is a movement so widespread and of such complex character that no succinct definition is possible. Various phrases, to be sure, have been used to describe it, and many of them do suggest certain of its features. For instance, the Renaissance is called the Revival of Learning. A new energy is evident in the fifteenth century; it dominates all fields pertaining to the intellect and to the arts and sciences. One might say that the great thirteenth-century wave of energy that had produced Gothic art was spent by the end of that period, and that the fourteenth century covers the time in which a new surge was gathering momentum to break only in the fifteenth century. Or, to change the metaphor, during the fourteenth century, Europe was catching its breath after the Gothic paean and before delivering its Renaissance oration.

But the Renaissance is neither exclusively nor exactly a revival of learning. No one today could regard the Gothic age as one of barbarism, though many men of the fifteenth century did think it such. An age that could produce a Roger Bacon, the vast knowledge of Vincent of Beauvais, or the abstract thought of Thomas Aquinas was neither ignorant nor barbaric. The difference is that the mind, ideals, and energy of the Renaissance were directed elsewhere. Late in the fourteenth century and early in the fifteenth, Italy rediscovered her classic past. The Roman remains were at her door, and had always tended to exert some influence on Italian thought and art. Witness the classicism of the Corinthian columns in Pisa Cathedral, or in the sculpture of Nicola d'Apulia. But the previous contributions from Rome had been accepted by instinct; now there was to be a conscious revival of the past, a deliberate return to Rome as the one acceptable source of civilization. This inspiration first manifested itself in the study of classic literature and in the avidity with which scholars vied with each other to rediscover ancient manuscripts. On the basis of these, they formed their own rhetorically pure

Latin styles, very different from the dog Latin of the Middle Ages. One group, the Ciceronians, carried to such an extreme their desire for purity and correctness in Latin diction that they would accept no word without the stamp of Cicero's approval in his known writings, even if other Latin authors, such as Horace, Virgil, or Quintilian, had employed it. The Roman Academy revived even the supposed manners and customs of Rome — unfortunately those of the Empire rather than the austere and moral customs of the Roman Republic.

The effect of this conscious revival on the arts, especially on architecture and sculpture, was profound. Even in philosophy, an attempt was made by the Neo-Platonists to reconcile classic philosophy to Christianity. With this new spirit abroad, to expect some revival of paganism is logical, but that one field, religion, remained unaffected or nearly so. The tendency of the humanists, as the classic scholars were called from their studies of the humanities, was to avoid the issue, or even, in north Italy, to champion Christianity wherever it came into conflict with paganism. However, the fervor of Christianity was not so intense as in the Gothic period, and the interest in questions of religion was less keen. Nevertheless, the fifteenth century and even the sixteenth, which marked the culmination of the Renaissance, hardly abated a jot in their adherence to the Church.

Humanism was the goal of the Renaissance, but the motive power was individualism. During the Middle Ages, man had looked at life on earth with reference to its bearing on the life eternal. In the Renaissance, man became concerned with the world as it bears on the life temporal. Therefore, the individual man gains importance whereas in the earlier epoch his individuality had been submerged. Now arises a desire for fame, a will to be known to one's fellow-man while alive and to be remembered after death. Aside from various illustrations in the careers of artists, the urge to individualism produced two remarkable manifestations. Portraits appeared, where they had been all but absent in the early Middle Ages, and moreover, often portraits of lifelike accuracy. Hardly a figure of any importance crossed the stage of Florentine life whose features do not look down at us from some sculptured bust or painting. Furthermore, biographies and autobiographies emerged. A few had been written during the Middle Ages, but most of them dealt with the lives of saints. Now Cellini wrote his autobiography, and Vasari compiled his *Lives of the Most Eminent Painters, Sculptors, and Architects.* Nor are these accounts necessarily edifying, however informative they may be. Vasari fills his pages with gossip about his subjects, which throws a flood of light on their personalities, even when his facts are not accurate; while Cellini, with a good conceit of himself, magnifies his own prowess in art, love, and war.

The best phrase to characterize the Renaissance is the Age of Discovery. On the one hand, it was the age of discovery of the classic past — humanism; on the other, of the dignity of man — individualism. This was the time when the world was discovered as it affected man's life on earth, both in the larger and in the smaller sense. The explorers of the fifteenth and sixteenth centuries, Columbus, Magellan, Vasco da Gama, and many others, enlarged the physical horizon. Similarly, men looked at the world with a more scientific attitude, a desire to prove for themselves rather than to accept statements on the basis of authority. To be sure, much that was believed then was incorrect, but such a man as Leonardo da Vinci conducted dissections to discover the structure of the human body. Long before him, the artists had begun to observe the exterior of the body. They studied human anatomy and zoology, botany and geology, as those subjects had never been studied before. True, the Gothic age had turned to nature but more as a manifestation of God than as field for scientific observation. ·

Of course, the return to nature cannot affect architecture, but humanism does. When Filippo Brunelleschi (1377–1446) was defeated in the competition for the bronze doors of the Baptistry in Florence, Vasari says that he went to Rome with Donatello, who was to become the dominant sculptor of the early Renaissance, and that the two young men spent their time drawing and measuring the fragments of classic architecture and sculpture in the Forum and elsewhere, until the Roman populace thought them mad. Characteristic too was Brunelleschi's determination to be first in one art, if not in the other. The stories Vasari tells of him present a vigorous and pugnacious personality with a zest to be famed for his achievements.

The dome of the Cathedral of Florence had not yet been built. Therefore, to prepare himself, Brunelleschi studied Roman construction, especially the dome of the Pantheon, as well as Roman design. When the committee for the cathedral had considered many expedients, some of them ridiculous in their unsuitability, they entrusted to Brunelleschi the task of building the dome, but one may imagine his chagrin to find himself yoked with Ghiberti as co-architect, the very man who fifteen years before had beaten him in the competition for the north doors of the Baptistry in Florence. Brunelleschi could not accept that as final. Vasari tells us how Brunelleschi, though he appeared to accept the situation at first, publicized Ghiberti's architectural incompetence until the latter was discharged and Brunelleschi left in sole charge; his, and his alone, remains the fame of designing and constructing the dome. In reality, the dome of the cathedral contains but little of the Renaissance in its forms (fig. 179). In a sense, its scale suggests a new desire for monumentality. And yet that size, almost the same as the dome of the Pantheon, is established by a plan that dates from the Gothic centuries. In structure, the dome is closer to the Tuscan Romanesque Baptistry of Florence than to the Roman Pantheon. Like the Baptistry, Brunelleschi's dome is pointed in section, not hemispherical; based on an octagonal plan, its ribs project at each angle on the exterior. Further, its minor ribs divide each side of the octagon into thirds. Unlike the architects of the Roman dome and of the Baptistry, Brunelleschi expected his vault to be imposing from the exterior as well as in the interior. The full curve is visible, while in the Pantheon (fig. 82) most of the curve is hidden within the mass of the building. Thus, though the dome has about it little that is specifically classic, except the lantern, built some years later, its spirit and the story of its building do typify the new energy and bespeak the architect's courage and imagination.

Brunelleschi first displayed the forms of the Renaissance in the façade of the Foundlings Hospital in Florence, dated 1419, but that design is less distinguished than his Pazzi Chapel, begun ten years later, beside Santa Croce in Florence. This little gem abandons the Gothic style save possibly in the vault, and even that differs from Gothic vaults. The square central area is covered by a ribbed vault, which looks like two Gothic apses set face to face and carried on pendentives, but at the sides barrel vaults rest on broad arches. These, in turn, spring from a continuous entablature supported by Corinthian pilasters whose slight projection hardly interrupts the wall plane. Except for the gray stone of these architectural members and of the frames of round arched panels between them, the walls are simply plastered. Thus, the effect of the interior is cool and restrained, and the basis of design has been changed from an expression of apparently revealed dynamic structure to a reliance on abstract proportion, scale, and composition.

On the exterior (fig. 180), the pinnacles and tracery, the buttresses and soaring lines of Gothic architecture, never strong in Italy, have been ruthlessly suppressed. In their place, a portico of Corinthian columns carries an entablature. Above them paired pilasters divide the wall into panels. The polychromy of the Gothic style, so pronounced in Tuscany, yields to monochrome. To be sure, Brunelleschi, for all his study and energy, had not yet mastered the Roman style. His design may be compared to the first exercises of a student of a new language; he has learned a few words but his accent and grammar are still inaccurate. His Corinthian capitals are stiff and wooden in their foliage, not plastic as in the best Roman examples. In larger matters the design, however delicate, is flat, as though conceived in line on a sheet of paper, not in the plastic forms of the past. The thin walls, light columns, and surface panels, despite their derivation from antiquity, produce a new style.

The Pazzi Chapel is small; San Lorenzo in Florence, designed for the Medici, is on a much larger scale. This remarkable family dominated Florence through most of the fifteenth century. Cosimo de Medici, called *pater patriae*, devoted his talents and his wealth from 1434 to his death in 1464 to the task of the government of Florence, as did his son Piero to 1469, and his grandson, Lorenzo the Magnificent, until 1492. Although the *de facto* rulers of the city, these generations of the family remained technically private citizens, and the forms of Florentine liberty were preserved. Each of them patronized the artists of his own day.

Brunelleschi's plan for San Lorenzo (fig. 181) turns to the Early Christian Roman basilica; he abandons the vault over the nave, and instead reverts to the simple wooden roof, thin clearstory walls, light nave arcade, and general arrangement of the early church type. However, Brunelleschi's design does not look like a basilica. It lacks the gorgeous color of those buildings, and its uniform colonnade, like that in the Pazzi Chapel, is inexpert in detail when measured by classic standards. That free-hand nonchalance of the basilica is admitted nowhere. Light in construction, delicate in detail, and almost monochromatic, San Lorenzo charms through its simplicity, which doubtless came to Florence as a welcome change from the colored and confused Gothic churches of the region. Thus, Brunelleschi's position in the Renaissance is that of originator and pioneer, who blazes the trails for others to follow.

Michelozzo, on the other hand, was almost a private architect to the Medici family. His plan for the Medici, or Riccardi, Palace in Florence (fig. 182) retains the disposition around a rectangular court typical of Florentine medieval palaces. This court serves as communication between the rooms; it lights them and tends to focus life around itself, as though to suggest that the street was neither attractive nor safe, both quite justified assumptions in those days.

Externally (fig. 183) something of austerity remains. Though the Riccardi Palace now has pedimented windows in the ground floor, those date from a century later than the rest of the building. This composition translates the medieval palace into a Renaissance vocabulary. The design of the second-floor windows, a double arch supported by a colonnette and framed within a larger arch, is inherited from the Gothic, save that the arches have ceased to be pointed. The massive rugged stonework, too, derives from medieval tradition. And yet an emphasis upon the horizontal, created by bands of classic moldings under the windows of the second and third floors, and especially the magnificent bold cornice that terminates the design show the Renaissance character of the work. Sensitive too are the proportions, the sequence in height of the floors from the tallest in the ground story to the lowest in the top story, and the wall treatment, which varies from smooth finished stones in the third floor to rugged rustication in the ground floor.

If Brunelleschi founded the architectural Renaissance and Michelozzo applied it to the palace, Leon Battista Alberti brought the scholarship and archaeology of the century to bear on building problems. Recognized among the humanists of his day, Alberti wrote extensively on architecture, basing his books on those of Vitruvius, the Roman architect, and through them influenced a long line of Renaissance theorists. This scholarship dictates his design of the Rucellai Palace in Florence (fig. 184), 1451–5, which differs from the Riccardi Palace in the application of superposed orders in pilaster form. A full entablature instead of a mere string course separates the stories. Consequently, the cornice at the top of the building must be proportioned to the uppermost order, and thus less effectively terminates the whole building than the dominant cornice of the Riccardi. The window forms too have changed; Alberti introduces a lintel on the colonnette below the arch, which tends to create the effect of a rectangular window. Some details of the Rucellai, such as the door jambs and a few moldings, betray a knowledge of Greek architecture unique in the Italian Renaissance, where Rome forms the almost exclusive source of inspiration. All in all, the Rucellai Palace exhibits its classicism not only in the use of the orders and in the windows, but in a certain articulation of the units of design, each part stated as a unit rather than submerging its individuality in the whole. Nevertheless, even here the sense of flatness and the linear appearance of the composition is Renaissance, not Roman.

In his remodeling of the exterior of San Francesco at Rimini, in 1447, though it was never completed, Alberti advanced farther on the road to Rome. The façade (fig. 185) adopts the compositional scheme of the Roman Arch of Augustus in Rimini, a Roman arch order repeated three times with engaged columns instead of the flatter pilasters. This gives the design a plastic character not hitherto found in Renaissance work, as do the deep arches along the sides of the building. The whole begins to mold itself in light and shade. In Alberti's design of 1470 for Sant' Andrea at Mantua, the motive of the temple front, with pilasters to support the unbroken entablature and pediment, combines with a triumphal arch. Also, in the interior, which was decorated later in the sixteenth century, the Roman barrel vault, with apparently solid supports and wide arches opening into the nave, grasps much of the Roman spatial sense. These marks of Alberti's style are just what one would expect of a scholar who built on the foundations Brunelleschi had laid, but who carried farther an understanding of Roman principles of design. In him, not only is the Roman architectural vocabulary more complete, but the rhetoric is more closely followed.

The seriousness and purity of the Renaissance during the fifteenth century is confined to Florence, its birthplace. What attracted the north of Italy, however, were not the larger elements of Roman design, its orders and arches, its volumes and its mass, but the decorative applied detail that the Romans had used in profusion and the north Italians now created in still greater quantity. The façade of the Certosa near Pavia (fig. 186), from the end of the fifteenth century, is appalling in its richness and confusion. Its designers considered it a legitimate field for exuberant detail, and plastered that detail, often exquisite in itself, over every possible surface. The colonnettes within the ground floor windows undergo all sorts of adventures between the base and the capital with floral designs, grotesque heads, and medallions applied to their surfaces. Decorative bands of delicate arabesques surround the window frames, with colored marble panels, sculptured heads or figures, or anything else that a bubbling fancy could suggest. No Florentine sense of restraint hindered these designers, Amadeo and others, from drowning their design in a sea of detail. If this sort of work did not promote the development of the Renaissance movement in Italy, its historical importance is immeasurable, since it was this style that the French, coming down over the Alps, first saw and admired, and which, therefore, afforded a principal root of the early French experiments in the Renaissance manner.

The abundant Roman ruins account for the influence of antiquity on Florentine architecture. In sculpture, also, a large corpus of Roman art was extant. However, the change in sculpture from Gothic to Renaissance was not quite so sudden as in architecture. For the jambs of the door of San Petronio at Bologna, Jacopo della Quercia (1374–1438) modeled a series of panels of the stories in the Book of Genesis. The Temptation (fig. 187) retains traces of the Gothic style; the lounging pose of the Eve is reminiscent of the curved posture of late Gothic figures. Also the tree, indicated by a stem with a few leaves on it, and the serpent with a woman's head derive from the medieval background. On the other hand, the bold modeling of the figures is Renaissance; so too is their abounding strength and energy. The languid Gothic pose is transformed into the vigorous conception of Adam remonstrating with his wife, as he twists his body and jerks his head around to speak to Eve over his shoulder. Indeed, that torsion of the body's axis, coupled with a reliance on the figure as a vehicle for expression, anticipates Michelangelo, who while still a young man was destined to work on this very portal a century later. The impression of monumentality gained by Quercia in these small panels is extraordinary; it derives from the fine sense of selection and amplification, and from the treatment of the parts as large units of design.

That monumentality and power of expression are even more evident in the allegorical Wisdom from the Fonte Gaia at Siena (fig. 188), damaged though it is. The voluminous masses of drapery fall in rounded folds, deeply modeled and quite distinct from the finicky linearism of fourteenth-century Gothic drapery. Indeed, Quercia's modeling approaches the generalized statement of classic statues. One of the world's great masterpieces of sculpture, the Tomb of Ilaria del Caretto in Lucca Cathedral, whether his or not, has an exquisite idealism of features and costume, while the children with heavy garlands of fruit along the sides is a common classic motive.

The competition for the north doors of the Florence Baptistry, whose loss turned Brunelleschi from sculpture to architecture, was won by Lorenzo Ghiberti (1378–1455). In view of its date, 1401, it is only natural that the competition should have required the shape of the panels, a Gothic quatrefoil, to be identical with those of the earlier south doors (fig. 159). Indeed, in a general view, the identity of their larger design makes it almost impossible to distinguish the two. The curved figures in the panels also retain much of Gothic tradition, including some architectural character, but exhibit a few pictorial elements, a trace of the new naturalism, and here and there a touch of the antique, especially in the borders to the panels and around the jamb of the doors.

The east doors, awarded to Ghiberti in 1425 without competition, show more understanding of the Renaissance point of view. Rectangular panels supplant the quatrefoils, and the molded frames cease to be Gothic. The number of panels is reduced from twenty-eight to ten and their size correspondingly increased (fig. 189). Of course, these changes affect the relation of the doors to the building, and in this respect one must admit that the earlier sets are more architectural and in better scale with the Baptistry. The larger size of the panels and their smaller number make it possible and necessary to introduce more than a single incident in many of them in order to satisfy the demand for narrative. In the story of Abraham (fig. 190), for example, the tent of Abraham is at the side, the patriarch welcomes the angels in the center, and the sacrifice of Abraham takes place at the top. To keep these incidents separate from one another calls for remarkable technical dexterity. Unlike most relief sculpture, in which the background lies in a single vertical plane, that of Ghiberti is varied in surface, sloping back in proportion to the distance at which the incidents are supposed to occur. Moreover, the depth of relief changes from the foreground figures, which are partly in the round, to those in the sacrifice, where the relief is extremely low. Thus an indication of depth results that impinges on the pictorial. Ghiberti resorts to a wealth of landscape details, rocks, bushes, and trees, which further add to a pictorial impression, as does the architecture that occasionally replaces the landscape setting, since the buildings are shown in correct perspective. The criticism that these doors are paintings in bronze has much justification. In almost every respect, these panels are conceived as three-dimensional pictures. And yet, though undesirable in theory, Ghiberti's handling is so subtle, his craftsmanship so exquisite, that no less a sculptor than Michelangelo could describe these doors as worthy to be the Gates of Paradise. Indeed, their success casts suspicion on the tenability of the theory. The subsidiary sculpture in narrow bands beside the panels and in the border on the door jambs illustrates the Renaissance scientific naturalism. The floral border, composed of a garland of the blossoms of Tuscany, quite recognizable and interspersed with squirrels, birds, and other fauna, parallels the enthusiasm for nature felt by such contemporary painters as Pisanello.

But the sculptor whose leadership really corresponded to that of his friend Brunelleschi in architecture is Donatello (c.1386–1466). Hardly a field touched and developed by the later men of the century was not surveyed by him. In him, both the classicism and realism of the Renaissance bear fruit. His bronze David (fig. 191) is the first important free-standing nude in European art since Roman days. It will be remembered that the Middle Ages clothed the body, but under the influence of his classic studies Donatello saw no reason to continue this practice. He could not fail to notice the frequency with which male figures other than portraits, and even some of these, were carved or cast in the nude by the Greeks and Romans. His study of the figure of David is quite deliberate, and to that extent must represent his ideal; nothing in the story of David calls for such a rendering; on the contrary, every indication points the other way. The body is further emphasized by the subordination of the head; that is, the hat, the brim of which projects over the lad's face and shades it, drives our attention from the head to the figure. Donatello conceives a boyish form whose anatomy might have been observed from nature, possibly from the youths of Florence bathing in the Arno. However, in this statue the sculptor holds realism in check. The details of the figure are selected to emphasize the youthful nature of the subject, and simplified for greater clarity of expression. The soft smooth surfaces and the sense of volumes in the figure are well adapted to the bronze medium. The lithe proportions, plastic modeling, and breadth are reminiscent of certain Hellenistic developments.

Donatello can, however, be brutally realistic. The statue on the Campanile of Florence called Lo Zuccone (fig. 192), which means The Pumpkin Head, is photographic as it follows the model. The insistence on the baldness that earned the figure its nickname, the modeling of the skull, the bony hands, and muscular arms are not beautiful in themselves but are powerful and individual. Even the drapery, whose amplitude creates a sense of volume sufficient to contain the figure completely, has caught the new spirit.

These two major strains in Donatello's work, his humanism and his realism, combine in the equestrian portrait of Gattamelata (fig. 193), the first free-standing equestrian monument since Roman days. Donatello conceives his figure in terms of a Roman Imperator, the extant equestrian statue of Marcus Aurelius, and gives him the Roman baton of command and the Roman short-skirted armor. The horse, also, resembles the famous horses of St. Mark's in Venice, whose precise origin is unknown but unquestionably classic. The scientific anatomy of this huge charger matches the realism of the eyebrows and wrinkles in the Romanized head. However, the small scale of the features makes it difficult to appreciate them from the ground. In one respect, Donatello's adherence to truth has betrayed him. The mass of the animal, necessarily large in comparison to the man, is so prominent that it detracts attention from his master, who has not quite the dominance that he should have. But such a criticism is carping when applied to so obvious a masterpiece.

All these monuments are in the round, but Donatello is no less original in relief sculpture. He probably invented and certainly popularized the mode called *rilievo schiacciato*, crushed relief, in which objects melt into one another and barely rise from the background, their outlines grooved into it. A good example, the Assumption of the Virgin in Sant' Angelo a Nilo in Naples, compels the greater or lesser projection of the figures to suggest not pictorial depth but spiritual importance. Though pictorialism is possible in this technique, Donatello's instinct is too plastic to admit a pictorial setting. This plastic quality helps to adapt certain of his compositions to the building in which they are placed. The gentle figures in high relief of the Annunciation in Santa Croce in Florence are framed in an architecture so rich that any larger amount of it would overwhelm the eye; as it is, these decorated moldings make an opulent accent in the church.

Sometimes Donatello's vitality so animates his scenes as to open to question their dignity as ecclesiastical fittings. An exuberant band of romping children streams across the breadth of the Singing Gallery he designed for Florence Cathedral. It is now shown to the public, with its sober companion piece by Luca della Robbia, in the Opera del Duomo in Florence. Which of these one prefers may be a matter of temperament. Donatello feels that the joyous dance of these children, however noisy, will not be unwelcome to God. Luca, on the other hand, illustrates the verses of the One Hundred and Fiftieth Psalm. His figures are not inert but they are less energetic, and their architectural setting plainer than Donatello's.

The shadow of Donatello fell over the other sculptors of the fifteenth century, as though they merely exploited the various attainments of the master. Some of these other men are conservative, or perhaps more justly are described as following the middle of the road; others seem absorbed in scientific realism. The Della Robbia family in their chosen medium of polychromed glazed terra cotta raised what is ordinarily a craft to the realm of sculpture through the fresh creative effort they applied to each product. A typical example by Andrea della Robbia is the Annunciation (fig. 194) on the Foundlings Hospital in Florence. Both the figures and floral border are freely modeled, with a good deal of realism in the latter, and in the former the plastic effect of simplified forms. If the medium has not the inherent monumentality of stone or bronze, it invites a simple color scheme that avoids the full polychromy of nature. The figures themselves are white, relieved against a vivid blue ground, with a few other colors in the border. Later members of the family unwisely sought greater realism of color, and thereby lost the effectiveness of the works by the first two important members of the family, Luca and Andrea. Such products as these, cheap because of their medium, win a legitimate popularity through their prettiness and their exploitation of refined sentiment.

Desiderio da Settignano, probably a pupil of Donatello, borrowed his master's technique, *rilievo schiacciato*, for his Madonna and Child (fig. 195). The figures seem sketched in marble with an exquisite subtlety, reinforced however by real firmness of structure. Realism, to him, might be subordinated to a soft gentle emotion conveyed through elegant forms and selected detail. At its best, such sculpture is capable of great charm; but without an underlying grasp of structure it can degenerate into weakness and routine productions, meretricious in appeal, like much of the popular work of Mino da Fiesole.

A magnificent example of the early Renaissance tomb is that of Leonardo Bruni, the Florentine humanist (fig. 196), by Bernardo Rossellino. The scholar's effigy rests quietly on his bier above his sarcophagus, within a niche terminated in a round arch supporting figures and heraldry above. Inside the arch, the lunette contains a Madonna and Child in low relief. Three red porphyry panels in the back wall of the niche accent the figure by contrast. This conception of a tomb is dignified, enshrined as it is in the wall, and yet prominent through its design and its architectural and sculptural decoration.

Among the more ardent realists, Antonio Pollaiuolo confesses his absorption with anatomy in movement in both the sculptured (fig. 197) and the painted versions of his Hercules and Antaeus. The subject, drawn from classic mythology, recalls the humanism of the century, but Pollaiuolo seems to make this particular selection because it affords an opportunity to represent powerful figures, their muscles strained to the utmost. The agony and last desperate effort of Antaeus to free himself from the python arms of Hercules involve every tense muscle and sinew. Hercules' legs betray the fact that they support the weight of both bodies, which reveals a close observation by the artist of the appearance of nature. For such realism, bronze is the obvious material, well fitted to convey his love of energy and violent movement.

Also at the end of the fifteenth century was modeled the second great equestrian monument of the early Renaissance, the Colleoni (fig. 198), by Andrea del Verrocchio (1435–88), whose very name, 'true eye,' suggests his observational powers. Of course, Verrocchio was familiar with the Gattamelata, but he rejected its classic features and developed and stressed its more realistic traits. The Colleoni wears the armor of the fifteenth century, explicit in every detail, with saddle and harness elaborated like goldsmith's work. The horse, with one foot lifted clear of the pedestal, is altogether a more detailed literal study than even the horse of Donatello. In the rider, the craving for individualism in portraiture gains salience. This deeply scored face gives every evidence of likeness to the features of the famous captain whom it represents. Its bold detail is larger in scale, and therefore easier to perceive from the ground than in the case of Gattamelata. Except in so far as realism is itself characteristic of Roman portraits, nothing of the classic remains. As often happens, the fifteenth century drew from the past only what was already part of itself; in other words, the spirit of the age demanded realism, but rationalized that urge as a revival of Roman civilization. The justifiable fame of the work does not rest wholly on its realism. We perceive the individual, but were that all, our interest in the statue would be aroused in proportion to our knowledge of Bartolommeo Colleoni, and therefore but slightly for most English-speaking peoples. Instead, Verrocchio creates a human type, the man of action, transcending time and space. The commanding pose and dominating glance express leadership, and are recognizable as such in our own day and in countries far removed from Italy. It is this grasp of something basic in humanity that gives the Colleoni its position in the history of art.

Sculpture and architecture feel the influence of antiquity more strongly than painting owing to the preservation of more copious examples of classic work in those two fields. Almost nothing of ancient painting was known to the Renaissance, so that the influence of humanism must be traced in other ways. The painters borrow their architectural backgrounds, if any are needed, from the classic past, or from the styles of contemporary architects themselves so affected by antiquity. The orders, the round arch, and other marks of Rome replace the pointed Gothic arches and frames that enrich the settings in paintings of Simone Martini, for example. Certain classic buildings seem to have been especially popular; the Arch of Constantine in Rome (fig. 84) recurs constantly with variations, as does the Colosseum (fig. 83). Fragments of architectural carving, such as arabesques and molded cornices, add their decorative value to the paintings. Some of the figures may be clad as Roman legionaries or centurions. Noted examples of classic sculpture inspire the artist; the Venus de Medici forms the basis for Botticelli's Birth of Venus (fig. 210). Also as in sculpture, an interest in the nude reveals the new spirit. Finally, the painters draw freely on the past for subjects. The themes of classic mythology, the labors of Hercules, for instance, or descriptions in classic poets may afford inspiration. However, these themes are metamorphosed when seen through the eyes of the fifteenth century. A Botticelli may turn to Horace or Lucretius for his subject, but what he paints has little in common with them.

The new interest in man prompts the development of portraiture. Through most of the century, the painters select the point of view that most clearly presents the individuality of their sitters, namely, the profile. In his beautiful portrait of Giovanna degli Albizzi (fig. 199), late in the fifteenth century, Ghirlandaio almost restricts himself to the silhouette, all that is needed to convey the likeness and to encompass decorative value. In the first part of the century, the subjects had usually been placed against a distant landscape background, but toward the end they were moved indoors. Ghirlandaio places his lady in front of a wall hung with strings of pearls and with a slip of paper pasted on it. The decorative quality of the painting is enhanced not only by the linear pattern, but even more by the extravagance of the fashionable costume, each detail of which the painter records with precision.

During the last quarter of the century, the profile in portraiture yielded popularity to the three-quarter-front view, wherein the subject looks out at an angle of forty-five degrees to the picture plane. In the so-called Condottiere (fig. 200), Antonello da Messina displays this new attitude, possibly imported from Flanders together with the oil technique that Antonello helped to introduce to Italy. This young man is rendered with Flemish realism, illustrated in his scarred lip and in the care devoted to each strand of hair. Sometimes a window in one corner of such a portrait produces a composition similar to that of the Memling portrait (fig. 178). The bit of landscape visible through this aperture hardly distracts the spectator's interest, as might the full landscape backgrounds in earlier portraits, to the detriment of concentration on the sitter. However, the realism and focused attention in the later examples involve some loss of decorative quality. Portraits also appear in religious paintings, sometimes as spectators, sometimes even as models for the principal figures.

But in spite of the corpus of examples illustrating individualism or humanism in their themes, the vast majority of fifteenth-century paintings remain religious in subject. Almost all commissions are given either by or for the church, to decorate its buildings or as public or private altarpieces. The devotion expressed in them weakens somewhat as the century progresses. At its outset, Fra Angelico revealed as serene a faith as any painter of the preceding epoch, but later the religious spirit was usually modified by other interests.

The techniques of fresco and tempera continue from the Gothic age unabated in popularity and, at least in the early fifteenth century, unmodified

in any important respect. However, some panels from the second half of
the century adopt the Flemish oil technique, either entirely or mingled
with tempera. This northern influence finds its way into the peninsula by
devious routes. For example, the economic connection between Venice
and Germany brought in its train a knowledge of German art, which employed an oil medium inspired by Flanders. Though this in itself bore
little fruit, it may have prepared the way for the rapid Venetian acceptance
of the technique when Antonello da Messina arrived in the city about 1475.
Whether this Sicilian artist visited Flanders or not, his method is northern
and its possibilities of realistic detail were welcomed by the Italians. In
Umbria at about the same time, Justus van Ghent, a native Flemish artist,
was active at the intellectual and artistic center of the court of Urbino.
And finally, some Flemish paintings found their way into Italy; the most
notable example, the Portinari Altarpiece (fig. 177) by Hugo van der Goes,
aroused tremendous excitement on its public exhibition in Florence about
1476. Its influence can be traced in several important Florentine paintings
shortly thereafter. However, this northern technique is only a minor variation, late in the century, on the established media of Italian painting.

The number and diversity of distinguished painters make the fifteenth-
century history of painting particularly difficult to organize. The simplest
plan is to group the artists in two categories: the experimentalists, and
those who are comparatively conservative, though no labels are satisfactory because the grouping itself is nebulous and artificial. By the former
term, we refer to those artists whose major interest lies in a scientific concern with the various technical problems of painting. It includes those who
experiment in their paintings with perspective, with anatomy of men and
animals, with the possibilities of rendering mass in their figures, and so
on. To these artists, the subject matter of their paintings is an opportunity
to expound any specific problem that interests them. On the other hand,
to those painters whom we reluctantly call conservatives, to express the
character of the subject is of greater moment than to develop the technical
sides of their craft. Some of these men are conservatives in the full meaning of the term, but many of them are alive to any contributions made by
their contemporaries; they seize upon each step toward realism taken by
the experimentalists and use it for their own ends. It is important also to
bear in mind that a painter in one of these categories may have some characteristics that belong in the other.

The painter who played the same role in his art as Donatello did in
sculpture and Brunelleschi in architecture, and who was an intimate friend
of both, was Masaccio (1401–28). His frescoes in the Brancacci Chapel in

Florence re-established the ideal of mass or solidity as a primary goal of painting, returning in that respect to the road laid out by Giotto. In the Expulsion from the Garden (fig. 201), he modeled two human beings to express their weight. Masaccio did not always attain his goal; his Eve is not convincingly solid, but the substantial figure of Adam looks not like an inflated skin, but a man of flesh and bone. To be sure, although the form is simplified, Masaccio observed the external masses of the body in more detail than his contemporaries. Also, he endowed his characters with human emotions: he underscored the tragedy of the Fall of Man by a wailing Eve and an Adam whose hands are pressed over his eyes in shame and despair.

Masaccio's monumentality is nowhere better revealed than in the Tribute Money (fig. 202). The apostles in a compact group around Christ are conceived as patriarchal figures, not at all pretty but with an epic grandeur in them; in the tax gatherer, with his back toward the spectator, you feel that you could grasp his calf and find it round and solid. By modulating his shade, Masaccio creates an image that appeals to our sense of touch, as though designed to convince us that these shapes rendered on a flat surface are three-dimensional volumes. This impression, though to a large extent gained by shadow, did not lead Masaccio to experiment with light and shade. The shadows are cast for the sake of the form they create, not to produce an effect of light.

So far, Masaccio attempted what Giotto had done before him, and carried it only a little farther in anatomy. But he also introduced aerial perspective in his background. He noticed in the hills around Florence that not only do objects appear to become smaller as they recede from the eye, but also they become indistinct in outline, and progressively lighter in value. The range of hills behind the apostles is clear near them but vaguer in the distance. The architectural value of the painting is not neglected either. The group of apostles fills a rectangle whose proportions are similar to those of the whole painting, and so brings it into accord with the wall area at Masaccio's disposal. In one respect at least Masaccio is immature. In his eagerness to tell the parable of the Tribute Money, he has squeezed three incidents into a single frame, just as Ghiberti did in the east doors of the Baptistry. In the center, the tax gatherer demands his money from Christ, on whose right hand stands St. Peter. At the extreme left, St. Peter takes the money from the fish's mouth. And finally, at the right he appears a third time to give the coin to the tax collector. Incidentally, it may be interesting to remember that Masaccio paints his own features for the apostle at the right of the central group.

Masaccio's great contribution of mass to Florentine painting did not prevent his fellow artists from availing themselves of the possibilities of line. In his own work to be sure, it plays a role subordinate to mass, but his successors made expert use of delineation as well as shading to indicate the form. The science of linear perspective, a tool essential to any artist whose purpose is optical realism, absorbed Paolo Uccello (1397–1475) throughout his life; he exploited its laws and became so enamored of its possibilities that he even wrote sonnets to his beloved perspective. One can hardly expect that his paintings will fail to display this passion. In the Battle of Sant' Egidio (fig. 203), the horsemen ride at an angle to the picture plane in order to introduce more complex perspective problems. A casualty obtrudes his feet toward the observer. Spears and shields bearing intricate devices, each of which affords another outlet for his absorbing study, litter the battlefield. In the background, the lines of partly harvested grain roll over the horizon. Such full use of linear perspective enabled the painter to indicate depth and space with greater success than had been possible hitherto. Therein lies Uccello's historic importance; but as an artist, whether because of or in spite of his use of perspective, Uccello realized a splendid decorative value. The constant interruption of the surface by his little problems creates a pattern in cool brownish tones to which the steps toward illusionism are subordinate.

Uccello's enthusiasm was quickly accepted by his contemporaries and successors in Florence and elsewhere. In his Resurrection (fig. 204), Piero della Francesca (c.1416–92), an Umbrian painter under Florentine influence, places a group of soldiers asleep in the foreground, some of them in profile but others propped against the tomb with their bodies and legs coming forward to the observer. Given the same standpoint from which the perspective is drawn, the recession of these forms carries conviction. Piero thinks out his design in stark monumentality. Like the figures in the Brancacci Chapel, but if anything more boldly, his gaunt Christ with the banner of the Resurrection in hand rises as a solid from the tomb to provide the culmination of the design up to which the soldiers lead. Piero does not concern himself with movement, even though the posture of some of his figures imply motion. The design itself is static, and gains impressiveness through the immobility of his figures, as though they were a sculptured group.

Piero's most famous pupil, Luca Signorelli (1441–1523), painted a series of frescoes in the Capella di San Brixio in the Cathedral of Orvieto at the close of the century. His conception of the Damned (fig. 205) betrays his enthusiasm for the body in vigorous movement. These naked souls who suffer the tortures of hell or are being hurled into it assume the most violent and contorted positions possible. Signorelli selects these attitudes not merely to portray the pains of hell, but to display his knowledge of muscular structure. Individually, the figures seem to have been flayed; they look as though the outer layer of flesh had been removed, the better to reveal the relation of the muscles beneath. Each sinew is strained to the utmost, as one unfortunate woman has her toes twisted by an energetic devil; a man nearly breaks his back as his satanic bearer hurls him down from the sky. The confused mass of figures interlace in a struggling knot. The Resurrection, another of the series, depicts humanity as it answers the trumpets of doom. As the dead arise from their graves and push themselves out of the ground, some skeletons in movement have not yet clothed themselves in flesh. Signorelli knew the body not only from inspection but also in its structure. If his overactive figures are too hard in surface and too angular to be convincing, still his concentration on anatomy helped to lay the groundwork on which Michelangelo would later build.

All of these men either belong to the school of Florence or are closely influenced by it. The same kind of inquiring spirit characterizes the north Italian painter Andrea Mantegna (1431–1506). His master, Francesco Squarcione, lay great stress on the drawing of mass; his pupils demonstrate that faculty in their paintings of garlands of fruit and flowers and fragments of classic decorative sculpture and architecture. The classic columns and entablature that frame the large San Zeno altarpiece in Verona, finished in 1459, form the front of a pergola, whose other sides Mantegna paints in perspective to establish a rectangular space wherein to place his saints and his Madonna and Child, raised on a pedestal in the center. Swags of fruit, each pineapple and grape rendered with the maximum solidity, festoon the architecture.

The persons in his St. James Led to Execution (fig. 206), one of a series of frescoes in the Eremitani in Padua (now destroyed), are painted with a full grasp of mass, which Mantegna enhances and stresses by his knowledge of perspective. The painting was to be placed in the chapel so that its lower edge was just above the eye level. Mantegna therefore conceived his characters as actors on a stage. The soldier in the foreground projects his heel in front of the stage; the sole of the foot is visible. As the actors move up stage, first their feet, then their ankles, and finally their lower legs disappear as though blocked from view by the front of the stage itself. Thus perspective begins to create an illusion of distance. Within the space, the setting is frankly Roman. Mantegna pushes his love of the classic to the verge of archaeology, to such an extent that Berenson says the humanist in him is always killing the artist. A Roman triumphal arch, rich with low reliefs, stands in the architectural background. The soldiers and some other characters are garbed Roman fashion, wear the short Roman armor, carry Roman shields and weapons. Of course, St. James lived during the Roman Empire, but the humanism of the Renaissance must explain this panoply of classicism.

The Gonzaga Palace in Mantua has several fine examples of secular art by Mantegna. On one wall, the Duke and Duchess are seated in the midst of their family and court. This family group appears to exist in an extension of the room itself. The ceiling of the Camera degli Sposi (fig. 207) takes a long step toward illusionism. Mantegna imagines the room to have a circular opening in the ceiling surmounted by a terrace or roof garden. Of course, a parapet or balustrade becomes essential for safety, but people on the roof may peep down into the room below. This parapet is drawn in perspective as though seen from the floor; cupids stand on the cornice within the balustrade; a tub of flowers rests partly on a bar, which crosses the void; and men and women crane their heads over the parapet to look within. Thus Mantegna does everything in his power to persuade the spectator that the room of his imagination is the room of actuality. And much about the painting is convincing, not to say deceptive. Still, a certain fifteenth-century hardness of rendering, obvious in the failure to indicate texture, coupled with the limitations inherent in the fresco medium, interferes with any achievement of an illusion as convincing as later and more sophisticated painting of the sixteenth and seventeenth centuries. Perhaps this is fortunate. One may wonder whether it is desirable to contradict the existence of the surface on which one is working. Mantegna does not do this, but there seems to be little doubt that he tried to do so and, moreover, that his day applauded the attempt.

Mantegna and Signorelli lived in the second half of the fifteenth century and into the sixteenth. To consider the so-called conservative painters, one must return once more to the beginning of the fifteenth century. Fra Angelico (1387–1455) is often described as an attractive but backward artist. His panel paintings, especially those executed early in his career, support this view of the Dominican monk of Florence. Even the mature Madonna dei Linaiuoli of 1433, though by no means flat, only partly realizes that enhanced statement of form that Masaccio expounded ten years before. The saints in the wing panels are more solid than the Madonna, to be sure, but the lesson of the Brancacci Chapel has not been well learned. Within the frame of this painting, Angelico sets those musical angels that today are so often reproduced on Florentine Christmas cards. None can deny the sweetness of these figures, the grace of their almost Gothic drapery, or the charm of the clear blue, pink, and violet robes flecked with gold. But however delightful these may be, they should not form the sole or even the principal basis for an estimate of Angelico's place in art. No great master has ever been judged by his picture frames.

His larger frescoes in San Marco in Florence prove Angelico to have been abreast of his time, and in some respects a leader in painting. His Annunciation (fig. 208), at the head of the stairs in the upper corridor of San Marco, is inscribed in Latin, 'When you come into the presence of a spotless Virgin, beware lest by negligence your Aves be silent.' It might have been Angelico's motto. To him, painting was an act of worship, through which could be confessed his unquestioning faith of an intensity almost unique in the Renaissance. His Gabriel kneels in reverence before the Madonna to deliver his message. The Virgin, a humble handmaid of the Lord, bends forward in submission. But this beatified monk, despite his cloistered life, is well aware of the new spirit abroad in Florence and is in sympathy with it. His scene is enacted in a cloister drawn from the up-to-date architecture of his own San Marco, which Michelozzo had just completed. The columns and arches recede in perspective. The figures have much feeling of roundness, not so powerful as that of Masaccio or Piero della Francesca, but by no means mere repetitions of the traditional shapes of late medieval painting. A study of Angelico's development shows that while medieval at the outset — since he began to paint before Donatello, the Brancacci Chapel, and the dome of Florence had started the Renaissance movement — his style grew with his time. Like his contemporaries, Fra Angelico has great interest in nature. The cloister garden of the Annunciation is spangled with blossoms, modeled and studied from the flora of Tuscany with many identifiable species. Moreover, he is one of the first to paint specific towns and landscapes in his backgrounds. Important as these contributions are, they do not absorb Fra Angelico's attention as completely as, for example, the study of anatomy does that of Pollaiuolo and Signorelli. These matters concern him less than the expression of devotion, and the character of his subject.

Active around the middle of the century, Fra Filippo Lippi (c.1406–69), though also a monk, has none of the devotional spirit of Angelico. Indeed Filippo is more excited by the visible world than by the invisible. The misfortune of his life was his entry into religious orders when hardly more than a child, since his spirit was anything but monastic. To go into the lurid details of his career is unnecessary. His tondo, that is, circular

painting, of the Madonna and Child (fig. 209) is admirably designed. Its
fine adjustment within this difficult shape is achieved by the lines of architecture in the background, a typical upper-class Florentine bedroom. In
view of its date, however, it is at least as conservative as Angelico. There
is better knowledge of perspective and the sense of form is surer. On the
other hand, all religious spirit is missing in his figures, who are human
types from the streets of Florence. Filippo loves and understands these
ordinary men and women; his slender long-necked Madonnas have the
features of his mistress, Lucrezia Buti, formerly a nun in the convent to
which Filippo was chaplain. His frescoes at Prato link the monumentality
of Masaccio with that of Ghirlandaio, foretelling the latter in portrait
groups to either side of the principal subject.

The style of Filippo Lippi is transformed to exquisite subtlety in the
hands of his pupil, Sandro Botticelli (1444–1510). This rare spirit admits
his enthusiasm for antiquity in his Birth of Venus (fig. 210). Not only is
the subject borrowed from mythology, but the pose of Venus is inspired
by the type of the Venus de Medici, a famous example of Hellenistic
sculpture. And yet, though Botticelli may have believed that he was being extremely Roman, it is safe to say that no Roman would have thought
so. This etherealized vision, based on an image Botticelli conjured up in
his own mind, has little to do with the past. It is, in fact, the purest Botticelli. A master of line unsurpassed in the Western world, he disregards the
Florentine interest in mass except in so far as it is asserted in delineation;
not that he could not accomplish it, but that he would not. For him, the
flowing curves of the silhouette, the V-shaped convention for the glittering waves, and the swirls of drapery combine to produce a subtle linear
pattern, which better meets his expressive needs. Indeed, with line Botticelli weaves the fabric of his designs.

His Primavera (fig. 211), an allegory of spring, he draws from Latin
authors. Horace describes how the three Graces, in loose transparent
dresses, danced before Mercury, and Lucretius tells of Spring's arrival,
preceded by the goddess of flowers, who strews her path with blossoms as
the west wind blows her forward. The pregnant Venus, symbol of nature's
fruitfulness in the spring, stands in the center. But the Graces of Horace
are not the nostalgic maidens painted by Botticelli. The Roman spirit was
far more vigorous than this scene, with its undercurrent of melancholy.
However, the artist's virtuosity in line is nowhere better revealed; through
it the movement, energetic in the west wind, changes to easy rhythms in
the Spring and to a sharp staccato vibrancy in the Flora. The quiet figure
of Venus almost concludes this garland of action, but her outstretched

hand just throws out a hint of it to be caught up in the lilting curves of the Graces and only stopped by the masculine Mercury at the extreme left. By means of such line, evanescent wisps of drapery or the solid structure of the male figures can be defined. The landscape is unreal, like the figures, and yet composed of elements that show that Botticelli is not indifferent to the prevailing interest in nature but makes it subservient to his own purposes. The foreground is lush with daisies, iris, and other botanically accurate blossoms, and a stream of them pours from the mouth of Spring to indicate her flowery breath. Not everyone will enjoy the highly personal art of Botticelli. It has not, with rare exceptions like the demonic St. Augustine in the Ognissanti in Florence, the vigor and masculinity of the experimentalists, but on the other hand they have not his refinement, his consummate mastery of delineation, or the nostalgia for a half-seen vision, which gives a peculiar charm to Botticelli's painting.

His contemporary, Domenico Ghirlandaio (1449–94), has none of this sheer lyricism. Instead, the frescoes by this industrious man, in the choir of Santa Maria Novella in Florence, are monumental but prosaic. Groups of Florentine socialites witness the stories or pay calls on St. Anne, who is recovering from the birth of the Virgin. Often they look down at the visitors to the paintings, anxious to be themselves observed. But if all interest in the spiritual has vanished, these worldly men and women in typical Florentine interiors are rendered with a fine grasp of form and a thorough understanding of the craft of fresco painting, which played its part in Michelangelo's training.

The fresh spirit of the closing fifteenth century may be symbolized by the spring-like landscape developed by Perugino (1446–1523). His mystical Crucifixion (fig. 212), in Santa Maria Maddalena dei Pazzi in Florence, is limited to a pair of figures against an idyllic background in each of three panels. The point of view toward landscape has altered radically since the days of Giotto. Perugino is not content to create an emblematic setting. He has behind him the studies of a century in natural forms, the landscape and flower experiments of Angelico, Baldovinetti, and Botticelli, to mention only three. Perugino grows up in the hills of Umbria with their quiet valleys. His trees are saplings with the pale green foliage of spring on their branches. The grass is clean, and hardly a breath of air disturbs the quiet fields, which roll out into the distance. This serenity created by the landscape pervades the peaceful figures and enhances their devotional spirit. On the other hand, although the figures stand or kneel on the grass, the landscape is conceived as background; the figures seem to be in relief against it, not placed in it, because of the relative absence of foreground details. Strong and clear in color for a fresco, the mystical Crucifixion is one of Perugino's most satisfying paintings.

In the city of Venice, Giovanni Bellini (c.1430–1516), though influenced at the outset by his brother-in-law, Mantegna, and later by Antonello da Messina to modify the usual tempera method by a partial introduction of an oil technique, provides something of a transition to the High Renaissance. This mundane city rarely produced religious painters, but Giovanni Bellini is the exception. His Frari Madonna (fig. 213), framed with pilasters, arches, and arabesques, proves that the city of the lagoons, like the rest of Italy, is well aware of the Roman past. Bellini designs three panels, but like Mantegna before him in the San Zeno Madonna, he imagines the space within them as one, as though the frame is but a screen, prolonged into the background of the painting itself. It might be the transepts and apse of a church that Bellini had in mind, with the Madonna enthroned in the center of the apse under its gold half dome and with musical angels below, while in the transepts stand subsidiary pairs of saints who look toward the Madonna. The form of these saints and the Madonna has a monumentality of expression conveyed in rich color, the Venetian heritage and glory. That grandeur is furthered by the pyramid of the central group, the very motive with which Leonardo da Vinci was experimenting during these years.

All in all, the complexity of the fifteenth century makes generalization about it hazardous. Its most engaging quality is its eagerness, that enthusiasm for the new, which may be the old as well, its exuberant plunge into the classic past, which it glorifies to its own satisfaction, and its joy in the world, which it studies so avidly. Sometimes the century is misled by its enthusiasm. In its laudable zeal for discovery and self-improvement, it occasionally overemphasizes the very qualities it brings to light. The organization of its pictures may be sacrificed to a love of detail; its realism at times defeats a sculptural expression. In his eagerness to prove himself classic, Brunelleschi is sometimes mastered by his own Roman details. But if the century is not always balanced, the youthful spirit of the Renaissance has its charms. When one sees artists struggling with new problems, to sympathize with their failures and to rejoice with them in their successes is both legitimate and human.

XII

The Sixteenth Century in Italy

THE Renaissance movement in art began in Florence and received its greatest impetus when the Medici controlled that city. Afterwards, when

THE HIGH RENAISSANCE IN ROME AND FLORENCE

certain members of that family rose to high ecclesiastical posts in Rome, first as cardinals and later as popes, the artistic center of the Renaissance also moved to Rome. Though other factors played a part in this shift of activity, the coincidence is singular. Broadly speaking, the High Renaissance, as the movement is called at the beginning of the sixteenth century, carried the tendencies of the early Renaissance to their logical conclusion. Individualism helped to crystallize the great personalities of Leonardo, Raphael, and Michelangelo. If each contained in his style much that was common to his generation, nevertheless each had his own personal mode of expression.

The attitude toward humanism, too, underwent a change. Less superficial, perhaps less obvious, the High Renaissance turned more to the underlying principles than to the externals of antiquity. Thus, the figures were idealized, the forms more monumental than they had been. The girlish fifteenth-century Madonna grew to womanhood with its more ample proportions. If these figures lost their youth, they gained in grandeur and power. The type was, so to speak, ideated by the artist, selected and dictated by his mind, not his feelings. It does not follow, however, that the High Renaissance failed to convey emotion; on the contrary, it did so powerfully, but by means and through forms evolved in the brain deliberately for such expression. This intellectuality was evident in the geometrical basis of the compositions. The scattered and apparently accidental arrangements of the early Renaissance were swept away in favor of the pyramid or some other geometrical scheme woven of interlocking forms, related to each other not only in height and width but also in depth. The greater plasticity or three dimensionality demanded a more visibly organized space.

Moreover, the scientific experiments of the fifteenth century in perspective, anatomy, and studies of natural objects also bore fruit. The artist of the early sixteenth century took such accomplishments for granted. He used them as his tools with no feeling that they were new and exciting discoveries. Therefore, his energies could be directed elsewhere. Occasional elaborate vistas in perspective were introduced, but their purpose was less to display the artist as a master of perspective than to serve the composition through convergence of line or to create the necessary space.

Similarly, the experiments and discoveries of Brunelleschi, Alberti, and other fifteenth-century architects prepare the ground for the more classical High Renaissance style, which centers in Rome. The key figure of the Roman school in architecture is Bramante. Though born in Urbino, his early career centered in north Italy. His remodeling of the Santa Maria delle Grazie in Milan, 1492–9, especially in the east end, is marked by the exuberance of Lombard detail, and also by its small scale, though neither quality is so extreme as in the Certosa at Pavia (fig. 186). When Milan fell to the French at the end of the century, Bramante drifted down to Rome, where he studied the remains of classic buildings and revolutionized his style. The Tempietto in San Pietro in Montorio in Rome (fig. 214) of 1502 shows to the full his mature academic manner. Backed by a thorough knowledge of the parts and relationships of the Roman orders, and by an archaeological acquaintance with such Roman round temples as that of Vesta at Tivoli, the Tempietto has none of the freedom of the fifteenth century. Each part of the Roman Doric order occupies its appointed place and fulfils the rules of disposition and proportion that apply to it, like a well-studied academic exercise, correct in every detail. Nevertheless, this is no copy of a Roman building. Circular in plan and surrounded by a ring of columns, the core of the building supports a dome whose full curve, unlike the dome of the Pantheon, rises visibly to climax the mass. The austerity and the grandeur of proportion give to the Tempietto a monumentality hardly to be expected in view of its small size. The concentration of the central type, symmetrical around a vertical axis rising through the center of the dome, is significant. Though examples of this basic scheme occur in the fifteenth century, its inherent monumentality brought it into favor in the High Renaissance. The outstanding example is St. Peter's itself, where Bramante and his sixteenth-century successors were to work variations on the theme. Since most parts of this building were modified and executed in the second half of the century, we shall discuss it later.

The church of San Biagio at Montepulciano (fig. 215), by Antonio da

San Gallo the Elder, is another illustration of the central type, built between 1518 and 1537, this time a Greek cross plan with shallow arms of equal length. The four arms of the cross support barrel vaults on broad arches, which help buttress the dome, or, more precisely, the pendentives on which the dome rests. Although the High Renaissance borrowed much from imperial Rome, it did not forget the late Roman or Byzantine structural innovation of a dome on pendentives. An engaged Roman Doric order breaks forward from the wall to carry the arches. Where the fifteenth century employed pilasters, the sixteenth turned instead to the engaged column. Consequently, a more plastic expression in the High Renaissance replaced the earlier linearism and went hand in hand with an increased spatial sense and a developed feeling for mass. These results are the architectural analogues of the plastic solidity and monumentality of sixteenth-century compositions in painting and sculpture.

The spirit of the new century, however, was not attained overnight. The palace form, exemplified in the Cancelleria in Rome (fig. 216), retains much from the fifteenth century. Though ascribed to Bramante, in spite of the fact that it was built at the end of the fifteenth century while he was still in the service of the Dukes of Milan, it seems closer in style to Alberti's Rucellai Palace (fig. 184). For example, the simple rustication and the superposed orders in pilaster form recall that building, but several significant changes are introduced. Instead of resting the pilasters of the upper orders on the entablature below, the architect of the Cancelleria inserts a pedestal between them, which serves both as a conclusion of the lower story and as a base for the upper. The origin of this transition member is, no doubt, the Colosseum (fig. 83). Thus the palace illustrates the archaeological spirit born earlier, but only developed to maturity in the sixteenth century. Moreover, the pilasters are no longer evenly spaced, as they had been in the Rucellai Palace. Those flanking the windows are set further apart than those between which no window occurs. Such an alternation gives a rhythm to the façade. The fenestration shows sequence, from the round-arched windows of the ground floor, through the arched windows enframed in rectangular panels with horizontal cornices on top, to the rectangular windows of the top floor. Finally, the façade is not designed in a single plane; instead, the corners of the building project a foot or two as pavilions, to terminate the design at either end. Such a use of accented corners is common in France and elsewhere, but most unusual in Italy.

The Cancelleria is not typical of the Roman school. On the other hand, the Farnese Palace typifies its period well. Designed by Antonio da San

Gallo the Younger, about 1520, its rectangular plan (fig. 217) surrounds an open court, entered through a colonnaded passageway. The rooms are ranged along the front and side of the building with little effort to provide means of communication to them save by passing from one room to another. The austere cliff-like façade (fig. 218), almost a hundred feet high, has one principal accent and only one, its door, colossal in scale, and emphasized by rustication. Similar accented blocks of stone recur at the angles of the façade to give visual expression of the strength needed on the corners of stone buildings. Though the orders on a large scale are abandoned, the windows prove that they have not been forgotten. Columns flank each window and support entablatures with alternate triangular and segmental pediments. No frivolous detail, nothing playful or accidental is allowed to disturb the sobriety of this design or to mitigate its scale.

The court (fig. 219) of the Farnese Palace best illustrates the new plastic feeling. Light columns support the court walls in early Renaissance palaces, but they are replaced by the Roman arch order with engaged columns on rectangular piers. Such piers make possible a greater mass at the corners, visibly to express strength there without loss of continuity. The rich shadows caught by the arcade and by the projecting orders convey the plastic character of High Renaissance buildings. This mode of architectural expression could hardly have been reached without the experimental archaeology of the fifteenth century, but nevertheless its severe monumentality opposes the delicate but slight linear compositions of Brunelleschi, Michelozzo, and even Alberti.

As one might expect, such palaces as the Farnese, and even fifteenth-century homes such as the Riccardi Palace in Florence, reflect the sophistication of the Renaissance in the greater quantity and variety of their furniture, as compared to medieval houses. Perhaps the chest, or as the Italians call it the *cassone*, still leads in importance, but its shape is more complicated and less structural, its surfaces enriched with arabesques, acanthus leaves, swags of fruits and flowers, and other decorative motives of classic origin, or its sides painted. The greatest artists of the Renaissance do not disdain to produce panels for these dower chests. Chairs are more plentiful, lighter in design, and varied in type; in the sixteenth century, cushioned seats begin to testify to an increased appreciation of comfort. Ornate carved tables no longer need, as in the Middle Ages, to be dismantled after each meal. Though still large, beds are lighter in design and neither enclosed nor built in. The sideboard, as distinct from the cabinet or dresser, and the chest of drawers put in their appearance.

The High Renaissance manner, so well exemplified in architecture by the Farnese Palace, is difficult to date precisely. Though it culminates early in the sixteenth century, it so happens that one of the men who does much to establish it in the arts in general spends most of his active life in the fifteenth century. Leonardo da Vinci (1452–1519) is the most amazing illustration in history of the universally talented man, a phenomenon common in a lesser degree in the Renaissance, when men felt that they might turn their hands and minds in many directions. We are apt to think of Leonardo as a painter, but he runs the gamut of the arts, including architecture, city planning, sculpture, literature, and music. Nevertheless, Leonardo himself and his own age regarded him primarily as an engineer and a scientist. Alike in hydraulics, aviation, and military engineering, in geometry, botany, zoology, anatomy, physics, mathematics, and astronomy, he led his age and plotted lines of development that were followed sometimes only after a lapse of centuries. His is the modern point of view, to reach truth by objective experimentation. Volumes have been written about Leonardo; it requires volumes to do him justice.

One effect of this versatility is the paucity of his paintings; another is that many of them were never completed. Perhaps Leonardo's interest in any task was sustained just so long as some problem remained unsolved; when he saw the way clear to that solution, rather than incurring the drudgery of completion, his mind sought other fields. He knew himself competent in the pictorial media of his day; as a young man he proved himself in them; why, then, spend his time doing what others could do? Leonardo's attitude is understandable, but nevertheless of doubtful wisdom, since a conception in art gains clarity through its completeness of expression. He seems to have lacked the mental discipline needed to finish his works. Pope Leo X says of him in despair, 'This man thinks of completing a painting before he begins it.'

At least twice in his life Leonardo defined the aims of painting, but very differently. In one place he says that the object of painting is to create an illusion of the third dimension, where none exists. Whatever the twentieth century may think of this definition, it states a cardinal aim of the fifteenth and sixteenth centuries. Indeed, the Madonna of the Rocks (fig. 220), painted in 1483, summarizes the accomplishments of the early Renaissance. The four figures are set in a landscape the details of which betray the naturalism of the fifteenth century and the scientific observation of Leonardo. In the foreground, the rocks are stratified; the flowers and low shrubs are meticulous. And yet it is doubtful whether the imagined setting as a whole should be described as natural. Its total effect, to say the least, is unusual, with a dramatic emphasis on a dark background against which the figures or parts of them may be relieved in light. The strong illumination is designed to model the figures, and to enhance the projection and recession of their parts. To that end, also, the poses are selected and drawn with masterful foreshortening, as in the Madonna's hand extended toward us, the light visible only on the fingertips. These gestures further serve to tie the figures together, to knit them into a related group, rather than leave them in isolation. However, Leonardo uses his light naturalistically. Where a lighted form is visualized against a dark ground, or *vice versa*, its outline is sharp. If, on the other hand, a portion of the figure be in shadow against a shaded background, the silhouette disappears as it would in nature. Thus the lighted features and breast of the Christ Child are prominent against the dark tones of the Madonna's robe, but the outline of His back is barely perceptible. This full chiaroscuro, or study of light and shade, in the Madonna of the Rocks fulfils Leonardo's first definition of the aims of painting. It creates forms on a flat surface which the eye interprets as three dimensional. This effect is reached by drawing in masses, not in line, and in value instead of color. Indeed, the color, though sufficient, is subordinate to the primary purpose of the painting. In the Madonna of the Rocks Leonardo also employs his famous Madonna type. Her smooth modeled features, soft cheeks, and small chin have a subtle reticence, a shyness and modesty stressed by the downcast eyes and by the faint half-smile on her lips.

But if this masterpiece is the culmination of fifteenth century art, it lacks the monumentality and the deliberate intellectuality of the High Renaissance. Those qualities are obvious in the world-famous Last Supper (fig. 221) in the refectory of the church of Santa Maria delle Grazie in Milan. Dissatisfied with fresco as a medium, because its necessary boldness of execution prevents the prolonged study Leonardo intended to give to each detail, and with tempera because it is unfitted to the scale at which he wanted to work, Leonardo experiments here with oil paints on a prepared surface of pitch and mastic plaster. The result was not successful, and the painting is in poor condition. It must be admitted, however, that to cut a doorway, which was later blocked up, through the lower part of the painting, and to store hay in the same room is not the proper treatment for a masterpiece.

As a result of its condition, one sees little more than the ghost of Leonardo's idea, only enough to perceive the composition and the artist's general approach to his problem. The painting covers the upper wall at one end of the refectory. Leonardo imagines that the upper room in which the Last Supper took place may be an extension of the space of the refectory itself. The plane of the side walls within the painting, therefore, prolongs the planes of the walls in the room. In the composition, everything accents the figure of Christ. First, through perspective, the receding beams of the ceiling, the tops of the tapestries along the walls, and the pattern of the floor all converge on a vanishing point within the area occupied by Christ's head. Next, the simple architecture of the room concentrates on the same purpose. Three windows in the back wall are rhythmically designed; the smaller ones are plain but the largest in the center enframes Christ, and through its size and its richer architecture draws the eye to Him. The segmental pediment above it curves from a center within the figure of Christ.

In the third place, the subsidiary characters focus attention on Christ. All twelve apostles as well as Christ sit on the further side of the table. Many earlier versions of the story had placed Judas alone on the nearer side of the table, as though to emphasize his isolation among the apostles and to bring him into that physical proximity to Christ demanded by the Scriptures. However, to do this is to make Judas, not Christ, the most prominent character. In Leonardo's painting, the apostles are arranged in two groups of three characters each on either side of Christ. By their poses and gestures, the apostles provide transitions from one triad to another without confusing the identity of any group. Thus St. Peter, his head second to the left from Christ, starts forward and carries the eye with him from the outer part toward the inner. At each side the action is subdued, but undergoes a crescendo toward the center. Finally, at that point Leonardo contrasts the quiet geometric form of Christ with the agitation elsewhere, and isolates Him visually from the figures of the apostles overlapping one another. This equilateral triangle of Christ focuses attention on itself, and particularly on its apex, the head of Christ, His light face surrounded by a band of dark hair, itself contrasted to the light background.

Furthermore, the Last Supper illustrates Leonardo's second pregnant definition of the purpose of painting: namely, that the greatest painting is that which through the motions of the body reveals the feelings of the soul. He advises painters to study deaf mutes to learn the expressive possibilities of gesture. Leonardo has characterized each individual as much by his action as by his face. To facilitate this, he chooses the most dramatic moment at the Last Supper, the instant after Christ said, 'One of you shall betray me!' To Christ, this was a simple truth, sad perhaps, but no occasion for surprise. Its effect on the apostles, however, was startling; so sudden an announcement of the existence of a traitor in their supposedly loyal group was perfectly calculated to expose their several natures. To the right of Christ, St. James Major draws back with outstretched arms as though to deprecate the possibility of such dastardy. Next to him, St. Philip leans forward, his hands pressed to his bosom as though to assure Christ of his own personal devotion. Behind them both, starting forward from the outer group but by his action brought nearer the center than St. James, is St. Thomas. Not for nothing has he been called 'doubting Thomas;' Leonardo reflects that his instinct would be to question Christ's accuracy, to ask for proof as though to argue the point, against the Master Himself if need be.

To the left of Christ, St. John, the beloved disciple, thinks only of the tragedy to his Saviour and slumps away from Christ as though about to swoon. Surely the action of St. John and St. James, by isolating Christ, symbolizes that within a few hours His closest followers will desert Him. Then St. Peter starts forward toward Christ, his head appearing next to St. John's. Always a man of action, St. Peter is angered at this disclosure; with never a thought that it might be himself, he proposes to discover the villain and to avert the disaster by direct action. One alone, beside Christ, knows the meaning. Judas, having a guilty conscience, feels himself exposed. His figure is tense; aware of danger, his emotions find their way through his fingers as though to strangle the money bag in his hand. Symbolically, too, Judas draws away from Christ, his elbow upsets the salt, and, as he turns away from the light, his face alone of all the apostles is in shadow. Finally, the other apostles, less vivid personalities in the Gospels, are grouped toward the ends of the table; their gestures reveal agitation, doubt of Christ's meaning, or whether they have heard Him aright. In view of its dramatic intensity and its pictorial unity, it is easy to understand why this painting has been from the moment of its execution the most famous version of the Last Supper. It has become the measure by which we gauge the success of other treatments, the last word, so to speak, on this theme.

A third pillar of Leonardo's fame as a painter is the Madonna and St. Anne (fig. 222), probably executed early in the sixteenth century. If the Madonna of the Rocks be a summary of the fifteenth century, the St. Anne is a prediction of the High Renaissance. Indeed, one might almost say the St. Anne is the High Renaissance. The figures abandon the slenderness Leonardo himself had preferred earlier, in favor of mass and monumentality. St. Anne's feet point to the left, her hips are frontal, but her head faces to the right; therefore, the axis of the body has turned through

ninety degrees. That torsion of the body, called *contrapposto*, produces
tension within the figure itself and gives to it a sense of balanced movement. Since the Madonna sits in her mother's lap and reaches forward
and downward to the infant Christ and the lamb, the three figures create
a pyramid as the composition. The outlines and surfaces of this geometric
shape are constantly repeated. The outstretched arms of the Madonna
and of Christ, the lamb's body, the line of St. Anne's shoulders and her
glance parallel one side of the pyramid, and are balanced by the lamb's
feet, the torso of the Madonna and of Christ, the legs of St. Anne, and so
on. Carried through with the completeness and intellectuality of a mathematical proposition, this type of composition reappears in many Raphael
Madonnas, and the reliance on geometry remains constant through the
first generation of the sixteenth century.

The most celebrated example of Leonardo's type is the Mona Lisa, a
portrait of the Neapolitan wife of Francesco del Giocondo. She had been
saddened by the loss of children, and it is said that Leonardo employed
musicians to charm a wan smile to her reluctant lips. Many have vaunted
to the clouds the beauty and mystery of Mona Lisa; others have found
her repellent; but one proof of her power lies in the strength of people's
reactions to her. No common portrait could provoke so much comment.
Whether one likes Mona Lisa as a person or not is unimportant. In this
painting, Leonardo once more demonstrates his power of draftsmanship,
his ability to create form, his analytical grasp of character, his accuracy
in natural objects, and his fertility in composition. These matters establish his position in the history of art, and from them come his contributions to the development of painting.

If Michelangelo's range of interests hardly compared with Leonardo's
versatility, the former's completed output in sculpture, painting, architecture, and literature was greater. During his long life (1475–1564), his
energy enabled him to accomplish colossal tasks in each of the major
arts. A giant in spirit, Michelangelo Buonarroti was physically small, and
his misfortunes darkened his already somber disposition. In him a deep
and almost medieval Christianity worked in opposition to his pagan love
of beauty in the body. He saw his beloved Italy become a battleground
of nations barbarous to him, and his native Florence, nominally a republic
in his youth, converted into a duchy. Moreover, he had to work for the
very men who subverted Florentine liberty, the later Medici, and for
ecclesiastics who were in large part to blame for the religious lethargy
of the Church in the early sixteenth century. His personal misfortunes
must be added to these — the unworthiness of his brothers and sisters

and their children to whom Michelangelo was, nevertheless, extremely generous; and his inability to complete his project for the Tomb of Julius II, which proved a thorn in his side for decades.

Though he learned to paint under Ghirlandaio, Michelangelo studied antique sculpture in the Medici collections and always considered himself primarily a sculptor. The subject of his first great triumph, the Pietà in St. Peter's (fig. 223), is a tragic one; nowhere have the lassitude of death and its pathos found more sympathy than is shown in this restrained group. The Madonna's sorrow is idealized in her face, and echoed in the sobriety of the broad folds of her costume. These polished surfaces retain something of the fifteenth-century spirit, but the High Renaissance mass of the pyramid, as in contemporary painting, forms the basis of the composition and compels compactness in the group. Moreover, Michelangelo alters normal proportions to suit his needs; indeed, through his whole career, he is the master of the figure, which in his hands becomes a vehicle for expression. In this case, Christ, though an adult male, is made smaller in mass than the Madonna on whose lap He lies, in order not to appear to crush her, or to destroy the pyramid of the group.

His colossal David (fig. 224) was carved a few years later from a block of stone that had been hacked by earlier sculptors and abandoned. Michelangelo again shows his preference for marble; his glyptic instinct contrasts with the plastic quality of most fifteenth-century work. His love of sheer size opposes the smaller scale of the early Renaissance. The body attests Michelangelo's already thorough knowledge of anatomy. Its powerful muscular structure, its features, and the veins and sinews of arms and hands are realistic in detail only. These forms are selected and, under the influence of the antique, given breadth so that they may be infused with his personal titanic energy. Michelangelo does not copy a human body; the head and the right hand are enlarged for expression. The pose, particularly that of the right arm, is similar to that carved by Donatello on Lo Zuccone (fig. 192). Like the Renaissance movement itself, Michelangelo's David seems to have grown to maturity; therefore, he is presented as older than the best-known fifteenth-century versions of the hero by Donatello (fig. 191) and Verrocchio. Also, where they had imagined David triumphant after the fight, Michelangelo chooses to present him grim with determination before the battle, as though such intensity were inherent in the sculptor himself.

These examples belong to the beginning of Michelangelo's career. The allegorical figures designed for the Tomb of Julius II come from his maturity. Because of the curtailment of that project, the so-called Bound Slave (fig. 225), which with its unfinished companion pieces may have symbolized the realm of nature as conceived in Neoplatonic philosophy, was dissociated from the final design. Here Michelangelo applies contrapposto to sculpture; this powerful figure struggles not against an outward adversary but within himself, muscle against muscle, the torture of a spirit. The completed tomb in San Pietro in Vincoli is the merest fragment of Michelangelo's conception. The Moses, its most important statue, is terrific; possibly he had just returned with the tables of the law under his arm to find that the Israelites in his absence had forsaken Jehovah; he rose, and in righteous anger threw down and broke the tablets. Michelangelo's figure has to the full the Old Testament energy, that expression of unmeasured will, Michelangelesque power, and anger, called terribiltà.

The Medici Tombs, for which Michelangelo designed the new sacristy of San Lorenzo in Florence, commemorate Giuliano, the Duke of Nemours, and Lorenzo, the Duke of Urbino. Each contains three figures, a seated man in a niche above, with a pair of nudes reclining on the sarcophagus below. The seated figures may be portraits, but if so they are generalized; though many interpretations have been suggested, it seems reasonable to believe that they symbolize in the Tomb of Giuliano (fig. 226) the active life, and in the Tomb of Lorenzo, the contemplative life. The nudes below, perhaps suggested by a hymn of St. Ambrose to St. Lawrence, represent four times of day: in the Tomb of Lorenzo, Dawn and Twilight, and in that of Giuliano, Night (fig. 227) and Day. This epic conception is matched by the design and execution. The architectural setting is arranged to afford a pattern of light and shade rather than to follow any laws of architecture. In fact, Michelangelo makes up his own laws as he goes along, and thus becomes the founder of the Baroque style.

In the Night, Michelangelo releases to the maximum extent his energy and sense of movement in sculpture. This tortured body, writhing in her dream, is known to reflect Michelangelo's dismay and disgust at the condition of the world around him, and particularly of Florence, bereft of liberty. Nevertheless, for all its movement, sculptural compactness persists. The original prismatic shape of the block is recalled by such devices as one arm thrown across the figure and by the crossed legs; these force the eye to travel from front to back or from bottom to top. Parts of many of these figures are unfinished, the chisel marks still visible in the stone. The pressure of circumstances and of other commissions compelled Michelangelo to abandon the project before it was quite completed. Certainly in the early Pietà, all the surfaces are finished, and in the Night also, which suggests that had he had time, he would have provided the same polish on all other figures of his composition.

His most famous production in painting is the barrel vault of the Sistine Chapel in the Vatican, executed under protest between 1508 and 1512. Thanks to his training with Ghirlandaio, Michelangelo was proficient in the techniques of painting, especially in fresco, but he affected to despise the art as fit only for women. He believed that his enemies had forced this commission on him with a view to discrediting him, a typically suspicious if unjustified notion. The project itself was colossal, and needed a gigantic imagination to solve it. The nine main panels, four large ones alternating with five smaller scenes, recount the story of the Creation and Fall of Man down to the Flood and the Drunkenness of Noah. They are framed in painted architecture. Twelve immense figures, seven sibyls and five prophets, flank each of the five smaller scenes or find space at either end of the vault. In the remaining areas, Michelangelo painted other Old and New Testament scenes and characters, and unified the whole arrangement with a series of decorative nudes, perched on the painted architecture to soften its lines and to afford transitions.

Michelangelo adopts a lighter color scheme in the center to call attention to the principal panels, since the eye seeks an area in higher values. A characteristic scene, the Creation of Man (fig. 228), displays Michelangelo's complete reliance on the figure. Landscape is reduced to a minimum; Adam lies on the earth, which is important only as a support and background for the man. Jehovah with his angels floats through the heavens, able to inspire life in the new-formed man by the bare approach of his finger. Adam looks back toward his Maker reluctantly, as though he realizes that the gift of life involves sorrow and tribulation. Two centuries before, Giotto had established the ideal of form or solidity as the goal of the Florentine school. Michelangelo here reaches that goal. His figures are massive; they speak to the mind through the sense of touch; their weight might be estimated accurately. And yet Jehovah can drift through the sky, when necessary, without seeming impossible. The superb Adam demonstrates Michelangelo's ideal of the body. He turns easily, his muscles rippling, with each mass selected and amplified to enhance the general effect. The artist is so familiar with anatomy that the body becomes a language to him; he does not copy figures, he creates them.

The Jeremiah (fig. 229) illustrates Michelangelo's love of sheer power. Such a figure seems worthy to be a patriarch of a great religion. It has been well said that these prophets must be immense because of the weight of thought they carry. Particularly the tragic character of Jeremiah must have been congenial to this artist; into it he has poured his own distress at the condition of the world as he saw it, and his own lamentation over the state of the Church.

The decorative nudes (fig. 230) bind these larger elements together. Many attempts have been made without success to discover some allegory in these figures. These splendid athletic youths are powerful conceptions. Michelangelo thinks instinctively in terms of the male figure. Even when the subject demands the female form, as in the sibyls, or in the sculpture on the Medici Tombs, he tends to endow it with the physique we associate with manhood. The variety of these nudes is amazing. Michelangelo once boasted that during his life in sculpture, painting, and drawing he had created ten thousand figures and had never repeated himself. One can believe it, since in his hands the figure is limitless in its possibilities and can be used to express the epic nature of his imagination.

Thirty years later, Michelangelo returned to the Sistine Chapel to paint the Last Judgment on the end wall. This immense composition, fundamentally Christ enclosed in a parenthesis of figures, is confusing. Massive as the individual characters are, they are nevertheless small in comparison to the total area. Even though combined in groups, so large a design cannot succeed with only small elements. By that time, Michelangelo had become embittered at his, and Italy's, misfortunes. He has lost none of his power of draftsmanship, but the exaggerated might of these figures defeats itself, and the result loses much of the grandeur of the ceiling. Moreover, his vision of the end of the world is hardly Christian. Michelangelo conceives the Saviour as He returns in anger on the day of wrath to hurl the souls of humanity to perdition, urged on in His purpose by naked saints around Him. Sober as is the ceiling, its view of man still retains a youthful hope of redemption, but the Last Judgment is hopeless, sinister, vengeful. The power of the ceiling has turned to vehemence, the movement to strain, the sorrow to bitterness. However great the Last Judgment, it has not the clarity or the universality of the ceiling.

The times had changed too. No protest was raised in 1512 against the nudes on the ceiling of this papal chapel, but in 1541 Michelangelo was absurdly accused of immorality in so representing the sacred characters, and was asked to provide these figures with decent clothing. This Michelangelo refused to do. One of his unfortunate followers, Daniele da Volterra, had to be engaged to drape Michelangelo's characters, and was promptly nicknamed the breeches maker.

Michelangelo's influence could not but be immense. So titanic a figure was bound to start a fashion. His overwhelming power aroused a taste for similar figures, but the secret of Michelangelo's greatness does not reside in his heavily muscled men and women. Such externals might be copied, but these colossal forms become effective only when they are imbued with a titanic spirit, and with the epic poetry of Michelangelo's own nature, something which could not be imitated. A Bandinelli in sculpture becomes ludicrous in his ineptitude. The bombast of the Michelangelesque painters is only tiresome, but the inadequacy of his successors highlights the genius of Michelangelo.

A more complete contrast of temperament than that between Michelangelo and Raphael would be hard to imagine. By nature, Raphael (1483–1520) was the soul and definition of geniality. His affability and urbanity were bound to make him popular among his contemporaries, and with reason. Where Michelangelo was admired and venerated, Raphael was loved. One might say too that if Leonardo foretold the modern spirit, and if Michelangelo's fervent Christianity recalled the Middle Ages, Raphael on the contrary was wholly of his own day. He could and did borrow from many, from Perugino, Pinturricchio, Leonardo, and Fra Bartolommeo; but, what was more important, he so fused their contributions with his own manner that they became his own, sublimated, personalized, and perfected to his own purposes. Indeed, the only artist from whom Raphael could not borrow with impunity was Michelangelo. Their spirits were too divergent; the power and tragedy of Michelangelo were impossible for the sunny nature of Raphael to absorb, and his worst failures were caused by his attempts to imitate Michelangelo's power.

Born in Urbino, his early work shows the influence of Perugino, one of his masters, in the quiet figures, as well as in the idyllic landscape of Umbria. Had Raphael died in 1504, he would have been an attractive but minor master. In that year, he moved to Florence, where he came into contact with the progressive and critical atmosphere of the metropolis. This gave him a feeling for structure and a monumentality absent from his earlier manner, but Raphael welded them to his own modesty of expression. During the next four years, a series of Madonnas came from his brush which have made his name remembered ever since. The Madonna del Cardellino (fig. 231) is named from the finch brought to Christ by St. John. The color is strong, fresh, and clear, yet simple; the dark blue and red of the Madonna's costume contrast with the light-blue sky and green grass. The landscape retains the peace of the Umbrian settings; young trees break into leaf under a fair sky; accurate in its details, the scene has all the serenity of a morning in spring. Some trace of Perugino lingers in both landscape and figures. But the type is Raphael's own, lovable and human. The figure is larger and more mature, the face a perfect oval with a broad forehead, widely set eyes, and a Cupid's bow mouth. These Raphael Madonnas are noble idealizations of womanhood. Under the influence of Florentine reality, he paints no figures that might not be of the earth, none of the winged cherubs, for instance, that occur in his production both before and after this period. Nevertheless, these paintings reveal their devotion with serenity and completeness. They gain monumentality through the pyramidal arrangement, borrowed from Leonardo's Madonna and St. Anne (fig. 222), but the difference between the two is the difference between the artists' personalities. The Raphael is less elaborate and less intellectual as a problem in design; here is the same contrapposto, but not so insistent. Though not untouched by them, Raphael subordinates scientific interests, movement, and power to admit more fully his sweet but never cloying spirit.

Later, after he moved to Rome, Raphael painted the Sistine Madonna. The intimacy of this painting is consequent on the motive, which allows the Madonna to approach the spectator down a path of clouds composed of the heads of cherubim. The composition is again geometrical, a rhomboid with the head of the Madonna at its apex, the figures of St. Sixtus, from whom the painting is named, and St. Barbara at its sides, and two cherubs resting on their arms at its base. The open-eyed Madonna has not the modesty of his best Florentine examples, and its intimacy involves theatricality, as though this tableau had been posed before the curtains were drawn. But although somewhat more pretentious than the Madonna del Cardellino and having less of its reality, the Sistine Madonna deserves its world-wide reputation.

Generally, when we visualize the Madonna, we do so in terms of Raphael. He establishes the standard for all time. But Raphael is also a master of portraiture; his portraits of Pope Julius II and Pope Leo X with his nephews betray his power of characterization. In the latter, Raphael introduces subsidiary objects, such as the exquisite chased bell, the magnifying glass, and the illuminated manuscript to expose the cultivated tastes of this member of the Medici family. The fleshy cheeks imply what is well known, that Leo loved the pleasures of a not too frugal table, but do not conceal his intellectual power. Somewhat simpler and not quite so famous is the portrait of Baldassare Castiglione (fig. 232), author of the

Book of the Courtier, a book of etiquette of his day. Castiglione was himself a gentleman and a close friend of the artist, and never did Raphael compose a more sympathetic portrait. The quiet color scheme in black and gray contradicts the brilliant color of many fifteenth-century portraits. Male fashions sobered down at this time, but none the less the costume is rich without ostentation — 'Costly thy habit as thy purse may buy, But not expressed in fancy, rich not gaudy,' Castiglione, like Polonius, might have said. That quiet restraint is well suited to Raphael.

But the greatest of Raphael's undertakings are the decorations of the Vatican Stanze, four rooms of moderate size. The first to be executed is the Stanza della Segnatura, whose paintings are almost entirely from Raphael's own hand. Next come in order the Stanza d'Eliodoro, the Stanza del Incendio del Borgo, and finally the Sala di Costantino. These show more and more of his pupils' work, until in the last the execution at least is wholly by his students. Raphael conceives the Stanza or Camera della Segnatura as a chamber of the faculties, with subjects that reflect theology, philosophy, poetry, and jurisprudence on the four walls. A rich ceiling includes roundels with allegorical figures of these studies corresponding to the paintings below. The School of Athens (fig. 233) is a symposium of classic philosophy. In the center stand the figures of Plato, carrying the *Timaeus,* and Aristotle with his *Ethics,* as the fountainheads of ancient thought. To the left of Plato, Socrates argues some proposition with a group of followers. Diogenes sprawls on the steps, while among the characters in the foreground can be identified Pythagoras with his mathematical table, Euclid drawing a geometric figure, Ptolemy and Zoroaster as astronomers, and others less positively recognized. Not only do these testify to an extensive knowledge of the classic figures in the realm of thought, but the way in which they are conceived has much of the breadth and idealism of classic times. These patriarchal characters, clad in large draperies and massive in form, achieve monumentality. The spirit of humanism more than its externals flows through this conception even in its wide architecture, which reflects Bramante's current scheme for St. Peter's, itself strongly classic.

In this composition, Raphael reaches his clearest and most complete expression of space as an element in design. With perfect assurance, he organizes his arrangement in three dimensions: the many figures create a ring or horseshoe, open in the foreground, to guide the eye around the group. The vast architectural background defines the space so clearly that it becomes almost tangible. Moreover, in spite of the movement around and within this volume, the symmetry of the whole design establishes a feeling of repose. Individual figures have possibilities of action, but the design is quiet, even static, its monumental equilibrium created by each part located in its appointed place. This clarity, completeness, and assurance is the essence of the High Renaissance in Rome.

WHILE Leonardo, Michelangelo, and Raphael fulfilled the destiny of the High Renaissance in Florence and Rome, an analogous but somewhat
VENETIAN PAINTING
modified development took place in Venice. This city, wealthy through its trade with the east, had acquired a character of semi-oriental richness, an exotic flavor unique in Italy. Although its problems in painting during the fifteenth century, like those of Florence, had been predominantly religious, the Venetian attitude toward the subject in the sixteenth century tended to become more secular. In spite of some masterpieces of religious painting, such as Titian's Assumption of the Virgin, it is hard to imagine a Fra Angelico or a Raphael in Venice. The Venetians were more attracted to splendor of costume, to elaborate architecture, to luxuriant physical types, and above all to color.

They adopt the Flemish oil medium, but modify it in the direction of modern practices, and thus develop a technique appropriate to their painterly approach. While they still underpaint their canvases, building them up layer by layer with a succession of semi-transparent glazes, they think in terms of the brush. The Florentines, with whom Vasari was familiar, never understood this point of view. The great Tuscan artists always design their paintings in terms of drawing in black and white; during the fifteenth and earlier centuries in terms of delineation, and later of form drawing in light and shade; but color is subordinate in a composition worked out with the pencil. With such a history, the looser Venetian drawing with a brush is bound to seem to the Florentines an indication of incompetence or carelessness, whereas in reality it is a different method and one much closer to the later painting. Venetian paintings rely on their color, which bears the same basic relation to the school of Venice that form does to the Florentine school.

The painter who in Venice introduced the later style is Giorgione da Castelfranco (c.1478–1510). His short career produced only a small number of canvases. The basis for a discussion of Giorgione's paintings is the so-called Tempest (fig. 234). The painting has also been named the Soldier and the Gypsy, and Adrastus and Hypsiphile. All of these titles are modern. Some definite subject always existed for earlier paintings; of course, an incident from the life of some minor saint may not be recognized today, but even then it is clearly a specific incident that the artist had in mind. In the Tempest, the narrative or illustrative purpose of the painting is minimized. The subject as such becomes of less importance because the painting deals with mood, which is intangible, not with a definite subject. The figures of a soldier and of a woman nursing her child have no obvious connection. They do not even look at one another; their whole appearance suggests contemplation, or day-dreaming in a moment of idleness.

The landscape, too, and its relation to the figures have changed. Throughout the fifteenth century, painters had experimented with landscape as a background. The figures had been dominant, and therefore were usually painted at a large scale in the foreground, where they were prominent in the composition. Now the figures occupy but a small fraction of the painting. Moreover, they are not in the foreground; the landscape comes forward to surround them, and a bush sends up its shoots in front of the nursing mother. Where previous artists had placed their figures on the landscape, Giorgione puts his in the landscape. Furthermore, the scene itself has altered. In place of the sunny, quiet, and panoramic landscapes of a Perugino, for example, the Venetian prefers the picturesqueness of a thunderstorm with its dark clouds ripped by lightning. He introduces ruins not for their archaeological interest, but for their pictorial possibilities. His trees grow in the foreground as well as in the background, and therefore only the trunks of some of them find space within the frame. In short, this landscape paints a mood appropriate to the figures. All of these considerations indicate that the point of view toward painting has changed; a visual and emotional approach has replaced the intellectual conceptions of the Florentine tradition. This alternate emphasis is neither better nor worse than the Florentine; it is merely different, and calls for a different type of appreciation.

The Madonna of Castelfranco, the principal altarpiece in the principal church of Giorgione's native village, is called by Ruskin the most beautiful painting in existence. Though the composition is symmetrical, like the fifteenth-century designs, the Madonna and Child, elevated on a high pedestal, form the apex of a triangle completed by the full-length figures of Saints Liberale and Francis. As in the Tempest, these figures are introspective, a peculiarity of Giorgione. St. Francis gazes fixedly at the ground, lost in thought, and if St. Liberale looks out of the picture, his eyes seem to see nothing.

Historically, Giorgione's Venus (fig. 235) is significant as the first example of the reclining nude female figure in Western painting, a motive exploited since then by almost every important painter. The landscape, as in the Tempest, creeps out to the picture plane to enclose the figure. The leaves, sod, and rocks are clear enough in general shape, but are not scientific or microscopic. The painter sweeps them in boldly; his brush leaves a band, indefinite as compared with Florentine panels, in which one color merges with another. The outlines of the figure in the landscape show this penumbra. The idealized Venus is sensuous but not at all sensual; its flowing surfaces melt into one another until the form looks as though it had been poured out on the landscape. This liquid conception marks the acme of lyrical visions of the human figure, asleep in an idyllic setting.

Giorgione and Titian were fellow pupils of Giovanni Bellini, but although a year older than Giorgione, Titian (1477–1576), in his early life, was nevertheless strongly influenced by him. During almost a century of production, this grand old man of Venetian painting passed through several modifications of style. With a keen eye to his personal comfort, but with a miserly eagerness, Titian begged for and received sinecures and pensions from the state and from various princes who patronized him. These positions freed him of financial worries, though indeed no painter of his ability in the sixteenth century would have gone unrecognized. Few artists have ever subjected their own work to more stringent criticism. On completing a canvas, Titian might set it aside in his studio till the first ardor of creation had faded, and perhaps months later re-examine it as though it had been painted by his worst enemy. Any defects might then be remedied, as an author corrects proof, and quite possibly the criticism and revision might be repeated several times. Such reworking commonly blurs the freshness of the original, but Titian avoided this too. As a result, his greatest canvases contained a balance and serenity, classic in the broadest sense of the term.

By 1518, the date of the Assumption of the Virgin (fig. 236), Titian had outgrown the early influence of Giovanni Bellini, and so digested his borrowings from Giorgione that they no longer betray their source. Thus, at the age of forty-one, Titian reached his early maturity. The painting glows with the golden tonality associated with Venetian art. The local colors are strong, but a superposed translucent yellowish glaze draws them together, as would a golden haze, to produce an effect of opulence and harmony. Like the High Renaissance paintings of Florence and Rome, the composition has a geometric basis, a circle supported on a horizontal base. The head of the Madonna marks the center of a circle composed of the semi-circular frame and the flight of child angels. The Madonna's followers stand below, but look upward or raise their arms; thus, by glance and gesture they visually join with the upper part, while their compact mass serves as a pedestal for the circle.

This dramatic conception reveals the temperamental difference between Giorgione and Titian. To Titian's lucid mind, the Assumption is the moment of the Madonna's triumph; naturally her friends are exuberant. All this is clearly and powerfully stated. Perhaps had Giorgione attempted this problem, he might have supposed that the followers of the Madonna, though jubilant for her sake, would feel some pangs at their personal loss. To Titian, such a possibility could never occur. It would be involved; it could not but confuse the main theme, and therefore should not be considered. Like the Raphael Madonnas, Titian's Assumption has become the standard for that subject.

Titian imagines Bacchus and Ariadne (fig. 237) as none of the various fifteenth-century painters of mythology could have done. His interpretation is vigorous, and the figures Olympian characters, robust and physical. They need no archeological costumes or attributes, because their lusty spirit is that of Mt. Olympus. Titian catches the fundamental quality of classic myths, a sensuous ideal of physical perfection. Therefore, he discards the display of humanism affected by his predecessors. The composition abandons symmetry; if Bacchus is nearly on the axis of the design, the lonely figure of Ariadne on the left is enough to balance the boisterous Bacchic band who stumble out of the woods to the right. Such a design gives a deceptive appearance of the accidental. Inspection shows that throughout the canvas Titian repeats forms and shapes for harmony; thus, though the unity of the composition is evident at a glance, the means of its accomplishment are not.

In addition to his mastery of mythological and religious paintings, Titian is one of the greatest portraitists of all time. The Young Englishman (fig. 238), sometimes identified as the Duke of Norfolk, is dressed in sober black, relieved only by the golden chain around his neck. The design is reduced to three spots of light against a dark background, the head and the two hands. Through an adjustment of size, shape, and emphasis, these accents establish equilibrium. So economical a composition eliminates every nonessential, and concentrates all on the man. Moreover, Titian so discusses the character of his sitter that one feels him to be an individual whom one knows whether he can be identified or not. Titian draws on his canvas not only a face but also a personality.

These paintings are High Renaissance in spirit; though contemporary, the Pesaro Madonna foretells a change in point of view. The plane of the huge columns recedes into the design, as do the planes of the figures. Instead of showing serenity and repose, the composition begins to become dynamic and incomplete, a foretaste of the future, but its promises were not to be fulfilled for some decades.

By about 1545, another change modified Titian's style. He was then sixty-eight, an age when most men have either died, retired, or are content to repeat the qualities of their maturity. The Rape of Europa (fig. 239) is much freer and looser in handling than Titian's earlier work; it testifies to a decline of interest in detail coupled with an increased concern with the whole. Details are suggested rather than defined. The pigment is spread broadly over the canvas. The design is now wholly dynamic; Europa riding on the bull duplicates in ideation a cupid sprawled over a dolphin; the abandoned movement of these figures slashes diagonally, with smaller diagonals in the flying cupids of the upper left corner. As in the Pesaro Madonna, these tendencies in the old Titian anticipate some of the elements of Baroque painting, as do some of the later works of Michelangelo. Titian's conception of color has changed quite as radically. In fact, he deserts color for tone; in place of the sonorous blues, reds, yellows, and greens of his early maturity, Titian's late palette is subdued, with silvery gray, blue, and old rose predominant.

Titian's place in painting is like that of Beethoven in music. His art is controlled and organized, with a grandeur of spirit, classic in its balanced perfection. Titian combines this visual structure and intellectual control with vigorous emotion. His works are not merely mental exercises in organization, though they are as complete as possible in that respect; nor are they unbridled spasms in paint, though they give an exhilarating stimulus to mood. They fuse the best of the intellectual and the emotional, to place Titian on the mountain top of pictorial achievement.

One might well think that having reached such a pinnacle, Venetian painting might have continued on that path, even if not at the same level. But art, no more than life, ever stands still. It is constantly changing, and one cannot state dogmatically that a change from even a Titian is necessarily a change for the worse. Any alteration of standards, or any adjustment of values in life, calls for a new interpretation. The geometric repose and the intellectual assurance of the High Renaissance began to crumble almost as soon as they were attained. Even in the hands of some of its most characteristic figures, we may see premonitions, at times, of the impending change.

More than any other man, the painter who underlined this change, long before Titian's death, was Antonio Allegri (1494–1534), a north Italian artist called Il Correggio from his native village. Active chiefly in Parma, Correggio must have been influenced by Leonardo, who had formed a school of devoted followers in Milan not far away. In the Madonna of St. Jerome (fig. 240), the disappearance of shaded contours against a dark background, which Leonardo had demonstrated in his Madonna of the Rocks (fig. 220), is carried further. The forms melt into one another, while the sweet types are cloying to the taste of the present day. Sentiment abounds, but whether this is objectionable or not depends on the observer. One thing is certain: in spite of its subject, this painting is not primarily a religious canvas. Correggio exulted in the beauty of human flesh, particularly feminine flesh. The Madonna, the Child, the angel, and St. Catherine are dangerous in their loveliness; the gaunt St. Jerome on the left seems out of place.

With this secular love of feminine beauty, Correggio should be at his best where the subject and his instinct work in harmony: for example, in the field of mythology. Fortunately, Correggio was commissioned to paint several canvases of the amours of Jupiter. One of these is the Io (fig. 241), whom the god visited enveloped in a cloud. This voluptuous canvas is the very ecstasy of love. The cloud, within whose mist the features of the god are barely visible, serves as a foil to set off the luscious pearly body of the nymph, a glorification of the feminine figure appealing to the senses. Nevertheless, these are not people, but passionate Olympians, classic in spirit. Such a vision is worlds removed from the young athletes Michelangelo spread over the Sistine ceiling.

That same sensuous physical exuberance pervades the Assumption of the Virgin, frescoed on the dome of Parma Cathedral. Correggio imagines the hemisphere of the dome as nonexistent, a void in which a rush of angels on beating wings transport the Virgin to heaven, while in the center Christ Himself descends tumultuously to greet her. Around the sides, within the painted balustrade, stand the apostles, and behind them a crowd of nude boys, like classic genii, hurry to and fro. These figures are all conceived as though they existed in space and were seen from the floor of the cathedral. While Mantegna on the ceiling of the Camera degli Sposi had tried to create an illusion of space, Correggio carries the idea farther than ever before. In the frenzy, the turbulence of the apostles, and in the more optical approach, Correggio becomes the prophet of Baroque decorations a century later. And yet Correggio was only a few years younger than Raphael, and died almost half a century before Titian, long before the latter developed his most Baroque anticipations.

Venice itself, however, shows the changing spirit of the times, partly in

Titian's later paintings, and partly in the younger men, all of whom are more or less influenced by the grand old man. Jacopo Robusti, better known by his nickname, Il Tintoretto (1518–94), for example, chose the motto, 'the color of Titian and the drawing of Michelangelo.' He achieved neither, though influenced by both. In spirit more violent and emotional than Titian, he has not the titanic character or the *terribiltà* of Michelangelo. His Presentation of the Virgin (fig. 242) is rich in color, with a predilection for golden browns; though sumptuous, the palette here has not the color range of the early Titian, or the subtle tonality of his last manner; it is Tintoretto's own vigorous combination. Light, too, has become prominent as a vehicle to enhance drama. The line of beggars on the steps of the temple is half concealed in shadow, while other rich passages of shade play over the pattern. The figures sway backward and forward, or swing from shadow into light with greater agitation than before. These muscular characters, influenced by Michelangelo, are often distorted with small heads on elongated bodies. Depth begins to play a prominent part in the composition. The little figure of the Virgin stands well back in the design at the top of the temple steps. An irregular ring of figures, including the beggars and several Venetian mothers with their children, reaches a climax in the Virgin and the High Priest silhouetted against the sky. The simple lines of a pyramid in front of the Virgin help to lead the eye toward her. Both light and perspective are merely means to dramatize this position of interest placed well back from the immediate foreground, whereas in Titian's paintings the center of interest is at the front or near it.

Moreover, the figures in Tintoretto's foreground bear the same relation to the subject that we do; they are spectators over whose shoulders, or between whom, we glimpse what is going on, as though it were an incident of current life. Thus the spectator is brought into intimacy with the subject. The scene is not presented to him; he is invited to become a part of it. This is true too in the Miracle of St. Mark. A naked Christian slave lies bound in the foreground, saved from execution by his patron saint. An eager crowd surges around him; its members push each other aside, or climb on columns to see better, but nothing impedes a clear view of the slave. Therefore, Tintoretto must have expected that the observers of his painting would imagine themselves as continuing the circle of curious spectators of the miracle. The color in this canvas has greater range than in the Presentation of the Virgin, and to that extent is closer to Titian. Also the foreshortening of St. Mark, poised in the air above his devoted follower, suggests the inspiration of Michelangelo. That influence is further illustrated by the figures, borrowed from the Medici Tombs, on either side of the pediment in the garden wall behind.

In these paintings, Tintoretto retains the geometrical basis of earlier compositions, but enriches and complicates it. The series of decorations in the Scuola di San Rocco, recently cleaned, displays his ability to handle complex schemes, notably in the Crucifixion. Here everything focuses on the head of Christ, though one hardly realizes why at first glance, so apparently casual is the disposition. The glances and gestures of the characters who form a ring of figures on the ground, a ladder lying near by but unused for the moment, the cross of one of the thieves, which is just being raised into position with ropes, and many other details establish lines that fan outward from the head of Christ. The effect of the scene is one of reality. Tintoretto makes no attempt to treat his subject with archaeological precision, but he imagines a heterogeneous crowd, including a small group of loyal disciples, executioners engaged in their tasks, members of the Synagogue come to gloat over their success in suppressing this dangerous man, and the idly curious, pausing to view a public execution. In other words, Tintoretto conceives the Crucifixion as history, not as a symbol of the Christian religion.

His Marriage of Bacchus and Ariadne (fig. 243), in the Sala del Anticollegio in the Ducal Palace in Venice, is arranged like the spokes and rim of a wheel. The curved arms of the three figures converge on the wedding ring proffered by Bacchus. The three bodies form similar curves; each starts inside one neighboring curve and ends outside the other. The elegant forms are powerful and idealized but not muscular. They have a full-blooded healthiness and physical vigor, which makes it easy to imagine them as denizens of Olympus. Notable too, especially in the Venus, is the influence of Michelangelo. Tintoretto is said to have made small models and suspended them from wires to assist him in learning to draw human beings in any position, including those which, by their very nature, could not be held by a model. Whether or not that is true, Tintoretto displays a mastery of the figure second only to that of Michelangelo himself.

In his paintings for the Ducal Palace, Tintoretto draws upon Venetian ceremonies for inspiration. The Marriage of Bacchus and Ariadne not only presents the classic myth, but by analogy symbolizes the marriage of Venice and the Adriatic. Annually, the Doge and his corps on the state barge *Bucentaur* were drawn into the neighboring sea on which the prosperity of Venice depended, and there deposited a gold wedding ring. In these superb decorations — there are three others by Tintoretto in the same room — the artist abandoned his customary drama in favor of a

Titianesque serenity. Different as they are, it does not follow that to love Titian prevents an enjoyment of Tintoretto. One may enjoy the drama of the latter, finely organized though less perfected and serene in form, just as one may relish some of the exuberance of Tschaikowsky without losing one's taste for Beethoven or Bach.

Finally, the fourth of the leading painters of sixteenth-century Venice is Paolo Veronese (1528–88). His most famous canvas, the Marriage at Cana (fig. 244), is religious in subject only. To Veronese, the magnificence of Venice sufficed; therefore, the scriptural subject becomes a mere excuse to record the panoply of Venetian life. This scriptural feast looks like a state banquet. The many guests are decked out in magnificent brocades of fashion; the setting is elaborate architecture, rich in light and shade, with the gorgeousness of contemporary Venetian buildings, such as the Library by Sansovino (fig. 245); waiters and pets circulate through the crowd, and a private orchestra provides incidental music. The players, it happens, have the features of Venetian artists, Titian with the double bass, Tintoretto playing the cello, Jacopo Bassano blowing the flute, and Veronese himself at the viola. The last, as his name suggests, is a native of Verona; his silvery tonality, like that of the north Italian schools, modified the golden tonality of purely Venetian artists. The architecture is designed either parallel or at right angles to the picture plane, to give the stateliness so formal a composition demands. Of course, when seen in perspective, that architecture focuses attention on the head of Christ, seated in the center of the table at the vanishing point of the principal lines. This composition is magnificent as decoration; on the other hand, one may look in vain for any deeper meaning in it. Veronese is uninterested in other matters. He displays the social glories of his adopted city as enthusiastically as any society journalist, but his characters have neither intellectual nor spiritual depth. The women in particular are stolid. A St. Catherine in another of his pictures has been described as having 'a heavy, placable nonchalance, like a performing cow,' and the characterization applies equally to many of his women. Everything is present that can be achieved by technique, perspective, color, composition, and external splendor, but that is all. His are magnificent paintings, nothing more; but perhaps it is enough.

These Venetian artists play a pivotal role in the story of European painting. Through their more painterly point of view, they link the earlier Italian schools to later European art. For centuries to come, almost all the major artists of the European tradition turned to Venice for inspiration. El Greco was trained here. Rubens and Van Dyck studied the works of these Venetians. Practically the whole English portrait school was affected by them, and painter after painter of the nineteenth century owes some debt to these masters. In view of their high level of accomplishment in composition, color, and decorative quality, there could have been no better school.

MEANWHILE, after the death of Raphael, Leonardo, and Giorgione, and even before that of Titian, Michelangelo, Tintoretto, and Veronese, the development known as Mannerism showed itself in Rome,
THE LATER Florence, and elsewhere. The traditions of the High
SIXTEENTH Renaissance masters could not continue unaltered, partly
CENTURY because of the human desire for change, partly because the ideals of that generation had been completely fulfilled, and partly because those ideals themselves could no longer be maintained under the new conditions. In particular, the outbreak of the Protestant Reformation in the north undermined the serenity and assurance of the High Renaissance. Though its impact on Italy at first was vague and distant, it brought with it in 1527 the sack of Rome by German mercenary troops. After that orgy of rape, loot, and desecration, though Rome regained some of her power, she could not recapture the carefree exuberance of her halcyon days.

The successors of the High Renaissance artists in the second third of the sixteenth century are of course much influenced by them, but their pictorial aim is not identical — which is quite obvious in Angelo Bronzino's painting of Venus, Cupid, Folly, and Time (fig. 246). For example, figures fill the foreground of this composition so as to choke the whole rectangle and eliminate much of the depth and the three-dimensional sense of Leonardo's and Raphael's pyramids. These figures seem too large for the space and must interlock in order to squeeze inside the frame. Though cleverly tied together, the composition sacrifices the clarity of an earlier generation. The figures themselves are conceived decoratively, with a sensuous feeling for the nude; their mincing grace has neither the spiritual import of the Michelangelo nudes, nor the Olympian robustness of Titian's mythologies. Perhaps the impulse to decoration is one reason for the elongated mannered proportions. Preternaturally tall, the figures sway to and fro, bend over backward, or turn in spirals as though searching elegance in pose, even at the price of affectation. Such mannered proportions and poses had begun to appear even in some of the men already considered. Certain paintings of the late Titian, and many of the works of

Tintoretto — for example, the mother standing half way up the temple steps in the Presentation of the Virgin (fig. 242) — testify to this development. But, to be sure, the late Titian and much of the career of Tintoretto is contemporary with the appearance of Mannerism. In color, also, the Mannerists tend to forego the sonorous primary chords of the High Renaissance, and turn instead to off shades, like lemon yellows, lavenders, steely blues, metallic colors, in place of the more straightforward tones.

Opposed to Mannerism in theory were the eclectic painters of the Bolognese Academy, founded in 1583 by the Carracci brothers, who thought to outdo their High Renaissance predecessors by borrowing from each those qualities in which each had excelled: the strength of Michelangelo, the color of Titian, the repose and balance of Raphael, and the sweetness of Correggio. It was a laudable ideal, but the difficulty lay in combining these divergent traits. Actually, Raphael and Correggio exerted the strongest influence, save perhaps in murals, where the Sistine Chapel ceiling was bound to inspire emulation. The Carracci altarpieces continue the types, motives, and color of the men they admire, but modify each of these contributions; the effects are strained, the sentiment a trifle obvious and cloying, and the composition too involved for clarity.

Their most prophetic work lies in the field of decoration. Annibale Carracci and his assistants fuse the effects of architecture, sculpture, and painting in the gallery of the Farnese Palace in Rome (fig. 247). Since the artist takes account of light sources within the room itself, and since his technical ability in perspective and modeling is more than adequate, one is often at a loss to know what is real and what painted. In fact, the whole ceiling above the cornice is painted, but the corners seem to open to the sky beyond, colossi in monochrome suggest sculpture, dark medallions like bronze reliefs contrast with the simulated marble, while here and there pictures are introduced in richly molded frames. The effect of illusionism carries added conviction, since sculptured figures at some points overlap the painted moldings of the frame or cast painted shadows around them. The mantle of Michelangelo falls on the heavily muscled figures as well as on the general conception of the ceiling. But the Sistine ceiling is illusionistic only to a mild degree, while the Farnese gallery partakes of the character of a trick, and so forms a half-way stage leading to the fullest development of illusionism and to the complete denial of the surface on which the artist works in the later Baroque of the seventeenth century.

In protest against the ideals of eclecticism arose the Realists led by Caravaggio (1573–1610). He rejected the idealized types the eclectics inherited from Raphael. In their place, Caravaggio peoples his Death of the Virgin (fig. 248) with characters drawn from the slums, some plain honest folk from the streets, and others from the tavern, the brothel, and the gutter. No longer are the apostles clad in rich robes, and the Madonna conceived as the Queen of Heaven. Instead, their clothing is poor, their features old, wrinkled, and often grimy. Such types do not belong in a palace or even a landscape; they are at home in a cellar, with a shaft of intense light streaming down from some open areaway and falling in stark brilliance on forms set against an inky background. The dramatic shadows of this *Tenebroso* style, as it is often called, almost reduce the scene to two planes, one of light and one of shadow.

Though Caravaggio and his followers are called the Realists, we may well question the justice of the term. Cellar lighting in its way is just as artificial as the diffused lighting of the High Renaissance masters. Also, there is room for doubt whether the types from low life, though more accurate in the narrow historical sense, are artistically preferable to noble types, which may indicate the importance of the scriptural char- acters as the founders of Christianity. Powerful as these paintings are, they lose something. Bald statements supplant the charm and serenity of earlier works, and, while helping to destroy the older conceptions, this substitute does not satisfy many people. Still, the influence of Caravaggio is extensive. His experimentation with lighting opens the way to the Baroque in that field, and ultimately to the more personal treatment of light by Rembrandt, while several of the Spanish masters, notably Ribera, are strongly affected by it.

Sculpture also displays the changing spirit. Jacopo Sansovino in Florence, in the first half of the sixteenth century, carves his Bacchus (fig. 249) in strongly classic style. The soft rounded forms of the figure and the generalized treatment produce as finished an academic expres- sion in sculpture as Bramante's Tempietto is in architecture. One of the few sculptors of his time not influenced by Michelangelo, Sansovino stands almost alone. He settled in Venice while still young, became an intimate friend of Titian, and is the sculptor who best expresses the classic ideals of that generation.

The voluble Benvenuto Cellini, on the other hand, is Mannerist to the core. His Nymph of Fontainebleau exhibits the elongated propor- tions and the affected grace of contemporary painting. Often brilliant in detail, thanks to his goldsmith training, most of Cellini's sculpture lacks the largeness of conception necessary to that art. His Perseus, of whose casting we read so exciting an account in his *Autobiography*, acquires a scale that the filigree adornment of the base and the complicated gore dripping from Medusa's neck cannot quite destroy. However, the artificial pose and modeling hardly justify Cellini's encomium on his own work.

The principal Mannerist sculptor, Giovanni da Bologna (c.1524–1608), also displays slender proportions in his bronze Mercury (fig. 250), an incarnation of light movement and a proof of technical skill. His academic Rape of the Sabines (fig. 251) shows sensuous naturalism in the modeling. The stone has become flesh, soft and yielding in the woman to the pressure of the man's fingers, but firmer in the masculine flesh. The problem itself is complex, as these three figures of different sexes and ages interweave and spiral upward. Where sculpture hitherto had been designed for the most part to be seen primarily from a single point of view, this group is interesting from all sides. The forms draw the eye from the front, around the sides, to the back; they demand a peripatetic spectator; one must progress around this group, one must see it from all angles to realize the purpose of the sculptor.

Architecture, too, gradually modifies its aims in design. The Library in Venice (fig. 245), by Sansovino the sculptor, under the influence of the Venetian love of richness already had abandoned in 1536 the austerity of the Bramantesque manner. This well-proportioned two-story building adopts the arch and column and enriches them by modeling the elements to create the richest possible design in light and shade. The open gallery of the ground floor has a severe Doric arch order. On the other hand, the second floor, with its deep window reveals, and its combination of arches and Ionic columns is exuberant. Carving almost buries the architecture with statues on the skyline, garlands in the frieze, medallions within the spandrels, and so on, and yet this façade is controlled as the fifteenth-century designs, such as the Certosa at Pavia, are not.

The Library in Venice has much in common with the High Renaissance, as does the earlier painting of Titian. However, the latter half of the sixteenth century prepares the way for the Baroque architecture of the seventeenth century, as Mannerism prepares the way in painting and sculpture. The man who fathered the Baroque style was Michelangelo. Thinking in terms of sculpture even when working in architecture, Michelangelo saw no reason to adhere to the rules of classic design. As he himself said, he intended to 'free architecture from the bonds and chains which she had laid upon herself.' He developed such forms in his buildings as seemed good to him, with an eye to creating patterns of light and shade, rather than with any consideration of their previous use. If a column embedded in an embrasure of a wall seemed to him effective, however illogical it might be, he did not hesitate to use it, as in the stairway to the Laurentian Library in Florence. Appointed chief architect of St. Peter's in 1546, he announced his intention of returning to the ideas of Bramante, though in practice he radically altered his predecessor's conception.

The idea of rebuilding the venerable Early Christian basilica of St. Peter's had occurred at least as early as the fifteenth century, but not until the pontificate of Julius II (1503–13) was any serious work done. He appointed Bramante in 1506 to begin construction of the new edifice. In the spirit of his day, with respect to classicism and scale, Bramante dreamed of piling the Pantheon on the Basilica of Constantine, thus choosing two of the largest Roman monuments to produce an even grander scheme. He planned a building of the central type (fig. 252), a Greek cross whose equal arms joined in the space covered by the great dome, almost the same in diameter as the dome of the Pantheon. The whole was to be inscribed in a square. With true architectonic feeling, Bramante retained enough smaller features in his design to convey its immensity. These elements, whose size could be measured against man's stature, were juxtaposed against the major portions, too large in themselves to permit such measurement. His dome was to have been a modification of the Roman type, higher and more prominent than that of the Pantheon, but still buttressed on all sides by rings of masonry around its base, and by a continuous colonnade. Bramante did not live to see much of his project executed; the foundations had been laid, and the building had just begun to rise when he died in 1514. After his death, a succession of architects were appointed to his post, each of whom drew up his own plans, many of them of the central type, which modified without rejecting the original project. Others, supported by cogent arguments, attempted to convert the scheme into a Latin-cross form.

When Michelangelo became chief architect, he so admired the monumentality of the central type that he returned to that idea. His conception of the dome required more concentrated supports than had Bramante's. Therefore, Michelangelo's plan (fig. 253) made the solids more solid, the voids more open. The four great central piers, like magnets, drew to themselves the smaller supports, which Bramante had left isolated. Perhaps the church was improved thereby, but certainly that change destroyed the sense of scale and made it impossible to appreciate at a glance the immensity of this building, particularly in the interior. Michelangelo's love of the colossal had betrayed itself.

One may still perceive Michelangelo's conception of St. Peter's around the apse or west end (fig. 254). An attic story crowns a colossal order of pilasters, almost a hundred feet high, as tall as many eight-story buildings. Windows and niches give scale to the exterior, which has a grandiose magnificence. The dome rises from a drum the perimeter of which is punctuated by pairs of columns engaged to solid masses of masonry. Each such mass buttresses, or seems to buttress, one of the visible ribs of the dome, whose full curve rises in soaring lines. To achieve this effect, so expressive of the unity and power of the Catholic Church in the Counter Reformation, Michelangelo thinks out his problem as a sculptor, searching for visual effectiveness with a disdain for structure.

To him, the engineering side of architecture is merely the handmaid of design, to execute what his eye demands, not to dictate the solution. The pairs of columns below are both illogical and inadequate to buttress the vast dome above: illogical, because a dome, in spite of the ribbed system, has a continuous thrust, which calls for continuous buttressing; and inadequate, because their mass is too small to resist any considerable thrust. The stability of this dome depends on chains embedded in the masonry, and even then has caused trouble. Giacomo della Porta constructed the dome in 1585–8, twenty years after Michelangelo's death. He altered the silhouette by raising the apex of the dome about twenty feet, while retaining the same diameter. This alteration probably produces the impressive effect that Michelangelo's model does not attain. Whether the dome is great architecture may be debatable; it depends on the relative emphasis placed on design and on structure; but few will deny the visual power of this culminating feature on the largest church in Christendom.

Early in the seventeenth century, Carlo Maderna was commissioned to complete the church proper by the addition of the nave, which found no place in the plans of Michelangelo or Bramante. There were several reasons for this change. The Latin-cross form adapts itself to the needs of Christian ritual better than does the Greek cross. The congregation and even most of the clergy cannot take part in the service from behind the altar, or even from the sides. But the nature of the Greek cross places three quarters of the area of the church behind or to the sides of the altar, since the architecture demands that it be placed under the center of the dome, lest it seem to be pushed into a corner. Moreover, immense as St. Peter's was to be, the Greek-cross designs did not occupy all the ground covered by the long nave of the Early Christian basilica. Centuries of use had hallowed that ground, and many were reluctant to see any part of it deconsecrated. In any case, the papacy, not the architect, decided on a nave.

Architecturally, the effect of this addition is unfortunate. The façade (fig. 255) is no higher than is necessary to cover the vaults of the nave behind it, vaults whose height was determined by existing portions of Michelangelo's building. Nevertheless, in its forward position, the façade conceals the drum and even some of the dome, except from a distance, and appears to tip the dome over backward. Therefore, from the front the dome cannot accomplish the purpose it so admirably fulfils for the west end, of pulling the lower masses of the design together. For the rest, Maderna could not but follow Michelangelo's executed work. The latter had planned a colossal porch of free-standing columns, but to have retained that feature with the new length would have accentuated the ill effects on the dome. The height of the single order and of the attic story was already determined. Maderna simply substituted pilasters for engaged columns, and his detail is less personal than that of Michelangelo; on the whole, however, the unsuccessful result of the façade is the consequence of the work of Michelangelo modified by the demands of the papacy.

The interior of St. Peter's (fig. 256) is vast indeed but, like much of the exterior, lacks scale. A barrel vault continues in dimensions and in general design the vaults with which Michelangelo surrounded his dome. Pairs of pilasters carry an unbroken entablature to support the vault. This order, almost as large as that of the exterior, has little to convey its size. Though added later, the child angels who support the stoups of water are young giants and consequently deceptive. However, this lack of scale can hardly be charged to Maderna, who merely continued the earlier design. From the entrance, the long nave prevents the immediate perception of the space within and around the great dome that both Bramante and Michelangelo had in mind, but this again was impossible for Maderna to avoid. Any nave would have had the same result. Here, as on the façade, Maderna followed the scheme Michelangelo had already built in such large part. He had, of course, to introduce windows in the vault, and he was able to lighten both vault and piers, since they did not need to support the mass of the dome. St. Peter's took a little over a century to build. Begun by Bramante in 1506, it was changed and carried further by Michelangelo, and the church itself completed early in the seventeenth century by Maderna, though its approaches and some of its fittings had still to be added in the High Baroque style. Whatever be its success, St. Peter's is the central monument of its time in Italian architecture.

Michelangelo, in his desire to overthrow the laws of architecture, was far in advance of his own day. Not until well on in the seventeenth century did the course of architecture catch up with him. Two architects of the latter half of the sixteenth century, however, exerted great influence later, as much through their writings as by their architecture. Andrea Palladio in his *Four Books of Architecture*, published in 1570, lays down his rules for the proportions of the various orders. These books became architectural gospels to England and thence to America. His style, as seen in the Villa Rotonda at Vicenza (fig. 257) in 1552, depends for its effect first of all on proportions, and second on restraint and formality. The Villa Rotonda is of the central type, square in plan, with a portico on each face and a domed chamber in the center. All sides of the building are, therefore, identical and gain additional monumentality from the flights of steps that approach their porticoes. Designed as a country residence, the regularity of its plan is not adapted to the asymmetrical requirements of a house. On the other hand, its stateliness is admirable as a background for a formal life, which helps to explain Palladio's popularity in Georgian England and America. The adherence to rule and the emphasis on correctness, which produce the academic flavor, are more Renaissance than Baroque, though in some of Palladio's buildings a hint of the later style can be detected.

The second of the late-sixteenth-century architects, Giacomo Barozzi da Vignola, is more advanced. He, too, wrote of architecture, but his volumes, *Rules of the Five Orders of Architecture*, 1562, have had their chief influence in France and also, through their use by the famous architectural school, the École des Beaux Arts, on those many Americans who received their architectural education in Paris. Though his books are not much less conservative than Palladio's his executed work shows more freedom. Vignola's church of the Gesù in Rome (1568–84) establishes a milestone in the history of Baroque architecture. The plan (fig. 258) is more compact than the three-aisled type. Short transepts hardly project beyond the rectangle of the church, and are much broader than they are deep. The nave is wider in proportion than had been usual. Instead of side aisles, a row of chapels lines the nave, and opens into it through large arches so that the space of the chapels seems rather an extension of the space of the nave than a separate volume.

Such a design suggests a different type of religion from that for which the medieval churches were built. It argues a growth in the importance of preaching. To be sure, there had been great preachers in the previous centuries, some of them so popular that they had to address their throngs out of doors. However, the medieval church was designed for the rich ceremonial preparatory to and connected with the Mass. That service was so familiar that it made little difference whether all within the church could hear distinctly, or whether they could all see the altar. On the other hand, ease of hearing and, only to a less extent, of sight are fundamental to preaching. Since the sermon plays a large part in the teaching of the Jesuits, their churches have to be so arranged that as nearly as possible the whole congregation shall have an unobstructed view of the pulpit. This functional requirement works toward the same result as the Baroque feeling for unity of space. The barrel vault springs from an entablature carried on paired pilasters (fig. 259). A half dome crowns the apse, while over the crossing a full dome is raised on a drum to let in a flood of light to the eastern part of the church. These unbroken volumes inaugurate a new conception of space, which played a central role in the seventeenth century.

The façade of the Gesù (fig. 260) was redesigned and erected after Vignola's death by Giacomo della Porta. Even Vignola displayed some Baroque freedom in his scheme, but Della Porta goes farther. This two-storied front is of a type that became standard for Italian church façades at this time and later. The lower story must be as wide as the nave and the lateral chapels, but the upper story screens only the vault over the nave, and is, therefore, narrower. A series of buttress-like masses rise along the sides of the church to support the barrel vault. Those are expressed on the façade in scroll forms at the sides of the second floor, and also soften the transition between the stories. Such a façade, while some of its elements reflect the building behind it, is predominantly a screen and can be treated as a problem independent of the building. One could hardly guess the existence of a barrel vault behind the upper story, and the freedom of design reflects a breakdown of architectural proprieties unknown in the High Renaissance.

The detail has not the correctness of a Palladio, but begins to exhibit the florid quality of the later Baroque. A single feature may suffice to illustrate the indifference to logic. Over the central door, Della Porta has set a triangular pediment inside a segmental pediment. This is preposterous. If the function of the pediment is to discharge rainfall to the sides of an opening, then one or the other pediment is useless. These architects do not pretend to logic; they are designing in light and shade, and if the pattern consequent on such a use of classic features interests the eye, to use them in this manner is justified. But although some straws point the direction of the wind, the Gesù has little of the plasticity of the Baroque. Only a few inches separate the planes of its façade, and no strong projections interrupt it; its flat members cast thin lines of shadow, with none of the boldness of seventeenth-century designs.

One of the most successful creations of Italy at this time is the villa. Its variety is infinite. The Villa d'Este at Tivoli has many characteristic features. Placed on the side of a hill to drain the utmost value from a stream that is diverted to feed the fountains, its paths lead the visitor down from level to level through ramps, alleys, and steps, shaded with trees and cooled by fountains. The balustrades, urns, stairs, and fountains are coarse in detail. Who would want the refinement of a drawing-room in features destined to be covered in time with moss and lichens? Playfulness and even broad humor find a legitimate place here. Jets of water once drenched any visitor who unwarily stepped on certain stones in the path, or on certain steps, though these booby traps no longer operate in our more fastidious days. But fountains are the glory of the villas. One never escapes the sound of splashing water as it spouts from a thousand jets, dribbles from one basin to another, or rushes down a cascade or over some constructed waterfall. In the Villa d'Este, the culmination is the Fountain of the Organ (fig. 261), where a series of great jets, like the pipes of an organ, contrasts with the plunging mass of water in the center. Such villas are pleasant places indeed to spend a warm afternoon in summer, and are among the most lasting contributions of the Italians to the history of art.

XIII

The Renaissance in the North

THE Gothic style was indigenous to the north; the Renaissance was not. By the sixteenth century, the Gothic energy had worn itself out so that the ground was ripe for something new. In the Renaissance, Italy gave birth to a civilization of greater sophistication, with a consequent emphasis on the amenities of life; forks, for example, were all but unknown in the north. The northerners slowly became aware of this refinement, though until the end of the fifteenth century its effects were hardly perceptible. Then, the series of Italian wars started, with the raid of Charles VIII of France into Italy in 1494, followed shortly by those of Louis XII and Francis I. Since many of the French aristocracy accompanied these excursions, the upper class was thrown into contact with the new style and civilization at the source, which they wanted to import immediately to their own homes.

The Renaissance style in France, therefore, grafts Italian elements on the native stock. The builders had been accustomed for centuries to work in the Gothic tradition. When their patrons called upon them for something entirely different, they were bound, at first, to take the superficial details of Italian art to adorn their works, while retaining much of the earlier tradition. To assist in the importation of the new fashion, Francis I and, to a lesser extent, his nobility invited to France such Italian artists as could be induced to come. Leonardo da Vinci, to whom Francis I gave the Château of Cloux near Amboise, where the great Florentine spent his declining years, is the most famous, though his productive days were already over when he went to France. Cellini, also, came to Paris and Fontainebleau for a brief time, but the greatest influence came from such men as Il Rosso, Primaticcio, and Serlio, who made Fontainebleau the training ground for the dissemination of new ideas.

The wing added by Francis I, in 1515 to 1519, to the Château at Blois (fig. 262) illustrates the peculiar combination of traditional French and imported Italian styles. It is, so to speak, the offspring of a marriage between the Jacques Cœur House at Bourges (fig. 152) and the Certosa at Pavia (fig. 186), one of the first buildings in the new manner the French saw on their Italian journeys. The former contributes the visible roof, the vertical continuity like Gothic buttresses, the mullioned and transomed windows, and the dormers in the roof. From the latter stem the translation of the buttress-like forms into classic pilasters, misunderstood in purpose but recognizable in design; the substitution of the round for the pointed arch; the decorative motives, like arabesques, carved wherever possible; and the rich cornice that replaced the parapet. There was in France the same misunderstanding of a new architectural language that hampered Italy at the beginning of the fifteenth century, but with this difference: the Italians at first mistranslate classic architecture to create the Renaissance; the French mistranslated Italian architecture and were therefore one step further removed from the classic. Their detail is coarser but no less profuse than the exquisite carving on the Certosa. However lawless, this style has an exuberant joy in life parallel to the richness and energy of Rabelais in the contemporary literature.

As time went on, the French became more at home in the new fashion, and the foreign details were naturalized. The château of Chambord (fig. 263), eight years later than Blois, is strictly symmetrical, though it maintains the courtyard of the medieval castle and the keep at one point in its walls. Tower balances tower, themselves French, but their regularity bespeaks the Renaissance influence. Thus the plan is reminiscent of bygone military needs, but the absence of fortifications and the many windows attest the new security. Each unit in the plan, each tower, and each building mass connecting them retains its independent roof as though the edifice were composed of associated elements, a peculiarity of French architecture at least until the middle of the seventeenth century. The effect is less vertical than in the earlier design at Blois; double bands above and below the windows in each story cross the structure, tower and connecting masses alike, and thus unite the whole. The detail has more of the Renaissance than previously — for example, the numerous but flat pilasters. The plan of Chambord and its broken silhouette thus distinguish it from any Italian design, while on the other hand its regularity and its detail separate it from the Middle Ages.

When in 1539, Charles V paid a visit of state to Francis I, the lack of any modern palace in which to receive his distinguished guest embarrassed the French king. He therefore commissioned Pierre Lescot to design a building to replace the medieval château of the Louvre in Paris. Though only a few parts of the existing Louvre date back to Lescot in 1546, those parts (fig. 264) demonstrate his evolution of a co-ordinated style from the charming but lawless vagaries and richness of the châteaux. This style is still French, with its visible roofs, its conception in terms of accented vertical pavilions alternating with less emphasized horizontal blocks, and its peculiar French feeling for elegance.

The vocabulary in which this style is expressed is now coherent and Renaissance. The orders are prominent both as engaged columns and as pilasters. A Composite order on the principal floor is superposed on the Corinthian order of the ground floor, each with a full and correct entablature. Every fourth bay makes a pavilion with bold membering, engaged columns instead of pilasters with an entablature broken forward above them, deep window reveals, rich ornament, and a dormer roof at the top a story higher than the neighboring bays. No one of these factors would call attention to itself, but collectively they distinguish these bays from the others, and so establish a rhythm in design. For the rest, round arched niches on the ground floor contain Renaissance windows, while pediments and pilasters enframe those above. The detail is rich but elegant, much of it carved by Jean Goujon and his assistants, and yet it takes its place in the design instead of running riot over the façade wherever room can be found. The humanism of the Renaissance, now better understood in architecture, also prompts the mythology of the Goujon decorations. In short, by the middle of the sixteenth century, France accepted the Renaissance but extracted her native version from it.

The diffusion of the Renaissance in other countries follows the same pattern. In Spain, the Plateresque, or silversmiths', style toward the end of the fifteenth century shows much the same exuberant energy in half-understood Italian forms as the earlier châteaux. Here, some trace of the Moorish gives its local flavor to the style. By mid-century, the Griego Romano, as its name suggests, parades the classicism of the High Renaissance with greater austerity than the contemporary work of Lescot in France. In Germany, also, the same course is pursued, with first the influence of the north Italian style being felt, then of the Bramantesque manner, and finally of the developing Baroque. The precise steps, however, are confused, and elements from more than one phase may exist in a single building. In general, the detail in Germany is apt to be treated in a heavy-handed and ugly manner.

Owing to local conditions, the story in England is a little different.

Early in the reign of Henry VIII occurred the same importation of Italian craftsmen that helped to establish the French style, but England, farther removed from Italy and with less to offer, could attract only third-rate artists, where the French could get at least second-rate men to serve them. The parts of Hampton Court built under Cardinal Wolsey in the first half of the sixteenth century show a similar application of Renaissance details to a Gothic building that one sees in the earliest French examples. Doubtless the English would have moved along lines similar to the French had it not been for the marital troubles of Henry VIII. Because of his divorce of Catherine of Aragon, a break with the Roman Church, though at first merely in church government, became inevitable. Since the papacy was virtually an Italian institution, the Italian colonies at London and Winchester dwindled and disappeared, and thus deprived the English of the source of Renaissance inspiration. The subsequent religious troubles under Edward VI and Mary engrossed the attention of the English too completely to permit much to be accomplished in the way of architecture. During the reign of Elizabeth, the art revived, but turned for inspiration to other countries affected by the Reformation — to Germany and the Low Countries. These countries were by then aware of the developing Baroque style, which they interpreted in a heavy-handed manner that became typical of Elizabethan palaces such as Burghley House in the second half of the sixteenth century. Much of the Perpendicular Gothic tradition is retained, for example the large multiple windows, but is coupled with such absurdities as Doric columns used for chimney pots. This fashion was better mastered in the Jacobean style under James I, early in the seventeenth century, though it was still apt to be heavy in detail.

The gradual assimilation of the Renaissance in the Gothic north is just as apparent in sculpture. A relief of St. George Slaying the Dragon by Michel Colombe, very early in the sixteenth century, treats the subject in much the same entertaining episodic manner as the International style in painting, discussed before. Remnants of its victims surround the dragon, itself a wondrous figment of the imagination. Like a playful puppy, it worries St. George's lance. The princess at the left prays for her champion; her type, her simplified drapery, and her partial idealization link her with the Détente. And yet Italian artists frame this late Gothic panel with Renaissance pilasters and an entablature embellished with north Italian detail, the same mixture of styles characteristic of the Francis I wing at Blois.

An urn (fig. 265) by Pierre Bontemps in the third quarter of the sixteenth century shows the results of the Italianate school of Fontainebleau, dominated by Primaticcio and Il Rosso. The scrolls, masks, nude children, and other decorative features concur with the Italianate subject matter and with the style to testify to the spread of this foreign manner among French artists. Bontemps attempts a modest contrapposto in the figures in relief, a problem to which his skill is not quite equal. The characters twist around in mannered poses and with the Mannerist proportions that mark the work of Cellini and Primaticcio, and indeed of the whole generation of Italian artists.

The influence of Italian Mannerism again molds the Nymphs from the Fountain of the Innocents in Paris (fig. 266), by Jean Goujon, a contemporary of Lescot, who couples it with a distinctly French quality. These slender figures in low relief create appropriate decoration. The drapery clings to and reveals the bodies, as they turn languidly in studied poses; the proportions are reminiscent of such mannered figures as Cellini's Nymph of Fontainebleau, with which Goujon must have been familiar. On the other hand, the linear design is more delicate, the conception exhibits a French elegance, and the type of face and figure is quite distinct from the Italian. Through such works as these, Goujon shows his subtlety and refinement.

Germain Pilon (1535–90) in his Christ of the Resurrection (fig. 267) is self-conscious in his attack on the problems of realism. His zest in detail conveys this desire for a literal summary of the form, and for precise anatomy to express the suffering of the saint in execution. The statue has power, though in its design, delicacy, and charm it seems unequal to Goujon's fountain. In the other countries in Europe, the same sequence of style, as in architecture, may be traced, running from slight modifications of the Gothic to more complete manifestations of the Renaissance and Italian point of view.

Much the most important development of painting during the sixteenth century outside of Italy took place in Germany. The technique practiced in the north derives from the oil painting of the medieval Flemish school, rather than from the Italian tempera or fresco methods. It offers the same opportunity for minute detail on a lacquer-like surface that existed for the Van Eycks and their followers. The earliest and greatest of these northern painters to be mentioned here, Albrecht Dürer (1471–1528), is still a medieval or at most a transitional figure. Little of the Renaissance affected his earlier work, and yet in his career as a whole something of the Renaissance can be detected. His love of microscopic detail is purely northern. On the other hand, his concern with perspective, the zest with which he seizes any opportunity to sketch exotic animals with fidelity, and occasionally the weight of his figures and his compositions imply that he had some familiarity with Italian Renaissance ideals, no doubt through the constant communication of the two countries at this time, even before his own trips across the Alps into Italy.

The commanding position occupied in Dürer's output by religious subject matter betrays his medieval origin. The Adoration of the Magi (fig. 268) is characteristic. The Flemish oil technique, but slightly modified, makes possible the polished surface and the clarity of detail. What joy he takes in the butterfly and beetle on the steps, the iris growing from a joint between the stones, the jeweled brocades of the costumes of his Magi, and the anthropological painting of the Negro! The Virgin, as always, adheres to the local physical type, in this case to the blond complexion, light hair, and tendency to fleshiness, which, rightly or wrongly, we associate with German womanhood. There is little of the Renaissance here. To be sure, the ruins in the background show round arches, but they are too elementary to be called classic or even Italian. The naturalistic detail, though typical of the early Renaissance, is equally if not more pronounced in the northern late-Gothic painting of the fifteenth century, and in itself can hardly be accepted as evidence of the Renaissance. The form of the Madonna and the largeness of conception, however, do suggest the existence of a new spirit creeping in to the northern schools.

The painting of the Four Saints, John, Peter, Mark, and Paul (fig. 269), being later, is more affected by Italian sources, though it does not lose its Germanic character. In this case, the sense of form is increased. A genuine monumentality inspires these figures, clad in ample draperies whose very plainness adds to the grandeur of the types. Naturalistic in detail though the heads are, some of them even prosaic, the avoidance of enrichment in the massive folds of the costumes lends a noble simplicity to this design. Dürer gave us here a microcosm of mankind, since the four saints symbolized the four temperaments or complexions, sanguine, choleric, phlegmatic, and melancholic, into which current belief divided humanity. For such a purpose, the elemental grandeur of these figures is vital.

Although Dürer never deserted the Catholic Church, he was not unaffected by the religious ferment that, during his lifetime, gave birth to the Lutheran Reformation. Criticism of the Church in Germany was widespread, and was expressed not only by the spoken and printed word, but in some respects with greater effect by graphic illustration. Dürer's master, Michael Wolgemut, for example, made an engraving of the Church in terms of the Whore of Babylon. The age called for serious thought on religious problems, though it is only the exceptional wood-block or print that is anticlerical. Dürer was even more important in the graphic arts than in painting. Two series, the Large and the Small Passion, revealed Dürer's medieval intensity of belief in the tragic incidents of Christ's trial and death. In the Four Horsemen of the Apocalypse, a woodcut, he showed the figures riding roughshod over the burghers of his native Nuremberg, artisan, merchant, and housewife alike. The engraving of Knight, Death, and the Devil shows a knight errant in sixteenth-century armor accompanied on his way by a skeleton, armed with scythe and hourglass, and followed by a devil whose horn and piggish snout seem unlikely to tempt anyone. These works prove how sober was Dürer's view of life. They also demonstrate him to be a great master in the graphic arts, with a power in black and white rarely equaled and never surpassed.

The same sobriety raised to the acme of religious mysticism dominates the celebrated Isenheim altarpiece by Matthias Grünewald (c.1485–c.1530). It builds up to its startling effect in all possible ways. The enamel-like surface enables the literal detail to be observed with unnatural clarity. The figures are posed with outlandish angularity. The dark sky throws them into prominence as they point toward the Crucifixion. But above all, the unearthly greenish tonality makes this painting look, as it was intended to look, like a scene from another world, gaunt, powerful, and tragic.

Very different was Lucas Cranach, the Elder (1472–1553), who lived in Saxony, the birthplace of the Reformation. Therefore, religious subject matter accounted for a smaller proportion of his work than of his predecessors, and what there was was somewhat affected by Protestantism. On the other hand, he was eager to keep abreast of the classic spirit of the Renaissance. His paintings of mythology, such as Venus and the Judgment of Paris, are laughable in their naïveté. These slender blond-haired German girls, who seem coy and a little embarrassed by their nakedness, parody Olympian characters. Such conceptions are worlds removed from the sensuous idealization given to similar themes by Giorgione and Titian.

Cranach's best paintings are straightforward portraits. In some, the costume of the sitters is amazing for its wealth of elaboration rendered with microscopic precision, but many of the finest are more plainly dressed. The Dr. Scheuring in the Brussels Museum, clad in a fur-trimmed robe, is typical of these half-length figures in its unpretentious presentation of the subject. Though not devoid of modeling, Cranach's portraits rely more on delineation, on a clean-cut silhouette against a background of a single tone of clear color, light tan, pale green, or most often robin's egg blue. The decorative value of this simple combination of color and line is undeniable.

Hans Holbein, the Younger (1497–1543), almost a generation later than Dürer and Grünewald, shows a quite different attitude toward religion. Born and trained in Swiss Basel, he belonged to the same cosmopolitan group as Erasmus and Melanchthon. He became a painter for the merchant class, and therefore religious subjects played an incidental role in his career. They were not wholly neglected, however, as the engraved series of the Dance of Death can testify. His most important painting, the Madonna of the Burgomaster Meyer, seems to prove that Holbein is indifferent to the religious characters. What really interests the artist are the kneeling portraits of that substantial citizen of Basel and his wives and family. One cannot help wonder whether Meyer's living wife relished the prominence given to his deceased and shrouded wife. Even the Madonna looks middle class. This secular attitude is much more Renaissance than Dürer's had been.

Further, where Dürer adopts a subjective attitude, and comments on his theme, Holbein is objective. No one more keenly analyzes the character of his sitters than Holbein, but his purpose is to show exactly what his sitters were like, rather than what they might be. Georg Gisze (fig. 270) is portrayed as a shrewd merchant of the German Steelyard in London, the establishment of the Hanseatic businessmen. In his office, Gisze is surrounded with the materials of his trade, a box of coins open on the table before him, ink, receipted bills, and other business documents on the wall beside him, and a curiously wrought container for a ball of string over his head. The texture of each of these details Holbein treats with objective realism, and their presence assists in the characterization of the individual. One feels that one understands Gisze better than if he were present in the flesh before us, because the portrait is not only a speaking likeness, but one in which the personality of the man has been underscored visually to bring out those traits of character which Holbein, the analyst, discovers in him. Without allowing his own personality to appear, Holbein concentrates his efforts on this objective presentation.

The Gisze was painted shortly after Holbein's arrival in England, partly to demonstrate his ability. It is therefore more elaborate in its setting than most of his portraits. The Jane Seymour (fig. 271) is simpler. While hardly less literal in effect, a linear style is adopted with very little shadow or modeling of the form. The result is an exquisitely finished, enamel-like panel. Each detail of costume or feature is precise from a graphic point of view. The plain background concentrates all attention on the features of the sitter. Such an analysis appears to be based on a quick but careful drawing in line, executed at a single sitting; this might then be translated into the finished portrait at the artist's leisure in his shop. Such details as those of the costume could be taken from whatever dress the subject chose to select and have sent to Holbein's studio, but the personality must have been established through a short period of observation, and especially through the artist's intellectual analysis of his subject.

The technique of Holbein, like that of Dürer, still continues the Flemish oil medium. The method proved equally applicable to the religious sobriety of Dürer, the merchant portraiture of Holbein, and the court portraiture of the Clouets in France. François Clouet, painter to Francis I and later to Henry II, in his Elizabeth of Austria (fig. 272), is quite similar to Holbein in technique and in his two-dimensional pattern-like approach. On the other hand, he differs from Holbein as one would expect a court portraitist to differ from an artist many of whose patrons belonged to the merchant class and whose point of view was colored by that fact. Holbein, to be sure, also painted members of the court of Henry VIII of England, but always with unsparing honesty. Clouet is less analytical and less frank. His portraits do not convey the same impression of a human personality dissected before us; rather his figures present themselves less as they are than as they would like to be. Perhaps Elizabeth of Austria was as handsome as she is rendered, but Clouet's portrait of her does not inspire the same feeling of authenticity as do Holbein's portraits, or the same power. Nevertheless, Clouet's portraits are exquisite in drawing, and have an egg-shell fragility in them fraught with infinite charm. The same elegance that characterizes Goujon's sculpture recurs here, and helps to give them their peculiarly French flavor. These portraits, like Holbein's, were based on quick sketches, but many such drawings were never intended to be used for paintings at all; they were collected as we collect photographs of our friends. Francis I and his successors loved to thumb through albums of these drawings, and sometimes to write remarks upon them concerning the sitters, compliments or frank and even ribald comments on the beauty, personality, or conduct of the subjects.

In Flanders also, the medieval school gradually became aware of the Renaissance. One man after another, such as Jan Gossaert, called Mabuse (c.1478–1533), made the pilgrimage to Italy, to return with more or less Italianism in his baggage. Others, less affected by the prevailing wave of southern influence, showed the spirit of the times in different ways. The extraordinary fantasies of Jerome Bosch (c.1450–1516) provided a precedent for the Surrealist painters of the twentieth century. Save for his sacred characters, he reveled in grotesque types, but even more fantastic are such details as a pair of enormous human ears pierced by an arrow and separated by a knife, or a body whose legs are gnarled trees and whose egg-like torso is broken to admit a glimpse of human figures within it. The inexhaustible wealth of his imagination nowhere found a fuller opportunity than in the Temptation of St. Anthony and The Garden of Earthly Delights; such paintings cannot be described; they must be examined in detail.

Pieter Bruegel, the Elder (c.1525–69), wove together the diverse threads of Flemish painting in the early sixteenth century in his epochmaking canvases. Like many of his predecessors, he traveled to Italy in 1553, but unlike them he made no attempt to borrow Italian motives. When he painted the Fall of Icarus, he relegated that incident to the background despite the inclusion of all the details of the story mentioned in Ovid's *Metamorphoses*. In their place, he substituted a Flemish peasant plowing a field. The influence of Bosch is prominent in the kaleidoscopic wealth of detail in such paintings as the Flemish Proverbs, or the Children's Games, compositions that show Bruegel's encyclopedic interest in the life of his time.

The canvases commonly called Huntsmen in the Snow, The Harvesters, The Return of the Herds, and others show Bruegel's grasp of the possibilities of landscape painting at varying seasons of the year. The many small Flemish figures, handled with great precision of detail and engaged in activities appropriate to the month, give some genre quality to these paintings, but that is subordinated to the larger conception of the landscape as a whole to such a point that Bruegel may be called the first great landscape painter in the European tradition.

Even more important was Bruegel's preoccupation with the vitality of Flemish life. To him, the common man offered all the opportunity he needed for his study of humanity; it was a passion that dominated his work whether the subject were mythology, a religious incident, such

as The Carrying of the Cross, landscape, or genre. The Parable of the
Blind Men was to him a file of beggars tumbling into a ditch, while the
Hireling Shepherd was a Flemish shepherd. His innate Flemish realism,
with a spirited emphasis on the awkward peasant types, found full play in
the Peasant Dance (fig. 273). A century before, Van der Goes had introduced Flemish peasants into his Portinari Altarpiece (fig. 177) as participants in a devotional scene. By Bruegel's time, the secularism of the
Renaissance left not a trace of religious motive in this genre subject,
based on daily life. How these burly farmers and their wives pound
through the vigorous movements of the dance, clumsy in person and
uncouth in clothing, but amazingly energetic withal! The lust for life
was strong in the sixteenth century.

Accurate as these figures are in essentials, the old microscopic detail has disappeared. Instead, the forms are enough simplified to yield
a pattern of shapes and colors. Great patches of red and blue, large
shapes and masses create a stirring arabesque of fine visual consequence.
The design is asymmetrical, as the nature of the subject demands, but is
none the less admirably balanced and adjusted. These clodhoppers
thump through space in their occupation, and also in their visual relation to each other. Surely Bruegel, both as a painter and as an observer
of the lusty vitality of life, still is not accorded a sufficiently high niche
in the history of art.

XIV

The Italian Baroque

To a considerable extent, the Baroque style, though it reaches its full development only in the seventeenth century, is the fruit of the Catholic Counter Reformation of the sixteenth century. Although that style made itself felt even in non-Catholic countries, such as England and Holland, the style developed in Italy and found its fullest expression in Italy, Spain, and Catholic Flanders. The sad condition of the Church, which provoked the Reformation in the north, did not pass unnoticed in Italy itself. Therefore, a small group of devout men, during the pontificate of the worldly Leo X, formed the Oratory of Divine Love to work for the purification of the Church from within. The reform movement grew with such landmarks as the establishment of the Dominican Inquisition, the Index, and the Council of Trent (1545–63), while the Jesuit Order, founded in 1540 by St. Ignatius Loyola on military lines, proved to be a powerful weapon in the hands of the Church in its fight against the spread of heresy. One product of the purification of the Church and its consequent strength was a renewed and almost arrogant affirmation of the authority of the Church and its unity. The scale and size of St. Peter's in Rome suggest that.

Another result was an emphasis on the sufficiency and the emotional nature of faith. The religious experience of such typical Counter-Reformation saints as St. Theresa of Avila is physical in its emotionalism and violence. Moreover, the renewed faith makes its appeal to the emotions through the senses more than through the mind. Hence one finds a growth in the dramatic conception of art, often a desire to astonish the observer by effects that seem unbelievable, or by a theatrical presentation in sculpture and painting of both miraculous and common events. Naturally, this leads to violent movement. Individual figures throw themselves around in excited gesticulation, enhanced by wind-tossed flights of drapery. Turbulence may at times help the intensity of expression; at other times, it becomes merely restless and tortured. Of course, this tendency is not found in the figures alone but in the composition as well. The geometric schemes of the Renaissance, the triangle, the circle, and the symmetrical shapes, which are, so to speak, complete in themselves, give way to asymmetrical designs that often emphasize the diagonal line, a motive in itself incomplete and dynamic.

Such a diagonal may cross the picture plane, or it may consist of movement leading the eye into the composition, accenting the depth of space the artist has at his disposal. The three-dimensional designs of the Renaissance, the ring of figures in Raphael's School of Athens (fig. 233), and the pyramid in Leonardo's Madonna and St. Anne (fig. 222), exist in space and have more or less distant backgrounds. But the spatial depth of the Baroque is more dramatic and important to the design; the movement in depth predominates over both lateral and vertical motion. The design opens up as though to imply the existence of still greater areas beyond and ever beyond, instead of being contained and complete in itself.

Coupled with this depth, and at times an instrument to attain it, is a fresh concern with light and shade and an extensive exploration of its possibilities. The Renaissance had confined its interest in light and shade largely to the modeling of the figures. Indeed, in many cases, though the light molds the objects, it casts little shadow. The Baroque, however, ranges from the personal treatment of light by Rembrandt, through the theatricality of Rubens' Descent from the Cross (fig. 289), to the naturalistic light of Velásquez (fig. 287). The same interest in light provokes the sculptors to undercut the drapery, and so to play with the surfaces as to induce a variegated design in shade over them. Similarly, the architects develop plastic arrangements, an opulence that creates a sense of movement through bold patterns of light and shade. In painting, this study introduces a painterly approach with an appreciable degree of optical realism. It does not follow that the results will be naturalistic, though they sometimes approach that, but simply that the appeal is visual. Hence, we find illusionism in some mural paintings, and a tendency to make other canvases credible in appearance, even when they deal with the miraculous or with the supernatural.

Such purposes call for a high degree of technical excellence, which becomes an end in itself — that is, virtuosity. Whether in architecture, sculpture, or painting, one is amazed at the dexterity of the performance. This may or may not be desirable; such facility may contribute to legitimate ends in the arts, or, if allowed to dominate, it may destroy the feeling for the material by playing tricks with it.

These various characteristics are not combined in every example of the Baroque, still less in all the works of the seventeenth century. Some of them are present in sixteenth-century artists, as for example, the cellar lighting of Caravaggio, or the turbulence of Correggio's frescoes. The late sixteenth century, indeed, leads into and merges with the Baroque. Also, local conditions modify the completeness with which the Baroque is adopted. At its purest in Catholic Italy, Spain, and Flanders, some elements of the style find their way into the contemporary art of France, Holland, and England in varying proportions and in different ways, according to the spirit of those countries and the background of the artists. Even in a single country, wide latitude is possible.

Although Michelangelo's desire to break down the laws of architecture reached its fulfilment in the High Baroque, it does not follow that all the monuments of that style are radical. When in 1656 Bernini was commissioned to create a setting for St. Peter's, he divided the space in front of the church into two parts. The portion nearer the façade, he treats as a trapezoidal piazza, which is, in turn, entered from an elliptical area outlined on the sides by colonnades four rows deep (fig. 255). The detail is conservative, though the proportions of the Doric columns are more slender than usual. Each column of the inner row is bound to be seen against parts of the columns behind it, a fact that tends optically to widen the diameter of the shafts; no doubt this suggests the lighter proportions of the columns to prevent an effect of too great heaviness.

On the whole, the design is austere. Those who consider that the Baroque is by definition florid and ornate must modify their judgment when faced with this monument, in which decoration is reduced to a minimum. The Baroque character of the design is unmistakable. Over each column of the inner row rises a statue to interrupt the skyline and to produce the broken silhouette so common in Baroque designs, though the motive can be found in the work of Palladio and Michelangelo. But above all, the plan establishes the Baroque quality. The trapezoidal shape, foretold in Michelangelo's group of buildings on the Capitoline Hill in Rome, lacks the regularity and geometric simplicity of the Renaissance. The oval of the front piazza is an unstable form; a dependent shape, it demands something else for its completion, in this case, the trapezoidal area and the façade of St. Peter's itself. Not only do these forms accentuate the great space, but they bring movement into the design, and, like great claws, pull the spectator forward.

Perhaps because of the quantity of Bernini's commissions, or perhaps because he is primarily a sculptor, he shows little interest in architectural detail and is content to follow precedent in this respect. Not so with Francesco Borromini; his interest is architectural, and few are the elements of that art with which his fertile imagination does not experiment. The Church of San Carlo alle Quattro Fontane, dated 1638–40, often called San Carlino from its diminutive size, is built on a tiny and irregular plot. Borromini displays the greatest ingenuity in adapting his solution to this recalcitrant site. Like Bernini in the colonnades of St. Peter's, Borromini bases his design upon an oval, but makes the long rather than the short axis dominant. Unlike Bernini, he does not stop with a simple shape, except in the dome, whose inner surface is paneled with crosses and irregular hexagons instead of the usual square or octagonal coffers. The oval in plan is not obvious at first glance, because of semicircular protrusions at the ends and semi-elliptical extensions at the sides. The entablature winds in and out of these shapes.

The serpentine façade of San Carlo (fig. 274) of later date recalls this undulating movement; composed of three bays, the central one on the ground floor is convex in plan, the lateral ones concave, but in the second story all three are concave with an elliptical sentry box in the center to provide the transition. Thus the whole façade is thrown into movement. At the top, flame-like curves replace the usual pediment. Engaged columns are preferred to pilasters, with a resultant enrichment of the light and shade patterns. The columns give an impression of verticality peculiar to much of Borromini's work, due partly to their exceptional height but more to the close spacing he prefers. Moreover, even the capitals are designed individually. Borromini is not content to repeat the time-honored members of the Corinthian order; he must turn the corner scrolls inward upon themselves instead of outward as usual. Or, in his remodeling of the nave of San Giovanni in Laterano, he alternates wide and narrow flutes in his pilasters. To the conservatives, such experiments are perverse license, calling forth the fulminations of such critics as Ruskin or Warren; but unless one assumes a sacrosanct immutability of the orders, they provide novel and even exciting variants on the norm, despite the fact that not all of these experiments are successful.

In spite of his originality, Borromini is overshadowed by the tremendous popularity of Bernini, so that his opportunities are none too many, and frequently on a small scale. The same is true of the sculptors. As the favorite of Urban VIII and of Alexander VII, Gian Lorenzo Bernini

(1598–1680) could choose his own projects and skim the cream of the commissions flowing from the papacy and elsewhere. His destined high fortune was stated by Urban VIII, who, on his election to the chair of St. Peter said, 'It is well for you that I, Maffeo Barberini, am become pope, but we are even more fortunate that the Cavaliere Bernini should live to decorate our pontificate.' Even when Bernini's star passed momentarily under a cloud during the pontificate of Innocent X, which separates the other two, he was able to win his way back into at least partial favor before the end of that reign. His fame brought from Louis XIV an invitation to Paris and Versailles to consult on the design for the Louvre; on his journey thither in 1665, he was received with honors generally accorded only to royalty. The cities through which he traveled turned out to do him honor, and built temporary triumphal arches over his route. Few artists have ever enjoyed such esteem.

As a young man, Bernini studied in the gardens of the Villa Borghese, and worked for that family. One of his commissions from them is the Apollo and Daphne (fig. 275). This prestidigitator of the seventeenth century would convince us that we do not look here at stone, but at many other more yielding substances. The texture of the male and female flesh is subtly distinguished and contrasted with the textures of cloth, bark, and leaves. Each surface is so handled that it almost deceives the eye, and creates a physical appeal.

Even more dexterous is the arrangement. The dynamic figures throw their arms about in actions that lead the eye on a diagonal out of the group rather than into it Sculptural compactness is not an aim here, nor is there the slightest indication of the original limits of the block of stone. Michelangelo had said that sculpture should look as if it could be rolled down hill without injury, and most of his work, however capable of movement within the block, retains that sense of compactness. The Baroque optical desire induced Bernini to select the dramatic climax, the very moment Daphne is being metamorphosed into the laurel to escape capture by Apollo. Everything must be momentary and in transition.

But that same movement occurs in portrait busts, where no story exists to explain it. Francesco d'Este (fig. 276) turns his head to one side, but such movement would be insufficient without the flight of drapery gratuitously swept around the shoulders. Why drapery over armor! Why, indeed, save that the metallic surfaces of armor seem to Bernini to need a contrasting texture, a pattern of light and shade that deep folds of drapery could supply, a suggestion of movement that conveys a counter action to the head. The finely characterized face breaks into undulations of surface to induce a dynamic play of light impossible to attain in simpler forms. The undercut curls of the wig complete the effect in texture, movement, and shadow.

These qualities remain paramount in sculpture designed for the Church. The religious spirit of the Counter Reformation receives full expression in the altarpiece of St. Theresa of Avila (fig. 277), in the Cornaro Chapel of Santa Maria della Vittoria in Rome. The whole chapel is arranged as a theater. A proscenium bent forward like the front of a stage frames the altar. Paired columns at the sides support concave bits of entablature, which then break back to permit a convex plan for the center of the entablature and pediment. This convex portion gives Bernini the opportunity to conceal a small window, whose light runs down gilded rays to the figures like the spot light of a theater. Even the side walls of the chapel play their part in the scheme; portrait groups in high relief of members of the Cornaro family attend the performance in boxes, some looking toward the stage, and others glancing around at the rest of the audience.

Such a setting calls for drama, and that the group of St. Theresa and the angel provides, an interpretation in white marble of the ecstasy of the saint. She tells how in her dreams an angel appeared to her and transfixed her body with an arrow. At that moment, she felt a combination of exquisite pleasure and of such agony as to cause her to swoon. Bernini translates this vision literally into stone. Momentary as the scene is, the story is told as though it were re-enacted for us by living characters. Every texture of flesh, cloth, and metal is suggested. The sensuous figures appeal to physical responses in the spectator. A spiritual orgasm is given expression in physical shape. The sweetness of the angel and the delighted suffering of the saint, fainting on a bank of clouds, tax our credulity. The Baroque dramatic sense thus couples with the Baroque wish to astonish the spectator. The sincerity of such visions has often been questioned, but although few people today are apt to experience religion with such intensity, there can be little doubt that the fervent faith of the seventeenth century evoked such emotions.

Equally dynamic and typical of the Baroque point of view is such a tomb as that of Alexander VII in St. Peter's (fig. 278). Four allegorical figures, whose gestures bear little relation to their meaning, begin the scheme, two in the foreground and two behind. A grim skeleton pushes aside the billows of fringed drapery carved in colored marble, and struggles upward to reach the kneeling pope at the top. Thus does the Baroque represent even death as a melodrama. The Renaissance feeling

of repose has given way to movement. Whether or not such a conception
be appropriate, this type of tomb remains the vogue until the end of
the eighteenth century.

The St. Theresa group and the Tomb of Alexander VII combine sculpture and architecture. One hardly knows whether to describe the Baldacchino of St. Peter's (fig. 256) as one or the other. This vast canopy has
to accent the high altar of the church, itself a small feature, and yet
must not block the vista down the length of the nave to Bernini's own
composition enclosing the Chair of St. Peter at the extreme end of the
church; it has to challenge the scale of the church without confusion
with the architecture. Dark bronze serves this purpose well; its color
contrasts with the lighter travertine stonework of the building, and yet
its strength allows the four twisted columns to rise as high as an eight-
story building. These vine-covered shafts, which enframe the altar between them, spiral upward in answering curves, the direction of turning
reversed in each pair. From their architraves hang bronze draperies,
embroidered and tasseled. The columns support angels, and scrolls that
join in the center to hold the ball and cross. Over all these architectural
members crawl thousands of bees, the heraldic emblem of the Barberini
family. Since the bronze for this monument came from the beams of the
Pantheon roof, the wits of the day coined the quip, 'Quod non fecit
barbari, fecerunt Barberini' — 'What the barbarians did not do, the Barberini have done.'

No single painter arose in Italy to challenge the position occupied in
sculpture by Bernini, though the art of painting was hardly less flourishing. Guercino's Burial of St. Petronilla (fig. 279) is characteristic. Here
is the same Baroque dexterity and command of resources, the control
over perspective, the figure, and the sense of depth. The design becomes
open by contrast with the closed designs of the Renaissance. Our eye
runs from the men who place the body of the saint in its grave at the
bottom, through curving masses that sweep to one side and back to the
other, always striving upward and inward. A succession of dynamic
diagonals carries the observer through the painting rather than permits
his attention to rest at any single point. The scene itself has the same
sensationalism, and the figures the same physical appeal as Bernini's
St. Theresa. It calls upon our faith for appreciation, and we must not
expect the moment represented to last. It is the dramatic climax alone
that absorbs Guercino's interest.

Similarly, in the ceiling of Sant' Ignazio (fig. 280), one of the huge

Baroque decorative schemes, Fra Andrea Pozzo gives us a glimpse of the Apotheosis of St. Ignatius Loyola. Here is illusionism carried to its conclusion. The vault of the church is imagined away. An elaborate ensemble of columns and arches, bits of entablature, and so on, rises apparently above the walls and in the plane of the walls; the whole center of the vault is open to the sky, and, within this void, Pozzo explodes a host of figures. Saints and angels with fluttering draperies rest upon clouds, sit on the painted architecture, or rise and fall in space. The perspective is calculated from a specific point on the floor of the church, and when one stands at that point, the effect is astonishing. So admirably has the problem been solved, so perfectly has Pozzo taken into account the light and painted shadows, that one cannot tell where the real architecture stops and the painting begins. These figures spill over on constructed parts of the building as well as on those that are merely envisioned. We may question the validity of this *tour de force* on the ground that a surface can hardly be decorated by denying its existence, but Pozzo and his contemporaries would not have admitted that the surface must be so respected, and if we accept his premise, the result could not be improved.

A testimonial to the force of Baroque decorative tradition lies in its continuation well into the eighteenth century. The Institution of the Rosary (fig. 281) on the ceiling of the Gesuati in Venice, by Giovanni Battista Tiepolo (1696–1770), retains the movement, the fancy, and the dynamic composition of its Baroque predecessors, but combines them with traditions in drawing and color inherited from Veronese. The explosive energy of the Baroque, however, lessens as the Rococo spirit of the new century lightens the motives it has inherited, and replaces gusto with a slighter vivacity. The color also betrays its date in its lighter value and softer quality. By this time, Venice had become in some degree a tourist center, catering to the taste for gaiety and entertainment. Such painters as Antonio Canale, called Canaletto, whose work was popular in England, and Francesco Guardi recorded the pageants and spectacles of Venice as well as its buildings, canals, and lagoons, while Pietro Longhi chronicled with fidelity the frivolous social life of the city. If these smaller and later Italian painters lack the stature and sobriety of their forebears, at least they portray the city and its society in their day.

XV

Some Spanish Painters

THOUGH Italy was untouched by the Protestant Reformation and remained the home of the papacy and the Church, it was too weak to play an important role in European politics during the late sixteenth and early seventeenth centuries. Therefore, Spain became the prop of the Catholic Church, and the real home of the Catholic Counter Reformation. It is significant that the Inquisition is associated with Spain in the popular mind, and that the founder of the order and many of the other early Jesuit saints were Spaniards. Spain has been characterized as the land of contrasts, of the subtropical coastal area with the bleak and arid plains of the center, of the fabulous wealth of the hidalgos and the abysmal poverty of the peons, of gaunt austerity and sentimental emotionalism.

Domenikos Theotokopoulos (c.1545–1614), the first Spanish painter of international importance, was born at Candia in the island of Crete. Like the rest of the Greek world, Crete was still Byzantine in culture; therefore, El Greco, as this painter was nicknamed, must have been aware from his childhood of the eastern willingness to distort the figures for the sake of either design or emotion. However, he received his training in Venice, probably from one of the Bassani family, contemporaries of Tintoretto and of Titian's old age. That training left its mark on his work for years afterward.

For example, the Purification of the Temple (fig. 282), though painted after he settled in Toledo in 1577, is still strongly Venetian. Its architecture betrays that origin, and so too does the sumptuous color, not yet personal to El Greco himself. Moreover, the figures and the calculated geometry of the composition testify still further to the thoroughness of Venetian training. The subject, too, has significance. El Greco repeats it at least six times during his career, though in earlier history the motive is almost unknown. Surely one is justified in recognizing here an allusion to the purification of the Church by the Council of Trent, one of the most important fruits of the Catholic Counter Reformation.

Indeed, El Greco more than any other artist becomes the painter of that movement; its mystic emotionalism, its fervid faith, find in him an interpreter. For example, the Burial of Gonzalo Ruiz, Count of Orgaz (fig. 283), records a local legend of Toledo. St. Lawrence and St. Augustine reappear on earth to lower the body into the grave. Dressed in the sumptuous vestments of the Spanish church, their identity has not yet become apparent to the noble friends of Orgaz or to most of the clergy. Meanwhile, the heavens have opened to receive the soul of this just man, an ecstatic vision witnessed by the priest in the right foreground. El Greco paints Christ in the center; below Him to either side, the Madonna and St. John the Baptist intercede for the soul of Orgaz, a vague form wrapped in swaddling clothes and borne aloft in the arms of an angel. El Greco does not hesitate to distort these heavenly figures; their proportions are elongated, in part through Mannerist tradition, and perhaps through some dimly remembered Byzantine conventions, but more as a personal and expressive element of El Greco's style. Here, too, his individual color scheme, characterized by a luminous white, is displayed. El Greco is attempting to express the supernatural by means of the unnatural.

The lower half of the painting forms a deliberate contrast. A portrait group of the Spanish nobility have gathered to attend the last rites of their friend. They stand in sober grief behind the group of priests and saints in the foreground. Neither the palette nor the proportion is unnatural in this scene, but then these figures are of the earth. Contrasted as are the upper and lower halves of this design, they are visually coordinated with magnificent success. Curved lines rise from the backs of St. Augustine and St. Lawrence through the angel into the rhythms of the upper part, and bind the two sections together. One may examine details of El Greco's painting in photographs, but such details never look complete. They always appear to need something else, so completely has El Greco subordinated each part to the whole. This cannot always be said even of great painters; one can sometimes find a part of a painting that is an entity in itself; but with El Greco, the building of the picture is so integrated that nothing can be added or taken away.

The Orgaz was painted within ten years of the time that El Greco had arrived in Spain. His later work, such as the Resurrection (fig. 284), is further removed from nature. By this time, his dynamic sense, foretelling the Baroque, has grown apace, and the forms themselves partake of the action. Especially is this conveyed through El Greco's peculiar light, a whitish light, which flickers over the forms where it is needed, not so much for its own sake as to increase the upward movement. That light helps to give El Greco's palette its unique flavor; his reds and blues, yellows and greens mold the forms they enrich, but each of them models toward this living whiteness found in the work of no other painter. One reason for the mysticism of El Greco's paintings and for their religious poignancy is the upward movement of the light. Not only are the forms elongated and accented by light, but they are piled one above another. The risen Christ with the banner of the resurrection ascends above a sprawling devil, whose arms and legs conduct our eyes up to the Saviour.

Though most of El Greco's work is religious, he does not confine himself to that field. The view of Toledo in the Metropolitan Museum is said to be the first pure landscape painting in the European tradition — that is, the first with no figures to provide an excuse for the scenery. A more dynamic landscape would be hard to find, as El Greco resolves the hill on which Toledo stands into a succession of swirling curves, which are answered in the stormy sky. The strong greens of the land create a base for the steely blues and whites above. Even in this field, his personality transforms the subject; landscape, religious themes, and portraits alike are filtered through El Greco's mystical nature.

In portraiture, too, he ranks with the best. The Niño de Guevara (fig. 285) is a solid painting of that leader of the Spanish Inquisition. His puritanical conviction of the justness of his cause, and his austere determination to prosecute it to the limit do not conceal the intellectuality of this head. The gorgeous crimson robes of the cardinal are set off against a background of yellowish tones, subdued in intensity. Significantly, El Greco places the sitter in an armchair neither facing the observer, nor in profile; rather the chair is at an angle, which introduces diagonal planes for the front and sides of the figure, and thus enhances the space by which the figure is surrounded. This is combined, however, with a linear pattern of curves in sequence, each leading to the head, a succession of drop-shaped loops to establish a harmony of line. The patterned leather background completes the design, so that even the incidental setting becomes an integral part of the scheme.

Very different from El Greco, and a generation later, is José de Ribera (1588–1656), who spent most of his active life in Naples, at that time under Spanish domination. His violent spirit vibrates between themes of sentimental piety, such as the St. Agnes, and ferocity, such as the Martyrdom of St. Bartholomew. The vigorous types and deep shadows attest the influence of Caravaggio and the Tenebroso style, and at best give his paintings strength akin to his own swashbuckling nature; but the shadows are apt to produce an unpleasant griminess of tone.

With but one important exception, El Greco had received no patronage from Philip II. That cold and bigoted monarch could not appreciate El Greco's fiery intensity. On the other hand, Don Diego Rodríguez de Silva y Velásquez (1599–1660) became court painter to Philip IV. Though he made two trips to Italy, he seems not to have been affected by the work of any particular artists he saw there. This is not surprising in view of his instinct for optical realism. Few painters have observed the facts of vision so clearly or recorded them so easily. The subtlest changes in light or atmosphere flow from his brush. Velásquez could paint anything that he could see; therein lies his strength and his weakness, for he lacked the ability to envision what he could not see. Whenever his subject deals with an unreal world, his imagination collapses, so that in his few Madonnas and mythological characters he is not at his best. In the painting called the Topers, Los Borrachos, an initiation of a follower of Bacchus, the god is the least effective figure of the group. On the other hand, the older devotees, as human figures, are magnificent. His Mars has been aptly characterized as an undressed policeman. A Spanish smithy serves for the Forge of Vulcan, with the sturdy blacksmiths at home but the god in his aureole of light distinctly out of place.

With this ability to catch the essence of visual reality, one would expect Velásquez to be successful in portraiture, and so he is. The portrait of Innocent X (fig. 286) in tones of red and white, a product of his second trip to Italy, shows an intensity of characterization rarely equaled. The intellectual force and strong personality of the pope are portrayed with a vividness at once faithful to externals and analytical. In pose, Velásquez seems here to be influenced by the Greco portrait of Niño de Guevara: Innocent X sits in an armchair placed at an angle to the picture plane as though to involve the sense of depth. But Velásquez does not compose his figure or its background with the richness of El Greco. He is content to leave the painting as a plain statement of the looks and character of his sitter, the fruit of his vision and his keen analysis. El Greco went on to synthesize his observations with the pictorial interest of composition.

Velásquez' zeal for optical realism has full scope in such canvases as the Maids of Honor, Las Meninas (fig. 287). This is a genre scene, that is, a painting of everyday life. It happened that Velásquez was busy painting the portraits of the king and queen, as he must frequently have been. The little Infanta, surrounded by her ladies in waiting, wandered in to observe the progress of the picture, and while there sent one of her attendants for a glass of water, which has just been brought. The princess stands in the center with her maids, nuns, dwarfs, and pets. To the left, the artist works on his canvas, while a courtier looks back from the open door on the scene he has just left, and finally the king and queen themselves are reflected in a mirror on the studio wall.

This incident has no particular significance, and yet Luca Giordano once referred to the Maids of Honor as a theology of painting. The handling is broad; details are summarized to record their visual effect. A few touches suffice to establish the flowered headdress of the kneeling lady in waiting, and the pleats and ribbons of the Infanta's gown. In such breadth, as well as in the emphasis on optical realism, Velásquez anticipates the nineteenth-century Impressionists. Space envelops the figures. One senses the volumes of air within the room, and even the visual effect of the atmosphere on distant as compared with nearer objects. In distinguishing no less than four planes of light within a small interior, by subtle gradations of values and intensities, Velásquez accomplishes a *tour de force* of painting. These planes establish the spatial relationships of the composition. Light from the window, the jamb of which is visible to the right, bathes the principal group. Being close at hand, these persons are most sharply seen. Farther back, a second plane, marked by a second window, includes canvases of Velásquez hung around the studio, and a mirror on the wall. Not much of pictorial interest occurs here, lest this zone compete with the main subject, though its recession is clear. Outside the door is a courtier, not merely smaller than the foreground figures, but with a thicker veil of atmosphere between him and our eyes. Finally, the king and queen reflected in the mirror, though they stand in the position of spectators to this canvas, are visually the farthest away. The light from their persons must travel to the further wall and back to our eye. Not only are they small through perspective but, though still recognizable, they are the least precisely painted characters in the whole canvas. To render four planes in the limitless spaces of out of doors involves a creation of great depth, but there the contrast between the several planes is large. Velásquez finds that contrast within the limited dimensions of an interior, and renders it with so sure a touch that the space has become real.

His feeling for space and his experimentation with light link Velásquez to the Baroque, but the religious side of that movement touched him not at all. Bartolomé Esteban Murillo (1617–82), however, exemplifies the sentimental side of Baroque faith in his Immaculate Conception (fig.

288), one of his many versions of a theme popular in his day. Once a general favorite, Murillo is now likely to arouse distaste. His compositions are satisfactory, with a predilection for the diagonal, here created by the attributes, and the angels who flutter around the Virgin. On the other hand, the drawing is weak, and the color, chiefly pinks and blues, suggests the tones of the nursery. These qualities go hand in hand with the pietistic sentiment revealed through the hands clasped on the bosom, the head thrown back, and the eyes rolling upward. Such sentiment comes close to the saccharine banalities of religious calendar art, which, one feels, has not infrequently been inspired by it. On the other hand, Murillo could be realistic, as in his genre paintings of the gamins of his native Seville. These brats, though not devoid of a sentimental appeal, are lively; their clothes are ragged, they are dirty and tanned, but they do have a vitality lacking in his sacred characters.

XVI

Painting in the Low Countries

DURING the early seventeenth century, the southern Netherlands was still under Spanish domination. Among the richest and most industrious of the Spanish possessions, Flanders remained within the fold **FLANDERS** of the Catholic Church, though it required the bloody persecutions of the Duke of Alva to stem the tide of the Reformation in those provinces. Also, an aristocracy continued to play an important role there; like the Church, it patronized the arts and so helped to form the character of Flemish painting. That character was embodied in the work of Peter Paul Rubens (1577–1640), the greatest Baroque painter of the north, if not indeed of Europe. As a child, Rubens served as page in the court of Margaret de Ligne-Aremberg, and received a schooling in court etiquette of great value to him in later life. That he knew how to behave in the presence of royalty was proved by his reception at the court of France, where Marie de Medici, then the Queen Mother, loved to watch him at work and to talk with him; and again in England, where Charles I did him the singular honor of commanding from him a self-portrait.

Rubens' training as a painter came at the hands of several minor Flemish masters. Going to Italy after he was trained, he spent eight additional years copying and studying the works of the Italian 'old masters.' This extraordinary length of what one might call a post-graduate course is worth observing by those who think they can learn to paint in a few years. On his return from Italy, Rubens opened a studio, which soon grew to the proportions of a picture factory. By 1611, two years after his return, he had two hundred painters and students active there. Apparently, too, there was a division of labor in this shop, with independent painters such as Snyders who specialized in animals, or Jan Bruegel, often called Bruegel de Velours from his interest in textiles. Rubens recognized this method in his scale of prices; so much for a canvas painted entirely by himself; somewhat less for one on which his students had carried out some of the work; and still less for products of the studio, untouched by the master. Such a system was financially successful. Rubens made two large fortunes during the course of a career of about thirty years in Flanders. The method was adapted to decorative work, and indeed that point of view dominated Rubens' style. Rich in color, which is inherited from Venice, his paintings, regardless of the subject, have vigor and a robust, sensuous, physical character.

The Descent from the Cross (fig. 289), painted not long after his return from Italy, is highly dramatic. Rubens slashes a spotlight across his scene; it follows the limp body of Christ, the diagonal sweep of the sheet on which He is being lowered, and the scarlet-robed Magdalen kneeling at the foot. The figures sway backward and forward, partly because of their roles in the incident, but more because of the Baroque love of movement. These men and women are strong and healthy, as yet without that exaggerated fleshiness that today in Rubens' paintings has repelled so many. They have a material reality that enhances their vigor.

The Rape of the Daughters of Leucippus by Castor and Pollux (fig. 290) shows this animal exuberance at its best. There is a robust grandeur in these characters who glory in their energy; such rousing love of being needs physical expression. The composition seems to be based on that of a lost painting by Leonardo da Vinci, the Battle of Anghiari, which is known through a sketch made of it by Rubens himself. But the diamond shapes have become dynamic. One point throws itself across the canvas to catch another, one movement sweeps into the next. The actors toss themselves around, possibly even more violently than the subject demands. Moreover, the forms are rendered in short quick curves; the abundant flesh of human beings and horses, the clouds above and the features of the ground below, all repeat this curving motive with variations. Such a design becomes decorative; it appeals less to the mind than to the eye. It is not so much concerned with telling a story, though it does that too, as with the sheer exuberance of these lush forms.

That sense of the decorative dominates even Rubens' portraits. Helena Fourment, Rubens' second wife (fig. 291), is sufficiently analyzed, but the painter is less eager to create a personality on canvas than to establish a decorative pattern of color and form. The full-length figure, with its rich costume, feather fan, and flowing hat, forms its own justification. Even half-length portraits, such as his Self-Portrait, Rubens paints in the same way, again with the broad-brimmed hat cocked at a rakish angle above his bearded face. These are brushed in with boldness in full color, a masculine technique, dashing and supremely confident of itself.

One measure of Rubens' greatness lies in his diversity. Religious paintings, mythologies, portraits, landscapes, and hunting scenes spring from his brush with equal readiness. His two principal followers each took up one or two fields of Rubens' activity, but could not match his scope. Jakob Jordaens (1593–1678) had much of his predecessor's vigor in his genre composition, The King Drinks. In this Flemish feast, the king of the banquet, usually the heaviest drinker, regulates the pace which his subjects must follow. The table groans, as well it may under such bounty, and if not all the gentlemen live up to standards approved by Emily Post, nevertheless good spirits overflow the picture. The gusto with which these vulgar people are recorded forms a seventeenth-century version of the zest for life seen earlier in this region in the peasant scenes of Pieter Bruegel. A sober piety of the middle and lower classes finds its way into Jordaens' religious compositions. In color, too, the warmth of Rubens' palette is continued and if anything exaggerated. It has been said that Rubens dipped his brush in blood, Jordaens in fire.

But where Jordaens accentuates his predecessor's animal spirits, Anthony van Dyck (1599–1641) concentrates on the courtly side of Rubens' nature. Van Dyck's religious canvases and his mythologies, though vigorous enough, have a restraint that deprives them of the exuberance of Rubens' paintings. He is, of course, best known for his portraiture, especially that of the court of Charles I of England. His Maria Louisa van Tassis (fig. 292) displays Van Dyck's exquisite drawing. The costumes and accessories retain something of Rubens' decorative quality, but without that passionate energy which lends power to Rubens' smallest work. Van Dyck's are society portraits at their best; as such they have neither the vitality of Rubens, nor the unsparing accuracy of Holbein. His court ladies are always seen to their best advantage. Surely not all these beauties were so attractive in person as they appear to be in Van Dyck's canvases. At its worst, this idealization may produce the vacuity of a routine society portrait, as it does in some of the beauties of the court of Charles I, even at the hands of Van Dyck himself. At its best, however, such an approach can create a sense of innate distinction, which sheds its social prestige over any room where the portraits are displayed. Very often these finely dressed men and women stand against a generalized landscape, or perhaps the pedestal and lower drums of a classic column, while a decorative sweep of drapery may fill in the canvas without too much distraction from the sitter. The color, influenced by the Venetians, is fresh, but not so intense as to violate the elegant but restrained technique that matches his characterizations. Through his creation of the society portrait, Van Dyck goes far to establish English portraiture, which reaches its finest native expression toward the close of the eighteenth century in the paintings of Reynolds and Gainsborough.

HOLLAND, the northern province of the Low Countries, during earlier times had been merely the poor sister of the Flemish school of painting. In the seventeenth century, local history molded conditions HOLLAND there, different from those in Flanders, which helped to give rise to an independent school of equal or greater eminence. For one thing, Holland had become predominantly Protestant. Therefore, religious painting was almost eliminated as subject matter for the artist, and a source of employment for him. When we reflect how large a proportion of the work of all previous painters had been religious in motive, we must realize how profound was the change when painting ceased to serve the Church. Rembrandt, to be sure, dealt with scriptural subjects, but both his choice and his treatment were inspired by a Protestant intimacy with the Bible, not by Catholic faith or dogma.

The spread of Protestantism in Holland drove the Dutch on to win their independence from Catholic Spain in the long wars that ended with the Peace of Westphalia in 1648. One might expect a school of historical painting with legitimate pride to commemorate the heroic incidents of that struggle. In reality, the Dutch were indifferent to historical painting, with very few exceptions. The burghers, who had fought that war, displayed their patriotism indirectly in their satisfaction with their own civilization. They admired painting that looked as much as possible like what it purported to represent. They were not interested in painting as a vehicle for the expression of abstract ideas, or in stories of mythological personages. What they wanted was portraiture, if one may use the term, not only of themselves, but of their lives and all matters that bore on them. They lived not in palaces but in comfortable houses, more or less of the size of our homes today, and their paintings were domestic in scale and in subject. The canvases could not be too large to hang in a room of normal size, and dealt with themes appropriate under these conditions.

Moreover, the Dutch burghers had the means to command such painting. Through her proverbial industry, her dairying, her printing, and above all her trade, Holland won prosperity for several generations. The Dutch captains sailed their craft far and wide. For a brief moment, they snatched control of the seas from England. Holland had a monopoly of the spice trade, then much more important than today, since before the days of electric refrigerators spices were not merely condiments but essential preservatives.

Thus, portraiture of individuals and of all the ramifications of their lives became the dominant production of the school. Most artists sought reputations for their handling of a given type of subject, and, willingly or otherwise, specialized in that field. That jolly soul, Frans Hals (*c.*1580–1666), was a portraitist, both of individuals and of groups. During the wars of liberation, many of the merchants had joined the civic guard to help maintain order, and the officers of these pseudo-military companies naturally formed clubs. These lived on, after the emergency had passed, as the businessmen's clubs of the time, analogous to the Lions, the Kiwanis, and the Rotary Clubs of America today. Such groups wanted records of themselves. Today, photographs of classes in school or college, of fraternity memberships, even of banquets testify to the same urge.

The Officers of St. Andrew's Company (fig. 293) is such a portrait group by Hals. Aside from the usual requirements of portraiture, this type of subject raises two special problems: first, at least reasonable importance must be allotted to each member of the group, without producing the monotony of serried rows of figures; and second, the artist must avoid if possible the posed artificiality that makes many group photographs today look stilted. In this painting, Hals masters these difficulties. He depicts the club around a table in the yard of their clubhouse. A natural light, free of theatricality, molds each member, but the trees and foliage in the background are kept dark and too vague in detail to obtrude themselves. The painter himself might have entered suddenly to utter a remark that caused many members to break off their conversations and turn toward him. Some do not. Many are seated, others stand and look back over their shoulders, while still others bend over the table, so that no rigid line of heads appears. Everyone's face has adequate space in the picture, and all are at ease, with one notable exception. One pompous individual has turned around and is posed very formally with his hands resting on his cane. Surely Hals paints him this way to enhance the characterization.

He is, of course, equally sure of himself in single portraits. The Jolly Toper (fig. 294) leans back in his chair, glass in hand, perfectly relaxed. Like most of the Hals portraits, the man seems in a right good humor. The joviality of the painter himself must be reflected in these merry individuals from whose expressions one might illustrate an encyclopedia of the laugh and smile. Such men would be out of place at court, but very much at home in a tavern or at a drinking bout. The technique is

suited to the problem. Hals indicates the necessary details, without drawing them. The pleats of his jerkin Hals sweeps in with a flowing stroke
of his brush, loaded with pigment. Such a stroke may be a quarter of an
inch wide but neither needs nor receives further definition. Like some
of the later works of Velásquez, notably Las Meninas (fig. 287), such
boldness of indication foretells the Impressionists of 1870.

Hals spent his life in Haarlem; Rembrandt van Rijn (1606–69), the
miller's son of Leyden, made the Dutch metropolis of Amsterdam the
site of his career. To him, light was the vehicle through which to reveal
his love of the variety of mankind. Where others had studied the effects
of this or that kind of illumination for its own sake, light was to Rembrandt only the means to an end. He was its master. During the ten years
of his first Amsterdam period, 1632 to 1642, he was fashionable and
prosperous. At this time, his style in painting coincided with the tastes
of his clientele. Although he produced only four group portraits, it so
happened that three of these marked milestones in his career.

Dr. Tulp's Anatomy Lesson (fig. 295), famous though it is, succeeds
only in part. The dramatic concentration of interest on the corpse, which
forms the subject of this demonstration, serves to produce a lively group
of portraits. And yet this concentration is produced at a price. Strong
light intensifies his center of interest, but to achieve this, Rembrandt
sacrificed the outer members of the group. Where the men close to the
corpse were painted in full light and color, those on the outskirts were
depicted in shade and in subdued tones, an obvious suppression of the
corners to stress the pictorial possibilities of climax. Moreover, Rembrandt
was not yet sure of himself in the matter of space. Those doctors leaning
over the cadaver for a better view are solid down to the waist, but there
seems hardly room for them to stand. Rembrandt appears to have forgotten the lower half of their persons. The artist himself attended the
lectures upon which this painting is based; it is therefore the more
curious that he should have represented the fingers of the corpse extended
almost flat on the leg when the tendons were raised by the doctor's
spatula. Rembrandt must have known that under these conditions the
fingers would flex more than in this painting. The explanation must be
that Rembrandt wanted to carry the diagonal toward the corner of his
design, there to stop the movement with the open book that cuts across
the angle. To permit the fingers to curve upward and inward would have
interrupted this movement. Rembrandt sacrificed what he must have
known to be true, to his desire for pictorial rightness.

On the whole, however, the Anatomy Lesson was sufficiently like the scene itself to satisfy his patrons. The portrait of his first wife, called Saskia in a Red Hat, reveals Rembrandt's aims at this time and the reasons for his popularity. The artist painted his subject's profile carefully and freshly. The bright carnations of Saskia's face, the richness of red velvet, feather, and embroidery, of necklaces and dress, are precise and descriptive. Each part invites inspection. Beautiful as the portait is, it can still be described as a painting of the surface, rich in color, and silhouetted against the dark background. Its objectivity, its gay tones, its accuracy, and its finish are enough to ensure a reputation to such paintings as this.

For ten years, Rembrandt was content to exploit this style, but the year 1642 marked a turning point in his career. Up till then he had been financially successful and happy. He owned a large house, accumulated a collection of works of art, and was a favorite portraitist of the wealthy Amsterdam merchants. In that year his wife, Saskia, died and he painted the so-called Night Watch (fig. 296), properly entitled Frans Banning Cocq's Company of the Civic Guard. The nickname can be explained by the personal treatment of light. Where Caravaggio had explored the possibilities of strong light contrasted with black shadows, Rembrandt made the shadows glow with reflected light. Instead of representing night illumination in this painting, Rembrandt showed the members of the club as they issued from the city gate in the morning to help welcome to Amsterdam Marie de Medici, the Queen Mother of France. Contrary to the common opinion, the painting was recognized from the first as remarkable, and was given a prominent position in the club house of the group.

Unlike most group portraitists, Rembrandt did not attempt to give nearly equal importance to each of the sixteen members of the company. To be sure, the captain in a red scarf and his lieutenant clad in a white-satin suit dominate the center, and other figures to the right and left are prominent, but the light and their positions to the rear subordinate a number of the members. That these matters improve the picture is undeniable. The composition assumes the form of an E arranged in perspective. A bar of four figures at the back forms the upright, from which three groups of members come forward, to the right, in the center, and on the left, with an opening between each of these groups.

The death of Saskia and the growth of his own pictorial sense opened the way to the introverted style of Rembrandt's later years. After 1642, he painted more and more for himself, to meet his own ideals rather than those of possible patrons. Like many another more recent artist, he separated himself from the public. A few trusted friends, such as the burgomaster Jan Six, still appreciated and helped him, but his fortunes declined.

Twenty years later, Rembrandt had a last opportunity to handle group portraiture in the Syndics of the Cloth Guild. Then he solved the problem, not only as a picture, but also as representation. Light falls evenly on the group. Each of the five men around the table is characterized, and even their servant who stands behind them can be seen as a subordinate. Their poses are natural, and yet Rembrandt produced a painting of great variety. Some of the syndics have their natural hair, others wear wigs; some are seated, others stand; and some look out of the picture, while others gaze at their companions. The painting is realistic enough to satisfy his patrons without any loss of artistic integrity.

It was in these later years that Rembrandt's sympathy for humanity reached its maximum. He turned to old age in The Rabbi (fig. 297) to develop psychological portraiture, which then absorbed his attention. This old man seems to have endured most of the experiences of life, and they have inscribed their record on his countenance. His haunting eyes try to look beyond the grave to everlasting peace. But this was not what the Dutch wanted; the successful merchants had no interest in these old men, most of whom were of no importance as the world measures importance. Nor are such portraits decorative as paintings. No vivid color and no picturesque costumes lend superficial attraction. A strong light plays over the faces as though to extract their personality and to suppress all else in the dark brown background. If one loves mankind for its own sake, in all its joys and sorrows, then these men and women become significant, for Rembrandt here explored a human soul through his own sympathy deepened by sorrow. Others may have dealt as well or better with objective appearance, but Rembrandt stands alone in his warm love of mankind.

He liked nothing better than to paint himself. A long series of these canvases, which reveal his instinct for self-dramatization, stud his whole career. He had a passion for dressing up and assuming some character, Rembrandt in a Plumed Hat, Rembrandt in a Steel Gorget, Rembrandt with Haggard Eyes, and here at the end, Rembrandt Laughing before the Bust of a Roman Emperor (fig. 298). His late method is very different from his earlier style of the Saskia. The impasto, or coating of pigment on the canvas, is heavier and its surface broken. No longer does it create the glitter of a smooth finish. Spread unevenly, it picks out the pictorially significant elements, as the heavily pigmented head emerges from the shadows behind. One likes to think that the self-dramatization, in this example, may be symbolic. By this time, Rembrandt had undergone heavier personal misfortunes than fall to the lot of most men. His fine house had long since been sold; his art collection and his studio equipment were sacrificed to his creditors; he had passed through bankruptcy; his son Titus had died; his devoted housekeeper and second wife, Hendrickje Stoffels, had died; he stood alone. But nothing could subdue that spirit. So long as he had brush and paints, or burin and copper plate, he could record the life he loved and let the rest go by.

Rembrandt was not typical of the Dutch school; he transcended it, though of course his style had many elements in common with his time. His interest in portraiture, his concern with light though of a much more personal quality, and the scale of most of his canvases fitted into the pattern of Dutch painting. But he was exceptional in the subjective analysis he substituted for the prevailing objectivity of vision, and in the range of his undertakings. Though the Dutch tended to specialize, Rembrandt did not. Portraits occupied a larger place in his output than any other single kind of subject, but he also handled still life, genre, landscape, and Biblical themes with equal aplomb, both in painting and in etching. He even experimented with the style of Indian Mughal painting, examples of which had come to Holland through the Dutch East India Company. The same diversity of subject marked his extensive production in the graphic arts. His mastery of light with its intrinsic perception of values endowed his work in this field with such distinction that Rembrandt has seldom been equaled and never surpassed.

Rembrandt alone would suffice to reflect glory on any country, but for so small a country in so short a time Holland also produced an extraordinary number of other painters. These artists had to be competent to meet the Dutch demands. Those who specialized in genre and who recorded the life of Holland have come to be known as the Little Masters. Each had his chosen field of subject matter. For example, Adriaen van Ostade deals with the lower classes, drinking or brawling in a tavern, lounging outside the door of an inn, or simply passing the time of day. Nicholas Maes, a pupil of Rembrandt, steals something of his master's light to display his servant girls peeling apples or active in other culinary and domestic pursuits. Gerhardt Terborch caters to the merchant class. His paintings show the wives and daughters of the well-to-do burghers at their music lessons, playing an informal concert, or washing their hands. The rooms in which these everyday scenes take place are not pretentious. Small, and furnished with chairs and tables, beds, stools, and clavichords, with pictures or maps on the wall, they established a familiar volume of space wherein the figures may live. The ladies dress in silks, satins, or velvets, exact in their appearance of texture. One can almost hear the satin rustle as the figures move; one can almost feel the softness of the velvet, or play with the long silky hair of the family spaniel. The paintings of Pieter de Hooch record Dutch interiors. The diffused light of indoors plays over them from some definite light source, such as a door or window. Strongest near the opening, the light fades away as the depth of the room is reached in imperceptible transitions.

Jan Vermeer of Delft (1632–75) is classed with this group because of his subject matter, the small size of most of his paintings, and his realism. The Girl with a Water Jug (fig. 299) reaches the climax of the mode of total visual effect. Every fact of vision is observed. The graded lighting models the forms with full appreciation of the existence of reflected light and reflected color. The blue dress prints a blue reflection on the pewter jug and modifies the other colors near it. The change of values and colors is accurate; a blue or yellow passage in light remains that same blue or yellow as it darkens into shade. And yet Vermeer is not photographic. He has a keen faculty for selection. The forms are simplified to retain only those elements pertinent to his purpose, that is, the visually significant parts. Though informal, the composition is nevertheless calculated. It has neither the geometry of the Renaissance nor the Baroque diagonals. Based on a series of rectangles created by the bits of wall, the pictures or maps hanging on it, and the shape of the table, Vermeer arranges these shapes to produce a design perfectly balanced and adjusted. Just enough curves vary this system to avert any touch of rigidity; the curves of the figure, or of the water pitcher serve as a foil for the straight lines of the rectangles.

Moreover, Vermeer's interpretation of his subject differs from that of the other Little Masters. None of them has the same intimacy of vision. He confines himself as a rule to only one or two figures, and they are so absorbed in what they are doing that they seem oblivious of any spectator. The ladies painted by Terborch are on their best behavior; they conduct themselves with full consciousness that others are watching them. The girls of Vermeer are too engrossed for that. Through that very absorption they seem to be accorded more respect, their privacy is unviolated. They are no mere decorative adjuncts around the house, attractive enough, but a useless luxury; Vermeer's women are the household, and through their occupations lend domesticity to the hearth.

If the Dutch are well enough satisfied with their society to want it painted, they are also proud of their country, its gardens and meadows, its canals and harbors. Therefore, a group of landscape painters is inevitable. Jakob van Ruysdael (1628–82) in The Mill (fig. 300) depicts an intimate bit of Holland. The scene with its water and its windmill serves as a symbol of his country. In this alluvial land, the sky is bound to bulk large in any normal view, and in Dutch landscapes it may occupy two thirds or more of the canvas. Billowing clouds roll in from the North Sea, and cast fleeting shadows on the ground. Certain devices are so regular that they may be called conventions. A shadow darkens the foreground, while the middle distance and the background are sunny. In this example, jetties and marsh grass lower the foreground values, but light focuses on the mill and the water. Possibly several planes of light and shade may succeed one another. In either case the result is to accent depth and space, and thereby to draw the eye from the foreground, with its large-scale detail, into the distance. Even in the paintings of the sea, one can often find this device of the dark foreground, where it is difficult to explain it on rational grounds. In color, though the range is considerable, the prevailing tone is apt to be brownish. The love of warm color, so common in the Baroque, impels these painters to record the shadows as brownish, the trunks of the trees in brown, and even the foliage as affected by the same tone. There is every reason why the artist should do this. Essentially he is painting a picture, not creating a landscape or even recording one, and if the adoption of a specific tonality aids in pictorial creation, then it belongs in his painting despite any conventional character it may have. In spite of these conventions, however, Ruysdael's picture looks like a particular scene. Though doubtless painted in the studio, not in the open, The Mill is not an abstract conception of landscape. The Dutch prefer the specific and therefore identifiable scene, and though the painting may symbolize the country, it still remains a view of a particular mill in the surroundings that building probably had.

Ruysdael painted landscape for its own sake, largely devoid of people and animals; Aelbert Cuyp, on the other hand, dealt with landscape and cattle. The lush meadows of Holland pastured sleek cattle, which contributed to the prosperity of Holland and which were portrayed with the same objectivity and with the same grasp of pictorial possibilities that one finds in the pure landscape painters or in the Little Masters. Others painted the sea and shipping, or buildings. Nowhere does the technical virtuosity of the seventeenth century find more vivid illustration than in the flower compositions of Jan van Huysum and others. These bouquets, convincing in themselves, are filled with naturalistic detail. Points of light glitter in crystal drops of water on the leaves or petals, while bees and butterflies pursue their activities among the blossoms. Still other artists specialized in piles of vegetables on kitchen tables, combined with culinary implements, with game, or poultry. Indeed, no facet of Dutch life escaped the attention of these painters. The school as a whole gives a picture of a civilization in all its aspects, a record as complete as that found in the reliefs and paintings of the Egyptian tombs, but even more vivid in that it is more realistic.

XVII

The Seventeenth Century in France and England

WHILE Dutch painting stemmed from its domestic background, its merchant patronage, and its democratic way of life, the art of France revealed the pre-eminence of the court and the growth of absolutism.

FRANCE   However, that concentration of power did not arise overnight. After the death of Henry II in 1559, his three young sons, who succeeded each other on the throne, were not strong enough to unite the country when Protestantism, at that time a disruptive force, was injected into the situation. The dismal story of the wars of religion and the massacre of St. Bartholomew's Day in 1572 need not be told here. Suffice it to say that these troubles exhausted France and brought the Renaissance to an end in that country. The civil wars were finally healed by Henry IV, Henry of Navarre, who began to recruit the resources of France and thereby laid the foundation on which Louis XIV in the last half of the seventeenth century could build his tremendous undertakings.

The architecture of Henry IV in its combination of brick and stone suggests the poverty of the country. The houses lining the Place des Vosges in Paris show that the style can be restrained, though it is affected by the early Baroque of Italy through the influence of Marie de Medici, the Queen of Henry IV. The successive French styles of the sixteenth, seventeenth, and eighteenth centuries are named from the kings, but do not coincide with them in date. Thus, the Luxembourg Palace in Paris, built 1615–20 for Marie de Medici after Henry's assassination in 1610, is one of the largest examples of the style of Henry IV. The queen directed her architect, Salomon de Brosse, to model the building on the newer parts of the Pitti Palace in Florence, which she had known in her childhood and drawings of which she had sent up from Italy. The rusticated columns, composed of alternate square and cylindrical blocks, come from that source. But De Brosse was a Frenchman, conscious of French tradition. Consequently, the Luxembourg retains the rhythmical pavilion and link scheme, with a central motive and wings that protrude from the plane of the façade and have their own semi-independent roofs. In plan, though the enclosed court still remains, one side has been lowered to a single story, and thus the palace is a more open design.

Under Louis XIII, the architectural pendulum swung in the direction of sophistication, restraint, and even classicism to a minor extent. The Pavillon de l'Horloge in the Louvre, next to Lescot's wing, was designed by Jacques LeMercier, 1624–30. Quieter than the work of De Brosse, it lacks the elegance of the very French buildings of François Mansart, not to be confused with his famous nephew of the following reign, Jules Hardouin Mansart. The Château of Maisons-Laffitte of 1642–51 testifies to Mansart's exquisite sense of proportion and composition. His style leads on into that of Louis XIV. At the same time, from the brush of Philippe de Champaigne flowed a stream of competent and somewhat Flemish portraits in a stately manner, well suited to such eminent personages as Cardinal Richelieu.

But the spirit of the century flowered under the personal rule of Louis XIV. This monarch ascended the throne as an infant in 1643, assumed personal command of the state in 1660, and fashioned French civilization in his own image until his death in 1715. His life covers the classic period of French art. The word classic is ambiguous; it may refer to productions that have stood the test of time, regardless of their style, as in the phrase the classics of literature; it may indicate the influence of antiquity; or it may describe a quality of restraint, an emphasis on the intellectual as contrasted to the emotional, and a prevailing control or reserve. As applied to the age of Louis XIV, it has all these meanings. This is the time of the great classic drama of Racine. That drama is, to some extent, modeled on the ancients, though the latter might not recognize the fact. Much of the subject matter of the painters and sculptors is borrowed from Rome. In art, the academic point of view with its respect for codified rules dominates. At their best, these productions are superb, their effects, and the means whereby these effects are realized, highly calculated and formal. Personal emotion yields to the demand for order and system, to regularization, which called into existence in 1648 the Academy of Painters and Sculptors under the royal protection, to match the Academy of Letters established earlier. But the arts do not submit themselves readily to such standardization; it tends to stifle originality and vitality, and if it adds in other directions, such as concentration and organization, it is questionable whether the gain compensates for the loss. However, to the people of that time, there could be no question that formality and order outweighed all other considerations.

The two greatest painters of France in the seventeenth century preferred to spend most of their lives in Italy. They matured before the Academy had gained the power it was to enjoy under Le Brun. Nevertheless, the spirit of the age was strong upon them. Nicolas Poussin (1594–1665) borrowed from Raphael, from Titian, and from the Carracci and their school, but a French logic and clarity of mind illuminate all he does. The Kingdom of Flora (fig. 301) draws its subject from classic mythology, but its prevailing quality is that of organization, thought out in terms of drawing. These are no lusty Olympian figures comparable to Titian's Bacchus and Ariadne; they are too sober to survive the hearty existence of Olympus. Instead, the spirit is restrained and ordered until as perfect an adjustment of the several parts as possible is achieved.

Classic, too, in subject is Et in Arcadia Ego (fig. 302), wherein four bucolic figures ponder the cryptic inscription on the tomb, which gives its title to the painting. Some of the actors hark back to antiquity, such as the woman on the right with her Greek profile, or the kneeling shepherd with his heavy curly beard. They are types, not individuals; they have that same abstraction one finds in the characters of Racine's dramas. Their actions, unimportant as movement, form part of the larger organization of the painting, or tie in with the generalized landscape. Nothing of the Baroque abandon disturbs the equilibrium of this composition in three-dimensional space. The arm of the kneeling shepherd tracing out the inscription carries the eye across to the younger man opposite, whose staff, in turn, parallels the leg of the first figure. The tree trunk behind continues the axis of the woman's figure, as the tree in the distance on the left prolongs the movement begun by the leg of the standing man on that side. It is, indeed, possible to discover some compositional and pictorial purpose in every part of this spatial design. A shape, so to speak, is presented on the canvas. From that, everything else follows inevitably, just as in the French classic drama a situation is stated and its consequences rigorously pursued to a conclusion. So organized a structure has something analytical in its cold intellectuality. It does not appeal to the emotions but to the mind. It offers no charm to the eye, no seduction of color, however much the latter may abet the structure of the design. Nothing unexpected can take place in this painting, which pursues its goal with the infallibility of a mathematical proposition. Whether such adherence to the demands of picture construction can command popular love and admiration or not, it has an abundance to offer to the painter. Hence, Poussin has been exceptionally influential. Artists have recognized his demonstrations of their own problems, and among the French he has found wide appreciation because of the lucidity of his mind, his feeling for logic and for abstract types.

Claude Gellée (1600–1682), called Claude Lorrain, had a wider vogue in England. As compared with Poussin, his mind is less dominant over his emotions. The structure of the picture, therefore, is not so fully developed. On the other hand, as his drawings testify, Claude had a poetic love of nature, which affected even his paintings. The Marriage of Isaac and Rebecca (fig. 303) does not attempt to be natural, although it is based on a profound study of tree forms. In it, two seventeenth-century conventions of landscape painting, the dark foreground leading out to the lighted middle distance, and the brownish tonality, are present, as they were in Holland. But unlike the Dutch landscape, this does not represent any particular scene. Claude is painting a landscape in the abstract, a formal conception of nature analogous in its sphere to the formality of Versailles. These wooded scenes leave an impression of tidiness, as though the ground keepers had just been through them to gather any dead branches and sweep up all the fallen leaves. Nature has had its face lifted to give it the order demanded by the spirit of the times. Figures are incidental to such designs and were often added by another hand, as though Claude felt so little interest in them that he himself could not bother to paint them. The stateliness of these landscapes derives much of its impressiveness from the feeling for deep space. Frequently, as here, the tree masses arrange themselves into a spiral, the largest and nearest in one corner, then sweeping across the dark foreground to the more distant trees on the other side, which, well behind the picture plane, lead the eye out to the background. All this is suffused with a glow of light, golden and warm, playing over trees, grass, and water from a sun that may often be seen in the sky just above the horizon. These serene creations, formal and ordered as they are, yet have a fine poetic quality.

The reign of Louis XIV found at least as full an expression of its love of order in architecture as it did in landscape painting, and a still greater opportunity to display its magnificence. Bernini's trip to Paris to consult on the design of the Louvre in 1665 proved abortive so far as that building was concerned. His scheme called for a Roman Baroque palace, which was not only foreign to the French spirit, but would have required the destruction of the already existing parts of the Louvre. Therefore, when he had returned to Italy, his design was shelved, and that of Claude Perrault preferred (fig. 304). The new scheme suited the taste of the day. Magnificent in scale, it had just the pomp and brilliance expected by the young monarch. Perrault's design can be described as a combination of French, Italian Baroque, and Roman classic elements, a mixture typical of its time. These three strains interweave with now one and now another predominant. A plain ground floor, whose solid walls are pierced by windows crowned with segmental arches, provides just the strong base needed by the richer treatment above. The colonnade in the Corinthian order is proportioned with classic correctness, a file of paired columns reflecting dignity or even majesty on the design. These paired columns in front of a gallery create a robust pattern of light and shade, and have something of the Baroque about them, while the cartouches with the reversed initials of the monarch surrounded by floral bands are unmistakably of that style. Some break in the French tradition occurs in the abandonment of the visible roof, which the earlier part of the century, like the French Renaissance, had maintained. The roof is now constructed with such a low pitch that in any normal view it is hidden behind the balustrade. And yet though the elements are borrowed, the colonnade of the Louvre is conceivable nowhere but in France. Its fundamental scheme adheres to French tradition; accented features at the center and at either end advance forward of the simpler mass of the colonnade as pavilions, and while they resemble the colonnade in design enough to compose with it, at the same time they differ from it enough to be distinct and articulate. The end pavilions, for instance, retain the order but not the gallery behind it, and the central accent is crowned by a pediment. The rhythmic disposition descends from the French châteaux in the style of Francis I, such as Chambord (fig. 263), which also has corner accents and a central motive, and beyond that in turn stems ultimately from the medieval castle.

The largest project of the reign was the Palace at Versailles. Louis XIV selected the site, on which a small hunting lodge already existed, partly because of the barren countryside, so that when his new work was completed it might be said that its splendor was his own creation, with a minimum of help from nature. To appreciate Versailles, one must try to understand the point of view of the seventeenth century, and of Louis XIV in particular. His phrase, *L'état, c'est moi,* succinctly stated his conception of France. His country might be compared to a pyramid, the firm base provided by the numerous lower classes, and each successive stratum of society, smaller in number, built up to the king at the summit. Never had such concentration of power been known in western Europe. If the monarch could not make all of the decisions of state himself, he could review them, and cancel or alter enough of them to keep control over affairs in his own hands. Granted his identification of himself with France, it followed that anything done to display his own magnificence shed glory on the country.

Unless we understand this point of view, Versailles must seem a monument to the unbounded egotism of the monarch. This vast design focuses on the bedchamber of His Majesty. In front, an avenue from Paris marks the axis of the palace, while other roads converge at balancing angles on the open Place d'Armes. Between these arrow-like avenues are the stables. A succession of axial courts, each smaller than its predecessor, forces the attention inward to the three windows that light the royal bedchamber. This insistence on the axis continues behind the palace between pairs of lagoons and along a canal, through formal gardens and woods designed by Le Nôtre, patterns of topiary work, sculpture, fountains, and straight paths leading to statues, more fountains, or garden pavilions, which close each vista through the woods.

The palace itself (fig. 305) is also symmetrical. Its state apartments in the central block provide an appropriate background for the grandeur of the Sun King, as his courtiers called Louis XIV. The principal access leads up a stairhall, monumental in its proportions and resplendent in polished marble, through one chamber after another, each more magnificent than the last, to the garden front. There only three rooms exist, the small Salon de la Guerre and Salon de la Paix at the ends, and the huge Galerie des Glaces (fig. 306) or Hall of Mirrors between them. This last chamber is the setting for state functions. Designed by Jules Hardouin Mansart, who built or remodeled much of the palace, and decorated in large part by Le Brun, the director of the Academy, it forms the epitome of the reign. Its mirrors reflect the arched windows opposite. A pilaster order, in which a Gallic cock modifies the normal Corinthian capital, punctuates walls enriched with marbles, gilding, and Baroque decorations, and supports a barrel vault whose surface is covered with gilded stucco and paintings of a warm brownish tonality. Individually, the paintings and the sculpture are not masterpieces, but as a whole they fulfil their function of completing the sumptuousness of the hall.

Nor is the furniture less ornate. Baroque scrolls form the arms or legs of upholstered chairs, in addition to providing a primary decorative theme. The shell motive, masks of human or animal heads, and acanthus leaves encrust beds, chairs, tables, cabinets, and chests of drawers. Inlaid designs of veined wood had developed in the Italian Renaissance; under Louis XIV, Boulle gives his name to a type of inlay or marquetry wherein tortoise shell and ormolu are employed. The latter is a composition of gold, mercury, and copper. Such opulent materials are capped by the solid silver furniture with which the Sun King saw fit to equip his halls of state.

To see Versailles properly requires an effort of the imagination. One generally sees it in company with a motley group of tourists in charge of some broken-down pensioner, who is eager to repeat his patter as quickly as possible. But one should try to envision Versailles as the setting for a court. Then, with the costumes, gorgeous in lace, silk, and velvet, and with powdered wigs and red-heeled shoes, lighted from thousands of candles redoubled in the mirrors, with hundreds of lackeys bustling about, and perhaps with incidental music from Lully's orchestra, the buzz of conversation hushed at the announcement that His Majesty is about to make his state entrance — in these circumstances, Versailles and its king must have been impressive indeed to the ministers of foreign states. What a tale they would take home of the power and glory of France! Such a life may be the last thing that we should wish, but such a life is the cause of Versailles.

In his desire to make his court splendid, Louis XIV drew the upper nobility into dependence upon himself, and forced it to attend his every act from the *lever du roi* to the *coucher du roi*. When one perceives the extent of Versailles as seen from the gardens (fig. 307), its dimensions are inexplicable unless one bears in mind that it is not a residence, even of a king, but the seat of the government of France. At its prime, Versailles housed ten thousand people in the palace. Men preferred to leave their own spacious estates to live in an attic bedroom in Versailles, because only by attendance in person could they obtain the royal favors. The garden façade of the building is, if anything, richer than the entrance front. Rustication marks each course of stone in the plain ground floor. The principal floor gains prominence by the application of the orders to it in pilaster form, but with three groups of free-standing columns, in the center, and near the ends. A decorative attic story tops the design. The roof is not visible, but Baroque accents enrich the skyline. The smaller of these accents are urns placed wherever the pilasters below them are paired; the larger, which repeat the corners of the colonnades, are trophies, piles of armor, cannon, shields, and other weapons heaped together and carved in stone; together, the urns and trophies recall in the silhouette of the building the rhythm its main design creates. This rhythm, fainter than at the Louvre, implies the fading of that traditional motive in French design.

The triple strains of classic, Baroque, and French occur also in the sculpture and painting of the reign. Pierre Puget's (1620–94) Milo of Croton (fig. 308) was a commission from the state. With academic formality, Puget creates a parallelogram whose sides are the torso and the tree trunk, the arm with its fingers caught in the cleft stump, and the legs, lines echoed in the lion and the bit of drapery that falls between the legs of Milo to the ground. A Baroque openness may be detected in this void in the center, in the movement of the figure turning its head around, and in the pictorial details that complete the group. And yet the effect is neither more nor less Baroque than is the effect of the Louvre. It is more controlled than the Baroque; it has more of the academic regard for rule; and in some respects, especially its anatomical treatment, its proportions, and its muscularity, it may recall the Hellenistic statue, the Farnese Hercules.

Puget preferred to work in Genoa or Toulon to Paris. Antoine Coysevox (1640–1720), on the other hand, spent most of his career in Paris and Versailles. His portrait of Le Brun (fig. 309) betrays obvious similarities to Bernini. The drapery, Baroque in its movement and in its undercut pattern of light and shade, contrasts in texture with the curls of the flowing wig. However, the movement is not as pronounced, the features not as animated as in the works of Bernini. Details are realistic, but the total effect is academic. Much more so, however, are Coysevox's decorative works at Versailles, such as the oval relief of Louis XIV in Triumph in the Salon de la Guerre. So powerful an organization as the Academy under royal control could dictate the kind of design in sculpture that the reign demanded.

Charles Le Brun (1619–90), as the leader of the Academy and dictator of design, in many ways vividly reflects the reign. His vast canvases are difficult to appreciate today, because of the disappearance of and lack of sympathy with the life they were painted to adorn. Gigantic in size, they need a palace as a setting. The subject of his Alexander Entering Babylon is superficially classic, but is intended to compliment Louis XIV, who impersonates Alexander riding in triumph. Great columns, elephants, burly men carrying loot compose a design no classic artist would have recognized. The lavishness of this design is artificial; the effect has a heavy-handed grandiosity, which the rich browns do little to relieve.

The state portraiture of Hyacinthe Rigaud, late in the reign, is as formal as the official art of Coysevox. Less staid than paintings by Philippe de Champaigne, his rendering of Louis XIV is more a record of an official position than of an individual. The king appears in his robes of state as he might have at some function; behind him is a sweep of curtain, the base of a column, and all the accoutrements common in official portraiture. These decorative accessories, the drapery and the column, originate in Venetian paintings of the time of Titian, and become stereotyped in these later examples. Vitality and individualism are less important here than pomp and circumstance.

WHILE these developments were taking place in France, England produced but little sculpture and painting. During the first half of the seventeenth century, Van Dyck painted portraits for the court of Charles I. During the Protectorate and after the Restoration, Sir Peter Lely and later Sir Godfrey Kneller, both German by birth and both trained in the Low Countries, continued the externals of Van Dyck's style, but without his strength. Some little-known native painters, such as Michael Wright, were more vigorous.

ENGLAND

In architecture, however, the century produced two of the greatest figures in the history of that art in England. The first of them, Inigo Jones, was equally eminent in stage design; he is credited with the development of the proscenium arch and of movable scenery, and his sets for Ben Jonson's masques were so ingenious as to steal attention from the masques themselves. He developed an enthusiasm for Palladio, which induced him to take at least one and perhaps two trips to Italy, and while there to spend his time chiefly in Vicenza, Venice, and Verona, where might be seen the works of his idol. When, in 1619, he designed the Banqueting House in Whitehall in London (fig. 310), he composed it in an academic and Palladian vein. This admirably proportioned building has no element that cannot be duplicated in one of Palladio's palaces. The plain basement supports two floors, which are treated with superposed orders of pilasters at the sides and of engaged columns in the center. The entablature of each order breaks forward, above every pilaster and column. A band of garlands of fruit and flowers enriches the second floor at the level of the Corinthian capitals. Triangular and segmental pediments alternate over the windows. A balustrade crowns the rusticated wall. These features reinforce the distinguished proportions, which really account for the success of the building. To say that this design is Italianate in origin is not to deny that it is also English, just as to recognize the Italianism of the Luxembourg Palace need not blind us to the French character of that structure.

To exaggerate the historical importance of the Banqueting House is impossible. The Elizabethan and Jacobean styles that had preceded it displayed a license in handling classic detail inspired through Flemish and German sources. Few Englishmen had ever had an opportunity to see what Italian architecture was really like. Its sophistication and its sense of order were diametrically opposite to the lawlessness of the Jacobean, and its Palladian purity to the florid ornament of its predecessor. Thus the Banqueting House was a revolution in English architecture that brought the island more or less up to date and in step with continental developments. Though its style would have been current in the last part of the sixteenth century in Italy instead of the early seventeenth century, it provided a closer approximation to the developments on the Continent than anything England had produced since the Middle Ages, or at most since the reign of Henry VIII.

The academic style of Inigo Jones had hardly got well launched when England found herself in the whirlpool of the Great Rebellion. Its disturbances particularly affected the cavalier classes, among which were most of Jones's patrons, and so minimized the opportunities for the spread of his style. When architecture revived with the Restoration in 1660, it assumed a Baroque quality in the work of Sir Christopher Wren. This remarkable astronomer, mathematician, and charter member of the Royal Society had much of the universality that appeared earlier in Leonardo da Vinci; his discoveries and interests ranged from new methods of sailing and better types of street pavements to improved forms of embroidery and a device for writing double. Wren always had an amateur interest in architecture, but after the Restoration his appointment to the committee in charge of old St. Paul's Cathedral in London led him to a closer observation and study of building problems.

The great fire of London in 1665 burned for a week and destroyed much of the medieval city. This offered Wren an unparalleled opportunity. First, he drew up a plan for rebuilding the city, one of several that were submitted. His plan, however, displayed a foresight into the problems of civic design far in advance of his day. Instead of imposing a geometrical pattern of streets, as did the other plans, Wren attacked the problem in terms of traffic routes, and planned residential streets thirty feet in width, business streets of sixty feet, and thoroughfares ninety feet wide, so disposed that passage through the city and to its principal centers would be facilitated to the utmost. Furthermore, at the intersection of avenues and wherever else a vista might be created, Wren reserved sites for public buildings, usually parish churches, while the two foci of the city, St. Paul's and the Royal Exchange, had splendid approaches to them. Modern city planners would not design as Wren did, but had his plan been carried out, it would without question have prevented many of the traffic jams that hamper London today. But although his scheme would have given to every landowner as much ground as he had before, and a site at least as desirable because of its accessibility, the lots could not in all cases be identical with the pre-fire holdings. The conservatism of the English was not to be overcome, and the city was rebuilt on its old lines.

Among the losses caused by the fire were many parish churches of London. As Surveyor General to the King, it was Wren's task and privilege to redesign them. Many of the old sites had been irregular, but that merely challenged Wren's ingenuity. The spirit of his time called for axial designs, and these Wren provided; in each instance, he adapted a regular plan to the limitations of the site with little sacrifice of available space. The variety in plan and elevation is amazing. Some of the churches are domed, others barrel vaulted, while still others are arranged with flat ceilings, or any conceivable combination of these and other forms, and with an equal variety in the type and arrangement of the supports. By this time, pews had come into general use, but since their seating capacity was small in proportion to the space they occupied, they prompted the addition of galleries to supplement the accommodation of the church. Although the altar is apt to remain in the center of the chancel and the pulpit to one side, the decline in emphasis on the service of Holy Communion allows a shallow chancel to replace the deep sanctuary of medieval times.

The towers and steeples of these buildings are often the only parts of the exterior visible from the street; the rest is hidden behind other buildings. The same fertility of imagination distinguishes these features in the Wren churches that marks his interiors. The steeple of St. Mary-le-Bow (fig. 311) in 1680 shows Wren's appreciation of the value of silhouette. A tower must be seen against the sky; therefore, the outline is its most telling feature. The tower is usually square in plan and severe in masonry; its upper story, where the bells are hung, is enriched by arches, columns, or in this instance, pilasters. The lowest stage of the steeple in St. Mary-le-Bow is circular, with a ring of free-standing columns. Baroque scrolls and urns soften the transition from the square to the circular form. Above that, more scrolls lead to a smaller colonnaded story, which supports a pyramid, a frequent conclusion of these steeples. St. Mary-le-Bow is exceptionally rich, but the steeple is only one of many Wren designs.

St. Paul's Cathedral, begun in 1675, is his masterpiece. Wren would have preferred a church of the central type, his model for which still exists, but English tradition called for length. The final arrangement combines the length, the western transepts, and the choir of the English medieval plan, with a system at the crossing suggested by the Sorbonne in Paris and other sources. Shallow transepts separate the nave and choir and create a crossing, which is covered by the great dome. In reality, the external dome is built of wood and lead, and expresses the existence of a much lower dome of masonry embedded within the drum. The visible dome dominates the exterior (fig. 312), its curve exposed and supported on the continuous colonnade of the drum. This suggests uninterrupted support and the buttressing needed by the domical form. The façade, influenced by the east front of the Louvre, has two stories of paired columns, the lower story somewhat wider, to indicate the presence of aisles as well as nave, whereas the upper colonnade corresponds to the span of the nave alone. Flanking towers enframe the dome as one looks up Fleet Street; like the steeples of Wren's parish churches, their free design is fraught with Baroque license in the treatment of the orders to provide the requisite interest in silhouette. Wren's towers and steeples are influenced by Italian towers of the High Baroque, familiar to him through publications, but the frequency with which they occur must be traced to the English tradition of tower building.

By comparison with St. Peter's, St. Paul's is more structural in the disposition of the dome and drum. In scale, St. Paul's, though smaller, is infinitely superior. On both the interior and the exterior, Wren incorporates small features to betray the size of his building, where the lack of these elements, human in scale, renders ineffectual the vastness of the papal monument. St. Paul's is unique in that it is the only one of the major cathedrals in western Europe to be carried out in its entirety by the man who had designed it. The final stone in the lantern atop the dome was set in place in Wren's presence by his son in 1710. All the other great churches took centuries to build, and involved the designs of several architects. What could be more appropriate, then, that when Wren died in 1723 his bones should be laid within the church that he had conceived? Above them is a simple inscription ending with the words, *Si monumentum requiris, circumspice,* 'If you seek a monument, look around you.'

XVIII

The Eighteenth Century — Rococo and Georgian Art

WHEN Louis XIV assumed personal control of France, his spirit was in accord with that of his day, but the old monarch lived too long. By 1715, the ideals and interests of France were changing beneath the surface. The repression of this new spirit by Louis XIV, under the influence of Madame de Maintenon during the closing years of his reign, made the reaction the more violent when he was succeeded by his grandson, Louis XV. The new century revolted against formality and heaviness in all matters. Whenever possible, society escaped from Versailles to seek diversion in smaller but elegant private mansions in Paris.

FRANCE

If the Hall of Mirrors symbolized the seventeenth century, the salon and the boudoir were characteristic of the early eighteenth century. In these smaller rooms, groups became more intimate, and their types of entertainment less pretentious. No age has ever been so influenced, not to say shaped, by woman as the age of Louis XV. She expected delicacy and politeness; the arts of the drawing room, sprightly conversation, and the *mot juste* met with her approval; etiquette dictated every word and action. She was the supreme arbiter of conduct, the dictator of society. Such a life was artificial. Indeed, in many ways pretense lay at the core of the times, and yet the simplicity of nature, as then conceived, had infinite charm. Later in the century, the affectation of society evoked a nostalgia for the natural man, who, free from the evils of society, pursued a noble and simple existence. But no group that had grown up in the atmosphere of Versailles could possibly become natural, as we understand the term.

The age of Louis XV rebelled against the rules and order of the seventeenth century. People craved pleasure, often frivolous in character; they wanted to be gay. They demanded freedom and license in art as well as in life, and to a considerable extent achieved them. The Italian comedy, which because of its salacious character had been banished during the closing years of the reign of Louis XIV, came trooping back into France. Amateur theatricals, pageants, and elaborate tableaux afforded an outlet to the craving for amusement that pervaded the age. And yet, however licentious the age might be, it was never coarse; its very immorality had an elegance about it.

Toward the end of the century, the freedom of the reign of Louis XV provoked its own reaction. Pleasure had sated society and immorality in itself had ceased to satisfy. Skepticism and rationalism ridiculed certain aspects of French life. The pendulum, which had swung to liberty, returned to sobriety. The style of Louis XVI began before his accession to the throne in 1775; it preserved the elegance of the earlier period, but the expression was better controlled, the effect quieter, as though the serious times of the French Revolution were casting their shadow before them.

In architecture, the classic strain of Louis XIV faded away. The boldness of the Baroque melted into the playful lightness of the Rococo. The full effect of this new manner was felt only on the interiors, at least in France. To be sure, in their enthusiasm for all things French, the Germans tortured the exteriors of their buildings, like the Zwinger at Dresden, with Rococo details, which had been devised for the salon and the boudoir; but in its native country the style is less marked externally. Though not abandoned, the orders lose their prominence, windows are apt to have segmental tops, and the whole project is generally smaller in scale. The Salon de la Princesse in the Hôtel de Soubise in Paris (fig. 313), designed by Boffrand about 1740, is characteristic of its time. A small room supplants the immense halls of Louis XIV. Such a chamber provides at once a setting for and an expression of sophisticated life and witty conversation. The orders have vanished; in their stead, delicate panels, whose upper and lower edges bend in free reversed curves, line the walls. The panels may be left in the natural surface of the wood, but more often they are painted white and the exquisite moldings gilded. The language of classic architecture is avoided, to such an extent that in extreme cases the panels become asymmetrical. In such instances, a panel in one part of a room may balance one in another part. Even the walls and ceilings of the rooms are no longer conceived as separate units; the upper moldings of the panels so interweave with the decoration of the ceiling that one can no longer say where the wall ends and the ceiling begins. This is especially true when the plane of the wall curves into that of the ceiling, as it does in this example. Such designs do not pretend to monumentality, or often to more than interior decoration, but they do have charm and delicacy partly through the very license of their design.

Asymmetry, lightness, and a rejection of classic motives characterize the design of Rococo furniture under Louis XV. The straight line almost vanishes as the legs of tables and chairs bend in sinuous curves, playful at the expense of sound construction, while the fronts of writing tables, commodes, and cabinets bulge to echo in their shapes the slender flowing scrolls of the wall and ceiling decorations. Tapestried upholstery, lacquer, marquetry, ormolu, and even porcelain inserts may add their beauties to designs that pushed to the point of virtuosity the master craftsmen of this time, whose skill, if not whose taste, has never been surpassed.

Just after the middle of the century, 1762–8, the Petit Trianon at Versailles (fig. 314) rejected that freedom and turned in the direction of classicism. A cornice or pediment crowns rectangular windows. The orders regain popularity, but they do not attempt the pomp of the preceding century. The Petit Trianon, by the architect Jacques Ange Gabriel, has such beauty of proportion that it deserves a place among the greatest masterpieces of architecture, small as it is. The relation of height to width, of sides to center, of solids to voids comes close to perfection. These beauties are reinforced by the exquisite delicacy of all detail. Without sacrificing any of the lightness of the Rococo, Gabriel introduced an element of control that gives to each smallest part its due place without overemphasis anywhere. It is no accident that in the days when architecture was taught, in part, by making measured drawings of the great monuments of the past, the Petit Trianon was almost invariably one of those selected for instruction.

Still later, and still more sober, is the church of Ste. Geneviève, in Paris, called the Panthéon (fig. 315), executed by Soufflot between 1764 and 1790. Just before the French Revolution, some members of French society turned their attention to England with enthusiasm; its political forms, its organization of society, its gardens, and its art all received the approval of an influential part of the French public. Hence, the dome of the Panthéon is inspired by the dome of St. Paul's. The ring of columns, which forms its drum, is based on Wren's masterpiece.

Even more important is the increase of classic influence. Remarkable activity in archaeology characterizes the second half of the eighteenth century, such as the excavation of the buried cities of Pompeii and Herculaneum, and the publication of scientific drawings of Roman and even of Greek monuments, though the latter do not begin to bear fruit until the next century. Under this influence, Soufflot designed the portico of

the Panthéon in the Corinthian order with a full entablature and pediment, as though it were the front of a classic temple. The archaeology of
this colonnade is not only purer than the Baroque — one might expect
that — but it is also much more classic than the Renaissance. When Roman
art was first revived, such artists as Brunelleschi permitted themselves
great freedom, partly through ignorance and partly through the vitality
of their period. Even buildings of the High Renaissance are not copies of
any Roman, still less Greek, edifice. The portico of the Panthéon, however, leads on to the still more archaeological adaptations of the early
nineteenth century. Its unbroken walls contribute substantially to this
sense of an increased classicism. As it was originally designed, Soufflot
had intended to have tall windows in those walls, but the amateur archaeologist, Quatremère de Quincy, forced his hand and made the building measure up to a standard of correctness more than it might otherwise
have done.

The increased sobriety of the age of Louis XVI makes itself felt in furniture design too. Straight lines reappear in the legs of tables and chairs,
in the paneling of walls, and in the sides of commodes and desks. The
lightness of the Rococo remains without its asymmetry and its extravagance. The decorative vocabulary in furniture is simpler and acquires
some restraint, to which fluting and other classic motives contribute.

The painting of the Fêtes Galantes corresponds to the Rococo in architecture. Antoine Watteau (1684–1721) is the most nearly perfect, if
not the most characteristic, painter of his age. The Embarkation for
Cythera (fig. 316) is the antithesis of the vast canvases of Le Brun. Painted
on a small scale, it is intended for a small and intimate room. The exquisite figures are hardly a foot high, and in many of his paintings are
still smaller. Their gay costumes are clear and fresh, sparkling like jewels
with flashes of green, blue, yellow, and lavender in place of the somber
browns of the previous reign. In spirit, too, the painting reveals the aristocratic society of its day. Here is no attempt to glorify the state, or to
compliment its ruler. These ladies and gentlemen of the court stroll
through a world of Watteau's imagination to Cythera, the enchanted isle of
love. A delicate undercurrent of eroticism colors the motive, but is always
refined. Moreover, this scene has no classic background. The characters
choose to go out of doors, but find themselves in a park. Their silks and
satins bespeak the sophistication of their lives; these dainty courtiers
transfer their activities for the moment from the salon to a well-groomed
wilderness, or perhaps a stage set. After all, the life they lead is itself

artificial, and though they, or their successors like Jean Jacques Rousseau, may talk of their love for nature and the natural man, it is at most a lip loyalty, a mannerism and a pose.

There is a tinge of melancholy beneath the frivolity of the scene, but that is Watteau's personal contribution, not present in other painters of his day. Gilles (fig. 317) is a character from the Italian comedy, its other players behind him. He is dressed as a clown, but Watteau's painting belies the comic costume. This clown, like *He Who Got Slapped*, is pathetic. Perhaps the painter had a premonition of his early death. In any case, the Gilles is exceptional in its scale, almost life size, and most instructive in that it demonstrates Watteau's ability to develop plastic forms at that size, and to conceive a figure who might serve as a monument to his own nostalgic spirit.

François Boucher (1703–70), the favorite painter of Madame du Pompadour, is more typical of the Rococo in that he is less serious. The Vulcan Presenting to Venus the Arms of Aeneas (fig. 318) has none of Watteau's sparkle, but then Watteau is one of the world's master draftsmen, with a lightness of touch only the best can equal. Boucher's drawing is adequate but undistinguished. His palette has the softness of the boudoir in its pinks and blues. This scene, though based upon mythology, might be a version of one of the tableaux enacted by society in some of its select parties. This Venus and her attendants could never survive the lusty life of Mt. Olympus. One cannot imagine her taking an active part on the battlefields of Troy and being wounded while defending her favorite, Paris. She represents the ideal of aristocratic beauty of her day, small of head and delicate in body, with powdered whites and pinks, fresh from the hands of the hairdresser. The swirling movement of the composition shows the Rococo to be a development of the Baroque, but in a lighter vein. Such designs as these, with their typical eighteenth-century cupids, set the type for tapestries and even for the applied arts in porcelain and other materials.

The character of the age was molded by the aristocracy, but the sturdy middle class was increasing in numbers and influence. Jean Baptiste Simeon Chardin (1699–1779), in addition to producing a series of powerful still lifes, became the painter of this group. The Blessing (fig. 319) has none of the frivolity of the upper class but rather the sober virtues of the middle class. The pause while the youngest daughter says grace before the noonday meal is restrained and dignified, ennobled into a type scene. This genre subject does not have the particular narrative character of the Dutch; however much it reflects its day, it also transcends time and place. The figures have a monumentality absent in the paintings of

Boucher. All details are conceived with accuracy and freedom. Less meticulous than in Dutch painting, the objects may be described as realistic but not naturalistic: that is, the essential character of each is enhanced and its accidentals of appearance suppressed. A superb control over his medium, a feeling for the brush in rich scumblings of pigment, a grasp of solidity, and a distinguished sense of composition in space mark Chardin as one of the soundest painters of his or any other time.

During the second half of the century, Jean Honoré Fragonard (1732–1806) seemed to prolong the spirit of the first half, even though that spirit was gradually changing. He represents the frenzied continuation of the quest for pleasure maintained by a dwindling group of the upper class. The Swing (fig. 320) was ordered and its subject dictated by a young nobleman. Watteau's delicate eroticism develops into open ribaldry. The fresh color, the drawing, and the technique raise a trivial theme into a painting of distinction. Elsewhere Fragonard exploits the possibilities of light and shade; he paints with strong color and impressionistic breadth such canvases as the Bathers.

Fragonard's willingness to accede to the amorous whims of his clients brought down upon him the condemnation of those, like Jean Baptiste Greuze (1725–1805), who pretended to be more serious and perhaps more moral. The latter's narrative compositions, of which The Return of the Prodigal Son (fig. 321) is painfully typical, are the worst banalities ever to win an undeserved reputation as great paintings. It would be hard to imagine a more trite rendering of this story, a more stilted gesture than that with which the mother calls her son's attention to his dead father, the extravagant sorrow of these gesticulating daughters, or the vulgar expression of remorse in the son himself. The characters are not acting their parts; they are overacting them. The sentiment of the story is revolting, especially in view of its evident insincerity. Greuze tops this type of work by a long series of young women who masquerade under such titles as Innocence, Girl with a Lamb, or The Broken Pitcher. They have little to recommend them beyond their youth. Often badly drawn, they assume a modesty that is belied by their costumes, disarrayed to reveal their charms. Fragonard may, at times, be suggestive, but at least he is frank; he does not pretend to be what he is not. In Greuze, we find a nasty hypocrisy, a decadent pandering under a guise of ingenuous charm. Far more than Fragonard, Greuze exemplifies the spirit that provoked the French Revolution.

The type popularized by Boucher recurs in The Bather (fig. 322) by his contemporary, the sculptor Étienne Maurice Falconet (1716–91).

Its slender figure, lithe and graceful, supports a small head with a fashionable coiffure, as though to express in marble the courtly ideal of feminine beauty. Though The Bather turns slightly, the movement is less violent than in the Baroque, while the modeling shows more of the naturalism of the eighteenth century. Falconet's equestrian statue of Peter the Great at Leningrad transfers that naturalism even to the pedestal, which deserts the usual architectural base in favor of an irregular, pseudo-naturalistic outcropping of rock. The horse, rearing on his hind legs, is balanced by a flowing tail, weighted with lead. Nevertheless, active as the group is, it does not lack characterization. Falconet also designed for bric-a-brac, which in view of its purpose may properly be more trivial than statues on a large scale. A frivolous interpretation of classic material, his Venus Spanking Cupid, for example, cannot and does not pretend to be serious; it is a light and amusing piece of genre intended for a casual glance, not for analysis.

Claude Michel, usually called Clodion, a generation later, formed one of a group that met the demands of society for this sort of thing. He modeled many terra-cotta figures and groups, like the Nymph and Satyr (fig. 323). Conceived and executed at a small scale, it mocks mythology by the triviality of the motive and by the amorous quality, which is more outspoken in these *objets d'art* than in most paintings and monumental sculpture. These nudes, overflowing with animal spirits and fleshy in physique, he conceives with dainty naturalism. Notable, too, is the momentary quality, a transitory impression appropriate to such a theme and on such a scale.

Many of these characteristics find their way even into the tombs of the century. That of Marshal Saxe (fig. 324) by Jean Baptiste Pigalle, dated 1756–76, developed from the Baroque but carried its movement and its pictorialism even farther. The drama of death is yet more extravagant than in Bernini's tombs, and finds its climax here. Such elaboration, like a table decoration in sugar, is ill adapted to our conception of the purpose of a tomb. Its sentiment, its mock drama, its naturalism of detail would be more appropriate on a small scale in the salon or the boudoir. Nevertheless, Pigalle is the incarnation of his century; its growing confidence in science finds expression in anatomical accuracy. His animated figures convey the graceful and feminine ideals of the Rococo as fully as do the paintings of Boucher.

At the very end of the century, France produced in Jean Antoine Houdon (1741–1828) a figure who ranks with her greatest sculptors of all time. The increasing sobriety of the age spared Houdon the necessity of catering to the less sculpturesque aspects of the Rococo, and the reviving classicism had not as yet progressed so far as to insist on archaeological correctness as basic to success. The Voltaire (fig. 325) is clad in simple drapery, which has none of the furbelows of the Rococo to disturb its sculpturesque lines. In fact, it is too general to suggest historic costume of any period. Its ample folds avoid the excessive naturalism of the mid-century, lest by superfluous detail they distract attention from the head and the hands, which convey the characterization. With consummate taste, Houdon selects for emphasis those details best calculated to reveal the personality of Voltaire, the vivacious eyes, the cynical twist of his lips, and the intellectual animation of his features. Voltaire leans forward, gripping the arms of his chair as though absorbed in conversation and as though he had just uttered one of his most provocative sallies.

The Rococo, on the whole, does not constitute a major style comparable to the Gothic, the Renaissance, and the Baroque. It is a vagary of style, slight and affected, and as such has been bitterly attacked by more sober times. Nevertheless, this boudoir style, however superficial in externals, has many admirable qualities. If it does not attempt to inculcate any moral and intellectual precepts, at best its proponents are exquisite draftsmen and delicate colorists, who display a sympathetic understanding of their media in sculpture and painting that may well be the envy of other generations.

MEANWHILE in England a different history was being shaped. The Georgian period was not exciting, and did not want to be. Its ideal was stateliness, serious and academic, but without the pomposity of the reign of Louis XIV, as it was also without the political absolutism of that age. A desire for rule and order affected everything, and compelled a sophisticated propriety. This sounds stuffy but the age does not lack interest; no century that produces a Dr. Johnson can be dull. In fact, the Doctor and his circle are typical of the time. Moreover, the very order of the century provokes occasional eddies of protest, a shadow of the Rococo, or perhaps the vagaries of the 'Chinese taste' or of the 'Gothick taste,' as the case may be. These are not serious studies of Chinese or Gothic art or architecture; they are variants, mostly of a flippant interior character, on the sober norm of Georgian architecture.

ENGLAND

The Baroque style of Sir Christopher Wren and his successors did not permit the academic rule demanded by the new age. Under the leadership of Richard Boyle, the Earl of Burlington, architecture in the first half of the eighteenth century turned instead to Inigo Jones and Palladio.

Burlington himself was an amateur, though he included in his circle many trained architects. Such amateurs, like Quatremère de Quincy in France at the end of the century, needed a formula they might discuss and by which they might measure architectural success as with a yardstick. In the case of Quatremère de Quincy, the standard was archaeological; for Burlington, it was academic. The proportions and members of the classic orders were all important; symmetry was to be achieved at any cost; imagination, less easily reduced to rule, was subordinate to regularity. Jones himself had been less narrow than this, while Wren was great enough to be law unto himself.

No outstanding architect appeared in this group, but many of its members were competent. Colin Campbell compiled the *Vitruvius Britannicus,* a collection of the best examples of English architecture as measured by the standards of the Burlington clique. Significantly, many of Jones's buildings were illustrated, but very few by Wren. The best Georgian designers were more independent, though they followed somewhat the same lines. James Gibbs was less academic and was, therefore, disapproved by the Burlington group. More than any other mid-eighteenth-century designer, he carried on Wren's Baroque manner, confirmed by his own trip to Italy and by the Italian stucco workers whom he brought back with him. To be sure, his portico on St. Martin's in the Fields in London, 1721–6, is Georgian in spirit, but the steeple would do Wren himself credit in its beauty of silhouette. Gibbs has great importance for Americans as the immediate source of inspiration for many colonial designs.

The best site to study Georgian domestic architecture is the city of Bath, which became a fashionable watering place at this time. Its regular lines and its blocks of houses of uniform design enable whole streets and squares to become units of design rather than individual houses. The quiet culture of Bath, in so far as it is expressed in and created by the architecture, is the work of the John Woods, father and son. Prior Park (fig. 326) near Bath, built from 1735 to 1743, shows the Georgian at its best. It was the country estate of Ralph Allen, who was the prototype of Squire Allworthy in Fielding's *Tom Jones,* and who promoted much of the new work in the city. The main block of the house is rectangular in plan and strictly axial; quadrant wings curve forward from each corner of the façade to connect with smaller blocks, which often functioned as kitchens and stables, their masses serving as a foil to the central building. This triple scheme can be traced back through designs of Inigo Jones to the Villas of Palladio. Its effect is stately, but presupposes a corps of servants and some sacrifice of convenience in the separation of the kitchen from the dining room. The spacious principal apartments are designed more for social functions and appearance than for domestic use as that is understood today. However, this impression that the house is designed for show is partly due to its monumentality. On the symmetrical façade, window balances window in number, size, and design. A free-standing portico, complete with entablature and pediment, accents the center, but it is important to notice that this feature is in the middle of the long side of the house, and the pediment does not, therefore, terminate the principal roof, as it did in classic art. Such a portico adds the final touch to the dignity and formality of the life within.

The smaller Georgian interiors, with their paneled walls, sometimes painted in quiet colors and elsewhere left in the natural color of the wood, were very satisfactory. Unfortunately, in the larger houses the academic desire for display led to the introduction of polished marbles and columns, pediments, and other such features, which were too large in scale and too public in character to be appropriate. Hence, toward the end of the century, the Georgian style, especially on the interior, gave way to the Adam style, created by the Adam brothers partly under the influence of increasing classicism. Robert Adam returned in 1760 from his travels in Italy, where he had shared in an archaeological investigation of the Palace of Diocletian at Spalato, which he later published, and also become familiar with the Roman domestic architecture recently unearthed at Pompeii.

The new classic vogue betrays itself on the façade of Kedleston in the disposition of the members like a triumphal arch and in the saucer-like appearance of the dome, but the Adam exteriors differ from the Georgian manner less than do other parts of their designs. In plan, the Adam style tends to vary the volumes of several rooms in a suite, from the square to the rectangle, oval, or circle, with large or small niches and exedrae to enrich the impression of each changing area. Lord Derby's House (fig. 327) in London shows the result of such a plan and also a substitution of elegance for grandeur. The forms become lighter and thus are better adapted to an interior than to an exterior. A rich vocabulary of small decorative features enlivens walls and ceilings alike. Rosettes, festoons of corn husks, slender urns, and floral motives modeled in plaster create an interior of sophistication and refinement suited to the polished life of this generation. A few touches of bright color, or perhaps decorative paintings by Angelica Kaufmann, enhance these details. The whole room assumes a similar character, thanks to the application of like motives in the furniture, and even in the locks, keys, and hinges. These were the fashionable interiors, which housed the social celebrities painted by Reynolds and Gainsborough.

The eighteenth century is recognized as the great age of English furniture. Walnut began to supersede oak as the favorite material of the cabinetmakers as early as 1660, to give way in turn to mahogany about 1725. However, these dates are approximations only, and walnut pieces were made long after 1725. Many familiar motives, such as the cabriole leg and the ball and claw foot, prevail in the first half of the century in both walnut and mahogany designs, characterized by vigor and restraint and executed with such skill that the unknown craftsmen need not bow to the celebrated cabinetmakers who succeeded them.

The first of these craftsmen to give his name to a style of furniture was Thomas Chippendale. Several types of design are associated with him, partly on the basis of the illustrations to *The Gentleman and Cabinet Maker's Director,* first published in 1754. He continued the cabriole leg and the ball and claw foot; he popularized the tripod support for screens and small tables; fretwork in either the Chinese or the Gothic tastes, as the eighteenth century called them, create playful variants; and at other times, the influence of the French Rococo style is paramount. Chippendale also worked for the Adam brothers after 1766, but in those cases the design is more theirs than his. The same decorative motives — corn husks, slender urns, and fluting — that characterize the Adam style in architecture also adorn the furniture that bears their name.

George Hepplewhite lived a few years later than Chippendale. His book, the *Cabinet-Maker and Upholsterer's Guide,* was published in 1788 after his death. Some features of his style include tapered legs; curved fronts for sideboards or commodes, perhaps with shutters; oval, shield, heart, or hoop-shaped backs of chairs; and sometimes light decorative woods in fine veneers. However, these characteristics, though most common in pieces designed in the manner of Hepplewhite, may occur also in furniture with which he had no immediate connection; the designers of the eighteenth century drew on the same traditions and also borrowed motives from one another.

Finally, Thomas Sheraton published *The Cabinet Maker and Upholsterer's Drawing Book* about 1791. Though he was scornful of the designs of his predecessors, his own manner draws on the same sources. In general, his models are a little simpler and more restrained, with less influence of the Rococo and more of the refined elegance of the developing classic fashion. Legs are usually straight, chair backs square or with quadrant corners, and although curved fronts are not eliminated, they become less common; perhaps even greater reliance than before is placed on the beauty of workmanship and veneers. The proverbial craftsmanship of men like Chippendale, Hepplewhite, and Sheraton faded during the nineteenth century with the rise of industrialism, mass production, and materialism, which led to striving for effect without taste. In protest, the arts-and-crafts movement of the late nineteenth century, led by William Morris, attempted to revive craftsmanship in printing, wall paper, textiles, and furniture. The Morris chair, with its adjustable back, was the most comfortable and functional piece of furniture developed during the nineteenth century.

Before the eighteenth century not much painting had been produced in England by native artists. Such portraiture as had been needed was supplied by foreigners like Holbein in the reign of Henry VIII, or Rubens and Van Dyck under Charles I, or Sir Peter Lely and Sir Godfrey Kneller under Charles II. These men established a tradition of aristocratic portraiture that was bound to have its effect. Some Georgian houses contained Baroque decorative paintings, perhaps in the stair hall by the Italian Verrio, or the Frenchman Laguerre. The dome of St. Paul's was decorated by Sir James Thornhill, a native artist, but on the whole, English decorative art is not important.

Aside from portraiture, however, the English spirit demanded narrative of its pictorial arts. William Hogarth (1697–1764), the first great English painter, deals with vivid narratives in pictures, the story told in a number of canvases as the story in a novel may develop in several chapters. Such a work is the Marriage à la Mode series. The first design (fig. 328) introduces the characters. The social position of the nobleman is to be bartered for the money of a wealthy tradesman. A gouty earl on the right points with pride to his position in his family tree, which traces his ancestry back to a knight in medieval armor. In exchange for this social eminence, he receives back the mortgage on his estate, and a cash settlement as well. The father of the bride-to-be inspects the marriage settlement with the same care and the same absence of emotion he might feel in reviewing a business contract. The engaged couple sit beside each other to the left, but Hogarth allows them to turn their backs upon one another. The young woman twirls her ring on her handkerchief and listens to the charming conversation of the lawyer in charge of this deal. With such a beginning, one can hardly expect a happy issue from this marrriage, and the remaining five pictures show the progress of the tragedy, the boredom of the couple in each other's company after marriage, the gaiety of the household, the infidelity of the bride leading to a duel in which the young nobleman is killed, and the subsequent death of his wife.

This and Hogarth's other series of paintings were made primarily to be engraved and the reproductions sold broadcast. Financially, they were very successful. The lucid story and its circumstantial detail would ensure that. These satires on social customs of Hogarth's day are historical documents of the first importance. They are often mistakenly described as moralistic. In a moral, the consequences of wrongdoing fall upon the heads of the transgressors, but Hogarth allows the chief culprits to escape untouched. The young couple have their union arranged for them, but they alone, and not their parents, bear the brunt of the tragedy. Rather than describe Hogarth as a moralist, one should recognize in him a realist, who takes a custom of his day and demonstrates its probable consequences without a trace of sentiment. These compositions may well, like the novels of Dickens in the next century, have borne their share in ameliorating the conditions they attacked.

But however biting their satire, and however vivid their narrative, these qualities alone could not make them great paintings, nor should success in these respects conceal Hogarth's power as a draftsman. If in these works he can be detailed, nevertheless, he is capable of extraordinary breadth, as in the Shrimp Girl, or of keen characterization, as in his portrait of Captain Coram. His composition appears to be accidental, or, more precisely, defined by the narrative exigencies of his subject. In reality, Hogarth shows a remarkable feeling for space, and for the coordination of the figures with the rooms they occupy. The pictorial strength of these designs rests on an organization that is none the less present for not being obvious.

But after all, it is the portrait school in the second half of the century that is most characteristic of the age. Its most important member, Sir Joshua Reynolds (1723–92), destined to be the first president of the Royal Academy, had studied for years in Italy. His rich color and even his lighting are affected by the Venetians, both directly through his own study, and indirectly through the Venetian influence upon Van Dyck and Rubens, who did so much to lay the foundations of English portraiture. Reynolds is often said to be at his finest in his paintings of women, for example, Mrs. Siddons as the Tragic Muse. He infuses that portrait with a histrionic character through the pose and lighting, appropriately since Mrs. Siddons was one of the great Shakespearian actresses of her day.

But Reynolds' best male portraits are more powerful than his female portraits. Dr. Johnson (fig. 329) could hardly be better characterized.

The painter and his sitter were intimate friends, as intimate, at least, as the spirit of the eighteenth century and the reserve of Reynolds himself would permit. The painter catches the ponderous intellectuality of Dr. Johnson perfectly. The Doctor might be formulating a definition of some word for his Dictionary, or characterizing in conversation one of the English poets. He looks the part of a dictator of English letters. Reynolds is at his best in these intimate portraits, concentrated against a plain background. In the more pretentious canvases, custom dictates such decorative accessories as the lower part of a column, a sweep of drapery, or a bit of landscape. Lord Heathfield, the hero of the defense of Gibraltar, is reinforced by a cannon and other details that allude to his profession. The lighting is generalized and makes no attempt to be natural. Sufficient to bring out the modeling, it comes closer to the diffused light of an interior than to sunlight on an exterior. Technically, the middle range of values in nature is recorded with nearly its actual contrasts, and therefore a suppression or crowding together of the very high and very low values becomes inevitable.

This English school is one of society portraiture. Thomas Gainsborough (1727–88) has a flair for infusing his characters with all the social graces. His portrait of the Honorable Mrs. Graham (fig. 330) looks as though she might just have come from a reception at St. James's Palace. She looks to the manner born, with that self-confident distinction caricatured in the March of the Peers in *Iolanthe*. The color, stronger and fresher than that of Reynolds, and the pictorial accessories of landscape and column create a sumptuous effect. The portrait sheds its richness and its social eminence on any room in which it may be displayed. Gainsborough is not so intellectual in his analysis of character as Reynolds. He was never, like Reynolds, able to make the trip to Italy, nor was he so influential in his day. On the other hand, Gainsborough is more brilliant as a painter; he has more of sheer genius. His dash and verve, his freedom, his pictorial instinct, and his virtuosity with the brush are more pronounced.

The danger of such brilliance of technique lies in its charm. A large group of painters in the late-eighteenth and early-nineteenth centuries follow the lines laid down by Reynolds and Gainsborough, men like Henry Raeburn, George Romney, and John Hoppner, to name only three. But these portrait manufacturers, as a more critical age has called them, lack both the intellect of Reynolds and the pictorial structure of Gainsborough. Sir Thomas Lawrence carries the school to its glittering extreme in sparkling color and virtuosity, but the means have become an end in themselves, and not much more than the shell of the school of Reynolds and

Gainsborough is preserved. At its worst, this school indulges in all the superficialities of society portraiture, and adheres to a pattern with monotonous regularity. In this formula, established by Van Dyck, a fashionably dressed figure painted in some detail is placed against a generalized background or one filled with vague accessories intended to hint at some achievement or interest of the sitter. However, even the weaker members of the group retain the decorative color and the social poise that typified the school.

XIX

The Birth of American Art

THE early settlements along the Atlantic seaboard were varied in origin; the largest colonies in Massachusetts, Pennsylvania, and Virginia were English, but the Dutch had settled in New York, the Swedes in Delaware, and the Germans in and around Philadelphia. Before the end of the seventeenth century, however, the English had absorbed all of these settlements, and their more diverse origins began to be submerged in the prevailing English culture. The colonists who came to this new land might have started afresh to lay the groundwork of an indigenous art appropriate to the new country and the new climate, based on the available materials and the new conditions of life under which they found themselves; actually they did not attempt to be original. Their change of conditions had some effect, but the fact that groups of settlers had sailed across the ocean from England did not in itself alter their traditions or their habits of thought. Inevitably, they attempted to build in the wilderness the same type of house that they had known at home, modified as little as might be by the circumstances they encountered in the new land. Consequently, the formative force in colonial art was its European background, generally English, but with some Dutch influence in New York and the Hudson Valley, and traces of other continental origins elsewhere on the Atlantic seaboard; and of course in Florida and the Southwest, the background was Spanish.

In 1620, the date of the settlement of Plymouth, English building traditions were still medieval. Inigo Jones, to be sure, had just begun the Banqueting House, but its influence was still in the future. The Renaissance had appeared in England a century before this, but, as we have seen, the classic side of that movement was only partly understood and its application was confined to the estates of the wealthy. It was not from such families that the colonists came. The houses of the lower and middle classes in 1620 were Gothic and continued to be so, probably even into the eighteenth century. Though much smaller and simpler than Compton

Wynyates, the style is fundamentally the same. Many of them were built of timber, or of half timber, which means just what it says, that the house was made half of timber and half of something else, the spaces between the timbers filled in with brick, or with clay matted on twigs. One does not expect vaults and flying buttresses, tracery and membered piers in wood construction, but a directness of solution and a frank exposure of structure are essentials of Gothic architecture, and these qualities characterized the village and cottage architecture of England at the time of the settlement of America and even later.

Thus, it is reasonable to say that the afterglow of the Gothic day, whose high noon had produced Westminster Abbey and Canterbury Cathedral, can be seen in the seventeenth-century colonial house. The only well-preserved examples of this type are found in the North, though there is good reason to believe the form was also common in Virginia. The Parson Capen House in Topsfield, Massachusetts, built in 1683, shows that the type remains unchanged through the whole seventeenth century. In plan, the house huddles around the single great central chimney, as though for warmth. It usually consists of two rooms only on each floor, one to either side of the chimney, with narrow stairs to the second story between the chimney and the door. These two rooms are not of the same size; therefore, the house, like most medieval designs is asymmetrical.

The forests, which had to be cleared anyway, provided a rich source of material. Rough-hewn logs compose the frame of the building, the half timber of English tradition, but experience soon showed the colonists that the colder climate of New England demands additional protection from the weather. Hence, the exteriors of these houses (fig. 331) are clapboarded, thin boards overlapping one another to create a blanket of wood around the house. Clapboards were commoner in seventeenth-century England than they are today in that country, but in New England they are almost universal. Consequently, the sturdy framework becomes visible only at the corners, and not always there, but it is often expressed by pendants that project below the overhanging second story. These pendants, the only enrichment of the house, recall the Gothic style, since they are structural members made decorative, rather than decoration applied as something distinct. A good deal of variety exists between the colonies and also between different houses in the matter of the overhang; sometimes it is found only on the front, sometimes only on the ends of the house, and at other times in both places. The idea comes from the Middle Ages, not only in England but in the timbered houses of France and Germany, where its purpose was probably to increase the room within the house by encroaching over the street in the crowded conditions of medieval towns. That reason carried no weight in colonial America, but tradition was strong enough to ensure its retention. A steep gable roof covers the mass. As the family expands, more space may be gained by adding other gables, as in the famous House of the Seven Gables in Salem, Massachusetts. Small casement windows are placed wherever light is most needed on the interior; no preconceived principle of symmetry dictates their arrangement. They are composed of multiples of small units; a single opening for small chambers, but two, three, or even more units to light the larger rooms — though none of the rooms were large by present-day standards. Leaded glass in rectangular or diamond-shaped panes is known from the earliest days of the colonies, but cannot have been universal, since letters advise prospective colonists to bring paper and linseed oil for the windows.

No porch mitigates the severity of these designs. The door of sturdy planks opens on the stair hall. The stairs are too narrow to permit more than one person to ascend at a time, and are dangerously steep. Each room centers on its fireplace, which warms it and where the cooking is done. Into such fireplaces one could roll a tree if necessary; like everything else in these modest houses, they are designed for a specific purpose, and their beauty is consequent on the directness with which they meet that purpose. The ceilings are so low for additional warmth that tall men cannot walk under the exposed beams and joists of the second floor without stooping. So, too, are the posts of the walls visible on the interior. But rarely do these builders permit themselves the luxury of sheathing the walls on the inside, and then usually only over the fireplace. In fact, when Winthrop sheathed the interior of his house with plain boards, the governor of the colony called him to task for such unnecessary ostentation, so that Winthrop had to explain that this sheathing was inexpensive and added to the warmth of his house.

The furniture is no less substantial in construction than the architecture. In the colonies, as in England during the seventeenth century, oak continues to be the standard material, although pine, being available, is also employed. The chest with plain carving, or adorned with Elizabethan or Jacobean motives and patterns, is perhaps the commonest single article, but sturdy stools, cradles, turned chairs, and high-backed settles eked out the furnishing of these small rooms. Simple as they are, nothing more functional has ever been built, or ever will be built than these seventeenth-century colonial houses and their furniture. In whole and in part they follow the needs of the day; they take no thought for their appearance, and perhaps in consequence achieve their homespun beauty, as sturdy as the men who built them.

The need for shelter made it inevitable that the house first should absorb the energy of the builders. And yet worship was so vital to them that it formed a major reason for their migration. Very few churches have been preserved from these days, but those few are instructive. St. Luke's, Smithfield, Virginia, in an Anglican settlement, was built in 1632 of brick and retained the plan and even the buttresses, pointed arches, and tracery of Gothic parish churches, though in simplified form. In New England, the Old Ship Meeting House in Hingham, Massachusetts, dated 1681, had the open frame construction of the houses but on a larger scale. The great curved timbers of the roof resemble the beams of a wooden ship. Its square plan, the pulpit centered on one wall, and a general openness reflect the democratic form of Congregational worship in contrast to Anglicanism.

By the beginning of the eighteenth century, conditions had so changed, at least along the seaboard, as to prompt an architectural revolution. The thrifty and enterprising merchants of the North and the Southern plantation owners alike had accumulated sufficient wealth to tempt them from the Spartan rigors of the days of settlement. The modest houses of their forebears could not accommodate the more genteel and formal life that now became possible. Luxuries and amenities, far from being suspect, were now sought. Of course, such a change did not occur overnight; an occasional house, like Colonel Hutchinson's in Boston, long since destroyed, foretold the change, but such mansions were rare before the eighteenth century.

With their greater wealth, the colonists turned to the mother country, not for traditions as hitherto, but for the latest fashions in building. Consequently, America jumped from the fifteenth century to the eighteenth, from the medieval to the Georgian. Floods of architectural textbooks, simple carpenter's handbooks, submerged the traditional style. Many of these were imported from England, but a considerable number, especially as the century progressed, were local products. These inexpensive volumes began with descriptions of the orders, went on to explain the intricacies of carpentry, and concluded with designs for windows and doors, staircases and fireplaces, in the latest fashion. Presumably when some well-to-do merchant determined to build himself a new house, he called in his neighbor, the builder, and together they thumbed through several of these handbooks to decide on the approximate model for the living-room fireplace, the balusters for the stairs, or the fenestration of the house.

These manuals establish the Georgian style as the model followed as closely in Massachusetts as in New York, in Philadelphia as in Charleston. Such differences as had existed in the seventeenth century because of divergent national origins no longer obtain. If one can distinguish separate styles in the several colonies, these are traceable to differences of climate and of available materials. The warm climate and plantation life of the South allows a more open design than the compact New England houses. Also, brick walls are more popular in Virginia than in Massachusetts, while the available ledge stone near Philadelphia colors the architecture of that region. Nevertheless, these differences are negligible in comparison to the unity of style displayed in the colonies. The same fundamental plan and the same principles of design govern the style from north to south, and one may even find identical details, inspired by the same handbooks in Virginia, Pennsylvania, or New Hampshire.

The sophisticated Georgian spirit not only demanded larger houses; it also required symmetry. Therefore, the typical house, such as Westover, Virginia, the Chew Mansion in Germantown, Pennsylvania, or the Royall House in Medford, Massachusetts, is a rectangle in plan and has four rooms, each larger than those of the preceding century, two on either side of an ample central hall. The latter serves the double purpose of giving space for the stairs and providing access to the rooms. Nothing, in plan, suggests the use to which these chambers were to be put. Since each room needs its own fireplace, a single chimney no longer suffices; two are possible, but more often four chimneys, two in each side wall of the house, indicate the rooms within.

This symmetrical plan dictates the exterior of the Isaac Royall House at Medford, Massachusetts (fig. 332), cited in the middle of the century as one of the grandest in the colonies. The roof is lower in pitch than in the seventeenth century, and occasionally is flattened at the top and, though not in this case, perhaps has a balustrade to finish the design. The orders in pilaster form accent the corners of the house, or in other instances the place occupied by the hall. Perhaps the Ionic order is the colonial favorite, but the Doric is almost as popular; though the Corinthian is known, its complexity forbids its common use. These builders, though influenced by an academic style, will not sacrifice much to it. Thus the pilasters carry blocks of entablature, but almost never do the builders allow more than the cornice to support the eaves of the house: to adopt a full entablature would interfere with the second-story windows.

Ordinarily, five windows of the second floor repeat four windows and a door on the ground floor. These symmetrical openings are larger than those of the seventeenth century, and the sash slides up and down in the plane of the wall. Leaded glass has given way to larger panes set in wood bars. In wooden houses, only a cornice may finish the second-story windows, but pediments, either triangular or segmental, enrich those of the ground floor. However, the door in the center focuses the design and gives character to the house. Here again, the orders with entablature and pediment express the dignity of the owners, though even now no porch offers shelter to the visitor.

A complete change remodels the interior also. The plastered ceilings, higher than in the seventeenth century, no longer expose to view the floor beams of the second story. At least the principal rooms are paneled, and may even admit the orders in pilaster form, especially around the fireplaces. Occasionally, native or imported wall paper takes the place of the panels. We are apt to think of these colonial interiors as white, though in reality a wide latitude in color prevails: dull blue, oyster gray, green, red, and even marbleized interiors are not uncommon, though too often the original color has been changed. The fireplaces are still large enough to be serviceable, but since most of them are no longer intended for cooking, they are less ample than before. Early in the century, a molding frames the fireplace, but in the decades just before the American Revolution, more elaborate mantels and overmantels establish the hearth as the focus of the room. The stairway is more commodious and its slope gentler than hitherto; a balustrade offers an opportunity for the carpenters to demonstrate their ability, and all manner of spiral turnings and still more complicated designs in the newel posts attest their skill. Such an interior suits the sedate existence of its day. Its rooms with their plastered ceilings and paneled walls match the change from the austerity of the seventeenth-century costume to the colorful garb of the colonial worthies portrayed by Copley.

So, too, does the furniture. Walnut and, later in the century, mahogany replace oak and pine; the designers turn to early Georgian models for inspiration, and the cabriole leg, ball and claw foot, and other motives of English cabinet work put in their appearance, along with spindle-backed Windsor chairs. As in architecture, the colonists accepted English developments a few years after the mother country, and before the Revolution the influence of Chippendale began to make itself felt. Though by no means plain, the American designs tend to be simpler than their English models.

As the colonies grew, they needed more public buildings, though such demands remained simple until after the Revolution. The Old State House in Boston and Independence Hall in Philadelphia are in essence enlarged private houses, bigger in scale to be sure, but with no fundamental change in conception. Time after time, local tradition points to a colonial church as designed by Sir Christopher Wren. With the exception of certain buildings at Williamsburg, Virginia, no foundation exists for these attributions. Like the houses, the churches of the eighteenth century are Georgian, some of them, such as the First Church in Providence, Rhode Island, inspired by the designs of James Gibbs. These white churches are distinguished by a tower, perhaps with a steeple built up in the manner of the Wren steeples, but much simpler and conceived in terms of wood. The interior of these meeting houses centers on the pulpit, which is raised well above the floor in the position occupied by the altar in a Catholic church. Even the Anglican churches of Virginia and elsewhere, such as Christ Church, Alexandria, or Christ Church, Philadelphia, subordinate the altar to the pulpit, and minimize the chancel. The exquisite craftsmanship, as demonstrated in the box pews and the pulpit, turns to the same basic motives and moldings as in the houses.

Sculpture in colonial America was negligible save for some naive tombstones and an occasional figurehead in wood on the ships. Civic life had not grown far enough to command monuments, and the cost of sculpture militated against its spread if fostered by private patronage alone. Perhaps the Puritan hostility to luxury acted more pointedly in sculpture than in painting; perhaps the unimportance of sculpture in England was responsible. Whatever the reason, the small demand for the representative arts was satisfied by painting, and even this only began to get under way by the middle of the eighteenth century.

Some of the limners, as they often styled themselves, were English trained, like John Smibert; others, such as Robert Feke of Newport, Rhode Island, were native products. In either case, their subject was portraiture. The colonial gentlemen had sufficient pride in themselves and their families to demand likenesses from their painters. Smibert's most important canvas, Bishop Berkeley and His Entourage, owned by Yale University, reveals his European training, among other ways in its sophisticated arrangement.

That this canvas influenced Feke's painting of 1741 of Isaac Royall and His Family, belonging to Harvard University, is obvious; the Feke portrait shows the same man for whom the Royall House at Medford in its present form was built, and is unusually elaborate. The rich costumes and the carpet table cover tell of the social position of the family, but the artist's desire has outrun his performance. Though his aim was realistic, his draftsmanship was inadequate; some of the characters are little dolls, though others are more at ease. The design leaves something to be desired, as though Feke was attempting a problem in composition that was too diffi- cult for him. Nevertheless, he had great native ability, and his painting shows an instinct for formal design, provincial though it be.

Beyond comparison the greatest of the colonial painters was John Sin- gleton Copley (1737–1815) of Boston. He painted Jeremiah Lee of Mar- blehead and Boston (fig. 333), carefully matching his colors to those of his sitter and his costume. There is little here of the fluency or the sophis- tication of a Gainsborough. Painting did not come easily to Copley; the form was well perceived and painstakingly rendered, but to achieve this result absorbed Copley's energy too much to permit him to fall into super- ficialities. The portrait has an unpretentious honesty about it. We have every reason to suppose that the sitter looked like this, and that Copley has not tampered with the reality of his task to give social graces to his models. Probably the independence of these portraits, their unwilling- ness to seem what they are not, may be due to the demands of the clients also. One is tempted to see in this sober honesty and this hatred of affecta- tion qualities outstanding in those men who laid the foundations of our country.

In 1774, just before the outbreak of the Revolution, Copley went abroad, and in the following year settled in London, where he was admitted to the Royal Academy, and where he lived for the rest of his life. Despite con- siderable success in his profession, at least down to 1800, the cosmopolitan atmosphere of the metropolis was not an unmixed blessing; what his style gained in facility, it lost in vigor. His later portraits lose the sobriety and sturdiness of his earlier work without achieving the brilliance of a Gains- borough or a Lawrence.

It is natural to suppose that the American Revolution broke our cultural relations with the mother country, but one may argue that in fighting the Revolution, we were being extremely English. Many of the revolutionary heroes maintained that they were defending their rights as Englishmen, and with them a large party in the mother country agreed. In any case, no abrupt break in tradition occurred. The period after the Revolution and down to about 1820 has been called the post-colonial or the early repub- lican, but the best name for the era is Federal. Culturally, the generation was dominated by the group that formed the backbone of the Federalist party in American politics, and the duration of the style almost coincided with the life of that party. Though some members of what we might call the colonial aristocracy belonged to the Democratic party, on the whole, and particularly in the North, the wealthier individuals of the community tended to be Federalist, and it was for them that the art of the time was produced. That class did not change its traditions with its allegiance.

When, at the outbreak of the Revolution, Copley went to England, he found Benjamin West (1738–1820), a Pennsylvanian, already established in London. In fact, West, despite his backwoods origin, or perhaps partly because that background made his modest achievement seem the more remarkable, won notable success in England. He became the historical painter to George III, and succeeded Reynolds as president of the Royal Academy. His painting is not inspired; in fact, one can almost agree with Byron's strictures about 'that dotard West, Europe's worst daub, poor England's best.' However, West was personally both genial and generous, and his home and studio became a center for American artists who had come to London to study.

Among them was Charles Willson Peale (1741–1827), who filled the gap between Copley and Stuart; if not inspired, he was enthusiastic about his art, so much so that he named several sons after old masters, such as Rembrandt and Raphael. It would be fortunate if our image of Washington were based upon his portraits by Peale, made when the first President was in the prime of life, instead of on those by Stuart, which were painted just a few years before Washington's death. In one of his finest paintings, a self-portrait, Peale lifts a rich red curtain so that the spectator may peep at the exhibits lining the walls of his museum in Philadelphia, devoted partly to painting and partly to natural history.

Although Gilbert Stuart (1755–1828) also studied with West in London, he was little influenced by him and became a far better painter. When Stuart returned to America in 1792, he was the best-trained painter in the country. His portrait of Thomas Jefferson (fig. 334) shows the cosmopolitan technique that his English experience had given him, as compared with the more provincial style of Copley before the Revolution. Painting came easily to Stuart; his brush flowed with a readiness that yields something of the decorative value of the contemporary English portrait school. His characters seem a little more aristocratic than Copley's, and their social poise is greater. They sit more easily, and the likeness is more gracious, but to reach this cosmopolitan style in place of the provincialism of the earlier men, Stuart has lost something. His portraits do not have the self-evident honesty of Copley's. His sense of structure is less powerful, and his figures a little flatter.

Stuart's famous portraits of Washington are too well known to need much comment. One regrets that this should be so, because the portraits of Washington are by no means the best of Stuart's work. Stuart had a faculty for putting his sitters at their ease by his flow of conversation, but something about Washington's innate dignity appears so to have awed Stuart that he could not himself be comfortable in the presence of the man he so admired. Also, Stuart had the opportunity to paint Washington only a few years before Washington's death, when physical vigor was beginning to fail and after the founder of his country had suffered from poor dentistry, a badly fitted set of false teeth, which gave a prognathous appearance to his jaw and lips.

A very different character from Stuart is John Trumbull (1756–1843), son of the revolutionary governor of Connecticut. An intellectual haughtiness revealed in the clear-cut features, with none of Stuart's geniality, characterizes both Trumbull and his sturdy portraits. Congress commissioned him to paint a series of historical compositions, battles of the Revolution and scenes of the formation of the Federal Government, for the rotunda of the United States Capitol. The artist studied each subject in detail; every character is a portrait, and therefore these paintings have great historic value. Moreover, they are direct, well drawn, and fresh in color, at least in the sketches preserved in New Haven, Connecticut. The few large paintings completed by him for the Capitol fail to preserve the same spontaneity, nor are they well adapted as murals.

This portrait school survived until well on in the nineteenth century, when American artists turned their allegiance from their English origin to Düsseldorf, Munich, and ultimately Paris.

The same English origin persists in the Federal style in architecture. This is woven of three strains: a continuation of colonial tradition, a strong influence of the Adam style, and a new archaeology, which reflects the incipient Roman revival. The elements of colonial design are more apparent in the early part of the period, and the Roman features later, though many exceptions to this generality can be cited. Books continued to be used, but the books themselves reflect the new ideals. More complex architectural needs arose, caused by the growth and independence of the country, and called into existence architects as well as builders. The style is consequently more architectonic than the colonial Georgian.

Even the houses catch the new spirit, though the absence of any single type makes generalization difficult. Protruding bays, or perhaps a salon bulging on the axis, complicate the simple rectangular plans. The rooms also cease to be always rectangular, as though the varied volumes of Adam interiors had won popularity on this side of the Atlantic, too. Furthermore, a niche to contain a sideboard or an alcove for a four-poster bed shows that some architects now had specific purposes in mind for such rooms. A balustrade or parapet at the eaves of the house often conceals the roof. Especially in the South, the two-storied portico dignifies the design, but, like those of the English Georgian, it is placed in the center of the long side of the house, not on one end. Since these colonnades reduce light in the second story, the North preferred a smaller porch, only large enough to shelter the door, whose composition is complicated by semicircular or elliptical fanlights above, in addition to rectangular sidelights.

The interiors of these houses have higher ceilings than before. Wallpaper, silk, or plain plaster replaces paneling in the popular esteem, though the latter is not unknown. Much of the detail, especially in the work of Samuel MacIntire of Salem, is strongly influenced by the Adam manner. No less exquisite in craftsmanship, often, in fact, even more dexterous, the sturdiness of the Georgian yields to a refinement that sometimes approaches virtuosity. The traditions of colonial times in cabinet work persist, but with traces of the styles of Adam, Hepplewhite, and Sheraton added to those of Chippendale and the earlier Georgian. In some work by Duncan Phyfe of New York, the influence of Hepplewhite is paramount, but his most characteristic output betrays instead a familiarity with Sheraton and a sympathy with the new-found classicism of the Federal period. His lyre-backed chairs and pedestal tables preserve to the full the integrity of late eighteenth-century craftsmanship.

The two leading architects of their time were Charles Bulfinch and Thomas Jefferson. Bulfinch belonged to the Boston aristocracy; he had traveled abroad, especially in England, and as a young man had expected to be a member of the leisure class, able to cultivate a gentleman's interest in architecture but with no need to turn his taste to financial profit. Unfortunate investments in real estate compelled him to become a professional architect to supplement his civic career as the Great Selectman of Boston.

The Boston State House, begun in 1795, the second of his three state capitols (the others being in Hartford, Connecticut, and Augusta, Maine), reflects his European travels. Traces of English and French influence suggest the more architectonic Federal approach, but it is his sense of proportion that gives to the State House its distinction. The white trim in wood and stone contrasts effectively against the warm brick of the walls. A noble colonnade above a high arcaded basement marks the original lower house of the state legislature. To the right was the chamber of the upper house, and to the left the offices of the administrative branch of the state government, though these uses have now been altered in part, owing to the growth of the legislature. The dome, though visually insecure above the pediment, nevertheless serves to tie the design together and to provide a dignified stateliness to the whole. One might almost say that the motive of the dome introduced here became standard for state capitols throughout the country. Bulfinch's design shows the conservative side of the Federal style. The proportions of the order are a little more slender than usual, and much of the interior detail shows the influence of the Adam style, which was still fashionable at the time of Bulfinch's sojourn in London. As yet there is little to suggest archaeology.

On the other hand, with Thomas Jefferson the case was very different. Like Bulfinch, Jefferson represented the cultured upper class, but his career left him with no need to become a professional architect. When he became enthusiastic about Roman architecture, he threw himself into the study of that style with consuming zeal. His design for the Richmond State Capitol, sent back from Paris in 1785, was modified in execution (fig. 335), but its main lines and proportions were retained. Jefferson studied the Maison Carrée in Nîmes (fig. 78), together with the French archaeologist, Clérisseau. To Jefferson, the little Roman temple was the 'model of cubical architecture;' no more fitting source than this could be found for the Virginia capitol. The exigencies of use compelled Jefferson to admit windows along the sides; the difficulties of execution presented by the Corinthian capital prompted the substitution of the Ionic order; but on the whole Jefferson followed his model closely.

Though not a copy of the Maison Carrée, the Richmond capitol demonstrates the renewed interest in the classic in that it revives not only the vocabulary of that style but also the type of building. This is the first application of the complete Roman temple form to a building intended for practical use anywhere in the world. Before this, some temples had been copied on a small scale as garden ornaments; after this, the temple form would be widely revived in Europe and America, and for such buildings Jefferson's design was pioneer. Whether such a borrowing from the past of complete types of building is desirable, and whether it does not entail too great a sacrifice to cram the diverse needs of a state legislature into the box of a Roman temple are debatable questions, but to Jefferson, the beauty of the form is a sufficient justification for its use, and after all the extent of the sacrifice involved can be easily exaggerated.

With his interest in architecture, Jefferson naturally used his own house, Monticello, near Charlottesville, Virginia, as a proving ground for his ideas. The plan is complex but ingenious and workable, and the building has been called the 'finest piece of proportion in America.' His last great design is the academical village for the University of Virginia at Charlottesville, dated 1817–26. Long colonnades flank the lawn on the east and west, and screen the student's quarters. These are punctuated at regular intervals by larger pavilions, which served at first as the homes of the faculty and the classrooms of the university. The colonnades approach the climax of the whole scheme, the library, whose source is the Pantheon in Rome (fig. 82), believed by Jefferson to be the 'model of spherical architecture.' Although, as in the Richmond capitol, windows had to be introduced and some other changes made, the library is almost a replica of the Pantheon at one quarter the size. The pavilions also are based on specific Roman temples, each on a different model, in part as demonstrations for the gentlemen students of correct designs. To Jefferson, a knowledge of architecture formed part of the education of every gentleman, and to him the only proper guide for young America was Roman architecture. That style he did his utmost to foster in this country.

XX

Neoclassicism in Europe

THE years in Europe corresponding to the Federal style in America, 1785–
1820 or somewhat later, witness the flowering of the Neoclassic, with
which indeed the Federal style itself may in part be classed. This new
revival of the classic past differs from the revival of Roman art in the
time of the Renaissance partly in its accuracy. The Renaissance had a
great enthusiasm for Roman times; it did revive the vocabulary and
something of the spirit of the past, but it modified both spirit and expression to suit its own needs. Later ages made even less of a fetish of
archaeology. Under Neoclassicism, on the other hand, success is judged
by archaeological correctness. Moreover, at least in later Neoclassicism,
a Greek inspiration, unknown to the Renaissance, challenges if it does
not supplant the Roman.

This new scholarship was rooted partly in the excavations carried out
through the eighteenth century at Pompeii and Herculaneum, cities that
had been buried by an eruption of Mt. Vesuvius in A.D. 79. The discoveries there showed an aspect of Roman architecture different from the
better-known monuments of the Roman forum. Moreover, scientific
archaeology, based on careful measurements, was eagerly pursued in
the later eighteenth century, and a series of important volumes were
published that familiarized the European world with the exact nature
of Roman architecture as never before. Robert Adam's work at Spalato,
already mentioned, was paralleled by Wood's studies at Palmyra, by
Clérisseau's *Monumens de Nismes*, and, most important of all for later
history, by Stuart and Revett's *The Antiquities of Athens*, which first
really opened the eyes of Europe to the difference in style between
Greek and Roman architecture.

The revival of the classic was not confined to the arts, by any means.
It was part of the spirit of the times. The growing republican sentiment,
rife in France even before the outbreak of the Revolution, sought a

precedent in the republics of Greece and Rome, however different they were in actuality from the civilization and background of Europe in the late eighteenth century. That enthusiasm for the past was sufficient to induce men to call one another after the names of famous classic characters, and at times to modify their costumes in the direction of classic garb. In literature, Mme. de Staël's *Corinne* was a pastiche of classic fragments, Walter Savage Landor became an enthusiastic proponent of Rome, and Keats was inspired to write an *Ode on a Grecian Urn*.

In architecture, Neoclassicism is marked by two strains, Roman and Greek. In general, the Roman revival is earlier than the Greek, and the latter receives its fullest development in those countries that had not formed part of the Roman Empire. But little of the Greek revival occurs in Italy, and almost none in France or Spain, whereas that movement is strong in the second quarter of the century in Germany, England, and America. One obvious reason why the Roman revival appears first is that, since the Renaissance, European architecture had been more or less derived from Roman architecture. The late eighteenth century witnessed a series of forerunners of Neoclassicism; the Adam style in England, the portico of the Panthéon in Paris by Soufflot, and Jefferson's Richmond State Capitol all herald the movement in their greater attention to archaeology or their increasing seriousness. The full character of the Roman revival appears in the Madeleine, 1806–42 (fig. 336), by Barthélemy Vignon, originally intended to celebrate Napoleon's victories. If we cannot visit a real Roman temple, we can still get an accurate idea of its external form from this building. Like a Roman temple, it is raised on a base and approached by a flight of steps across the front. A colonnade surrounds the building, and supports an unbroken entablature and pediments, which terminate the low pitched roof. The Corinthian order is correct, like an academic study. And yet, like such a study, the Madeleine is cold and precise; it is like a mummy from the past, lacking the life that the best Roman buildings display. Furthermore, it fails to be consistent. No one would guess from the exterior that the building is roofed by three consecutive domes, and on entering the visitor always sustains a sense of shock: the design of the interior and the exterior are not co-ordinated.

At best, the Madeleine has an icy dignity, but the Roman revival is not always so rigid in its archaeology. The Arc de Triomphe in Paris, built by Chalgrin from 1806 to 1836, though inspired by a Roman triumphal arch, is like no known example of Roman work. Its superb scale, the suppression of the orders, the reliance on sculptured groups for enrichment, and the boldness of proportions give Chalgrin's arch a degree of vitality not approximated in the Madeleine. The latter relies on archaeological correctness for its success, but the Arc de Triomphe has a more architectural basis. As a matter of fact, Chalgrin's masterpiece touches a higher peak of architectural distinction than any similar extant Roman edifice.

By the 1820's the Greek temple form begins to be the motive for houses, churches, and public buildings. The Walhalla at Regensburg, built 1830–42 by Leo von Klenze, is based on the Parthenon, save in its picturesque setting. The absurdity of a Greek temple dedicated to Norse heroes seems to have bothered nobody. Langhans's Brandenburg Gate in Berlin, an exceptionally early example, dated 1788–91, derives from the Propylaea. These two sources, with the addition of the Erechtheum, the Choragic Monument of Lysicrates in Athens and the Temple of Poseidon at Paestum comprise the direct inspiration of almost all of the Greek revival works, and can be recognized over and over again. However, some features of the Brandenburg Gate, such as the arrangement of the triglyphs and the separate bases for the columns, betray a modification of the pure Hellenic style by Roman models. The details of the Walhalla, on the other hand, or of Thomas Hamilton's Edinburgh High School of 1825–9, adhere rigidly to Athenian precedent.

As with the Roman revival, not all the Greek revival monuments are so strict. In the Bank of England, 1788–1835, Sir John Soane borrows at will from the Roman Temple of Vesta at Tivoli and the Erechtheum in Athens, but conceives parts of his design in geometric volumes, often almost stripped of detail, and thought out, like the works of some modern architects, as designs in abstract shapes. The simplified detail of his own house, now the Soane Museum in London, hardly interrupts the surface; therefore, the block-like masses dominate any traces of archaeology. In fact, the end of the Greek revival so purifies its designs that they have style without styles; they are conceived as architecture, not as Greek architecture, and through this elimination of historic precedent they parallel certain developments of modern architecture.

Similarly strict and free phases, Roman and Greek precedents, influence Neoclassic sculpture. The Italian Antonio Canova (1757–1822), at the outset of his career, retained much of the very late Baroque spirit. His Hercules Hurling Lichias into the Sea incorporates turbulent energy. The open design has a violence and an interest in pictorial detail, handled with some realism, that testify to the extended influence of

Bernini. The heavy bearded type of Hercules and its muscularity and proportions may be inspired by the Farnese Hercules, a famous Graeco-Roman statue, but as a whole these early works are no more than transitional to Neoclassicism.

On the other hand, his later work, after the beginning of the nineteenth century, is purely Neoclassic. The Perseus (fig. 337), ordered by the Vatican to replace the Apollo Belvedere, which had been stolen and transported to Paris by Napoleon, is inspired by that statue. The movement of his earlier manner has gone. In its place, we have a quiet Neoclassic work, its surface generalized to such a point that all interest has been eliminated, in spite of a trace of eighteenth-century softness of modeling. The affected grace of pose, derived from its model, has a deliberately 'artistic' character, which misses its mark; but Canova's statue is no worse than its dull Hellenistic prototype, once so extravagantly admired.

If Canova represents the Roman revival, Bertel Thorvaldsen (1770–1844), the Dane, prefers an emasculated Hellenism. For all his study of the monuments of Athens, and despite his borrowing of motives and details from them, he fails to catch the Greek breadth and freedom of spirit. His Jason again restudies the Apollo Belvedere, but with even less vitality than Canova. In him is nothing of the majesty of Hellenic idealism, none of the largeness of conception or the feeling for the material Greek art had demonstrated in its earlier and more vital periods; only the hard and empty shell remains.

Both sculpture and architecture had a wealth of precedents to which they could and did refer. Painting was more fortunate in this respect. With the exception of Greek vase paintings, which were really drawings, and of a few second-rate mural compositions mostly on the walls of Pompeii, nothing of ancient painting had been preserved. Consequently, the painters were not hampered by direct comparison, nor could the dead hand of the past stifle originality. None the less, Jacques Louis David (1748–1825) had the evangelist spirit, and the will to enforce, if necessary, the tenets of his creed on a world that was, however, ready to receive them as an antidote to the frivolity of the Rococo. An ardent Jacobin, high in the councils of the Revolution, he reorganized the old Academy as the *Institut de France* and formulated a code on the basis of the seventeenth-century academic formula, which was to be the accepted doctrine for a generation.

First and foremost, art must be noble and public. Anything that smacked of triviality, however charming, fell under the ban. Dutch genre paintings and the frivolity of the Fêtes Galantes could not meet this goal. But nobility of subject matter to David meant subject matter drawn from the classics, preferably themes of Roman or Greek history or mythology, invested with the stern virtues of the Roman republic. Nature was not fitted to be a direct source of inspiration, but only the most beautiful aspects of nature were worthy of the artist's attention. Painting was like poetry, and unfortunately the painters allowed the poets to select for them from the bounty of nature. Clarity of statement was essential and could best be achieved by drawing; color, therefore, must be subordinated. Though it could not be abandoned, color became something to elucidate the drawing, which told the story or described the scene. It became, as it were, an afterthought instead of being the principal medium of the painter.

The Oath of the Horatii, first exhibited in 1785, is the ultimatum of this new style. The figures, rounded by cold light, are firmly drawn. Only in the group of women to the right is there a trace of eighteenth-century grace. The severe architecture has already assumed the guise of the Roman revival. The men seem inspired by grim determination; they might well become Jacobins, pledging themselves to the cause, so austere is their zeal and so high are their principles. Such a painting is too anxious to preach its lesson ever to relax its severity. Its cold intellectual approach forbids any emotional expression.

This is the type known as a historical canvas, on which David expected his reputation to rest in later ages. Another example is the Death of Socrates (fig. 338). It is hard thus to visualize the scene after reading the Platonic dialogue of *Phaedo*, on which it is based. However, the histrionic attitudes, the jailer who covers his eyes as he hands Socrates the fatal cup of hemlock, the philosopher who blandly accepts the cup and points upward to indicate the immortality of his soul, which he has been discussing, and the mourning of his friends may all find their excuse if not their feeling in Plato. These characters do not ring true; their sentiment is too obvious and so fails to carry conviction to the spectator. However clear its didactic lesson, the whole scene is badly conceived. Each form is modeled as though cast in plaster. The drawing is accurate but academic. In spite of the reds and blues, the impression is that these tones have been applied to a design in black and white by some later process; they do not form an integral part of the conception, so that the painting hardly suffers in a monochrome reproduction.

Occasionally, David is shocked out of his academic ivory tower. The assassination of his friend Marat provoked a realistic design, stark in its contrasts of light and shade, and hard in its modeling, which in this instance enforces the expression of gaunt tragedy. To some degree, portraits evoke this power of realism, since the necessity of adhering to the sitter's appearance helps to blast David loose from his formulae. Charlotte de Val d'Ognes (fig. 339), dressed in the costume of the day, a fashion simplified through the classic influence, sits sketching with her back to the window. Her face, therefore, is seen in reflected light, and her gown modeled by a fringe of light around the edges while most of it remains in shadow. That David can observe and record visual phenomena when he chooses, we may see in the broken window, where the slight distinction of sky seen through the glass or through the break is well preserved. To many, the portraits and the handful of David's other works in a realistic vein are more stirring than those official canvases he himself believed to be his masterpieces.

Whatever be the final judgment of David's painting, its historical importance is enormous. Not only does it reflect the civilization of his day, its aims and ideals, but it lays the tracks on which the Academy and official art were to run through the nineteenth century. To be sure, not even the Academy preserved indefinitely David's kind of historical painting. The pressure of later developments and new tastes drew the Academy further and further away from its origins. But the pseudo-intellectualism and the insistence upon drawing as basic to success in painting characterize official art for the whole century. They helped to turn this influential group, the Academy, into a reactionary force to oppose each new movement of the nineteenth century. By investing official patronage in this conservative body, which popular opinion is apt to follow, David made unnecessarily difficult the path of progressive painters for many generations.

XXI

Romanticism

In its underlying aspects, Romanticism may be defined as an escape mechanism prompted by the sordid conditions of the nineteenth century. The phenomenon known as the Industrial Revolution, the substitution of machine power for handicrafts, together with the rise of the factory system and therefore of large cities, had been manifest through the eighteenth century, especially in England, and in some occupations even before then. It is significant that Romanticism took deep root in England and that it first appeared there. Whatever advantages may have accrued to humanity in the long run from the Industrial Revolution, it brought in its train chaotic, overcrowded, and unsanitary cities, grimy with smoke and filth.

There were three possible ways to escape these conditions, mentally at least. First, past centuries, in which life was very different, offered to the imagination the chance of vicarious adventure and romance. Second, exotic lands were enchanting and alluring through distance. Finally, the mind might turn into the realm of the subjective, and to flights of fancy without connection with reality. To these three possibilities and in certain ways connected with them, must be added a renewed interest in nature, its freshness and cleanness in contrast to the dingy cities, its beauty as opposed to sordid urban reality. Probably all periods would claim to love nature in some degree, even the age of Louis XIV, but under the impulse of Romanticism nature was accepted more nearly as she is, in her slighter manifestations and intimate details as well as her larger effects.

On the surface, no two movements can be much further apart than Neoclassicism and Romanticism in the visual arts. In architecture, it is the gulf between the Roman and the Greek revivals on the one hand, and the Gothic revival on the other. In painting and sculpture, the Romantic movement assaults the subject matter, the style, and the very purpose of painting as laid down by David, an attack that was to leave its mark on the Academy itself. And yet, the more thoughtfully these two movements are examined, the more surely the conclusion is reached that they are parts of a single movement, the obverse and reverse of the medal, or two leaves growing from a single stem. The roots of Neo-classicism reach back into the eighteenth century; so also the origins of the Gothic revival occur at least as early as 1750. An archaeological note is common to both, though the archaeology of the Middle Ages, without the background possessed for the study of antiquity, is slower to mature. Often the same persons contributed to both movements. In literature, Keats not only admired the classic in the *Ode on a Grecian Urn*; he also loved the Gothic as in *The Eve of St. Agnes*. Most significant, if Romanticism be an escape in time or place, or both, the reversion to Rome or Greece constitutes as much of an escape as the return to the Gothic.

The Gothic revival started as a playful variation on the Georgian, no more serious than the *Chinoiseries*, those wallpapers, bits of china, and decorative carving which the eighteenth century loved to call Chinese, though no oriental would recognize the kinship. The fad of working in Gothic, at first taken up by the *nouveau riche*, became socially respectable when Horace Walpole began to play with the style at Strawberry Hill about 1752. His interest lay in the details of Gothic, in its picturesqueness, but not at all in its principles or in its construction. The Gothic details are a mere stage setting, and often frankly a sham, to such an extent that absurdities like sham ruins are actually built. The eighteenth century considered Gothic buildings as a setting for a mood, a background for self-dramatization. Some fortunate individuals owned estates on which the crumbling walls of a medieval abbey remained, but for those whose property was not so well equipped there was always the possibility of beautifying the place by building a ruin. William Mason perfectly describes this curious point of view in his poem, *The English Garden*.

Fonthill Abbey (fig. 340), designed by Wyatt at the turn of the century for the eccentric millionaire, William Beckford, was not built as a ruin, though it shortly became one. It is simply the most extravagant of the manifestations of this urge to the picturesque. This must have been the most inconvenient house ever built. Its four great wings consist chiefly of corridors, which lead to nothing. The entrance hall, with a broad flight of thoroughly un-Gothic stairs, is big enough to accommodate larger crowds than the house itself could hold. This hall exaggerates the proportions of a Gothic church, its doors and windows tall and narrow. Externally, the silhouette is irregular in the extreme. The picturesque asymmetry of the Middle Ages here becomes a goal, instead of resulting from the requirements of the building or the site. Such a building denies the principles of Gothic construction and its unself-conscious spirit. Wyatt gave thought to his effect; indeed he thought of little else. It is fortunate that Fonthill Abbey should have vanished. We can revisit the building only in imagination, in which realm its inconvenience and its flimsy construction can be calmly overlooked. Built as a fantasy, Fonthill Abbey should be enveloped in a haze of unreality.

Neither Wyatt nor Beckford, nor for that matter Walpole, were hampered by much knowledge of the medieval styles. Indeed, their day had not realized that the Middle Ages produced more than a single style. Still archaeology, in this case the result of antiquarian interest, gradually collected the basic information essential to any serious version of the style. Thomas Rickman produced the first intelligible classification of the medieval styles; he demonstrated their sequence and made it impossible thereafter to combine Early English, Decorated, and Perpendicular elements naively in the same building. Then men like John Britton disseminated a popular knowledge of the style through volumes of fine engravings, sold extensively because of the growing interest in and enthusiasm for Gothic architecture. Finally, the elder Pugin published plates of measured drawings of such details as arches, piers, tracery, ribs, buttresses, doors, and windows, which gave the architect who had to design a Gothic building the information he needed. A new church or castle cannot be designed on the basis of general views, however picturesque, but Pugin, himself an architect, knew just what sort of information was requisite.

These men and others laid an archaeological foundation on which the sober maturity of the Gothic revival could be reared. That movement was fostered by the identification of Gothic as a national architecture, at a time when nationalism was beginning to be powerful in England. The belief was widespread in England that the Gothic was a purely English style, whereas the Roman and the Greek were foreign in origin. It had not yet been realized or admitted that however native the Gothic became, it was originally imported from France to England.

Even more influential was the identification of Gothic as Christian architecture, whereas Greek and Roman were pagan. The revival within the Anglican Church, known as the Oxford Movement, provided a stimulus to faith and worship that turned to the ritual of the Middle Ages for expression. That ritual needed a setting, and thus the power of religion reinforced the Gothic revival. Therefore, its point of view changed from one of superficiality and picturesqueness to one of sobriety and seriousness comparable to a Quest of the Holy Grail.

The most famous building of the Gothic revival in England, where the movement was strongest, is the Houses of Parliament (fig. 341). Designed by Sir Charles Barry in the middle of the century, but with its Perpendicular Gothic detail supplied by the younger Pugin, the Houses of Parliament is still transitional to the maturity of the revival. Barry is by training and preference a classicist. If his plan and mass are not classic, neither are they pure Gothic. Probably this is fortunate: the plan has a coherence no Gothic revivalist of the time could have achieved. However, the silhouette is so picturesque that the Houses of Parliament has long been a goal of painters, but its style, the Perpendicular, was identified at the time with the decay of Gothic architecture, and went out of fashion even before the building was completed. A. N. Welby Pugin's own work, such as St. Augustine's at Ramsgate in 1842, prefers the Decorated or sometimes the Early English style. His profound knowledge of medieval architecture and his religious spirit enabled him to withstand better than his contemporaries the tendency to display. At their best, his buildings are not merely correct in detail, but sound in construction and devotional in character.

If Romanticism in architecture is best realized in England, its effects in sculpture and painting, save in the field of landscape, can better be illustrated on the Continent. The group by François Rude (1784–1855) called the Departure of the Volunteers (fig. 342) on the Arc de Triomphe in Paris is transitional. The presence of the nude figure carries over from Neoclassicism, and yet even here the proportions and the modeling to bring out the tenseness of the forms are not academic or classic. Moreover, the armor is Romantic, based upon French armor of the sixteenth century. The group as a whole has an exuberance of emotion and a surging movement that Neoclassic sculpture abhorred. Under the patriotic stimulus of the *Marseillaise*, this band of volunteers leaving for the front has inspired an emotion in the artist never found in the cold intellectuality of Neoclassicism. Rude becomes completely Romantic in the portrait of Marshal Ney (fig. 343). Neoclassic portraits had been generalized; they were robed in anachronistic togas or some garb that would identify them with well-known examples of classic sculpture, such as Canova's portrait of Pauline Bonaparte Borghese as a semi-nude Venus Victrix. Rude, on the other hand, dresses Marshal Ney in the uniform of the Napoleonic armies. He is rendered not as a type but as an individual. His upraised arm, with sword aloft, and mouth open as though shouting a command to charge involve movement in the composition. This dramatic moment of action helps to characterize the figure.

In the actuality of Marshal Ney, the Romantic return to nature manifests itself. So too, but more pungently, does it appear in the animal sculpture of Antoine Louis Barye (1796–1875). His Jaguar Devouring a Hare (fig. 344) testifies to his study in the Paris Zoological Gardens and his measurements of the exotic animals to be seen there. Though Barye never saw these creatures in their native habitats, no one has so grasped their Romantic wildness and ferocity. The style is at once realistic and broad. No detail is present that might not be found in reality, but many details that do exist in nature are suppressed by Barye with a view to greater emphasis on the essential and the expressive. Through such a treatment, Barye creates a succession of dynamic and sculpturesque animal groups. His understanding of character in animals is unsurpassed. The action of the big cat with ears laid back, its tail flicking to and fro, and its tense crouch while feeding can be observed in even so humble a representative of the family as the domestic cat, but is, naturally, increased in scale. The exotic nature of these creatures and the selection of a moment of feeding or combat to emphasize their wildness are fundamentally Romantic traits. No animal sculptor has ever reached the height scaled by Barye, partly through his combination of realism and the sculpturesque, and partly through his use of animals to parallel human emotions. We, as humans, respond to the qualities Barye discovers in his subjects.

The painters of Romanticism, like the sculptors, reject Neoclassic doctrine. They refuse to respect the formulae laid down by the Academy, and turn to subject matter of greater range. Not only do they exploit the history of the Middle Ages — in fact, they do that only to a limited extent — but they also turn to their own day to utilize material that touches their lives and provokes in them an emotion they can convey to their audience. Thrills, excitement, horror, not born of the mind but rather of the emotions, replace the aridity of Neoclassicism. Such an altered purpose demands a change of technique. Therefore, the insistence on drawing, and especially on delineation, must be reduced.

In its place, the emotional possibilities of color once more come into their own. Although the color and vitality of Rubens had been anathema to David, the Flemish painter exercised great influence over the foremost Romanticist, Delacroix.

One important forerunner of the full-blown Romantic movement calls for comment. Francisco Goya y Lucientes (1746–1828) was as turbulent by nature as were the days of the Napoleonic occupation of Spain through which he lived. Strongly erotic — he almost lost his life in consequence cf one of his ill-starred escapades — Goya was probably never happier than when embroiled. The best Spanish painter since Velásquez, he became portraitist to the decadent court of Charles IV. It is astonishing that Goya should have been able to retain this post unchallenged. His realism enabled him to characterize to the point of caricature. Goya painted the queen as a sensual vixen, and the king as a moron — characterizations that might be accurate, but we suspect that only the inability of the court to recognize their truth prevented these paintings from being suppressed and Goya with them. In many of his early works, Goya is not above criticism. His figures are often stiff and wooden; they do not stand firmly, nor have they much atmosphere around them, as though he painted them in a vacuum.

The Maja Desnuda (fig. 345), the same fundamental motive as Giorgione's Venus (fig. 235), is entirely representative of Goya. No more sensual or naturalistic portrait of the female figure can be discovered in the annals of great painting. Everything is done in drawing, in color, and in pose to make the figure as alluring as possible. Nevertheless, Goya does not neglect the exigencies of composition. The figure strikes the diagonal of the canvas, and the arms, folded behind her head, provide a counter movement to stop the action in that direction. Goya once said, 'Lines, always lines, and never body. But where do we see these lines in nature? I see only forms which advance, forms which recede, masses in light or in shadow.' Clearly then, Goya was not in sympathy with the delineation stressed by the Academy, and intended to turn from it to methods that correspond to the observed appearances of nature.

To a man of his temperament, the incidents of the Napoleonic occupation of Spain gave a perfect opportunity to dramatize the horrible. The Execution of Madrileños (fig. 346) depicts a military execution of those who resisted the French occupation. They say that Goya came upon the scene the morning after the execution, when the bodies were still lying in the gutter, and dipped his handkerchief in the pools of their stagnant blood to make his first sketch of this composition on a near-by wall. Whether this be true or not, it is just the sort of thing that Goya would do. A dramatic light brings into prominence the group of victims filled with the horror of impending death, and silhouettes the soldiers with their leveled rifles in the foreground. Here Goya expresses his interest in 'masses in light, and masses in shadow, planes which recede, reliefs or backgrounds.' None of these figures is delineated; that would have lost the turbulence, and therefore the emotional horror of the scene.

This macabre strain in Goya finds extensive expression in the series of etchings called Los Desastres de la Guerra, and to a much lesser extent in the series, La Tauromaquía, a sort of history of the bull ring. His wild fancy and his sarcasm prompt the other two series, Los Caprichos and Los Proverbios. A single plate, Hasta la Muerte (Till Death) (fig. 347), shows his grim humor. The age-old desire to retain the habiliments of youth long after they have ceased to be appropriate receives here a sarcastic commentary, with figures verging on grotesqueness. If in these etchings are humor and entertainment, there is also present much that is less pleasant to contemplate, as Goya dissects the foibles of humanity with pitiless accuracy.

The French Academy naturally never had the force in Spain that it enjoyed in Paris. Hence, an independent spirit like Goya could arise in Spain at the very height of the Neoclassic movement. The rise of Romanticism in France comes a little later and more slowly. It is dimly foretold in Baron Antoine Jean Gros, who in 1815 succeeded David as leader of the Academy when David was exiled as a regicide to Brussels on the occasion of the restoration of the Bourbons. Baron Gros concurred in the ideals of historical painting set down by David, but Gros had served with Napoleon during the Egyptian campaign and at other times, and the military life of his own day interested him, not the wars of Hannibal or the battles of Marathon and Thermopylae. Napoleon in the Pest House at Jaffa (fig. 348) has first of all the interest of a historical event known to Gros. The members of Napoleon's staff wear their full military regalia. Nothing of the classic in subject matter can find a place in such a scene. Perhaps the nude man in the foreground may recall the academic concentration on the figure, but a strong and natural light falls on the central group in the foreground and defines the planes of the buildings in the distance, a very different effect from the cold lighting of the Death of Socrates (fig. 338) for example.

Also transitional, but further along on the road to Romanticism, is

Théodore Géricault (1791–1824). Because of its military glory, the Academy might condone the Napoleon at Jaffa, but the Raft of the Medusa (fig. 349) came as a grenade to the Salon of 1819. It happened that the ship *Medusa* had been allowed to leave port in an unseaworthy condition and had foundered at sea. After days of suffering on an open raft in mid-ocean, a few survivors were picked up by another ship and brought to port. Many had died of exposure and starvation on the raft; others had gone insane. Their tales of horror invoked a wave of sympathy, and of criticism of the Government, which seemed partly responsible for the disaster. Géricault was among those who were stirred. He was accused of criticizing the Government in this picture; that such was his intention is by no means certain, but there can be no two opinions about the dramatic horror of his painting. The moment is that when the rescuing ship has just been sighted on the horizon, and the strongest survivors, led by a Negro, struggle upward in hysterical joy at the prospect of rescue. The old man at the left has lost all hope of deliverance, and perhaps all desire, as he drops his hand in a protecting gesture over the corpse of his son. The survivors have not strength enough to clear the raft of their comrades who have already died, such as the body dragging through the waves to the right. No one in 1819, with the tragedy still fresh in his mind, could look at this painting unmoved. Its gruesome tale inspired pity in all who saw it. On the other hand, no one feels emotionally aroused by David's historical designs, whether they be accepted as great paintings or not. This is why the conservatives of the Academy condemned the Medusa. It is not especially foreign to their traditions in color; the prevailing tonality is still brown. The large size of the painting is not different from academic standards. The emphasis on drawing and the academic love of the figure are still present, as Géricault uses to the full the opportunities afforded by his theme for a study of the nude. The contrasts of light and dark, however, are more dramatic than in Neoclassic paintings. With that exception, the technique remains conservative in this painting of Géricault, but the spirit of Romanticism is already rampant.

Had Géricault lived, he might have become the leader of the Romantic rebels. His premature death in 1824 allowed the torch to fall into the hands of Ferdinand Eugène Delacroix (1798–1863). An exceptionally well-informed and intelligent man, Delacroix was anything but revolutionary by nature. It was not his desire to head a movement with whose excesses he had little sympathy, no matter how fully he himself might adhere to the less radical sides of the new development. Already, in his Bark of Dante in 1822, Delacroix had proclaimed his willingness to turn to a theme of the Middle Ages drawn from the *Inferno*, and with something of its horror paramount in the result. Nevertheless, the browns and the academic interest in the nude still remained, though with heavier modeling of the forms. As in Géricault, it was more the spirit than the forms that had altered.

A few years later, partly under the influence of Rubens, Delacroix's color and forms began to change. The Massacre of Scio (fig. 350), like the Raft of the Medusa, came from a contemporary event. In this case, the source was the Greek war of liberation from Turkey. The prosperous island of Chios had not joined that revolt, but an abortive raid by the rebels caused the Turkish governor to lose his head and permit the Janissaries to massacre thousands of the defenseless civilian population. Liberal sentiment in western Europe was appalled at this new act of dastardy committed by the 'unspeakable Turk.' Sympathy for the Greeks already existed in western Europe, where it stimulated the Greek revival; Delacroix's epic vision of the Greek war illustrated that sympathy. The painting is handled with restraint; in the foreground, a group of Greeks, men and women, wait their turn for slaughter, helpless and hopeless. They do not even struggle against the inevitable. The scenes of tumult are relegated to the background. Nor are the Janissaries more violent; their mission, foreordained by Allah, is to slay these Christian pigs; they complete their task with contempt but with little more emotion than a butcher plying his trade. Horrible as is the subject with its accent on pathos, the expression seems controlled merely to heighten its grimness through contrast. No longer does delineation dominate; the brownish tonality has been modified in favor of richer color than obtained hitherto. The use of complementary tones, such as violet shadows on a yellow passage, or green to serve as a foil to red, probably came to Delacroix through observation, though it did exist in paintings by some of the 'old masters' with whose works Delacroix was conversant and in Constable's contemporary English landscape paintings.

More riotous in color, with an evident influence from Rubens, is the Death of Sardanapalus. The subject of this large and sensational canvas is drawn from Byron, that is, from English Romanticism. What an opportunity it affords Delacroix to study the female figure, as the eunuchs put to death the women of the harem lest they become part of the booty of the king's enemies! The theme gives Delacroix a chance to develop action, rich contrasts of light and shade, and sumptuousness of color.

Delacroix returns to French life for inspiration in Liberty Leading the People, an event that occurred 28 July 1830 (fig. 351). In it he creates an apotheosis of the July revolution, which ejected Charles X, of the older branch of the Bourbon dynasty, from the throne of France and installed the younger branch in its place in the person of Louis Philippe, who promised to be favorable to the business classes. In the center, the allegorical figure of France bears the banner of the revolution. On the right is irrepressible youth who, like a traditional western cowboy, strides over the barricades with both guns swinging, a splendid interpretation of a type, to whom the ends of the revolution appear to be less important than its excitement. The lower-class support of this palace revolution inspires the man at the extreme left, but that figure is shadowed, while next to him is an eminently respectable businessman. One expects sideburns, a frock coat, and a top hat on 'change;' they look anachronous in the confusion and melee of street fighting. And yet the class he represents controls this political upset; they want a government favorable to their interests; but they do not want another social upheaval like the French Revolution; that would be very bad for trade. This solid businessman seems to have picked down from above his mantel an old fowling piece, which looks as antiquated as he himself is unexpected in these surroundings. The dramatic lighting, the color, the contemporary scene, and the excitement in the painting make it a landmark of Romanticism as well as a document of great historical interest.

During the 1830's, France began to expand into north Africa. The Moorish civilization there and the exotic wild life of the region attracted artists like Delacroix. As a member of a mission to the Sultan of Morocco, he had first-hand knowledge of this part of the world. Lion hunts with turbaned and burnoosed Bedouins provide Delacroix with an opportunity to achieve the movement and color that he finds in Rubens. Here, too, he begins to exploit the peculiar qualities of paint, and therefore his draftsmanship becomes looser or, more precisely, free. The old linearism is deserted. Nor does he restrict his themes to animals and the hunt. The Algerian Women (fig. 352) is at least as exotic as his paintings of lions. The hot stillness of this inner room, its oriental color in the pink, orange, black, and white tiled wall echoed in the costumes, and the life represented in this scene is as foreign as it well could be to life in France. Such a scene is alluring, especially when seen from a distance through the medium of painting. It provides those elements of romance that were fast disappearing from European civilization and whose want the painters might help to correct. Moreover, such paintings attest the European interest in colonial expansion under economic and imperialistic stimuli.

Delacroix's fight for recognition of the Romantic point of view met the opposition of Jean Auguste Dominique Ingres (1780–1867). Older than Delacroix, Ingres had been a pupil of David; later he spent many years in Rome, supporting himself, in part, by a series of exquisite pencil portraits. These tight drawings are sharp in detail around the face, but more sketchy in their indication of costume. Essentially linear, Ingres suppresses shadow. A few small areas, under the chin or below the nose, suffice to establish the form of the head. The passages fade so subtly into white that the pencil strokes are imperceptible and suggest a waxy smoothness of surface. Such elegance and refinement recur from time to time in French art, in the paintings of the Clouets, and the drawings and paintings of Watteau, as though they were sympathetic to the French temperament. These little drawings testify to Ingres' consummate skill as a draftsman, and are often fresher than his paintings.

They suggest that draftsmanship lies at the basis of his style. When Ingres became the recognized leader of the Academy, he modified the ideals of that body and, even more than David, determined its character for the rest of the nineteenth century. By his time, the spirit of the day had changed so that the historical subjects of David could no longer maintain their position of dominance. In their place, Ingres substituted the human figure, sometimes male but more often female, as the prime requisite of painting. His Odalisque (fig. 353) already represents the type. The figure is not individualized; on the contrary, the form is generalized, the principal divisions of the body accurate enough, but with all sensuous details eliminated. His control of line tends to emphasize delineation; we are first aware of the outline of the figure developed with lyrical beauty and clarity. The figure as such means nothing. It is an excuse for Ingres to display his proficiency as a draftsman. Such a nude may be posed in any number of ways, though in fact the poses are almost invariably quiet; it may serve to represent Truth or Venus, a Fountain or an Odalisque. The title changes but the essential figure does not. Through such works as this, Ingres established the academic nude as the primary subject of official art for the rest of the century, and, by reason of his insistence upon delineation, draftsmanship became the prerequisite for academic recognition. 'Anything that is well drawn is well enough painted,' he once said. Therefore, color is an afterthought, and from then on the Academy produced a series of coldly academic studies, which, however adequate in draftsmanship, look like tinted drawings. A man of less breadth of mind than Delacroix, Ingres' narrow spirit restricted official art for generations.

The Romantic interest in nature, as a palliative for urban conditions, is bound to have far-reaching results in landscape painting. The new point of view went back into the eighteenth century in the work of the English watercolorists, some of them amateurs who dabbled in landscape, but who dealt with specific scenes. More important is Richard Wilson (1714–82) who, though he retained the conventional dark foreground and brownish tonality inherited from the French classic school of Claude Lorrain, turned by preference to the rugged aspects of nature, to Cader Idris and the Welsh mountains, for example. He substitutes the beauty of the picturesque and the unexpected for the well-groomed, carefully constructed landscapes, traditional in his day. Somewhat later, Thomas Gainsborough, who preferred landscape to portraiture, gave vent to his lyrical spirit and his pictorial power in a series of magnificent designs, like the Market Wagon, which his own time failed to appreciate.

However, it remained for John Constable (1776–1837) to effect the revolution in landscape painting. He stated his aims, which may be taken as the creed of Romantic landscape painting, in saying, 'There is room for a natural painter.' Though his finished compositions, such as the Hay Wain (fig. 354), may be executed within his studio, they reject the traditional scheme of landscape painting. The dark foreground and lighted distance and the brownish tonality are tossed into the limbo of antiquated notions. Instead of areas of solid color, Constable breaks up the masses of foliage into sparkling green passages, broad and free in handling, and far closer to the vibrancy of nature than are the traditional solutions of the problem.

Like the Dutch, he turns to the specific, not the general, in landscape; the Hay Wain represents a bit of his native Suffolk. In composition, we are at first unaware of the existence of a deliberate scheme. The painting appears to be well adjusted, but even more strongly the house and the group of trees near the foreground on the left seem to be placed there because in this particular scene that is where they happened to occur. Though this casualness of arrangement may be, and in this instance is, more apparent than real, nevertheless such informality underscores Constable's acceptance of the actual scene. He so loves nature that he clings to her not only in the structure of his trees, his cloud formations, and all the other elements of landscape, but even in their arrangement. Therein lies both his strength and his weakness. Few better grasp and render the scenes before them, but at times his passion for actuality leads him to forget that after all he is painting a picture, not creating a landscape. His scope is limited, through his very naturalism, to those scenes he had himself observed, and since he seldom traveled, the range of his material is restricted. Nevertheless, Constable does select his subject and modify it enough to construct pictures without loss of naturalism, while his serious study of the structure of natural forms gives to his work a solidity seldom rivaled and never surpassed.

As much cannot be said of Joseph Mallord William Turner (1775–1851). More fluent as a draftsman than Constable, he relied too heavily on such facility, to the detriment of those qualities of honest structure that empower all of Constable's paintings. Turner had an unbounded admiration for Claude Lorrain, and in his earlier career especially, for example, Crossing the Brook, he retained the composition and something of the restricted palette of his great forebear, but combined them with the Romantic love of nature. He obviously thought his work better than that on which it was based, since he bequeathed to the British nation several paintings by Claude, on the condition that they be displayed in conjunction with some of his own. His idea was at once to acknowledge his debt, and to demonstrate his superiority. His own day believed him; today critics realize that he had little of the pictorial ability so marked in the French artist. Facile as they are, his trees become stereotyped and have none of that lyric love of nature evident even through the conventions of Claude's paintings.

As his style developed, Turner became more and more absorbed in color, and, toward the end of his life, in atmosphere, which he approached emotionally with swirling masses of unco-ordinated color and pigment. Often at this time, he tended to lose his sense of structure and his contact with nature, without offering in their place any compensation in the way of pictorial values. The Fighting *Téméraire* (fig. 355) appeals to sentiment; who does not feel the tragedy when some fine old ship, ennobled by its associations, is towed away to destruction? That drama is heightened by the contrast of the picturesque man-of-war and a most unromantic tug. Such an appeal to sentiment may be legitimate, but in other respects the painting is not. The ship has become a ghostly galleon, a veritable *Flying Dutchman,* with no feeling for structure at all. The sun perversely sets in the darkest corner of the sky. Turner has begun to dump his paint pot upside down to call attention to his canvas, which is full of anachronisms.

His celebrated canvas, Rain, Steam, and Speed, purports to show a train crossing a viaduct in a fog. The tangible subject dwindles to a mere excuse for a study of atmosphere, in which forms dissolve in a haze of smoke and mist, unsubstantial and unscientific by comparison with later atmospheric studies of Claude Monet. A recent critic calls his work a parody of nature. However, it seems probable that the current condemnation of Turner is excessive, perhaps as false as his extreme adulation by his own day. No doubt he suffers from the quantity of his work on display, much of it mediocre or worse. Still, it is wiser to judge a man by his best work, and Turner is capable, if not of Constable's soundness of structure or Claude's pictorial brilliance, of effective canvases, which were to play a historic role as an influence on Impressionism a generation later.

On the other hand, Constable's influence, injected by his paintings into the Salon of 1824, is profound on the Barbizon school, a group of landscape painters who, in the 1830's, sought refuge from the cost of living in Paris at Barbizon on the outskirts of the forest of Fontainebleau. Théodore Rousseau (1812–67), called the eagle of the group because of his strength, turns to the *paysage intime,* the same kind of pastoral and intimate bits of landscape that Constable loves. He discards the picturesque and the scenic. The Oaks (fig. 356) occupy and block the center of the composition and so confine our attention to the foreground. Such distance as may be necessary to establish this grove in space is relegated to the sides. The tufts of grass in the foreground are more important to Rousseau than a vista of great distance, and the structure of the trees more significant than either. There is nothing epic in the scene, save its power of observation. This delight in the smaller aspects of nature and this confidence in their pictorial sufficiency did not meet the approval of the Academy; so consistently were Rousseau's paintings rejected by the juries of the Salons that he was nicknamed 'le Grand Refusé.'

Strictly speaking, Jean Baptiste Camille Corot (1796–1875) does not belong to the Barbizon school, though he sympathized with its members and helped them to the best of his ability. His own characteristic manner is easily recognized in La Matinée (fig. 357), sometimes called the Dance of the Nymphs. These idyllic figures might be the dream children of the landscape itself, which has an unreal and imaginative appearance. In actuality, Corot has an understanding of nature and its structure, a lyric love of the country, which pervades these songs in paint like odes in honor of his goddess. His strict limitation of color and values suppresses extreme darks and lights, and vivid colors in preference to silvery grays or gray greens. An occasional touch of stronger color serves to accent the quietness of the scene. These canvases, so characteristic of Corot, contrast with his early work, such as the Honfleur (fig. 358), more architectural scenes with planes of strong light and shade, blocked in with a structural sense of pictorial possibilities. This same sturdy construction marks his few but powerful figure paintings. After we have become sated with the repetition of his better-known works, such designs as these come both as a surprise and a relief.

The Barbizon group is primarily one of landscape painters. With them, Jean François Millet (1814–75) allies himself, but applies their directness and their unpretentious modesty to the figure. By birth a Norman peasant, Millet fully understood the types for which he was to become known. The Sower (fig. 359) pursues his vocation in the time-honored way, strewing the grain over the fields by hand. The setting is reduced to a minimum; merely a plane of brown to indicate the plowed ground, and a line for the horizon. Against this background, Millet creates an epic type, a symbol of the farmer of all times and places, in his constant struggle to wrest a livelihood from the soil. This is no musical-comedy peasant with a picturesque costume; he is dressed in rough but serviceable garments, adapted to heavy wear. The technique of painting is as rough as the costume and the figure, as though to insist on the bulk of this monumental character.

In these types, Millet created an apotheosis of the class he knew and loved, as he understood it. In his lifetime, he was accused of social propaganda; to later ages, he reflected their own attitude that the underprivileged were oppressed by the exploitation of the upper classes. Such interpretations were totally foreign to Millet. He was amused that his own day could discover propaganda in his paintings; he would be astonished that anyone should think of his peasants as 'stolid and stunned, a brother to the ox,' as Edwin Markham wrote. On the contrary, if the peasant's lot be hard, Millet believed he had the strength to bear it. His characters exult in the importance of their calling; they are, in fact, the group upon whom the strength of France is based, and their elemental power lends them majesty. Theirs is no message of despair; it is a magnificent tribute to the people whom Millet knew so well.

XXII

The Later Nineteenth Century in Europe

As the nineteenth century progressed, Paris became more and more the center of the art world. It was there that new artistic ideas were born and new developments took place. Its atmosphere fostered informal discussion and the existence of a large group of artists in Paris, as well as other advantages, drew still more artists from all over the European world to that metropolis. Consequently, each new step in French art was reflected in the art of other countries, and of course academic art continued in Paris and elsewhere to supply at once an accompaniment and a foil to the new ideas, each of which had to battle itself into recognition against the persistent conservatism of official bodies.

The Academies in painting paralleled the École des Beaux Arts in architecture. This school laid stress on drawing and on the effectiveness of a design on paper. Such an emphasis inevitably focused on the pictorial possibilities in design, and although structural training existed in the curriculum, if one may call it that, and was expected to appear in the drawings, the position accorded to it was apt to be insignificant. Also new materials, however great their implicit possibilities, had to overcome a strong academic prejudice, based on the supposition that they were ill adapted to monumental architecture.

This is a difficult era to discuss, because all manner of different styles coexist. Eclecticism is the guiding thread. The word means freedom of choice; as applied to the arts, specifically freedom to select from among the styles of the past. Either the architect or his client or both may decide in what historic style the building shall be dressed. Eclecticism did not really obtain during the earlier Greek and Gothic revivals, though its germs were present even then. Many factors may influence the choice; some of them intelligent, others so minor as to be merely silly. The association, however speciously, of a given type of building with a given style, as for example, the identification of church architecture and the Gothic, may determine the selection. The supposed existence of a national historic style is sometimes a governing factor. The training of the architect selected, or his or his client's whims or tastes, which may or may not be rational, are but too frequently the only reasons for adopting one style rather than another. All the styles tend to be crass, whether it be some modification of the classic or the Victorian Gothic, which often turns from English and French sources to Italian or German Gothic. The architects feel equally free to borrow details from where they will, and to mix elements drawn from one style with elements taken from another; their confidence in their ability to effect such a combination is supreme if unjustified.

Nevertheless, from this unpromising ground sprang a few distinguished architectural monuments. The Bibliothèque Ste. Geneviève in 1843–50 by Henri Labrouste derives from the early Italian Renaissance, and owes some debt to Alberti's design of the flank of San Francesco at Rimini. Severe arcades enclose the windows of the second-floor reading room, and only small arched windows and a band of garlands break the plain stone wall of the ground floor. These fifteenth-century motives lead to nothing; more prophetic is the reading room (fig. 360). Among its other qualities, the nineteenth century fostered a phenomenal growth in science, a corollary to its materialism; so far as it affected architecture, this is reflected in the increased use of metal as a structural material. Iron and bronze had been employed from time immemorial for the decorative details of architecture, but the cost of metal had hitherto prevented its structural use. During the eighteenth century, it began to appear in bridges, for example, the Severn Bridge, constructed in 1775–9, and from there it spread to utilitarian buildings. In 1801, it appeared in a cotton mill in Manchester, and in 1824 in the market hall of the Madeleine in Paris.

Up to the middle of the century, however, tradition had hampered its adoption for monumental buildings, as did the Beaux Arts' emphasis on historic styles. Labrouste wanted his reading room to be free of heavy interior supports. He might have vaulted it in stone, but to do so would have necessitated heavy walls, which in turn would have curtailed the light. To cover this span with wooden beams, even if it were possible, would result in a lack of monumentality and permanence. Therefore Labrouste turned to iron in the form of arches and slender columns, whose light proportions were possible in no other material. As always when a new material is adopted, the design is conceived partly in terms of other materials. The slender iron columns retain the details of the Corinthian order. Moreover, the utilitarian arches are disguised with waving foliate designs, as though Labrouste were ashamed of his material or perhaps had not yet found a solution in design for it as acceptable to the public as the solutions so readily at hand with the older building materials. On the other hand, in the utilitarian stacks, the architect takes full advantage of iron. The open grilled floors allow penetration of light and create a frank expression of intersecting planes.

Architects are often unjustly condemned for their conservatism, and derisive comparisons are drawn between them and engineers. In that connection, it is fair to remember that adequate designs for the automobile were not immediately discovered by the engineers, who at the outset designed their cars in terms of wagons; it took more than a generation to reach the beauty of contemporary automobiles. Much the same can be said of the locomotive, the steamship, and the airplane. Moreover, the architect experiments with his client's money, and the latter will usually prevent any solution of a new problem, however appropriate, which departs too radically from the buildings known to him. One cannot test buildings on a proving ground, since their cost forbids their immediate destruction and redesign, even when lines of improvement become obvious at once. Such a scheme as Labrouste's, then, though it has some precedent in utilitarian buildings and parallels contemporary exposition architecture, such as the Crystal Palace in London in 1851, represents a bold experiment with a material, not yet respectable in academic circles, whose perfected expressions, such as the Eiffel Tower in Paris or the skyscrapers in America, could arise only later.

If the Bibliothèque Ste. Geneviève derives from the Renaissance, the Paris Opera House of 1861–74 (fig. 361) by Charles Garnier stems from the Baroque. The well-organized plan testifies to the thoroughness of the Beaux Arts training, as does the controlled richness of the Baroque façade. Such opulence of arches and columns, cartouches and sculpture, lends a festive character to the building. The Baroque sumptuousness of opera, quite understandable since opera is a Baroque form, seemed to call for this kind of display. Garnier's success is tragically evident when contrasted with many an American theater, whose designers were tempted to walk in the paths of the mighty without adequate training for such an exercise. It requires an architect with a thorough understanding of composition to master so rich a style. The stairway of the Paris Opera (fig. 362), with its Baroque curves and bulging balconies, not only communicates with the boxes and seats; even more it affords a setting for the social panoply opera inspires.

On the other hand, the church of the Sacré Cœur in Paris, begun in 1873, is Romanesque in style and the quintessence of Romanticism in feeling. Its architect, Abadie, had remodeled the church of St. Front at Pé-rigueux, an example of the half-Byzantine Romanesque of Aquitaine, crowned with five domes. No doubt this suggested the new design, but Abadie has piled up turrets and dome in a picturesque manner, far more extravagant in effect than the medieval building. Crowning the heights of Montmartre, this church has a fairy-tale unreality about it, something un-believable, like an illustration for the *Arabian Nights.*

The same eclecticism is prevalent in sculpture — at times, even the same styles that inspire the architects are used. Jean Baptiste Carpeaux's (1827–75) group of the Dance (fig. 363) on the Paris Opera House is as Baroque as the building. The subject involves a momentary expression of violent movement. The action of these figures, even though they form a ring, often leads the eye out of the central mass. Thus the composition has the complexity of the Baroque, its openness, and its turbulence. Much picto-rial detail finds room here. The whole design, though executed in marble, is in fact conceived for the plasticity of clay.

Just as the painters of Romanticism turn to Rubens for inspiration, so too do Carpeaux and, even more, Jules Dalou. In the latter's Silenus in the Luxembourg Gardens, the fleshy figure, the movement and abandon, the naturalism of the modeling, and the pictorial accessories may well jus-tify a description of the work as a modeler's version of a Rubens mythol-ogy. Like all sculptors of their day, Carpeaux and Dalou build up their compositions in a soft material, which may be molded under their fin-gers into naturalistic details. The model can then be transcribed into bronze or stone, and each modulation of the clay surface preserved. To achieve monumentality under these circumstances is all but impossible; effects appropriate in clay are too readily at hand to be avoided, even if the sculptor tries to retain in his mind the qualities of the final material in which the work will appear.

These considerations go far to explain the style of Auguste Rodin (1840–1917), the outstanding sculptor of the second half of the nineteenth cen-tury. He concludes the development from the break-down of Neoclas-sicism at the hands of Rude and Barye through the pictorial modeling of Carpeaux and Dalou. That Rodin is capable of amazing naturalism is ap-parent in the Age of Bronze. This figure of a young Belgian soldier caused Rodin to be attacked by his fellow sculptors, who accused him of trying to palm off a life cast as an independent work. Rodin was able to free himself from this charge, but the accusation would never have been made at all had not his statue been so like the human figure in every detail. The group called the Burghers of Calais is only less naturalistic. These five figures, who commemorate an incident of local history, are each individualized, their faces stern if not haggard, their bare arms gaunt and sinewy, and their sackcloth pictorial. Rodin wanted to dispense with a pedestal, and place them on a plinth only a few inches high. Had this been carried out, the effect when one encountered the group in a city square would have been startling.

These works were cast in bronze, but his most common type of sculpture is in marble and may be illustrated by The Kiss (fig. 364). The surfaces of these intertwined figures undulate to induce a play of light and shade over them. This concern with light effects recalls the contemporary Impressionist preoccupation with that field, and hence permits a description of Rodin as the foremost Impressionist sculptor. The fluid surface modulation, however, is not so broken as to violate naturalism; on the contrary, it is calculated to give the stone the animation of living flesh. Rodin's love of the body is sensuous, and often frankly erotic, as these figures interlock in their passionate embrace. The soft texture of flesh contrasts with the rough block of stone on which they sit, the marks of the chisel still apparent on its surface. Very often Rodin resorts to the device of allowing part of his figures to emerge from an unfinished block, as Michelangelo had done before him. In the case of the great Florentine, the lack of finish is probably due to pressure of other work; in Rodin's hands, it becomes meretricious. It does not even express a feeling for the material. The sensuous naturalism and his modeler's conception and methods leave him typical of nineteenth-century sculpture in both respects.

When he was commissioned to do a portrait of Balzac (fig. 365), Rodin's patrons were outraged at the result and rejected it, though by then he had won recognition. Rodin conceives Balzac wrapped in his dressing gown and striding about the room in the throes of literary composition. A powerful head tops a chaotic mass. The bulk of the great body, though simple in its larger outlines, like some outcropping of nature, fritters away its form in meaningless bosses and hollows, rough and broken clay-like surfaces, until it becomes amorphous. The interpretive portrait, with its beetling eyebrows and heavy features, is intended to be lighted from above to accentuate to the utmost its sensationalism.

Whatever importance the architecture and sculpture of the time may have, the dominant medium of art of the late nineteenth century is painting. So pronounced is this pre-eminence that many people today confuse the terms art and painting, or use them as synonyms, and thus fail to realize that art comprises many other media. However, there is something of the painter's attitude in Rodin's pictorial interest in light and shade, and, in fact, many of the sculptors of his day either started as painters or practiced that art in addition to their own. Perhaps even in architecture, the eclectic tendency to design for effect and to deny, conceal, or at the very least minimize the importance of structure may be traced to the same attitude. Possibly the methods of education in all the arts by means of the Academies combine to produce this result. However that may be, the fact remains that painting is as pre-eminent in the arts during the nineteenth century as sculpture had been in Periclean Greece and architecture in medieval Europe.

Moreover, the Industrial Revolution, against whose results Romanticism had protested, called into being a crass materialism in a large section of the public. Progress became identified with bigger and better production, and success measured in terms of money. Whether or not such a scale of values is desirable, it is impertinent as applied to painting and sculpture, and hardly relevant in architecture. Thus the values that the artist recognized, the public rejected, and *vice versa*. The success of a painting cannot be measured by its dimensions or by the quantity and cost of the pigment expended on it. Therefore, the artist became separated further from the public in aims and ideals. If the notion that the artist is a queer and impractical fellow did not originate at this time, it did gain currency.

This separation of the artist from the public, and his consequent rebellious attitude, could not but affect his work. The fact that without a market for his paintings the artist might starve is in some respects a minor matter, however vital to him. His enemies could retort that inability to earn a livelihood in painting did not close the door to other gainful occupations, and if the artist chose to suffer in a garret rather than work in a factory, that was his own affair. During earlier centuries, the upper class, either the aristocracy or the church, had cultivated a genuine interest in the arts, and passed it on as a tradition from generation to generation. Their ideals were susceptible of interpretation in paint or stone with no loss of artistic integrity; moreover, the artist's public sympathized with, understood, and enjoyed his products. With the materialistic ideals of the nineteenth century, the artist could not compromise without losing his integrity. Furthermore, through the new economic developments, a new wealthy group had come to the fore. These men had no inherited appreciation of the arts. They lacked the background and traditions that had sustained painting in earlier days. At the same time, they realized, or some of them did, that patronage of art was one of the perquisites, if not a social requisite, of their position. In an unknown field, to whom should they turn for guidance if not to official art and the Academies?

By reason of their control of the annual salons, the Academies wielded tremendous power. Their juries could and did reject not merely the incompetent but the new and original, and indeed anything that failed to meet their conservative standards. By refusing to exhibit the works of a painter, the Academy could deprive him of the opportunity to become known to that part of the public interested in art; in other words, it controlled his most legitimate form of publicity. Through its awards, it set the stamp of mastership where it chose, and by so doing increased the probability of sale of that artist's work. The artists were aware of these considerations and therefore tried so to paint that their canvases, displayed on the walls of the annual salons, would catch the public eye. This they might accomplish by sensationalism in subject or color, but sheer size of canvas was the most direct means. No matter how clearly we realize that size is irrelevant to quality, if a very large picture and others of medium and small size are hung on a single wall, it is human nature to examine the large one first. Also, the largest painting is inevitably placed in the center; it can hardly be pushed into a corner. Irreverent artists nicknamed these great compositions 'machines.' Quite aside from any other consideration, their size alone made it certain that no private patron would buy them, since they required a palace for their display. They were painted to be sold to the Government as 'great art' after winning their medals and acclaim in the salons. One example will suffice, the Romans of the Decadence, painted by Thomas Couture in 1847, master of the 'well painted bit.' The canvas measures 15 feet 3 inches, by 25 feet 5 inches. The subject itself is sensational, an orgy, on which the statues of worthy ancestors look down as with disgust. The work is facile and competent, but though influenced by Veronese in its architectural setting, its interest lies in its subject.

Through its ability to make reputations, the Academy could open the door to portraiture, the one really lucrative field in the arts. Those who could afford to have their portraits painted turned to known artists; the more wealthy the individual, the more certainly would he patronize officially recognized masters. If their portraits are tight, such men as Léon Bonnat are well trained, according to their lights. The draftsmanship is precise, the pigment applied as though figure and drapery were waxen, and the personality and likeness are well caught.

However much they might covet the security that academic success could assure, a few painters, and among them the most serious of their generations, insisted that the goals of the Academy and of the public were insufficient, and that the expressive possibilities of painting as an interpretation of life were more significant. Honoré Daumier (1808–79) stands alone in his day in his Gargantuan human sympathies. His professional activity lay in the field of the graphic arts, where his pungent caricatures got him into trouble with the state. In such a cartoon as Gargantua (fig. 366), Daumier invited hostility on the part of the Government. The ministers of Louis Philippe collect taxes from the people in panniers, which they convey to the insatiable maw of Gargantua, personified as the monarch. From under his chair issue privileges and monopolies to benefit the business classes in whose interests, under the *laissez-faire* theory of economics, his government was conducted. The taunts of this satire were too sharp to be forgiven. In a series of lithographs and paintings based upon his observations in the law courts, Daumier dissects for all to see the conduct of the legal profession, the lawyers' impassioned pleas for unworthy clients, or their hobnobbing around the halls of justice. His representation is not flattering to them either as individuals or as a group, but his grasp of the essentials of characterization is superb.

Perhaps his training as a caricaturist in the graphic arts gave him a feeling for the economy of essentials and for the elimination of the accidental, and also a realization of the power inherent in values. The Washwoman (fig. 367) is immense in monumentality. The action and mass of the figure are fundamentals to which detail can be sacrificed. Little is visible within the outlines of this dark figure silhouetted against the buildings on the other bank, as the mother stoops over to help her child up the last steps. Here is nothing of narrative; no story is conveyed by these figures. No individualism of characterization mars Daumier's preoccupation with the general. His effort is concentrated in the simplified forms that transcend time and space to become types of humanity always recognizable and forever understandable.

In his day, Daumier was hardly known as a painter. Gustave Courbet (1819–77), on the other hand, took pains to reach notoriety. When in the Exposition of 1855 his works were refused, he arranged his personal exhibition opposite the Exposition grounds. He coined the term 'Realism' to describe his style. Once he shouted at a friend, who had urged him to paint a picture from his imagination, 'If you show me an angel, I'll paint one!' In brief, Courbet's interest lay in the visible world, and he considered it his function to record it as it was. His style is not photographic; in actuality, it shows a keen sense of selection of what to paint among the innumerable details of nature to give the essentials of his subject.

Sentiment and idealism find no place in him. The Burial at Ornans (fig. 368) is matter of fact, too much so for the taste of his day, which was appalled at this unvarnished statement of reality. In this painting, Courbet seemed to say what everyone knew to be true, that the priest reading the burial service was performing his routine duties in a routine way, that the acolytes attendant on the scene might yet pay no heed to it, and that the presence of friends and relatives was more socially expected than prompted by real and lasting grief. These matters were familiar to his time, but no one liked to have the pretty veils, with which society had surrounded such events, torn down. Mankind preferred a sentimental, if false, view of such things; Courbet gave his observations bald objectivity. He neither condemned nor satirized, but painted what he saw.

In reality, the Burial at Ornans is a great portrait group, its members individualized and characterized. Any one of the forms on close examination turns out to be simplified in order to bring out what Courbet believed to be its essentials of form or character; the incidental or accidental is suppressed despite an informality of pose. Such a procedure prevents loss of monumentality. The color creates a chord of gray, red, and violet against the gray blue of the sky. The composition consists of a series of verticals created by the group around the open grave, tied together by the long horizontals of the cliffs and horizon. For emphasis, the one break in the cliffs occurs above the center of action, where the priest performs his office, and at the only point at which the verticals carry upward in the crucifix outlined against the sky.

If Courbet could be so matter of fact in figure composition, he could have no reason to be less so in the field of landscape. Sometimes his paintings represent deep woods, for Courbet was an avid out-of-doors man. Other landscapes record the shore around Ornans. The Wave (fig. 369) glances along the coast at an angle, with a dory drawn up on the beach, and a great comber about to break. The diagonal planes pursue each other with fine consistency, to build up an asymmetrical composition whose accidental appearance is belied by its underlying structure. In addition, a perception of the forces of nature gives vitality to this design. What Courbet does is to take the modest accuracy of the Barbizon painters, their delight in the intimate aspects of nature and their reliance on the sufficiency of her beauty, and then to intensify those aims. He gave to them monumentality, and stormed his way into public recognition. The Barbizon school was winning its position slowly, but Courbet's temperament was more forceful and impatient.

His influence on Edouard Manet (1832–83) is profound. Especially at the beginning of the latter's career, a series of studies of form in light and shade show the same absorption in reality. Manet went to Spain in 1865, but even before this he had come into contact with a group of Spanish dancers, some of whom posed for him. Moreover, he was enthusiastic about Goya and even more about Velásquez. The 'men of 1870,' as they were called, admired the Spaniards and also Frans Hals, the more because they found in them the qualities toward which they were themselves working. To say that the course of French painting was changed by the new familiarity with Velásquez is incorrect; that is the result rather than the cause. From this renewed interest in visual reality, it was an inevitable next step to Impressionism, which became more pronounced in Manet's later work.

The term Impressionist was coined by a journalist to deride the unconventional work of a group of younger artists. The manner of painting this described has a number of characteristics related to one another. It is, however, important to observe that these qualities occur in varying degrees in different artists, and that not all need be found in the painting of any one man for him to be placed in this group. Most of them are landscape painters, but the techniques and approach can be applied to other fields as well. Beauty exists for these painters not in any particular subject, but in the eye of the beholder. Therefore the subject, as such, ceases to be important; a railroad station or coal barges may be as worthy the artist's attention as a noble panorama or a bucolic scene. Furthermore, older renderings of landscape, even those of Constable, do not quite succeed in catching the appearance of sunlight. Their canvases tend to be dark when hung on a light wall. Hence the Impressionists, for the first time, take their easels out of doors. Other men had sketched from nature, but the finished paintings had always been studio products; now the artists complete their works before the subject itself. This in turn stimulates a close observation of conditions of light and atmosphere. However, these qualities in nature are anything but constant; they change with every hour of the day. Therefore, if the artist is to catch these fleeting impressions, some method of quick notation has to be adopted, a sort of short-hand brushstroke that will convey the principal elements of light and atmosphere quickly and accurately. Finally, the strength of color in nature prompts experiments in the application of pigments, called broken color.

Most of these characteristics result from the Impressionist desire to deal objectively with the facts of vision. Consequently, Impressionism has been defined as the cult of the eye. Much was said of the innocent eye, that is, of vision as nearly as possible divorced from memory. We have all become accustomed by experience since our cradle days to translate what we see into what we know. A ball with some shadow on it we say looks spherical to us. What we mean is that we know it to be spherical, though we see it as a circle with a pattern of light and shade upon it. What the Impressionists try to do is to record what they see, where other painters alter the visual appearance by what they know about the objects.

Moreover, they represent in their paintings just as much as the eye can take in at a glance and no more. If we look at a painting by David, the artist expects us to let our eyes wander over the canvas, to examine each figure and each part of a figure separately; we may see the painting as a whole, but we may also inspect its details, and to do this the point of focus of our vision must change. When we look at a figure, while our gaze is focused on the head, we are conscious of the costume and of certain details, but we do not perceive those details sharply until we change the point of focus of our eyes from the head to the details. The Impressionist summarizes the scene for us with short-hand brush strokes and a broad indication of detail. When Velásquez painted Las Meninas (fig. 287), he was content to indicate the flowers in the hair of his lady-in-waiting, and expected the observer to be satisfied with their general appearance in form and color but did not ask him to examine them. From close at hand, those flowers are mere blurs of pigment indistinguishable in detail. Were this point of view carried out to its conclusion, one should expect a center of interest where the detail is sharp, surrounded by less precise zones, but in an Impressionist canvas the painting is considered as a whole, and the whole may therefore be painted with equal breadth. Taking all these factors into consideration, Impressionism may be described as optical realism carried to its logical conclusion.

Only one of these matters is clear in Manet's Olympia (fig. 370), namely the respect for appearance under specific light conditions. This painting represents a nude woman lying on a couch, her black cat at its foot, and her Negro servant behind, flowers in hand. The diffused light of the interior falls evenly on the forms, and visually flattens them out. Very slight shadows under the breast and along the edges of the figure hardly change it from a two-dimensional image to a three-dimensional form. Manet observes that under these conditions of light, the form, though solid, appears to be almost flat, and paints it that way. Through the influence of Courbet, Velásquez, and Hals, he becomes engrossed in the possibilities of the brush and pigments, in short in the peculiarities of his medium. His flowing brush delights in the warm white tones of the flesh, the ivory of the scarf beneath the figure, and the bluish white of the linen sheet. The textures of each part are suggested for their general appearance, not to render each thread in the material. Such clear, fresh, and direct painting outraged the Academy.

Ostensibly, this masterpiece dealt with a theme that was common in the Salons, the nude female figure. Manet was surprised and more than a little hurt that so few people appreciated the brilliance of the painting. Doubtless the conservative strictures were to some degree prompted by jealousy, but they bit none the less. However, the similarity to the academic nude is more superficial than real. In spirit, Olympia contrasts at every point with the vacuity of official art. Where their figures are soft and idealized, Manet's is hard and realistic; his study of flesh is firm, while theirs look as though the skin is stuffed with cotton. Where the academic nude is no one in particular, Manet's figure is individualized and recognizable, a portrait of a well-known model of the day. Where the academic nude is surrounded by objects or a setting purporting to give the figure some ideal explanation such as Truth or Spring or September Morn, Olympia's household connotes her character only too well, the servant with a bouquet from some admirer, or the black cat always associated with the sinister in womanhood. The cat creates a series of short verticals necessary to stop the compositional movement of the figure from escaping at the right, but such a pictorial purpose, however justifiable, does not lend itself to journalistic notice. There is no comparison in strength between the Manet and the academic nudes; the former has an assurance and a visual integrity that they lack.

Twenty years later, in the Bar of the Folies Bergères (fig. 371), Manet carries farther his concern with the summary indication of form. The bottles on the bar are swept in with bold strokes of the brush; Manet deals only with essentials, not with detail as such. One might suppose that such optical realism would approach the photographic. Actually, the selectivity of this technique, its very indication rather than definition of detail, leaves a wide gulf between this and what we understand as the photographic. However much Manet may dwell upon the facts of vision, he does not forget for one moment that he is painting a picture, and is willing to sacrifice even the visually possible to better his design. Behind the barmaid, a mirror reflects a fashionable throng in the distance, and near at hand the barmaid and her patron of the moment. But no possible arrangement of the mirror could produce these reflections seen from a position in front of the girl. Manet arbitrarily moves his reflections to one side for pictorial interest.

The subjects of Impressionism may be unimportant in themselves, but collectively they suggest the influence of the upper middle class in Paris. Manet himself was well to do, and, to judge by his paintings, one would say that urban entertainment and a holiday spirit had affected his selection of material, especially in his later works. That point of view was common to the Impressionists as a group. They sought in the country what delighted the city dweller on vacation, a stream on whose banks one might while away an afternoon, a boating party, yachting, or fields that promised repose. In the city, the theater, the boulevard, the dance hall, and the racecourse recurred in the paintings of these men, the favorite entertainments of the upper middle class.

In his later years, Manet was influenced by Claude Monet (1840–1926). Though he painted figures at times, Monet's primary concern was landscape. The scientific research of the nineteenth century here impinged upon problems of painting. Such physicists as Chevreul and Helmholtz and Professor Rood of Columbia University were experimenting at this time with the natural laws of color. They were observing that disks, painted alternately in red and yellow, when revolved appeared to be orange. The original colors reflected to the eye in such rapid succession could no longer be distinguished, but instead the two colors were added together to produce a third quite different tone. A painter cannot use a series of moving disks; but he can obtain a similar result from small touches of different colors placed side by side on the canvas, since, from a short distance, the eye fails to perceive the individual colors and blends them for itself. There is reason to believe that such artists as Claude Monet discovered the technique of broken color independently of the investigations of the physicists, but it is typical of the late nineteenth century that similar experimentation should occur both in art and in the natural sciences. Broken color permits more vibrancy of tone and a greater freshness than can be obtained by a mechanical mixture of the same pigments upon the palette. However, this technique entails some sacrifice. The beauties of brushwork must be abandoned, and the surface becomes rough in appearance. At times, heavy bits of pigment may even project so far from the surface as to cast their own shadows on the painting, and thus make it necessary to regulate the direction of light relative to the canvas.

Coupled with this new technique, which is partly anticipated in the work of Constable and Delacroix, is a more or less scientific approach toward the phenomena of light and atmosphere. Where Turner had painted atmosphere from the emotional Romantic point of view, Monet was absorbed in rendering the subtlest changes in weather conditions with scientific realism. To that end, he takes from his studio to the site selected half a dozen or more canvases. Then he begins to paint the pair of Haystacks (fig. 372), or more exactly to paint the light, color, and atmosphere within which those haystacks are seen. The subject, in the usual sense of the term, remains important to the artist only in so far as it provides a background for his main purpose. As those conditions of light change, Monet changes his canvas and paints many versions of the same scene, each with all the accuracy of observation of which he is capable. A contemporary painter once said that Monet was only an eye, and added, but what an eye! Degas, on looking at an exhibition of Monet's paintings, turned up his coat collar in mute tribute to the artist's success in rendering the weather.

And yet for all their accuracy, Monet's landscapes are full of lyrical beauty. A profound love of nature as it appears to him colors his work and transcends its scientific aspect. The composition is so informal as to seem accidental; coupled with the brushwork, it gives to these canvases the casual quality of sketches. His color scheme becomes lighter in tonality than that of any previous school. In many museums, the visitor may look from a room in which older paintings are exhibited into one devoted to the Impressionists and remark this contrast, that where the older landscapes make dark spots against the light background of the wall, Impressionist paintings on the contrary bring a bit of light into their surroundings. Though not necessarily brilliant in color, their effect is that of cheerfulness.

Not many Impressionists carry these matters as far as does Monet. Pierre Auguste Renoir (1841–1919) paints landscapes in broken color, but he seems less absorbed in the problems of atmosphere and light. His primary concern is with the figure, more specifically with Parisian womanhood of the lower middle class, the forms well rounded and feminine. The Moulin de la Galette (fig. 373), a gay scene in an open-air dance hall, shows a moderate use of broken color for its own sake. The Impressionist study of light is prominent as sunlight filters through the leafy trees overhead and flecks the blue dresses of the ladies, or their features. These very French men and women tend to be flattened out by the light, which is scattered and diffused as it sifts through the foliage.

As Renoir developed, he studied light less and buxom form more zealously, as in the Seated Bather (fig. 374), one of his many versions of that subject. To the end of his long life, Renoir preserved the broken color of the Impressionists but used that technique for its brilliance of tone, in touches of vivid reds, yellows, violets, and blues. Instead of a two-dimensional image, he stressed volume more and more as time went on. Though simplified and well clothed in flesh, the structure and movement of his figures remain basic. Something of Rubens reappears, but bathed in the deep well of Renoir's imagination to emerge as more delicate and unmistakably French. Though Renoir must be classed with the Impressionists, more than most of them he retains elements of the earlier French tradition, which link him in spirit to the great painters of the past, to Delacroix, to Fragonard, and to Boucher.

Nor is Edgar Hilaire Germain Degas (1834–1917) entirely typical of the new movement. The exquisite draftsmanship of Ingres, even in its linearism, lies at the basis of Degas' work. A man of independent means, Degas painted to satisfy his own taste, which disdained anything pictorially vulgar, and instead sought the unusual and the unexpected in color and composition. No one knows better how to exploit dissonance in color. The tones of some of his ballet scenes, or his bathing women, startle, if they do not shock, the observer. He may select a vivid arsenic green and combine it with touches of brick red and of lavender, which many would say could not harmonize, but which do in his paintings. These dissonant colors must have seemed perverse discords to his day, but now our eyes have become more accustomed to such effects, as our ears have become attuned to the music of Wagner, which sounded discordant to Degas' day.

That zest for the unusual marks both his compositions and his choice of models. In feature and in pose, he avoids the pretty and prefers the awkward. The Ballet Dancer on the Stage (fig. 375) too well embodies the fleeting beauty of such entertainment to be typical. But when one examines this composition, one realizes that the dancer is far off to the right of the picture, and yet the painting is balanced. We are at first perplexed at this, until we observe that Degas has introduced the dark blur of the ballet master in the wings, just important enough to re-establish the balance. In essence, such a design builds up from the disposition of a number of spots or areas, carefully chosen in size and shape and precisely placed in relation to each other. Almost all Western painting has relied upon a series of leading lines or movements to carry the eye from one point to another, and to tie the forms together in compositional unity. Whether the basis of the design was geometrical as in the High Renaissance paintings of Italy, or informal as among the works of the Dutch masters, some visual connection of the parts had been established. In the art of the Far East, on the other hand, a tendency to build the design in a series of well-chosen, perfectly adjusted accents is traditional. Also, the Orientals recognize the value of the open space and take advantage of it; they are content to arrange a few flowers or other motives within a rectangle, and rely on their placement to make the design seem complete, (fig. 570).

The generation of the Impressionists discovered the Japanese print as they had discovered Velásquez, because they were ready for it, and more directly because of an exposition of Japanese prints in Paris in the 'sixties. Degas borrows none of the superficial externals of Oriental art, but his own compositions betray its influence, so absorbed as to become part of his own style. To that end, he is ready to omit part of an object, even what might be considered the most important part, if the remainder provides the shape he needs. The ballet master, as we have observed, produces the dark accent needed for asymmetrical balance, but his head would add nothing; therefore, Degas allows the scenery to conceal it. Thus his painting seizes upon the unexpected, and is, consequently, refreshing to the eye.

Instead of arranging his subject in normal perspective, he prefers to see it from an abnormal point of view. At times, he seems to look down upon his subject; elsewhere, the figures act upon a stage and are rendered as though perceived from below. This selection of the unusual angle of vision admits a wide new range of pictorial effects, such as one may see exploited in modern photography. Degas has not the popular appeal that has made Renoir beloved. One suspects that he would have avoided such popularity, had it seemed imminent, as unworthy of his aristocratic and esoteric nature. And yet his paintings improve with familiarity; we learn to expect the unexpected, and to relish the spicy dissonances of his color.

Neither Renoir with his interest in form nor, still less, Degas' exquisite draftsmanship and subtle compositions fit neatly into the pattern of Impressionism. It was not long before some painters, other than academic conservatives, toward the end of the century began to contradict the very premises upon which Impressionism was reared. Was the sole purpose of painting to record the fleeting aspect of the moment, an ever-changing atmosphere, or transient, if not accidental, conditions of light and shade? Should not the painter attempt greater permanence? Above all, should he not concentrate on structure and form rather than on appearance, however attractive that might be? Some painters, at least, began to think so, and among them was Georges Seurat (1859–91). His painting of Sunday on the Grande Jatte (fig. 376) corresponds to Impressionism in subject matter. This Parisian resort on a sunny afternoon is visited by respectable people with their pets, and its waters are alive with pleasure craft. In technique, also, broken color persists, but with a basic change. Seurat's technique, called *pointillisme,* tends to reduce to a formula the method of broken color, and to give it an almost mathematical regularity as each dot, like a piece of confetti, is placed in position, and graded in intensity to create space organization in depth. Monet's method has none of this calculated quality, but Seurat carries the technique even into the frames of his pictures.

Still more significant is the insistence on form, which is so highly simplified as to approach abstraction. All accidentals of shape and costume are swept into the discard. In their place is an austere preoccupation with simplified outline and with the geometrical mass it contains. These forms are not chosen primarily as a setting for light and shade; in so far as the latter play a part at all, it is to mold those forms into solid volumes and to establish the successive planes in space. Movement is abandoned in favor of nearly static shapes, like the monumental figures of Piero della Francesca (fig. 204), as though permanence and solidity were of the greatest artistic value. Their function as forms is dual: to state the essential and timeless elements in the objects themselves, conceived with sculpturesque simplicity, and to assist in constructing the picture. The apparently accidental arrangements of the Impressionists give way to a design wherein each shape is calculated with regard to every other shape in size, in location within the frame, and in color. The design is as carefully constructed as a Poussin, and as formal.

In spite of the immature age at which Seurat died, he still formed one of the pillars on which modern art rests. Another was Paul Gauguin (1848–1903), who turned to painting comparatively late in life after considerable success as a banker in Paris. This son of a French father and a Peruvian mother rebelled against the tame mores of his day, both in life and in painting. Though influenced by the heightened color of the Impressionists, his instinct sought those primitive cultures as yet but little affected by contact with Western sophistication. In Brittany, the childlike faith of the peasant women prompted such a composition as the Yellow Christ, in which the form of the Crucified is as distorted as the twelfth- and thirteenth-century crucifixes of the early Italian painters. Gauguin makes no attempt to render Christ realistically; on the contrary, his version in line and areas of flat color, like stained glass, may be called expressionistic or symbolic. The white-linen headdresses of the women provide an arabesque of flat shapes, each outline filled in with a single tone.

But Brittany proved to be only a stepping stone in Gauguin's return to the primitive. A trip to Martinique in the West Indies confirmed his bent, and led to longer sojourns in Polynesia. His escape from civilization becomes complete in Manao Tu Papua (fig. 377). The subject rebels against the mundane material of Impressionism, to exploit the exotic because of its strangeness and mystery. Realism ceases to be an end. In place of plastic solids, Gauguin returns to a two-dimensional scheme. Each shape and area is outlined and painted with a flat tone of strong color, without model-ing. For expression or for decorative effect, Gauguin is quite willing to distort the proportions of his figures, to give up or to modify perspective, or to sacrifice representation for local color. The sonorous tones he em-ploys have often been likened to medieval stained glass; a better analogy would be late-medieval tapestry. Intense as his tones are, their prevailing value is not high; their richness is increased by their depth. Through his personal arrangement of these shapes, as in Mahana No Atua (fig. 378), Gauguin achieves the fullest decorative expression.

One debatable question concerning Gauguin arises in regard to the extent and the honesty of his return to the primitive as an escape from the oversophistication of modern life. The linearism of native arts and their lack of perspective are due partly to their indifference to realistic methods, and partly to their identification of forms and shapes with religious pur-poses. For a Parisian of the 'nineties, is there not an element of affecta-tion in Gauguin's return to the primitive? Is not Gauguin deliberately sen-sational? In his life the answer must be in the affirmative. He craved adulation, and would sacrifice anything, do anything, to become the lion of the hour. Nevertheless, so far as his painting goes, the affectation is less apparent, if it exists at all. Gauguin accepts from the primitive whatever best suits his pictorial purpose, but he cannot be said to imitate primitive art. For all their unreality, his are not the forms of Polynesian art. Even the subjects are often Occidental, and merely expressed in terms of native models. In spite of the apparent simplification, Gauguin's paintings betray in every direction a sophisticated amalgam of the decorative and non-representational attitude of semi-civilized peoples with the spirit of the Paris of his own day.

The inspired madman, Vincent van Gogh (1853–90), threw himself with uncontrolled energy into every field that caught his attention. Like Gauguin, Van Gogh did not at once begin to paint. As a clerk in the shop of an art dealer, Goupil, he proved unsatisfactory because of his persistent attempts to force his tastes upon prospective patrons. He turned thence to religion, and served with missionary zeal, first in the degrading slums of Whitechapel in London, and then among the miners of Le Borinage in Belgium. It was typical of Van Gogh that he should feel it necessary to live under even worse conditions than those to whom he would minister. When in the last five years of his life, he turned his full attention to painting, he threw himself into that pursuit with the same unnatural energy; he painted like mad, as though he had to get these records on canvas before death or insanity should interfere.

At one time, he came into contact with Gauguin, who claimed to have influenced him. The method of line and flat tone that Gauguin uses is again approximated in La Berceuse (fig. 379), though even here there is more feeling for mass than in most Gauguin's. The color is somewhat lighter in value, and much more intense. Above all, Van Gogh creates a fiery and passionate portrait, expressive of the subject filtered through the screen of his own personality. He is not concerned with abstract beauty, but with emphasizing what, to him, is significant about his subject. The primary importance of woman is her role as mother of the race; hence, the deliberate enlargement of the breasts and hips. The neck offers few possibilities of expression, and therefore Van Gogh allows the head, again enlarged, to rest directly on the shoulders, with a heavy and rather coarse indication of the features. The eyes and mouth are magnified as centers of expression, but other parts of the face are comparatively neglected.

Van Gogh does not always paint in such an arabesque of tones, however vivid they may be. His own incandescent energy activates his Landscape at Auvers (fig. 380) to such an extent that even inanimate objects acquire vitality. The pigment is slapped on and around these things in streaks, perhaps applied with a brush, but often smeared on with a palette knife, and, to judge from the intensity of color, he used paints as they came from their tubes with no mixing of tones on his palette at all. The landscape itself has become emotionally excited; the trees flicker in green flames, the ground undulates, and the sky and sun are tormented in swirls of line and color. No wholly sane mind could have imagined such an ensemble, but perhaps no such mind could have achieved the visual excitement or the frenzied brilliance of his paintings, either.

If Gauguin's foremost quality is decorative, and Van Gogh's expressive, Paul Cézanne's is structural. At the outset, Cézanne (1839–1906), who was somewhat older than the other two but developed slowly to his maturity, exhibited with the Impressionists, though he has none of the fluency, the virtuosity of brushwork, that Manet commands. In fact, Manet describes Cézanne's early work as 'foul painting.' At that time, he loaded his pigment on the canvas in patches. But Cézanne, though he admitted the value of some of the Impressionist contributions, such as their feeling for color, rejected the transient nature of their conceptions. His goal, unappreciated in his lifetime, was to combine their ideas with the firm picture construction he noticed in the 'old masters' in the museums.

A Still Life (fig. 381) offers opportunity for prolonged analysis. Cézanne constructs the composition in an architectonic vein. The front of the table parallels the picture plane, the drawer of the table is drawn out to repeat that plane, the objects on the table recall it again, and in the background a chest of drawers finally stops the series. Horizontal planes separate these vertical planes one from another and create the necessary recession. Such a system requires the implied permanence of geometric forms. The apples are in essence spheres; to insist upon that shape, several concentric strokes of the brush may repeat its circular silhouette. Conservatives accuse Cézanne of bad drawing, and point to the top of the vase in proof. That aperture is, of course, a circle, and everyone knows that a circle in perspective is visually an ellipse. But Cézanne does not draw it so; he squares the circle. The oval shape in itself lacks the architectonic character of the rest of his design. Therefore, Cézanne modifies that ellipse, flattens its upper and lower edges, and even straightens out its sides until it becomes a rectangle with rounded corners. It is absurd to suppose that this can be owing to inability; the veriest tyro can sketch a better oval than Cézanne has painted. We must conclude, then, that the artist has done this deliberately, for the sake of his composition. Whether the result justifies that modification may be another question; whether the composition is improved by it can, dialectically at least, be challenged. To most people of his day, the shock was too great to be condoned on these or any other grounds; to most people today, little doubt remains that Cézanne was right to make such modifications.

Mere visual appearance seemed to Cézanne negligible. However pretty may be the texture of an apple, or the play of light and shade over it, such matters are insignificant in comparison with the fundamental nature of the fruit and its pictorial possibilities. Apples in general approach a spherical shape, though in any individual apple accidents may have injured the perfection of the form. To Cézanne, however, these accidents were to be disregarded; he sought its permanent and universal aspects. The creation of solid form on a two-dimensional surface of panel or canvas had been a common aim of Western art from the time of Giotto. But Cézanne wanted to encompass this form, not so much by modeling in light and shade as by means of color. He realized that some colors seem to project, others by comparison to recede; through this visual phenomenon, he can model his forms solidly by color and establish successive planes by pure tone. In this attempt, Cézanne surveyed a new path. He has often been compared to Giotto, and in this respect with justice; Cézanne is a 'primitive' in the sense that he has a conception, an aim, a *petite sensation* as he himself says, to which the road has not yet been explored. That Cézanne sometimes failed to reach his goal is but to be expected. He fumbled his way forward, and often sacrificed to his main purpose other matters of less consequence to him; but in the best of his still lifes, Cézanne succeeded, as Giotto had succeeded in the Arena Chapel in Padua.

This concentration on structure and modeling in pure color lies at the basis of Cézanne's painting and of his importance in the history of art. The same point of view dominates his landscape painting. Mt. Ste. Victoire (fig. 382) is typical. The landscape is analyzed into planes, each of which plays its appointed role in the picture. At first, the observer is inclined to feel that these landscapes are too unnatural in appearance to have much contact with reality. In fact, photographs have been made of the sites in and around Aix en Provence found in Cézanne's paintings. As one would expect, these are more detailed than Cézanne's canvases, but the important point to realize is that every line in Cézanne's landscapes existed in the scene before him. Evidently his method is the same as in his still lifes; he analyzes the scene before him with the utmost care to extract from it those elements susceptible to pictorial and architectonic composition, and then omits the rest. The branch of the pine in the foreground, which repeats the profile of the mountain and the horizon, is a case in point. We have every reason to believe that such a parallelism existed, and that Cézanne seized upon it to help unify the design by tying together the foreground and the background. As in his still lifes again, Cézanne prefers the general to the particular, such as the cylindrical mass of the tree trunk or the characteristic silhouette of the mountain, and therefore emphasizes them as essentials of the objects before him.

If he applies these principles in both still life and landscape, it would be strange for him to depart from them in his figure composition. His problem in dealing with figures is complicated by their animate nature. An apple will pose motionless for him, and will remain so for any length of time, until he is satisfied with his painting. So will a landscape. But human beings cannot be static indefinitely. Even a quietly posed model must be permitted to relax and can seldom return to the identical position. If this complicates the artist's problem, the distortion of the figure is always more difficult for the public to accept than a corresponding departure from appearance in landscape or still life. This distortion in Cézanne sometimes results from selection and simplification, in which case, however unnatural in appearance, it is not strictly distortion; but in other instances he alters the size and proportions of the parts of the human body. An extreme example of this is the Bathers (fig. 383). One of Cézanne's expressed ideals was 'to do a Poussin before nature:' that is, to regain the pictorial structure of the old master and combine it with the color of the Impressionists. The composition here is singularly geometric. The trees tip inward to establish an equilateral triangle with the group. Its sides are repeated in the forms of the nude women. Anatomical accuracy is insignificant in comparison to the requirements of the pictorial scheme. Moreover, these figures begin to be analyzed into geometric forms, just as in landscape the tree trunk becomes cylindrical, or in still life the apple becomes spherical. But the geometry of the human figure is more complex, and to reduce the head or the breast to spheres, the arm or the thigh to cylinders, violates the usual notions of the figure.

The charge of distortion, leveled against Cézanne as though it were a crime against art, is absurd, at least in its simple form. Art always involves distortion; the range of color in pigments does not equal that in nature; forms are three dimensional and the painter must translate them as best he can on a flat surface, and present them in some pictorial medium. Even more important, the artist is not a divinity who can create nature, or even a human being who copies nature. He is first and foremost painting a picture, and, in spite of the old cliché, nature does not present perfect pictures. All artists, then, have distorted to a greater or lesser degree, even the most naturalistic of them. Thus, such a charge leveled at Cézanne means little in itself.

However, the debatable question arises, how far the artist may contradict appearances. Dialectically speaking, the artist may depart just as far as he sees fit in order to increase his compositional unity, his decorative result, or his expressive possibilities. If this be true, we may then ask whether the result in one or more of these directions justifies the means in any particular case. Of course it does, if improvement is effected thereby. In El Greco's case, or in that of many non-realistic painters, such as Duccio, the expression and the decorative brilliance is undoubtedly enhanced by their unreality. On the other hand, many of the greatest painters, such as Titian, Michelangelo, Rembrandt, and Rubens, distort only to a minor extent. Have their works less compositional integrity, less expression, or less decorative value than those of more recent artists, who carry distortion to such a point that it calls attention to itself? Have not the 'old masters' reached as fine pictorial qualities as the moderns? Indeed, have they not outstripped the moderns in these very respects by so restricting their departure from appearances that those departures, by not calling attention to themselves, thus leave the observer free to enjoy more important pictorial matters? To these questions no categorical answer can be given. Conservatives will answer in one way; enthusiastic modernists in another. Probably no sweeping answer will ever be satisfactory. Each painting should be considered on its own merits.

If it were a choice confined to Cézanne and to the contemporary academicians, there could be only one intelligent selection. Although Cézanne longed to be recognized by the Academy, he could not but feel contempt for many of its leaders. His paintings protest against the non-intellectual and non-structural approach of the Impressionists, and the vacuities of academicians such as Bouguereau. The latter's Birth of Venus (fig. 384) typifies what has been called the bar-room nude, the ideal of high art held by a stockbroker of the black-walnut generation. These slick, soft, and spineless figures are well drawn from the academic point of view. The linearism of Ingres marches on with faint eclectic traces of Botticelli and Raphael. By its lights, the painting is competent — but its lights are a little dim. A less critical and less pictorially conscious generation, with some literary but little artistic background, accepted it because of its superficial purity, its prettiness, and its high finish. The more powerful paintings of Cézanne have none of these qualities. The difference is that Cézanne's paintings are loaded with pictorial consequence, whereas Bouguereau's have nothing to say, like the covers of certain popular magazines. They are pretty enough, but artistically dumb.

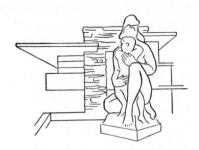

XXIII

The Growth of American Art

IF American art through the Federal period can be described as a provincial version of English art, its subsequent growth also has continued to be influenced by European civilization. Each major movement on the other side of the Atlantic has found its faithful echo on this side, though the source is no longer predominantly English. However, the inspiration is not in every case foreign. At times, a local spirit wells up to hide, if not to eliminate, the imported factors. These local developments can justly be called American in the fullest sense of the word, but it does not follow that the derivative art is un-American. The artistic manifestations of our civilization have been neither more nor less indigenous than our culture as a whole.

Neoclassicism, and especially the Greek revival, took a firm root in this country. The latter movement, extending in America from 1825 to 1850, received great impetus from the American sympathy for the Greek revolt against Turkey, a sentiment also felt by the liberal groups of western Europe, but the keener in this country because the United States was a republic and to some extent considered the ancient Greek republics as its prototypes. Moreover, our country has always tended to sympathize with the 'underdog,' and we have been very open to appeals based on sentiment. One can almost trace the settlement of the country from 1800 to 1850 by the classical place names. Athens, Ithaca, Sparta, Ypsilanti, and hundreds of other frontier or near frontier towns thus signified their admiration for the Greeks. The contrast between such settlements and Periclean Athens might be startling, but who could tell how these rude villages might grow? Classical allusions and quotations stud the political orations of the time, and the almost exclusively classical curricula of the colleges point in the same direction. Both in date and to some extent in spirit, the development links up with the rise and power of Jacksonian democracy. The older styles of English origin were tinged with an aristocratic background; the Greek was believed to be democratic in background.

Andalusia (fig. 385), on the banks of the Delaware in Bucks County, Pennsylvania, was the estate of Nicholas Biddle, the first American to travel in Greece. Under his instructions, Thomas U. Walter, later to become famous for his completion of the United States Capitol in Washington, dressed one wing projecting toward the river in a pure Greek Doric portico in 1836, with a full entablature and pediment, derived in proportions from the Parthenon. Very tall windows testify to the increased story heights on the interior. The walls become simple planes as far as possible, with plaster or smooth boarding; such un-Greek devices as shingles or clapboards are avoided in the purest examples. That the portico is designed for effect, few will deny. Obviously, some sacrifice must be made to force the requirements of a house into the form of a Greek temple. The very perfection of that form for its original purpose implies its imperfection for other purposes. The windows, especially those on the second floor, lose much of their effectiveness when thus hidden under the portico. Through the influence of books, detail was simplified. Greek architecture had been adapted to stone; its members were, therefore, bold. In order to translate these forms into wood, the exquisite richness of Federal detail yielded to simplification. At least during the early part of the Greek Revival itself, craftsmanship remained at a high level. Nevertheless, the simpler demands made upon the woodworkers, and the pressure upon them to give to their work not the character appropriate to wood, but that suited to stone, helped to undermine the native traditions in the former material.

But even if these charges are just, much may be said in praise of the Greek revival. Great mansions like Andalusia undoubtedly do what they set out to do; they are imposing, even magnificent in their way. We sing of our 'templed hills,' and the phrase is no empty figure of speech, as witness the Lee Mansion in Arlington, across the river from Washington. Andalusia is stately with lawns, which slope down to the river bank; the Lee Mansion crowns its height. Nor should one conclude that most of these houses slavishly follow the temple form. It happens that both these examples have wings that break the usual lines of the temple. These extensions are not emphasized from the front; they may even be concealed from that point of view, but they add to the commodity and flexibility of the house.

Still more important, the vast bulk of the work in this period is far less archaeological than these famous houses. In reality, the best of the architects and the builders throughout the country adapted the style to local conditions and problems, except when forced to do otherwise by the client. They retained its noble simplicity, its repose, its restrained dignity, but they so far modified its vocabulary as to make it American Greek. In the course of time, this simplified version came very close indeed to becoming a vernacular. A Phidias or an Ictinus might no longer recognize it; it might be naive, even provincial, from a cosmopolitan point of view; but these manifestations of the Greek manner, still extant in quantity in every village from Maine to Florida and west to the Mississippi, have a better claim to being American than much that we have built since that time. Generally speaking, the less elaborate it attempts to be, the more indigenous the style becomes.

The same can be said of sculpture, especially of the more pretentious statues. Ships' figureheads and local crafts are purely native, but more formal sculptors imitated their European colleagues and went to Italy, where the techniques of sculpture still lived. Horatio Greenough (1805–52) of Boston was commissioned to create a monumental statue of Washington, intended to be displayed under the dome of the Capitol. When the statue arrived in Washington, it proved to be too large to pass through the Capitol doors; they had to be enlarged to admit the figure. Then it became clear that its great weight was endangering the floor, and it was moved outside the building, where it sat for many years facing the east front of the Capitol. Finally, in 1908, it was transferred to the Smithsonian Institution to protect it from further weathering. So large a figure needs room around it, something not possible in the crowded floors of the Smithsonian. In its present cramped quarters, it looks as out of scale as a giant in a baby carriage. The statue (fig. 386) is pompous to the point of absurdity. The idea of Washington, that Virginia gentleman, tricked out in terms of an Olympian Zeus seems incongruous to the present day. Such an identification would not have appeared so to the men of Greenough's time. The trite gesture accords with the fulsome orations of the time. Nevertheless, it is only fair to remember that the dry execution and the dull over-generalization of the form are defects of the day and are not peculiar to Greenough. He is, in fact, no rival to Canova, but he is neither better nor worse than most sculptors of European Neoclassicism.

Nor was the academic admiration for the figure without its exponent among American sculptors. Hiram Powers won notoriety by his statue of the Greek Slave. It says much about America in the 1830's that before the statue was exhibited, a committee of clergymen in Cincinnati visited it to pass on the purity of its morals. (Purity Leagues and Watch and Ward Societies are not twentieth-century inventions in America.) The gentlemen concluded that since her hands were chained, and her un-draped condition therefore irremediable, she would not endanger public virtue. In another case, men and women were admitted separately to an exhibition of casts of Greek sculpture, as to a *Sala Pornographica*. The Greek Slave is in fact a better than average version of the figure sculp-ture of its generation, graceful in pose and slick in surface, but quite lifeless. It owes its fame more to its subject than to its quality.

During this period, painting still concentrated on portraits by late followers of the school of Benjamin West. These continued to respect the Federal traditions, which faded away as the influence of the cultured class in the community waned. Little true Neoclassic painting was done in America or by Americans, save perhaps for the heavy pomposities of Washington Allston. This worthy gentleman had unbounded en-thusiasm for Michelangelo, whence came the grandiose scale of his canvases and the bulk of his characters; but most of his paintings were as drab in color and as dull in execution as the mediocre work of David's followers in France.

The foundation of the National Academy of the Arts of Design in 1826, the first important attempt to write the annals of American art, namely the *History of the Rise and Progress of the Arts of Design in the United States,* by William Dunlap, published in 1834, and countless critical articles in magazines testify to the enthusiasm for the arts in eastern centers. Nevertheless, the spirit of the country, thanks to the influence of the frontier, was hostile to painting as well as to sculpture. Art was a useless occupation in a frontier community, and therefore pressure developed during the expansion of the country to divert men from it to practical activities, such as mechanical invention. Robert Fulton is known to every school child in America, however wrongly, as the inventor of the steamboat; Samuel F. B. Morse of the telegraph; but few realize that both of these men had been successful painters before their energy was diverted to other channels more congenial to the tastes, and perhaps to the needs, of their day.

At least by the 'forties, the universality of the Greek revival was challenged by the Gothic revival, which had left some examples even of its earlier phase in America. Bulfinch, in the Federal Street Church in Boston in 1809, had tried his hand at Gothic with results marked by as complete misunderstanding of the style as the faddish stage of the movement in England. The real change in spirit to the mature Gothic revival, with its purer archaeology and, above all, its revival of a liturgical style, occurs in the Episcopal churches of Richard Upjohn. Trinity Church, New York, 1839–46 (fig. 387), marks the turning point. Though by no means copied from any known building, it is sympathetic to the spirit of an English parish church. Its deep chancel, the first in America, is significant, since it proves the influence of the Oxford Movement in the Episcopal Church, which compelled a form not only closer to the medieval, but better adapted to the ritual of the high-church party. Richard Upjohn, himself English born and English trained, knew well the architectural character appropriate to this problem. The nave and aisles, the piers and Gothic arches, the traceried windows, the tower and soaring spire are all admirable. At only one point does the church contradict the spirit of the style in which it is designed. The vaulted roof is not built in the stone its forms postulate, but evidence exists to show that the architect would have preferred the more straightforward and structural wooden trussed roof; this was supplanted by the sham vaults only on pressure from the building committee. Elsewhere the church respects its material.

Not many other buildings of the Gothic revival in America reach the point of monumentality achieved in Trinity Church. Many of Richard Upjohn's other churches reveal less of archaeology but even more sympathy with the demands of construction in either wood or stone; these are usually country parish churches, smaller and simpler than Trinity. The Perpendicular style of Trinity Church, like the same style in the Houses of Parliament, was abandoned as an improper source after the completion of Trinity; instead, the Early English or the Decorated styles served as inspiration. As in the Greek revival, the country builder simplified his version of the Gothic so far as to approach a vernacular. Even Richard Upjohn's design for a country church in wood bears only a remote resemblance to his larger work, though in fact its straightforward carpentry and adherence to the problem have a Gothic directness. His design for a wooden Gothic church, published in 1853, can be recognized, sometimes with local modifications, in hundreds of towns scattered through every state admitted to the Union before 1870.

On the whole, houses and other types of buildings are less affected by the Gothic revival than churches, partly because the prototypes, if they existed at all, are less well known, and partly because the leader of the new style, Richard Upjohn, identified it with the new movement in the Episcopal Church and refused to profane it by turning it to secular use. Nevertheless, the Gothic Villa, of which Alexander J. Davis designed many notable examples, is an application of pseudo-Gothic detail to plans of great complexity. The motive in such designs is less archaeological than imaginative, a decorative exploitation of a style that once was structural. A generation ago, at least one example might be found in almost every village up and down the Hudson Valley; today, unfortunately, so many of them have been destroyed that this type is approaching extinction. A pilgrimage to Sunnyside, Washington Irving's home near Tarrytown, will reward anyone who wants to see how picturesque this type can be.

As the architects turned away from the Greek revival, so also the sculptors rejected the arid Neoclassic formulae in favor of a fresh naturalism. The statue of Washington (fig. 388) by Henry Kirke Brown (1814–86) is not the first equestrian portrait in American sculpture. That distinction must go to Clark Mills's portrait of Jackson in front of the White House in Washington, finished in 1853, a month before Brown's monument. In this laughable rendering the great democrat raises his hat, presumably to a cheering throng, while the horse rears on its hind legs. One can hardly admit Mills's monument as serious sculpture, but the enthusiasm that greeted it — Congress more than doubled the amount of the sculptor's commission — testifies to the uneducated taste of the country, and perhaps to its new-found and somewhat unjustified self-confidence. Brown's Washington is more monumental. Though indebted to Verrocchio and Donatello, it copies the famous monument of neither. Clad as a general of the colonial army, Washington commands his troops. The selection of historical costume, instead of the Greek garb that Greenough chose, recalls a similar decision by Benjamin West in painting, and by François Rude for the Marshal Ney (fig. 343). The strongly modeled horse remains subordinate to its rider. In technique, Brown is competent but not facile; his surfaces lack the vitality of more cosmopolitan sculptors, but neither have they the dullness of Neoclassic productions. Brown turns to nature for his model and inspiration, but by no means sacrifices the sculpturesque to it. Sober, unpretentious, and dignified, his statue may not be a masterpiece of world art, but it has in it much of which to be proud and nothing that is unworthy. Somewhat later, John Quincy Adams Ward (1830–1910) continued this vein, with greater precision in his statue of Washington on the steps of the Subtreasury Building in New York. The emphasis here rests on Washington's civilian achievements, but as in the equestrian portrait, no trace of affectation mars the honest effort to convey the grandeur of his personality.

These sculptors reject the European; they reflect the growth of a national spirit in this country, a supreme faith in its destiny, a new pride in themselves and, at times, an unwarranted confidence in their ability to solve any problem that may arise. They form a counterpart to the literary development that flowered in New England in the days of clipper ships, when the American merchant marine reached its height. The spirit continued in the decades after the Civil War, until other conditions compelled a change. In minor works, and sometimes even in more important productions, sentiment plays a considerable role. John Rogers (1829–1904) became famous for his groups, reproduced in plaster and sold broadcast. Some of the subjects commemorate the Civil War; others are sentimental genre scenes, like Checkers Down at the Farm, or Coming to the Parson (fig. 389), which might be an illustration for Lowell's poem, 'The Courtin'.' The use of dialect in verse and of episodic detail in these figures reveals an appreciation of the country for itself not unmixed with humor.

Painting, meanwhile, though it did not neglect the possibilities of genre, as in the canvases of William S. Mount (1807–68), turned to landscape, just as did Romanticism in France and England. However, the cult of the wilderness finds no parallel in Europe; it must be traced to the proximity of the frontier and its effect on American life. Virgin land had long since vanished in Europe, but it lay at the back door of America. Its influence on the poetry of Bryant and on Cooper's Leather-stocking Tales is obvious. So, too, in William Doughty, at times even in Thomas Cole, and especially in Asher Brown Durand (1796–1886) can be found the lure of the wild. In the Woods (fig. 390) is a glimpse into the depth of a primeval forest. Man has not yet left his mark anywhere. Each tree and branch, each rotting log half damming the brook, is incredibly naturalistic, studied with crystal clarity, but with little regard for pictorial structure. The scene details the deep woods. Elsewhere, these and other painters select panoramic views up and down the Hudson Valley, allied to the cult of the wilderness in a topographical attitude but based upon more settled regions.

The early landscape school culminated in George Inness (1825–94), whose youthful work retains much of the naturalism and topographic quality, but who developed toward greater breadth. Autumn Oaks (fig. 391), rich in color, shows him aware of the need of picture construction. These sturdy trees produce a sweeping curve in silhouette to draw the eye into the distance over the spacious country. His concern with atmosphere increased as his style matured; thus his first paintings correspond to the Barbizon school, while his later work parallels the Impressionists, but is less scientific in approach.

Somewhat different and a little younger is Winslow Homer (1836–1910), who served as a correspondent illustrator for *Harper's Weekly* during the Civil War, but settled in 1884 at Prout's Neck on the Maine coast. A native product, he was little affected by European art. From this fact came both his strength and his weakness. He had little feeling for texture; in All's Well, a lookout aboard ship, the sou'wester is as metallic as the ship's bell. On the other hand, those qualities that spring from a study of nature, his unaffected realism and his frank observation, empower such canvases as Northeaster (fig. 392). The strong color, the sense of the surging sea, and the broken rocks of the coast attest his love of the shore. Though informal, the composition is well organized, with an effective use of repeated diagonals.

Homer's contemporary and counterpart in figure painting was Thomas Eakins (1844–1916) of Philadelphia, who took the regular medical courses in anatomy at the Jefferson Medical College to perfect his knowledge of the body. Such a painting as the Gross Clinic, an actual operation, is a documentary record of medical practice, strange to modern surgeons but accurate to the last detail. Several of his paintings, such as Between Rounds, are based on prize fights in the old arena in Philadelphia; the pugilists offered Eakins an opportunity to exhibit his knowledge of the figure, and yet they are more than anatomical studies. The forms throughout are solid and structural. Furthermore, his serious nature leads Eakins to the heart of his subject, nowhere more so than in The Thinker, a portrait of his brother-in-law, so absorbed in a brown study that his awkward pose with hands thrust deep in his trouser pockets is indifferent to superficial grace.

The native qualities of this era were soon to be submerged by a new wave of foreign influence. In fact, Homer and Eakins, both of whom lived on through this later period, gained in stature by their independence from it. The climax of the Gothic revival in America, as in England, was short lived. After the Civil War, the full blast of later nineteenth-century eclecticism shattered any lingering consistency of style. The Gothic revival turned into Victorian Gothic, sometimes restrained, sometimes extravagant, as in the Hartford Capitol by Richard M. Upjohn, son of the architect of Trinity Church, New York. The uninspired Baroque descendant of the Paris Opera rears its ugly head in the old State, War, and Navy Department Building in Washington by the Government architect Mullet, who had his foot in many another government design, such as the old Post Office in New York. Tallmadge well describes this time as the Parvenu period, when ignorance is bliss. The vulgar display of many buildings in the Philadelphia Centennial Exposition of 1876 suggests the unschooled desires of men whose fortunes piled up in the unbridled expansion of the country after the war. Many of these men of wealth rose from the ranks, with no tradition behind them to help them distinguish richness and magnificence from glitter and sham. They were bound to confuse size with scale, novelty with originality, and to demand a crass ostentation in their surroundings. The flashy landscapes of Albert Bierstadt and Frederick Church won acclaim, not through their quality as paintings, but because of the fame and scenic beauty of their subjects, such as Niagara Falls, Cotopaxi, or the Yosemite Valley. Cast-iron Indians began to hunt the stag through the shrubbery on the lawns, while within the houses such mechanical advances as central heating and bathrooms helped to compensate for the lush opulence of overstuffed rooms. During this heyday of the pressed flower, the stuffed bird under a glass canopy, the gas chandelier, and the whatnot, high-ceilinged rooms were as disorderly with excessive furniture as the outside of the house was with too much of what passed for architecture. With luck, one might escape the obtrusive points of the central marble-topped table, only to trip over the bear-skin hearth rug, and fall into a Morris chair, the one comfortable piece of furniture in the house.

From this chaos, Henry Hobson Richardson took steps to free us. One of the first Americans to study in the École des Beaux Arts in Paris, Richardson returned to this country shortly after the Civil War. His design for Trinity Church, Boston (fig. 393), won the competition in 1872 and gained him a national reputation. To Richardson, the rugged strength of the Romanesque styles expressed a young and growing nation like America better than any other style, Gothic or classic. He fuses in Trinity Church elements borrowed from the Romanesque of Auvergne, of Provence, especially in the porch, and of Spain. In particular, the source of his tower or lantern is that of the old cathedral at Salamanca. These matters imply that Richardson is merely one more eclectic architect, distinguished by the style he selects and perhaps by the genius with which he handles it. But Trinity is more than another monument of eclecticism. Its rusticated masonry is not characteristic of the Romanesque; on the contrary, it is personal, and reveals Richardson's feeling for the rugged power of stone. But rarely in the nineteenth century has material played so prominent a part in design, or its qualities received such sympathy. The superficial results of the Beaux Arts training, as in the matter of historic styles, are sloughed off, but its valuable contribution, namely its training in composition, remains. This design is conceived in terms of mass and developed in three dimensions, not the two dimensions of the drafting board. One great bulk leads to another, to pile up with monumental concentration.

The success of Trinity Church, Boston, and Richardson's other early designs took the country by storm. They gave birth to the Richardsonian Romanesque with its progeny in every city of the country. But the followers could grasp only the externals of the master's manner, the contrast of granite and sandstone, without his ability in composition. While they become Romanesque-minded, Richardson himself grew away from that style. His eclecticism, even in Trinity Church, is of minor importance; the Marshall Field Warehouse in Chicago (fig. 394), of 1885–7, has rejected it. This design is thought out in architectural terms, a frank use of materials, an effective search for the character of the building, and a composition that relies on mass and on a vertical sequence in the fenestration. The number of windows in each bay decreases from top to bottom, but the size increases. Such designs as this earn Richardson the proud title of pioneer of modern architecture. Nor is his contribution restricted to stone. The years of extensive application of metal to building began just after his death, but in wood, that time-honored American material, he worked wonders. His shingled houses have the same basic qualities, the same grasp of the fundamentals of architecture that distinguish the Field Warehouse. The Stoughton House in Cambridge, Massachusetts, creates a vernacular in shingles, founded upon volume and proportion, with nothing of historic precedent or of meretricious ornament in a time when both of these were rife.

The World's Columbian Exposition in Chicago in 1893 put an end to the Richardsonian Romanesque. Although Daniel H. Burnham of Chicago, an able administrator, was a perfect selection for architect in charge, he was influenced, one might almost say awed, in matters of design by Charles Follen McKim from New York, who, like many other architects of his generation on the East Coast, had been trained in Paris. McKim's silver tongue and his fine taste, that is, his sense of proportion, organization, and style, dictated first that a uniformity of style be mandatory for all buildings on the great Court of Honor; second, that that style should be 'Modernized Classic;' and third, that external color should be expunged. The result was the 'White City,' which so impressed America and so distressed foreign visitors, who looked to the new country for something original. There was reason for both. Few Americans had ever had an opportunity to see so large a group co-ordinated in design and dominated by a sense of order. A uniform cornice line, sixty feet high for buildings on the central court, helped to tie them together as parts of a larger whole, and the total effect must have been imposing. Its virginal purity was timid, but at least it had not the blatancy of so much bad Victorian color. The Agricultural Building (fig. 395) by McKim, Mead, and White well illustrates the style. It differs from Neoclassicism in that it rejects the fetish of archaeology; correct and academic though the elements are, they are adapted with sympathy and freedom. The design is admirably proportioned and marked throughout by good taste.

The 'Modernized Classic,' derived from the architecture of imperial Rome, reflects the imperialism of business enterprise. The same wide extent, the same power, the same ramifications, and the same colossal wealth typified the business empires of the end of the century that marked the centralized government of the Roman Empire. The success of the style in expressing the ideals of one of the largest contemporary forces is the real reason for the influence of the Chicago Fair. It fixed upon America for a generation the 'Modernized Classic' as the only mode for the design of civic and commercial buildings. State capitols, court houses, memorials, banks, department stores, and even skyscrapers fell under its spell. The memory of its beauty that America carried away from the Fair, and its lessons in the possibilities of planning and of consistency of style were lasting. Austere critics of the twentieth century deplore the falsity of the Fair, its monumental architecture designed for stone but built of wood and plaster, and its arctic whiteness splashed on with a squirt gun. That the Fair was designed for effect is indisputable; but at least it succeeded in that purpose, and, if it had something of stage scenery about it, an exposition should be theatrical. Even more than that, it was probably for the best that America should undergo another generation of disciplined academic study. Not so much the architects, though even they could profit from such study, but especially the public at large needed this opportunity for further experience of architecture, even if it was an architecture of taste, lest in a premature attempt to try his wings the American Icarus should fall into a sea of undisciplined novelty. However, it does not follow that this influence should continue today. Now we have had our period of training, and we may hope to be better prepared to stand on our own feet in architecture.

Even in 1893, a few were ready to desert eclecticism in any form, and to design architecture instead of styles. European visitors to the Fair recognized in the Transportation Building (fig. 396) the hand of an original genius, Louis Sullivan, of the firm of Adler and Sullivan. In opposition to the whiteness of the main buildings, the golden door rioted in color. Though influenced by Richardson, the building had no obvious character of either Romanesque or 'Modernized Classic.' Sullivan had announced his creed that in architecture 'form follows function,' that each problem, large or small, contained the germ of its own solution, and that the task of the architect was to uncover this solution. Like the others, his building at the Fair was constructed of wood and plaster, but, unlike the rest, it was made to look so. This did not imply something mean or shoddy, but rather that its design should be appropriate to and expressive of its materials. If a projection over the entrance was desirable, the wooden rafters might project sharply beyond the face of the wall below. In a stone architecture, bed moldings must be present to support the overhanging blocks that make the cornice; these were unnecessary in wood and were therefore omitted. Plaster, obviously decorative and not structural in appearance, encased the rafters. The entrance needed dramatization; concentric arches rich with shadows and sumptuous surface ornament forced the eye down to the portals. These must be wide to allow freedom of communication, but they did not need to be high. They were proportioned to the human scale, but brought into relation to the scale of the building by the arches above. The originality of Sullivan's design and its lessons in the principles of architecture were lost on America in 1893, but not on Europe. The path he helped to cut has been the path of architectural development, and amply justifies his title as prophet of modern architecture.

For a generation, his was to be a voice crying in the wilderness. Apparently eclecticism had won the day. Modern eclecticism differs from that of the nineteenth century not in essentials or in point of view, but in results. The scholarship in historic styles is sounder, the possibilities of adaptation better understood. The best of our twentieth-century eclectics do not copy any specific building. On the contrary, they write their architectural essays in the language of the past with a facile understanding of its grammar and rhetoric. The best buildings replace with vitality the dullness of much nineteenth-century work; in the better examples, fine craftsmanship supplants hard and mechanical detail. One is tempted to suggest that the spread of photography is responsible for this. The nineteenth-century designers had to depend on engravings, accurate but metallic and, by their very nature, linear in effect; these qualities reappear in nineteenth-century eclecticism. Only a few photographs brighten the pages of architectural periodicals before 1900, but later they flood in, less to supplant the information engravings and measured drawings must provide, than to supplement it by more complete and plastic illustrations of historic buildings. Today hardly a cottage exists in the countries of western Europe that has not been photographed from all angles.

A consequence of this fund of information is great diversity of style. Even before the Chicago Fair, McKim, Mead, and White designed the Public Library in Boston in the Italian Renaissance manner, with a strong influence from the Bibliothèque Ste. Geneviève in Paris. In fact, they adopted the composition of Labrouste's exterior, but refined it and perfected its proportions. More recently, in 1923, the Lincoln Memorial in Washington (fig. 397) by Henry Bacon turned to the Greek, but the design does not copy a Greek temple. Bacon was the master of the style, not its servant, and he modified it at will, for example, in the entablature. He made the short axis of the building primary, and substituted an attic story for the sloping roof and pediments of the Greek temple. Adaptation likewise transformed the modern version of medieval styles at the hands of such men as Henry Vaughan and Cram, Goodhue, and Ferguson at almost exactly the time of the World's Columbian Exposition. Bertram Grosvenor Goodhue especially, in the Chapel of the Intercession and in St. Bartholomew's, both in New York, showed a freedom based upon profound understanding of the past, whose suggestions he so modified as to approach a modern style. That tendency to simplification he carried further in the Nebraska State Capitol at Lincoln, begun in 1920, one of his latest works, which has thrown overboard completely the baggage of eclecticism.

For better or worse, modern eclectic design dominated the 'nineties and the early twentieth century in America. A generation whose cultural leaders turned to London and Paris for guidance would borrow in architecture and in the other arts as well. That generation was still going to school in the old world. Today, to attack eclecticism is fashionable. It can be done only too easily, and sometimes with justice. In fairness to the past we should examine the charges leveled at any specific eclectic building, and test them narrowly to be certain they apply. The Orientals have a proverb to the effect that when you stand on a man's shoulders, you should try not to spit on his head. To say that eclecticism sacrifices convenience and practicality to its fetish of historic style is easy and often correct. Perhaps it is always true to some extent, but in the better examples any sacrifice of convenience to style is negligible. Nor does the statement that eclectic buildings cost more than comparable structures in a modern style always hold true, even if expense were pertinent in aesthetic criticism. In truth, up to the present time, the advantage in this matter has rested more with the conservatives than with the progressives. One may urge that the traditional activities of our lives may as reasonably claim expression as those parts of life in which we differ from our ancestors. Nevertheless, the trend of architecture is leading away from eclecticism. That is well, since there is reason to hope that the change is based on principles of architecture, not on principles of style. The substitution of a 'modernistic style' would bring little or no improvement. Let us avoid that by concentrating on architecture that bears directly on our lives, and not on 'style,' ancient or modern, which touches us not at all.

Most of this could be said with equal pertinence about sculpture. While the architects were going to the Beaux Arts, the sculptors also turned to the Paris ateliers. Augustus St. Gaudens (1848–1907) dominated his generation in America. He was, of course, a modeler, like his European contemporaries, but he was an expert with fine taste and, at best, a sculpturesque power of conception. The monument to Admiral Farragut in New York (fig. 398), he designed in collaboration with Stanford White, of the firm of McKim, Mead, and White. The pedestal is flanked by curved benches in stone, with allegorical figures in low relief at either end. These young women who look so frank and healthy represent the ideal of his generation. Irregular slashes in the stone suggest water and seaweed, appropriate enough to the subject, who stands with legs apart, as though on the deck of his flagship. Though the figure is not remarkable for its mass, it is by no means devoid of sculptural plasticity. Farragut looks capable of movement, but his action stays within bounds and inside the composition. More sophisticated and less direct than portraits by Brown or Ward, the surfaces are marked by greater vitality. St. Gaudens does not attempt the undulations of surface that we find in Rodin, but he introduces enough variety to give interest to his modeling. The kind of sculpture for which he stands is wholly that of his generation. Daniel Chester French, Frederick MacMonnies, Lorado Taft, and many others worked along the same lines without St. Gaudens' refined taste or his sculptural quality.

The painters, too, went to school in Paris. James McNeill Whistler (1834–1903), though American born, spent most of his professional life in London. The Japanese influence, found in Impressionism, is strong in him. Many externals such as costume and still life in his paintings are Oriental, but more important is the exquisite delicacy and the sense of selection that strips each canvas down to a few well-chosen, perfectly arranged accents. The pier and roadway of Old Battersea Bridge (fig. 399) at twilight create within the frame a pattern relieved by twinkling lights reflected in the river. Such extreme simplification outraged the public in England and embroiled Whistler, to his delight, in his famous lawsuit with Ruskin. The critic referred to the artist as an impudent coxcomb who flung a paint pot in the face of the public, and Whistler sued for heavy damages. He won his case, but the damages awarded to him — one farthing — exactly expressed the injury to his reputation. At his best, his paintings are fantasies, so balanced that each accent, even to his butterfly signature, must remain exactly as he placed it. Nevertheless, this consciously esoteric aesthete, like his friend Oscar Wilde, sometimes allowed cleverness to beguile him into mistaking shadow for substance.

The most popular painter of his day was John Singer Sargent (1856–1925), a society portraitist. The techniques of painting came easily to him; he relied upon dash and verve for facile effects. The temptation to snap out flashy likenesses, flattering to his sitters, must have been great, since they accepted them so eagerly, and one cannot suppose that all sitters would stimulate him enough to compel a study of structure and character. Some of his earlier portraits, like those of the Wertheimer family, are among his best. The Daughters of Asher Wertheimer (fig. 400) are characterized with satirical bitterness. Sargent's fame during his lifetime was inflated, but in their eagerness to remedy that error many modern critics have gone to the opposite extreme. He is not a great painter, but his best canvases on which the future will base its estimate of him have some structure and decorative value as well as the fluency of their technique to recommend them.

The most unique American contribution to the history of art in the World's Fair generation is the skyscraper. This problem originates in the desire of American businessmen engaged in the same field of enterprise to be as near one another as possible. It is not due to scarcity of land, at least in the ordinary sense of the term, nor to high land values, of which indeed it is the cause rather than the result. The skyscraper was born in the Middle West, not in New York as is commonly supposed. Two developments had to take place to make skyscrapers possible. First of all, some means of vertical transportation was essential, before the economic limits even of stone construction could be reached. By the middle of the century, passenger elevators began to be introduced, at first in hotels, and later in office buildings. The early elevators were slow and not too reliable, but when they were sufficiently improved to make access to the tenth floor, for example, as easy as to the second floor, the tall building could and did appear. Each increase in the height of skyscrapers coincides with an improvement in elevator design.

But if the elevator made the skyscraper practical, metal construction made it possible. As already noted, the nineteenth century explored the structural possibilities of metal. It remained for Leroy S. Buffington of Minneapolis to design a multi-story building wherein a masonry wall rested on iron supports. He thereby transformed the building from one in which the walls supported at least their own weight, if not also the floors within, to one in which the framework of metal beams and columns carried the entire load of floors and outer walls as well. Buffington claimed that he conceived the notion of a braced metal frame with iron shelves to hold the masonry as early as 1882. His claim is supported by drawings, but the dates on them have been questioned. In any case, some buildings, both in Europe and America, had already grasped this principle in part, notably the Menier Chocolate Works at Noisiel-sur-Marne in France in 1871-2, but none realized the possibility of great height inherent in this method. On the basis of this idea, Buffington designed a twenty-eight story building (fig. 401) to elucidate his principle and its possibilities. His design is remarkable for its grasp of the aesthetic opportunities of the form. Though some details bear the imprint of the Richardsonian Romanesque, such as the round arched entrances and the heavy rustication, and though the pointed roof seems archaic today, nevertheless Buffington's design is far ahead of his time. He places the piers slightly in front of the plane of the windows and makes them continuous to create sweeping lines and to tie the whole design into a vertical unity.

Buffington never had an opportunity to build a skyscraper, since his project remained only a design. The honor of first doing so belongs to William L. B. Jenney of the firm of Jenney and Mundie of Chicago in the Home Life Insurance Building, designed in 1883 and occupied in 1885, which employs skeleton construction. Granite walls in the two lower floors carry the external weight, but iron beams bolted to cast-iron columns support the walls at the fourth, sixth, ninth, and tenth floors. However, the brick wall has still to be substantial, since no other provision is made for lateral bracing. Jenney hardly realized at the time the advantages of light, speedy, and flexible construction implicit in the new method, nor did he grasp its possibilities in design. Not for nothing were the early skyscrapers ridiculed as packing boxes on end. Jenney piled his ten stories, to which two more were added later, on top of one another, some of them grouped in pairs or threes, but each unit as distinct as a part in a sectional bookcase. He nodded to the architectural amenities with an occasional pilaster, molding, or cornice, eclectic features that in this instance could have been omitted without damage to the design.

Perhaps Jenney was more engineer than architect, but even those who claimed to be designers failed to solve this problem. In an eclectic age, a proper solution for a new problem was not instantly obvious. Burnham and Root designed the Masonic Temple in Chicago in 1892, a twenty-two story edifice, the half dozen upper floors of which are conceived in terms of a German medieval town hall with steep roof and small windows. These stories, considered by themselves and placed on the ground, would make a decent if not distinguished eclectic design. They seem preposterous perched atop this mass as though a gigantic flower stalk had germinated under them. Of course, after 1893, the 'Modernized Classic' prevailed. Skyscrapers might confess their architectural allegiance by columns or pilasters, arches and entablatures draped around the upper floors and a similar scheme around the ground stories, with a plain shaft in between, the only successful part in such a building.

One man alone perceived the possibilities of the new problem, and accepted the challenge it offered. In the Wainwright Building in St. Louis (fig. 402), dated 1890, Louis Sullivan vindicates his belief that the skyscraper needs no apology if rightly conceived, but that it may become a 'proud and soaring thing.' The mass of the skyscraper can be dramatized, and its height stressed to create a composition. The outer piers, uninterrupted from basement to roof, should be so devised as to look continuous. The walls, whose only functions are to exclude the weather and to fireproof the steel, must not counterfeit supporting members; between the windows in each vertical band, the wall is treated decoratively to deny any structural significance in it. The cornice projects abruptly to reveal the presence of a flat roof, but without any trace of historic precedent to interfere with a demonstration of the new material and the new method of construction. Floors that serve a similar purpose are identical in design, but contrast with floors that have different functions. Therefore the bulk of this building, devoted to office space, is uniform; but the ground floors allotted to shops, and the top floor to services common to the whole, are distinct. Sullivan is too much of an artist to idolize consistency; in the Wainwright Building, the supporting steel rises only in every other pier. That is clear at the bottom, since the intermediate supports do not descend through the windows of the ground floor, but in the mass of the building nothing distinguishes one pier from another. Such objections are insignificant in view of the fact that the Wainwright Building, unlike most skyscrapers for the next twenty-five years, is a co-ordinated and expressive design.

That the verticality of the skyscraper should not have turned more of the eclectics to the one historic style that had stressed the vertical, the Gothic, is curious. It must be attributed partly to the hypnotism of the Chicago Fair, and partly to the opinion that Gothic should be confined to churches, or at least that it was not appropriate for business buildings. A few examples do exist, and among them the most distinguished eclectic skyscraper previous to 1916. The Woolworth Building in New York (fig. 403), completed by Cass Gilbert in 1913, was for years the tallest building in the world. To call it Gothic is misleading; its effectiveness comes not from its Gothic tracery, its canopies, and its pointed arches in terra cotta, but in spite of them. The one Gothic feature that helps the design is the verticality. Large and small piers rise in rhythms, as they could hardly do in the classic styles, and reveal the location of the principal supports. The tower with its successive stages creates an effective silhouette against the sky. But one must always remember that the result comes more from the mass than from the Gothic details.

By this time, it had become evident to the public at large that the skyscraper had brought with it many problems, especially a chaotic effect on land values. Moreover, the difficulty of the traffic problem, attributed to it somewhat unjustly, its obstruction of light and air, and its conversion of the streets into canyons made some form of regulation inevitable. The New York Zoning Law of 1916 provided a model that spread throughout the country, its principles sometimes accepted with little change, though at other times different methods of control were preferred. In addition to restricting certain activities to specified parts of the city, the zoning law prescribed partial height limitations. The city was divided into districts, each with a number to describe it, ranging from ½ to 3½. This figure signified that on any piece of property in a '1½-times' district, for example, the owner might build a vertical wall to a height 1½ times the width of the street. A building could rise beyond that height, but only if its upper part were contained within a line drawn from the center of the street through the top of the vertical wall.

These factors operated to produce what the law described as the mass envelop, the legal maximum of building on any given site. A number of exceptions in detail complicated the law, but none of them need be mentioned here except that a tower of unlimited height might be added, its area not to exceed ¼ of the area of the plot. Hugh Ferriss illustrated the provisions of the law on a theoretical city block in four drawings, the first of which showed the mass envelop (fig. 404), the second the excision of light courts in that mass, next the walls of each story within the crowning pyramid made vertical, and finally these set-back stories grouped for simplification of construction. In spite of all its restrictions on property rights, the law was accepted with little criticism, a proof of its soundness, though it was later simplified in some respects. The architectural world soon realized that the law contained and in large part compelled a satisfactory solution of the aesthetic problem of the skyscraper.

Consequently, its principles were incorporated in almost all skyscrapers, even in cities where they were not yet compulsory. However, our entry into the First World War, and the minor depression after the war, prevented much building previous to 1922. That year saw the next milestone in the story of the skyscraper, an open competition for the Chicago Tribune Building. Many of the foremost architects of the country, and indeed of the world, entered. From the date the competition was announced, the *Tribune* illustrated the masterpieces of world architecture, each of which bore the caption 'Will the new Tribune Building look like this?' Had they been able to foresee the results, they might well have asked that question. The most amazing range of designs were submitted, borrowed freely, not to say blatantly, from all styles of the European tradition. The absurdity of many of them would have been laughable had it not been tragic. The winning design by Howells and Hood was a sensitive piece of eclecticism, influenced by the Tour de Beurre of Rouen Cathedral, but well composed and in no sense a copy. It was obsolete, however, even before the building was finished. The second prize design (fig. 405) by the Finnish architect, Eliel Saarinen, overshadowed it. Developed in terms of verticality and mass, with no correspondence to any historic style, Saarinen's design soared aloft, while its rhythmic piers and corner accents flowered into admirably proportioned setbacks at the top.

The solution exemplified here set the type for the skyscrapers of the 'twenties, for example, the Chicago Daily News Building (fig. 406) by Holabird and Root, or the Barclay-Vesey Telephone Building in

New York (fig. 407) by McKenzie, Voorhees, and Gmelin. By then, architects had realized that their buildings were so enormous that the older types of architectural elements, like doors and windows, no longer counted in the general result. Instead, they must rely upon masses, each as large as entire buildings of the past. The blocks, projected above the main mass to form the buttresses and foundations of the tower, would each, if placed on the ground, be a structure of considerable dimensions. As it is, they form mere units of the whole. Detail, as it had been conceived through the centuries, could no longer tell. The decorative conclusion of the building at the top must be designed on bolder lines. Moreover, the increasing cost of skilled labor made the traditional types of decoration prohibitive. More and more, ornament was forced to become repetitive, and thus capable of being produced in part at least by machine. The result is magnificent in mass, overwhelming in scale, and strongly vertical in consequence of the projection of each pier in front of the windows. Skyscrapers of this type adorn all the large cities of the country, and testify to the popularity of the skyscraper idea and to the success of this solution.

A few buildings, but very few, under the influence of European modernism and of what has been called the International style, have rejected this solution. The best of these is the Philadelphia Savings Fund Society Building (fig. 408) by Howe and Lescaze. Where the designers of the standard skyscraper have not availed themselves of the possibilities of the cantilever principle, these architects exploit them. On the main front, the face of the wall projects beyond the last supporting piers, and each floor overhangs the columns on which it rests. Therefore, since the supports are withdrawn from the face of the building, the entire wall area can be converted to continuous windows stretched from corner to corner, and even around the corners. The result is that this face of the building becomes a series of bands, alternately light and dark. Moreover, the elimination of the wall as a structural feature produces this change in the conception; that wall and windows together become a skin drawn over the frame with only the slightest projections and recessions. The thin wall is made to look so by the absence of any shadows, which might create an impression of its thickness and so of its weight. Such a design expresses the structure of the building, betrays the existence of each separate floor through its bands of windows, and utilizes the possibilities of steel construction on the cantilever principle; on the Twelfth Street side, however, the vertical columns are visible.

Though less radical in style, Rockefeller Center in New York, built between 1931 and 1939, is the last word in skyscrapers. So large a project called for collaboration in design; its architects included Corbett, Harrison, and MacMurray, Hood and Fouilhoux, and Reinhard and Hofmeister, though many others contributed designs for shops and so forth. They developed a group of tall buildings related to one another. Generally, it is difficult if not impossible to see a skyscraper in its entirety, because it is surrounded by other buildings, which partly conceal many of the lower floors and tend to minimize its height. In Rockefeller Center, on the other hand, low and high blocks are so disposed that each shall admit to the group as much light, air, and visibility as possible. The open space in front of the seventy-story RCA building allows dramatic expression to the height of this climax of the ensemble. Its thin book-like mass is based on the satisfactory depth of an office and the access to it; as each bank of elevators rises to its limit, the space it occupied is no longer valuable and a setback occurs; thus, Rockefeller Center represents as nearly scientific an approach as is possible in the art of building.

But while eclecticism was continuing even in some of the skyscrapers, and more commonly in other buildings, some architects were pursuing their personal ideals. Frank Lloyd Wright, who calls Sullivan his *lieber meister*, is the only living American architect who can claim world renown. While the rest of the country was building its Gothic churches and 'Modernized Classic' banks, Wright designed the Unity church in Oak Park, Illinois (fig. 409), just after 1900. Considering the problem on its own merits, Wright backed the auditorium against the main street and raised its windows high in the wall to avoid noise and interruption from heavy traffic. The chief source of light is a skylight, invisible from the ground, which bathes the interior with more than adequate illumination. Partly under pressure of economy, Wright chose poured concrete as his material, and evolved a design in that material proper to it. Up to this time, concrete had not been admitted to the Social Register of architecture as a monumental building material. Wright won it that standing. The austere rectangular forms, not only of the chief masses but of the smaller members as well, betray a grasp of the true character of concrete. The medium is often called plastic, because of its fluid state while being mixed. However, since it must be poured into rigid forms to hold it in place until it sets, rectilinear shapes express the substance better than curved, plastic surfaces. Of course, concrete can be poured into a form of any shape, such as the weird curves of the Einstein Tower in Potsdam, by Erich Mendelssohn, but the solution hit upon in the Unity Church is earlier, simpler, and more direct.

The abrupt right angles that limit these abstract shapes foretell later continental developments.

The so-called prairie house, like the Coonley House of 1908 in Riverside, Illinois (fig. 410), comes as a relief after the usual residence of its day, not because it lacks any eclectic features, but because its horizontality conveys repose instead of the restlessness of its contemporaries. The extremely complex plan is difficult to read, even for those who have had wide experience in architecture. This rambling house throws forward a room here into the lawns and gardens, or draws one back there, as though to pull the exterior within the house. The inside and the outside fuse so that it is difficult to say where one begins and the other stops. To this union of the house and its setting, assisted by the horizontal composition, must be credited the exceptional charm of Wright's buildings. He abandoned the idea that the house must consist of cubical volumes called rooms; instead, by eliminating partitions wherever privacy was unnecessary, he allowed his enclosed space to flow from one area to another, and for that matter to flow from inside the house to the outside and back.

On the exterior, the low-pitched roof overhangs the wall below so that it shades the windows. Its long horizontals echo those of the projecting balconies, or of window boxes shaggy with growth. His multiple windows give an openness to the house, and yet the roofs and balconies curtail much of the light that might come through them, even when the undersides of these projections are treated in some light-toned material. The picturesqueness of these houses is thoroughly romantic in spirit, as is their emphasis on individualism, Wright's outstanding personal characteristic. Many of Wright's enthusiastic admirers praise the logic of his work, and try to adduce practical explanations for every peculiarity. Such an attempt is not only hopeless, since his designs are not always logical, but is quite unnecessary. Wright, in fact, is too much of an artist not to be ready at any time to depart from, or to contradict, logic for the sake of architectural effect, or even for some jolly architectonic joke.

Since the early years of the century, he has continued to work in his own individual vein. The Millard Residence in Pasadena, California, built in the 'twenties, gives a decorative expression to precast concrete blocks, another ordinarily drab material. In each block, he casts a simple pattern in shadow, one design for the ordinary wall members and another for the narrower supporting members. He adapts his solutions to the spirit and traditions of the region in which he finds himself, without resorting to historic styles. The Barnsdall Residence in Hollywood, California, is no modern version of adobe architecture in poured concrete, but its blocky masses and bold scale seem allied and sympathetic to the older architecture of southern California. Perhaps it would be fair to say that it is closer to the past in spirit than the twentieth-century versions of Spanish mission architecture. Or again, Wright injected an oriental tinge into the Imperial Hotel in Tokyo without contradiction of his own Occidental background.

Wright is not a 'modern' architect, as that nebulous term is used today. He does not subscribe to the International style, but expresses his opinion of it in caustic terms. Indeed, his underlying romanticism compels hostility to that style. But some of his more recent work appears to have developed along similar lines. The Kaufman House at Bear Run, Pennsylvania (fig. 411), built 1937-9, exploits concrete and cantilever principle, but combines them in a design appropriate to its romantic site overhanging a roaring brook.

Still more recently, in 1945, Wright designed the Modern Gallery (fig. 412) for a proposed museum of abstract art. The main exhibition space consists of a spiral ramp lighted from a court covered by a dome of glass tubing supported on stainless steel. Whether the structure will be built of reinforced concrete or of welded steel remains to be seen. No such museum has ever been built — but neither was there precedent for the Unity Church, the Millard Residence, or the Imperial Hotel. However extravagant Wright's projects may seem, his completed buildings have always fulfilled his expectations and confounded his critics; we must learn to expect originality from genius. Until recently, America has ignored Wright; he has had but little influence here, but in Europe, especially in Holland, his genius has long been acclaimed. The openness of his plans, the freshness of his houses, his sense of materials, his avoidance of eclecticism, and his powerful originality helped to formulate the architecture of the past four decades in Europe. If its course has turned away from him in certain matters, he has not been forgotten or left without honor.

Eclecticism, so dominant in architecture during the early decades of the century but declining in recent years, pursues a similar course in sculpture. Conservatives, like Paul Manship, born in 1885, continue to design with exquisite craftsmanship in the older, more or less archaeological styles. His small bronze Centaur and Dryad in the Metropolitan Museum has borrowed the decorative patterns of archaic Greece. The Dancer and Gazelles of the Corcoran Gallery in Washington has something of the East Indian in its stylization. On the other hand, his portrait of his infant daughter, marble enframed in wood, reverts to the Italian Renaissance. We can hardly refuse admiration for the delicacy of these works, slight in dimensions and small in scale, like table ornaments, or fail to recognize the linear design upon which they rely.

More progressive sculptors deny the legitimacy of eclecticism as a goal. Like contemporary Europeans, they turn to a direct study of their materials, and re-examine the basic elements of sculpture. Gaston Lachaise in his Dolphins shows an admirable feeling for movement and for design in simplified curving volumes. In his Statue of a Woman (fig. 413), he so departs from normal proportions as to outrage the conservatives. The sex characteristics of the woman are emphasized for expression, as in Van Gogh's La Berceuse (fig. 379), only much more so, carried to an almost psychopathic extreme. His purpose in this and many similar figures is to build up a series of expressive sculptural volumes.

Others, like William Zorach (b. 1887), abandon the nineteenth-century practice of works modeled in plaster and then transcribed into stone. The Mother and Child (fig. 414) was cut directly in pink marble with only a small model to guide him; even then, he departed from his sketch as the conception grew in stone under his hand. The design of such a statue as this is calculated from all points of view, though in this instance some views of the back are less successful than others. On the whole, each part in the mass is sculpturally related to every other part. The compact enclosed design marks and echoes the limits of the block from which these figures have been released. It dramatizes the weight and massiveness of stone in volumes sufficiently similar to the human body to be self-explanatory, and yet simplified and abstract enough to yield a sculpturesque treatment. Zorach is representative of American sculpture today. He is neither eclectic nor academic, nor is he radical in the direction of abstraction. He appears to walk in the middle of the road in his search for the possibilities of his material and of sculpturesque monumentality through working directly in stone, without a complete sacrifice of recognizable forms.

Meanwhile in painting, George Bellows carried on the realistic vein of Homer and Eakins until his death in 1925, but, as one might expect, simplified the forms. His large canvas of Dempsey and Firpo (fig. 415) selects the dramatic moment when the 'wild bull of the pampas,' as the sports writers called Firpo, knocked Dempsey out of the ring. The exciting action of the figures builds up to Firpo, whose widespread legs complete a pyramidal composition. The individual forms are highly simplified. Bellows does not stress details of anatomy; rather he prefers the semi-abstract geometric shapes into which the body and the parts thereof can be reduced. The heads of the spectators and officials in the foreground are almost ovoid, and firmly modeled as such. Both color and value are strong and fresh, but handled with the same stringent selection and the same simplification as the forms themselves. Such painting as this is certainly not conservative or academic, nor is it representative of the more extreme movements toward abstraction, which play so obtrusive a part in any panorama of twentieth-century painting.

But America has not been unaware of those movements. Even in Bellows, the tendency to simplification testifies to their influence. Up to 1913, America at large remained oblivious to the existence of such developments, but in that year a group of painters in New York organized the now famous Armory Show, where, among others, such radical experiments as Cubism, marked by Marcel Duchamp's notorious Nude Descending the Stairs, aroused widespread attention. The interest in abstraction and the willingness to experiment with it allowed McDonald Wright and Morgan Russell to form what was called the Synchromist movement, one of many minor phenomena of the current European progressive vogue. This country in general has not taken very kindly to these experiments, at least in their extreme forms, but their emphasis on design and their partial if not complete suppression of representation in painting has played its part in the compositions of Georgia O'Keefe, as well as in some of the more analytical paintings of Charles Sheeler and Arthur Dove, to mention only a few.

Rather less willing to tread the road to abstraction is a large and distinguished group of men who may be called painters of the American scene, for want of a better term. In general, the panorama of American life has attracted them. The Bowery, or perhaps Negro life in Harlem, may provide material for Reginald Marsh. His High Yaller, a garishly fashionable Negress, is not only typical of Harlem in subject but also in spirit. The bargain basement, Coney Island, the water front, restaurants, Greenwich Village, and slums provide grist for such painters as John Sloan, 'Pop' Hart, Glenn Coleman, Kenneth Hayes Miller, and Edward Hopper. Hopper's painting, Lighthouse (fig. 416), shows the same grand simplification, the same sturdy grasp of structure, the strong color and values that appear in the mature work of Bellows. These men and many others, however much they may differ from one another, are not unaware of the developments toward abstraction, nor are they uninfluenced by them; but they reject the more radical features of these movements. They deal with what they know from experience; they analyze it in detail and characterize it succinctly. As a group, they are concerned but little with theory and rely on more concrete things and on their own unpretending ability.

For mural painting, the progressive artists reject those vapid allegories, once popular, as they also contradict the idea that a mural is merely an easel painting affixed to a wall. A return to true fresco painting by certain Mexican artists, notably Diego Rivera and José Clemente Orozco, lends to their work a greater sympathy with the wall than oil paintings can achieve. Though it is quite possible to develop some mural quality in oils, most nineteenth-century examples were not distinguished for this quality. Much of Rivera's wide notoriety is due to his leftist political views and their frequent prominence in his paintings. Regardless of the merits or defects of his cause, such propaganda is not pertinent to the success of his works as paintings. In all aesthetic matters, Orozco (b. 1883) seems far superior. The latter's decorations in the Dartmouth College Library reach their culmination in the Risen Christ, a terrific conception of the Saviour returned to earth to destroy His cross because of the mountain of military equipment behind Him. Through its simplification, and especially through its composition, the design fits the wall without any sacrifice of the modern brilliance of color.

Different from this but allied to it in their willingness to modify appearances are the murals of Thomas Benton (b. 1889). In such a painting as the Arts of the West (fig. 417), he combines figures and scenes, which through their associative images create a sort of composite picture of that region. Cowboys, gambling in a saloon, horseshoe pitching, oil wells, and Indians succeed one another in rapid and bewildering succession. Such compositions may be too complex, and yet they have some diffused decorative value, and certainly one cannot deny the wealth of topical interest in them. The forms are simplified, but not in the direction of elementary geometric volumes. It is perhaps better to describe them as stylized in undulating dynamic shapes animated with restless energy.

The question is bound to arise how justly we may call our arts 'American.' Even a cursory survey makes it clear that each European movement from 1700 to the present day finds its faithful reflection in America. Much of it is distinguished by a provincial flavor, as one would expect. Our civilization is bound to be European; we are not descended from the American Indian, but from the stocks of all the European countries, and particularly of Great Britain. As each has left its strain in our cultural life, so each is bound to be represented in the arts. But in so far as we have created a civilization that is distinguishable from the European, exactly so far also have we expressed that difference in our architecture, sculpture, and painting. If we tend to be a sentimental people, we produce a John Rogers and our painters and sculptors of the World's Fair generation, as well as the Longfellows, Whittiers, and Lowells. We have not been much attracted to theory or to the abstract, preferring in all lines some more concrete outlet for our energies. We like to think of ourselves, deservedly or not, as a practical people. The formative influence of the frontier in American life, where practical results were vital, has colored our whole outlook. Affectation may have some place in a cosmopolitan society, but it has none in a pioneering community. The result is that the most purely American artists have been characterized by sober honesty, an utter freedom from pretense, which one finds in Copley and Bellows, in Hopper and Inness, Brown and Zorach, Homer and Eakins. So recurrent a quality we have every right to call American. That does not mean that it cannot be found elsewhere, or that other elements may not be present in American art; but on the whole, this seems to be the central thread around which is twisted the pattern of our painting and sculpture.

What if the American past has been provincial? We have no more reason to be ashamed of or to apologize for this background than for the traditional career of the farmer's boy or backwoodsman risen to wealth and power. On the contrary, we may look on what we have accomplished with justifiable satisfaction, and feel no need to measure it with a European yardstick. If we can preserve this straightforward attitude and the openness of mind that goes with it, we may expect our art to grow more and more distinct from the European. Let us not disregard what others have done and are doing, even though under different conditions; they may offer us valuable help in solving our own problems. However, a weak strain in our art has appeared whenever and wherever we have consciously tried to be European. For all his brilliance, Stuart lacks the homespun strength of Copley; the American Homer is much more powerful than the cosmopolitan Sargent. In short, we have been at our best when we have been most native, most completely ourselves. So long as we continue to adhere to these traditional American traits — not to external forms, for that would in itself be false to this spirit — we need not fear for the future of American art.

XXIV

Twentieth-Century Art

THE rapid tempo of modern life results in a series of abrupt and seemingly chaotic changes in the arts. Every few years, from the beginning of the century to the present day, some new development has arisen in painting or sculpture that flourished for a day, was given a new label, and either disappeared or was modified in yet a newer style. A few, such as Cubism, have lasted longer. Throughout the earlier history of art, movements had risen gradually and had subsided as slowly. The apparent chaos of modern art can be partly attributed to its being too close to us; time has not yet winnowed what has been of real significance from what has been a passing whim and novelty of the day. Eventually, historians will doubtless combine under more general headings artists and styles that now seem diverse to us. Probably every period has seemed more complex to itself than to its descendants.

That the progressive artists of the twentieth century revolted against their predecessors is obvious. On the whole, the nineteenth century had tended to overstress subject matter in art. Some painters of the English Academy guarded their subjects like trade secrets until the annual exhibition opened, lest some fellow artist steal them. Obviously, they found the literary values of their paintings more absorbing than the pictorial, and of course the spectators felt the same way. Such pictures as the Shepherd's Last Friend, by Sir Edwin Landseer, a dog mourning over his master's coffin, stood or fell on the basis of the story they told, rather than on their aesthetic quality. Though this example is extreme, to a slighter degree a similar point of view held good in the French Academy; even among progressive French painters of the nineteenth century, such as Courbet, Manet, Monet, and Degas, the representational point of view, if not the narrative, remained dominant. At the end of the century the Post Impressionists, like Seurat and Cézanne, Gauguin and Van Gogh, rebelled against this point of view, and their lead was followed and carried much further by their twentieth-century successors. One may speculate whether improvements in photography, by making possible representation mechanically more accurate than the most literal painting, may have prompted the artists to re-examine the bases of painting and sculpture; but more important in provoking this reconsideration was the nineteenth-century overemphasis in one way or another on representation. Certainly though representation and subject have been significant in the past and may still be so today, they are not now believed to be the nucleus of the artist's problem.

A group of painters, including Matisse, Derain, Rouault, and others, accepted the name *Les Fauves*, the wild beasts, after they had been called that in derision by a critic. Like ferocious animals, they threw themselves on the alleged laws and traditions of painting and tore them to shreds. Rejecting the validity of those traditions, especially that too common standard of superficial resemblance, they maintained that the indispensability of representation was inimical to the best interest of progressive artists trying to express themselves and their beliefs about art in paint or stone. The subject from the point of view of representation or narration becomes insignificant, incidental, and subordinate to color, to composition, and to dynamic movement often expressed through line. Henri Matisse (*b*. 1869) in The Dance (fig. 418) takes greater liberties with the human figure than any recent artist has dared. The swinging action of the dancers Matisse conveys primarily by long curving lines. The axes of the figures as they turn and twist in the dance follow these curves. The same motive also defines the parts of their figures, the thighs and arms, heads and torsos, different in size, position, and direction, and creates a dynamic harmony through repetition. Like many of these artists, Matisse is well informed, not merely of the European past in his own art but of many other fields. The sparkling color of Indian miniatures, the feeling for pattern in Persian textiles have both played their part in helping him to form his own sense of design, which comes out in the many versions of the Odalisque, but these later paintings are no longer Fauvist in character. Rich and integrated in design, they add to their pattern a fresh concern with color.

The most publicized artist of our time is Pablo Picasso (*b*. 1881), about whom violent controversy has raged time and again. Like all of the more important artists, Picasso is capable of painting a figure realistic enough to satisfy the most academic spirit. The charge of incompetence so often leveled at modern artists because of the unnaturalism of their works is utterly groundless in his case. Though by no means realistic, The Spring (fig. 419), from Picasso's so-called classic period of about 1920, is far from abstract in purpose or result. The figures have a sculpturesque dignity and repose. The artist rejects all minor elements and concentrates on the larger features. The head is austere, heavy of countenance, and serious with a sobriety and mass parallel to classic sculpture. Indeed this figure is more justly described as classic than many of the pseudo-classic productions by the Bouguereaus and Alma Tademas of the academies.

Early in his career, Picasso endured a time of great financial difficulty, when he often did not know where to find his next meal. A series of half-starved mountebanks and clowns from the circus, haggard mothers with their children, and old guitar players absorbed his attention at that time, 1901–4. These he painted in shades of blue, perhaps to express the tragedy of their lives. They created a sensation, but Picasso turned from blue to rose in 1905–6. During these years, he carried distortion no farther than many of his predecessors and certainly no more than necessary to express the bitterness of life. In 1907, the newly discovered sculpture of the African Negro excited the Parisian art world through its indifference to natural appearance. The result is Picasso's Negro period. The violent distortions of the Young Ladies of Avignon issue from this source. While the figures remain recognizable as such, their features are blocked out in line, and the pattern is by no means confined to normal appearance. Enlarged eyes stare out above a nose curved laterally, while a twisted mouth has moved off the axis of the head — if one can speak of an axis in such circumstances.

But Picasso is best known for his experiments leading toward abstraction, beginning about 1909 in his work and that of Georges Braque. Cézanne had remarked in a letter to Emile Bernard that all forms in nature could be reduced to terms of the sphere, the cone, and the cylinder. This letter Bernard published in 1907. Perhaps the Cubists took their cue from that; they were influenced by Cézanne, and particularly by his later work. In the Fernande (fig. 420), Picasso has analyzed the head into a series of planes, each defined by straight lines. A certain pattern results from these facets of more or less uniform character. Then it occurred to the artist that it might be interesting to see what would happen if these planes were shuffled around in a kaleidoscopic fashion. In the Still Life (fig. 421), the subject can no longer readily be identified. Here is a bit of newspaper, and there a few circles might suggest grapes to an imaginative mind.

It should be evident that Picasso's conception of painting and his purpose have changed. He has so immersed himself in problems of organization of shapes that color is almost suppressed and representation avoided.

It is a serious mistake for the observer to examine these Cubist compositions as though they were puzzle pictures of the sort familiar to childhood — find the cat hidden among the trees. The artist is not representing a still life; he is creating an arrangement. One might well ask, then, whether it would not be less confusing, at least to the lay mind, to describe these paintings by abstract titles, which would not appear to invite the observer to identify some known visual objects. Such a device might be wise, but the title does have its purpose even here. It suggests the springboard, the point of departure upon which the artist has built his arrangement; it gives the source of his visual analysis; but it does not imply an attempt or a desire on Picasso's part to represent in the older sense of the term.

Music is commonly divided into two groups, program music and pure or absolute music. In the former, the sounds may parallel a story, as in the case of Strauss' *Till Eulenspiegel,* or suggest a scene or phenomenon in nature, as in Beethoven's Sixth Symphony or Chopin's 'Raindrop Prelude.' But even in these examples, the effect of the music is not reached through the image, vague at best, evoked in the mind of the listener, but in the organization of musical tone. We must admit that the ordered sounds of a Beethoven symphony or a Bach fugue have an intense emotional power, which may be felt by the listener, as well as a brilliant intellectual structure, which may be perceived through the mind. If these results can be accomplished by sounds speaking to the ear with no particular and identifiable images suggested by them, in other words by abstract relationships, may it not be possible to appeal to the emotions and the intellect through the eye by an arrangement of lines, shapes, and colors of equally abstract character? It seems unreasonable to deny to the eye powers of enjoyment that everyone accords to the ear without question. We have become so accustomed to the abstract in music that we do not demand anything else. We have become even more trained in the visual arts to expect to identify shapes and colors with known and concrete objects. In justice to the painters and sculptors who have been experimenting with abstraction, it is only fair to approach their works with the same open mind that we grant to the sister art. Whether the paintings of Cubism have succeeded in creating adequate visual interest of arrangement is another question, one that can be settled only by each observer before each example. But it is a question that can never be decided reasonably unless the spectator is willing to grant some such premise as this, and to school himself not to expect in the painting something which is not there.

Like every new development, the movement toward abstraction has met with hostility, more violent as its departure from visual reality is more pronounced and thus more foreign to our experience. The bulk of commissioned work still goes to the conservatives. The radical painters have preferred, instead of the more or less veiled dictation of the client, freedom to conduct their experiments as they choose. When one of these artists reaches a certain point of promise, his work may be sponsored by a dealer, who helps give it the needed publicity and who will display it to the interested public in his gallery. Perhaps later some wealthy individual may help the artist with his patronage, but these possibilities touch only the most important artists.

Cubism, which developed before the outbreak of the First World War, was not absolutely abstract, though it so far deserted objective appearance as to open wide the gate to a flood of other innovations. If the design in abstract facets was all important, there could be no prescriptive reason to create such shapes only in paint on canvas. Any material that offered the precise tone and especially the texture needed by the artist should be legitimate. Hence *collage* appeared, derived from the French word for glue, and referring to compositions made from the contents of the wastepaper basket pasted on a surface. In one instance, irregular newspaper clippings combine with fragments of a playbill, the artist's calling card, a cigarette, and other scraps, though these usually supplement pigments.

In so far as design is concerned, collage stands or falls with Cubism. To it, however, this objection may be raised; the materials from which it is made in many cases appear not to have the possibility of permanence. Modern newsprint is poor in quality; it yellows and eventually powders on exposure to light and air. This makes it probable that the existence of much collage is threatened by time to an extent not true of competent oil paintings. Even if means should be discovered to prevent the disintegration of collage, this may be urged against it; if, for purposes of argument, we grant the adjustment of shapes and visual tones in the collage to be perfect as originally arranged, the change of tone in the paper, not equaled by changes in the painted parts, must eventually throw the composition out of adjustment. If it was right when new, it must be less satisfactory as it changes. Sensational though it was, collage after all was but a minor phase of Cubism.

The short-lived Futurist movement of Italian origin just before the First World War attempted to analyze movement. Thus, Balla painted a dog walking with each leg in half a dozen positions, each more or less sharply indicated. Others, like Russolo, tried to express action through abstract lines and shapes. In the Dynamism of an Auto, he drew the shape of a speeding car, but the suggestion of movement is accomplished more by superimposing on it a series of angles all pointing in the same direction, and each more acute than the last.

In these and other developments, some trace of subject may remain. During and after the war, Cubism itself changed its character somewhat. It combined non-representational shapes with several aspects of a figure or scene, viewed at different angles but presented simultaneously, and fused to convey the totality of the object's significance. Thus, Picasso may choose to draw the same head in profile and in full front, one super-imposed on the other, or perhaps one half of the head as seen from the front and the other half from the side. After the war, the movement turned to brilliant decorative color. In Russia, just after the war, the Suprematists, such as Malevich, abandoned reality. The elements of their compositions and the titles too are absolutely abstract. Squares and circles may be present and perhaps nothing else. Simplification and selection are car-ried to their logical conclusion, as in White on White, a white square laid upon a slightly less white rectangle. Such a work, like The Wonderful One Hoss Shay, may be a *reductio ad absurdum*.

But abstraction need not be so reduced. The Neo-Plasticists, starting in Holland but closely allied to the Bauhaus group in Germany, are no less abstract than the Suprematists. A typical Neo-Plasticist composition (fig. 422), by Piet Mondrian, is divided into rectangles by narrow dark lines. At best, admirable proportions and patterns may be created in these abstract shapes. Whether such work as this is great painting, or even whether it can be called painting at all in the older sense of the word, need not be answered here and is not important. These patterns have been adopted in the applied arts, for example in linoleum and textiles, while their influence on commercial design and advertising has been eminently beneficial. Their abstraction and particularly their two-dimensional char-acter make them well suited to such uses. Indeed, the higher standards of design in the applied arts today, as compared to those of a generation ago, are traceable to the experiments in abstraction painters have been conducting these many years. The flat surface of a floor or textile de-mands such two-dimensional designs rather than those that compel us to crush printed flowers or trip over apparent projections and recessions in rugs and carpets. The close resemblance of these compositions to the International style in architecture fits them well to collaborate with that style. This similarity partly derives from the intimate association of crea-tive designers in the Bauhaus group, composed of painters, architects, and craftsmen working in close collaboration.

The charge is often made that anyone can do this sort of thing. Shams have been foisted upon critics and the sympathetic section of the public on occasion, but often prove nothing more than the gullibility of the critics. Though it is true that anyone with a ruler and a sheet of paper can map a Neo-Plasticist composition, not everyone can attain a satisfactory proportion and adjustment of the resulting shapes. In any case, this charge is demonstrably false with respect to the Surrealists. This group paints detail as sharp and naturalistic as any Flemish primitive. Indeed, it is almost microscopic. Far from being avoided, perspective is accented to increase the depth of the scene. Each object is modeled in cold, clear light, which leaves nothing to the imagination. The link with abstraction lies in the forms created and in their relation to one another. Some of these shapes, though definite, are not to be found in our experience. Others are recognizable, but both kinds are so juxtaposed and given such surroundings as to appear irrational. In the Persistence of Memory (fig. 423), by Salvador Dali (b. 1904), a watch lying on a horizontal plane becomes pliable and hangs over the edge of that plane in limp undulations. In his Specter of Sex Appeal, a little boy with a hoop looks up at what we must call a figure, whose left leg ends with a ragged bone at the ankle, whose exaggerated breasts are tied up in sacking like great sausages, and who leans on a crutch. The Surrealists are said to have turned to the subconscious for inspiration under the influence of Freudian and other modern psychological studies; their paintings have both the painful clarity of dreams and their irrationality. If it is true that they exploit the subconscious and that the subconscious bears a ratio to the conscious of 8 or 9 to 1, the Surrealists have found a large field to develop.

Modern sculpture to a large extent has followed the same course of development as painting. A re-examination of the bases of sculpture led to the same rejection of representation as an adequate purpose. The special emphases in sculpture come to be, first, a new and increased feeling for design, not necessarily abstract but often founded on the designs of primitive sculptors, devices which for the modern sculptor form a shorthand to expression. Secondly, and just as important, the sculptors tend to reject the modeler's technique and conceptions of the nineteenth century, and to think and work more directly in the final material of the statue. It does not follow that all even of the progressive sculptors invariably follow the *taille directe*, that is, each sculptor cutting his block of stone in person; but when he does not, he tries to think in terms of the problems and qualities of his material.

The Seated Woman (fig. 424) by Aristide Maillol (1861–1944) rejects the Rodinesque pictorial style. Nothing remains of Rodin's undulating surface with its liveliness of light and shade. No involved movement or sensual textured flesh detract from Maillol's preoccupation with mass. It looks as though his first and last thought was that stone is a hard heavy substance, and therefore that the forms must develop to the full their possibilities of weight and mass. Each shape approximates a geometric solid; the breasts are generally spherical, the thighs cylindrical or conical, and so on. Minor divisions of anatomy vanish to preserve the sculpturesque relations and design. Or in Emile Antoine Bourdelle's (1861–1929) relief, The Dance (fig. 425), these same simplified forms are arranged to produce a design as sculptural as a Greek metope, and like it with no distracting pictorial elements. Such work, though it has no obviously Greek motive, comes close to the classic in style.

Somewhat later the Jugoslav sculptor, Ivan Meštrović (b. 1883), retains and reflects the half-barbaric vigor of his people, in types and in subjects drawn from their historic past. The Maiden of Kossovo (fig. 426) was the Molly Pitcher of Jugoslav history, who, when her man was wounded, took his place at the gun. This work, directly carved by the artist, turns to the primitive not as a revival but for the qualities of design and expression inherent in primitive art, for example, in the repetitive pattern-like treatment of the hair. Meštrović does this without denial of the accumulated knowledge of his day. The anatomy of the figure is accented; each muscular mass intersects its neighbors in sharp lines and is not modulated into the surrounding surfaces. Even such details as the veins of the arms play their part in the pattern. The chiseled features, high cheek bones, heavy nose, and coarse protruding lips add to the vigor of the whole. The woman's hair is described by a linear pattern of wavy lines terminated in a roll of similar treatment over the forehead. Nothing of pictorial detail mars the concentration on the sculpturesque preoccupation with the figures as elements of design.

These older sculptors, while they depart from the realistic styles of the nineteenth century, do not closely approach abstraction. With Alexander Archipenko, the Russian sculptor now active in America, the case is different. The Dance reveals the same simplification of the figure in the direction of Cubist forms and planes that one might look for in some of the early work of Picasso or Braque. Each part of the two figures is blocked out in simple rhythmic planes, legs, knees, and torso, while the head has become an unimportant boss of conical form at the top. The same rejection of reality and the same reliance on the visual possibilities of abstract shapes in a co-ordinated design lie behind this work that lie behind Cubism in painting, and with the same degree of justification. The action crosses from figure to figure, and leads the eye through the composition of repeated angular planes.

Analogous to collage in painting is the use of materials hitherto strange to sculpture, but with this difference. The new materials selected by many sculptors, Archipenko among them, give promise of longer durability than newsprint and cigarettes. Where historic sculptors were confined to a few materials, chiefly stone, bronze, and wood, and occasionally terra cotta for less monumental work, modern sculptors have turned to the vast array of both fabricated and natural materials provided by modern science and industry. The machine-smooth surfaces of many metals, such as tin, aluminum, and chromium steel, offer new possibilities for exploitation. Glass, either molded or in planes, and fabricated materials can be and have been utilized as media in whole or in part. Archipenko's Medrano (fig. 427), a figure inspired by the Medrano circus in Paris, has the knees formed by red balls of manufactured material, while other parts are in tin or wood, thereby introducing polychromy into sculpture. Certainly there is no good reason why sculptors, like architects, should not avail themselves today of these new substances, and thus reach new and appropriate expressions sympathetic to the spirit of our times.

Finally some sculptors, like some painters, have verged on complete abstraction. Leda (fig. 428) by the Rumanian sculptor, Constantin Brancusi, carries abstraction to that point where nothing remains but an ovoid form resting on a cylindrical base. The smooth surfaces of the form may be subtle, so subtle they can best be appreciated through the sense of touch as one's fingers wander over the surface, but it is difficult for most people to concentrate attention upon them for long with profit or enjoyment. The patterns they cast in light and shade may have some transient interest, even some emotional significance to sensitive individuals, but will probably never arouse much response from the many, save perhaps idle and unsympathetic curiosity. Or in the Human Concretion (fig. 429) by Hans Arp, the curvilinear shapes are vaguely organic, like protoplasm. These abstract protrusions find a balance and adjustment without symmetry, a harmony through the consistent use of similar shapes.

The new materials of modern times offer wide possibilities in furniture. In this field in particular, the functional philosophy of the Bauhaus group and its emphasis on the influence of materials on design have proved beneficial. Tubular metal furniture, at best, is as structural as the finest traditional designs in wood, with the additional value of sympathy with its own age. The spring of metal adds to the comfort of chairs, and its strength enables the occupant, if he so desires, to tilt backward in a manner hazardous in wood chairs of older types. But wood has not been neglected; among others, the Finnish architect, Alvar Aalto, has produced chairs in plywood (fig. 430) bent to almost any desired shape. For those who feel that metal furniture in a home is cold and hard, Aalto's designs have a warmth and even luxury, which adapts itself to modern interiors. Such furniture is eminently practical, its smooth surfaces offer no shelter to dust, and it promises to be as durable as can be desired.

The rejection of eclecticism in architecture corresponds to the rejection of realism in painting and sculpture. Though this prepared the way for something new, it alone would not have been enough. No great style in architecture has ever been born of a deliberate search for novelty. Architectural styles result from one or more of three factors: first, the emergence of new problems, which include not only new building types, such as railway stations, airports, power plants, and so on, different from any problems hitherto faced by architecture, but also an altered spirit imperiously demanding a fresh form of expression. Second, new materials, if basic and widely enough used in architecture, can create a new style by themselves as appropriate solutions are discovered for them. Today steel and reinforced concrete as well as a host of manufactured substances, not to mention glass in large sheets or in the form of translucent bricks, offer countless opportunities for new effects. Finally, new methods of construction play their part. The cantilever principle has been known and used for centuries, but its application in the traditional materials of stone and wood is limited. On the other hand, its results in steel or reinforced concrete can be astonishing. Moreover, the substitution of machinery for handwork in the production of building materials and, to a lesser extent as yet, in the prefabrication of the building as a whole or in parts has led to the adoption of repetitive designs of clean-cut units, dependent for their effect upon precision instead of upon the subtleties of craftsmanship. Therefore, the proportion of manual labor in building has declined, a change accelerated by the constantly rising cost of skilled labor. The prominence of all three of these conditions since the late nineteenth century was bound to give birth to a new style.

A gradual elimination of eclecticism by progressive architects of all countries opened the way. The steps taken in that direction by Richardson, Sullivan, and Wright in America are the same as those made by their leading contemporaries in Europe. Some of the houses by Sir Edwin Lutyens in England show the same frank acceptance of materials, the same informality, and the same direct solution, for example in the size and location of windows, that characterized late Gothic architecture such as Compton Wynyates, and yet without the architectural vocabulary of that style. In such a house as Deanery Gardens at Sonning, at the very start of the century, Lutyens thinks first and last about the needs of the house, practically and as they pertain to expression, but not at all in terms of historic style. If the small building has elements of tradition about it, they come more from the use of traditional materials than from subservience to the past. The northern European countries in particular were active in stripping away eclecticism. The City Hall in Stockholm, begun in 1912 by Ragnar Ostberg, and the Gruntvig Church of 1927, in Copenhagen, by Jensen-Klint, borrow somewhat from the architecture of the Baltic region but with a freshness of interpretation. The widespread ignorance in America of Scandinavian architectural history makes these and other similar buildings seem to many Americans less eclectic than they really are.

More advanced in style is the Postal Savings Bank in Vienna by Otto Wagner, built in 1905. Not only has it discarded eclecticism but, equally significant, the façade no longer looks like a heavy wall. Its decorative diaper patterns bespeak some light substance enclosing space, as the silk of a balloon confines its gas. Moreover, the window glass is almost flush with the wall surface. Therefore, the band of shadow at the top and side of the window, which in a masonry aesthetic expressed the thickness and therefore the firmness of the wall, no longer exists, and by its absence furthers the impression of light construction. On the other hand, these windows are still vertical rectangles, taller than they are wide, a shape inherent in stone architecture. Thus the full implications of the new conditions are not yet apparent.

None of these buildings, most of which were designed before the emergence of Cubism in 1909, can be described as more than transitional. Just as pure abstraction was reached slowly in sculpture and painting, the full change to the modern point of view gradually became apparent in architecture. The Bauhaus at Dessau (fig. 431), designed by Walter Gropius in 1925, demonstrates the new style in all its scientific rationalism. Glass encases the workshop above the ground floor, and the whole exterior surface of the building on this side is cantilevered, overhanging the ground story by several feet. We can see some of the concrete columns and floors through this screen of glass. The maximum of light thereby admitted is less important than the demonstration of the new principles of structure and the dramatization of lightness in construction. The plane of the wall, if one must still use that term, looks like a skin drawn over a frame, as thin both in actuality and in appearance as possible. The fundamental concept of the building has changed from that of a mass to that of an enclosed volume. The elimination of the wall as a weight-bearing member in itself has lightened the building and permitted an additional lightening of its component parts. Moreover, the essential rectangles, the units of this design, are horizontal in such steel or concrete construction. Finally, the severe cubical shape parallels the Neo-Plasticist compositions of Mondrian (fig. 422), which are allied to it.

The charge is often made that the International style, so-called because of its emergence all over the world during the 1920's, is too scientific and exact to be capable of charm. The Tugendhat House at Brno in Czechoslovakia, designed in 1930 by Mies van der Rohe, disproves this. The plan (fig. 432) first of all betrays the light construction. Compared with buildings designed on a masonry aesthetic, this plan seems to have no supports at all. A very slender metal column or two, and strips of thin wall here and there are sufficient to carry the light flat roof. No partitions divide the living quarters into rooms; screens, some of them movable, indicate that a given area is intended primarily for one purpose but is not restricted to that purpose. The volume enclosed within the house flows from one part to another with a minimum of interruption. This sense of openness and of flowing volumes stems ultimately from the work of Frank Lloyd Wright, which exerts profound influence on European architecture.

Then too the house turns its back on the street. An overhanging slab shelters the entrance, with broad sheets of translucent but not transparent glass to admit light but to preserve privacy. On that side of the house are the necessary services. The owner may drive his car into the garage without that tedious process of backing and starting so often necessary in suburban homes in America where the garage is placed at the back, a process, be it said, hazardous both to the car and to any neighboring shrubbery. Here, these occupants are less attracted to the street, with its noise and public character, than to the magnificent view behind, where the land falls away and where is located most of the property belonging to the house. If all is utility on the street front, the back (fig. 433) is a delight. The whole wall plane is converted into a sheet of glass, which hardly separates the interior from the exterior and which allows the maximum advantage to be taken of the view. This window, if one may call it that, extends around the corner, and a porch and steps lead down to the lawn. The flat roof involves the application of the cantilever principle. Thus the house seems composed of block-like formations in horizontal rectangles, easier to see than in the Bauhaus. These are asymmetrically disposed from the standpoint of utility and interior convenience.

This arrangement is dictated by a careful, almost scientific examination of the needs and purposes of the house and of its several parts. In designing a modern house, the architect should consider the probable routes of prospective occupants pursuing their daily occupations, and so arrange the house that these paths shall intersect as little as possible. In fact, the idea applies on a small scale some of the principles that govern modern highway design to minimize friction and interference. To this end, the open interior (fig. 434) greatly assists. It also offers communion with nature in perfect comfort. The owner or his guests may either be in the open air under partial shelter in the porch, or on cooler days enjoy the beauty of the outdoors from within. Under some circumstances, so large a glass area might admit more light than would be desirable, but this condition can be controlled by draperies, whereas the maximum natural light is left for overcast weather. Comfortable furniture, based on modern materials and also designed first from the point of view of its primary purpose, fits such an interior as this.

Of course, the candid observer will admit that not all of the advantages lie on one side. This open interior offers a world of adaptability, of light, freedom, and spaciousness. But at certain times, such complete openness may not be desirable. If one member of the family chooses to listen to the radio, another to play the piano, and a third to read at the same time, arguments may ensue. We can visualize many occasions when the traditional division into rooms, several of which are available for general living purposes, may be preferable to such large unbroken areas. Screens may not always provide sufficient privacy. Like all complex problems, ideally each house demands a solution adapted to the needs of the prospective occupants and designed to serve and express those needs. Where such variety exists, dogmatic statements can seldom be made that this solution is right and that wrong. But of one thing we can be sure, that the use of modern materials, modern methods of construction, and a rational determination of as many factors in the problem as possible need not result in a cold scientific product devoid of warmth and individuality.

The arts from the days of Egypt on down have always written a faithful and tangible record of their civilizations. No less true is that of the arts of the twentieth century. The adoption of modern materials in sculpture and architecture in itself has created forms of expression open to no previous generation. The constant searching and turmoil of modern life, the impact of the machine and of modern science, and the willingness to experiment in any and every direction have all left their imprint on the arts of our own times, as these same forces have been modifying our lives. What the future may bring forth no one can predict in the arts any more than in other fields. Indeed, dependent as the arts are upon civilization, we would have to know what the future will demand from life in order to imagine what its manifestations may be in the world of art. We can be sure in this matter of only one thing: since humanity demands them for enjoyment and expression, if not for existence, the arts will continue to live and to change as long as man continues to exist and to change. As the future alters man's needs, real or imagined, so too will the arts develop, and continue to reflect in the future as in the past whatever manner of culture man may shape for himself.

XXV

Persia

In the land lying between the Tigris and Euphrates rivers, and to the east of it, in the plateaus and sandy valleys of Iran, or Persia, archaeologists

THE ANCIENT NEAR EAST have unearthed pottery that dates back into the prehistoric period, about 4000 to 3000 B.C. From Samarra, Susa, Tell Halaf, Mussian, and Reshahr they have taken vessels fashioned by the hands of early inhabitants which are so homogeneous that they indicate a civilization opposed to that of near-by Babylonia. The ancient swastika pattern, Maltese crosses, lozenge designs, the ibex (fig. 435), and the serpent are popular, as are life-giving water (indicated by waving lines) and hills of patterned triangles. Trees in that arid land are already an important motif, as are birds, bulls, and sheep. Man plays a somewhat minor role, often reduced to geometric form portrayed by simple angular or curving lines. Cult figures of gods and goddesses, especially those latter who might grant children, were modeled in the round, and were found with the usual weapons and instruments of flint, stone, and clay. In these early objects, as in their later art, we are impressed by the skill in design demonstrated by these people, a wonderful sensitiveness in stylizing forms derived from the world around them, making unforgettable patterns of animals, birds, trees, mountains, and sky.

Bronze-age craftsmen, who began casting metal objects as early as 2700 B.C., used many of the same motifs in the cheek plaques, bridle ornaments, weapons, and jewelry made in Luristan. These metalworkers, using a technique that may have had its origin in Armenia as early as 3000 B.C., fashioned all kinds of trappings and gear for the Lur horsebreeders who lived east of Samarra and Susa, showing a technical skill and artistic talent unsurpassed in the ancient Near East.

Gilgamesh, hero of the epic poem, or his counterpart, grasps lions in a strangle hold, symbol of man the powerful hunter, who was the ideal of these and later generations; composite animals, winged or horned, confront each other in perfect balance (fig. 436), or pursue each other in the eternal combat that seemed as inevitable as day following night, and, indeed, became the symbol of daylight devouring darkness. Lithe, elegant, and spirited, filled with life though simplified to pattern, they gave a hint of the particular genius that will always illumine Persian art. Even their weapons were ornamented with these vigorous and expressive animals, and their bowls and cups, dating as late as the ninth century, have similar designs in repoussé.

THIS metalwork of Iran, in its emphasis on balance and stylization, differs from the art of the migratory people who ranged from the eastern part of
THE ART OF THE MIGRATORY PEOPLES: STEPPE ART Siberia to the steppes of the Black Sea area in Russia. Nomads and hunters, shifting from place to place with their tents, carts, and possessions, seeking respite from the bitter winds of winter and the blazing sun of summer, swooping down on their more settled neighbors, they left no records other than the metal objects placed in their tombs or dropped in combat. Weapons, tools, and bits of ornament must serve instead of books to give us some idea of their culture. In the proto-historic period, an Indo-European group of Iranian race, called Scyths by Greek historians and Saka by the Indian, occupied the lands north of the Black Sea and eastward to the Altai Mountains and Minussinsk on the Ienissei River. Some other Indo-Europeans settled in the oases of the Tarim River basin, from Kashgar to Kutcha and Karashar. From the beginning of the Christian era the movement was reversed; the pressure was from East to West, as the Hsiung-nu (Huns) pushed from the borders of China into South Russia and Hungary, followed in the sixth century A.D. by the Avars, a Mongol people, and successive waves of Turks and Mongols through the thirteenth century.

Between 750–700 B.C. the Scyths had dispossessed the Cimmerians north of the Black Sea, retaining mastery until the fourth century B.C. when the Sarmatians in turn conquered them. Though classed as Indo-Europeans in race, their customs resembled those of other nomadic people, the Tungus, Turks, and Mongols, in their predatory existence, their killing of sacrificial victims, the burial alive of serving people and horses around the body of the chieftain. According to Herodotus, who wrote in the fifth century B.C., to express grief they slashed their arms, foreheads, and noses, and they drank the blood of their victims; they were understandably classed by the Greeks as complete barbarians. Near Maikop on the southeast steppe in the Kuban area, and in the Ukraine, they lived and left the graves of their leaders, placing in them magnificent ornaments in gold and bronze — such as necklaces, bracelets, gold plaques made to be sewn on their leather garments, masks, beaten gold sheaths for arrow quivers, ceremonial axes, shield ornaments, belt buckles, shallow ceremonial cups, and other gear and insignia. Their favorite designs were of animals common to that part of the world — bears, boar, deer, and moose, panthers, birds of prey, and other creatures they knew very well in the hunt. They showed them in combat or in pursuit of each other, or glancing backward toward some possible danger as they were awakened, their feet still drawn up under them (fig. 437). They are modeled with skill, vigor, and simplicity by the artists who worked for the huntsmen and who infused the forms with so much life that this is often referred to as the 'Animal Art,' very different from the contemporary Greek art, which was also found in the tombs.

The hunt, pursuit, and combat were so much a part of their lives that even in their belt buckles we find animals attacking and devouring one another, designs so compelling that they were copied in bronze by less skilled workmen far to the east, in the Ordos on the borders of China, and far to the west in Europe — in Hungary, Bulgaria, Germany and the Scandinavian countries — as the migrations moved in that direction. They were copied, too, in embroideries and in woven textiles by other nomads of Central Asia, especially the Hsiung-nu (Huns), who occupied the Altai region about 200 B.C. Twisting, interlacing forms, sometimes of the whole animal, sometimes of a part of an animal, detached and woven into a pattern, drawn directly from nature, or exaggerated into a grotesque, are to be found alike in the jades and bronzes of the Far East and on the manuscript pages and church façades of medieval Europe.

We know what some of the Scyths looked like, for Greek metalworkers made portraits of them on vases found in the Crimea and Ukraine. They wore peaked caps with ear flaps, leather tunics and trousers, the appropriate clothing for a horse-riding people who lived in a cold, windy country. We see them, too, in the processions of Persepolis among the Immortals who brought gifts to the Achaemenid kings at the New Year festival in the fifth century B.C. (fig. 440).

By 900 B.C., an invasion had taken place on the Iranian Plateau by Aryan people, a people who came from the vast plains of the Oxus and Iaxartes westward to the area south of the Caspian Sea. Their language was one branch of the Indo-European family, akin to the Germanic, Slavic, Greek,

and Celto-Italic tongues, and developed into Old Iranian, Sanskrit, Śaka,
Sogdian, and Ossetic. They came with new gods and new ideas of a
society divided into caste groups, which left
THE ARYAN INVASION their mark on Persian culture as on that of
AND HISTORIC PERSIA north India, where some of them settled. The
first Iranians to be of importance historically were the Medes; in 612, their
king Cyaxares took Nineveh and destroyed the Assyrian Empire, as his
in turn was conquered in 550 by Cyrus, the Achaemenid. From that time
until the conquest of Alexander the Great (334–327 B.C.), the Achaemenids
ruled over an empire unrivaled in size and importance in the ancient
world, from Lydia south of the Black Sea to the Oxus on the east, the Indus
bordering India, and the Nile of Egypt, including the Chaldean or Baby-
lonian Empire with its Syrian dependencies on the Mediterranean. They
organized and welded together peoples of divergent tongues and religious
practices, holding them by a despotism more humane than any known
before their time.

Cyrus, Cambyses, Darius, and Xerxes were the conquerors and builders
of that empire, failing only in the conquest of Greece in the fifth century.
Their tombs, palaces, rich robes, and jewels were the wonders of their time
and set a standard of splendor that still colors our imagination when we
think of the Oriental potentate. Out of the cliffs rising above the sandy
Iranian plains they had tomb chambers cut, as the Egyptians had, so that
the body of the emperor would lie inviolate. The tomb of Xerxes at Naqsh-
i-Rustam near Persepolis is of this type (fig. 438), consisting of a façade
ornamented with relief sculpture of the ruler standing before a fire altar,
supported by men representing thirty nations of the empire, representing
but not portraying their real appearance, for they look like a string of identical paper dolls pasted upon the face of the rock, symbols of majesty
and power, timeless and durable as the rock itself. Inside the rectangular
chamber the body of the king was laid in state, clad in magnificent garments, protected by his weapons, but without all the food, utensils, and
favorite furniture that would have been buried with an Egyptian king,
for, unlike the Egyptian rulers, he did not expect to return to the tomb;
he was a monotheist, a follower of the god Ahura-Mazda. Of the many
Deva and Ahura (or Aśura) in which the early Iranians believed, one,
Ahura-Mazda, the 'wise lord' was recognized by the ruling house as the
greatest of the gods, and was worshiped to the exclusion of all others. He
is shown, in sculpture, as a human figure emerging from a disk that forms
the center of a bird's body, similar to the winged sun-disk of Egypt, and
he holds a circlet, symbol of power, in his hand. As the principle of Light,

or Goodness, he was also represented by fire, so the fire altar is another important element of Achaemenid culture in architecture and sculpture. It takes the place of spacious temples necessary in the more elaborate rituals of their contemporaries, the Egyptians; for these makers of the Persian empire, their altars, palaces, and tombs sufficed.

Differing from the rock-cut tomb, the free-standing sarcophagus of Cyrus (fig. 439), ancestor of Darius, is built of stone blocks. It had been placed near a great palace at Pasargadae, consisting of wide courtyards and colonnades; but it is, in contrast, like a small, compact gabled house set upon a platform of six steps; the rectangular chamber is, therefore, at the seventh level, an auspicious number. It was a treasure house as well as a mausoleum, for Cyrus had been buried with pomp and magnificence.

More sumptuous than the tombs were the palaces, especially those of Persepolis and Susa, built by the hands of the conquered people, using materials brought from all corners of the empire. Until they were burned at the time of the conquest of Alexander the Great, the palaces of Persepolis were among the most stately ever erected by man, and the tall, slim columns (fig. 440) still rising above the sands are monuments, even today, to the 'king of kings,' who ordered them built. Darius left his inscription:

This country of Persia which Ahura-Mazda gave to my safekeeping, this country which is beautiful, rich in men and horses, according to the will of Ahura-Mazda and mine, King Darius, will not tremble before any enemy. I, Darius, the Great King, King of Kings, King of Countries, King of this great land, by the grace of Ahura-Mazda I have built this citadel, and I have built it complete and beautiful and perfect, as I have wished. May Ahura-Mazda and all the Gods keep me with it.

Actually it was not complete in his time. He started it about 520 B.C., and work was still being done in the reign of Artaxerxes I in 460, but judging from the elaborate system of conduits and drains hewn in the rock platform, the plan of halls and dwelling quarters must have been made by his architects.

A stairway of 106 steps, low enough for horses to walk up, led to a great gateway, the 'Gateway of the World' (fig. 441) of Xerxes, through which passed the bearers of gifts at the New Year festival. At that time, tribute was brought by men speaking many languages, clad in the costumes of the far provinces. On the gate were outer and inner doors, faced with bronze, about 30 feet high. These were flanked by winged guardians, bulls with human faces like the Assyrian monsters of the Sargonid palaces, but the Achaemenid sculptors carved them with a grace and purity missing in the Assyrian prototypes, and eliminated the fifth leg favored by the older artists. Within the building were benches for the guard and space for archives; outside, to the north, were small fire altars.

Beyond were the royal buildings, all of the same type, based on the old Iranian hypostyle house. The façade consisted of an open portico, the side walls were of brick, and the interior supports were limestone or wooden columns. These halls follow the same orientation, with spacious courtyards between them, which must have been filled with trees and shrubs. The effect of space, freedom, and height was increased by the clever use of open stairways outside of most of the halls, which added to the impressiveness of processions at audience time. The Apadana (audience hall) of Xerxes (fig. 440) must have been the scene of many such pageants; it was a square hall, with walls of sun-dried brick, 15 feet thick, a ceiling 60 feet high supported by slim columns, a great throne room which could hold 10,000 people. There were flights of steps on the north and east sides, and both stairs were adorned with sculpture of tribute bearers, the figures done in three registers, each measuring about 270 feet in length. The Medes in conical caps and the Persians wearing crowns brought lotus blossoms, while the Syrians brought gold vessels, ornaments, and a chariot drawn by Arabian horses. The Lydians, too, brought gold vessels and garments; the Scythians, those horse-riding barbarians from north of the Black Sea, bore gifts of gold and a stallion; the Sattagydians from the hot Punjab of India led a humped bull; the Bactrians (fig. 442), coming in from the deserts to the east, brought a two-humped camel; Ethiopians from Africa offered a giraffe and tribute ivory; Elamites led in a lioness snarling in anger; Cilicians brought more placid rams, and garments. These and the others of the twenty-five nations are shown facing the stair, each group separated from the next by a cedar tree, the ancient Tree of Life, here shown as though split through the middle, with trunk and branches visible from the top to the bottom and as symmetrical and elegant as an ancient bronze. All faces, hands, and feet are directed toward the focal doorway, suggesting the procession, but the figures are as rigid as those of Egypt, without any indication of bodily motion. Unlike Egyptian sculpture, though, the arms and torsos are seen from the side, so that there is an increasing realism; the sculptors were careful, too, in observing each racial type and costume of the gift bearers, but they are types, not individuals. The details of head-dresses, hair, weapons, and garments are done as meticulously as in Assyrian art, and they are as patterned, but there is no emphasis here on brutality, on bulging muscles, or on constant combat; the sculptors achieved an ordered purity and clarity, a stability that may reflect the stability of the Empire. The figures project at the same level from a background that is kept bare. There is no attempt to indicate locale or to suggest space; the carvers respected the wall as a limiting member, primarily architectural. In the brilliant sunlight of Persepolis, every clearly cut line and every shadow are effective parts of the dignified, majestic pattern.

In contrast to the men, who stand expressionless in their frozen world, the animals are endowed with emotion and personality. The lioness, camel, horses, and rams react to their captivity with varying degrees of anger or exasperation. In the angle of the stairs, flanking the spear holders, are two scenes of a lion attacking a bull (fig. 443). Though the effect from a distance is one of heraldic grandeur, on close inspection one sees the fury in the lion's face and claws, made more dramatic by linear patterns cut sharply in the stone, which, by contrast, bring out the subtle and simple planes in the head of the bull. Though the same theme of attack was used so often by the creators of the Animal Art of the steppe country, the stylization of hair and muscle as seen here at Persepolis marks a difference in concept. The various registers are separated by bands of rosettes repeated horizontally, each one a perfect copy of the other, clear and pure in contour, and interesting because of repetition rather than because of variety, such as one would find in the medieval carving of Europe. Another decorative motif is the ziggurat, the stepped pyramid, here used as a crowning member on stairs and platforms.

Within the halls, columns of wood or stone broke the space into small units. Some of the capitals and imposts, consisting of young bulls placed back to back, carried the beams that upheld the flat ceilings. These bicephalic impost blocks (fig. 444) are carved with the same precision, love of pattern, and symmetry that marked the relief sculpture. The shafts of the stone columns are relatively taller than those of the Greeks, some 60 feet high, and are cut by more flutes; the shaft is separated from the capital by an intervening member ornamented with volutes and rosettes. These elements, combined with a high base (fig. 445), are so characteristic that they are referred to as the Persepolitan Column, showing a unique development in Achaemenid art, which borrowed frequently from other countries, as we have noted, but produced a result unlike anything assembled in Egypt, Assyria, or Greece.

The living quarters, like the audience halls, emphasized spaciousness and beauty of detail. The Tachara (winter house) of Darius (fig. 446), which was also raised on a platform, had doors, windows, and niches of stone, which survived the burning by Alexander, though the walls of brick have disappeared. The Egyptian influence is so strong here as to suggest that the architects were Egyptian. The Hadish (men's quarters) of Xerxes was placed on the highest level of the terrace, from which stairs led down into the near-by dark rooms of the Harem (women's quarters). In all of the buildings the dark limestone was polished with great care, giving it a uniform smoothness, clarity, and grace. This is noteworthy because it is the work of many hands of the men of various nations.

Within the walls of brilliantly colored brick there must have been splendid feasts and gatherings. The metal bowls, pitchers, drinking horns, and cups give evidence of the same love of beauty that marked the arts of building and stone carving. A winged ibex handle (fig. 447), typical of the gold and silver work done for these monarchs, still charms us with its look of swift alertness and by the exquisite modeling of its body from the tips of its graceful horns to the hoof of each delicate foot. This was a consistent part of a world destroyed by Alexander the Great, in the fourth century B.C., as he swept through on his conquest to India and reduced the Achaemenids and their monuments to ruins.

That conquest left an impression of Hellenism on Iran through the succeeding period, the Seleucid, 323–250 B.C., but it did not smother the flame of creative Iranian spirit. After the intervening rule by the Parthians, 250 B.C.–A.D. 226, who were the 'middlemen' in the profitable silk trade between the Romans and the Chinese, a new Persian dynasty came to power, the Sassanian, which lasted from A.D. 226 to 642. Ardashīr, Shāpūr, Bahrām, and Chosroes are among the illustrious names of the Sassanian rulers who sought to encourage a flowering-again of the arts practiced by the Achaemenids. Like their forebears, they became world famous for their sculpture, metalwork, textile weaving, and architecture.

Unlike the palaces at Persepolis and Susa, which had flat roofs upheld by columns, the Sassanian peoples used arcuated forms — domes, vaults, and arches — which made for a great uncluttered interior space in contrast to the Achaemenid, which had been broken into small units by the many supports. A typical palace built for the Sassanian kings is the one called Tāq-i-Kisrā (Arch of Khusrau or Chosroes) at Ctesiphon (fig. 448). In the mild climate of Mesopotamia, on a site chosen by the first of the line, Ardashīr, the winter residence was erected by Shāpūr (A.D. 242–72) after his defeat of the Roman emperor Valerian. A big barrel vault with a span of 84 feet runs through the center of the building; smaller rooms and chambers are placed on either side, with thick outer walls in which arcades are the ornamental feature, as they are on the façade. We have to imagine the brick and rubble walls as they once looked, covered with smooth stucco and relief sculpture painted in gay colors. Since the native mortar contained a large quantity of gypsum, which sets quickly, the huge central vault was made without centering; it was classed as one of the wonders of the world. Beneath its majestic curve the kings held audience with a splendor rivaling that of Darius and Xerxes; even the carpet on the floor, called the Springtime of Chosroes, was famous.

Another of the palaces, at Fīrūzābād, demonstrates the ingenious use of squinches, which were built out in radiating arches from the angles of the square central chamber to meet the circle of the dome that topped it. They were used here for the first time and were to become an integral part of Moslem architecture later on, as well as an important contribution to the art of building in Europe. In the same audience hall the traditional Egyptian cornice was placed over the doorways, showing the Sassanian love of the old and the new, pride in their inheritance from the past and skill in working out new solutions.

In their sculpture they show the same respect for the past and eagerness for the novel. Like the Achaemenids, the Sassanian rulers had huge images carved in the cliffs near Persepolis, Naqsh-i-Rustam, Naqsh-i-Rajab, and Bishapur (Shāpūr), as well as farther north at Tāq-i-Bustan. These, too, serve as monuments to the glory of the kings, but not as a part of tomb ornament, rather as independent works of art commemorating investiture, victory, or the king supreme in combat and the hunt. The investiture of Ardashīr I (fig. 449) emphasizes the relation between god and emperor as Ardashīr receives the diadem from Hormuzd (Ahura-Mazda). They face each other on horseback, each trampling upon his enemy; Ardawān's head is under the hoof of Ardashīr's horse, and Ahriman's under that of Hormuzd. Thus the founder of the dynasty overcomes the last of the Arsacids, as light and goodness overcome darkness and evil — the king rules by divine right. The two face each other in a composition as symmetrical in plan as that of an ancient bronze from Luristan. The heads, shoulders, waists, knees, and feet of the men are at the same level, as are the heads, bodies, and feet of the horses. That love of symmetry inherited from the past and the profile head and full-front torso technique are in contrast to the new elements — a soft modeling in surface modulation in which there is great variety in projection from the background, the flying ribbons, the hanging foot, and the awareness each of the other combining to give an impression of monumental grandeur.

Near by is carved the triumph of Shāpūr I over the Roman emperor Valerian, one of four such scenes made after his capture in A.D. 260. The Roman, wearing a short skirt and billowing cape, kneels before the majestic conqueror, who sits astride his horse as his ancestor did, ribbons flying behind him, his hand grasping the broad sword hanging at his waist, his foot hanging almost to the ground. He, like other monarchs of his dynasty, wears a crown so individual that it helps to identify him in the rock-cut sculpture and on his coins. Even more vigorous is the carving of Bahrām II, A.D. 276–93, in combat. Riding full tilt at his opponent, in the flying gallop, he unseats the adversary as easily as a great monarch should, showing a third-century version of a technique that will sweep over Europe a thousand years later in the Age of Chivalry.

Antedating the use of chain mail in Europe, flexible, protective armor made of rings of metal joined together was worn by the kings of the Sassanian period. It is to be seen in the large portrait of Chosroes II at Tāq-i-Bustan. There, deep in the Garden Arch carved in a cliff that rises above an artificial lake on the royal hunting preserve, he is shown in high relief in full armor, with helmet, lance, and shield, seated upon his richly caparisoned horse. On either side of this equestrian, on the inner surface of the arch, some hunting scenes were carved, showing him in action and giving us a good idea of the royal sport as practiced in the seventh century. In one he pursues deer, and in the other, wild boar; he is accompanied by ladies playing on musical instruments, by elephant riders, and camels, but his is the largest figure in the compositions, as befits a king. The game, driven out of enclosures and swamps by the beaters, is picked up, limp and lifeless, after the ruler has proved himself a mighty hunter. These scenes, smaller in scale than the Persepolis carvings, are considerably broader in scope. Men, women, animals, and vegetation are suggested in an atmospheric setting, in which light and shade play an important part though perspective and focus in the Western sense are lacking. They are charged with emotion, full of tumult and excitement. The animal forms, especially, are done with sensitiveness and understanding: the heavy elephants moving through the underbrush, which they trample with their big feet; wild boar racing across the compound; deer in the flying gallop, heads held high, or crumpling as the arrows of the king find their mark; all are remarkable studies of individual animal forms and all are a part, too, of dramatic narrative.

Roman influence had made itself felt in the other sculpture on the same site. The large arch of the Grotto is not unlike a triumphal arch in size, though it is carved in living rock, not free-standing. Angels of victory, the winged Nikes inherited from Greece, were to fit into the spandrels; one was finished, a western-looking goddess with curly hair and a flowing classical robe, who holds a cup of pearls and a circlet of sovereignty. As in much of the other Sassanian sculpture, the change from

Achaemenid times is evident in the more careful modeling of the body beneath the drapery, a more realistic anatomical study. Below her, leafy ornaments were carved, the leaves resembling prickly acanthus but adapted to a symmetrical tree-of-life pattern, which shows the ancient Iranian love of the motif and the Iranian pleasure in fine surface decoration.

Many of the designs cut into the cliffs in monumental sculpture were used by metalworkers in the gold and silver bowls, cups and pitchers for Sassanian feasts. The figures are raised from the background in various levels of projection, as in the sculpture, and show the same interest in surface modulation. The contrast of human and animal forms, the excitement of the hunt (fig. 450), the calm majesty of the ruler enthroned, looking directly out, 'assailing the onlooker by his glance,' and surrounded by his nobles, moon symbols and sun symbols, natural animals and composite creatures, all were pictured by the craftsmen, often in conjunction with leaf and flower patterns, and pearls. One of their favorite motifs was the senmurv, or si-murgh, a fabulous animal who sometimes had the head of a dog, a fox, or even a camel, the claws of a beast of prey, the tail of a peacock or rooster, and the wings of a barnyard fowl, the whole generally framed by a circlet of pearls or leaves.

These designs were used also as architectural ornaments, judging by the stucco reliefs placed over the bricks and rubble of palace walls. The senmurv, the boar's head surrounded by pearls, the king hunting, the tree of life, and other motifs must have adorned the walls of the impressive domed edifices of the kings. They invaded the field of textiles, too. Evidently every symbol of power and sovereignty had to be displayed in every available space, even on clothes, carpets, and wall-hangings. We can imagine how dearly these fabrics were prized when we find that some were preserved in the sands of the desert along the Trade Routes, others served as inspiration for Chinese textiles still to be found in the eighth-century Shōsōin collection of Japan, and still others are now in the museums and churches of Europe, small fragments of tissue, gold and blue, green and red, subtle combinations of design and color — all monuments to the Sassanids as much as were the great domes and arches and rock carvings. The fragments now in European collections are bits from fine silken wrappings for the bodies of early Christian martyrs, which were placed in the church treasuries where, until recent times, they were shown as wonders from the Holy Land. Among the patterns of these ancient textiles are the senmurv and cocks, horses, hunting scenes, the tree of life, the rose, the pearl, all done in heraldic splendor (fig. 451).

Having revived the glory of the Achaemenids in an art that touched all of the civilized world, the Sassanian princes weakened, then crumbled, before the onslaught of Islam, which came in the seventh century.

MOHAMMED was born in Mecca, Arabia, about A.D. 570, and began his teaching in his early manhood, urging his fellow Arabians to follow his leadership toward an inspired monotheism. This **ISLAMIC PERSIA** offended the pagan aristocracy, who sensed a threat in his desire for change, and he was forced to flee to Medīna in 622, which marks the beginning of the Moslem calendar — the year of the Hegira. He built a house that was also used as a mosque in Medīna, and set about the political reform of the rest of Arabia, coupling it with his religious fervor in winning converts to his belief in Allah, the One God; in ten years of struggle and warfare he accomplished his task. Arabia was unified politically, and the majority of the population were followers of the Prophet, fired with enthusiasm to bring the rich neighboring countries under the domination of the Arabs and Islam.

The first caliphs lived simply as Bedouins, but, as the northern countries were brought under their sway, the Byzantine ideas that permeated Syria began to influence the internal organization of the Mohammedans, and there was an increasing splendor surrounding the leader, who was established at Damascus. Finally, in the eighth century, the capital was moved to Baghdad, and a rich material civilization came into being, which became legend throughout the world.

Even when the court was in Damascus the caliphs had wished to rival Byzantium and had instructed the architects, who were brought in to build their mosques, to make them on a scale comparable to Christian churches, in richness if not in size, so there is a marked influence of East Christian form and ornament in early Moslem architecture. The mosque (Masjid or Jami') was their first concern; it consisted of four porticoes (liwan), each covered with a flat roof supported by columns and arches, which enclosed a courtyard in which there was a fountain for purification. On the side toward Mecca the liwan was more impressive than the others, for it contained the Mihrab, the prayer niche marking the direction of Mecca, and the preacher's pulpit. Towers, called minarets, or mināra, were erected beside the large rectangle so that the muezzin could call the faithful to prayer (fig. 462). As in Byzantine and Syrian churches, the ornament usually consisted of intricate surface decoration in mosaic, colored marbles, metalwork, and carved wood (figs. 452, 453).

As Sassanian power was overthrown in the seventh century, Islam spread throughout the land and Iran became a stronghold of Mohammedanism. By 747, a princely Arab family, the 'Abbāsids, revolted against the caliphs of Damascus (the Ommayads or Umayyads) and set up the 'Abbāsid dynasty, which marked a triumph of the Persian element, for they considered themselves 'Moslem Sassanids.' Like the line of kings before them, these caliphs became enthusiastic patrons of the arts, particularly those of building, metalwork, ceramics, carpets, and bookmaking.

Under them and their Turkish sultans, the mosques (figs. 454, 455) developed into splendid monuments, which combined some of the features of old Sassanian architecture adapted to the needs of the Mohammedan congregation, with new motifs. Structurally, the builders used the pointed arch, the dome, and the squinch. Over these they used stucco ornaments, glazed tile, and brick. Honeycomb elements of increasing complexity were developed in the squinches, breaking the surfaces with pockets of light and dark, and the interior space was broken by columns and arches; the effect was one of shadowy coolness kept from seeming overpowering and aloof by ornamental patterns and inscriptions. In both Persia and Turkestan the ceramic artist and the architect worked together to create magnificent structures, arched and domed, gleaming in various shades of blue, yellow, and rose under the clear blue skies. Their palaces, too, kept pace with the mosques in ever-increasing complexity and beauty of detail.

Pottery bowls, pitchers, and vases were made to imitate metalwork in a less costly medium; the ceramic artists discovered how to make lusterware that gave the effect of gold or silver. Other potteries made full use of blue, green, yellow, and other strong colors in their designs. Some in both pottery and metalwork were based on old Sassanian motifs (figs. 456, 457), notably of the king hunting and holding audience, though in later examples he began to have a very Turkish cast of face, with slanting eyes and long black hair. Writing done by master calligraphers was considered a handsome ornament on plates and on the Mihrab of the mosque. Thus old Persian elements were combined with Arabic and Turkish ideas under the influence of Islam to form a rich and decorative art.

Literature, too, flowered under this patronage. In the eleventh century, in Afghanistan, Firdausī wrote the *Shāh-namah*, the Book of Kings, which he dedicated to his patron, the Sultan Mahmud, in A.D. 1010. He had gathered together fragments of truth and legend about the ancient rulers and heroes of Persia, and fused them into one of the world's great epics.

Rustam, the central figure of the poem, extricates the mythical Kaiyānī rulers (Achaemenids) from their difficulties and dangers, such as wars, intrigues, betrayals, and even magic practices. Dārā (Darius) is among them, and Iskandar (Alexander the Great) in their various adventures; other episodes deal with Bīzhan, Rustam's nephew, and with the Sassanian hunter, King Bahrām Gur, and his lady musician, Azada, and with Suhrāb, Rustam's son, who was killed unknowingly by the father. It marks the beginning of a great literature and serves as a favorite text for calligraphers and painters in succeeding centuries.

The practice of making fine books went well back into the past. One of the most renowned artists of the book was Mani, leader of the religious sect of the Manichaeans, who had lived in the third century A.D. in Persia. Influenced by both Christianity and Mazdaism, filled with religious fervor, and inspired by a vision of a heavenly messenger who bade him to go out and proclaim his teaching, he tried to win converts at Ctesiphon but met with little success. He was regarded by orthodox Zoroastrians as a heretic, just as he was so regarded by Christians, and he was forced to go east into the desert and oasis settlements to spread his gospel. There he met with great success, and founded communities of lay followers and clergy, who were willing to adhere to his very strict rules of conduct and obligation. Being a gifted painter, he wrote out his scriptures and illuminated the pages with brilliantly colored figures of the men and women of the congregations, of the heaven they would reach by right living, of the demons of the world of darkness, and of flowers, fruits, and other lovely things on this earth. This attractive way of recording and spreading his teaching seemed to infuriate his opponents as much as did his doctrine, so Manichaean books were burned whenever they were found by his enemies. Modern scholarship knew of them only by reputation and hearsay until the German expedition of Grünwedel and Von Le Coq to Chinese Turkestan in the early twentieth century. There, in the dry sands of the desert, they found a number of fragments of the precious texts, written in beautiful script and still glowing with color. They had been made probably for the Uighur Turks, who were ardent followers of Mani and who had established houses of worship for themselves not only in the oasis cities but also in China, when they were staunch allies of the Chinese in the eighth and ninth centuries. These texts date from before the tenth century, and bespeak the long tradition of miniature illumination encouraged by the followers of the first teacher.

The figures in the Manichaean texts are quite Turkish in type, with slanting eyes and straight black hair, very much like those painted on pottery in the twelfth and thirteenth centuries in Persia, especially at Raiy (Rhages) (fig. 457). The heads are big, and the hands very expressive; costumes are painted in great detail, but the setting is often ignored. These two creative streams — of painting on pottery and of illustrating religious texts — seem to have nourished the ground from which grew the superb art of book illumination in Persia.

Under the 'Abbāsids, many treatises were translated on natural history, properties of herbs, mechanical wonders, studies of the stars, et cetera. They were illustrated in a style similar to Syrian work derived from Greek and Byzantine art, as well as to the pottery and manuscript painting of Central Asia and Persia. The Dioscorides manuscript (fig. 458), showing two physicians cutting a plant, gives us a good idea of the figure style and composition used by the early thirteenth-century painters. The men face each other, separated by a large plant which one of them is cutting, a plant as symmetrical in form as the ancient tree of life as portrayed at Persepolis or on a Sassanian textile. In fact, the balanced arrangement of men and plant reminds us, too, of the Luristan bronzes, expressing a feeling for design almost as old as art itself in Persia. The faces, hands, and feet of the men are shown in profile, as they were at Persepolis, and their garments are as rich in pattern as those of Chosroes at Tāq-i-Bustan; they even have floating scarves like the Sassanian kings, and they exist in space untouched by cloud or shadow. Only the eyes and hands give some indication of Near Eastern vivaciousness, and bring life to a composition that might otherwise be too static for illustration, as this was intended to be. Primary opaque colors were favored, as simple as folk embroidery and as direct. Not all of the Dioscorides illuminations are as simple as this, but it is quite typical of the figures scattered through the text; the miniature does not occupy a page by itself, it is incidental to the writing, and fitted into whatever place was left for it by the calligrapher. It differs from Greek manuscript illumination in that much of it seems to have been painted for the sheer pleasure of having it there, since the illustrations are not very explicit as diagrams to be used by doctors.

Another text illustrated several times in the thirteenth century was the *Maqāmāt* written by al-Harīrī, a kind of *Canterbury Tales* of the Arabs, done in rhyming prose. In his illuminations, which are gaily colored and lively, the painter al-Wasiti brings a freshness and boldness to the tale that is quite appropriate to the adventurous hero. Even when he is painting camels, and not some fabulous creature, he lets his imagination play and sets down colors that are delightful and quite unrelated to nature — pink and mauve as well as tan, vibrant tones that give as much life to the camels as the lines of their bodies. He states already one of the purposes of the Persian illustrator: though not bound by the appearance of things as he sees them, to give them such beauty of form and color that they seem more vivid to the beholder than do the natural objects from which they were derived.

Fables, too, were popular in the thirteenth century. Coming probably from India where young princes were instructed by their tutors in this pleasant and indirect way by hearing stories about animals who had human characteristics that won them favor or lost them their heart's desire according to the virtue or vice involved, these stories had great charm for the Persians and Turks who were patrons of the painters. Two jackals, Kalīlah and Dimnah, had a remarkable series of adventures pictured in a thirteenth-century manuscript, which has liveliness, color, and expressive narrative style. Trees and flowers are like motifs in carpets, and the animals remind us a bit of Persepolis, but their heraldic forms are softened by humorous expressions that are nearly human. A bull may be red or yellow, a fox pink or lavender, trees may be colored like flowers and flowers like trees; each illustration is vivid and complete in itself.

In the thirteenth century a political change came with the Mongol invasion of Jenghis Khan and his followers, which was bound to affect the arts profoundly. Baghdad escaped until 1258, but eastern Iran was overrun in 1220 in an appalling destruction, and welded into the Mongol Empire, which stretched from the seacoast of China through most of Asia (except India) into Russia and eastern Europe. With a genius for organization that rivaled the ancient Persians, these nomads held their wide territory together and opened the trade routes that allowed much freer traveling between eastern and western Asia. Culturally it brought together the two important civilizations of the East and West, the Chinese and the Arabo-Persian. Men from each section were sent to the other by the ruling khans whenever they were needed to assist in warfare and administration or to bring pleasure to the palaces. The Mongol khans soon learned to live as patrons of the arts, and began to have books illuminated as had the caliphs and their courtiers.

The Manāfi' al-Hayawān (a natural history describing the characteristics of animals and their properties useful to mankind) was painted under the Mongols in the last decade of the thirteenth century, and shows the mingling of Chinese and Persian methods. The stag and doe (fig. 459) are not placed symmetrically within the border of the miniature, but are placed diagonally; the tree, instead of being in the exact center, with an even number of leaves and flowers or fruit growing to the right and to the left, is also diagonal and to one side, like a Chinese plum in a Sung painting. Above and to the left is a Chinese cloud scroll — one of the first cloud and shadow effects to be used in a thirteenth-century painting — which does not, to the Western eye, suggest much space, but it is an attempt on the part of the artist to deal with atmospheric effects. The ground plane is more of a suggestion than a real description of locale, but, thanks to the graded tone and shading and to the Chinese hills on the right, it gives an impression of a foreground on which the deer stand. The love of surface decoration on the bodies of the animals, the patterned treatment of legs and heads, and the careful delineation of little plants are still Persian. The text recommends powdered horn for cleansing the teeth, and avows that ashes of horn will remove freckles, while 'the flesh, minced, seasoned, and melted in fat is good for rheumatism.' Another of the illustrations is of the senmurv (si-murgh), which looks much more like the pheasant (fêng) of Chinese art than the composite creature on Sassanian silks and metalwork. A critic was prompted to write on the margin, 'Thou fool, since thou hast never seen the senmurv, how canst thou portray it?'

In the early fourteenth century, painters were still trying to combine Chinese and Persian ideas in their illustrations. In Rashīd-al-Dīn's *History of the World,* written for the Mongols, the illuminators had a wonderful opportunity to let their fancy rove, for the history dealt with India, China, the Near East (including Bible stories), and the other countries brought under Mongol suzerainty. As David is summoned to be king (fig. 460), we note the Arabian costumes, the checkered carpet that extends vertically up the page, the detailed painting of fruit and leaves on the trees, the use of the architectural arch with its floral ornamentation, placed next to two trees that are quite Chinese in their irregular form, and all done by a painter trained in the Chinese method of handling a brush, making lines thick or thin to suggest volume and shadow. Here, line rather than color is dominant in most of the illustrations.

Gradually, as the period wore on and the conquerors took on more and more Iranian characteristics, the painters allowed the Persian elements to overshadow the Chinese, and by the fifteenth century the most accomplished and splendid miniatures came into being. The word miniature describes them properly, for the ideal was one of infinite care, painstaking detail, compositions planned with exactitude to give the most dynamic effect, and color of the most precious and exquisite tones. The subjects illustrated lent themselves to this kind of interpretation: the Shāh-nāmah was still popular, and the poems of Sa'di, Nizāmī, and the other lyrical and mystical writers of verse, dealing with rose gardens, nightingales, lovers separated and mournful, the comfort of the wine cup, the excitement of victory, and speculation upon life and death, could be illuminated by the painters in an art almost intoxicating to the senses.

Though political change and destruction had come with the second great conquest by a Turkic horde (that of Tīmūr or Tamerlane in 1369), one of the most renowned artists worked in the fifteenth and sixteenth centuries: Bihzād, the greatest Persian painter, who lived at the eastern center of Herāt and later at Tabriz. Both there and in Samarkand beyond the Oxus there was a ferment of artistic production.

Bihzād and his contemporaries painted the courtly, poetic, or mystic scenes suggested by legends of the past or revels (fig. 461) of their time. Faithfully portraying the costumes, carpets, flowers, wine bottles, and intricate architectural ornaments, they may serve as records of that society, and so in a sense they do; but they exist in a world of the imagination more vivid than what the mortal eye sees. An entrance door topped by an arch and encased in enameled tiles as brilliant in design and color as the architecture of the mosques (fig. 462), allows one to step into a scene of feasting and drinking inside a garden wall. Surrounded by flowering trees, a flaming plane tree and a poplar, and with the sound of music in the distance, the sultan and his friends are partaking of food and wine so freely that one member has to be assisted out; it might be a bawdy or gross scene, but it is so exquisite in detail that the whole thing is delightful. When we see Tahmīna entering the chamber of Rustam at night (fig. 463), we are so intrigued by patterns, colors, and appointments of the room, and by the shy tilt of her head, the dramatic gesture of the attendant as he lifts the curtain and holds the candle for her (the only indication that it is night, for the painter would not be so foolish as to darken his singing colors by making the room black), by the interested expression of Rustam as he turns in bed to see who his unexpected caller may be, we are transported into the realm of poetry. Even when the out-of-doors is painted fantasy enters in. Darius, when out hunting, almost injures one of his herdsmen (fig. 464), who walks up to the King of Kings, builder of Persepolis, and reproves him for not being better acquainted with a faithful servitor. Bihzād, like the makers of neolithic pottery and Luristan bronzes, uses trees, mountains, running water, and animals as his motifs, but he paints trees more exquisite than those one would see on a day's outing, and flowers are scattered through the grass as though they were on a carpet, each one painted so that the beholder gets full impact of form and color. Rocks (still a bit Chinese) are like the inside of a shell of opalescent hues of mother-of-pearl; horses are pink, lavender, maroon, and even sky-blue; the stream was once silver, but is now black owing to oxidation, the only pigment that has suffered with the passage of time; the men, dressed in garments of many colors, are not entirely natural in pose, but their expressions are drawn from life; the horses are done by a man of acute observation; the flowers and trees are based on things Bihzād had seen though he has chosen to arrange and color them to suit his needs in the picture. He and his fellow painters had elevated the art of illustration to such a degree that they were on a level with the calligrapher, and were allowed a whole page for the miniature, not just a random corner unoccupied by the writing. They, and the patrons who furnished the precious materials of which these superb books were made (fig. 465), have won the gratitude of lovers of beauty down the ages.

As conditions changed in the Safawid period, the patrons could not always afford such luxuries, and the tendency in the late sixteenth and seventeenth centuries was to concentrate on single figures (fig. 466) or on brush sketches left uncolored. Again Persian art came close to Chinese, but the idiom was quite strongly Iranian by that time. Much of the old power was gone; the taste seemed to be for languid men or women delicately posed. It was not illustration of epic or the glorification of kings: the lyric, poetic character, and effete refinement of a civilization nearly stagnant were reflected by the painters. The makers of textiles and carpets, however, were more faithful to the old themes, and borrowed motifs and colors from the earlier, brilliant miniatures (fig. 467) to weave them into the silken rugs of Persia, which are the most precious in the world. They had not lost the glory, nor was it dead in painting and architecture; it was transplanted into India by the descendants of Tamerlane, the Moghuls (Mughals), after their conquest in the sixteenth century.

XXVI

India and Southeast Asia

In the Neolithic period, 3000 B.C., people in India, like those in the Near East, south Russia, and China, were busy making pottery (fig. 468)

EARLY INDIA and weapons. Excavations at the sites of Mohenjo-Daro and Harappa in the Indus Valley have thrown much light on the way men lived in the region some 5000 years ago, and show that there was actual contact between them and their neighbors in Mesopotamia. Seals discovered at Tel Asmar, near Baghdad, show elephants and humpbacked bulls of India like those from Chandu-Daro and Mohenjo-Daro (fig. 469). The dating of the Tel Asmar finds at about 2800 B.C. is the key to the chronology of the Indus Valley cultures.

The thirty acres of ruins at Mohenjo-Daro have yielded rich materials from those early days. It proved to be a city, one of the first showing 'city planning,' with streets laid out north and south, east and west, to catch the prevailing winds, which swept and ventilated it. Houses were made of burnt brick of a quality superior to those used in Mesopotamia and Egypt. Some of the buildings on the streets were designed with rounded corners so that pack animals could pass without dislodging their loads. The dwelling places and shops seem to be spacious but of a moderate size, and uniform to the extent that no palaces or homes of nobles are indicated. Within were pleasant rooms, open courts, and separate bathrooms, connected with sewers, as tall as a man, in the side streets. We may deduce from this their emphasis on cleanliness, and picture as well a society so well organized that community plans could be made and carried out.

The largest edifice in the center of the city is a bathing pool, 39 by 25 feet, with an outer wall 8 feet thick, and a row of chambers on the east side. Since other temples and sanctuaries are lacking, it is probable that this pool, fed by a well, was the gathering place for purification and healing, even as the Ganges is today.

Water, which cleanses and makes growth possible, is still associated with the conoid vertical linga stones and the circular yoni, which in Neolithic years as well as the twentieth century mark a phallus-worshiping people. The power of male and female, of generative force, already is evident in the art of India.

Among the human figures carved and modeled by the early people are some very striking examples of men and women that have a particularly Hindu character, such as a splendid sandstone torso from Harappa (fig. 470), which has an inflated look and stresses plumpness as a mark of beauty; a slim dancing girl (fig. 471), nonchalant, angular and bejeweled, from Mohenjo-Daro; a solemn priestly male wearing a gown covered with trefoil patterns, contemplating the tip of his nose like a good yogi, from the same place; and the countless mother goddesses, begirdled and coiffed. There is already, in Indian sculpture, a sensitive awareness of plastic form and a manifest gift for endowing form with life.

Typical of India, too, is the love of animals displayed in the clay toys and in the seals. In contrast to the Near East, where combat and pursuit were so often shown in sculpture, the feeling here is of affection, and when humans wear animal masks, even of identity. There are no evidences that these people admired warlike traits or sought war; instead, their energies went into the domestication of animals, in which they succeeded very well, for ponderous elephants are shown before mangers for the first time in either history or iconography. Men subdued animals by an inner spiritual force rather than by weapons, it would seem, as the beasts bow down before the man, who is their lord, or serve as vehicles for gods and goddesses. Rhinoceros, tiger, elephant, and humped bull are carved with unequaled beauty on the steatite seals, done with knowledge and skill quite lacking in those of human figures and trees, though they bow before the tree and the tree spirit. Here, as in the Near East, there is tree and serpent worship, and here, too, composite animals are symbols of power. So compelling were these ideas that they survived the Aryan invasion and flowered again in popular Hindu imagination much later, in the medieval period.

The Aryans had come down to the Indo-Gangetic plain from Iran, probably in the early part of the second millennium B.C., long after the Indus Valley civilization came to an end, for reasons unknown to us. These people brought their own religious ideas with them, but also gained much from their predecessors, the Dravidians, who had apparently had a highly developed culture. It was the fusion of these two elements that was to produce the basic Indian culture of later times. Society had been divided in pre-Aryan days into three castes, the Brahmans who served as priests, the warriors, and husbandmen. To these, the Indo-Aryans added a fourth, the serfs. The priests officiated at the ceremonies to their many gods of the firmament, the middle air, and the lower air by chanting and singing hymns, the Vedas, to the Shining Ones, or Devas. The hymns of the Veda probably came into being about 1500 B.C., and these were followed about 1000 B.C. by the Brāhmanas, which set forth the rules for ritual and sacrifice, and later by the Upanishads, which were speculative philosophical treatises on the nature of the universe, the gods, et cetera. In these works, and in the later mythological texts, the Purānas, are the roots of all Indian religion, Hindu, Jain and Buddhist. We have little to guide us in imagining what their buildings looked like, or any of their visual arts, but the poetry of the Vedas is magnificent. Their hymns to the Dawn, to Sūrya (the sun), to storm and wind and cosmic order, even to the fire of sacrifice, are among the most moving that the mind and heart of man have ever conceived.

In the sixth century B.C., India, like China and Greece, produced some great thinkers and masters, leaders who have profoundly influenced their fellow men far and wide. In India the two most important were Mahāvīra, founder of the Jain sect, and the man named Gautama, who was to become the Buddha. The latter was born Prince Siddhārtha, heir to a noble family of Kapilavastu, Nepal. His mother had a dream in which a white elephant descended and entered her body, and this was interpreted as meaning that she would have a child who would be either a world ruler or a Buddha. She went into a garden at the time of his birth, when, touching a tree with her right hand, the child issued from her side. All the world rejoiced at that moment: other young things were born, flowers appeared miraculously, the air was scented with fragrance, and all the birds sang. Siddhārtha was received by the ancient Vedic gods, Indra and Brahmā, and was given his first bath. He took steps in the four directions, symbolizing his universal sovereignty, and lotus flowers sprang up beneath his feet.

From this auspicious birth, his life was a protected and fortunate one. He was married to a beautiful girl when he was sixteen, winning her hand by proving his prowess in many contests. Ignorant of the sorrows of the world, his life in the palace was one of ease and pleasure. Though this was managed deliberately by his father, he did finally become aware of human suffering in three experiences: when driving out through the streets he saw an aged man; then, later, a diseased man; and, still later, a corpse. The realization that old age, sickness, and death existed made him impatient of the life of pleasure. He resolved, when he saw a mendicant friar, to renounce the world.

Out of the palace he stole at night assisted by his groom and by dwarf earth spirits (Yakshas), who upheld the hooves of his horse so that no one would waken to stop him. Safely outside, he took off his princely robes, cut his long hair, and began his life of asceticism. Six years of it convinced him that he was still far from illumination, that he must find it by meditation. Later, when he felt that the moment was near, he sat down beneath a fig tree, where he was tempted by the demon Māra, whose evil cohorts and beautiful daughters could not shake him from his contemplation. Māra offered to make him a chakravārtin, or wheel turner, wielding temporal power, but he remained unmoved; falsely accused, Siddhārtha touched the earth, calling it to witness in his behalf. Then, having resisted temptation, the moment of enlightenment, Bodhi, came, and thenceforth he was a Buddha.

In near-by Benares, in a deer park, he preached his first sermon, expounding the Four Noble Truths. It had come to him that suffering must come to all living things; that the cause of suffering is desire; to eliminate suffering, one must eliminate desire; to achieve that, one must have good thoughts, good words, and good deeds. That was the beginning of a long life of preaching, which took him over most of northern India, where he urged compassion upon his fellow men, and performed many miracles to win adherents. He established monastic foundations for men and women, insisting that they take the vows of poverty, chastity, and obedience, and go, like him, out into the world with only a begging bowl.

In the year 483 B.C., when he was 80, he felt that death was near, and called his favorite disciples around him. After giving them final instructions, he passed into Nirvāna. His body was cremated as the nations of the earth mourned, and the relics were distributed, some to be placed beneath earth mounds, or stūpas, as he had directed.

As the years passed, there were more and more adherents to the doctrine he had preached. In the reign of Aśoka (264–c.227 B.C.), one of the kings of the Maurya dynasty, all his subjects were urged by the monarch to become followers of the Compassionate One. His edicts recommending the teachings of the Buddha were inscribed on various stones and on tall pillars similar to those of Persepolis. The pillar at Sārnāth (fig. 472) was topped by four lions, symbol of the Buddha as leader, or lion, of the Śakya clan, and on the abacus below were carved wheels, symbols of his teaching when he set the Wheels of the Law in motion, and the lion, elephant, horse, and humped bull, symbols of the great rivers of India, the whole representing the Law as spreading in all directions in time and space. The upper part was a seed pod, a lotus, symbolizing Mt. Meru, the home of the gods. To the faithful these edict pillars had a holy significance, for merit was to be gained by walking around them. As in the Indus Valley sculpture, the animal figures display unusual technical skill and a profound understanding of the forms.

Aśoka, according to legend, sent missionaries far and wide — to Ceylon, Burma, and the East Indies, even into the Mediterranean world, and often when they went they carried with them the first civilizing forces known to those countries. Symbolic art, in that it could teach unlettered tribesmen about the Buddha, was one of the powerful agents in conversion and worship, and so from Mother India ideas and formulas for building monuments and making images spread, and gave rise to some of the most beautiful and the most significant art in all the Eastern world.

In the Ganges Valley, the stūpas of Bhārhut and Sānchī are particularly fine, the stūpa no. 1 at Sānchī being especially well preserved (fig. 473). It consists of an outer stone railing pierced by four gateways, set at the cardinal points of the compass. Within is a terrace, then the hemisphere of earth and stone, and the crowning member, a platform and parasol stand, which was both axis and symbol of kingship. The gateways, or torana, which were done in the first century B.C., are crowded with narratives and symbols related to the Buddha, done in relief that reminds us of ivory carving, as well it might, for a guild of the workers in ivory probably had a hand in it. In all the richness and profusion of human beings, animals, trees, and flowers, it is notable that the Buddha is never shown in human form, though he is suggested countless times by symbols — by the wheel, lotus, lion, empty throne, Bodhi tree, and by his footprint. His followers are there, and donors, as well as the animals who loved him as men did, and the spirits of the air, earth, and waters who had come into the Buddhist hierarchy from Vedic days. Swinging out from the East Gate is a Yakshī (tree spirit) (fig. 474), who embodies the ancient tradition of the ideal feminine form, the dancing girl adorned with bracelets, lithe, sinuous, full-blown. In contrast to her voluptuous grace is the male guardian of mineral treasures, a Yaksha, who is solid, ponderous, and earthy, conforming to the male ideal of the ancient Harappa torso, having the same 'inflated' look. Persian art, we recall, glorified kingship, but these slabs show commoner and king, man and animal, on much the same footing, for all were beloved by the Buddha.

At Sānchī, and earlier at Bhārhut, there are stories in stone of previous existences of Gautama, the *jātakas*, which begin: 'Once upon a time the king of Benares . . .' and continue to tell wonderful tales of the Buddha when he was king of the monkeys, or a six-tusked elephant, or a deer in the forest, always rescuing his friends and repaying evil with good, done with a narrative gift that seems particularly Indian. At Bodhgayā, too, on a railing similar to that of Bhārhut (figs. 475, 476), there are spirits, symbols, and the ancient gods, including Sūrya, god of the sun, driving his chariot across the sky (fig. 477). The railing marked the path of the walk taken by the Buddha when he rose from beneath the sacred fig tree after the Illumination.

The believers worshiped in temples carved into the living rock, the Chaitya Halls, found in western India in Bedsā, Kārlī (figs. 478, 479), and elsewhere near Bombay. Though no structural support was needed, beams were chiseled out of stone like wooden ribs, and columns spaced along the sides as though to hold them up. Light was admitted through a clearstory window in the façade set under a double-curved arch, which must have been one of the most characteristic features of early Indian architecture. Inside, the focal point for the worshiper was the stūpa carved in stone at the far end of the sanctuary — a smaller version in sculpture of the great mounds of Sānchī and Bhārhut. Here, too, merit was gained by walking around it in a sunwise direction.

Out in the border province of Gandhāra, beyond the Indus, the Good Law had spread. Monasteries had been established, stone carvers were busy. The ruling house, the Kushāns, an Indo-Scythian or Śaka people who dwelt there from *c.*A.D. 50–320, were ardent Buddhists. On the coin of King Kanishka (died A.D. 160) the Buddha is given human form, shown as a standing figure wearing a flowing robe, more like that of a Greek orator than an Indian mystic. Greek influence was strong here, in a tradition that went back to the conquest of Alexander the Great and was strengthened by the occupation of north India by the Bactrian heirs of Alexander, who, in turn, left a Hellenistic legacy to the Kushāns. Up in the foothills of the Pamirs, in the Punjab and down the Indus Valley, these men of Greek heritage brought new forms and ideas to the service of Buddhism. Tritons, Atlantids, Herculean men with bulging muscles, women as wise as Athena and as ample as Demeter, cupbearers, boys holding garlands — even the Trojan horse — appear now associated with the Buddhist hierarchy.

It is a hybrid art, more interesting than beautiful, showing a late flowering of the antique Hellenistic seed in a remote place, infused with a spiritual power born of India, giving rise in time to strange and wonderful creations in the sands of Central Asia, the rock caves of China, and the temple confines of Japan. Here and at Mathurā in the Ganges Valley, Buddha and Bodhisattva were carved in stone as majestic men, no longer simply suggested by symbol.

On the Casket of Kanishka (fig. 480), as well as on his coin, and on votive stele (stone memorials dedicated by the faithful) and among the figures in the round found by modern archaeologists in ruins of monasteries, the Buddha is a sturdy, compelling figure, clad in a flowing robe. Often, as in the third-century figure from the Guides' Mess of Hotī-Mardan (fig. 481), his features bear a resemblance to Apollos of the Praxitelean type, his hair curls back in waves from his forehead like a Greek god's, and the body under the drapery is carved in the Graeco-Roman tradition. But the mark between the eyes, the ūrnā, is Indian, as is the protuberance on top of his head, the ushnīsha, for both are marks peculiar to the Buddha indicating especial virtue. The long ear lobes remind us of his days in the palace before the Renunciation, when he, like other princes, wore heavy earrings.

Even more Indian in form are the Bodhisattvas (fig. 482) those beings who had attained the essence of wisdom but not full Buddhahood; Gautama had been one before he sat beneath the sacred tree and received enlightenment. Instead of the robe covering the whole body, they wear the dhotī cloth wrapped around the waist, leaving the torso bare, as was natural in a hot country. Jeweled turban, bracelets, earrings, anklets, floating scarves, and beads are among the 'thirteen precious objects' that distinguish them. Heavy lids droop over languid eyes, a small mustache often shadows the full lips, and a fold of flesh rolls above the dhotī. These are princely beings, not monastic followers of rule and discipline.

The hands of Buddha and Bodhisattvas are often shown in particular gestures, mudrā, which have an especial significance. These mudrā were used by the sculptors to indicate various attitudes, and were recognized by the beholders at once; they go with Buddhism into Greater India, Central Asia, China, and Japan. The hand up, palm out (Abhaya) meant, 'Do not fear'; the hand pendant, palm out (Vara or Varada), was extended in charity; one hand laid upon the other, palm up, was the mudrā used when engaged in contemplation (Dhyāna); hands held before the breast, fingers touching, was the teaching mudrā (Dharmachakra), turning the Wheel of the Law; in discussion, one hand was raised, thumb touching second finger (Vitarka); hands together in adoration was 'Angali'; and when the Buddha was seated yoga-fashion, legs crossed and soles of his feet turned up as he sat under the Bodhi tree, he touched the earth with his hand extended, palm in, calling the earth to witness (Bhūmisparśa) when Māra the demon assailed him.

There were lesser beings, too, used by the sculptors as they fashioned votive stones: Apsarases, the music-making angels; Lokapala, the guardian kings of the Four Directions; Vajrapāni, the thunderbolt bearers; Yakshas, dwarf dwellers in the underground world of mineral treasures; Nāgas, serpents living in rivers and lakes; their enemies, the Garudas, birds of the air; and Gandharvas, sky minstrels. These, too, will go wherever Buddhism goes, changing a bit when done by a carver of Cambodia or Java, or Siam.

Some of the most beautiful Buddhist figures were made of stucco, in molds, discovered by members of the French Delegation to Afghanistan when they dug in the ruins of Hadda. Dating probably from before the fifth century A.D., when the Epthalite Huns swept through, destroying everything in their path, they show an expressive power and a love of individuality quite rare in an art that tended to become stylized in Gandhāra. All the minor deities and characters are done as great portrait studies. There are Apollonian youths, a lad playing the pipes of Pan, angelic beings who might have come from a French Gothic cathedral, and diabolical ones who might be ancestors of gargoyles long before gargoyles were thought of. There is a tribesman in a long coat (fig. 483), a beseeching, Mongoloid person sometimes called Māra, and there are languid, graceful people who are purely Hindu; it was a meeting place of many types, all brought to the service of the Buddha, fashioned by the hands of great sculptors known to us only by the fragments that remain.

In near-by Kābul and the surrounding country the French Delegation unearthed Syrian glass, metalwork from Rome, ivory from India, and Sassanian works of many kinds from Persia. Throughout the countryside there are abundant proofs of the international quality of the art of the area, largely owing to caravan trade and to pilgrimages made by the Buddhists. In Bāmiyān the faithful had carved two colossal Buddhas (fig. 484) in stone cliffs overlooking the valley, one 175 feet high, the other 120 feet high. On such a huge scale, the work is impressive rather than beautiful, and bears witness again to the enthusiasm of the devotees who came there. In the photograph, we can see the damage done to the sculpture by Moslems who were offended by these images and destroyed their faces in target practice from across the valley. We should suppose that carving the enormous figures in the living rock, and attaching folds of drapery to wooden pegs set in holes drilled in the rock, would be task enough for the makers, but the Chinese pilgrims, Fa-hsien, who went through the valley in the fourth century, and Hsüan-tsang, who went through in the seventh, speak of the great statues gleaming in the sun, so metal must have been used as well. The niches were covered by layers of plaster, and frescoes were painted there, Buddhist in inspiration, but international in style, Sassanian, Hindu, and Hellenistic motifs predominating.

Down in the Ganges Valley parallel developments were taking place. At Mathurā (Muttra) another great center of religious sculpture had been flourishing, probably from pre-Buddhist times, and even when Buddhism was dominant there are evidences that the Jains were strong there, too. The stūpa art must have been contemporary with that of Bhārhut and Sānchī, while the practice of making Buddhas and Bodhisattvas in monumental forms was common there under the Kushāns as it was in Gandhāra. One of the most important of these is a standing Bodhisattva dedicated by Friar Bala (fig. 485) in the third year of Kanishka, or A.D. 131–2, a figure 8 feet high, or, to give it in Hindu measurements, 8½ tala, which was the ideal according to the Indian canon of proportion. In every respect the Indian ideal is followed, without the Graeco-Roman influence we have seen in the art of the Indus area; it has the torso of a lion, the arms of a hunter, the long supple legs of a deer. The drapery, too, is of the native type, consisting of the dhotī, low girdle, and scarf thrown over one arm, leaving one shoulder bare, all of a light transparent material, rather than of the heavier cloth that made such prominent folds in the Hotī-Mardan Buddha. The relatively small head, with its round, wide-open eyes and smooth hair brushed back from a sloping forehead, has none of the Greek-god softness noted in the Gandhāran type. There was Graeco-Roman influence in Mathurā, to be sure, in Bacchanalian scenes, and Olympian heroes (fig. 486), but they are expressed in an Indian idiom, in the local red sandstone.

Far to the south, on the east coast, another fine group of Buddhist sculptures were found, at Amarāvatī, on the Kistna River. Perhaps because the material, a greenish marble, was better adapted to the carvers' needs, perhaps because it was farther away from foreign invasion, it is in many respects the most beautiful of all. Slabs once used on stūpas, since burned and looted, suggest that the southern sculptors were most accomplished in their handling of human and animal forms. With an effortless ease the whole panorama of life is portrayed, crowded streets, palace interiors, sacred monuments, even the realms of the Tushita heavens whence came the white elephant to Māyā, the mother of the serene Buddha. Bodily tensions and movement, utter relaxation, drama and calmness are there (fig. 487). Compositions are sometimes unbearably crowded, sometimes done with an almost mathematical precision. Lithe and energetic, the men and women seem to pulsate with life, a splendid expression of an Indian ideal, which was to be able to show in sculpture the difference between a dead man and a sleeping one. The relief is generally high and well-rounded (fig. 488), designed by artists who had an excellent understanding of light and dark values in expressive sculpture. Gradations are more subtle than at Bhārhut and Sānchī, indicating a more mature approach on the part of the carvers.

In architecture, too, there is a marked originality. The stūpa, as we see it in the small slabs of relief sculpture, was surrounded by a railing, but there were no gateways as at Sānchī. A moonstone was placed at the entrance, and five slender columns were set inside at the terrace level, both features we shall see in Ceylon. Sculpture was used lavishly, rich in symbolism, suggesting the Buddha by the empty throne, the riderless horse, the parasol, the wheel, lotus, lion, et cetera, and later by showing him in his monk's robe. (Drapery, in the latter figures, is conceived of in smooth volume cut by delicate lines.) The evolution at Amarāvatī from the Age of Symbol to the Age of Representation is so gradual that we are hardly aware of it, just as we feel no shock of transition from this art of the Āndhra period (220 B.C.–c.A.D. 300) to the classical art of the Gupta (A.D. 320–600).

The Gupta kings, natives of Bihār, who extended their rule throughout the Aryan north, were not Buddhists, but their attitude toward those who were was one of tolerance, so there was no checking of the impulse to build and carve and paint in honor of the Buddha. Sculptors were busy in Mathurā, Sānchī, Bodhgayā, and Sārnāth making images that became the models for later artists and for the carvers in faraway lands. The Preaching Buddha of Sārnāth (fig. 489) is a superb example of the ideal as it had become crystallized by this time. The seated figure is finished with a smooth perfection that bespeaks the infinite care lavished upon every detail by the maker, and the spiritual expression reveals the attitude of the Indian sculptor toward his art, that of making God manifest in stone, present in all things, as the number one is present in all numbers. The crisply carved brows, eyelids, mouth, hands, and feet have a grace and tenderness of form that seem almost paradoxical. The whole figure is majestic, aloof, withdrawn, but not haughty or arrogant; compassion is there, and a serene wisdom. Just as there is the Indian emphasis on the spirit, so the very proportions are Indian, based on other natural forms; the head is oval as an egg, the shoulders strong as a lion's, the waist slim as a wasp's, and the lotus pose, the padmāsana, is one taken by followers of yoga as they seek to free the mind for contemplation. The hair is a series of tight snail-shell motifs, the ear lobes are extended, and the drapery is so light that we have to look closely at the incised lines at the neck, the delicate folds at the wrists and ankles, to become aware of it at all. Behind the subtle curves of head and shoulders a great halo is placed, richly ornamented with floral and leaf patterns, beads, and, at the edge, a minute scallop design that had been used earlier at Mathurā. The smaller attendants, flying above, or kneeling below at the turning wheel, are similar to the lithe Amarāvatī men and women. Whatever had come to India from other lands has been absorbed and changed so that the result is now the perfect vehicle for her aesthetic ideal.

Out in the western regions, inland from Bombay, at Ajantā, some mendicants had gone in the rainy season and had taken shelter in caves above the Waghora River. A religious community had been established gradually in the jungle country, which had, according to legend, once belonged to a Nāga king. In the solid rock above the bend of the river 29 halls of worship (chaitya) and monastic quarters (vihāra) had been hollowed out and adorned with painting and sculpture from c.200 B.C. to c.A.D. 500, some of the best work having been done in the Gupta period. The façade of cave XIX (fig. 490) gives us a very good idea of the rough stone in which so many intricate and delicate figures were carved, and shows, too, that the chaitya window still dominates the architectural design. Beautiful as the architecture and sculpture are, and marvelous when we consider their remoteness from other art centers, it is the paintings that cause unbounded admiration. In caves I and II especially the walls are covered with such a variety of forms, so vibrant with life, that the earliest Europeans who saw them could not believe that they were religious. In glowing browns — reddish, greenish, chocolate, and almost black — set off by lapis blue, pearly white, crimson, and green, men, spirits, and animals crowd about the walls in great rhythmic patterns. In cave I the central chamber is 64 feet square, a huge space to hollow out of solid rock, and contains countless figures, the most famous being the Beautiful Bodhisattva (fig. 491), which is 5 feet 9½ inches from the crown of the head to the knees. He is the lotus holder, Padmapāni, who dwells now on earth, performing the functions of Gautama until the Buddha of the Future, Maitreya, has come. He is shown as a prince of noble birth and breeding, wearing the jewels of the highborn, aloof but not detached from the beings who crowd around him, seeking salvation. As in the Sārnāth sculpture, the proportions of the ideal of manly beauty have been followed, strong, graceful, and supple. High lights are brought out in skilful gradations of tone, giving volume by shading from dark to light within the limited color range.

In the narratives that relate to the life of the Buddha or his previous existence there are rich panoramas of palaces, gardens, processions, audiences, incidents of many kinds, all separated by cleft rocks and architectural motifs into horizontal units. Rocks and architecture seem to come forth from the walls toward the beholder in a perspective that is quite startling to the western eye accustomed to a convention that pretends to penetrate the wall. Up on the ceiling are lovely patterns (fig. 492) of flowers, birds, children, lovers, and fantastic forms fitted into carefully regulated spaces, all showing the vitality, grace, and imagination that characterize the art of the many anonymous painters who worked on the plaster of these walls. Perhaps they followed the scheme of a master planner, for transfers were used, the outlines pricked to allow red or black chalk rubbed over them to cling to the rough plaster beneath the finely burnished surface in which the pigment was incorporated. Working in the large, dark chamber by torchlight or light reflected from the doorway by holding a white sheet there, these men can be imagined striving to express the ideas and methods handed down from generation to generation in their guilds, and with such superb success that Ajantā became the mother school for Central Asia, China, and Japan. It is almost the last great moment before a rising tide of popular Hinduism will engulf most of India in forms more violent than those approved of by the followers of the Compassionate One.

As we have seen, Gupta kings were not Buddhists but Brahmanists, in whose reigns there was a revival of the old Vedic worship, bringing

MEDIEVAL INDIA a need for new temples, and new tasks for the sculptors who must give form to a new pantheon of gods. No longer were the forces of nature, the storms, winds, rains, et cetera, thought of as impersonal phenomena to be addressed by priests in ritual; they now became gods who dwelt in their temples, who had to be anointed with oil and cared for, who delighted in gifts brought to the temples, and who had to be propitiated, so that they would not bring evil into the lives of their followers, fearful of their wrath and craving their love. Brahmā, soul and creator of the universe, was rarely represented, but in traditional iconography has four heads and four arms (which hold the four books of the Vedas), is seated upon his particular vehicle, the goose (hamsa), and is accompanied by his consort, Sarasvatī, goddess of eloquence and music.

More popular with the masses were the two other members of the Trimūrti, Vishnu and Śiva. Vishnu, known also as Hari and Mārāyana, was the great hero who appeared in various incarnations (avatārs) to save the day for fellow gods and humans. He had been an ancient deity of the sun, and his color, blue, still suggests his heavenly association. He is generally represented with four arms, the hands holding a mace, conch shell, lotus, and disk. His vehicle is the garuda bird, and his consorts are Lakshmi, goddess of beauty and fortune, and Bhūmi-devi, goddess of earth. He appears also in his ten avatārs: as a fish, tortoise, boar, lion, horse, dwarf, Buddha, Brahman hero Paraśurama, Rāma, the bowman, and Krishna, the herdsman, all part of a rich legend, which could be used dramatically by painters and sculptors. In a brief account it is impossible to give more than a small selection of the attributes and aspects of Vishnu and the other Hindu gods; to do them justice would fill volumes.

Śiva, developed from the ancient storm-god Rudra, had to be placated by sacrifice, for he was a destroyer; at the same time, in his power, he was god of generative force, represented by the linga stone, and was shown associated with his vehicle, Nandi, the bull. In making this complete cycle he was the ideal of many Hindus. He was also lord of beasts, and dwelt upon Mt. Kailāsa, sometimes as an ascetic, his emaciated body covered with ashes, or, at other times, as a consort of Pārvatī, protecting her tenderly. His power is shown, too, as the dancer, Natarāja, performing his divine dance of creation and destruction (fig. 493). His wild locks swing out in the dance, and on his head are a skull, a crescent moon, the goddess Gangā, and sometimes the fifth head of Brahmā. In one of his four hands he holds a drum (the first sound in the universe), in another the flame of destruction. One hand is raised in the Abhaya mudrā, with a serpent wrapped like a bracelet on the arm; the other hand points down to the dwarf on whom he dances, one of the many enemies overcome by this lord of death. In addition to two human eyes, he has a third vertical eye in the middle of his forehead. To the devotee, the dance, Tandava, took place within himself, bringing release and freedom to come.

Śiva's consort is as full of contradictions as he is. As Pārvatī or Umā, she is the daughter of the mountain, wild and gracious (fig. 494). She is the mother of Skanda, god of war, and of Ganeśa, the elephant-headed god of mischief and good luck, familiar to all travelers in the Orient. As Durgā, Chandi, or Kālī (fig. 495) she is a scourge, bloodthirsty and insatiable, wearing a necklace of skulls, devouring men. She is attended by seven goddesses who spread disease, all dreaded by terrified believers. But with her power as a destroyer, she can also destroy demons, and rescue her followers from care and want, and so she is hailed as a saviour.

Among the early medieval monuments inspired by these gods of popular Hinduism are the monolithic 'raths' at Māmallapuram down on the southeastern coast near Madras, and the famous relief of the Descent of the Ganges carved on a cliff near by (fig. 496). This is 30 feet long and 23 feet high, filled with figures of gods and men and animals who witnessed this marvelous event. It is a seventh-century rendering of the legend that explains how the river Ganges came to water the dry plains of north India. The goddess of the river, which flowed only in the celestial regions, took pity on a pious king who had subjected himself to austerities for 1000 years, and she agreed to come down to earth to help his subjects. Śiva, realizing that the shock of the descending torrent might destroy the earth, stood to receive it on his head, allowing the water to trickle through his locks, and so come gently to the parched earth. Magnificent elephants stand below divinities of the sky who fly above; all manner of birds and beasts are gathered there for the great event, even an ascetic cat, aping the good king who stood for so long with his arms raised above his head! Mystics and genii cluster around the stream (which is an outlet for a reservoir above), while the sovereigns of the water, the Nāga king and queen, accept their homage with calm majesty. In scale, in breadth of conception, as well as in beauty of detail, it is one of the most impressive of the early medieval monuments, and it is, as well, a worthy part of the long tradition of Indian sculpture going back as far as Mohenjo-Daro.

At Elūrā, in the Ajantā area, in the seventh and eighth centuries, a series of rock-cut cave temples and monolithic carvings were made belonging to three sects, Buddhist, Jain, and Brahman. Of the last named, one of the most remarkable is the Kailāsa Temple (fig. 497), a representation in solid rock of the great peak atop the Himalayas, which the demon Rāvana tried to take from Śiva. As we notice the small figure mounting the steps near the center of the picture we become aware of the tremendous scale of this temple, cut 100 feet deep into the side of the natural rock. Architectural details are splendid, delicately pointing up the massiveness of the whole.

The sculpture, which blends harmoniously with the architecture, demonstrates the skill of the carvers engaged here. Rāvana, shaking the mountain, trying to dislodge Śiva and Pārvatī (fig. 498), is seen in the half gloom of a subterranean grotto, a many-headed and terrible demon brandishing his several arms in a powerful representation of an energetic figure in motion impelled by envy and fury. Sure of his eminence, Śiva sits above, languid and graceful, while Pārvatī leans upon him, frightened, clinging to her lord. All the forms are rounded, cut out in high relief, and show a singular understanding of the dramatic possibilities of light and shade on the part of the sculptor.

Mystery and power are suggested in another early medieval temple, the eighth-century Elephantā, out in the Bay of Bombay. In the subterranean caverns the worshipers of Śiva could approach by torchlight, coming into the presence of the god in a thrice-terrible aspect; for deep in a niche the three-headed one looms up, becrowned and jeweled, cruel, sensual, self-contained (fig. 499). Near by they could pay tribute to him as god of generative force by bringing gifts and offerings to the linga stone in its own chapel.

There are, besides these rock-cut temples with their unique sculpture, a number of structural houses of worship, which show the evolution of the Hindu type in the north and south. Going back to Buddhist architecture in the Ganges Valley, we find that one of the most remarkable monuments there is the Mahābodhi Temple at Bodhgayā, which may have been built first as early as the fourth century A.D., though in its present state of restoration (fig. 500) it looks much later. It consists of a four-sided tower set upon a high base, flanked by smaller towers at the angles of the platform, all carefully oriented, and symbolic of the word of the Buddha spreading in all directions. The sculpture has its symbolic significance, too, and gives a fine surface decoration to the pyramidal mass of the tower, or śikhara, which is topped by a curving finial, the kalaśa. Early Hindu temples show a tendency to combine the tower with the rectangular hall of the type found at no. 17 at Sānchī (fig. 501), as may be seen in the Durgā Temple at Aihole (fig. 502), which has an outer porch where the faithful might circumambulate, and then go within the flat-roofed cella to the sanctuary where the god lived and where the image was kept. By the eighth century we see that the tower becomes increasingly important (fig. 503), and begins to curve near the top in a melon shape, while the finial is mushroomed to a flat support for the bronze symbol of the god to whom the temple is dedicated, such as the trident, wheel, or disk. The emphasis is still on mass, but the surface is cut horizontally by countless sculptured reliefs, also indicating the god who lives there. The cella seems almost an afterthought attached to the tower. By the tenth century, as the Lingarāja Temple at Bhuvaneśvara demonstrates (fig. 504), the melon-shaped śikhara becomes the dominant and characteristic feature, adorned with myriads of small sculptured ornaments; the cella is now beneath the tower, 19 feet square. In the same period is the Jaganātha Temple at Purī, quite similar to the Lingarāja; each year at the time of annual pilgrimage, a model of the central tower is made of bamboo (which suggests a possible origin of the shape, as the bamboo poles can be bent into graceful curves very easily) and is carried out on a cart pulled through the streets by the faithful. Excitement runs so high that some in their frenzy try to throw themselves under the heavy cart, the Juggernaut, which is a symbol, even in Western thought, of inevitable, crushing fate.

The temple as a cart was translated into stone in the Black Pagoda of Konārak (fig. 505), a thirteenth-century building, dedicated to the ancient sun god, Sūrya, who drove his chariot across the sky. This elaborate and splendid structure, of which the cella alone remains now, is mounted on a platform on which are carved giant wheels (fig. 506) ornamented with a delicate surface carving that suggests the ivory technique.

A later development, in the seventeenth century, of the Dravidian type noted in the Raths at Māmallapuram, is to be seen in the southernmost part of India in the temples of Madura, Tanjore, and Conjeeveram. They are pilgrimage centers, designed to take care of hundreds of Hindus who hope to wash away their sins or fulfil vows made to the Brahmanical gods. Each is a complex group of buildings consisting of gateways, pools, sanctuaries, pavilions, and private quarters, constructed of local stone. They are dominated by the high towers at the gates, called gopura (fig. 507), four-sided pyramids so covered with sculpture that one is conscious only of a surface ornamented with so many forms that no single one stands out. Power is expressed by multiplicity rather than by the energy of individual figures. These carved stone deities have none of the serene sweetness of those made in the Gupta and Pāla periods, nor have they the tenseness and potential movement of the medieval bronzes — they are often awkward or lifeless representations of the gods who were supposed to live there, placed on the gopura, the columns and in the sanctuaries. They are overwhelming in number, as the intention of the builders was that those who enter the home of the gods should be overcome with awe.

THIS emphasis on profusion, natural enough in a jungle country, was characteristic of southern India. In the north at the same time, that is,

MUGHAL AND RĀJPUT INDIA

the seventeenth century, a very different development took place. Conquerors of Persian and Mongol descent, the Moghuls or Mughals, had come into India in the sixteenth century and had established themselves at Delhi and Agra. Under them, creations of unparalleled beauty came into being in architecture and the book arts. Of course there was a strong Moslem influence even when the sovereign was not an orthodox follower of Mohammed, and their buildings have a character much influenced by Iranian mosques, but the materials of India, marble and semi-precious stones, gave a permanence, purity, and elegance the colorful faïence of Persia had lacked. The first of the Mughal line, Babur, conquered Delhi in 1527, and his five successors, Humāyūn, Akbar, Jahāngīr, Shāh Jahān, and Aurangzīb, took nearly all the rest of the country. Though they were warriors, they were also great patrons of the arts, and directed their builders and painters with a sure taste and high ideal of excellence.

Palaces, mosques, and tombs were erected in the Delhi-Agra area on a scale that outshone the magnificent buildings of the seventeenth century in Europe, even the palace of Versailles. The arch and dome were used extensively, particularly the bulbous, onion-shaped domes, which differed in profile and construction from the spherical Byzantine type. Columns and piers used as supporting members broke up the interior space into small units; they were sometimes joined by curving brackets like those used in Jain temples on Mt. Ābu (fig. 508), where white marble had been used in the eleventh- and twelfth-century temples — a soft marble when first quarried, which allowed intricate and delicate carving.

The tomb of Humāyūn in Old Delhi, built in the sixteenth century, stood on an arched platform made of red sandstone inlaid with marble, and was topped by a dome of marble. It was the first to be enclosed in a park or garden, and shows the combination of old Persian features with fine Indian stone and stonecutting. Akbar's tomb was equally splendid, and the huge palace built by Shāh Jahān in Delhi, consisting of a great portal, entrance hall, courtyards, bazaars, audience halls, and music halls, baths and gardens, almost staggers the imagination.

Fine as they were, it is the seventeenth-century mausoleum erected by Shāh Jahān in memory of his wife that still charms everyone by its matchless beauty, the Tāj Mahall (fig. 509). Placed between two red sandstone mosques, it gleams white and pure, reflected in the Jamna River, which flows beside it. Set on a platform 18 feet high, with tall minarets flanking each angle, a great dome crowns the central square, rising 200 feet above the platform. The entrance in each face is of the usual recessed type, consisting of pointed arches set in square frames, and inside them pierced marble screens allow a dim and subdued light to reach the interior. The proportions of platform, entrances, and dome are in perfect harmony, as are the light and dark areas of surface penetration. Equally lovely is the contrast of white marble against the green accent of the formal gardens that surround it, the slim dark spears of cypress reaching toward the minarets, and the low masses of the planting along the shallow reflecting pool reminding us of the old Persian concept of the garden as a place for cool refreshment, with the sound of running water and welcome shade more important than brightly colored flowers. Only after we become fully aware of the skilful design of the building and the excellence of its setting do we begin to notice the exquisite detail of the inlaid work in onyx, jasper, agate, bloodstone, cornelian, and lapis lazuli, worked into the base of the dome and above the pointed arches. Inside and out, graceful patterns of flowers and arabesques were set into the spaces cut in the marble to receive them, thousands of exactly fitted pieces of semi-precious stones set in by the workmen, some of whom came from Italy. Moslems, Hindus, and Europeans joined together in designing and building this monument to Mumtāz Mahall, the 'Elect of the Palace,' who was given immortality by her husband in this marvel of Mughal taste and skill.

Of the mosques, the Moti Masjid, 'the Pearl,' also in Agra (fig. 510), is surely the most exquisite. Built in the period from 1646 to 1653, it, too, is made of white marble. Unlike the Tāj, it is topped by three domes of equal importance, which rise above the entrance pierced by five openings framed in cusped arches. The emphasis here, too, is on beauty of proportion, fine spacing of light and dark areas, and detail work showing great restraint and finesse. Though the first impression is of delicacy, it is not a small mosque, for the court is 150 feet square, and the corridors inside are long and spacious.

As patrons of the arts, the Mughal rulers had in their households calligraphers and painters who copied and illustrated Persian poems, Hindu literature, scientific treatises, and books inspired by the various forms of religion that interested them. Humāyūn had spent a year with Shāh Tahmāsp in Persia, in one of his fifteen bitter years of exile away from India, and in that time he saw how the arts were encouraged in the Persian traditions. He had visited the great cities, where he saw the mosques and palaces and gardens; he saw the painters working in the royal palace, in the tradition of Bihzād and other masters; and he even visited the ruins of Persepolis. When he returned to India in 1555 he brought that ideal with him, and so firmly planted it in the mind of his son, Akbar, that the lad carried it with him in spite of his early years of turmoil and battle. Though Akbar never had the opportunity to learn to read, for he spent most of his time in the saddle, from his accession to the throne at the age of thirteen throughout his reign, he collected an enormous library and paid readers to be in constant attendance. He loved to discuss doctrine with Christians, Hindus, Moslems, and the Zoroastrian Parsees; he worked out a monotheism of his own and tried to establish it among his subjects. But he did not force it upon them, and they, being content with their many gods, did not accept it. One of his wives was a Rājput princess, of the great line of sovereigns in northwest India, and their union brought together two traditions, the native and that of the conqueror.

The Rājput country had seen the continuance of a vital development in painting, dating from the time of the glory of Ajantā. With some of the fresco technique still in their memories, as well as the narrative style used by Jains in illustrating the life of their leader, Mahāvīra, the local craftsmen had evolved a method of painting that was quite unique. They were especially fond of the Rāgmālā form, which united a musical mode, a poem, and a painting, all conveying the same mood. They were male and female, Rāga and Rāginī, and were composed to express the most delicate shadings of emotion and sentiment. They were appropriate to certain seasons and times of day or night; at the top of the page there was a strip of 'weather' — blue and gray for a melancholy dark day, drops of rain for the rainy season, snake-like lines of lightning in yellow and red for storm, clear yellow for a bright day, shades of rose for sunset, et cetera. A man or woman was often shown playing upon a musical instrument (fig. 511), charming peacocks, fawns, snakes, and birds who came close, even as the animals had done in the Mohenjo-Daro seals. Sometimes the mood is of utter despair, at other times of rejoicing, or even of the serene peace of yoga contemplation. Like the Jain manuscript figures of the fifteenth century, the Rājputs are usually shown in profile, with prominent noses and receding chins, and expressive hands extended in significant gestures. They are symbols rather than flesh-and-blood men and women, for it was not the purpose of the painters to strive for reality. The designs are splendid, done with a breadth of concept that stems from the mural tradition of Ajantā, though these paintings are page-size. The colors, too, remind us of wall painting, confined to a palette of dark blue, olive green, lemon yellow, tomato red, and chalk white. It is a folk art, handed down from generation to generation.

In the seventeenth and eighteenth centuries there are, besides the Rāgmālā, a great many Rājput paintings dealing with Hindu gods, myths, and legends. Vishnu is a favorite, especially in his incarnation as Krishna, the herdsman, and as Rāma, the bowman, hero of the Ramāyāna. All aspects of the Krishna story are portrayed: his early years, when he was hidden among the dairymaids for safety; through his young manhood, when he began to charm his former playmates, and chose one, Rādha, for his constant companion; through his various adventures as the saviour of his friends, both human and animal. In the minds of the Rājputs, he and Rādha were personifications of their own emotions, the anguish of separation felt by the lovers, or the joy of reunion, being their own anguish and joy. To them, seeking union with their god and finding it was like this joy of reunion. Another popular series was the Siege of Lankā, illustrating the epic of Rāma, the huntsman, whose wife, Sitā, was stolen by the demon Rāvana, who took her to his fortress on Lankā (Ceylon). Aided by his brother and by monkeys and bears, Rāma laid siege to the fortress and won his wife back, after enduring hardship that would have destroyed a man less powerful than Vishnu, in a human incarnation. Śiva and Parvatī were painted, too, sometimes as a loving couple happy in their home on Mt. Kailāsa, other times in their terrible, destructive aspects.

When the Mughals came and established their courts at Delhi and Agra, they brought painters and calligraphers from Persia trained in the arts of bookmaking, in graceful lettering, miniature illumination, and exquisite leather tooling. At first the subjects chosen were the characteristic Iranian ones, glorification of the king as huntsman, warrior, and courtier, and the romances and mystic poems of Persia. Gradually the costumes became increasingly Indian, as did the weapons and architecture. Then, as native painters were summoned to court, a mingling of styles resulted. There was still the delicacy of Persian line, the love of decorative detail, the use of Chinese rock and cloud motifs, which had been used in Persia since the Mongol invasion of the thirteenth century, the careful delineation of flowers and trees, the radiant color of the Safawid masters, all of which were tempered finally by their contact with the vigorous native style. Even in the Hamza-nāmah (fig. 512), started under Humāyūn and continued in Akbar's reign, there is more power than subtlety in the color, and two new elements are evident — interest in shading, and perspective. Akbar not only encouraged the native painters in a special effort to honor the Rājputs; he also was keenly interested in books and gifts brought from Europe. He had received a Jesuit mission, and was delighted by the pictures of the Virgin Mary, as well as by Plantyn's Royal Polyglot Bible, brought to him in 1580, in which there were engravings by Flemish artists of the sixteenth century.

This European element in Mughal painting continued to be important under Jahāngīr. He received Sir Thomas Roe as envoy from James I and, like his father, welcomed the religious teachers from Europe. Portuguese and Dutch traders played their part, too, in bringing Western methods and motifs to India, just as they carried tales of India back to Europe. We know that Rembrandt saw and sketched from album pages owned by the president of the Dutch East India Company as well as from those in his own collection; and that Archbishop Laud had put his name and the date 1640 in a book of Indian drawings now in the Bodleian Library. Now, for the first time in India, there is an interest in the appearance of things, a searching for reality for its own sake, a desire to show shadow and cloud, and objects diminishing in size and clarity in the distance.

Among the subjects painted for the albums of Akbar, Jahāngīr (fig. 513), and Shāh Jahān were Durbars (daily audiences of the rulers), which meant, of course, many portraits of attending nobles; single portraits of advisers and relatives; equestrians; abnormal people like Inayat Khan, the opium-taker (fig. 514), who was sketched by order of the emperor just before he died; sages and poets, musicians and mystics, garden scenes and hermits' retreats. Studies in natural history were made, birds drawn with such clarity and precision that every feather could be studied, or flowers enlarged so that one could examine the root system, buds, and blossoms. All of these are done by painters who stressed objectivity and purity of form rather than fantasy or poetry, and they are rendered in clear colors and fine lines, which had to come up to the standard set by imperial patrons who demanded the best from their builders, painters, and artists of all kinds. Not until Aurangzīb took the throne in 1658 was there a falling off of power in this Mughal school, and then it was because he was a strict Moslem who thought that painting a portrait was a sin (man was trying to imitate God in his creative skill), and royal patronage was withdrawn. Painters were then no longer a part of the imperial household, protected and guided by the sovereign, nor were the fine paper and beautiful pigments available.

Up in the foothills of the Himalayas, small native schools continued to flourish into the eighteenth century, part of the Rājput tradition with strong Mughal influence. At Jammu, Chamba, Tehri-Garhwal, and particularly at Kāngra, Hindu themes inspired by native poems and religious thought were painted in a style that has still much of the early Rājput vigor, combined with the delicate line and shading popular at Delhi; but it is essentially a romantic art, having little of the realism of the court products, and none of the talent for psychological portraiture developed there. It is poetic, moving, concerned with the spirit rather than the outward appearance of things (fig. 515).

The arts of weaving and making weapons, which had been well developed in India before the Mughals came, were carried to new heights under the northern emperors. Printed or stamped cottons ornamented with designs that showed a combination of Persian and Hindu motifs were valued all over the world, and their guns, daggers, swords, and shields are still sought for museum collections. Jewelry, too, was produced by some of the most skilful artisans the world has known, using the rubies, emeralds, pearls, and other precious stones abounding in India in exquisite settings. In all these arts there is such a high level of taste and beauty of workmanship, whether in tomb, mosque, palace, painting, fabric, bracelet, or sword, that we recognize it at once as Mughal.

Ceylon: The energy and power that went into the creation of Indian art for so many centuries was bound to have a profound influence on the lands within traveling range, and so it did,
GREATER INDIA spread by missionaries, conquerors, and traders. Ceylon, lying off the southeast coast, became a stronghold of Buddhism in the third century B.C., converted, according to legend, by Mahinda, son of the King Aśoka, who went down with several companions bearing relics of the Buddha, and was welcomed by the ruling monarch and his subjects. Buddhism, which died out on the mainland about A.D. 800,

has remained strong there until the present day, so, fortunately, monuments and texts have been well preserved; here the Hīnayāna (the
Lesser Vehicle) is largely followed, with its emphasis on Buddha as a
man, on his doctrine, and on the community of monks living under strict
discipline. The rich hierarchy of gods and beings of the Mahāyāna
(Greater Vehicle), which inspired the northern sculptors of Gandhāra,
Mathurā, and Amarāvatī to carve the Bodhisattvas, Nāgas, Yakshas, and
all the other creatures included in the more elaborate theology accepted
there, was not popular on the island, but the Buddha, his followers, and
his symbols were.

As in the time of Aśoka, a stūpa was built to receive relics and to
symbolize the Buddha as teacher and leader of men. The mound differs
a bit in construction and symbolism in Ceylon, where it is called a thūpa,
or dāgoba. With the instructions in mind of Gautama when he placed
his begging bowl upside down on his cloak and laid his staff beside them,
the Sinhalese used a platform, a great mound of earth, sometimes covered
with brick, crowned by the harmikā, or platform, which had sun and
moon symbols on it, and topped by the chattra, the parasol element
condensed into a solid cone. The stūpa was a reliquary with all the
qualities of divinity, a combination of a thing both royal and divine. To
worship it was to gain merit; to build it was even more virtuous. The
location was determined by magic formulas related to directions used by
builders on the mainland, for it was most important to place it propi-
tiously. The stūpas of Ceylon did not have the sculptured railing and
gateways, like those of Sānchī and Bhārhut; little narrative sculpture
was used; and the habit of placing colonnettes, slim and ornamental like
those of Amarāvatī, was characteristic. Some of the dāgobas are enormous. The Ruwanveli, built about 100 B.C., has a dome 254 feet in
diameter at the base, and rises 270 feet high; it is set upon 3 circular
terraces about 7 feet wide, and is raised on a platform 500 feet on each
side.

The city of Anurādhapura, in which it was erected, was colossal,
extending at least eight miles in diameter, comparable in its day to
New York or London. It was filled with imposing buildings — temples,
palaces, and stūpas — lovely pools, and homes of all those who thronged
the streets of the capital. Recent excavations give evidence of a flourishing trade with Greece and Rome and other Mediterranean cities; perhaps
the grandeur of Rome was challenged here, for architecture and sculpture were conceived on a large scale.

The most notable painting is to be found at Sígirya, a citadel about twenty miles west of Polonnāruva, a great stone rising about 600 feet above the tilled fields, which was used as a refuge in the late fifth or early sixth century by the parricide king Kasyapa I. There are murals in two irregularly shaped 'pockets' in the west cliff; one pocket is a little over 40 feet long, the other nearly 27. In them there are processions of ladies and their serving maids, carrying lotus flowers in their hands, who are painted as if moving toward a Buddhist temple to the north of the hill. They are sometimes compared to the frescoes of Ajantā, though they differ in color and composition, red, yellow, and green being the dominant colors in Ceylon, where little blue is used; and there is none of the tension of forms, no narrative, no contrast of figure and background, which marked the great wall decorations of the mainland. The women have the long oval faces and long noses of the south, and they suggest a languid tempo in the relaxation of pose of heads, bodies, and hands. They seem to have been done free hand rather than to have been transferred by pounces, as were the Ajantā paintings, and the gauze of their jackets and skirts, and the gaiety of color lack the intensity of the Indian mother school, though they are equally graceful and appealing.

The sculpture is imposing rather than moving. Most of the Buddhist figures are more than life-size, and carved with a certain stiffness not improved by the weathering they have undergone. Even so, the ideal of the Buddha as a being withdrawn in contemplation is successfully conveyed in large 8-foot seated images.

The capital was moved south to Polonnāruva when a Tamil invasion came in the eighth century, and again, temples, stūpas, and palaces were erected on a grand scale, throughout the thirteenth century. Trade with the Arab world, with the Chinese, and with the nearer neighbors in Indo-China enriched the culture and spread the influence of Ceylon beyond its island shores. The dāgoba form of stūpa was carried up into Tibet, and finally into China itself by the Mongols and Manchus. There were round temples (wata-dā-gē), rectangular ones approached by wide staircases, and stepped pyramids, which were symbols of Mt. Meru, mountain of the gods. Sculpture, too, follows the tradition of the early period in scale and spirit. One of the most remarkable pieces is of the Buddha reclining at the moment of Nirvāna (figs. 516, 517), 46 feet long, heavy but serene. Quite a few figures were made in copper and bronze in the medieval period, usually of the Hindu gods, for Śiva (fig. 518) and Vishnu found devotees in 'Lankā' as well as on the mainland, and their images are done with the same lithe grace as in the mother country.

*   *   *

Java: Farther out in the East Indies the island of Java had its own great art based on that of India. The early records, including the diary of the Chinese pilgrim Fa-Hsien of the early fifth century, indicate that the people at first worshiped the Brahmanical gods, while conversion to Buddhism came later. By the late seventh century the kingdom of Śrīvijaya had been established in Sumatra, Java, and the Malay Peninsula by the Śailendras, 'Kings of the Mountains,' who seem to be descendants of the Pallavas of north India; they were Buddhists, and encouraged the worship of Buddha among their subjects. In the late eighth century, in 778, the Chandi Kalasan was dedicated to Tārā, female embodiment of the ideal of compassion.

Under these same kings a wonderful and unique monument was made on the Dieng Plateau, the Barabudur (fig. 519). Among the palm groves and volcanic mountains it rises over 100 feet, covered with sculpture, the most elaborate expression of Buddhist doctrine and instrument of worship made by the followers of the Compassionate One. It is perfectly orientated to the cardinal points of the compass, the east gate being the main entrance for the worshiper, who could begin a circumambulation more extensive than any other in the Buddhist world. There are six square terraces topped by three circular ones, making nine in all, a propitious number. The lower ones are galleries lined with panels of relief sculpture, illustrating narratives inspired by Buddhist texts. First, on a level once hidden, are scenes of violence and suffering, the hell of torment, the earthly desires that must be buried as the sculpture was buried; then comes the life of Gautama as given in the Lalitavistara Sūtra and jātaka stories, and higher up, miracles of the Bodhisattvas. As the pilgrim ascends the sculpture becomes less narrative, until he reaches the three circular terraces where there are figures of the Dhyāni Buddhas carved in the round — he has left the world of action behind and has reached the world of the spirit. The Buddhas were placed in small shrines of the dāgoba type, perforated so that one could see them inside, and the whole great stūpa was crowned by a dāgoba. The last of the Buddhas was left unfinished by the carver; purposely, no doubt, for the pilgrim who reached the highest stage needed no more than a suggestion to spur his imagination.

It has been estimated that if all the sculpture, nearly 1000 panels of reliefs, were placed end to end it would reach 3 miles, and there are as well some 432 niches containing images of the Buddha a little more than life-size (fig. 520). Cut out of the dark gray, pitted volcanic rock of that area, a most unsympathetic material was used to create beings of the utmost beauty. We do not know the name of the designer of this great symbol of the Law, which has all the clarity of a holy chart, or Mandala, nor do we know the names of the countless carvers who filled their panels (fig. 521) with gracious figures, lovely trees, flowers, birds, and animals. They are done with a tenderness and sweetness that surpasses anything done in India itself. Based upon the Gupta ideal and canon of proportion, but less remote, they mark the culmination of the Indian ability to produce spiritual qualities in sculptural and architectural forms.

In the medieval period, especially from the eleventh through the thirteenth centuries, both Buddhist and Hindu gods served to inspire the image makers whose works are touched with the same violence that had marked medieval sculpture on the mainland. Śiva with his three eyes, Vishnu riding on his Garuda vehicle, Durgā lifting her arms to strike, Ganeśa the elephant god, looking sleepy and beguiling but seated on skulls — all are done with a love of elaborate detail, prompted by the medieval desire for richness. Even the Buddhist sculpture shows the same tendency toward profusion: jewels are intricate, many deities have several arms, and are surrounded by flowers and attributes, though the faces have a serene sweetness reminiscent of Barabudur.

Cambodia: In the ninth century a Śailendra prince went from Java into the country of the Khmers, which we call Cambodia, and established himself as devarāja, 'god-king,' Jayavarman II. The cult he instituted to make himself stronger was based on the principle that the king is to his kingdom as God is to the world, and he, by ceremony, allied himself with Śiva. He left Java to go to a country that already had a splendid art tradition based on that of Gupta India; it had come with the commerce of the direct sea routes to the Indian coast, and by land through the Môn state of Dvāravatī (Burma). He found the Khmer people divided into two kingdoms — Chên-la of the Land, and Chên-la of the Sea — which he united and welded into a strong state.

From the pre-Khmer art, which followed the Indian rules so closely, there developed new forms in architecture and sculpture, which still make the world marvel, the best known being the Angkor Vat and the Angkor Thom. In sculpture we can see the change taking place as we look at the majestic Hari-Hara (fig. 522). It is a combination of Vishnu and Śiva in one body, the Śiva side distinguished by the 'wild locks' (reduced to waving lines on the tiara) and a trace of the third vertical eye in the middle of the forehead. It might well be a portrait of a local chieftain, tall, poised, with head held high. He looks out with a steady gaze, eyes wide open, and with his mouth set in a straight line under a light mustache. The several arms are unfortunately broken, and we notice the stumps with surprise, for the rest of the man looks so normal the extra growth from the shoulder is almost shocking. His drapery is noteworthy, a very light loin cloth folded over to form a flap of crisply cut, flat pleats.

The evolution from the ninth century on is toward a heavier, more massive form. In the tenth century, the hair was reduced to a pattern of snail-shell motifs, fitting the head almost like a skullcap, which meets the forehead in a sharp horizontal line, with an equally horizontal emphasis on brows and mouth. The cutting around the eyes was sharply and cleanly done, as it was on the mouth, with its strangely compelling smile. The lips, brows, and mustache are often outlined in two thin lines. The Indian ideal of the oval head and delicate nose has been influenced by the racial characteristics of these people who had wide, flat foreheads, flat noses, and thick lips. In the eleventh (fig. 523), twelfth, and thirteenth centuries the massiveness gives way to suppleness and grace, and, in the Buddhist images, a more profound spirituality, particularly in the Buddhas in meditation. One of their favorite themes is that of the Buddha raised above a flood by the Nāga king in the period following the Illumination; the body of the snake is coiled beneath the Blessed One, who is completely oblivious of the world, and of the many cobra heads forming a protecting halo behind him. The smooth volumes of the central figure and the minute scales of the serpent heads form an interesting contrast of textures.

Worship of the Nāgas dates far back into the past of this country and Burma, and is still important to remote tribes. Small wonder then that so many snakes are used as sculptural and architectural motifs. In both the Angkor Vat and the Angkor Thom they are to be found as balustrades, fountain heads, and decorative finials. Rising out of the jungle, reflected in countless pools, it is appropriate that these monuments should have so many reminders of the kings of the waters, who were supposed to be the legendary founders of the race.

The capital and residence of Jayavarman's line was the Angkor Thom, the 'Great City,' started in the ninth century and used until the wars with Annam and Siam in the fourteenth. It was planned as a huge square, surrounded by a moat and walls 192 yards long on each side. In the exact center, in the late twelfth and thirteenth centuries, the great mass of the Bayon rose, a world-mountain in stone, tower piled upon tower.

Each of the 51 square spires is ornamented with masklike faces, many of them 9 feet high, facing the four directions (fig. 524). They were Buddhist under Jayavarman VII (c.1182–1201), who had identified himself with Lokeśvara (Avalokiteśvara, Bodhisattva of Mercy); then, under the later kings who worshiped Hindu gods, they were dedicated to Śiva. Whether regarded as Buddhist or Śaivite, they are completely Cambodian, broad, flat, and smiling, the expression of composure surviving the damage of time and the cleavage of individual stones on which they were carved.

A mile and a half south of the present city a temple was started in the middle of the twelfth century, the Angkor Vat, the last of the tremendous undertakings of the Khmers and renowned all over the world (fig. 525). Though we know now that it is part of a gradual growth in the art and science of building, preceded by numerous smaller and less ambitious temples based on Indian prototypes and not sprung miraculously in the jungle, it is a supreme achievement of Khmer genius. An outer gate on the west side allowed entrance to the worshipers of Vishnu and the kingly representative, for this is Brahmanical, not Buddhist — it was the home of the god and the tomb of the king. Down a spacious roadway, 220 yards long and over 25 feet wide, bordered by a Nāga balustrade, the visitor walks toward the finely proportioned mass of the temple. Directly ahead is the stately central tower, which rises 200 feet above the top step, with smaller towers at each angle of the rectangular central shrine, consisting of terraces and covered galleries and steps rising toward the tower, each level being twice as high as the one below it.

There is genius in the building, and genius in the sculpture that lines the corridors and graces the towers. Vishnu in his several avatārs, Śiva, the kings and their consorts, processions, battles, slaves, dancing girls and palace attendants, humans and spirits, animals, birds, trees, and flowers, all carved with great decorative skill in the sandstone that faces the laterite core of the temple. The reliefs lining the corridors, miles of them, are cut so delicately into the stone that the effect is like an embroidery or tapestry, but there is so much energy in the figures that they are far more powerful than anything produced by the tedious needle arts. One of the most impressive is the Churning of the Sea, the Battle between the Aśuras (demons) and Devas (gods), who wrapped the world serpent around Mt. Mandala and had a tug of war, each side hoping to gain possession of the amrita, sacred beverage, which they intended to churn up. At one time a terrible poison came up, which would have destroyed them, but Śiva saved the day by drinking it. A white elephant came up, and a goddess, Lakshmi, who became the consort of Vishnu. Finally the amrita appeared and was snatched by the Devas, which gave them ascendency forever over the Aśuras. Vishnu is present in his tortoise avatār supporting the mountain, and in heroic form above. His arms, brandishing his attributes, seem almost to move, his knees wide apart (the legs looking very much like a frog's legs) and his ankles bent at an unbelievable angle give the impression of an elastic springiness characteristic of many of the other figures, too. Whether they fly or tug they are possessed of enormous tension, suggested largely by the use of curving lines in all parts of the bodies and costumes, and by poses of extreme angularity, which were related to the dance.

In contrast to these beings of the spirit world, some slaves are shown in another section: thin, drooping, hardly able to stand under the weight of the yokes around their necks, they are driven mercilessly by guards, who hold their whips high with an energy as terrible as the gods'. Perhaps the stones used in building the temple were brought through the steaming jungle by just such pitiful captives. Then there are the kings riding out on elephants, surrounded by men and women of the court in magnificent processions, which, seen here, can also be read about in the account of the Chinese traveler Chou Ta-Kuan, who was there in 1296 and saw such pageantry as he had not dreamed of.

Among the narrative reliefs the story of Rāma is recorded in a peculiarly Cambodian way: though the Rāmāyana is faithfully followed, the idiom used in telling it is so different from that of the mother country that we hardly recognize it as the theme so popular among the Rājput painters. Rāma, going out to shoot the golden hind, stands with his knees wide apart and pulls his bow with a magnificent gesture worthy of a dramatic dancer; the trees show a finesse and grace reminiscent of Persian miniatures, each leaf meticulously done. Rāvana in his chariot, with his many heads and arms, is more terrible than in any other representation, filled as he is with the incredible energy of the Khmers. Even in their dramatic episodes a very low relief is used, and the modeling is flattened within that slight projection. The effect is more like the Achaemenid reliefs of Persepolis than any of the medieval Indian sculpture, which is closer in time and space to Cambodia, but this has a sophistication and grace reminiscent of late Persian art.

Facing one of the pools, a frieze of dancing girls or devatas (fig. 526) was carved in a somewhat higher relief than the narrative sculptures.

Their long supple bodies are lightly covered with transparent dhotīs, folded over flat girdles in the crisp Cambodian fashion. Their head-dresses look like miniature versions of the Angkor Vat, amazingly intri-cate towers rising above their elaborate coiffures, which lend a vertical touch to their flat, horizontal faces, and are quite unrelated to their earth-bound feet. Again we are reminded of the time, eight hundred years ago, when harem and court existed in the present wilderness in a splendor and color that can only be hinted at in the red sandstone. This great temple, and the Bayon, and some lovely bronze figures were the last expressions of Khmer power in art, which faded away, as did their political power, before their conquerors, the Siamese.

Siam and Burma: Siam, like these many other neighboring nations, received its early art impulse from India when Buddhism was intro-duced. The first images were of the Gupta type, having come directly from Amarāvatī, and show the power of the Gupta ideal in sculpture. Then gradually local racial characteristics change the canon in Siam, and we witness another delightful variation from the Indian classic norm. The sculpture faithfully reflects cultural and political changes to a re-markable degree.

To the trained eye the changes may be noted after the fifth century, when Môn characteristics appear; the faces become rounder than the Indian oval, the eyebrows are arched high over a long, aquiline nose, and a smile, almost of disdain, is given to the Buddha figures. The Môns came from near-by Burma, and the sculpture and architecture of the two countries have, at times, great similarities. From the seventh through the twelfth centuries the Hindu-Javanese influence made itself felt, as the Śailendras extended their power from Sumatra and Java and finally became leaders of the Khmers; from the tenth through the thirteenth centuries, in the peak of Khmer power, the broad, flat faces of these Cambodians, the double line used to define the mouth with its strange smile, become a part of Siamese art; some of these developments took place in art centers quite close together, differing because of local reli-gious tradition and trade affiliation. Finally, from the eleventh through the fourteenth centuries at Chiengsen and Suk'ot'ai, a new group from southwest China, the Tai people, established themselves; then the true Siamese style emerges. Again the long nose is considered beautiful, as it was in Ceylon, and, as in Ceylon, a flame is added to the ushnisha mound, making the face vertical in emphasis; all that remains of the Khmer ideal of beauty is the double line around the mouth. Bronze figures of the period (fig. 527) are slim and burnished and have an aristocratic aloofness bordering on hauteur. Drapery is shown clinging to the body, defining curving volumes and smooth surfaces that catch the light, for the metal is highly polished, and all textures — hair, skin, and cloth — gleam with equal brilliance.

In both Siam and Burma, architecture at first shows dependence upon India, and in both countries the Buddhist stūpas are close to the dāgoba type of Ceylon; in the temples (fig. 528), however, they develop an exuberant style, using richly ornamented cornices and curving roof lines more exaggerated and fantastic even than those of China, which they resemble in some respects. There is a fancifulness and a gift of ornament, which have rightly made Bangkok and Mandalay synonymous with the color and romance of the East. Though the temple is still essentially a reconstruction of the cosmos in miniature, as it was in India, the airy grace of pinnacles and roofs show the mark of a genius that is non-Indian and local.

Tibet: In the highest country in the world, Tibet, art and Buddhism come together. The early native religion, Bön or Pön, had been one of nature worship, with emphasis on sacrifice to demons, both human and animal sacrifice, made by sorcerer-priests. Two young princesses were sent to Tibet in the seventh century A.D. to be consorts of the king — one from Nepal, and one from China. Both were Buddhists. Together they won the king away from sorcery and demon worship and persuaded him to accept the Eight Fold Path. Thanks to their success in that conversion they were regarded as earthly incarnations of Buddhist deities, the Green Tārā and the White Tārā.

Even in India there had been a certain emphasis on spells and charms in Buddhism; the Buddhist believed that the repetition of formulas (dhāranis or mantras) and the achievement of a meditative state through yoga would put him in touch with some of the deities of the Mahāyāna pantheon. There had also been a belief, influenced by Hinduism, that male gods had female consorts, sisters, even dual aspects (śakti). Tārā was a female manifestation of the merciful Bodhisattva Avalokiteśvara, and was much beloved by Buddhists of north India, who held to this Tantric type of worship. In the Pāla empire, which controlled northeast India from A.D. 750 to 1197, and in Nepal in the medieval period, some sculpture and painting of singular beauty had come into being (figs. 529, 530). The figures were slim and elegant with the heads almost heart-shaped and gracefully tilted; like Hindu images, they frequently had four or more arms. This was the type of painting and sculpture carried into near-by Tibet by the missionaries and teachers, who went in to convert the mountain people in the eleventh and twelfth centuries.

In the eighth century a monk from Nepal, familiar with Tantric formulas, was summoned to the court. This Guru Padma Sambhava proceeded to subdue local demons, perform miracles, and establish the system of Lamaism, the Lama being a superior man, the principal leader in a monastery. He became so adept at charms that, instead of dying, he disappeared into the air and was never seen again. In temple banners he is always painted as wearing a flowing red robe and a peaked red cap.

Though he came to Tibet to drive out magic practices, he had adopted quite a few himself, and the Buddhist church there had begun to sponsor devil dancing, exorcising, and rituals undreamed of by Gautama Buddha and his orthodox followers. By the eleventh century reform was very much needed, and a southerner from Sumatra, Atīśa, came up to purify the corrupt church. Contact with the Mongols came in the twelfth century, and through them, closer contact with China. When the Mongols conquered China, Lamaism became popular under Kubilai Khan, and there was an interchange of art motifs between the two countries, as well as a popular acceptance of demons and spirits that still colors Chinese folklore and practice. Even when the Ming rulers came to power and had driven the Mongols out in the fourteenth century, the emperor of the Yung-lo period summoned the most noted Tibetan teacher, Tsong-kha-pa, to discuss doctrine with him.

Tsong-kha-pa, like Atīśa, was a reformer. He instituted celibacy for the monks, and founded the Church of the Yellow Caps, Ge-Lugs-Pa, with headquarters in Lhasa, which had been the home of the king of Tibet. The head of the church became chief of state, combining temporal and spiritual power. He introduced the two-Lama system. The Dalai Lama (Great Lama), who was believed to be a reincarnation of Avalokiteśvara, had a fortress-palace in Lhasa, high up in the mountains, called the Potala. The present one was built in the seventeenth century. The second Lama, the Panchan Lama, had headquarters in Tashilhunpo.

Since there was little carving on a grand scale in the palaces, the walls were hung instead with painted banners, brilliant in color, rigidly conventional in composition. It is difficult to date Tibetan paintings, because the rules for making them were handed down unchanged from generation to generation, and so a nineteenth-century work may look very much like a fifteenth-century one. Pounces, pricked patterns, were used over and over again to transfer the designs to the silk or other cloth, on which flat colors were then filled in — strong blues, reds, greens, yellow, and gold. Texts had to be carefully followed in narrative detail, and canons of proportion set the figure types. Here, as we might suppose, ideas from India and China met. The form of the banners is Chinese — vertical wall hangings which can be rolled up — and they are often mounted on Chinese brocades and silk. Details (which could be done with some freedom by the individual painter) were often Chinese, especially flowers, cloud scrolls, and architectural motifs. The most usual subjects were: the life of Gautama as given in the sūtras; deities of the Mahāyāna pantheon (showing the tutelary one in the center, and lesser ones in medallions joined by rainbow-hued ribbons to him or her); the eighty-four sorcerers, alchemists, or church fathers, often done in a tree-of-life design; and still another, the Wheel of Life, a chart of man's existence divided into segments, a mandala used by sorcerers.

Even the monks could coerce spirits. Each monk chose his own divinity, which he could bring, by spells and charms, to do jobs for him. In moments of ecstasy he could assume attributes and become identified with this divinity, who might have male or female form. Ritual objects include the prayer wheel (a cylinder in a box with prayers attached, which could be turned by a perfunctory worshiper who gained merit at each revolution of the wheel); the vajra or thunderbolt, bell, dagger, horn, conch shell, and a drum made of a human skull with skin stretched over it. Human bones were used as rosaries and ornaments of various sorts.

In sculpture the Nepalese style was largely followed, especially in the casting of small bronze figurines, which were made in great numbers. They are notable for grace of form and contour, for the heart-shaped faces of north India, and for their elaborate jewels. The White Tārā was made with a third eye in her forehead, holding a lotus, and the Green Tārā shown seated in 'royal ease' with one foot hanging down. Their male counterpart, Avalokiteśvara, was often done in his eleven-headed aspect; having promised to heed all the cries of the distressed in the world, his head split into many pieces, which were gathered together by Amitābha and assembled into ten heads, topped by Amitābha's own image. The Bodhisattva usually has many arms, which reach out to carry souls to Amitābha's Western Paradise, or hold comforting symbols of mercy.

Since even the gentlest being is thus shown in a rather terrible way with his many heads and arms, we are not surprised to find demons and demon-quellers done with a fierceness born of mountain winds and snows. Yamāntaka (queller of Yama, king of hell) has many heads, the principal one being of a bull or boar. He has thirty-four hands, grasping various attributes, and holds his śakti (female essence) in a close embrace, being incomplete without her; like Śiva, he tramples upon a dwarf. Indeed, there are so many Hindu elements in this art it seems much more Śaivite than Buddhist, a weird step-cousin of the serene figures from Sārnāth and Barabudur, tempered by storms and fury, and the ever-present threat of death. Out of the compassionate teachings of the Buddha this Lamaistic, Tantric form has grown and still flourishes in Tibet, while in the Ganges Valley Gautama is forgotten.

China

THE early Neolithic culture of China is much like that of the same age in America and Eurasia — men hunted and fished, raised grain, made tools

ANCIENT CHINA and weapons of stone, used the bow and arrow, made baskets and cloth and pottery, and domesticated the pig and dog. Pottery of those early days has been discovered in sites widely distributed over North China, from Kansu in the West to southern Manchuria and Shantung in the East. A great variety of clays were used in the different localities to produce wares that were either plain or decorated with incised or painted designs.

Among the most striking examples are the large, thin, well-potted jars from Kansu (fig. 531), painted with broad swirling lines of black, red, and purplish chocolate brown on the reddish-buff clay. The powerful sweeping curves and geometric patterns of this ware show a number of similarities with early pottery from the Near East, though actual contact between the two regions is still a matter of conjecture. In Honan, pots of heavy, coarse gray clay have been found, sometimes with mat impressions, while from Shantung more delicate pieces have been recovered, made of thin, fine-grained black clay with a highly polished surface. Of the many shapes used, the hollow-legged tripod, *li*, is peculiar to China and unknown in any other culture area that flourished at the same time. The earliest examples of these Chinese potteries probably date from before 3000 B.C., and the Neolithic cultures continued to flourish in the outlying regions until about 500 B.C., long after the Bronze Age had come, and Chinese civilization had been developing for many centuries in the Yellow River plain.

In the historic period, called Shang-Yin (*c.*1766–1122 B.C.), a white clay was used to make handsome pieces with designs carved on the surface. The patterns were linear, geometric versions of insect and animal forms, of which the cicada or locust (symbol of immortality), birds, and dragons were often used on the body of the vessel, while masks suggesting the heads of water buffalo, rams, tigers, and deer were raised in relief. The background was filled with abstract fret meanders called cloud-and-thunder. Bone, ivory, jade, and marble (figs. 532, 533) were carved with the same delicate and intricate incised lines, and bronze ritual vessels with similar patterns were cast from molds.

The Shang people had the highest standards of craftsmanship, great imaginative power, and a rich and complex symbolism, of which, so far, we understand almost nothing. Their material culture has gradually been revealed to us since 1929, when systematic archaeological excavations were started on the site of the last Shang capital (c.1350–1122 b.c.), at Anyang in Honan. The palace of the king, houses for the nobility, and workmen's quarters were discovered. The walls of these buildings were made of pounded earth; in the finer structures, painted wooden beams were used, and bronze fittings. The royal tombs had been carefully prepared down under the earth, and yielded every evidence of elaborate funeral ceremony and burial, including the sacrifice of human and animal victims. In these tombs, as well as in the countless smaller pits used for the less important burials, the excavators found bronze vessels, pottery fragments, tortoise shell, cowrie shells, gold, jade, and silk. These were products of a feudal society, in which the king and his nobles hunted, engaged in battle, held court, and performed sacrifices; artisans, who lived in a special district, made most of the beautiful objects used by the highborn.

From inscriptions on oracle bones, which are the only historical records of the time, and from the Book of Poetry, the Shih Ching, written down a little later, as well as from a study of the tomb relics, we can re-create a picture of the Shang people. They could already express ideas in a pictograph writing, so developed that it gives evidence of having been started long before, in the legendary times of the Hsia. They asked advice of the spirits of departed ancestors, who could bring success in hunting, war, agriculture, and other activities, or could plague them with sickness and misfortune. Therefore the living served them with food and sacrifice, and consulted the diviners, who wrote questions on the oracle bones and interpreted the answers from the spirit world. Ritual and ceremony, the music of drums and 'sonorous jade,' the rustle of silk robes of state, the fragrance of sacrifice on the altars formed an important part of the basis of early Chinese life.

On the altars were vessels made by the bronze casters, who were the greatest masters of the craft the world has ever known. Chariot fittings, weapons, personal ornaments, and household objects were made in the artisan's quarters as were also the vases, tripods, cups, and containers of ceremonial usage; and similar pieces must have been made in other parts of China. The evolution of the different types of vessels is a rewarding but intricate study, which we can only touch upon here, examining the most common. In nearly all of the graves, the *ku* (fig. 534) and *chüeh* (fig. 535) were found, one used as a libation cup, the other for heating liquid over the fire. The *yü*, a bucket shape with a handle, was also associated with liquids. A sturdier container for meat or cereal was the *ting* (fig. 536) with its three legs joining the body at abrupt angles, and with a decoration called the *t'ao-t'ieh* on the body; this ornament consisted usually of arched eyebrows or horns, wide-open eyes, a nose and upper lip, but with the lower lip omitted. The *t'ao-t'ieh* was used on many objects, sometimes in high relief, sometimes in low, and it seems almost to change expression as one looks at it. It was infused with the dynamic power that inspired all Shang design, and which makes a group of vessels brought together on the family altar (fig. 537) compelling in vigor, mystery, and beauty of form.

Having reached a high degree of culture, devoted more to the cultivation of the arts than warfare, the Shang people were set upon by the Chou, who occupied the western borders. Anyang was destroyed. The conquered people fled in different directions, though some stayed to keep alive their traditions and to tutor the barbarians, who established a dynasty that lasted from c.1122–256 B.C. Early Chou art follows Shang models carefully, and the Chou conquerors soon adopted the laws, ceremonies, and precepts of the more civilized inhabitants of the Yellow River country. Chou bronzes are marked with longer inscriptions, which tell the ancestors of their marriages, of honors come to the family, and of all kinds of changes and events appropriate to these memorials that were to last forever.

In the latter part of the Chou period, texts were gathered together and written down, which, for more than two thousand years, constituted the bulwark, the very life blood, of Chinese culture. The *I Ching*, Book of Changes, was a record of divination practices, telling (among other things) about the use of milfoil in long and short pieces, which represented respectively the male (Yang, light, fire, spring, summer, power, and strength, the active principle), and the female (Yin, dark, moon, earth, water, cold, autumn, winter, the receptive, passive principle); the long, or Yang lines coupled with two short, or Yin, lines, could be arranged in eight sets of three, and are called the *pa kua*. Another way of representing Yang and Yin is by a circle divided into two parts by a waving line, the Yang part colored red, the Yin all black. As in India, the Chinese thought

the male incomplete without the female and *vice versa,* but they chose
abstract linear symbols, not human beings embracing, to suggest these
dual modalities, the positive and negative elements.

The other classics of history, poetry, etiquette, and ceremony were re-
cited and sung, learned by priests, politicians, and tutors. The king had to
be well versed in rites and ceremonies, for by acceptable sacrifice he could
bring to all his subjects prosperity, good crops, and favorable seasons.
High-ranking nobles made sacrifices to mountains and rivers, and heads
of clans and families had their ritual duties to perform, all for the purposes
of protection. A large class of men who assisted in these rites, perhaps
descendants of the Shang diviners, went from place to place, not engaging
in manual labor, but keeping tradition pure.

Probably about the fourth century B.C., one of China's greatest philosophers, Lao-tzu, taught that men should be humble, simple, close to nature,
and should avoid the distractions of public office. His teaching of the *Tao,*
or the Way, was based on a retreat from life to solitary places, where the
individual might discover himself akin to other living beings, in harmony
with the laws of the universe. A somewhat earlier philosopher, Confucius,
believed the good life could come only to those who fulfilled all their
moral obligations, i.e. to the state, the community, and the family, relying
on ceremony, etiquette, and precepts from the past for guidance. Confucius and his followers and opponents lived in a time of great literary activity, the period of the Spring and Autumn Annals (722–481 B.C.), after the
Chou capital had been moved from Ch'ang-an to Lo-yang, a time that
profoundly influenced Chinese life for centuries to come.

In the ritual bronzes there had been a decline in technical ability and
imaginative power after the early years. Toward the end of the Chou
period, as smaller states broke away from the weakening ruling house,
there was a renaissance, a new cycle of creative activity among the bronze
casters. New shapes became popular (fig. 538), as well as new versions of
the old; new patterns appeared on the surfaces, intertwining dragons, serpents, and birds, twisting and turning with so much energy that parts of
their bodies became detached and appeared in unexpected places. The
t'ao-t'ieh still is used, with eyes popping out like a Pekingese dog's. Much
of this dynamic design is contained within bands or registers, done in
delicate surface patterns of knobs and dots not unlike embroidery stitches.
Bronze bells and gongs of various sizes, often richly ornamented, were
cast in great numbers for ritual use. Circular mirrors (fig. 539) were polished on one side and adorned with designs in relief on the other; some
were carried by priests as part of their regalia; others were used in every-

day life. Jade was carved in designs similar to the bronzes, often done in a circle, symbol of heaven and of the king, the holder of heaven's mandate on earth (fig. 540). Buckles and hooks and other personal ornaments were made of jade, and of bronze inlaid with gold and silver, all intricate, curving and energetic, done by master craftsmen who used traditional Chinese designs as well as newer, barbaric motifs introduced by the neighboring nomad tribes. Many of these small ornaments were given to barbarian chieftains as marks of esteem, and by them were taken all over north Asia, and even into Europe when pressure drove them to the West. Certainly the animal forms, the interlacing patterns, the delicate fancifulness of design, all of which resulted from the fusion of Asiatic cultures, seem to have inspired some of the medieval art of Europe.

ONE of the warring states, the Ch'in, absorbed weaker states and overthrew the last Chou king in 249 B.C. Again the sturdier westerner con-

IMPERIAL CHINA quered and began a period of consolidation and reform (221–207 B.C.) that laid the foundation for the Chinese economy and administrative organization for centuries to come. The head of the ruling house for the first time assumed the title of Emperor, Shih Huang-ti, and he used every means possible to bring unity to China. He joined together and built up isolated local fortifications into the Great Wall. He had canals built, roads widened, better communication systems established, and, for himself, a fabulous palace erected. Though what he did was for the power and unification of China, he was not loved by the people. He taxed them unmercifully for his great projects; he offended them by burning the books, which were their treasured links with the past, and by throwing their ritual tripods into the river. Later, when he wanted to think himself one of the long line of hereditary rulers rather than an innovator, he tried to recover the bronze vessels so that he could perform the kingly sacrificial ceremonies, but, according to legend, a dragon cut the cord being used to haul out the *ting*, and it dropped back into the river, safe from the hands of the usurper.

Shih Huang-ti's vision of glory for China was passed on to the next dynasty, the Han (207 B.C.–A.D. 220), especially under the Han emperor Wu Ti (140–87 B.C.), who extended the limits of China west and south, sent his soldiers to subdue the Turkic tribes of the Hsiung-nu and other nomads of the Tarim basin, colonized Korea, and attached Tongking near Cambodia.

The tomb of one of his generals, Ho Ch'ü-ping, a veteran of the Hsiung-nu wars, is near Wu Ti's tomb in Shensi, and is an interesting combination of Chinese and barbarian forms. It consists of an earth mound 50 feet high (the Emperor wanted it to look like part of a mountain range, but it is smaller than his own 140 foot tumulus), with great boulders at its base, some carved, some waterworn and smooth, the largest weighing 15 tons, all of them brought from quite a distance. Originally they must have been placed in pairs to line a spirit path guarding the approach to the tomb, much as sphinxes were in Egypt and Assyria; but the forms are barbarian rather than Near Eastern. The most striking is that of a horse trampling a warrior beneath him (fig. 541), massive, heavy, quite unlike the fanciful and graceful figures in other parts of China. Both man and animal are of a Central Asiatic type, the man undoubtedly a Hsiung-nu Hun, who grasps his curved bow in his hand as he lies beneath the horse. The idea of a conquered person being trampled upon is more extensively used in Western Asiatic art than in Central or Eastern Asia; it is known to have been used by the Hittites, and later, by the Sassanian Persians, in their investiture scenes (fig. 449). The other carved stones suggest Turkic and Scythian ideas of combat and struggle, animals with their feet drawn up under them, and animals of totemic significance. Since a bull and a rat are among them, they may have been related to the Duodenary cycle of the Hsiung-nu, who divided their days and nights into the hours of the horse, bull, rat, et cetera, as the Chinese learned to do from them.

In Western China, too, in Szechwan province, a number of tombs and memorials still survive from this period. The pillars of Shên (figs. 542, 543) are very handsome, and quite Chinese in form and decoration. The stone shafts are carved to imitate the tile roof and wooden brackets that were normally used in the Han house; three sides are marked with symbolic creatures of the directions — the Red Bird on the south, the Dragon on the east, and the Tiger on the west. The *t'ao-t'ieh* appears, and all manner of strange pixy people, fantastic birds, and animals. The inscriptions (done in beautiful Han calligraphy 'powerful as brandished lances, or waves of the sea blown by the wind') indicate that Shên was a prefect and military governor of Tongking.

In the eastern peninsular province, Shantung, there are other famous monuments of this period. One, the offering chamber of the Wu family called Wu Liang Tzŭ (fig. 544), is especially well known because of the many rubbings that have been taken from it. In registers that remind one of late Chou bronzes, stories of all kinds are told with a wonderful animation and skill, the particular product of Chinese genius. Both Confucianism and Taoism are represented by historical scenes, by pictures of virtuous persons of the past, and by imaginative worlds of sky and water inhabited by deities who personify forces of nature.

In a very low relief that projects less than half an inch from the background, the men and women in long robes bow ceremoniously to each other, or attend banquets, or watch Shih Huang-ti try to fish the ritual *ting* out of the river; one is such a loyal son, that, though he is in his sixties, he plays about on the floor like a child to make his eighty-year-old parents feel young again. Of the spirit world, the storm-god orders his minions to roll out the lightning or pour rain out of bowls, the deity of the Great Dipper rides high, and Hsi Wang Mu, Queen Mother of the West, receives the King of the East in her pavilion, or watches her heavenly guardians, who protect the peach tree of Immortality. Mortal men ride in chariots, pulled by spirited horses, the famous horses of Han, heavy of body, with delicate feet and arching necks, while the immortals in their own realms ride fantastic sky and sea creatures. Though the figures are flat as silhouettes, and the carvers are not interested in spacious backgrounds, there is throughout a feeling of life, vitality, and the tension of carefully related forms.

The other famous Shantung slabs are from the Mount of the Hall of Filial Piety, the Hsiao T'ang Shan. They are also from an offering chamber, and are as flat in projection as the Wu group, with figures incised into the background. There, too, long-robed men bow to each other, or ride high-stepping horses, or engage in very realistic warfare, hanging up the severed heads of their enemies by their long hair; or they go out to hunt rabbits and deer with hounds at their heels. Again we have an excellent way of studying their dress, weapons, and practices.

By this time burial customs called for clay figurines, which were put into the tombs to represent the people and things beloved by the departed spirits. Thus, in miniature, we see the essentials of Han life. The Chinese house (fig. 545) was a tiled-roof structure, consisting of several pavilions or wings that formed a compound and courtyards, set off from the street by a wall. The central building, in which the head of the family lived, faced south. It was approached by a ramp or steps, recalling the ancient practice of building above flood level in the Yellow River region. The sloping roof was upheld by posts and brackets that became the essential feature of Chinese domestic and religious architecture in the centuries to come. Inside, in the home of a well-to-do Chinese, the rooms were spacious; furniture consisted of chests, small tables, or arm rests, and movable bedding rolls, which were put away in the daytime. The kitchen was below the first floor or in a separate wing; the second floor seems to have been the women's quarters. We know that the exposed wooden beams were gaily painted and lacquered, and that pictures were painted or hung on the walls, though we know it only through literary references, for no large Han paintings have survived to the present day. Bronze fittings were carefully designed and made; even the smallest fragments are treasured still for their beauty or humor.

Out in the courtyard pigs, dogs, chickens, and children added to the color of the household. The clay figurines of the period, and the stamped tiles depicting Han animals, birds, and people, give such a lively picture of Chinese life two thousand years ago that they are sought today as great works of art, rather than as minor products of an ancient civilization. That civilization was carried by Han public servants into far provinces and distant lands. In Korea, in the tomb of the Chinese governor and his wife, the excavators found beautiful lacquer boxes, toilet articles, and ornaments, the lacquer work painted red, yellow, green and black in patterns so full of energy and fantasy that it is hard to believe a human hand produced them. Out on the deserts of Central Asia, on the trade routes, other fragments of Han life have come to light, including some woven tapestries of complex colors and designs, as fanciful as their sculpture and painting, showing a blending of forms akin to the Near East and the purely Chinese dragons and spirits.

They felt very close to the world of spirits then. Taoism, which had originated as a movement to simplify the life of the individual, had now developed into an elaborate mystical cult involving magical practices of all kinds and peopled with a great variety of immortal beings with miraculous qualities. The Taoist priesthood sought immortality by compounding drugs, tried to turn base metals into gold (one of the ingredients of the Elixir of Life), and engaged in alchemy, as popular then in China as it would be a thousand years later in Europe in the Middle Ages. Magic writing and charts were in vogue, and had their influence on the patterns of bronze mirrors (fig. 546), which were turned out in considerable quantities, especially those carried by the priests and used in burial ceremonies. Even ritual vessels were ornamented with fairy forms, clouds, and heavenly beings. Among the smaller bronze objects, contact with the 'barbarians' is reflected in animal combat scenes similar to those found in South Russia, Siberia, and the Ordos area just north of the bend in the Yellow River. Animals common to those places — bears (fig. 547), panthers, moose, mountain goats, mules, etc. — were woven into the intricate patterns of belthooks, incense burners, and weapons.

It was a time of political and of creative power, drawing from the past, enriched by many contacts outside the Middle Kingdom. Silk was carried halfway across the world to Rome, palaces were filled with beautiful objects brought from far away, hands were busy making jades, bronzes, lacquers, silks, potteries, pavilions, and gardens unrivaled elsewhere — small wonder that a modern Chinese still calls himself a Son of Han.

The Han emperors had heard of the teachings of the Buddha with interest, and Buddhist texts had been translated from Sanskrit into Chinese soon after A.D. 150, but Buddhism had not deeply touched the lives of average Chinese until the troubled times of the Six Dynasties period (A.D. 317–589), when all of north China was overrun by Tatar tribes. As they established themselves in their new territory, they brought their own religious practices and beliefs. Wanderers though they were, they had been converted to Buddhism by Central Asiatic missionaries, who taught them that they would gain merit by making images and fashioning sanctuaries in the name of the Buddha. One group, the Wei, were particularly active in western and northern China.

Up in Shansi province, just south of the Great Wall, they began, in A.D. 414, to hollow out a sandstone cliff at Yün-kang, near Ta-t'ung, making grottoes that they filled with Indianlike sculpture following directions given in texts brought from India to this new land over the Central Asian tracks. They had, as well, small bronze and clay images of Buddha and other Buddhist deities, the Bodhisattva, the lesser deities, and the stūpa, all somewhat changed when made by the oasis artist who had not seen the Indian originals. As the Tatars and their Chinese subjects attempted to follow models and written rules, they produced results at first that were neither Indian nor Chinese (fig. 548). All of the essentials were there — the ūrnā and the ushnisha, the long ear lobes, the hands in the appropriate mudrā, the long robe, the smooth torso — but none of the Indian fluidity of form of an organism infused with life was there, or the spirited energy of China. They are simple, massive symbols of ideas, with faces and drapery cut according to formulas, not copied from nature. There is a great Buddha 32 feet high set in front of a flaming mandorla (fig. 549), and there are literally thousands of smaller ones of different sizes, in high and low relief, all originally colored. Gradually Chinese characteristics creep in — the eyes become more slanting; in architecture the tile roof replaces the Indian arch; and Chinese dress is used instead of the dhotī cloth, thus covering more of the body by drapery, which falls in flat patterned folds.

In the middle of the fifth century, persecutions were ordered by an emperor who was influenced against Buddhism by Confucianists, but toward the end of the century there was a new burst of religious activity. The capital was moved south to Lo-yang in Honan province, and the caves of Lung-mên were started, the dark marble-like limestone hollowed out into grottoes adorned with all the gods of the Mahāyāna Buddhist hierarchy. As it was a better material to carve in than the sandstone of Yün-kang, and the ideas were not quite so strange by that time, the results were finer in quality than at the earlier caves. Some of the most exquisite representations of heavenly beings ever carved were made there (fig. 550), touched by a delicate, tender spirituality. It was estimated that nine out of ten families had been converted by that time, for Buddhism offered to the common people a vision of good things in the next world. Emperors and empresses were donors, too, appearing with their courtiers to inspect the work and bring offerings (fig. 551), and they encouraged the study of the sūtras at court. The monk Fa-hsien was sent to India on a perilous journey that lasted 15 years. He returned with Sanskrit books, which were translated into Chinese, and he told of the marvels of strange lands in his diary. He was the first of many monks who risked their lives to go to India and to contribute to the Indianization of Chinese art, philosophy, and learning.

Even in the south where the Chinese had established a capital at Nanking, and strove to preserve their ancient culture menaced by the barbarians in the north, the worship of the Buddha spread, and great teachers were invited to discuss the doctrine. Ideas were interchanged, and by A.D. 500, the Wei emperor issued an edict prohibiting the use of the Tatar language, culture, and customs in favor of the Chinese. By 589 the country was united again under the Sui Dynasty (A.D. 589–618) and Buddhism continued to play a dominant part. The first Sui emperor ordered the construction of 3,792 temples, caused 1,508,904 images to be repaired, and 106,580 new ones, large and small, to be made in various materials — gold, bronze, stone, sandalwood, lacquer, and ivory.

A lovely altar group in the Museum of Fine Arts in Boston (fig. 552), cast in bronze in A.D. 593, shows the development in religious worship and artistic expression taking place as Buddhism became more and more Chinese. It is of Amitābha Buddha (O-mi-t'o Fo), who presides over the Western Paradise, receiving the souls of all who call upon him or his attendant Bodhisattva. It was not necessary to be learned, or wealthy, or highborn to seek salvation through him; he heard the prayers of all sincere believers who said his name. No longer were the common people condemned to suffer the Wheel of Existence; they could now find release from it even as monks and scholars had, who had been able to lose themselves in contemplation and project their minds, guided by the sūtras, into the realms of the infinite; even the ignorant could have faith and reach the Blessed Land. In this shrine, Amitābha sits majestically upon a pedestal, a lotus throne. He is attended by monks who were mortal and therefore done as realistic portraits, and by his two Bodhisattva, who stand worshipfully on lotus flowers. Lions, guardian kings, an incense burner, and music-making angels complete the whole as now exhibited by the museum. The Indian elements are still there — the yoga pose, snail-shell hair, Hindu torso, and hand gestures of Amitābha, the thirteen attributes of the Bodhisattva, the lions and guardians as prescribed by texts; but the Chinese maker added pendants, a flaming halo, and a winsome slimness of figure. The Bodhisattva, Avalokiteśvara (Kuan Yin in Chinese), and Mahāsthāmaprāpta (Ta Shih Chih) wear the high jeweled crowns, the necklaces and scarves of young rajas, but they have none of the masculine heaviness of their Gandhāran prototypes; they are sexless, with a feminine daintiness of gesture, and show the Chinese lack of interest in anatomical studies. This was now the proper shrine for the family altar, taking the place of the ritual vessels that held food for sacrifice in the ancient days. Spirits of the departed were still important, and Taoist monks tried to rival the Buddhists in influence; but most of the carving, casting, and painting was done in the service of the Buddha (figs. 553, 554).

Again the Chinese began to expand, sending armies into Annam, Korea, and Central Asia. The Sui emperor was displaced by the Duke of T'ang, who had equally ambitious ideas. So the dynasty changed, but Chinese conquest continued unabated, and a new era rivaling the Han came to the Middle Kingdom. Warriors, diplomats, and patrons of the arts, the T'ang rulers ushered in another epoch of political and creative power, which lasted from A.D. 618 to 907.

One of the outstanding rulers, T'ang T'ai-tsung (627–49), defeated the Turks who tried to take Ch'ang-an, the western capital. By conquest or treaty he began to control the oasis cities of Central Asia — Turfan, Kucha, Karashar, Khotan, Kashgar, Yarkand, Bokhara, and Samarkand. Gifts in great numbers were exchanged back and forth, Turkish and Uighur princes were invited to attend court and serve as officers in the Chinese army, and princesses were given in marriage to consolidate these ties. One, as we have seen, was sent to Tibet, for the Tibetans proved to be very troublesome at this time. Though silk was no longer a monopoly of China, the old silk road was kept open by Chinese garrisons for active trade between the Byzantines, the Arabs, Indians, and Chinese. Water routes were as important as land routes, and the seaport towns were thronged with foreigners, as were the two capital cities of the north. Travelers, merchants, astrologers, entertainers, healers, monks, students, and soldiers poured into China from all directions. They brought new gods to worship, new fashions in dress, music, medicine, food, and entertainment. The old Chinese were shocked by the ready acceptance of 'barbarian' ways by court and commoner, but their reproofs did not prevent the building of temples to the strange gods, nor did they keep the ladies of the palace from riding horseback, playing polo, or going about without hats. Chinese arts, like Chinese life, underwent considerable change.

The clay figurines still used in tombs give us a vivid picture of the times. They include many foreign ethnic types: camel drivers (fig. 555), grooms who were sent in with the tribute horses, dancing girls, Negroes, dwarfs, clerks, warriors, merchants, musicians, rascals, and holy men. Bronze mirrors, too, show Western influence; stone slabs are ornamented with Persians wearing the long tunic of the Sassanian period; textiles are woven with so many Sassanian motifs that it is somewhat of a shock to find Chinese characters on them; pilgrim bottles and other pottery forms have strong Near Eastern influences in design; and Buddhist art is injected with a fresh, direct impulse from Gupta India.

There are few architectural remains of the T'ang period in China. Except for a rare octagonal pagoda of brick or stone, little can be seen of the era; only in Japan wooden structures based on Chinese models have survived (fig. 593). The cave temples, however, had not been severely damaged until modern times; before the great harm done them in the twentieth century, some were studied and photographed by experts who have reconstructed the Buddhist places of worship well enough for us to see that there was a gradual evolution in architecture, sculpture, and painting toward the cosmopolitan Chinese ideal from the simple beginnings of the Six Dynasties period. In north and eastern China, in Yün-kang, T'ien-lung-shan, and Lung-mên, work had gone on from the fifth century; in southwest China, archaeologists have recently discovered many more sites. The farthest outpost of all, Tun-huang, the place where caravans stopped on entering or leaving the country for the overland desert route, had been a center of religious activity since the fourth century. A monk had been led by a vision to that place; he had hollowed out grottoes in the mud cliffs above a dry stream, having in his heart the ideal of his dream, a concrete representation of the Thousand Buddhas, one of the miracles of Gautama. Other helpers had come, and as the years passed there were many temples hollowed out, their walls covered with scenes of the life of the historical Buddha, and the heavenly worlds to which the faithful might go (fig. 556). The donors who contributed toward this great undertaking, and all who brought offerings are pictured there, too, in their finest clothes. The Turkish donors are especially brightly colored, for the women wore richly embroidered robes and high headdresses of flowers and elaborate hairpins, and their cheeks were painted with crimson circles. All the walls vibrated with color, and the sculptured figures placed against them were equally brilliant.

The mother school for all this was Ajantā, and Indian proportions were faithfully followed, as were the texts telling how the various scenes must be arranged, but many changes had taken place; Central Asiatic artists had worked out the themes, and their methods naturally influenced the Turks and Chinese, who must have been most active in the making of this outpost shrine. In the oasis cities of the northern and southern Trade Routes there were flourishing Buddhist communities, and many monasteries, so that the local kings, the lay believers, and the monks had all been patrons of art, or artists themselves, making countless images in clay (for stone was scarce), and adorning walls with frescoes in the Indian tradition. Central Asia was a meeting place for many peoples, as Huns, Turks, and Mongols sought better pastures for their flocks, and town dwellers engaged in the commerce of caravan trade. Persians, Armenians, Syrians, Hindus, Scyths, Tocharians, Uighurs, and many others came and went, each contributing something to the art of the area. The subtle shading of tones used by Ajantā painters was translated by oasis artists into bands of primary colors; a kneecap, for instance, which had been modeled in light and dark shadows, was here reduced to a circle of blue, green, or yellow, making a pleasant pattern, if quite an unrealistic one. With the coming of so much activity to the Buddhist shrines of China, owing to the overland trade and missionaries, the desert and oasis art made a profound impression there.

Tun-huang is a rich mine for the student and explorer, not only because of its wall paintings made from the fourth through the tenth centuries, and its T'ang sculpture (fig. 557), but also because of the countless votive banners painted on cotton and silk (fig. 558), and the texts in many languages found by the English archaeologist, Sir Aurel Stein, and the French sinologist, Professor Paul Pelliot. The first printed book in the world was found in a walled-up library where many precious things had been hidden, a paper scroll of the Diamond Sūtra (Buddhist text) dated A.D. 868.

It was a time of literary and intellectual activity. Poets sang the praises of their emperors, of palace beauties, of the great festivals, and of the lonely men who were garrisoned in the far-flung outposts controlled by China. Courtiers and scholars discussed the classics, and called upon monks to expound the doctrine of the many religious foundations in the capitals — Zoroastrian, Manichaean, Nestorian Christian, Moslem, and Buddhist. Students and learned men came and went, quite a few to India to the University at Nālandā, the most famous of the travelers in the seventh century being the Master of the Law, Hsüan-tsang. His diary with its vivid descriptions of oasis cities, of desert suns and mountain winds, of the marvels of India, is one of the most delightful travel stories in any literature, and served as a guide to modern archaeologists in their discoveries of many important sites rich in Buddhist remains. He came back to China with Sanskrit texts which had to be translated and interpreted, as did other monks who took similar journeys, so the monasteries were busy centers of learning.

Symbol of the law and doctrine and intellectual aspect of the church was Vairocana Buddha (Lu-shê-na), a celestial being who had not lived upon the earth, but in a paradise eons of years away, where he sat upon a lotus throne, the power of his mind emanating spiritual rays that inspired confidence and hope in believers. At Lung-mên, near Lo-yang, the eastern capital, the Buddha was represented in a colossal image 85 feet high (fig. 559), carved in the solid rock. It was dedicated in an impressive ceremony in the reign of T'ang Kao-tsung in A.D. 672. Remote and awe-inspiring he sits upon his throne, with a great halo containing the Seven Buddhas of the Past carved in relief behind him. The colossus is flanked by Bodhisattva and monks, and protected by muscular guardians of the law (fig. 560), who stand 50 feet high. The sculptors had to portray many different qualities in the various beings prescribed by the Buddhist texts — symbols of wisdom, compassion, kingly majesty, mystical rapture, austerity, brute force — all conceived on a scale that would have been impossible to less gifted men, but in art as in politics, nothing seemed impossible then to the Chinese. Poised, mature, and benign, even the small images are imbued with greatness (fig. 561).

In painting as well as in sculpture there was a ferment of activity, and a level of accomplishment to which later generations pointed with pride. Painters were hired by the hundreds to adorn the walls of Buddhist grottoes and sanctuaries, monks and nuns became painters, and, in secular life, at court and among the scholars, painting was regarded as a fine art. Buddhist banners and murals, of course, were made according to rules developed in India, and reflect as much Indian and Central Asiatic influence as the sculpture does, but there was, as well, a native tradition that stemmed from the Han period.

Though there are no scrolls in existence as old as the Han, we know from historical records that painting played an important part in the lives of the people of that era. Portraits of the virtuous and great were hung on the walls, and the beams and supports of palaces and temples were richly decorated. In fact, the Wu Liang Tzŭ motifs (fig. 544) are so nearly like descriptions of palace ornamentation in a contemporary poem that it is quite likely that the flat silhouettes in low relief were derived from painted figures. Lacquered objects (fig. 562) and painted pottery that have survived are witness to the skill and dexterity of brushwork developed in that early period, a brushwork that was well suited to the fanciful subjects favored then. Chang Hêng, for instance, a painter who lived from A.D. 78 to 139, preferred to paint ghosts and demons, for he thought that real objects were difficult to represent and the realm of the unreal was infinite.

A renowned copy of a scroll by a fourth-century painter, Ku K'ai-chih, was based on a text called the *Admonitions of the Imperial Preceptress* (fig. 563). As its title suggests, it is courtly and Confucianist in theme. The young ladies of the palace were urged by their imperial tutor to learn proper deportment by imitating the famous heroines and beauties of the past. The horizontal silk scroll is designed in a series of scenes, each one carefully labeled, illustrating an incident or moral precept. Loyalty to the emperor, the folly of vanity, the desirability of a large family and of telling the truth are illustrated in a delicate brush style. There are reminders that whatever rises high must fall — as the sun rises, so shall it set, as the moon waxes, so must it wane. And again, 'No one can endlessly please,' a piece of worldly advice based on the experience of hundreds of beauties who were brought from all over China to please the Emperor, but who held power for only a brief moment. Each episode is a unit to be looked at and enjoyed separately. The figures are irresistible in their delicate charm, floating almost in an undefined space, fragile and exquisite as the flowers for which they were named. Quite unlike the voluptuous Indian beauties who wore much jewelry and a few diaphanous scarves, the Chinese ladies were clothed from head to foot in long silk robes that give no hint of the body underneath; their appeal is subtle, sophisticated, as tenuous as a faint perfume. They are painted in true Chinese fashion by means of brush and ink on silk, in which forms are suggested by thickening and thinning lines. Some color was used, but line would be sufficient without color, it is so filled with life and rhythm, so carefully placed. Like the calligraphy labeling each scene, the brushwork demonstrates that the painter-writer had mastered one of the most difficult disciplines in the world of art.

The writer, or painter, by control and dexterity, could make a thin line or a thick one while using the same brush. Depending on his skill, imagination, and personality, he could, in a few strokes, suggest the power of an ocean wave or the delicacy of a butterfly's wing, even in a written character or pictograph. The shape of a character and the spacing of its parts were of as great concern to the writer as were the arrangement of mountain peaks and waterfalls to the maker of pictures. To both writer and painter, no matter what the subject might be, the quality desired above all was a rhythmic vitality, a suggestion of the form of life itself. As early as about A.D. 500, in canons written by Hsieh Ho, this came first on his list of directions for producing great paintings. The last canon is as characteristically Chinese as the first: he suggests that by copying the old masters one might reach toward a greater creative activity.

Many of the poets were painters by the T'ang period, adding that highest accomplishment of the gentleman and the scholar to their poetic gift. They were founders of the tradition of the philosopher-poets, the scholar-painters, who were not bound by rules as were the craftsmen working on religious subjects, but were free to paint any subject that served their purpose, once they had mastered the discipline of 'good brush.' By it they had a further means of expressing their attitude toward nature or their fellow man, and they did it in true Chinese fashion, seeking to convey much by the simplest means, realizing that the unsaid is as important as the said, that a suggestion is more challenging than complete statement. It meant setting down the essence of the subject, which could come only after a devoted study of it. Therefore, as they tell us, they watched each flower as it grew, opening in the dew of the morning, advancing from bud to blossom to seed pod. They noted all kinds of trees, each with its own root system, trunk, branches, and characteristic leaves, and watched them change appearance in the different seasons. Mountains and rocks, the flight of birds, the fall of snow, a fisherman, a spray of bamboo — all of nature was their guide and tutor. Remembering Hsieh Ho's first canon, they imbued their paintings with life and vitality instead of making objective, scientific studies, which might have served as illustrations to bird or botany books; they had looked deeper than the surface, and had caught the rhythm as well as the appearance of things in the world about them.

Landscape was a favorite theme with the poet-painters, and landscape consisted primarily of mountains and water. Like their poems, the paintings are made of mist and mountains, and reflect the mood of the artist. Wang Wei is one of the outstanding masters of poetry and scroll painting in the T'ang period. Though we know of his painting only from copies or from descriptions and remarks made by contemporaries, he could serve well as the representative of the unhampered Chinese style of delicate color, ink, and shading on silk or paper, in contrast to the religious paintings of Buddhist caves and sanctuaries, with their strong Indian and Central Asian influences.

In Tun-huang, especially, the wall paintings and banners of the T'ang period give us an idea of the splendor and magnificence of Mahāyāna Buddhist art as it developed in China (fig. 556). The walls were prepared with a fine coating of plaster, which was applied over rougher layers, and on it the designs were laid out according to Indian formulas, the Buddha usually in the center, largest in scale, and Bodhisattva arranged radially around the central deity, somewhat smaller. Then came pavilions of attendants, holy men and women, and, at the base, near the floor, usually a procession of donors in Chinese or Turkic dress. The central scheme was worked out by using chalk on string; the body of the Buddha served as the starting point, and, once his measurements were correct, and a circle made for the halo behind his head, as well as a larger mandorla behind the body, the craftsman then placed the Bodhisattva at intervals, snapping the chalk against the plaster to establish radial lines. The outlines of the figures were drawn freehand or made by using pounces; each one had to be made in the proper proportion and with the proper garments, hand gestures, and attributes, according to Indian texts. Colors, too, were assigned to certain figures. They were much more vivid than the browns, blues, and greens of Ajantā (fig. 491), the mother school of Buddhist mural painting, for the Central Asian communities and the Chinese had different pigments and different interpretations of the texts. The primary colors, red, blue, and yellow, with some brilliant secondaries, were popular in Tun-huang.

When Sir Aurel Stein and Professor Paul Pelliot investigated the hidden library there, they found countless banners as well as texts. Some of the banners were painted on silk and cotton (fig. 558), other votive pieces were woven or embroidered. Some had already been dedicated to the Buddha or one of the Bodhisattva, others had been prepared but the dedication had not yet been written in the space designed for it. They vary in workmanship from the marvelous in color and composition to the poorest provincial copies and handiwork. Some are as magnificent as the wall paintings in scale, others are small vertical hangings with a few hastily sketched figures on them. Good and bad, they are authentic, and they reflect T'ang ideas in religious art; we must turn to them, and to a few pieces preserved in Japan, for our knowledge of the period. It is an invaluable group of materials for our study of Chinese art, and also of Tibetan art. The Tibetans occupied Tun-huang at times under the T'ang, and they came and went at all times from the outpost city nearest their own territory. It is natural, then, that they took some of the banners home with them and brought their own to dedicate to the Thousand Buddhas; a number of the Tun-huang banners show Tibetan influence, and in the earliest Tibetan paintings are vivid halos, streamers of radiance or cloud in rainbow colors, Chinese flowers and architectural motifs, which stem from T'ang painting.

In the banners as well as the murals the painter had some opportunity to use his own ideas and let his imagination guide him in the small *jātakas* (tales of previous existences of the Buddha) and in episodes from the life of the historical Buddha or the Bodhisattva. These themes were much smaller in scale than the big Buddhist Heavens, and they were narratives, not hieratic schemes of glorification. In them we see a blending of the foreign and the native styles, and the introduction of Chinese costume, architecture, landscape motifs, even of the playful, fanciful sprites and demons of old Chinese art, into Buddhist religious painting. Though they are small and sometimes badly preserved, they are among the most important and delightful treasures of the Caves of the Thousand Buddhas.

Mural painting on a grand scale was continued in China in the succeeding periods, but the most sought-after paintings are those done in the native tradition on silk or paper, the small album pieces or the horizontal and vertical scrolls.

When the next dynasty came to power, the Sung (960–1279), one of the emperors, Hui-tsung, chose to become one of the poet-painters, as well as a great collector of masterpieces of the past. He was the patron of artists who were called to the capital to be a part of the Academy he directed. Members of the Academy wore special robes and insignia, and were expected to maintain a high level of excellence in their painting. The Emperor specified the subjects to be portrayed, and rewarded the best competitors. Some of these subjects seem more fitting for poets than painters and were a great challenge to the ingenuity of the artist: 'The hoofs of his steed returned heavily charged with the scent of the trampled flowers,' or 'A boat lying idle the whole day long as nobody wishes to cross the river,' were solved by the winners by showing butterflies clustering around the horse's hoofs, and by a boatman daydreaming with his flute beside him.

Hui-tsung copied a T'ang design of Ladies Preparing Newly Woven Silk (fig. 564), faithfully depicting costume, textile patterns, coiffures, and beauty marks, but ignoring any specific setting where the thread drying and ironing might be taking place. His Five-Colored Parakeet (fig. 565) is typical of the album painting beloved at that time, the bird perched on an apricot branch, with an inscription in delicate calligraphy beside it, and seals of approval above. Instead of showing the whole tree or shrub, by choosing a few branches that come up dynamically from a place outside the limits of his silk, he suggests the whole growing organism. Tiny buds, some beginning to open, and some full-blown blossoms cluster together as they would on a growing fruit tree, developing in a cycle as inevitable as spring itself. A firmer brushstroke was used on the branches and twigs, for 'old branches are like dragon's horns, young ones like angling rods,' and the parakeet clings confidently to the longest. As we study it we become aware of the subtle repetition of curves in the body of the bird and in the branches, and of the importance of the unpainted areas. Though it looks like a simple and unpremeditated design, it is deliberately unsymmetrical and carefully planned. Only an artist who had observed the parakeet and apricot for a long time could thus catch the inner character of each, and only a skilled painter could paint on the silk without a preliminary sketch, never erasing line or color, and seem to do it so effortlessly.

Even before Hui-tsung's time some great landscapes were painted, both as album pieces (fig. 566) and horizontal scrolls (fig. 567). These long compositions were as carefully planned as the little circular or rectangular studies, and gave fuller scope to Chinese genius, with its longing for infinity and space. The two characters that make up their word for landscape are mountain and water, both suggesting vastness, solitude. Man occupies a small part of that vastness, so we have to look closely for him in the valleys if we are to find him at all; he is usually a traveler carrying a pack on his back, or a boatman, or a donkey rider. He is all men on their journey through life, with their burdens, their hills to climb, their stony paths, their streams to cross, their visions of beauty beyond as the mist clears, their comfort in an inn at the close of day. He is not so great as a mountain, nor does he live as long as a pine; he is beaten low by storms, but he goes on his way. He belongs in the scheme of things, as birds do, and clouds; he does not tame nature; he accepts his place, patiently and with humility, a being at home in his universe. Through him, and through the world about him, flows a vibrant life, movement and change and rhythm. In the Clear Weather in the Valley by Tung Yüan (fig. 567), the landscape elements of rocks, trees, mist, man, and mountain are arranged in changing groups of motifs woven together horizontally, with vertical accents rising or falling behind them. If we follow from right to left, seeing only a few inches of the scroll at a time as it is slowly un-rolled, we find that we are actually in a moving picture; but our eyes are doing the moving, not the objects painted on the paper, drawn up, over, down, and across by a constantly moving focus, by variations on the themes that are broken occasionally by moving water. After showing the majesty of mountains with evergreens crowning their summits, the sturdi-ness of light trees and dark trees in the foreground, leafless branches, cleft rocks, distant land, tiny men in boats, open stretches of river, and bubbling streams, the painter closes his composition with a repetition of his opening harmonies — and yet he does not close it, for we must imagine the rest of it, as the river flows down to the sea.

While the Emperor and his masters of the brush tried to capture the fragrance of a flower and the delicate pattern of bamboo reflected on silk in the moonlight, the barbarians closed in again from the northwest. Hui-tsung fled, giving up his collection of over 6000 scrolls and other precious possessions, but he was taken captive and killed by the Golden Tatars. Kao-tsung, his successor, went south to Nanking, but could not escape, and in 1141 signed a treaty with the invaders giving them most of the northern provinces. The Tatars made their capital in Peking, while the Chinese court was established in the south at Hangchou, a lovely city among the lakes, which later charmed Marco Polo. The imperial pottery makers moved south with the Emperor, courtiers, and painters, and some of the finest works of art ever produced by man were done in the southern Sung period. It was a time of sorrow for most of China, when they could do little more than dream of the past or face the hard work and bitterness of the present. More than ever the poets found beauty in small, exquisite things, in the sound of rain, or the jade-white petal of a flower, or the melancholy music of the flute. They retired to their bamboo groves, as did former statesmen; for the time being, the teaching of Lao-tzu, with its emphasis on nature, seemed more in key with the times than the pre-cepts of Confucius.

The pomp and color of Mahāyāna Buddhism, and all the texts and rituals began to pall. A more philosophic, personal approach had been introduced in the sixth century by Indian teachers who believed in the efficacy of contemplation (dhyāna, Ch'an in Chinese, an offshoot of yoga) in which each worshiper had to find the Buddha in his heart. No one could intercede for him, nor would the building of temples, shrines, or memorials increase his merit; he had to rely on himself, with the guidance of a few masters who could only suggest, not prescribe, how he might find

the Way. Thus Ch'an Buddhism and Taoism grew into a form of religion
very agreeable to the Chinese temperament. Monasteries had been established near Nanking as well as in the north, and were run by abbots who,
though enlightened, might be quite unlettered. Menial tasks were assigned
to the novices, for Illumination often came while chopping wood, drawing
water, or fishing. If it seemed slow in coming, a box on the ear or some
other unexpected shock might bring it about. Teachers talked in riddles,
for 'the Tao of which one can speak is not the Tao' (Ch'an Buddhism made
this saying of Lao-tzu its own).

Painters in these monasteries no longer decorated walls with huge,
formal pictures of the heavens of the future, with Buddha in the center
and Bodhisattva on either side, jeweled and draped like Indian kings.
Now the painter-monks retired to their cells, cleared their minds of distracting thoughts, and set to work with brush, ink, and paper. Even light
color was discarded, for the ink painting was more of a challenge to the
imagination, leaving much to the observer to fill in. Instead of painting
each leaf or rock carefully, the brush swept quickly over the paper, giving
an impression of the forms. Thus Liang K'ai did a masterly portrait of the
famous T'ang poet, Li T'ai-po (fig. 568) with the fewest possible strokes,
and in a staccato style he painted Hui-nêng tearing up sūtras (fig. 569),
showing the Ch'an monk discarding the old Buddhist scriptures in a frenzy
of energy since he believed that the only way to Illumination was through
self-reliance and contemplation. The motion of Liang K'ai's brush must
have been as abrupt as if *he* were tearing the sūtras; he put the ink on the
paper in quick angular lines, and made a pine branch up above shoot like
a rocket in a diagonal across the scroll. As in the early ink paintings, these
figures exist in a very real but entirely anonymous space. A fellow monk-
painter, Mu Ch'i, showed equal skill in suggesting much through simple
means; his paintings of persimmons (fig. 570), very daring in its simplicity
of form and shaded tone, looks more like a work of the twentieth century
than one of the thirteenth. Landscape, containing so much symbolic significance, was a favorite theme for the Ch'an philosophers, and was
painted with the same freedom of brush. A detail of Ying Yü-chien's
Mountain Village in the Mist, with a bridge in the foreground, jagged
rocks, and two travelers pushing up toward the houses shrouded in mist, is
done in a manner more impressionistic than the Tung Yüan scroll mentioned above (fig. 567); it is all tone, a shading of the ink from dark to
light, carefully controlled by the artist, however carefree it may seem at
first glance.

This is the great moment of painting in China. Future generations will

look to the Sung masters of the brush and collect their works with as
much love as they have lavished on the classics of literature and ancient
ritual bronzes, which were catalogued and venerated in this period. Famous names abound as they do three centuries later in the rich era of the
Renaissance in Italy.

Ma Yüan, in an album piece (fig. 571), shows a tiny traveler, his possessions tied to a stick held over his shoulder, as he approaches a bridge
flanked by willow trees. We enter the picture with the small figure in the
lower right-hand corner and identify ourselves with him as he nears the
tall, graceful willows with their curving branches, which must be about
to put out the pale yellow-green buds of early spring. The timber bridge
lies ahead, with water flowing under it, and, once safely across it, he may
go through a bamboo grove to the house nestling in a cove. The damp
mist is rising, almost obscuring the bamboo and the house, cloaking the
base of the mountain that rises majestically in the distance. There is the
mood about it of the twilight hour at the end of the day, of a journey almost done, of the need to hurry before the fog settles to hide the bridge
and the house. The curve of willow branches, of the bridge, and of the
mountain are in perfect harmony with the circle of the silk on which
Ma Yüan placed his ink. The dark accents of the lower right, repeated
near the bridge, in the tree tops, and on the mountain ridge, add to the
impression of a vibrant radiation, which gives life to a scene composed
of undramatic elements. The design of these parts, of the light and dark
areas, of the empty spaces and the filled, was done by a master hand, sure
and subtle.

Fan K'uan also chose the circular, fan-shaped silk for his album piece of
A Temple Among the Snowy Hills, and like Ma Yüan he emphasized the
curving patterns of rock, shore line, tree trunk, bamboo, and mountain
(fig. 566). He, too, places the heaviest elements in the lower right-hand
corner, and expands his design radially from there; his elements, too, are
of the utmost simplicity — rock, tree, rooftops rising above bamboo, a
boat almost hidden in a cove, a traveler walking toward the huts, a crag
crowned with sparse vegetation, and the temple between foreground and
middleground almost projecting out of the picture on the far right. But
the mood of his snow scene is quite different; there is a suggestion of the
soundless chill of winter, of a world blanketed in white. Contours are
sharp, contrasts more striking. Man is still small, he still labors toward
shelter and peace, but this time with a hat as big as an umbrella, and, as
he bends into the wind, he lifts his feet to get through the heavy drifts.

More violent and tempestuous in mood, free and powerful in brushstroke, Hsia Kuei's Rain Storm is another Sung masterpiece (fig. 572). The vertical, hanging scroll gave the artist more scope and space, but he is careful not to fill the space with insignificant details. Far down in the right-hand corner, the traveler is about to leave the solid bank to cross a rickety bridge, and he, too, braces himself against the wind that roars through the gully, tearing autumn leaves off the trees. He almost crouches under his umbrella, and will have to be careful of his footing before he reaches his friends in the pavilion across the river. A bold cliff juts out on the left side, to which the trees cling, their roots cutting into it like dragon claws. Everything is unsteady, designed in sweeping diagonals. Hsia Kuei's brushstroke is free and forceful, his ink is rich and black, or shaded to thin wisps. The mass of foliage on the trees is done by a few quick dabs of the brush loaded with ink — not the meticulous description of each leaf, as was done by Tung Yüan — and even the leaves blown by the wind are small, bold dots. Behind the trees, the mist comes in — mist that may be there only momentarily — obscuring a hill that appears high up in the picture. A small sapling growing from the mountain is mercilessly beaten by this autumn wind, which blows from nowhere and into nowhere, a force to be endured, not tamed.

Equally original, Mi Fei became famous for his technique of placing small 'blobs' of ink in varying tones close together, a twelfth-century 'pointillist' approach in monochrome (fig. 573). The effect is one of softness and subtle shading, well adapted to the portrayal of mist, mountain, and trees that have a vaporous, undulating quality, and are so interesting in themselves that no human figures are needed. Though the method of painting was original and unorthodox, Mi Fei achieved the serene peacefulness that was the ideal of more academic painters.

One of the academicians who moved south after the collapse of Hui-tsung's regime was Li T'ang. He was inspired by the beauty of the Hang-chou hills to paint bold landscapes, and he was equally inspired by rice wine. His Man on a Water Buffalo Returning Intoxicated from a Village Feast (fig. 574) might well be a self-portrait done with humor and realism. The pitiful figure of an old man who has had a wonderful time is kept astride his lowly steed by a faithful retainer walking beside him. A ragged boy pulls the unwilling beast, who had doubtless had a hard day's labor in the fields. They are all unkempt, stooped, and dejected; the old man had tried to forget the sorrow of the Sung, the shame of China, with the barbarians flourishing in the north. Li T'ang, the former court painter, was meticulous in his brushstroke. Every tiny willow leaf is done carefully, and the hair of the buffalo is equally fine in texture. The willow trunks are covered by rough, detailed bark, and the bamboo leaves are painted with smoother, even contours. Hundreds of delicate lines indicate the rippling surface of the river flowing beside the slow-moving procession.

The quietness of winter and the loneliness of a gray day are expressed by Ma Lin in his painting of Ling Chao-nü Standing in the Snow (fig. 575). Daughter of a good Taoist who did not believe in disturbing his spirit by mingling in the bustle of worldly affairs, she had to go out to seek food and firewood as a dutiful child should. Though there are cracks in the silk, which is 700 years old, and it has yellowed with age, we are still touched by the mood evoked by that artist so long ago. The slim figure of the girl, the leaves blackened by frost, branches broken and bent, the path, stones, and tree trunks blanketed by snow suggest a stillness and a solitude unbroken even by the song of a bird.

Something of the same melancholy is conveyed by an anonymous painter of the twelfth century who did a narrative scroll of Lady Wen-chi's captivity in Mongolia and her return to China (fig. 576). Illustrating a favorite story of Han times, he showed the delicate Chinese girl as she was taken out into Mongolia by her captor, who made her his wife. She had to live in a tent and grow accustomed to the uncouth ways of nomadic people, which she gradually learned to do. Finally money for her ransom came, and she was to be returned to her civilized world, but she parted sorrowfully from her husband and the children she had borne him. She arrived back in the Chinese capital, bewildered by crowded streets and the rush of many peoples, as she mounted the steps, clad in the white robes of mourning. We look down upon the scene of her return, into a picture cut by diagonals of roof lines into small segments filled with people of all kinds — courtiers, priests, grooms, merchants — a vivid portrayal of twelfth-century life. As in many Oriental paintings, the lines suggest space extending out from the picture plane toward the beholder, and they create a simple setting for the lively panorama of street and palace.

Dragons were regarded as particularly beneficent creatures, as we have seen: they served as symbols of the East, they were the bringers of rain, of thunder and lightning, and so the bringers of good crops. They lived in lakes and pools, or in the Eastern Sea, and they could rise like the mist, disappear into a cloud, become invisible at will, moving like lightning. Though it would seem almost impossible to portray a creature of sky and mystery on a piece of silk or paper, the painters often devoted themselves to dragon subjects. One of the greatest was Ch'ên Jung of the thirteenth century, a magistrate, and later a governor of Fukien, who painted as a hobby. Like Li T'ang, he was often inspired by wine, and was known to shout as he flung his ink on the paper, probably feeling as powerful as a dragon at the moment. Part of a 36-foot horizontal scroll (fig. 577), done in ink with light color on bamboo paper, is a detail of one of his master-pieces, full of fury and spirit.

Some of the painters who specialized in birds and flowers preferred to do long scrolls rather than album pieces of the academic kind. Ma Fên of the late eleventh century undertook an ambitious project when he painted The Hundred Geese, showing them flying, settling down on the water, swimming, feeding, always varied and full of life. A copy of his scroll (fig. 578) is one of the most delightful ink paintings in the Sung style, sure in its brushwork, beautifully spaced, done with understanding and acute observation of the birds.

This freedom of expression that came with the Sung period affected even the religious painting mode of orthodox Mahāyāna Buddhist subjects. One of the Ten Kings of Hell (fig. 579) sits like a Chinese magistrate at his desk, interviewing the wicked who are brought before him. Though the flames of Hell burn near by in this thirteenth-century painting by Hsi-chin Chü-shih — and they are vivid red flames touched with yellow — the King goes calmly about his judgments, full of ceremony and etiquette in good Chinese fashion. All of his attendants, even misshapen demoniac guards, are portraits, and they are individuals. We are aware of what a great change has taken place as we compare this with the T'ang painting of Buddhist worlds (fig. 556), where deities existed in a remote heaven, personifications of virtue or learning, attended by spirits of superhuman, hieratic aspect, each placed at a prescribed distance from the Buddha.

In the series by Chou Chi-ch'ang and Lin T'ing-kuei of the twelfth century (fig. 580), there is the same interest in portraiture and individuality. The sages, or Arhats, are shown as men of supernatural power drifting down toward the earth, clad in monk's robes, but they look like prosperous Chinese citizens bestowing alms on the ragged and miserable beggars below them. There is a striking contrast between the misshapen, grotesque ragamuffins who are almost caricatures of misery, and the bland, plump Immortals scattering their bounty. The Chinese artists have rebelled against the strict formality of composition dictated by the Indian sūtras, and show their figures in unsymmetrical groups: clouds, trees, and rocks are cut by the border of the picture, suggesting more than what is held within the picture plane, an infinity of space and movement.

Buddhist painters showed a tendency to break away from the grand and magnificent crowded composition and to prefer the solitary monk, particularly when he is engaged in contemplation. Lu Hsin-chung of the thirteenth century painted Vanavāsi Gazing at a Lotus Pond (fig. 581), so intent in his concentration that he is not aware of an attendant who has approached with a tray. He is oblivious of ducks playing among the lotus, and of the wind in the willows; he is completely lost in thought. Unlike the Ch'an paintings, which were monochrome, black and white, these Mahāyāna Buddhist paintings are colored. Vanavāsi wears a red and gold brocaded priest's robe over a green undergarment; his attendant wears a blue gown tied with red cords about his waist, the ducks are brown and blue-green; the lotus blossoms a fragile pink, and the lotus leaves and willow leaves are green. In this, as in other paintings of the same series in Boston, the artist shows a master's skill in arranging forms, textures, and patterns, which give a magical quality to the work, demonstrating his interest in the concrete world and the realms beyond reality.

These are a few of the many Sung paintings preserved in monasteries, palaces, and private collections, guarded as precious treasures, stamped with seals of approval. These are a few among the great names of the Sung painters. Figure painters, landscape artists such as Li Kung-lin (fig. 582), specialists in birds, flowers, dragons, and bamboo — all were splendid in their chosen lines. Many were innovators, experimenting in techniques and styles that have influenced Chinese painting down the ages, and still set a standard for all the world to admire.

This is the great moment in the ceramic arts, too. Based on the tradition handed down from Neolithic times, reaching a high point under the Han and T'ang, pottery making in China now outstripped that of other lands in refinement, beauty of shape, and glaze. The imperial family took a great interest in its production, choosing the rarest and finest pieces for the palace or for honored guests. Shapes were modeled on the bronze ritual vessels, or were designed especially as flower holders, tea ceremony dishes, or for some other practical purpose. The thickness of the body varies from heavy stoneware to delicate porcelain that rings when flicked by the finger, some of it fired at high temperatures. Glazing advanced well beyond anything known before; the potters learned how to make crackle in the glaze at will, and to control the size and direction of the cracks. Most of the Sung ware is monochrome — white, cream, blue, moss green, or purplish black, described by their Chinese names in a truly poetic way, 'blue as the sky after rain,' 'ice crackle,' 'fish roe crackle,' 'onion green,' 'hares' fur,' or 'palm eyes.' Sometimes a design was cut into the body before glazing, or was painted in the glaze, done with as much skill as in calligraphy or painting on silk. The bowl of Ting ware (fig. 583), glazed creamy white, is as delightful as an album painting. The curve of the bowl is repeated in the curve of the grasses, the bodies of the swans, and the waves that buoy them up. It is graceful, exquisite, and a miracle of restraint.

THE southern Sung Dynasty, always uneasy politically, came to an end with the Mongol invasion. Under Jenghis Khan, the hard-hitting nomads had harassed the Tanguts and Chin in the north, and

LATER CHINESE ART

had established themselves there by 1234. The Chinese attacked them, and started a conflict that lasted forty-five years, ending in the subjugation of all of China, so that that large territory was added to most of Asia already under Mongol rule. Another era of contact with other countries was ushered in: Chinese were sent to Mesopotamia, and tribesmen from all parts of Asia flocked to Peking, Kaifeng, Canton, and other big cities. Under Kubilai, who was the Khan of China from 1260 to 1294, Peking was proclaimed the winter capital, and was rebuilt over a thirty-year period under Moslem direction. Many halls, pavilions, gardens, orchards, and even a zoo were in 'Khanbaliq,' as it was called, and Marco Polo was not the only traveler to report on its charms. Since Kubilai was interested in all kinds of strange and wonderful things and people, we can imagine how its streets looked as the caravans came in from the desert, bearing gifts from Persia, Russia, and Damascus, or when traders came up from the south with spices, jewels, and rare animals. Tibet and Lamaism played important roles in the life of the north and west, for the Mongols supported that sect, as well as allowing the established Buddhist Church, Taoism, and Confucianism to continue.

Painting followed the Sung tradition for the most part, as the 'non-collaborators' tried to ignore their conquerors and lived in solitude apart from the cosmopolitan bustle of Mongol cities, but some of the most gifted artists were patronized by the newcomers. The 'barbarians' liked paintings of horses and the hunt, those which tended to emphasize vigor and strength rather than delicacy, refinement, and sophistication; but the most renowned names are those of artists who followed the principles of the past. Chao Mêng-fu and his son and grandson were so famous as painters of horses and animals that nearly every Yüan (Mongol period) scroll that has a horse in it is ascribed to this family. Chao's wife, Kuan Tao-shêng, is one of the few women who rank high in the Chinese records of their painters; she was known as a specialist in bamboo painting (fig. 584). Wu Chên, basing his ink painting on the Sung ideals of life, rhythm, and simplicity of form, did many studies of bamboo, of which the one in the Museum of Fine Arts in Boston is considered a notable example. Another traditionalist is Ch'ien Hsüan, whose Early Autumn scroll in the Detroit Institute of Arts would have pleased the Sung emperor-painter Hui-tsung.

Many lovely landscapes were painted, often in the old styles, but there were several innovators who tried out different brush techniques, and by a few strokes suggested rocks, trees, water, and mountain without encircling mist or melting tone. As might be expected in a time when parts of Europe and Asia were under the same rule, the Chinese concept of space began to undergo changes; hills and mountains at times diminished in size in the landscape, instead of rising majestically in the distance, as they so often had in earlier painting. Ni Tsan (fig. 585) and Huang Kung-wang were among these experimenters, bringing a new power and originality to the main stream of development in landscape painting. The former, particularly, won for himself an honored place in the history of Chinese painting by pioneering in the dry-brush technique. By it he achieved a solidity of form in rocks and trees that formed the basis for some of the great Ming painting to follow.

Owing perhaps to their contact with other civilizations where realism was stressed, the Mongols had portraits made of the khans and their wives. Their jewelry, gay embroidery, and high headdresses are similar to those seen in paintings of Turkic people of Central Asia done in the T'ang period. In style, the Ming ancestor portraits followed the same painstaking meticulousness for the next several centuries.

Much of the Buddhist painting of this period follows the past tradition, but some of it shows Mongol influence. Of the scroll painters of this group, Yen Hui is one of the most interesting, reflecting in his work the popular belief in folklore, spirits, and genii, for Chinese fairy folk were joined by Tibetan demons and Persian djinns in the minds of the common people. His Immortal (fig. 586) is one of the dwellers in hills and forests who lived on dew and nuts, who had been given the secret of immortality by the Queen Mother of the West; his astral body issues from his mouth, soaring up into the air, while he remains sitting above the abyss as the mist closes in. He looks like an unkempt foreigner, with bushy hair, flat, knotty fingers, and a Persian pilgrim bottle hanging at his side. Largely through the artist's skilful use of tone, he is endowed with a magic quality equal to that of the Sung arhats.

In the decorative arts, as in painting, there was a considerable exchange of ideas and motifs with the outside world, particularly with the Near East. From Russia, which was also under Mongol domination, the art of cloisonné enamel was introduced as practiced by Byzantine craftsmen. Thus China, joined later by Japan, became a great center for the making of highly colored vases and dishes.

Like other conquerors of the Chinese, the Mongols were unable to maintain their sovereignty long. Strong as they seemed, they, too, weakened and were driven out by forces from the south in 1368. A Buddhist monk of humble origin, leader of the Chinese army, established a new dynasty, the Ming, which lasted until 1644. At first there was a great expansion by land and sea, for the Chinese were victorious in military campaigns and had impressive fleets plying the coastal waters, and voyaging to India and Africa.

The early capital of the Ming Dynasty was in Nanking, but in 1403 it was moved north to Peking, which was rebuilt on the plan we know today by the Emperor of the Yung-lo period. Except for the imperial tombs near Nanking, the northern capital affords the best examples of Chinese genius in planning and building imposing edifices. The imperial palace (Tzu-chin-ch'êng), the 'Forbidden City' of later days, contains three courtyards around which are grouped pavilions, halls, terraces, gardens, and ornamental waterways. Like the ancient house in fundamental plan, but expanded to magnificent dimensions, it has been called the grandest palace building in the world. The tile roof is still used, supported by brackets that branch out from vertical supports, but the roofs are colored blue, green, gold, and red rather than a somber brown or clay, and the bracket system has grown increasingly complex with the passing of years. The courtyards and walls are laid out symmetrically according to definite concepts of order and auspicious direction inherited from the past, but the material of which the walls are made, white marble, marks a break with tradition. Walls, terraces, and balustrades of the marble blend harmoniously with the colors of tiles and ornaments. The Altar of Heaven (fig. 587) consists of three circular terraces with their balustrades joined by imposing stairs and ramps that were used by the emperor when he went there in the early dawn to perform his sacrificial rituals. Like the jade symbol of heaven, the *pi* (fig. 540), the circle of the altar suggested completeness that was both heavenly and imperial.

In Peking there was a revival of the arts and a renewed activity in the making of encyclopedias, books on crafts and agriculture, and fine editions of religious and philosophic works. Increased trade carried Chinese porcelains, silks, carved ivories, and jewels to other parts of the world, where 'chinoiserie' later became a great vogue, especially in the seventeenth and eighteenth centuries, and China, in turn, became acquainted with products from the Western world. Then, in the seventeenth century the Chinese were forbidden to go abroad, and trading on a large scale was not encouraged; the Chinese more and more turned their eyes on the glorious past.

While some of the Ming painters studied the past with love and reverence, others produced works notable for their originality and power. So great was their versatility, in fact, they are difficult to classify in limited compartments. One group, the Chê, consisted for the most part of court painters. They had as their particular models the Sung masters, Ma Yüan (fig. 571) and Hsia Kuei (fig. 572). Though some of them produced copies more remarkable for love of detail and precision than for freshness and boldness, their leader, Tai Chin, was free, imaginative, and original, capable of working in several different methods. His interpretation of nature shows the sensitiveness, humor, and understanding that we look for in the best of Chinese painting. In his scroll of fishermen bringing their boats to harbor in a hard blow (fig. 588), the brushwork is strong, demonstrating how expert he was in that exacting medium. The handling of tone, which he graded from light to dark to suggest volume, shows how well he knew that much could be expressed by simple means if every brushstroke counted. Like the masterpieces of former days, the painting is filled with life and rhythm; one follows the moving focus through the horizontal scroll, from scene to scene, each a part of the other, and each perfect in itself. The wind, bending trees and shrubs, filling the sails, and blowing travelers before its irresistible force, has rarely been painted so successfully. Hsia Kuei would have looked upon it with delight.

Of the non-professional painters, the Wu school of literary men produced versatile and worthy amateurs; Shên Chou, poet, court favorite, and gentleman painter, was a real leader among them. With delicate humor and fine brushwork he gave an engaging individuality to both album pieces and large compositions. Whether he painted persimmons, silkworms, or majestic landscapes, he did them with a mastery of technique and unfailing charm that set him above the hundreds of painters of the period. He followed the Yüan masters, especially Ni Tsan (fig. 585), taking the dry-brush method and adding color. Of his pupils, T'ang Yin is noteworthy for his swift brushwork, his delicacy of perception, and his humor and Wên Chêng-ming for his independence and versatility. In the sixteenth century Tung Ch'i-ch'ang was outstanding; he was a scholar, statesman, art critic, and a friend of Matteo Ricci, the Jesuit priest who took such an interest in Chinese painting. Chu Tuan, another important Ming painter, produced traditional subjects in the freer Ming style (fig. 589).

The use of color is one of the important contributions of the Ming artists to the history of Chinese painting. Many of them loved the exquisite festivals of the court, and the refined entertainment, which took place behind walls that shut out the noisy city in a charming setting amid exotic rocks, dwarfed pines, weeping willows and curving bridges, for the courtiers and ladies who feasted there. Ch'iu Ying gives us a good picture of such entertainment. Everything is cultivated; no longer do the moods of nature touch these people. They and their music live in a protected world, painted in subtle tones of mauve, vermilion, and blue-green.

While the name of Ming has long been familiar to students and collectors of Chinese porcelain, it is only in the last decade or so that we have come to know the really great examples of Ming ceramic wares. At Ching-te-chên, which had been a former center of activity under imperial patronage, the factories were re-established in 1369. From that time on, in unbelievable quantities, came the finest porcelain the world has ever seen. For almost three centuries they produced vases, bowls, basins, bottles, platters, cups, saucers, teapots, pitchers, and boxes of all shapes and sizes. Never was the porcelain more purely white, the glaze more flawlessly translucent. Among the greatest achievements were the vases decorated in underglaze blue with cobalt imported from Persia, the so-called Mohammedan blue, and the pieces similarly decorated with red derived from copper.

Monochrome ware was equally fine. Shapes of unparalleled purity and beauty were enhanced by reds, yellows, greens, and other colors. It was at this time, too, that the famous 'five-color' enameled wares were made, the enamels applied over the glaze, both in combination with underglaze designs and alone. Floral designs, good luck symbols, the god of longevity, dragons, court beauties, butterflies, and sages were some of the popular ornaments for Ming porcelains. The 'three-color' wares were usually heavy pots, big bowls, bottles, and garden seats, and the technique consisted of walling off from each other the patterns of colored glazes by means of cloisons of clay or by incisions in the paste, so that in firing there would be no intermingling of colors; some of these were carved in openwork designs called *kuei kung*, devils' work. Aside from the standard wares, the beautiful creamy white called *blanc de chine* was made in Fukien province; in I-hsing, west of Shanghai, were made the teapots and small articles for the scholars' tables, of unglazed clays in chocolate brown and shades of red and yellow, sometimes intricately carved. Other regions, too, had their specialties.

Ming porcelains have been so skilfully imitated that the placing of a piece in its proper period is an extremely complex and puzzling task, and, in spite of a voluminous literature on the subject in European languages, we are still very much in the dark. The vases of at least ten of the seventeen Ming reign periods can be distinguished by a careful study of the quality of the paste, glaze, color, and type of design, but finding the mark of a Ming ruler on a piece of porcelain may mean nothing more than that a copy was made by a later workman emulating the honorable past.

Wood-block printing was used extensively in this period in the making of encyclopedias, in the illustration of religious texts, and in copybooks used by art students. The color print had been developed into a thing of exquisite beauty by Ming craftsmen. Embroidery, which has always kept pace with the major arts of China, assumed a new importance as Ming rulers demanded splendid robes for state ceremony and sacrificial rituals, ornamented with symbols handed down from prehistoric times. These robes were so much admired by the conquerors of the Ming, the Manchus, that they adopted many of the symbolic designs for their own imperial costumes.

In 1644 the Manchus, who later conquered Turkestan and Tibet, infiltrated into north China and took Peking for their second capital, which it remained until 1912 when the Republic was proclaimed. For forty years they waged campaigns in the south, and finally extended their power to Indo-China, bringing all of the country under their rule which they called the Ch'ing Dynasty. They readily adapted themselves to Chinese law, manners and customs, and brought years of peace in which the arts could flourish. Since they admired so much of what had been done under the Ming, it was natural that they should encourage writers, painters, porcelain makers, furniture craftsmen, jewelers, textile workers, men of letters, and artists of all kinds. More than ever the past was admired and copied, and a love of skill for its own sake came uppermost, especially in painting.

Brushstroke types were classified and made into copybooks, which were studied more earnestly by apprentices than was nature herself; as a consequence countless painters proved to be proficient, but their work was dry, academic, and lifeless. They were charmed by meticulousness and were inclined to overload their compositions, often stressing the decorative values at the expense of power and vitality. Though they turned to the Sung period for instruction, they failed to capture the majesty, simplicity, and grandeur that had been a part of the heritage of that time. The eighteenth- and nineteenth-century painters were often frame-conscious, allowing the borders of their scrolls to serve as a real stopping place for the imagination, instead of suggesting much more than was included in the picture; they ran their mountains up to astonishing heights to fit them into the vertical composition, and arranged other motifs to suit themselves

within the pattern; they were fascinated by different textures, and by mul-
titudinous objects that could be squeezed into the composition. Man did
not occupy a humble place any longer; portraits were popular, especially
if rank could be indicated by 'mandarin squares,' the embroidered insignia
indicating the exact status of civil and military officials. Lovely ladies were
shown swooning in delicate melancholy (fig. 590), and courtiers in their
richest robes in audience with the emperor. Men gathered in pavilions for
sociable meetings, and the painters delighted in depicting every detail of
serving cups, musical instruments, flower arrangements, textile designs,
and furniture.

In spite of the popularity of copying, and the widespread worship of the
past or of the materialistic present, some Ch'ing painting shows a freedom
and spontaneity that marks a real progress in the long development of
brush techniques. Because they retained inherited discipline, there is still
vitality, strength, refinement, poetry of line, subtlety of form, and sly
humor, especially in the work of Chu Ta, Tao Chi, Yün Shou-ping, Chu
Hao, and the renowned Four Wangs. They are interested in the variety
in nature, rather than in its uniformity. Some made careful descriptive
studies, trying to capture what the eye sees, but, unlike their copybook
contemporaries, they drew from nature and endowed their studies with
personality. A bird on a branch, by Chu Ta, for instance (fig. 591), is done
with the fewest possible strokes of the brush; each stroke is essential,
placed in exactly the right relation to the other strokes, and, what is more
important in Chinese painting, in the right relation to the unfilled areas.
This painting seems to have been more rapidly done than similar studies
painted in the Sung and Ming periods, and is very modern in its freshness, directness, and bold simplicity. Men of this caliber are the true in-
heritors of the past and the guardians of the future. It is their work, rather
than the mannered, graceful, decorative pieces that inspired 'chinoiserie,'
which link a stirring twentieth-century China to her creative tradition of
the dynasties long since gone, a heritage unrivaled by any other nation in
the modern world.

The wood-block print again was used extensively to illustrate treatises
and literature. We can turn to them for a picture of the times, for they are
faithful genre scenes, now valuable to the student of porcelain, furniture,
naval architecture, and even of warfare. A series of prints, the Conquests
of the Emperor, were engraved on copper in France, and other prints were
designed in China and printed in Europe or vice versa. Naturally there
was more European influence than ever before to be found in perspective
used in the Western manner, in costumes, and in racial type that appear

in Ming and Ch'ing art. An Italian monk, Castiglione, combined both Western and Oriental ideas in his painting of the Ch'ien-lung period, and won great favor with the emperor. The flourishing trade with the United States and Europe in the eighteenth and nineteenth centuries had a profound influence on those lands, as carved ivories, lacquer work, portraits on glass, embroidered shawls, painted fans, and Canton enamels were shipped out in quantity to grace the homes of seafaring men. Ceramic wares from China were in demand everywhere, and foreign influences were registered in that art as in so many others, but pieces made for the imperial household had to meet the rigid standards of imperial patronage just as they had in the past. The reigns of the K'ang-hsi emperor (1661–1722) and the Ch'ien-lung emperor (1736–95) are noted for their beauty in many things, but especially for the porcelains. Those emperors were great connoisseurs, collecting some of the finest Sung pieces, which now bear their poems or marks of approval, and they demanded the best from their own workers in the imperial factories at Ching-tê-chên. Blue and white ware was still made, though of a more mechanical perfection, and more standardized than in the Ming Dynasty. Among the enameled wares, some of the most popular in Europe were those called by the French collectors 'famille verte, jaune, rose,' et cetera, if the ornamentation showed a preponderance of those colors. Monochromes came into favor again, with magnificent vases glazed 'mirror black,' *sang de boeuf* (copper red), 'apple green,' Imperial yellow, 'peach bloom,' *clair de lune,* 'coral red,' 'iron rust,' 'tea dust,' 'turquoise blue,' and 'camellia-leaf green.' Shape and glaze were superbly suited to each other, so that a delicate vase the color of moonlight seemed really to capture the fleeting beauty of a summer night.

By the twentieth century corruption in high places, especially in the palace, marked the downfall of the Manchus in China. By the time the dowager empress had been laid away, pressure was brought on the boy emperor to retire from public life to the sheltered precincts of the Forbidden City, and in 1912 the Republic came into being. For the last time an emperor of China had climbed the marble steps of the Altar of Heaven (fig. 587), and the sacrifices were discontinued. There on the white platform surrounded by its three tiers of balustrades, the ancient rituals had been performed for the last time.

Japan

THE islands of Japan lying off the east coast of Asia were the last to receive
the stream of Asiatic culture that was carried there from India and China
particularly, and to a lesser extent from the Near East.
EARLY ART   Hokkaidō in the north, the large island of Honshū stretching south and west, with Shikoku fitting into a curve of its southern shore,
and Kyūshū almost due east from Shanghai are a beautiful group of volcanic lands that naturally inspired the early inhabitants to a worship of
mountains, streams, and trees. We know nothing about their culture before
about 500 B.C. and have no written records until Buddhism was introduced
in A.D. 552. Their myths and legends of the creation of the islands, which
were under the special protection of the sun-goddess, Amaterasu-Ō-
Mikami, and her earthly descendants who form the imperial house of
Japan, indicate the love and pride felt for their country by the aborigines
and the peoples who may have come up from the South Seas and the mainland to join them. According to legend, the Three Precious Things — a
jewel, a sword, and a mirror — were given in 660 B.C. to Jimmu Tennō,
who is supposed to have founded the empire.

There is some pre-historic pottery showing the use of the potter's wheel
and a variety of interesting patterns in bowls and vases, as well as pottery
figures of hollow tile. These were set around the graves, not placed inside
them as in China and Persia, but set on stems that were pushed into the
ground. They were of men, women, and horses for the most part, about
3½ to 4 feet high. Though not great works of art, they offer the student a
chance to study early costume, especially the armor, and they indicate the
Japanese preference for things that are 'bright and clear' in their simplicity and doll-like appeal. We are impressed at once by the difference
between this and Chinese art, which embodied the forces of nature and
dealt with mysteries that stirred the souls of men.

Early bronze articles are less accomplished in casting than many mainland pieces; Daitoku bells, which are very thin, have quite primitive designs in their panels of matchstick men, animals, hunting scenes, and houses. Some Chinese influence came via Korea in the Han Dynasty, bringing the mirror form and ornament, to which they added jingles similar to those used in Siberia.

Judging from early clay models of houses, and from houses built in the traditional manner in remote districts today, the high, pitched roof with spreading gables was the most characteristic feature of archaic dwellings. No doubt the 'palace' erected by the descendant of the sun-goddess in western Japan was of this type, which is still followed in the famous Shintō shrine at Izumo (fig. 592). Like most Indonesian houses, it is set up on a platform of posts and planks, and is almost dwarfed by the great roof, which should serve to protect it even in a torrential downpour; the roof is thick, made of layers of cryptomeria bark or thatch, originally kept in place by the crossed timbers on the ridge pole which are retained now as a decorative feature. In this, as in later Japanese construction, the post and lintel are the basis of design and support, rather than the wall. It is a splendid and clear development, using wood as the vital material, an excellent fusing of function and design. Wood, the only material at hand for the early builders, was appropriate, too, because of the emphasis on purity and simplicity in their ritual. Some of the modern shrines are rebuilt on these traditional lines every twenty or thirty years, so that there is no decay; they are not adorned with color, plaster, or clay; the wood speaks for itself. Inside the shrine there was one chamber, almost divided in two parts by a partition; there were no images at first, only a matting on the floor and an altar; the worshiper did not go inside.

The entrances to the early places of worship, which were generally in groves of trees or on mountains, were marked by simple gateways made by placing a horizontal log on two vertical tree trunks. This practice is continued in modern times in Shintō shrines in the erection of the *torii*, though the simplicity of ancient days has been discarded; the bark is stripped off of the logs, the surfaces are smoothed and frequently painted, and the topmost horizontal piece often is curved. The *torii* is used, for instance, at the famous shrine of the sun-goddess at Ise, and at the shrine of the Emperor Meiji in Tōkyō, and those of other deified members of the imperial family. Shintō, the 'Way of the Gods,' which was so closely associated with creation legends and the sacred groves of nature spirits, embraces the ruling house of Japan, and those who give their lives to protect the emperor and nation. In the nineteenth and twentieth centuries this relationship has been used to inspire patriotic fervor in the people, who were promised immortality through the sacrifice of a life in the line of duty. Whether in an isolated place like Ise, with its clear, bubbling streams and giant trees — a rustic setting for the simple wooden shrine and a fitting place for a goddess — or in a modern bustling city like Tōkyō, where elaborate edifices have been erected to the patriots, the Japanese recognize the *torii* as a symbol of the things they have revered most as a nation.

Except for the South Seas influence in architecture and in some of the early bronzes, the chief source of arts and crafts seems to have been Korea. In the Han period Korea had become a Chinese province, and thus had received her lacquer, bronzes, jade, pottery, and other material things from the Middle Kingdom, as well as laws and Confucian ideals. These made their way gradually into Japan. Then, in the fifth century, when the Tatars swept over north China and a ferment of activity began in the service of the Buddha, Korea shared in that, too. Image makers, temple builders, and painters followed missionary monks as the Law spread north and east.

The King of Paikche (a kingdom of Korea) sent an image of the Buddha to the Emperor of Japan in A.D. 552, with sacred texts, and a letter recommending the adoption of the new religion to his fellow ruler. The Emperor, being unable to decide so important an issue alone, submitted the problem to his ministers, who were torn between the old and the new; they could not agree, and thus was caused a prolonged cleavage at court, nobleman set against nobleman in that feudal society. In spite of dissension and suspicion, Buddhism gradually took hold in Japan. Its early days were stormy; sometimes it was in favor, sometimes out, but the missionary zeal of the believers did not flag. Though scourges of illness were attributed to the foreign god, and persecutions took place in which even the high-ranking converts suffered, the practice of the Law became more and more widespread toward the end of the sixth century. As the demand grew, more holy relics were brought over from Korea, priests and monks hastened to instruct the 'children' of the Land of the Rising Sun, temple carpenters came, as did skilled painters of images, carvers in wood, and sculptors in bronze and clay.

In 593 a woman, the Empress Suiko, came to the throne following the murder of the reigning emperor. In her time, inspired largely by her regent, the first art period begins (Suiko, A.D. 552–646). This regent, her nephew, who was known posthumously as Shōtoku Taishi, 'Sage Virtue,' was one of the great men of Japan in the early historic period. In 604 he gave a Code of Laws to his people, incorporating much of Buddhist and Confucian doctrine in it. He recognized in Buddhism a civilizing agent of prime importance to his country, and therefore encouraged the building of temples and sanctuaries and the translation of texts (in which Chinese characters were used, since up to that time the Japanese had had no written language), and made use of the knowledge of the monks in practical affairs in the development of agriculture and crafts in his native land. By the end of A.D. 624, there were 46 temples, 816 priests and monks, and 569 nuns.

One of the temples, the Hōryū-ji, still stands today, the oldest wooden building in the world (fig. 593), and one of the best examples in Japan of the early seventh-century style which closely followed Chinese lines. Since there is nothing so well preserved in China itself, it takes on an added significance. It served both as monastery and seminary, a training school for monks, a seat of learning especially dear to Shōtoku Taishi. The various buildings are enclosed in a rectangle by a wall, on the south side of which is the Great South Gate, the Nandaimon. Within are the Golden Hall (Kondō), the five-tiered pagoda (Go-jū-no-tō), the lecture hall (Kōdō — illustrated by the one at Tōshōdaiji, fig. 594), reading halls, priests' quarters, and the Hall of Dreams (Yumedono), which was added later in the eighth century on the site of Shōtoku's palace. The roofs are of tile, not thatch, showing the change from the old Japanese system to the fashionable Chinese type. The weight of the roof is carried by wooden beams that rest on tall, mast-like posts, and on the brackets, or corbels, of the wall, which were derived from the Han Dynasty supports (fig. 545); the wall itself is of wood and plaster. It is an excellent example of the simple and honest construction of the time, in which the materials were used to the greatest advantage for space and beauty, appropriate to the setting. The walls, buildings, pine trees, sand, and surrounding hills blend in a harmonious whole.

Early sculpture, like the architecture, is close to Chinese and Korean models, which perforce had followed Buddhist texts written in India. Akin to the images of the Wei and Sui periods of China (figs. 550, 552), the figures are somewhat rigid, faces and robes seem to have been based upon patterns rather than living models, and in them the spirit shines forth serenely.

Though plagues of illness were attributed to followers of the Buddha who had broken with the nature gods, miraculous cures were credited to him by those who prayed to him in his healing aspect, called (in Japanese) the Yakushi Buddha. Several of the most notable figures of the Suiko period are of Yakushi, or of the Bodhisattva of Mercy (Kwan-non). The historical Buddha, Śakyamuni of India (Shaka in Japanese), inspired many more dedications. Chinese and Korean masters, both wood carvers and bronze casters, taught their native pupils all the secrets of their arts, and the pupils proved to be so apt that the Suiko period and following eras produced some of the finest masterpieces in Nip-ponese sculpture. We cannot say now with authority which were made by the teachers and which by their apprentices; the motherland, China, has so little left in wood or monumental bronze of the same time that we can only be grateful for the Japanese examples.

Of them, one of the most precious in the eyes of Buddhists and con-noisseurs is the Yumedono Kwannon (fig. 595), shut away from most mortals in the Hall of Dreams of the Hōryū-ji, a favorite place of retire-ment for the prince-regent. According to popular belief, the tall, slim, six-foot wooden figure was based on that of Shōtoku, who must have been taller than his countrymen if the tale is true. The Bodhisattva (Bosatsu) holds a flaming jewel of immortality, and looks out with a benign smile for those who call upon his mercy. He is crowned with a diadem of pierced bronze set upon the flat waves of his hair, which follows the neckline, and descends in regular curls over the shoulders. This type of diadem, the long, stylized curls, and drapery arranged in rigid folds are characteristic of most of Suiko sculpture. The Indian prototype has been followed to the extent that the ūrna between the eyes is included, and long earlobes, and the dhotī, scarves, and jewelry of a prince; but they show Chinese influence in the flattening of vol-umes, the lack of interest in the body beneath the drapery, and the flowing robes, which are like Six Dynasty and Sui dress. The halo, too, seems to be a combination of Indian and Chinese ideas, as it extends upward in a flame, ornamented with lotus flowers and the stūpa sym-bolizing the Buddha.

Within the simple, spacious interior of the Kondō of the Hōryū-ji (which is not gilded, though it is called the Golden Hall), there are other splendid figures of the Suiko period. Two gilt bronze groups are attributed to the sculptor Tori of the early seventh century, one of Yakushi with attendants, and one of Shaka and two Bosatsu (fig. 596). Like the Yumedono Kwannon, some necessary Indian features in icono-graphic details are retained, but the character of the whole is much nearer Chinese Six Dynasty work, especially in drapery treatment. The stylized folds flow over the pedestals in sharply marked patterns of curving lines, which serve to emphasize the smooth modeling of each

face and throat as they emerge from the upper garments with architectonic simplicity. Another, called the Kudara Kwannon (fig. 597)
because it was reputed to be from Kudara, Korea, was carved from a
solid tree trunk, and painted. The paint has worn off in places, revealing
the sure stroke and sweep of the carver's knife. Side drapery runs parallel to the body, rather than at right angles to it, allowing the spectator
viewing it from the front to see the thin profile of the folds, which are
in marked contrast to the full, long arms, and the rounded volume of
the vase holding the dew of immortality suspended from the left hand.
Placed in the four corners of the room are the guardians of the Four
Quarters (fig. 598), the kings who safeguard followers of the Buddha,
each of whom holds his weapons and attributes in his hands, and stands
upon a miserable creature who is his vehicle. Later versions of these
guardians will be full of fury, movement and power, but at this early
stage the sculptors were content to make them majestic, as stiff and
unyielding as the tree trunks from which they were carved, massive,
yet crowned, as were so many other Suiko figures, by delicate, pierced
bronze diadems.

In the Chūgū-ji Nunnery in Nara, a seated Bodhisattva is enshrined.
The nuns have taken such excellent care of it in these thirteen hundred
years that it looks as though it were made of polished bronze rather than
wood (fig. 599). The bare torso of the Indian rajah has been retained,
but two knobs adorn the head instead of one; the pose may be seen in
countless figures taken from the caves of Yün-kang and Lung-mên in
China, but the true Japanese style begins to manifest itself in the marked
feeling for decorative folds and sharp, linear rhythms of hairline, ears,
and shoulder curls. Because the body is heavier and nearer the human
form in modeling, it is sometimes attributed to the following period.
Without knowing anything about its place in the mainstream of Japanese sculptural development, or even what it represents, thousands
who have seen it, or a photograph of it, have felt its appeal; the gentle
smile and subtle carving have made it, for many people, the most beautiful figure in Japan.

Almost as famous as these pieces of sculpture is a small painted
shrine, called the Tamamushi. The various panels represent scenes from
the life of the Buddha, or holy men, or symbols of Buddhist worship.
They are framed by strips of pierced bronze under which are impris-
oned iridescent beetle wings, which give the shrine its name. One of
them (fig. 600) illustrates an event in the life of the Buddha in which
he gave his life to save some starving tiger cubs. He is shown, in the

upper section, standing on a cliff, hanging his garment on a small tree; then he plunges through space, and we see his lifeless body in the lower part of the panel as he is being devoured by the hungry beasts. Delicate bamboos serve to mask the stark painfulness of this latter part, however, and they serve, in the composition, to balance the heavier upper areas. Colors are laid on in the 'banded style' of the early T'ang painters of China. The upper part of the shrine is a fine scale model of a Chinese temple, as interesting to architects as the panels are to students of the history of painting, especially for the rafters and roof supports.

Direct contact with China in the early years of the T'ang Dynasty wrought a change in Japanese art, as did the maturing gifts of native artists. The Hakuhō period (646–710) was enriched by contact with mainland cultures, as students, missionaries, priests, and travelers of all kinds flocked to the great T'ang cities. As we have seen, the western capital, Ch'ang-an, was a truly cosmopolitan place, a revelation to the Japanese, who became acquainted there with other Asiatic people and with the sumptuous wares offered for sale in the bazaars. Their art at home began to take on a more mature aspect, becoming richer and heavier, close to T'ang sculpture, painting, and architecture.

In Buddhist art Amidism, with its idea of salvation for the masses, had a profound effect. In one of the best examples of Hakuhō art, the shrine of the Lady Tachibana (fig. 601), Amida (Amitābha of India) occupies the central position in a bronze triad. The three figures sit or stand upon lotus, which seem to grow from a pool in his heavenly paradise. The saviour, benign and welcoming, sits in Indian fashion upon his flower pedestal, flanked by standing Bodhisattva. Features, hair, drapery, and hand gestures are integral parts of circular and oval linear rhythms, which serve to enhance the massiveness of their ponderous, cylindrical bodies — an effect that is unusual in small scale sculpture, for they are only a few inches high. Throughout, the shrine shows the utmost care in design and execution, even in parts not visible at first to the onlooker. The pool is made of bronze, a sheet of the metal ornamented with patterned waves and lotus, which one can see only by standing above the little group; a delicately designed halo nearly hides a screen (fig. 602), which is an exquisite portrayal in low relief of the souls of the blessed. They, too, are seated on lotus, which seem to grow up from the pool, guarded by the waving tentacles of an octopus, and clad in scarves that float lazily upward in their watery world.

Amida is one of the four impressive deities painted on the walls of the Kondō of the Hōryū-ji (fig. 603). These murals, about ten feet high, mark the easternmost flowering of the Buddhist fresco tradition, which had stemmed from Ajantā, then changed in the hands of Central Asiatic artists and the Chinese. In magnificence of conception, purity of line, and beauty of color, they are among the finest wall paintings in all of Asia.

Plumpness of cheeks, neck, and hands, so much admired in T'ang art, and a certain languid grace associated with India are to be found in the big black bronze Yakushi of the Yakushi-ji in Nara (fig. 604). The healing Buddha sits upon a pedestal ornamented with motifs borrowed from Sassanian Persia, India, and China. There are clusters of grapes nestling in grape leaves in the upper border, jewels surrounded by pearls, and, on each of the four sides, the quadrant animals — the Dragon, Red Bird, Tiger, and Tortoise in combat. Strange dwarf people with kinky hair and protruding teeth look out from caves in the lower sections, and yakshas hold ornaments over their heads, which divide the panels in two parts — symbols of civilization and barbarity are brought together to serve the Buddha. He sits cross-legged, and gazes into space, ignoring his two attendants, Nikko and Gakko, who stand on either side. All three figures have survived several fires that destroyed the temple building, fires that might have melted other images; and their survival has been attributed by the Japanese to magical qualities in the bronze. There is a large amount of silver in the alloy, which has turned black with the passage of time; this blackness and the smooth round volumes of faces, necks, and hands catch the light and give a richer appearance than the simple wood carvings of the earlier era.

A similar black bronze figure is housed near by in the pagoda. This three-storied pagoda (fig. 605) is an outstanding architectural monument of the period, for it has the splendid subtlety of proportion and the honesty of construction found in the Hōryū-ji buildings, plus a grace and lightness that mark later Japanese design. From the central mast (fig. 606), the horizontal beams extend to support the roofs, five in number, which form an interesting and uneven pattern in silhouette. A nine-ring soren serves as a crowning member, recalling the parasols that topped the stūpas of India, the source of inspiration for the pagodas of China and Japan.

The later Nara period, called Tempyō (710–794), was one of constant activity. The capital was established in Nara, laid out on lines similar to the Chinese capital, Ch'ang-an. The court became entirely Buddhist, modeling itself on the Buddhist hierarchy of gods; courtiers were referred to as Bodhisattva, and sūtras were read by every cultured person. Many new monasteries and temples were built, in which members of the royal family and nobility retired to a life of contemplation. As a climax to the building and making of images, the dedication of the huge bronze Buddha of the Tōdai-ji in 752 was unequaled for pomp and ceremony. The building itself, later destroyed by fire, was the largest wooden building in the world, and the 53-foot-high Buddha had kept the bronze casters busy for months. In answer to many prayers of the devout, gold was discovered miraculously in the north — just enough gold to cover the colossus. Amid great rejoicing, the Emperor called out his whole court to see him as he painted the pupil of the eye, which was the finishing touch. Like the big stone Buddha at Lung-mên (fig. 559), this was dedicated to Vairocana (Roshana) the Illuminator, the source of all wisdom and law.

The Tōdai-ji became a center of Buddhist learning, and a favored temple of the royal family. An illustrious Chinese monk was invited to establish a *kaidan* (platform for ordination) there, and did finally succeed, though he survived perils that would have stopped a less determined character. It was on his sixth attempt, in 754, that he reached Nara, after having been delayed by pirates, storms, shipwreck, and the Chinese authorities. Blind and feeble, this Ganjin held his first triumphal consecration ceremonies at the Tōdai-ji, in which he received more than 400 persons into the church, including the Empress Dowager. A portrait of him (fig. 607) made after his death is one of the finest in Japanese sculpture.

One of the most devout Buddhists of the royal family, the Emperor Shōmu, had abdicated in 748 to become a monk. His wife thereupon gave his extensive art collection to the Tōdai-ji, where a special house, the Shōsōin, was built to receive it. He had collected things made in all parts of Asia — textiles, musical instruments, furniture, masks, saddles, screens, glass, lacquer, paintings (figs. 608, 609), wearing apparel — a priceless group of treasures brought together before the mid-eighth century, which has not been augmented since, a fact that also adds immeasurably to its value in the eyes of the student of Oriental art.

In the Tōdai-ji, too, some of the outstanding contemporary sculpture is housed. Tempyō sculptors were, on the whole, modelers rather than carvers. Clay and lacquer were used, which allowed more variety of pose and greater freedom in surface modulation than was possible in the carved wood of the Suiko period. Building out from a wooden armature, the clay — or cloth dipped in lacquer juice — could be molded quite easily into folds of garments (fig. 610), or protruding muscles and veins (fig. 611), or even whirling draperies and scarves. Just as in China, where Indian ideas had come in a fresh wave in the T'ang period, Tantric formulas proved to be popular. Kwannons with eleven heads and many arms were made according to directions, but the Tempyō sculptors failed to give them the inner fire and energy notable in India; on the whole, the Japanese examples of thousand-armed Bodhisattva are overwhelming because of the sheer conglomeration of forms, not because of tension and power (fig. 612). The lacquer Aśura (demon — fig. 613), enemy of the gods, looks bewildered and rather dismayed at having spidery projections coming out of his armholes, and shows no affinity to his fellow demons of Cambodia or Tibet. Like other contemporary religious images, he wears a carefully painted garment, for the Japanese love of textile patterns begins to enter all their art.

So many members of the royal family retired to monasteries and continued to exert influence on national policy from a distance, and so
MEDIEVAL   much land was declared tax-exempt because it had
                passed into the hands of religious foundations, that
JAPANESE ART   an edict was issued removing the capital from Nara
to Kyōto or Heian-kyō, 'the capital of peace and tranquility,' where a new palace was made ready in 795. For the next ten years there was building on a grand scale, for smaller palaces had to be prepared for distant members of the royal family and the nobles, and a university devoted to Chinese studies, mathematics, and law, consisting of three large faculty halls, was erected near the South Gate. Kyōto, like Nara, was modeled on Ch'ang-an, symmetrically divided by broad roads into squares, and subdivided by narrow roads. By each was a moat; in fact, water from near-by Lake Biwa flowed into most of the gardens of the fine houses. Since there were many shrines already in Kyōto before it became capital, the Emperor Kwammu issued an edict soon after his accession (782) limiting the number of temples and restricting the admission of priests to holy orders; but soon the hillsides were covered with monasteries and sacred halls, and a hot rivalry sprang up between the various sects. Warlike monks proved to be a greater menace than anything dreamed of in Nara. Intrigue among the high-ranking clansmen in the palace kept the people in a turmoil; there were fires and ambushes, plots and counterplots, so the name of the city was more of an ideal to work toward than an actuality.

Some of this restlessness is reflected in the art of the Jōgan period (A.D. 794–897) and the patronage of the monasteries tended to encourage it, for mystery and terror were a part of this Buddhism, touched by Hinduism, which replaced the tender and protective teaching of the Suiko days. Instead of Shaka (who had come into the world to lead men away from pain by his Eight-fold Path), Yakushi the healer, Kwannon the merciful one, Amida the savior, and Miroku the leader of the future, all benign, there were Fudō and Dainichi, stern and remote, chastisers of the wicked, symbols of mystic forces of the universe. Kwannon becomes forbidding, almost repulsive, a strange combination of courtly elegance, dainty hand gesture, and a Tantric head with a mouth as cruel as Śiva's. The Red Fudō from Mt. Kōya (fig. 614) was considered too terrible a painting for average mortals to look upon: he sits in his fiery cavern, holding a thunderbolt and sword entwined in serpents, and a lasso to catch the wicked, attended by two youths who look more frightened than vengeful and have a cast of face that is decidedly Japanese, even to the prominent teeth. It belongs to one of the big monasteries founded in the ninth century adhering to the Shingon sect, established by Kōbō Daishi. He had gone to China to study, and returned in 807, imbued with the doctrine of the Mahā Vairocana or Dainichi Nyorai, the primordial and eternal Buddha from whom emanate all other Buddhas, who is to be approached by incantations (mantras), magic formulae (tantra and Dhārani), and ritual gestures. In sculpture (fig. 615) and painting, he is depicted as holding the forefinger of one hand in the five fingers of the other, a pose called the mudrā of the six elements, each finger standing for an element – earth, water, fire, air, ether, and wisdom. He was the Great Sun surrounded by flames, the highest vehicle of mystic union.

A rival institution, the Enryaku-ji monastery on Mt. Hiyei near Lake Biwa, had been founded in 805 by Dengyō Daishi, who adhered to the Tendai sect. He, too, had gone to China to study, at the T'ien T'ai monastery, and was learned in the Lotus Sūtra, which stressed meditation, self-discipline, and esoteric projection.

One of his monks, Genshin, found this too remote, and started a more popular worship of Amida (Amitābha). He reassured his followers by emphasizing faith, not deeds, and he reminded them that the Buddha of Boundless Light had vowed not to save himself until all who called on him were saved. If they said 'Namu Amida Butsu' often enough to reach his ear, he would assure their rebirth in his Western Paradise, the Pure Land (Jōdo). This comforting philosophy appealed much more to laymen than the difficult studies and magic of Tendai and Shingon.

Not far from Kyōto, at Uji, a nobleman had built a charming country house, which later was given to the church and dedicated to Amida. The courtiers of the Fujiwara period (897–1185) were very cultivated ladies and gentlemen, given to a study of literature and the arts, and the making of gardens, the writing of poetry, and dedicating their lives to proper etiquette and ceremony — all, surprisingly enough, in the midst of constant strife among the clans. This country house (fig. 616), true to the taste of the time for fantasy, was designed in the shape of a phoenix (pheasant, the Chinese fêng), the body and tail a corridor stretching out behind it, and the wings spread on either side. It is in the early tradition of post and lintel construction, using the simple bracket inherited from the Chinese. The proportions are exquisite, and the sloping tile roofs a delight to the eye, twice lovely because they are repeated in the lotus pool that reflects the temple. High on the roof of the central pavilion the bronze male and female phoenix face each other, graceful and full of style. Within the hall, now a sanctuary, the Amida Buddha presides (fig. 617), calm and majestic, a gilded wooden figure attributed to Jōchō, done in 1054. The high lotus pedestal, the stiff spareness of the Buddha, and the elaborate halo, canopy, and wall decoration are characteristic of the period. The ceiling is inlaid with mother-of-pearl and painted in flower medallions of rose, green, and blue. On the side walls a joyous throng of Bosatsu (Bodhisattva), carved in wood, seem to sweep down, playing on musical instruments and sporting on clouds. The sweetness, tenderness, and elegance of this are in perfect contrast to the brooding and terrible figures of Kōyasan. The inner facing of the wooden doors was painted with more Bosatsu and with a few bits of landscape, which mark the beginning of a style uniquely Japanese, decorative, resplendent, almost like a textile pattern.

This Tosa style of painting was started by a Fujiwara nobleman, and it reflects the ideals of Japan so perfectly that it has been labeled Yamato-e (Yamato being the homeland of Japanese culture, comprising the Ise-Nara-Kyōto area, where Jimmu is supposed to have settled). It is used to illustrate the Tales of Genji, the *Genji Monogatari* (fig. 618), written by a lady-in-waiting, Murasaki Shikibu, in the early eleventh century. It is a remarkable romance, one of the world's great books, which we may read in English in the fine translation by Arthur Waley. Genji was a courtier, a man of tender sentiment and a roving eye, who left a trail of broken hearts behind him in Kyōto and in his places of frequent exile. Lady Murasaki was one he loved and left, but she manages to remain detached enough to tell her tale with charm and vivaciousness. Written on tinted paper flecked with gold, in a script as delicate and graceful as the heroines it tells about, it is a perfect reflection of courtly refinement so much admired at that time. The scenes that illustrate the narrative are painted in tones of violet, green, rose, gold, and beige, set off by clear black lines. The perspective angle is from above and to one side, so that we seem to be looking into palace rooms made roofless for our inspection. As in other Asiatic painting, the lines come toward us instead of vanishing to some point within the picture plane. The background is established by the use of sliding panels and screens (actually used in the house of that era), and by emphasizing the diagonal lines of the floor matting. There are no cast shadows, the whole thing is done in the same clear light, space being linear and not atmospheric. Figures are cut into segments and patterns by the screens; it makes little difference whether one looks at the scroll right side up or upside down — the pattern is always striking. The ladies sit on the floor dressed in their court robes of brocade, with sleeves so wide and stiff that they look like butterfly wings, and their long, straight black hair is brushed to the hem of the garment, a mark of especial beauty. Their oval faces are all of a type; there is no individuality among them. All have tiny rosebud mouths, infinitesimal noses, small slanting eyes, and very heavy eyebrows. They are well named — Wisteria Blossom, Cherry, Chrysanthemum — sentimental and adorable participants in poetry contests and moon-gazing parties, as adept at intrigue as are palace beauties all over the world. The men, too, wear heavy brocaded robes and a characteristic tall black hat; they seem to be accomplished eavesdroppers, troubadours, and sportsmen, engaging in sallies of wit or arms with equal aplomb. In design the scroll reaches a high mark in Japanese art. The intricate spatial relations and color areas are the work of a great master who would feel perfectly at home in twentieth-century painting.

The pompousness of court and religious ceremony proved to be too tempting to the abbot of a monastery for him to resist poking fun at them. Toba Sōjō — or some other monk well skilled in brushwork — painted a series of scrolls caricaturing the occupations and games of his contemporaries. These four scrolls, hidden for years in a hollow lacquer statue, now belong to the Kōzan-ji monastery. As we roll them out and chuckle over the incidents — monkeys, frogs and hares (fig. 619), acting like courtiers and priests, ragamuffins and bums playing games with zest and disturbing the peace — we can readily understand why they had to be hidden. Luckily they were found, allowing us to see a different side of the Japanese personality of the time, and to enjoy the different scenes that are so skilfully done, superb in line and satire. The whole of each scroll in the set should be seen to get full enjoyment out of them, for the time element in the unrolling is important, but even a fragment is delightful. In one part, beneath a tree worthy of a Sung master, we see a monkey garbed as an officiating priest making an offering to the Buddha — and Buddha is a frog. His legs are folded in yoga fashion, his hands raised in the right mudrās, his smile as benign and blank as some temple image, his halo of large leaves and his cushion of a lotus leaf are as correct as a courtier's hat. In the next scene another priest-monkey is receiving gifts of tiger skins, fruits, scrolls, and other good things, checking them in with a pious smugness, which was probably all too familiar to the painter. Long before Walt Disney, a Japanese discovered the joys of poking fun at man and his foibles in the guise of animals. There is no text, nor is there need for words — the pictures speak for themselves.

These, and the three scrolls of the Shigisan Engi, which are done in light color and with a brush as remarkable as the Kōzan-ji set, and other scrolls of demons, diseases, and wars mark the beginning of a secular art that grew and developed one day into the wood-block prints of the eighteenth and nineteenth centuries. The Tosa style became so popular that it even intruded into the religious field; the sūtras dedicated to the Taira family are as gay as fans and as delicate as dew on a cobweb. They are far removed from the solemn spirit of dedication of the man whose words they are supposed to be. Kichijōten (Lakshmi in India), goddess of beauty and fortune, is no longer a goddess but a court lady (fig. 620) and a colorful Japanese one.

The frivolous, cultivated court was shaken from its dreams when Yoritomo, conqueror of the Taira clan, established himself as Shōgun (Barbarian-quelling Generalissimo) in 1192 in Kamakura, the ancient seat of his clan, the Minamoto. The real government then moved north, though the emperor was allowed to keep his court and nominal power in Kyōto. Military men took over the actual running of the country, which left the court nobles with a beautiful, elaborate, and empty etiquette to maintain. The glorification of war and some of its terror were depicted in a set of scrolls dealing with the Heiji wars: one scroll, the Burning of the Sanjō Palace, is in the Museum of Fine Arts in Boston (fig. 621). This last detail, which follows a tumultuous and vivid continuous picture of hurrying crowds, flames, and smoke billowing from the palace, as courtiers, nuns, and attendants were trampled under foot and horsemen rushed through the palace, comes as a tense and quieter moment in all the excitement. The Emperor is being protected by his guard, who go forward gingerly, expecting an ambush. After the crowded ovals of frantic, milling people, this makes a final wedge-shaped pattern pointing toward the equestrian on the black horse and the archer who almost tiptoes toward the unknown. It is one of many splendid narrative scrolls based on the lives of national heroes, churchmen, and men of letters (figs. 622, 623, 624).

Religious painters were as active as secular artists, still doing the large, magnificent vertical scrolls that were hung in the temples or carried to the bedside of those about to die; such paintings of Amida, resplendent in gold, were thus taken as a kind of extreme unction to the faithful, a reassuring vision of the Western Paradise where they would be reborn. Jizō, special protector of little children (fig. 625), was a popular figure in painting and sculpture, portrayed as a young monk in a rich robe, carrying a staff. He was a boyish and pleasant youth especially dear to the Japanese. Even a Shintō god of war (for Shintō now had to compete with Buddhism in image making) is shown as a mild monk (fig. 626).

One of Japan's greatest sculptors was active in the Kamakura period — Unkei, son of Kōkei. He and his relatives, Kōben his son, and Tankei and Kōen his grandsons, went to Nara to restore some of the Suiko period figures and so lived with some of the splendid sculpture of the past. They, too, worked in wood, but they preferred joining pieces together rather than carving from a solid trunk, a method that allowed far more freedom of action and pose than the Suiko sculptors had achieved. It is a period of realism and dynamic power. They made the two guardians that are placed inside the great gate at the entrance of the Tōdai-ji monastery in Nara, muscular, fierce, with exaggerated veins and tendons, bulging eyes, and widespread fingers, worthy descendants of the fiery Chinese guardians of Lung-mên made in the T'ang period. In a quieter vein there is the portrait of Muchaku (Hsüan-tsang, the Chinese pilgrim and scholar), an interesting character study of the traveling monk and Master of the Law (fig. 627). One of Unkei's followers carved a full-length figure of the Indian teacher Vasubandhu (Basu-sennin) who looks as lean as a Donatello St. John the Baptist, or St. Mary Magdalene, the miserable flesh hanging on his bones, eyes sunk in their sockets, and his rags flapping on his bent body (fig. 628). Another, Jōkei, did a muscular guardian with swirling drapery (fig. 629), which must have pleased the military leaders of the period. Most of the wooden sculpture had crystal eyes (fig. 630) set in to make the faces more natural, and one figure (fig. 631) was left nude so that it could be clothed in brocaded garments. The Japanese feeling for pattern and simplicity of form is demonstrated in the carving of a courtier, Uesugi Shigefusa (fig. 632), which looks to us more like a twentieth-century piece than one of the thirteenth century. It is rather a pity that one of the inferior works of this magnificent period is the best known, the Great Amida in Kamakura (fig. 633), admired by all tourists, and copied in desk size for the curio seeker. The temple housing it has been destroyed so often that there have been no more attempts to rebuild it, and Amida now sits in the midst of beautiful trees, a sanctuary in itself.

Kubilai Khan had tried to open peaceful relations with Japan in 1268, but threatened war if his proffers were refused. Japan ignored his envoys and threats, and in 1274 a Mongol army, reinforced with Koreans, set forth from Korea in 450 ships. When these were destroyed by storms, he tried again in 1281, but this time his fleet was smashed by storm after his men had landed and engaged in battle. Thus the Japanese, like the Indians, escaped the Mongol domination that spread over most of the rest of Asia. But Kamakura power was waning, and there was restlessness in Kyōto where intrigue reached its height when five ex-emperors, all of whom had abdicated, tried to exercise the authority belonging to a ruler. By 1330 two lines were in conflict, and Daigo II of the junior line was victor; Kamakura was captured in 1333 and destroyed by fire. Kyōto again became the seat of government, though the Emperor entrusted the administration to the Ashikaga family, who were appointed Shōguns, and they were the actual rulers from 1392 to 1568.

Numbers of Chinese had moved to Japan when the Mongols destroyed the Sung Dynasty, and they continued to follow the philosophy that emphasized self-reliance and meditation, the Ch'an form of Buddhism, called Zen in Japan. The simplicity, rugged individualism, absence of pomp, and disregard for involved metaphysics appealed to the military minds of the Ashikaga or Muromachi period. Zen priests were placed in key positions; they were important politically, and their practice and teaching influenced all of the art and life of that time. They controlled trade, and they brought 'modern' spoken Chinese to Japan, where the language of China of four centuries before was still used.

Following the inspiration of the Sung Dynasty artists, many of whose masterpieces had been taken to Japan, there was a furor of artistic activity as soon as peace and order were restored in Kyōto. Turning their backs on their own rapidly developing styles and idioms, Japanese painters and other artists received this direct Chinese influence with enthusiasm. Many new temples were built, gardens were constructed to look like Chinese scenery in miniature, flower arrangement became the pastime of monks and military men alike, the tea ceremony offered a welcome change from the battlefield or affairs at court, and priest and courtier tried brush painting in black and white with such good results that it is hard to tell some of the Japanese painting from the Chinese.

The third Shōgun, Yoshimitsu, built the Golden Pavilion in 1397, and ruled from there like a retired emperor; he had abdicated two years earlier, but remained influential. The Pavilion (fig. 634) is a three-story house made of fine woods in the simple manner dictated by Zen. The balustrades, supports, and walls are unadorned, and the only curving lines are to be found in the roofs and the windows on the third floor; even the proposed gilding was confined to the third story, where few traces of it remain. It is reflected in a pool, and surrounded by austere gardens consisting largely of pines, rocks, and sand.

The eighth Shōgun, Yoshimasa, was equally active in encouraging the arts during his rule from 1449 to 1474. He built the Silver Pavilion, and had its gardens laid out by the famous painter Sō-ami, who created Chinese waterfalls, rocks, mountains, and trees on screens (fig. 635) as well as in miniature in the gardens.

Japanese painters learned to suggest more in the black and white paintings than was actually described, in true Zen fashion. Jōsetsu, at the end of the fourteenth century, did the Catfish and Gourd (fig. 636), which is composed of bamboo, river grasses, running water, misty mountains, and a ragged fisherman, who looks, in the Chinese manner, like a child of nature trying to catch his lunch; but it is actually a symbol of man's endeavors in which he reaches beyond himself. It is as hard to catch a slippery catfish in a small gourd as to be a true follower of the Tao.

Since it was a period of great artistic activity, there are many names that should be included in an exhaustive study; but one outshines all the others — that of Sesshū. Oda Tōyō, for that was his real name, lived from 1420 to 1506, most of his life a Zen priest. In training for the priesthood he had the opportunity to learn to paint, and proved to be so promising that he became a pupil of the distinguished priest-painter Shūbun (fig. 637). As he studied the Chinese masters whose works had been taken to Japan in considerable numbers, he was fired with the ambition to go to the land that had inspired them, to see the rivers and mountains for himself. He went to China from 1467 to 1469, and was received with honor in Chinese monasteries. He traveled extensively, steeping himself in the landscapes that had had such a profound influence on the painters of the Sung period, especially the rugged, dramatic places that might have served as models for Hsia Kuei, whose work he particularly admired. On his return to Japan he devoted himself to perfecting a similar style (fig. 638) by which he could portray the crystalline hardness of rocks, the tortuous twisting of tree branches and roots, the rough thatch of a cottage roof, with a few vigorous brushstrokes. A human being could be done in ten strokes. Among his more ambitious works is the horizontal scroll, 51 feet long, now in the possession of Count Mori. This he did in his sixty-seventh year, a masterpiece of sustained effort. If we compare it with the Chinese scrolls, we find that there is less grading of tones, less poetry in his painting, less interest in actual space, and more in the relationship of forms, which he handles in a personal and exciting way; portions of it would seem to be forerunners of Van Gogh. Like other Japanese, the decorative qualities interest him. He worked in three styles, and toward the end of his life seemed to prefer a free and powerful tonal painting, done with unbelievable speed and sureness, a *tour de force* of dexterity, leaving so much unsaid that the imagination is called into full play. Of his many followers, one, Sesson, learned to use his ink with freedom and power, and a marked feeling for decorative design (fig. 639).

WHILE priests and scholars were trying to paint in the Chinese way, courtiers continued to love the Tosa style (fig. 640). Thinking to combine the good qualities of both, a group of professional painters formed a school called Kanō, led by Masanobu and his son Motonobu. They were much

LATER JAPANESE ART

in demand as painters of screens, especially for the Kyōto monasteries. They decorated the sliding panels that separated one room from another, and large six-fold or eight-fold screens, which could be placed against the wall; appropriate subjects were the changing seasons, sages and leaders of the past, and the birds and flowers, symbols of men's virtues. Since they were to be seen from a distance, they had to be boldly designed and executed, using definite lines, brilliant colors, and gold leaf laid on in squares (fig. 641).

In the following period, the Momoyama (1568–1615), civil wars again troubled Japan. Military men had influence even in the world of art. They erected big castles and fortresses in the European fashion, built of stone with strong foundations (fig. 642). To bring warmth and color to the severe walls they used big, magnificent screens, much as Europeans of the Middle Ages had used tapestries. The taste of the military did not run to the delicate and subtle, so the Kanō makers had a splendid opportunity to give free rein to the Japanese genius for striking design. A six-fold screen attributed to Sanraku (fig. 643) of the Bridge at Uji has been much admired as a characteristic example. The background is covered with gold leaf, willow trees with reddish brown trunks and branches droop over the bridge that sweeps across the panels in a bold and distorted pattern, dominating the whole design. The water under the bridge flows in patterned waves, bronze-colored, and seems to mingle with clouds on the right, which are equally patterned.

By this time Buddhist art was on the decline, and Tosa was almost dead; it was the great moment for the decorators and the few who still worked in the Chinese manner. Of the latter, one of the most interesting is Tōhaku. He is particularly renowned for his screens (fig. 644), which are quite different from the brilliant Kanō products, being usually black and white, or in light colors, relying on soft tone and brushwork rather than striking pattern for their appeal.

As the church and nobility ceased to be patrons, the way was paved for a popular, plebeian art to come into being, something gay, rich in color, and not too profound. In the next period, the Tokugawa (1615–1867), just such an art developed. Painters made designs for pottery, screens, and panels, men like the Ogata brothers Kōrin (fig. 645) and Kenzan (fig. 646). They and the lacquer makers, porcelain manufacturers, makers of theater posters, calendars, and wood-block prints had an opportunity at last to make their wares completely Japanese in style. Some of them co-operated with architects to make the sumptuous buildings of the seventeenth and eighteenth centuries.

The famous shrines at Nikkō (fig. 647) reflect the change from the simplicity of the past to the richness of the Japanese Baroque. In a setting of magnificent trees and streams, which would have been shrine enough for worshipers in earlier times, they erected gates, pagodas, outbuildings, and halls of prayer so elaborately carved, lacquered, and gilded that it would take days to study all the panels. A brilliant red-lacquered bridge was reserved for the use of the royal family, but all pilgrims and tourists could enter the gate, with its several curved roofs and its many corbels, flanked by corridors adorned with carved, painted panels of birds and fish. Among the temple buildings was the sacred stable, and there the famous monkeys of 'Hear no evil, see no evil, say no evil' were carved and colored green, brown, white, and gold. Moving away from the dazzling forms and colors of the temple, the patriot could go up a long simple flight of steps to the mausoleum of the Shōgun Ieyasu, a peaceful and austere place guarded by giant cryptomeria trees, more like the original Shintō shrine.

One of the eras, the Genroku (1688–1704), was a time of great luxury, famous for lacquer work, textile weaving, porcelain making, and other decorative arts. The nobility became alarmed at the prosperity of tradesmen and other plebeians, and had laws passed that forbade them to own things as elaborate as those of the hereditary families, but even these sumptuary laws were circumvented by the people who were rapidly taking the fortunes from the nobility, and wanted some of the bright and tempting things to be seen in the shops of Yedo (Tōkyō), the new capital.

Farmers and travelers came to the city from other parts of Japan to see the sights, especially of the theater and the Yoshiwara district, where the ladies of the Green Houses lived in a tempting world of their own; and they wanted pictures and souvenirs to take home. The inexpensive wood-block print proved to be the means of satisfying them. The process had been perfected in China, where it was being used extensively at this same time, but the Japanese made of it an art that has not been rivaled by any other country.

In the late seventeenth century, Moronobu made a series of prints of occupations in Tōkyō, as well as single sheet pictures for visitors to take home with them, pictures of a Floating World (Ukiyo-e). They were usually small in scale, some of them page size, not unlike the book illustrations that had been made for centuries, except that he recognized more than anyone else the possibilities of the woodcut. Some were colored by hand, but most of them were patterns in black and white in which there were no cast shadows, no grading of tone; space was established by diagonals set against curves, and by the placing of the figures. They are animated, gay, sometimes satirical. Though we think of the Ukiyo-e masters as being primarily interested in prints, which are better known because of their great numbers, they did paintings as well, a considerable body of which survives.

Moronobu's pupil Kiyonobu was a sign painter for the theater, accustomed to big designs and swirling patterns, ample curves and splendid textile design in the garments of the actors. He began to do these in the wood-block technique, and became the founder of the Torii school specializing in theater work. His eldest son, Torii Kiyomasu, worked in a style so similar that it is not easy to tell their prints apart (fig. 648).

As the trade became more profitable and interesting, all kinds of refinements were thought of; the simple prints were enriched with gleaming black lacquer, water colors, and gold, and gauffrage began to be used — a kind of relief, made by raising the surface of some areas. The next step was the use of separate blocks for printing color; at first, pink and green, or other simple two- and three-color prints were made, and finally, under Harunobu (1725–70), the art of printing many colors was brought to its highest point, using as many as eleven separate blocks to print the 'brocade' colors, which he started in 1764.

From that time on, he experimented, regarding the medium as one possible of producing delicate and subtle prints of great artistic merit. Instead of drawing his subjects from the crowded city streets or the theater, he concentrated on young girlhood with all its moods and fancies, the refined and lovely daughters of the well-to-do, graceful and appealing. In their most casual occupations, reading at home, admiring cherry blossoms, doing their hair, he found subjects worthy of his most painstaking care. He liked to emphasize their frailty by showing them buffeted by wind and rain, walking through the snow, crossing a bridge, or standing beside a building much larger than they. One is wearily going up the temple steps; against the strong diagonals, she looks unbelievably small, with hands and feet too tiny even for her body. Another, called the Crow and the Heron (fig. 649), is of a white-robed girl and her escort, who is swathed in black, as they walk through the snow, stepping softly on their high wooden shoes and holding an umbrella on which the snow is white and heavy. The mood of winter, the feeling of a winter day, is brought out by his restraint in handling the little genre scene, in the delicacy of color and line. He purposely distorts his figures for effective design, and uses the traditional contrast of diagonals and curves, as well as color, to indicate space.

His success was so great that the other print makers almost stopped work in discouragement. Two of his pupils, however, Koryusai and Shunshō, strove, as their master had, to develop the color print into a great art, and succeeded nearly as well. Shunshō specialized in doing actors of the popular theater in their favorite roles. As in the time of Shakespeare, men were the only actors on the stage. They took women's parts, having been trained from childhood to do it, spending their lives acting and speaking like women, even off the stage, practicing a mincing walk that made the flowing kimono move in graceful lines, and speaking in a falsetto. They were so proud of their art that they handed the tradi-

tion from father to son, or to an adopted child who was brought up to
be a specialist in these certain parts.

Toward the latter part of the eighteenth century another master of
the Torii line, Kiyonaga, brought out prints in still a different style
(fig. 650). He liked mature women, tall, classic, and poised. Their
kimono and the obi tied around the waist are of varied patterns and
colors, which are shown to advantage on their ample figures; their elaborate coiffures are a special study in themselves. He preferred spacious
backgrounds, the grand sweep of riverside or garden, as a setting for
them; sometimes he found one piece of paper too small, and made a
design that was printed in three parts, a triptych of eighteenth-century
Japanese life. He was inspired by breadth and grandeur rather than by
the delicacy and frailty Harunobu loved.

At about the same time two other artists of unusual talent came to the
public eye — Utamaro and Sharaku. Utamaro considered himself the high
priest of the ladies of the Green Houses (fig. 651); he gloried in showing
every pose, gesture, coiffure, and mood of the famous beauties, who
were often cultivated and gifted women. The half-length figure appealed
to him particularly, for it allowed him to concentrate on the face, throat,
and shoulders, the delicate hairline or tiny ear. His outline is so tenuous
that it is hard to see; at times he dispensed with the black line entirely,
and had colors printed side by side. He and some of his contemporaries
enriched the whole print by using powdered mica on the background,
giving it a sparkling quality. This seemed to make it too precious in the
opinion of the nobles, so sumptuary laws were passed, forbidding it. By
some he is considered one of the greatest of the Ukiyo-e masters; by
others, a decadent practitioner of an art that lacks dynamic quality or
nobility of theme.

Sharaku, the mystery man of the whole group, appeared like a comet
and disappeared as quickly. In the year 1794, in a few months, he
designed 130 prints caricaturing actors of the popular drama (fig. 652),
caricatures of such power and venom that it is hard to believe that they
were done by an amateur. We know only that he was an actor in the
classical Nō drama, attached to a nobleman's household, and therefore
forbidden to mingle with actors in the Kabuki (plebeian) theater. So far,
no early works have been discovered that could help us to account for
these accomplished satires; we are reminded of Toba Sōjō and his rebellion against the pompousness of the Fujiwara court and church (fig.
619), expressed in biting or humorous sketches, just as we know that
the masks worn by Nō actors were made by carvers who were specialists

in exaggeration, and that old religious sculpture — of guardians particularly (fig. 598) — might have inspired a painter by their energy and
fury — they could have been a part of the heritage of any Japanese of
the time. All that we know about him is that he is the master of the
expressive eyebrow, the pig-like eye, the hooked nose, and the vicious
mouth; and the master, too, of interesting hands and of elegant, simple
robes, in which he used the actor's crest (*mon*) very effectively. He
stopped as suddenly as he had started, and retired, perhaps to the sheltered world of an aristocratic household. Whether it was done by choice,
or by order of his lord, or through pressure brought to bear on him by
the popular actors he lampooned, we do not know.

In the late eighteenth and early nineteenth centuries the color print
was used by two outstanding landscape artists, Hokusai and Hiroshigé,
to picture the whole of Japanese life and most of the beauty spots of
Honshu, the main island of their country. Hokusai, the 'old man mad
with painting,' lived to be 89 years old, and at his death his only regret
was that he had neglected to make more pictures of his homeland.
During his long life he illustrated books and poems, made single prints
of birds and flowers, and did series of views, the best known being the
Views of Fuji. He included everything he could in his landscapes —
peasants working in the rice fields, or poling boats on the river, doing
carpentry, going to festivals, or fishing. In his famous print, The Wave
(fig. 653), he gives a vivid impression of the life of those who go out on
the sea in frail boats. In a composition of sweeping curves, he shows
the boatmen almost swamped by the overpowering ocean, their heads
hardly larger than the fingers of foam that reach toward them. There are
the surge of the sea, the mist rising from it, and Fuji in the far distance,
all done in tones of blue with a suggestion of yellow in the sky. The
energy with which he did this — and almost every subject imaginable —
is characteristic of him and his unfailing zest for life.

Hiroshigé, too, did series of landscapes (fig. 654), and bird and flower
prints. Like Hokusai he succeeded in recording the most typical and
beautiful aspects of his country from one end of it to the other — the
post road from Kyōto to Tōkyō, lakes, temples, mountains, and rivers.
Even today, wherever the traveler may look he is sure to see a bit of
the land that reminds him of a Hiroshigé print. Unlike Hokusai, who
liked to include many details in his compositions, the younger man
learned to leave out some of the nonessential, if picturesque, elements,
and thus gave to his work a breadth and subtlety that are a constant
delight. He relied more on color and tone, less on line, for his interesting

effects; the Japanese had become acquainted with European art and perspective techniques by his time, and his work shows that he had studied them, though the total impression is entirely Oriental. He not only pictured specific places, he caught as well the moods of nature, the changes of season, the insignificance of man, and the majesty of mountains; his was a poetic expression. Rain pouring down, making of bamboo and hillside a study in tones of gray, geese flying across the moon, the fox spirits gathering in the gloaming, a bridge at sunset — all are done with singular beauty.

He and the others mark the final development of a unique art, which struck nineteenth-century Europe as a fresh, lovely, and admirable thing. These prints served as ambassadors of good will to a world waiting for something new — but what they expressed was not new; it was as old as civilization itself, growing out of the infinite riches of the Orient. The poetry of Persia in all its brilliant color, the intellect and emotion of India made visible in stone and bronze, the secret harmonies of nature echoed in the rhythms of Chinese art, the youthfulness and boldness of Japan — all are ours now to enjoy and study. We can take pleasure in them without knowing more than that the design and color are appealing, but that pleasure can be increased immeasurably by learning something of the peoples and places that produced them, for there is no art for art's sake in the Orient. The disciplines of the various crafts were perfected to serve the glory of man or god; therefore we must look beyond technical facility to the inner vision that inspired it, enriching ourselves as we reach toward that greater understanding.

Glossary

Abacus The uppermost member of a classic capital; a simple plinth in the Doric, the abacus becomes a thin slab, sometimes decorated in the Ionic, and in the Corinthian order a molded block with concave sides.

Acanthus A Greek plant that served as the inspiration for the foliage of the Corinthian capital and other architectural motives.

Acroteria Figures or decorations placed above the angles of a pediment.

Adobe A method of construction using dried clay, especially associated with southwestern United States.

Aisle A longitudinal division of a plan separated from other parts of the building by colonnades or arcades; especially the narrower lateral divisions of church plans.

Ambulatory The semicircular or semipolygonal aisle encircling an apse.

Anta A thickening of a wall provided with a plain capital and base, to receive the end of a beam. Somewhat similar to but not to be confused with a pilaster, the anta is simpler and its capital and base plainer than that of the order with which it is to be used.

Apadana An audience hall.

Apsaras Angel.

Apse A semicircular or polygonal part of a plan, particularly one terminating the main axis of a church.

Arabesque Originally signifying the rich surface patterns of Mohammedan art, the word has come to mean any elaborate scroll pattern in paint or low relief.

Arcade A row of arches supported by piers or columns.

Arch A device for spanning an opening, consisting of wedge-shaped blocks called voussoirs.

Arch Order An arch, enframed by engaged columns or pilasters and entablature, developed in Rome, but also used in the Renaissance and in the derivatives of either style.

Architrave A beam, particularly the lower of the three principal divisions of a classic entablature.

Archivolt An architrave turned into an arch; a group of moldings adorning and emphasizing the curve of an arch.

Arhat or Lohan A disciple of Buddha.

Armature A frame of wood or metal serving as the support for the clay of a statue while the sculptor models it.

Arris A ridge formed by the intersection of two planes; particularly the ridge that separates flutes in a Doric column.

Ashlar Cut stone masonry; in regular ashlar, the blocks are rectangular and uniform in size; in random ashlar the blocks vary in size.

Atrium   An enclosed but unroofed forecourt such as those found in Roman houses and in Early Christian and later churches.

Attic   (1) A low story placed above a cornice. (2) The uppermost story of a house, curtailed in volume by the slope of the roof. (3) Pertaining to the land of Attica; i.e. Athens.

Axis   An imaginary central line around which a design or any of the parts thereof is balanced.

Baldacchino   The word comes from the canopies carried in religious processions; hence, a free-standing architectural canopy over an altar.

Barrel Vault   A semicylindrical vault.

Bas Relief   Low reliefs; sculpture in which the roundness of the forms is expressed by planes projecting slightly from a flat background.

Basilica   A hall-like structure flanked by aisles; Roman basilicas served as business buildings; the Early Christian basilicas were churches.

Batter   An inward slope of the surface of a masonry wall, used to add strength.

Bay   The space between the centers of adjacent supports, and thus a unit of design.

Beam   A horizontal member to support a weight over an opening.

Bodhisattva   Saintly Buddhist beings who deny themselves eternal blessedness to save others from misery.

Bond   The interlocking of stones or bricks in a wall by laying one unit over parts of two or more other units. The commonest bonds in brickwork are (1) American Bond, one course of headers (the short ends of brick exposed) out of every six or seven courses of stretchers (the long side of the brick exposed; (2) English Bond, alternate courses of headers and stretchers; and (3) Flemish Bond, alternate headers and stretchers within each course.

Cartoon   The final full-size preliminary drawing for a painting.

Cartouche   An ornament in paint or low relief carving, composed of scrolls, heraldry, or foliate designs.

Caryatid   A sculptured female figure used in place of a column.

Casement   See *Sash*.

Cella   The sanctuary of a classic temple.

Cement   A material that when mixed with water will dry into a stonelike mass. Cement should be carefully distinguished from concrete, of which it is one of the ingredients; cement is also used in some mortars.

Centering   The temporary mold of wood or metal used to support an arch or vault until construction is completed; the centering is then removed.

Chaitya   Hall for worship, India.

Chamfer   A diagonal plane cut from the corner of a rectangular member, such as a square pier, or a window or door opening.

Chancel   The area of a Christian church around the high altar, reserved for the clergy; the sanctuary.

Chapel   A small church; also a part of a larger church housing one of the secondary altars.

Chevet   The complex of apse, ambulatory, and radiating chapels in medieval churches.

Chiaroscuro   Light and shade in painting.

Choir   That portion of a church between the altar and the nave or crossing reserved for the lower clergy, especially the singers. Occasionally the liturgical choir may extend down into the architectural nave.

Chryselephantine   Of gold and ivory, as was the Zeus of Phidias.

Cire Perdue Lost wax; a method of bronze-casting wherein the shell of the statue is duplicated in wax which is then replaced by molten bronze.

Clapboard A thin board nailed horizontally to the frame of a house; clapboards overlap one another like shingles.

Clearstory Part of a building raised above the roof of a neighboring part to admit light.

Cloister A rectangular courtyard beside a medieval church to provide a sheltered walk for the clergy.

Coffer A decorative panel sunk in the under surface of a vault or ceiling; most coffers are rectangular or octagonal but they may be of any shape.

Collage Compositions created by glueing bits of paper, cloth, cigarettes, and other scraps on a flat surface; parts of the design may be painted.

Colonnade A row of columns supporting beams or lintels.

Colonnette A small column.

Column An architectural support, round in plan or nearly so, and composed of a base, shaft, and capital.

Compound Pier An architectural support composed of colonnettes, and rectangular members around a masonry core.

Concrete A building material similar to stone when dry but semifluid while being mixed. The ingredients are cement, sand, crushed stone or gravel, and water.

Contrapposto A torsion of the axis of the body to produce a sense of balancing movements within the figure, as when the shoulders face in a different direction from the hips.

Corbel A stone or brick whose face projects beyond that of its support to serve as a bracket. A Corbel Table consists of a series of small arches resting on corbels. A Corbel Arch is composed of stones laid in horizontal courses, each corbelled out in turn until the opening is covered.

Cornice The uppermost division of a classic entablature, projecting sharply to support the edge of the roof; any similar molded projection.

Course A horizontal layer of stone or brick in a wall.

Court An area open to the sky but enclosed on three or four sides by walls or blocks of building.

Crocket A projecting stone, usually carved with foliage, on the edge of a gable or the angles of a spire.

Crossing The space in churches occupied by the intersection of the nave and transepts.

Crown of an Arch The apex of an arch.

Crypt The basement of a church, not necessarily underground, often containing some of the relics.

Cyclopean Masonry Large, irregularly cut blocks of stone built into ponderous walls.

Dāgoba See *Stūpa.*

Dentil A small rectangular block; a molding composed of such blocks, commonly used to support a cornice.

Dhotī Draped skirt, India.

Diptych A painting composed of two balancing panels.

Dome A hemispherical vault.

Dormer An attic window with its roof and enframement projecting through a sloping roof.

Drum A cylindrical block of stone to form part of the shaft of a column; also the cylindrical wall on which a dome rests.

Eaves   The portion of a roof overhanging the walls.

Echinus   The cushion-like member of the Doric capital immediately below the abacus.

Elevation   A scaled architectural drawing portraying the front, back, or side of a building.

Engaged Column   A column part of whose diameter is incorporated in a wall.

Engraving   A process in the graphic arts in which the design is scratched on a metal plate; ink wiped over the plate will remain in the scratches and thus enable the design to be printed.

Entablature   The portion above the columns and below the roof on the exterior of a classic temple, consisting of the architrave, frieze, and cornice; these same members may also be used to terminate a wall.

Entasis   The slight vertical curve or bulge in a shaft when compared with a straight line run from the top to the bottom. Most columns taper somewhat, but this is not entasis.

Etching   A graphic process wherein the design is scratched through a film of wax onto a metal plate; the plate is then bathed in acid which attacks the metal wherever the wax has been scratched off; after the acid has been washed off, and the remaining wax removed, the plate is inked and prints made from it.

Façade   The front of a building.

Fenestration   The arrangement of windows in a building.

Fêng   "Phoenix," bird of pheasant type in Chinese art.

Fillet   A narrow flat molding.

Flute   A groove, usually vertical; especially that in the shaft of a column or pilaster. Collectively these grooves are called fluting.

Flying Buttress   A half arch supporting a diagonal course of stone to transfer the thrusts of the nave vault over the aisle roofs to the pier buttress on the outer wall of the church.

Fresco   A technique of painting on wet plaster. See p. 164.

Frieze   A horizontal band, sometimes sculptured, especially the middle third of an entablature.

Frontality, Law of   Figures in which the axis of the body is not twisted or curved laterally are said to obey the law of frontality. The action of the arms or legs of such figures, however, need not be identical in pose.

Gambrel Roof   A roof with two slopes in each half; the upper slope comparatively gentle, and the lower one steeper.

Gandharva   Sky minstrel, India.

Gargoyle   A waterspout, frequently carved as a grotesque in mediaeval architecture.

Garuda   Bird enemy of Nāgas, India.

Gauffrage   Relief printing without color.

Gesso   The layers of plaster mixed with glue applied to panels to provide a smooth surface for the pigment.

Girder   A strong horizontal member supporting the beams of a floor or roof.

Groin Vault   A type of vault created by the intersection of two barrel vaults of equal span, the ridges of their intersections being called groins.

Half Timber   A form of construction in which the spaces between the heavy timbers of the frame are filled with brick or other material.

Hatching   Repeated small parallel lines frequently adopted to provide a transition from one value or color to another in early paintings. Cross Hatching refers to a crisscross of such lines.

Haunch   Roughly the middle third of the height of an arch.

Hīnāyāna   Lesser Vehicle of Buddhist doctrine.

Hip Roof   A roof that slopes up from three or four sides of a building, as distinguished from a gable roof which rises only from two sides.

Hypostyle   A colonnaded hall, particularly those in Egyptian temples.

Iconography   The identification of religious characters, incidents, and symbols in the arts.

Illuminated Manuscript   A hand-written book in which designs are introduced to adorn the text, such as initial letters, decorative borders, or even miniature paintings.

Impasto   The layer or layers of pigment in a painting.

Impost Block   A block placed between the capital of a column and the arches or vaults it supports.

Intercolumniation   The space between two columns.

Isocephaly   Heads of figures on the same level, as in a frieze.

Jātakas   Tales of previous existence of the Buddha, India.

Joist   A small beam to support a floor or ceiling.

Kakemono   Vertical scroll painting, Japan.

Keystone   The central stone in a round or segmental arch. As a rule, there is no keystone in pointed arches.

Kōdō   Japanese, lecture hall.

Kondō   Japanese, Golden hall.

Ku   Chinese ritual vessel.

Lantern   A cupola placed at the apex of a dome or roof to admit light.

Lean-to   A roof with a single slope; a shed roof.

Li   Tripod with hollow legs; Chinese ritual vessel.

Linga   Phallic stone, India.

Lintel   A beam over a door, window, or intercolumniation.

Lithography   A graphic process in which the design is drawn on stone or metal with a greasy pencil. The stone may then be inked to permit printing of the design.

Liwan   A chamber or hall opening on a court, usually with a vaulted passage giving access to the interior, Persia.

Lokopala   Guardians of the four directions, India.

Mahāyāna   Greater Vehicle of Buddhist doctrine.

Makemono   Horizontal scroll painting, Japan.

Mandala (*Mandara,* Jap.)   Holy chart, India.

Mastaba   An Egyptian tomb form, rectangular in plan, low, flat-topped, and plain externally.

Metope   An approximately square slab in a Doric frieze between two triglyphs, sometimes enriched with sculpture.

Mihrab   Prayer niche in mosque, Persia.

Miniature   A small painting.

Modillion   A bracket-like form, often carved with an acanthus leaf, supporting the overhanging members of Corinthian or Composite cornices.

Molding   A small band used singly or in combination with other moldings to decorate or divide architectural members.

Mortar   A mixture of cement or lime with sand and water to provide a cushion for stones or bricks in masonry.

Mosaic   A design composed of small cubes of stone or glass set in mortar to decorate floors, walls, or vaults. The designs may contain figures, or they may be floral or abstract.

Mudrā Significant hand gestures, India.

Mullion A vertical bar of stone or wood subdividing a window.

Nāga Serpent kings, India.

Narthex The vestibule of Early Christian or Byzantine churches.

Nave Architecturally the central aisle of a church, and by extension, the entire western arm of a church. Liturgically, the portion of a church assigned to the laity.

Nave Arcade The arches that support the triforium and clearstory, and therefore mark the separation of the nave and aisles.

Necking The lowest portion of a capital which serves as a transition from the shaft to the upper members of the capital.

Obelisk A tall, tapering rectangular monolith with a small pyramidal top, commonly used in front of Egyptian temples.

Obi Sash worn by Japanese women.

Order A formal system of base, column, and entablature in classic architecture.

Organic Architecture An architecture in which ribbed vaults concentrate their weight and thrust at isolated points and are logically and visibly supported and abutted.

Patina A discoloration of the surface of bronze, or by extension of stone sculpture, acquired through time or artificially induced.

Pediment The low triangle at the end of a building corresponding to the pitched roof; a similar motive used over a door or window for accent or to discharge rainfall to the sides of the opening.

Pendant A projection below the architectural member to which it is attached; pendants sometimes mark the junction of ribs in late Gothic vaults, or the lower ends of structural timbers under the overhanging second floor in early colonial houses.

Pendentive A triangular section of a vault used to support a dome; four pendentives enable a dome to be supported over a square area.

Peripteral Surrounded on all sides by free-standing columns.

Peristyle A colonnade surrounding a building or within a court.

Perspective The science of graphic presentation of the relative distances of objects. Linear Perspective resorts to line and relative size for this purpose; Atmospheric Perspective relies on the relatively sharper definition of nearby objects.

Pi A circle, symbol of heaven and heaven's mandate held by the emperor of China.

Pier An isolated architectural support, especially one whose plan is not circular. Pier is a more general term than column, but should be reserved to refer to those supports that cannot be called columns.

Pietà A representation of the Virgin holding the dead body of Christ.

Pilaster A columnar form flattened against a wall.

Pinnacle A decorative turret projecting above a surface. Pinnacles appear in late Gothic buildings at the apex of gables and around the base of the spire, or above the buttresses along the parapet of a roof.

Plastics Any of a number of fabricated precast or premolded materials available today for architecture and sculpture.

Plinth A flat rectangular block; particularly the lowest unit of the base for an Ionic or Corinthian column.

Pointing   A mechanical method for reproducing in stone from a plaster model at any desired size the shape of a work of sculpture.

Polyptych   A painting of many panels.

Portico   A porch whose roof is supported by columns or piers.

Post and Lintel   A basic system of construction in which vertical supports carry horizontal beams.

Predella   In painting, the row of small panels below the principal panels of an altarpiece.

Pseudo-peripteral   Having a free-standing colonnade on one side, continued by pilasters on the remaining sides.

Pylon   A pair of solid masses of masonry flanking and forming an entrance; particularly in an Egyptian temple.

Quadripartite Vault   A four-part vault; a vault supported by ribs with the two diagonal ribs dividing the rectangle covered by the vault into four triangles.

Quoins   Alternate long and short blocks of stone at the corner of a masonry building for strength and accent.

Raking Cornice   A cornice following the sloping lines of a pediment.

Reinforced Concrete   Concrete in which steel bars have been embedded to add to the tensile strength.

Relief   Projection from a plane; particularly sculpture whose figures or objects are represented by their relative projection from a background.

Rib   An arch used to support a vault.

Rilievo Schiacciato   Crushed relief; very flat relief in which the forms seem to melt into the background; popularized by Donatello.

Rinceau   A pattern composed of a series of connected spirals of floral design.

Rustication   A treatment of stonework in which the individual blocks are accented either by leaving the exposed surface undressed, or by cutting back the edges of each block.

Sanctuary   The area in a religious structure especially consecrated to the god.

Sash   The frame of a window holding the glass; the earlier type of sash was the Casement either fixed in place or hinged; late in seventeenth-century England the Double Hung Sash became popular, in which one or both halves of the window may slide up or down in grooves.

Senmurv or Si-murgh   Fabulous composite creature, Persia.

Set Back   Upper stories of smaller area than lower stories which therefore break back from the plane of the lower walls; particularly the upper stories of skyscrapers treated in this way.

Sexpartite Vault   A vault whose ribs divide the surface into six compartments, common in late Romanesque and early Gothic buildings.

Shaft   The portion of a column between the base and the capital comprising most of the height of the column.

Soffit   The exposed under surface of an arch or beam.

Soren   Crowning member of pagoda consisting of metal rings, Japan.

Spire   A tall pyramidal form placed over a tower.

Splay   A diagonal plane commonly used in mediaeval architecture to enlarge the areas of doors or windows.

Springing   The point at which an arch begins to curve.

Squinch   A device to support a dome over a square area; it may consist of an arched niche, or blocks placed diagonally across the corners of the square.

Steeple   Similar to a spire but different in that a steeple is composed of several distinct stories or stages whereas a spire is a single more or less enriched pyramid.

Stele   Memorial slab or tablet.

Stilting   The vertical portion of an arch between the impost or capital and the point at which the arch begins to curve. In Gothic architecture, stilting may be so pronounced that it requires a colonnette above the main capital. This is not true of Roman, Romanesque, or Renaissance arches, many of which, however, are slightly stilted.

String Course   A horizontal molding used to mark primary divisions in a wall.

Stūpa   Memorial mound, sometimes a reliquary, India.

Stylobate   The top step or platform of a classic temple on which the columns rest.

Sūtra   Buddhist scriptures, India.

Swag   A carved garland of fruit and flowers, commonly used in Roman art and its Renaissance and later derivatives.

Taille Directe   Direct cutting in stone of the final statue by the artist himself, instead of the nineteenth-century practice of turning over a plaster model of his work to a stonecutter for conversion into stone by pointing.

T'ao-t'ieh   Ornamental monster mask consisting of animal head with lower jaw missing, China.

Tempera   A technique of painting on a plaster-covered wooden panel. See p. 160.

Terra Cotta   Baked clay. Both architectural and sculptural forms can be molded in clay and then baked to become hardened; they may also be colored and glazed before baking.

Thrust   The lateral pressure of an arch or vault.

Thūpa   Pali for Stūpa.

Tie Rod   A rod of wood or metal whose ends are anchored in the springing of arches or vaults to counteract thrust; Italian architecture resorts to tie rods so regularly that painters introduce them into their paintings, but northern peoples tend to look on them as a subterfuge and to prefer the more structural masonry buttress.

Ting Vessel   Tripod for food offering, China.

Ting Ware   White glazed ceramic ware, China.

Tondo   A circular painting or relief.

Torana   Gateway to Buddhist shrine, India.

Torii   Gateway to Shinto shrine, Japan.

Tracery   The interlocking bars of stone subdividing Gothic windows and supporting the glass.

Transepts   A transverse unit of a church plan projecting beyond the walls of the aisles and usually of the same height as the nave.

Triforium   That gallery in churches between the nave arcade and the clerestory, corresponding in height to the lean-to roof over the aisles.

Triglyph   A group of vertical members alternating with metopes in the frieze of the Doric order.

Triptych   A painting with three panels; the side panels are often one half the size of the central panel and hinged to it so that they may be folded over it like doors.

Trumeau   A post supporting a tympanum within an arch and dividing a doorway into two doors.

Truss   A structure of wood or metal members, based on the rigidity of a tri-

angle, and devised to support a heavier load or cover a wider span
than is practicable with beams or girders.

Tympanum   The surface below an arch and above a door, often sculptured.

Ukiyo-e   'Pictures of a floating world' — popular Japanese art.

Ūrnā   Buddhist mark between the eyes, India.

Ushnisha   Buddhist protuberance on top of head, India.

Vajrapani   Thunderbolt-bearers, India.

Vault   A method of roofing an area based on the principle of the arch. See
Barrel Vault, Dome, Groin Vault, Quadripartite Vault, Sexpartite Vault.

Veneer   A thin layer of material applied as surface decoration for its beauty
of color or texture.

Vihāra   Monastic establishment, India.

Volute   A scroll, such as the spirals at the sides of Ionic capitals, or the large
scrolls flanking the second-story façades of Italian late sixteenth- and
early seventeenth-century churches.

Voussoir   One of the wedge-shaped stones of an arch or vault.

Wainscot   A treatment of an interior wall, especially of its lower part, with
paneling.

Web of a Vault   The mass of a vault as distinguished from the ribs.

Woodcut   A graphic process in which the design to be printed is left on the
surface of a block of wood by cutting away the portions intended to
be left white.

Yaksha   Guardian of mineral treasures of the earth, India.

Yakshi   Nature spirit, tree guardian, India.

Yamato-e   Painting in true Japanese style.

Yang and Yin   Symbols of male and female elements in Chinese art.

Yoni   Symbol of the female in India, a circle.

Yü   Bucket-shaped ritual vessel for carrying liquids, Chinese.

Ziggurat   A Mesopotamian temple tower of stepped form, built of brick.

Zoning Law   A legal restriction on building imposed in many communities
to limit the use and size of buildings within specified areas.

Suggested Reading

GENERAL

Abbot, E. R., *The Great Painters in Relation to the European Tradition,* New York, Harcourt, Brace, 1927.
>An adequate survey of the history of painting in Europe and America from the Middle Ages to modern times. Illustrated.

Chase, G. H., and Post, C. R., *A History of Sculpture,* New York, Harper, 1925.
>The best one-volume introduction to the subject. Illustrated.

Cheney, Sheldon, *A World History of Art,* New York, Viking, 1937.
>An exciting, if biased, version of the history of art, brilliantly written by an outspoken advocate of modern art. Illustrated.

Craven, T., *Men of Art,* New York, Simon and Schuster, 1931.
>Popular and readable, but inclined to a journalistic and, at times, prejudiced point of view. Illustrated.

Fry, R., *Transformations,* London, Chatto and Windus, 1926.
——, *Vision and Design,* London, Chatto and Windus, 1920.
>Two volumes of unusually thought provoking essays on miscellaneous problems in the theory and history of art. Illustrated.

Hamlin, T. F., *Architecture Through the Ages,* New York, Putnam, 1940.
>A splendid interpretation of architecture in civilization by one of the leading American architectural historians. Illustrated.

Kimball, F., and Edgell, G. H., *A History of Architecture,* New York, Harper, 1917.
>A good introduction to the subject, valuable for handy reference. Illustrated.

Post, C. R., *A History of European and American Sculpture from the Early Christian Period to the Present Day,* 2 vols., Cambridge, Harvard University Press, 1921.
>A comprehensive survey but insufficient illustrations.

COLLECTIONS OF ILLUSTRATIONS

Phaidon Press.
>A series of volumes, chiefly of illustrations that are exceptional in quality. The principal periods and personalities covered to date include Ancient Egypt, Roman Portraits, Donatello, Botticelli, Leonardo, Michelangelo, Raphael, Titian, Dürer, El Greco, Velásquez, Rubens, Hals, Rembrandt, Vermeer, The Impressionists, Rodin, Cézanne, Van Gogh, and Chinese Painting.

Propylaeen Kunstgeschichte.
>Twenty-three volumes on successive art periods. Although the brief

text, captions, and index are in German, the illustrations are copious and of excellent quality. The chief defect lies in an overemphasis on German art.

The University Prints.

An extensive and admirable (in view of the very reasonable price) collection of photographs covering architecture, sculpture, and painting, and some of the minor arts in Europe, America, and the Orient. The prints may be obtained individually, in sets covering particular art periods, or, in some cases, in bound volumes.

THEORY, ICONOGRAPHY, ET CETERA

Bulfinch, T., *The Age of Fable,* new ed., Philadelphia, McKay, 1898.
An old standard reference book on classic mythology. Illustrated.
Ducasse, C. J., *The Philosophy of Art,* New York, MacVeagh, 1929.
A well-balanced and critical discussion.
Hamlin, T. F., *Architecture, An Art for All Men,* New York, Columbia University Press, 1947.
An unimpeachable presentation of the elements and theory of architecture for the layman.
Jameson, Mrs. A., *Legends of the Madonna,* Boston, Houghton Mifflin, 1896.
——, *Legends of the Monastic Orders,* Boston, Houghton Mifflin, 1897.
——, *Sacred and Legendary Art,* 2 vols., Boston, Houghton Mifflin, 1897.
A group of indispensable reference works on Christian iconography. Illustrated.
Ruskin, J., *Modern Painters,* new ed., New York, Merrill and Baker, 1873.
An epoch-making examination of Renaissance and later landscape painting. Illustrated.
——, *The Seven Lamps of Architecture,* Orpington, Allen, 1880.
A literary classic providing a Victorian moralistic theory of architecture.
Scott, G., *The Architecture of Humanism,* 2nd ed., New York, Scribner, 1924.
A penetrating examination of architectural theory and the fallacies that have crept into the criticism of architecture.
Sullivan, L., *The Autobiography of an Idea,* New York, Norton, 1934.
A picturesque account of Sullivan's life and of his formulation of the functional theory of architecture.
Wölfflin, H., *Principles of Art History,* 7th ed., trans. by M. D. Hottinger, London, Bell, 1932.
Hard reading, but widely recognized for its discussion of basic art problems. Illustrated.

PRECLASSICAL ART (CHAPTER II)

Baikie, J., *The Sea-Kings of Crete,* 3rd ed., London, Black, 1920.
More readable and popular than Hall, but less reliable and informative. Illustrated.
Hall, H. R., *Aegean Archaeology,* London, Warner, 1915.
A careful but dry summary of Aegean civilization. Illustrated.
Handcock, P. S. P., *Mesopotamian Archeology,* London, Macmillan, 1912.
There is no satisfactory brief account of this field. This book is perhaps the best but makes only dull reading and is too old to take into account the more recent discoveries. Illustrated.
Maspero, G. C. M., *Manual of Egyptian Archaeology and Guide to the Study*

of Antiquities in Egypt, 6th Eng. ed., trans. and enl. by A. S. Johns, New York, Putnam, 1914.

> An old but still valuable handbook providing an excellent introduction. Illustrated with drawings only.

Smith, E. Baldwin, *Egyptian Architecture as Cultural Expression,* New York, Appleton-Century, 1938.

> By far the best book on this field; a thorough and scholarly presentation of the causes, characteristics, and growth of Egyptian architecture. Well illustrated.

Greek Art (Chapters iii–v)

Anderson, W. J., and Spiers, R. P., *The Architecture of Ancient Greece,* new ed., rev. by W. B. Dinsmoor, London, Batsford, 1927.

> An old standard brought up to date by the foremost archaeologist in America; thoroughly reliable and comprehensive. Illustrated.

Dickinson, G. L., *The Greek View of Life,* 15th ed., New York, Doubleday, 1924.

> An admirable commentary on the interrelation in Greek life of religion, the state, the individual, and the various forms of artistic expression. Not illustrated.

Gardner, E. A., *A Handbook of Greek Sculpture,* 2nd ed., London, Macmillan, 1924.

> Dry but comprehensive; recommended chiefly for reference. Meager illustrations.

——, *Six Greek Sculptors,* New York, Scribner, 1915.

> Essays on the personalities and works of Myron, Phidias, Polyclitus, Praxiteles, Scopas, and Lysippus. Very readable and contains most of the literary references to these men. Illustrated.

Richter, G. M. A., *The Sculpture and Sculptors of the Greeks,* New Haven, Yale University Press, 1929.

> A well-illustrated and scholarly volume on the whole field of Greek sculpture.

Warren, H. L., *The Foundations of Classic Architecture,* New York, Macmillan, 1919.

> Covers ancient architecture from Egypt through classical Greece; recommended, despite its conclusion, for its stimulating discussion of the origin of the Doric order. Illustrated.

Roman Art (Chapter vi)

Anderson, W. J., and Spiers, R. P., *The Architecture of Ancient Rome,* rev. by T. Ashby, London, Batsford, 1927.

> The standard in this field.

Walters, H. B., *The Art of the Romans,* London, Methuen, 1911.

> Satisfactory general account of Roman architecture, sculpture, and painting. Well illustrated.

The Arts of the Early Church (Chapter vii)

Dalton, O. M., *Byzantine Art and Archaeology,* Oxford, Clarendon Press, 1911.

> The most satisfactory work in one volume on a field not well covered by publications in English. Illustrated.

Lowrie, W., *Art in the Early Church,* New York, Pantheon Books, 1947.

> A sound handbook on Early Christian art, covering iconography, archi-

tecture, sculpture, painting, and the minor arts. Chiefly for reference purposes. Illustrated.

Rivoira, G. T., *Lombardic Architecture; Its Origins, Development, and Derivatives*, 2 vols., new ed., trans. by G. M. Rushforth, Oxford, Clarendon Press, 1933.

> The outstanding opponent of Strzygowski; this book carries on through the Romanesque period. Though prejudiced in favor of Italy, especially in the matter of dates, it is well illustrated.

Strzygowski, J., *Origin of Christian Church Art*, trans. by O. M. Dalton and H. J. Braunholtz, Oxford, Clarendon Press, 1923.

> An attempt to trace the origin of Early Christian art to the eastern Mediterranean and beyond; its hypothesis finds less favor today than some years ago. Illustrated.

Swift, E. H., *Hagia Sophia*, New York, Columbia University Press, 1940.

> An exhaustive and eminently scholarly examination of the principal monument of Byzantine art. Illustrated.

ROMANESQUE AND GOTHIC ART (CHAPTERS VIII–X)

Bond, F., *English Church Architecture*, 2 vols., New York, Oxford, 1913.

> A remarkable scholarly analysis of the development of the several elements of English medieval architecture in the Romanesque and Gothic periods. Well illustrated.

Clapham, A. W., *English Romanesque Architecture After the Conquest*, Oxford, Clarendon Press, 1934.

> The last word on a very significant branch of the Romanesque family of styles. Well illustrated.

——, *Romanesque Architecture in Western Europe*, Oxford, Clarendon Press, 1936.

> The most satisfactory general discussion of Romanesque architecture. Well illustrated.

Conway, M., *The Van Eycks and Their Followers*, New York, Dutton, 1921.

> Standard; although many of the attributions have been questioned, the book is fully illustrated and contains much valuable information.

Edgell, G. H., *A History of Sienese Painting*, New York, Dial Press, 1932.

> A well-written discussion of the major and minor personalities of Sienese painting during the Middle Ages and the Renaissance. Plentiful but mediocre illustrations.

Gardner, A., *Medieval Sculpture in France*, Cambridge, Cambridge University Press, 1931.

> A fine and comprehensive survey of the early Romanesque through the later Gothic periods. Illustrated.

Mâle, É., *Religious Art in France; XIII Century*, 3rd ed., trans. by D. Nussey, New York, Dutton, 1913.

> The classic discussion of medieval iconography; two other volumes covering the earlier and later Middle Ages have not been translated. Well illustrated.

Moore, C. H., *Development and Character of Gothic Architecture*, 2nd ed., New York, Macmillan, 1904.

> Presents the thesis that the origin of Gothic architecture lies in its solution of structural problems. Although this thesis is well presented and the chapters on French Gothic architecture are recommended, the book fails to consider the aesthetic qualities of Gothic buildings, and its thesis

distorts the discussion of Gothic architecture outside of France. Illustrated only by drawings.

Morey, C. R., *Medieval Art*, New York, Norton, 1942.

A scholarly discussion of iconography and style from Early Christian times through late Gothic art by America's foremost medievalist. Well illustrated.

Porter, A. K., *Medieval Architecture*, New Haven, Yale University Press, 1912.

A distinguished presentation of the major problems of Romanesque and French Gothic buildings, with a brief introduction to the architecture of the early church. Illustrated.

Prior, E. S., and Gardner, A., *An Account of Medieval Figure-Sculpture in England*, Cambridge, Cambridge University Press, 1912.

A fine reference work, with unusually copious illustrations.

Sirén, O., *Giotto and Some of His Followers*, 2 vols., Cambridge, Harvard University Press, 1917.

A recognized standard on Florentine painting of the fourteenth century. The second volume contains the illustrations.

Ward, C., *Medieval Church Vaulting*, Princeton, Princeton University Press, 1915.

A clear analysis of a complex subject. Well illustrated.

ITALIAN RENAISSANCE ART (CHAPTERS XI, XII)

Anderson, W. J., *The Architecture of the Renaissance in Italy*, 5th ed. rev. and enl. by A. Stratton, New York, Scribner, 1927.

A standard handbook. Well illustrated.

Burckhardt, J., *Civilization of the Renaissance in Italy*, New York, Oxford Press, 1944.

Presents the background and character of the movement, indispensable to both the student and the general reader. Illustrated.

Castiglione, B., *The Book of the Courtier*, trans. by L. E. Opdycke, New York, Scribner, 1927.

Imaginary discussions by a contemporary of the characteristics of ladies and gentlemen in the early sixteenth century. Not illustrated.

Cellini, B., *The Autobiography of Benvenuto Cellini*, trans. by J. A. Symonds, New York, Macmillan, 1929.

A highly colored account of his personal prowess and artistic achievement. Not illustrated.

Cook, H. F., *Giorgione*, London, Bell, 1900.

Satisfactory and short. Illustrated.

Cruttwell, M., *Andrea Mantegna*, London, Bell, 1908.

Brief, but satisfactory. Illustrated.

——, *Donatello*, London, Methuen, 1911.

A good account of his life and works. Illustrated.

Freeman, L. J., *Italian Sculpture of the Renaissance*, New York, Macmillan, 1927.

The leaders of late medieval and Renaissance sculpture from the Pisani to Michelangelo with briefer reference to minor artists. Illustrated.

Hausenstein, W., *Fra Angelico*, trans. by A. Blake, London, Methuen, 1928.

Well illustrated.

Horne, H. P., *Alessandro Filipepi, Commonly Called Sandro Botticelli*, London, Bell, 1908.

Definitive life and criticism. Illustrated.

Mather, F. J., *A History of Italian Painting*, New York, Holt, 1923.
> A readable account of the development and character of Italian painting from Giotto and Duccio through the sixteenth century with a brief conclusion on later painting of the seventeenth and eighteenth centuries. Illustrated.

Moore, T. S., *Correggio*, New York, Scribner, 1906.
> Illustrated.

Muntz, Eugene, *Raphael*, new ed., trans. by W. Armstrong, New York, Armstrong, 1888.
> An old but informative account of his life and works. Poorly illustrated.

Osmond, P., *Paolo Veronese; His Career and Work*, New York, Macmillan, 1927.
> Illustrated.

Phillips, E. M., *Tintoretto*, London, Methuen, 1911.
> Life and work. Illustrated.

Ricketts, C., *Titian*, London, Methuen, 1910.
> Life and work. Well illustrated.

Schmeckebier, L., *A Handbook of Italian Renaissance Painting*, New York, Putnam, 1938.
> An extremely valuable volume in its concentration on the facts pertinent to Italian Renaissance painting. Not illustrated.

Sirén, O., *Leonardo da Vinci, The Artist and the Man*, New Haven, Yale University Press, 1916.
> The literature on Leonardo is so extensive that selection of any one book is difficult. This volume on the whole seems the most satisfactory for general purposes. Illustrated.

Symonds, J. A., *Life of Michelangelo Buonarroti*, 2 vols., 3rd ed., New York, Scribner, 1925.
> A sympathetic account by a master of English prose and a recognized scholar in the Italian Renaissance. Poorly illustrated.

Vasari, G., *Lives of Seventy of the Most Eminent Painters, Sculptors, and Architects*, 10 vols., trans. by G. D. de Vere, London, Macmillan, 1912–14.
> This classic, though often inaccurate, is still worth reading for its exciting gossip about the leaders of Italian art in the late Middle Ages and Renaissance. Many editions and translations are available.

The Renaissance in the North (Chapter XIII)

Blomfield, R., *A History of Renaissance Architecture in England*, 1500–1800, 2 vols., London, Bell, 1897.
> Illustrated.

Dickinson, H. A., *German Masters of Art*, New York, Stokes, 1914.
> A survey of the German school in the late fifteenth and sixteenth centuries.

Dimier, L., *French Painting in the Sixteenth Century*, New York, Scribner, 1911.
> Standard in this field. Not illustrated.

Hueffer, F. M., *Hans Holbein the Younger*, London, Duckworth, 1914.
> Illustrated.

Huxley, A., *The Elder Peter Bruegel*, New York, Willey, 1938.
> Brief but thoughtful and well written. Illustrated.

Mather, F. J., *Western European Painting of the Renaissance*, New York, Holt, 1939.

Though less distinguished than his book on Italian painting, this book discusses painting in western Europe outside of Italy in the sixteenth and seventeenth centuries. Illustrated.

Panofsky, E., *Albrecht Dürer*, 2 vols., Princeton, Princeton University Press, 1943.

The most recent discussion. Well illustrated.

Ward, W. H., *The Architecture of the Renaissance in France*, 2 vols., 2nd ed. rev., London, Batsford, 1926.

French architecture from the late fifteenth to the early nineteenth century. Illustrated.

The Seventeenth Century in Europe (Chapters XIV–XVII)

Beruete, A. de, *Velázquez*, London, Methuen, 1906.

Illustrated.

Brown, G. B., *Rembrandt, Study of His Life and Work*, New York, Scribner, 1907.

As usable as any book in the vast literature on this artist. Sparsely illustrated.

Dillon, E., *Rubens*, London, Methuen, 1909.

Life and work. Illustrated.

Dircks, R., ed., *Sir Christopher Wren; Memorial Volume*, London, Hodder & Stoughton, 1923.

A collection of essays on the life of Wren and on certain architectural problems faced by Wren. Illustrated.

Hartley, C. G., *Record of Spanish Painting*, London, Scott, 1904.

Illustrated.

Norton, R., *Bernini and Other Studies in the History of Art*, New York, Macmillan, 1914.

A sensitive critical appreciation. Illustrated.

Rutter, F., *El Greco*, London, Methuen, 1930.

Illustrated.

Sutro, E., *Nicolas Poussin*, London, Medici Society, 1923.

Illustrated.

Wilenski, R. H., *An Introduction to Dutch Art*, London, Faber, 1929.

Sound criticism, with lists of important paintings of each master. Illustrated.

Rococo and Georgian Art (Chapter XVIII)

Dilke, Lady E. F., *French Painters of the Eighteenth Century*, London, Bell, 1899.

Old but still standard. Illustrated.

Wilenski, R. H., *English Painting*, London, Faber, 1933.

A history of English painting from the Middle Ages through the nineteenth century. Illustrated.

The Nineteenth Century in Europe (Chapters XX–XXII)

Clark, K., *The Gothic Revival*, New York, Scribner, 1929.

A well-written examination of the bases and growth of the movement, hampered by a paucity of illustrations.

Duret, T., *Manet and the French Impressionists*, Philadelphia, Lippincott, 1910.

Sympathetic commentary on the men of seventy. Illustrated.

Fry, R. E., *Cézanne; A Study of His Development*, 2nd ed., London, Leonard & Woolf, 1932.
> A brilliant critique by an ardent admirer. Illustrated.

——, *Characteristics of French Art*, London, Chatto & Windus, 1932.
> Six critical essays covering the story of French painting from the late Middle Ages through the nineteenth century. Illustrated.

Hoeber, A., *The Barbizon Painters; Being the Story of the Men of Thirty*, New York, Stokes, 1915.
> A conversational introduction to the group. Poorly illustrated.

Holmes, C. J., *Constable and His Influence on Landscape Painting*, Westminster, Constable, 1902.
> Ponderous in format but not in treatment. Large illustrations.

Mather, F. J., *Modern Painting, A Study of Tendencies*, New York, Holt, 1927.
> Although unsympathetic in its treatment of the men after the Impressionists, its discussion of the earlier nineteenth century movements is effective. Inadequate illustrations.

Meier-Graefe, J., *Modern Art; Being a Contribution to a New System of Aesthetics*, 2 vols., trans. by F. Simmonds and G. W. Chrystal, New York, Putnam, 1908.
> Though spotty, and overloaded in the second volume with German painters, its treatment of the Impressionists and Post-Impressionists is excellent. Illustrated.

Wilenski, R. H., *French Painting*, Boston, Hale, 1931.
> French Painting from the Middle Ages to the twentieth century. Illustrated.

——, *Modern French Painters*, New York, Reynal & Hitchcock, 1939.
> Excellent on the Post-Impressionists. Illustrated.

AMERICAN ART (CHAPTERS XIX AND XXIII)

Burroughs, A., *Limners and Likenesses; Three Centuries of American Painting*, Cambridge, Harvard University Press, 1936.
> Brief but stimulating. Well illustrated.

Hamlin, T. F., *Greek Revival Architecture in America*, New York, Oxford, 1944.
> The last word on this field; a splendid treatment by an outstanding scholar.

Hitchcock, H. R., *The Architecture of H. H. Richardson and His Times*, New York, Museum of Modern Art, 1936.
> Authoritative. Well illustrated.

——, *In the Nature of Materials; The Buildings of Frank Lloyd Wright*, 1887–1941, New York, Duell, Sloan, and Pearce, 1942.
> Well illustrated.

Isham, S., *History of American Painting*, new ed., with supplementary chapters by Royal Cortissoz, New York, Macmillan, 1927.
> The best general history and one of considerable critical quality. Some illustrations.

Kimball, S. F., *Domestic Architecture of the American Colonies and of the Early Republic*, New York, Scribner, 1922.
> A detailed analysis of Colonial and Federal houses. Illustrated.

LaFollette, S., *Art in America*, New York, Harper, 1929.
> The major arts from colonial days into the twentieth century. Illustrated.

Morrison, H., *Louis Sullivan; Prophet of Modern Architecture*, New York,

Norton, 1935.
> Well illustrated.

Mujica, F., *History of the Skyscraper*, Paris, Archaeology and Architecture Press, 1929.
> Adequate on the skyscraper through 1925. Chiefly illustrations.

Mumford, L., *Sticks and Stones*, New York, Norton, 1933.
> Critical essays on American architecture in civilization. Not illustrated.

Taft, L., *History of American Sculpture*, new ed. rev., New York, Macmillan, 1930.
> The only serious work on this field, but the geniality and eclecticism of its beloved author hamper its critical quality. Some illustrations.

Tallmadge, T. E., *The Story of Architecture in America*, New York, Norton, 1927.
> An entertaining account of the development of American architecture. Highly recommended despite its few illustrations.

MODERN ART (CHAPTER XXIV)

Giedion, S., *Space, Time, and Architecture*, Cambridge, Harvard University Press, 1941.
> The growth of modern architecture in structure and aesthetics from the late Baroque style in Europe to the present. Many unusual illustrations.

Hitchcock, H. R., *Modern Architecture, Romanticism and Reintegration*, New York, Payson, 1929.
> The most thorough account of the growth of modern architecture from the early nineteenth century to the present. Illustrated.

Le Corbusier, *Towards a New Architecture*, trans. from the 13th French ed. by F. Etchells, London, Rodker, 1931.
> A leader of the modern school expresses his concepts of architecture and its future. Illustrated.

Museum of Modern Art. Catalogs, especially those on 'Picasso' (1939), 'Cubism and Abstract Art' (1936), and 'Fantastic Art, Dada, Surrealism' (1936).
> Both the brief introductions and the abundant illustrations are admirable.

ORIENTAL ART, GENERAL (CHAPTERS XXV–XXVIII)

Binyon, L., *The Spirit of Man in Asian Art*, Cambridge, Harvard University Press, 1935.
> Excellent introductory essays. Not illustrated.

Grousset, R., *The Civilizations of the East*, trans. by C. A. Phillips, 4 vols., New York, Knopf, 1931–5.
> The arts of Persia, India and Greater India, China, and Japan. Well illustrated.

Hackin, J., and others, *Asiatic Mythology*, London, Harrap, 1932.
> A useful handbook. Illustrated.

PERSIA (CHAPTER XXV)

Arnold, T. W., *Painting in Islam*, Oxford, Clarendon Press, 1928.
> Interesting text. Illustrated.

Dimand, M., *Handbook of Muhammadan Art*, New York, Metropolitan Museum, 1944.
> Illustrated. Bibliography.

Gray, B., *Persian Painting*, London, Benn, 1930.
> A good summary, including a discussion of techniques. Illustrated.

Herzfeld, E., *Iran in the Ancient East*, New York, Oxford, 1941.
> Persian art from prehistoric times through early historic periods. Illustrated.

Pope, A. U., ed., *A Survey of Persian Art*, 6 vols., New York, Oxford, 1938–9.
> Recommended for illustrations.

INDIA (CHAPTER XXVI)

Anand, M. R., *The Hindu View of Art*, London, Allen & Unwin, 1933.

Binyon, L., *The Court Painters of the Great Moguls*, New York, Oxford, 1921.
> An account of Mogul court and art. Illustrated.

Brown, P., *Indian Architecture*, Bombay, 1942.
> Illustrated.

Codrington, K. de B., *An Introduction to the Study of Mediaeval Indian Sculpture*, London, Goldston, 1929.
> Recommended for later Hindu art. Illustrated.

Coomaraswamy, A. K., *History of Indian and Indonesian Art*, London, Goldston, 1927.
> For reference and bibliography. Illustrated.

——, *Rajput Painting*, 2 vols., New York, Oxford, 1936.
> Illustrated.

Gordon, A. K., *The Iconography of Tibetan Lamaism*, New York, Columbia University Press, 1939.
> Good reference book for beginners. Illustrated.

Khandalavala, K., *Indian Sculpture and Painting*, Bombay, Taraporevala, n. d.
> Introductory. Color plates.

Mackay, E., *The Indus Valley Civilization*, London, 1935.
> Résumé of prehistoric art. Illustrated.

Mehta, N. C., *Studies in Indian Painting*, Bombay, Taraporevala, 1926.
> Text and color plates.

Vogel, J. P., *Buddhist Art in India, Ceylon, and Java*, Oxford, Clarendon, 1936.
> Excellent handbook. Illustrated.

Zimmer, H., *Myths and Symbols in Indian Art and Civilization*, New York, Pantheon, 1946.
> Illustrated.

CHINA (CHAPTER XXVII)

Ashton, L., *An Introduction to the Study of Chinese Sculpture*, London, Benn, 1924.
> Still good for the beginner. Illustrated.

Binyon, L., *The Flight of the Dragon*, London, Murray, 1943.
> Distinguished essay on Chinese art. Not illustrated.

——, *Painting in the Far East*, London, Arnold, 1934.
> A standard work. Illustrated.

Creel, H. G., *The Birth of China*, New York, Reynal & Hitchcock, 1936.
> Recommended for the early arts of China. Illustrated.

Driscoll, L., and Toda, K., *Chinese Calligraphy*, Chicago, University of Chicago, 1935.
> Good historical account. Illustrated.

Getty, A., *The Gods of Northern Buddhism*, Oxford, Clarendon, 1928.
> For reference. Illustrated.

Goodrich, C., and Fenn, H., *A Syllabus of the History of Chinese Civilization and Culture*, New York, Chinese Society of America, 1941.
> For reference and bibliography. Not illustrated.

Grousset, R., *In the Footsteps of the Buddha*, London, Routledge, 1932.
> Translations from the diary of a Chinese monk of the seventh century, containing an account of life in China, Central Asia, and India. Illustrated.

Guest, G. D., and Wenley, A. G., *Outlines for the Study of Far Eastern Art — China*, Washington, Freer Gallery, 1946.
> Annotated bibliography on China and Japan. Illustrated.

Kuo Hsi, *An Essay on Landscape Painting*, trans. by S. Sakanishi, London, Murray, 1935.
> Not illustrated.

Leach, B., *A Potter's Book*, London, 1940.
> Excellent on techniques.

Nourse, M., *A Short History of the Chinese*, Philadelphia, Blakiston, 1944.
> Recommended for beginners. Not illustrated.

Sakanishi, S., *The Spirit of the Brush*, London, Murray, 1939.
> Not illustrated.

Silcock, A., *Introduction to Chinese Art and History*, New York, Oxford, 1948.
> Recommended for beginners, with helpful maps and tables. Illustrated.

JAPAN (CHAPTER XXVIII)

Binyon, L., and Sexton, J. J. O., *Japanese Colour Prints*, London, Benn, 1923.
> Reference. Illustrated.

Ledoux, L. V., *An Essay on Japanese Prints*, New York, privately printed, 1938.
> Colored illustrations.

Minamoto, H., *An Illustrated History of Japanese Art*, trans. by H. G. Henderson, Kyoto, Hoshino, 1935.
> Recommended for beginners. Copious illustrations.

Okakura, K., *Ideals of the East*, London, Murray, 1905.
> Essays by a man acquainted with both Oriental and Western traditions.

Paine, R. T., *Japanese Screen Paintings*, Boston, Museum of Fine Arts, 1935.
> Illustrated.

Sadler, A. L., *Cha-no-yu*, London, 1934.
> Description of the tea ceremony.

Sansom, G. B., *Japan, A Short Cultural History*, rev. ed., New York, Appleton, 1943.
> Excellent for the student of history and art.

Soper, A., *The Evolution of Buddhist Architecture in Japan*, Princeton, Princeton University Press, 1942.
> Good text and illustrations.

Toda, K., *Japanese Scroll Painting*, Chicago, University of Chicago Press, 1935.
> Text. Illustrated.

Tsuda, N., *Handbook of Japanese Art*, Tokyo, Sanseido, 1935.
> For reference. Illustrated.

Warner, L., *The Craft of the Japanese Sculptor*, New York, McFarlane, 1936.
> Popular treatment. Illustrated.

Index

COMPARATIVE CHRONOLOGY FROM 1300 - 1650

Dates	Italy	Periods	France	Periods	English Periods	England and Germany	Spanish Periods	Spain and the Low Countries
1300	c. 1255 · Duccio · 1319 c. 1266 · Giotto · 1336 c. 1283 · Martini · 1344 1330 · South doors, Baptistry, Florence	Late Gothic	1318 · S. Ouen, Rouen	Rayonnant Gothic	Decorated Gothic	c. 1326 · Nave, Exeter Cathedral	Gothic	1316 · Gerona Cathedral
1350	1348 · Black Death · 1350 c. 1308 · Orcagna · 1368		1339 · Hundred Years War · 1453 1348 · Black Death · 1350 1373 · S. John's Chapel, Amiens 1395 · Well of Moses, Champmol		Perpendicular Gothic	1348 · Black Death · 1350 1351 · Cloisters, Gloucester 1386 · Bodiam Castle		1348 · Black Death · 1350
1400	1378 · Ghiberti · 1455 c. 1420 · S. Lorenzo, Florence c. 1401 · Masaccio · 1428 1386 · Donatello · 1466 1387 · Angelico · 1455 1433 · Cosimo de Medici · 1464 1397 · Uccello · 1475	Early Renaissance	1437 · S. Maclou, Rouen 1443 · Jacques Coeur House, Bourges	Flamboyant Gothic		1446 · King's College Chapel, Cambridge	Flamboyant Gothic	1401 · Seville Cathedral Hours of Chantilly c. 1366 · Hubert Van Eyck · 1426 c. 1385 · Jan Van Eyck · 1440 c. 1399 · Van der Weyden · 1464
1450	1444 · Riccardi Pal., Florence c. 1406 · Filippo Lippi · 1469							

556